# of ANTIQUES
& COLLECTIBLES

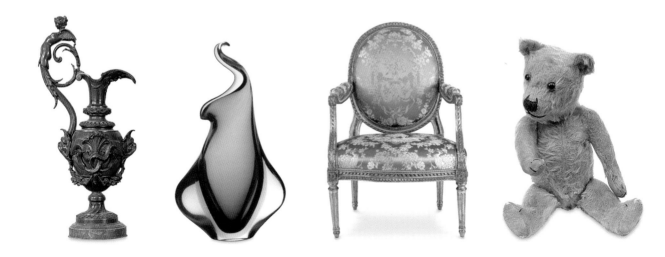

# of ANTIQUES
& COLLECTIBLES

JUDITH MILLER

LONDON, NEW YORK, MUNICH,
MELBOURNE, DELHI

A joint production from DK and
THE PRICE GUIDE COMPANY

DK INDIA

Design Managers Arunesh Talapatra,
Romi Chakraborty
Designers Mini Dhawan, Gunjan
Ahlawat, Ivy Roy
Editorial Manager Dipali Singh
Editors Aditi Ray, Saloni Talwar,
Alicia Ingty
DTP Coordinator Pankaj Sharma
DTP team Preetam Singh,
Dheeraj Arora
Art Director Shefali Upadhyay

DK LONDON

Project Editor Nicola Hodgson
Senior Art Editor Silke Spingies
Managing Editor Julie Oughton
Managing Art Editor Christine Keilty
Publisher Jonathan Metcalf
Art Director Bryn Walls
Publishing Manager Liz Wheeler
Production Editor Tony Phipps
Production Controller Linda Dare
Picture Researcher Claire Bowers
US Editor Christine Heilman

THE PRICE GUIDE COMPANY

Publisher Judith Miller
Chief Contributors Mark Hill, John Wainwright
Publishing Manager Julie Brooke
Managing Editor Carolyn Madden
Editor Sara Sturgess

First American Edition, 2008

Published in the United States by
DK Publishing
375 Hudson Street
New York, New York 10014

07 08 09 10 11   10 9 8 7 6 5 4 3 2 1

ID047—February 2008

Text first published in *The Illustrated Dictionary of Antiques and
Collectibles* © Judith Miller 2001, this revision copyright © Judith Miller
and Dorling Kindersley Limited 2007

Published in Great Britain by Dorling Kindersley Limited.

A catalog record for this book is available from the Library of Congress

ISBN: 978-0-7566-3385-1

DK books are available at special discounts when purchased in bulk
for sales promotions, premiums, fund-raising, or educational use.
For details contact: DK Publishing Special Markets, 375 Hudson Street,
New York, New York 10014 or Special Sales@dk.com.

Printed and bound in China by
Hung Hing Printing Offset Company Ltd

Discover more at
www.dk.com

FOREWORD

Over the past 30 years, two major developments in the collecting world have made this *A–Z of Antiques and Collectibles* a necessity for collectors. The first is the increase in what is classified "antique." When I started to collect "old plates" during my student days in Edinburgh, an antique had to be at least 100 years old and many dealers and fairs would only accept items from before 1840. This meant that "newer" items were condemned to a lower status and consequently could be found in junk shops. They were also considered less worthy of research. This has changed dramatically—especially in the past few years—with many items from the 20th century now eagerly collected and valued highly. The result is a far greater choice of items for people to collect and discover— many of them with strange names and even stranger terminology.

The second, and possibly more important, factor is the vast interest in antiques and collectibles fueled by many successful television series such as the *Antiques Roadshow* in both the US and the UK. Today more and more people want to find out what Grandma's vase is and when was it made. The family says that chair was made by Charles Eames, but who was he? What does it mean when something is described as Rococo? And what was a tsuba used for?

As soon as you start to use this book, you will find it is so much more than a simple dictionary. The information has been checked by a team of the top experts in their field to ensure that it is of use to both the experienced collector and someone just starting out. It explains the different styles and periods, discusses the great craftsmen and women, describes what a piece is, how it was used, and when it was most fashionable. Methods of construction and decoration are also explained. Influential names in the world of antiques—from kings and queens to architects, inventors to religious sects—are set in context and their impact assessed.

This book aims to provide a single essential, authoritative, and accessible source of reference for anyone who is interested in unlocking the fascinating world of antiques and collecting.

Judith Miller.

CONSULTANTS

Each of the consultants involved in the checking and compilation of this book is an authority in his or her own field. They are also experts on the BBC *Antiques Roadshow*, where they give advice and valuations on antiques and collectibles brought to them by the general public. In 2007 the show celebrated its 30th anniversary of broadcasting.

John Bly – Furniture

John Bly is an antique dealer who worked with Sotheby's in London for four years before joining his family business, which was established in Tring in 1891. In 1991 he opened premises in the West End of London. He is also an author, a lecturer, a Fellow of the Royal Society of Arts, and a Liveryman of the Worshipful Company of Goldsmiths. He is a former Chairman of the British Antiques Dealers' Association.

Marc Allum – Modern classics

Marc is a generalist with over sixteen years' experience in the auction business. As a former director of major London auctioneers, he has a wide range of interests. His personal favorites include antiquities, South American Art, Georgian glassware, and the Grand Tour. He spends much of his time at Chateau Coye, his home and lecture venue in southwest France.

Bunny Campione – Automata, dolls, soft toys, and textiles

Bunny Campione worked at Sotheby's in London for 23 years in the Furniture and Collectors' Departments and for five years at Christie's as a Senior Consultant. Since 1988 she has run her own antiques consultancy company. Bunny specializes in subjects including automata, birdcages, textiles, corkscrews, dolls, pre-Victorian and miniature furniture, and soft toys.

John Axford – Continental pottery and porcelain; oriental

John Axford worked for Phillips Auctioneers in London before joining Woolley and Wallis Fine Art Auctioneers, Salisbury, in 1993 to become Head of the Ceramics, Glass and Oriental Departments. He is now a Director of the company. He also writes and lectures on ceramics and oriental art and has acted as a consultant on several books.

Bill Harriman – Arms and armor

Bill Harriman is Director of Firearms for the British Association for Shooting and Conservation. He is also an independent consultant specializing in all firearms, ballistics, and general weapons as well as the law relating to them. In 2002, he was appointed to the British Home Office Reference Panel for historical firearms. Bill writes widely and is the editor of the *Classic Arms and Militaria* magazine.

Hilary Kay – Collectibles and toys

Hilary Kay is an independent consultant, lecturer, writer, and broadcaster on antiques and collectibles, and she joined the *Antiques Roadshow* in 1979. She worked for Sotheby's in London for over 20 years as an auctioneer and Senior Director before setting up the corporate entertainment company *Antiques Roadshow Lecture and Conference Services*. Hilary also appears regularly on television and radio.

Eric Knowles – Decorative arts

Eric Knowles began his career in northern England in the early 1970s. He came south to join Bonhams, the London auctioneers. He went on to set up the Art Nouveau and Art Deco departments and become a Director of the company. Eric has written numerous books and articles on Victoriana, Art Nouveau, and Art Deco.

Andy McConnell – Glass

Andy McConnell is a writer and historian specializing in glass. He is the author of several books including *The Decanter, An Illustrated History of Glass from 1650*. Andy owns a vast collection of glass dating from 1650 to the present day and he is as interested in examples that can be bought for a small amount, as those that command thousands. He has worked as the glass consultant on several books and writes on the subject for magazines.

Geoffrey Munn – Jewelry and *objets de vertu*

Geoffrey Munn is the Managing Director of a long-established London jeweler and has a particular interest in 19th-century jewelry and metalwork. He has organized many special exhibitions, including the 2002 Tiaras exhibition at the V&A Museum, London, and has written books about jewelers and jewelry.

Henry Sandon – British pottery and porcelain

Henry Sandon is regarded as the world authority on Worcester Porcelain and was curator of the Dyson Perrins Museum, Worcester, for many years. He has a wide knowledge of pottery and porcelain of all periods and countries. He is the author of many books dealing with Worcester and other porcelains and lectures frequently on the subject.

Clive Stewart-Lockhart – Fine art and ceramics

Clive is Deputy Chairman of Dreweatt Neate fine art auctioneers in Berkshire, where he specializes in pictures, works of art, and oriental ceramics. He started at Sotheby's in London in 1973 and after short spells at Bluett and Sons, Oriental dealers, and Bonhams, he moved to Dreweatt Neate 25 years ago.

8

Aalto, Alvar ■ (1898–1976) A Finnish architect and designer considered one of the giants of 20th-century design. A leading exponent of the MODERN MOVEMENT but with a Humanist outlook, Aalto favored an organic approach to design. One of his most highly regarded architectural projects was the Paimio Sanitorium for Tuberculosis in Finland (1929–33), where he also designed the interior furnishings of the building, including the notable Model No. 41 Paimio bentwood chair.

Aalto's furniture met with great acclaim abroad when it was shown in London at Fortnum & Mason in 1933. His popularity abroad was furthered with his design for the Finnish Pavilion at the 1939 New York World's Fair. Aalto formed a production company called Artek in 1935 with Harry Gullichsen, Nils Hahl, and his wife Aino Marsio Aalto, to produce his designs. Finmar was established to import Aalto's furniture designs into England, while Wohnbedorf was established in Switzerland for other European imports. Although renowned primarily as an architect and furniture designer, he also designed the famous Savoy glass vase for Karhula-littala, Finland, in 1936. It is characterized by an asymmetrical form and organic appearance, and has the same fluid outline as Aalto's chairs.

Aaron's rod A term used by plasterers in the 18th and early 19th centuries to describe a leaf-entwined staff. It can also refer to the caduceus, a winged staff coiled with two serpents. In Classical mythology it is an attribute of Mercury, the messenger god of the Roman pantheon (in Greek, Hermes).

Abacus The flat molding on the top of a capital that supports the entablature. Occasionally the abacus has simple ornament such as chamfered borders or slight indentations.

Abalone ■ A species of edible shellfish (mollusks), the hard shells of which have a decorative lining ranging from iridescent silvery white to green-red MOTHER-OF-PEARL, to combinations of pinks and reds with blues, greens, and purples. Since the RENAISSANCE notable uses have been in jewelry, an embellishment of metalware, and since the 17th century as an inlay for furniture.

Abbotsford style Furniture of the 19th century inspired by the decoration of Abbotsford (1824), the Scottish home of Sir Walter Scott, and characterized by ELIZABETHAN and GOTHIC motifs such as STRAPWORK, cusps, and spiral columns.

Abraham, Robert Frederick (1827–95) An English painter who studied in Paris and Antwerp and exhibited at the Royal Academy from 1846 to 1851. He went to COALPORT in 1855 as a porcelain decorator. In 1863 he left Coalport and went to Hill Pottery. In 1865 he became art director at COPELAND AND GARRETT.

Abrash Variations in tone and saturation found within a single color in a carpet. It is

ALVAR AALTO

Finnish designer Alvar Aalto used natural birch and laminated birch plywood rather than modern materials such as tubular steel because he felt they were more sympathetic to the physical and psychological condition of people. He characterized these needs as "psychophysical."

Tea cart
Modernist birchwood tea cart, designed by Alvar Aalto for Artek, Helsinki. c. 1936.

Abalone
French abalone-shell-covered souvenir pin case. c. 1890.

Birch chest
Early Alvar Aalto birch chest.

Lounge chair
Alvar Aalto lounge chair with closed loop birch frame and blue fabric upholstery. c. 1950.

caused by slight variations between different batches of wool, which are dyed at different times, and is most obvious on large, single-color areas.

Abstract Expressionism A term first used in 1919 to describe certain paintings by Wassily Kandinsky. It is applied today to a movement in American painting and studio ceramics from around 1942, which was highly influential in the 1950s and early 1960s. The work of potters Peter Voulkos and John Mason is notable. Features include apparently random compositions with gestural marks and holes.

Abtsbessingen A town in Thuringia, Germany, with a factory that produced a fine, white-glazed FAIENCE. In business from 1747 to 1791, it was one of the best 18th-century faience factories. Painter Joseph Philipp Dannhofer worked in Abtsbessingen for three years. The usual mark was a motif like a tuning fork, sometimes with the decorator's initials.

Acacia A durable hardwood ranging in color from pale yellow to golden brown with darker brown markings. Although employed primarily for INLAY and BANDING, it was also used for the CARCASS of some rustic furniture in the 18th and 19th centuries.

Acanthus ▪ A Mediterranean plant with fleshy, scalloped leaves. From antiquity it was widely used as an ornament such as in decorative moldings and Corinthian and Composite capitals. In the 18th century it was a popular motif for furniture and metalwork.

Accordion pleat A series of folds like those of the bellows of an accordion, particularly fashionable in 1950s dressmaking.

Achromatic lens A triple lens combination discovered in the mid-18th century that removed the color fringes and spherical distortion from images seen through telescopes. This also allowed telescopes to become smaller and more portable. Patented in 1758 by the Englishman John Dollond, the combination was applied at the end of the century to microscopes.

Acid polishing A process used from the late 19th century on cut glass to achieve a lustrous, shiny surface. Instead of using hand and mechanical polishing methods, the cut piece is dipped into a mixture of sulfuric and HYDROFLUORIC ACID to create the smooth finish.

Acid etching ▪ A technique that was popular from the 1890s to the 1930s for decorating glass. The pattern is marked out and the areas around it protected by an acid-resistant wax. The vessel is then submerged in HYDROFLUORIC ACID, which eats into the unprotected glass. The longer the piece is exposed to the acid, the deeper the relief. The principle is the same for PRINTS, except that the medium is copper, zinc, or mild steel sheets.

Acier, Michel-Victor ▪ (1736–95) A French sculptor and modeler of groups and figures at SÈVRES, appointed to the MEISSEN Porcelain Factory in 1764, and pensioned off in 1781. His favorite themes were children, and allegorical and mythological scenes, sometimes sentimental in feel, which he set in a style between ROCOCO and CLASSICAL.

Acoma pottery 19th-century Native American pottery from the US southwest, in unglazed terra-cotta, painted with geometric patterns in earth tones.

Acorn ▪ The fruit of the oak tree, it symbolized fecundity and immortality in Roman, Celtic, and Scandinavian art and ornament. The acorn motif features widely on JACOBEAN oak furniture, and in the form of brass drop handles on late-17th-century and American furniture. It was also prominent in the GOTHIC REVIVAL, and remains to this day a popular form for turned, wooden pulls for blind and curtain cords.

Acorn cup An English silver STANDING CUP with a bowl and cover in the form of an acorn and a tree-trunk stem, made from around 1580 to 1620.

A
9

Acanthus
leaf carving

Acanthus
George III carved giltwood armchair by Thomas Chippendale. c. 1770.

Acid etching
A Steuben acid-etched green jade bowl. c. 1925.

Acier, Michel-Victor
Meissen Putto-Figure by Michel Victor Acier. c. 1770.

Acorn
Detail of chair back with carved acorn splat, by Paul Follot and Laurent Malcles. 1920s.

A

Acorn flagon An English, particularly Yorkshire, pewter flagon, mostly made from about 1700 to 1750, with a wide base and tapering bulbous body like an acorn. It usually has a domed cover.

Acorn knop A finial on the end of silver or base-metal spoons taking the form of an acorn. It is seen on some of the earliest forms of medieval spoons, from about 1300 to 1500, and was also popular in the early 20th century with silversmiths such as Georg Jensen.

Act of Parliament clock See TAVERN CLOCK.

Acupictura A term for embroidery that imitates painting. Sometimes called needle painting, the subject is represented in the most accurate detail achievable.

Adam, Robert ■ (1728–92) A Scottish NEOCLASSICAL architect, interior decorator, and designer, and son of William Adam, a notable Scottish architect. Together with his brothers, John and James, Robert inherited his father's practice in 1748. In 1754 he embarked on an architectural GRAND TOUR. During his stay in Rome he cultivated potential aristocratic patrons and became an accomplished draftsman, absorbing the principles and motifs of Roman antiquity and the NEOCLASSICAL style that he studied assiduously. In 1758 he set up as an architect in London, and by the early 1760s had become the leading British architect of the day, also designing interiors, architectural fixtures— ranging from chimney-pieces to door handles and ESCUTCHEONS—and all types of furniture, metalwork, and textiles in the light, delicate Neoclassical style that bears his name. His designs were executed by INCE & MAYHEW, and Thomas CHIPPENDALE also made Adam-style furniture. The furniture, often painted, gilded, or applied with marquetry, depended more on ornament than form for effect. Wall mirrors, pier tables, commodes, and girandoles were decorated with Classical motifs such as rams' heads, husks, palmettes, and festoons. The popularity of the Adam style peaked in Britain in the 1760s and 1770s. *Works in Architecture* by Robert and James Adam was published in Britain from 1773 to 1779, with a third, posthumous, volume in 1822, and helped to spread the style to France and the US.

Adams & Co. A late 19th-century American glassmaker, established in Pittsburgh in 1851 as a union of two older firms: Adams, Macklin & Co. and Stourbridge Flint Glassworks. Till 1891 Adams made mostly clear pressed and engraved FLINT GLASS of heavy type; subsequently it became a factory taken over by the US Glass Company.

Adams, George (1709–72) An English craftsman producing fine-quality precision instruments. He established his workshop in 1734 and gained a good reputation. In 1746 he invented the New Universal Single Microscope, which incorporated the system of using single lenses of various powers set in a revolving disk under the barrel. Adams also provided both the East India Company and the Ordnance Department with instruments and authored a number of important scientific treatises. He and his son George Adams Jr. were appointed to the positions of mathematical instrument-makers to George III in 1760 and produced a number of scientific instruments for the king's collection.

Adams, Robert (1809–80) An English firearms designer. In 1851 he was in partnership as Deane, Adams & Deane and obtained a British patent for a solid frame, self-cocking percussion REVOLVER. Shown at the GREAT EXHIBITION in 1851, it was used by officers during the Crimean War (1853–56), as the gun's mechanism allowed it to be fired more rapidly than other models, such as the Colt. In 1856 Adams cofounded the London Armory Company and his revolver became an official revolver of the British army, being used in the Indian Mutiny in 1857 and in the US Civil War. Production declined in the early 1860s, but it was still used until the 1880s.

Adams, William There were several potters by this name during the 18th and 19th centuries in Staffordshire, all closely

Adam, Robert
George III giltwood open armchair, in the style of Robert Adam. c. 1775.

Adler glass
Enameled vase, with a crucifix over a double-headed eagle. 16th century.

Adler glass
Bohemian enameled humpen with historismus decoration dated 1645 (falsely). c. 1865.

Aegricanes
Detail of George III mahogany table, with ram's head (aegricanes) terminals.

or distantly related to one another. The first recorded William Adams established Adams & Co. in 1769 in Greengates, Tunstall, and made EARTHENWARE, BASALT, and JASPER until 1800. Another William Adams was based in Stoke and made blue printed earthenware between 1804 and 1840. Toward the end of the 19th century another company called William Adams & Co. produced COMMEMORATIVE WARE.

Adler glass ■ A tall, cylindrical German glass drinking BEAKER or HUMPEN, sometimes with a cover, also called in German *Adlerhumpen* (eagle beaker) or *Reichsadlerhumpen* (imperial eagle beaker), with enameled decoration of a double-headed eagle with the symbols of the Holy Roman Empire on its wings. Made in Germany and Bohemia from the mid-6th century, such glasses were used to drink toasts and were much reproduced in the HISTORISMUS movement. See also HUMPEN.

Aedicule From the Latin *aedicula* (small shrine). A shrine within a temple, framed by two COLUMNS supporting a pediment and entablature and containing a statue. The term is also applied to the frame of a window, door, or niche formed by two PIERS, PILASTERS, or columns supporting a PEDIMENT and an entablature, gable, lintel, or plaque.

Aegricanes ■ In Classical architecture, the head of a ram or goat, a motif most frequently used in temples. Swags or garlands are often attached to the horns, sometimes curving into VOLUTES reminiscent of an Ionic capital. Revived as an ornamental motif in the Renaissance, the aegricane was a popular device in the 18th century, combined with festoons for repeating frieze decoration in the style of Robert ADAM. Aegricanes were also used for handles in ceramics and metalwork, and on furniture combined with cloven hoof MONOPODIA for tripods and side tables.

Aerography A technique employed since the 1890s, in which a colored ground is applied mechanically to lesser quality porcelain or pottery, using a mechanical atomizer or sprayer such as an AEROGRAPH, instead of a more traditional method such as employing a carefully moderated layer of oil to hold the color to the surface.

Aesthetic Movement ■ In the late 19th century a number of English artists, architects, and critics reacted against the art and design popular at the time, which was based on realism or meant to convey moral values, in favor of works of art whose only justification was their intrinsic beauty. The movement was largely an English phenomenon, although it spread to the US, and in its turn, influenced both the ARTS AND CRAFTS and ART NOUVEAU styles. Both the movement and the names popularly associated with it—the American painter James Abbott McNeill Whistler, the writer Oscar Wilde,

A

11

AESTHETIC MOVEMENT

Prevalent from the late 1860s to around 1901, the Aesthetic Movement rejected the essentially Victorian notion that art or artifacts should either be useful or have a moral purpose, or both. Rather, the worth or value of something lay in its intrinsic beauty.

Minton plaque
Minton buff earthenware plaque. 1877.

Silver drop handles

Gnarled branch handle

Celadon glaze

Ebonized chair
Aesthetic Movement ebonized chair, in the manner of Godwin. Late 19th century.

Metal jug
Aesthetic Movement silver-plated metal jug. Late 19th century.

Moon flask
Royal Worcester Aesthetic moon flask.

Gillows cabinet
Anglo-Japanese mahogany writing cabinet by Gillows. Late 19th century.

A

12

and the architect E. W. GODWIN—received much newspaper coverage, with both Whistler and Wilde involved in famous court cases.

The sources of inspiration of the movement were diverse and included JAPONAISERIE, Egyptian and Moorish, the GOTHIC REVIVAL, and the QUEEN ANNE REVIVAL. The leading architect whose work clearly shows his appreciation of Oriental simplicity and subtlety was E. W. Godwin. The work of the English illustrator Aubrey Beardsley also shows a marked Japanese influence. The Queen Anne Revival was attributed to the architects Richard Norman Shaw and William Eden Nesfield, along with William MORRIS. The Gothic style, brought to prominence by A. W. N. PUGIN, also had some impact. Egyptian influences can be seen, for example, in a THEBES STOOL made by LIBERTY & CO. Japanese art had a major influence on Western art after Japan opened its doors to the West in 1853.

Commercial pieces in ceramic or silver may be Oriental-looking, made as if from bamboo, or have conventional shapes with Oriental decoration with flowers, birds, and insects. Furniture was often ebonized and featured spindles, gilded highlights, or painted panels. In the US the influence of the Aesthetic style can be seen in the early interior decoration of Louis Comfort TIFFANY, the silverware of the GORHAM MANUFACTURING COMPANY, and in ART POTTERY by various makers, including ROOKWOOD POTTERY.

Affleck, Thomas ■ (1740–95) A Scottish-born American cabinet-maker and chair specialist active in Philadelphia from 1763. Affleck's work is among the most highly prized of all American Chippendale furniture. Typical pieces include mahogany chairs carved in the manner of early George III examples, showing a restrained Rococo influence.

Afshar rugs ■ Carpets from a Turkic-speaking nomadic and partly settled tribal group based in southeastern Persia (Iran) near Kerman, who made (and continue to make) fine and coarse rugs with geometric designs in which jewel-like shades of red and blue predominate. Products include pile rugs, KILIMS, and SOUMAK carpets.

Agate ■ An opaque and banded variety of chalcedony, agate is a member of the quartz family and has been used as an ornamental hardstone for centuries. Frequently stained, the layers of contrasting browns, oranges, blues, grays, and greens are ideal for carving into cameos. The black and white variety is called onyx, while the red and white kind is called sardonyx.

Agate glass See LITHYALIN GLASS. An opaque, marbleized, and striated glass that was used to imitate costly and rare vessels made from semiprecious stones such as agate, chalcedony, and jasper. Produced from Roman times, it was made by mixing together two or more colors of molten glass such as green and purple. It was further

developed in the late 15th century by Venetian glassmakers who developed "chalcedony" glass. It was refined still further in the 19th century by Bohemian glassmakers such as Friedrich EGERMANN, and John Ford in Edinburgh, and, later, Louis Comfort TIFFANY.

Agateware ■ A ceramic imitation of agate and marble, and made either by kneading together variously colored clays, or sometimes by painting an imitation of the finish. When kneaded, the striations of color go through the BODY and this is called "solid agate." Particularly made by WEDGWOOD and other Staffordshire potteries in the 18th and 19th centuries, it was also produced in continental Europe, notably at the APT factory.

Agra carpets Agra was the capital of the Mughal Empire in the 16th and 17th centuries and an important carpet-weaving center from about 1850 to 1910. Carpets, mainly with wool pile, were made in commercial workshops and in the city's jail. Formal curvilinear designs are based on earlier Persian Classical models. The traditional red and blue threads are dominant in the design; ivory ground carpets are also seen but are rare.

Aide-mémoire Fashionable in 18th-century France, and popular generally throughout the 19th century, these memory aids were decorative cases on clips or chains, which open to reveal ivory

Affleck, Thomas
A Chippendale mahogany side chair, designed by Thomas Affleck, Philadelphia. c. 1765.

Afshar rug
Afshar rug, from southwest Iran. c. 1900.

Agate
A gilt snuff box with inlaid Scottish agate plaques, c. 1770.

Agateware
Teapot and cover, with a serpent-modeled handle and lion knop. c. 1740–50.

leaves (later, paper) and a pencil for jotting notes. They were often housed in gold or silver cases and decorated with enamel, jewels, and tortoiseshell.

Aigrette The French word for egret or heron. A decorative hair ornament in the form of, or made to hold, a feather or feathers. They were especially popular in the 18th and 19th centuries, but worn earlier with turbans in the Middle East. Mounted in gold or silver and frequently set with diamonds, gems, or pearls, the most popular designs included feathers, plumes, and sprays of flowers.

Air "beading" A decoration most commonly used in the stems of 18th- and 19th-century wine glasses, in the form of small bubbles or "beads" of air of similar size that form a continuous line.

Air twist ■ A decoration used in the stems of 18th-century English drinking glasses in which bubbles of air were deliberately introduced into the glass, pulled into thin columns, and then twisted as necessary to form an internal, often spiraling, pattern.

Ajouré A French word meaning "allowing light through." *Ajouré* is a term for metal objects with a pierced openwork pattern, made by using punches, drills, and chisels. It is used for both functional reasons and decorative effect, especially in jewelry.

Akstafa A village in the Caucasus, the name being applied to a distinctive type of rug made by tribal weavers in the region in the 19th and early 20th centuries. The rugs are finely knotted, with cotton weft and woolen warp. They are immediately recognizable by the presence of large fan-tailed birds (possibly peacocks), which always flank a column of star-shaped medallions, supported by flowerheads and zoomorphic motifs. Designs are always geometric and multicolored with extensive and effective use of white.

Aksu A region in East Turkestan known for the production of carpets and rugs. See KHOTAN and YARKAND.

Alabaster ■ A fine-grained, marblelike form of gypsum. Mostly white, yellow, or red in color, and translucent when thinly cut, it is easily carved and can be polished to a waxlike finish. Although primarily used for small sculptures, especially religious statuary prior to the 17th century, other notable uses have included pedestals and vases.

Alabastron The Greek name for a small bottle or flask used for storing ointments, oils, and perfumes. It had a rounded base, slightly elongated form, and usually two small loop handles on the sides. Early glass examples from around 300 BCE to 100 CE were CORE FORMED and often had colored trailed decoration. See PERFUME BOTTLE.

Albany pattern First mass-produced in the 1880s, this popular style of silver FLATWARE and cutlery is characterized by fanned and fluted handles. They were an affordable alternative to the 18th-century ONSLOW pattern.

Albany slip ■ A rich brown glaze added to the interior of an American CROCK to render the vessel impervious to liquid. It was named after the upstate New York capital city, but was used throughout the northeastern states.

Albarelli ■ An Italian word of obscure origin given to pharmacy jars, usually of a waisted cylindrical shape. Probably originating in the Middle East, they were made from tin-glazed earthenware in Italy, Spain, and the Netherlands from the 15th century onward. They usually had a label bearing the name of the drug contained inside, and were often made in sets for the pharmacies of monasteries. Some had a groove around the neck so that a parchment cover could be tied on.

Albert A metal watch chain with a bar at one end for securing in a buttonhole, and a swiveling attachment at the other to hold a pocket or fob watch. The article was given its name in 1845, when a jeweler presented an example to Prince Albert, Queen Victoria's husband. An Albert could also have held a small watch or clock key or a small mechanical pencil.

A

13

Air twist
Wine glass, on multi-spiral air twist stem. c. 1750.

Alabaster
German bust of a child in alabaster, c. 1910. 6¼ inches (16 cm) high.

Albany slip
Albany slip glazed jug, impressed "E. Norton & Co. Bennington, Vt." c. 1880.

Albarelli
Pair of Sicilian blue and white albarelli. 17th century.

A

Albert pattern Named after Prince Albert and produced from 1840 onward, this classic style of silver FLATWARE and cutlery has a curving border of scrolls around the handles, which terminate in foliate motifs.

Albisola potteries A northern Italian center of MAIOLICA and FAIENCE production that started in the 17th and 18th centuries with the nearby towns of Savona and Genoa. Although little is known of their products, the Grossi, Corradi, and Levantino families are known to have worked there, producing wares decorated in a free and flowing way, with polychrome figures in landscapes with flowers and trees. In the early years, blue and later HIGH TEMPERATURE COLORS were used. The mark was the Pharos (lighthouse of antiquity in Alexandria). Maiolica is still made in the area.

Album quilt ■ Also known as friendship or autograph quilts, album quilts were made in the US during the mid-19th century. They were made up of a number of separate sections of appliqué patchwork, each worked by various individuals. Often each block was designed by its creator. The finished quilt was frequently presented as a token of friendship, support, or love.

Alcaraz An important carpet-weaving center from the mid-15th to the end of the 17th century in southwest Spain. It was famous for the 15th-century Admiral

heraldic carpet, woven for Don Fadrique Enriquez, 26th Admiral of Castille, bearing his armorial in three square panels. Typical features include Anatolian geometric motifs, kufic script, and armorials of Spanish nobility. Turkish carpets from the 15th and 16th centuries were also imitated. Examples exist with Holbein designs. In the 16th century patterns became more European in character, featuring wreaths of oak leaves and acorns, vines, and crowns. Italian and contemporary 16th-century textiles were also a great influence. Deep reds were used in the 15th century, which became lighter in the 16th, with yellows, blues, and ivory being typical later colors. The knot in these carpets is distinctive and is tied around alternate single warps in offset rows.

Alcock, Samuel & Co. ■ Based at Cobridge, Staffordshire (1828–53), and at Burslem (1830–59), this firm made general pottery and bone china and some good PORCELLANEOUS animal models. It used printed, painted, and impressed marks of Samuel Alcock & Co., S.A. & Co., and S. Alcock & Co.

Alcora pottery ■ This Spanish factory started by making faience around 1727, and the French potter and painter Joseph Olerys from MOUSTIERS worked there from 1727 to 1737. Lustered pottery was made from 1749 to a recipe brought from Manises in Valencia. A great variety of wares was produced, the

earliest being in the style of Moustiers, particularly Bérain, including table centerpieces, candlesticks, CORNUCOPIAE, statues, animals, and table services. The factory continued to make faience until 1780, when it moved into the manufacture of cream-colored earthenware in the English style. In the 19th century the factory switched production to TRANSFER-PRINTED ware, but it eventually closed in 1895. The mark was a capital "A," impressed and painted in red, brown, and black. Another mark, "Fab. De Aranda A," in colors is also known.

Alder A durable hardwood from a wetlands tree native to northern Europe. Pale brown in color, it carves well and was employed, most notably, for TREEN and 18th- and 19th-century country furniture.

Ale glass ■ A type of flute-shaped English drinking glass, designed to hold small quantities of the very potent ale of the 17th to early 19th centuries. Early examples had short stems and were known as short or dwarf ale glasses. From the late 17th century they became taller with longer stems. The bowls are often engraved with barley or hop motifs, and can be WRYTHEN or contain an air twist.

Ale warmer A copper or brass pan with a wooden or iron handle that was put in a fire to warm ale or prepare mulled ale. It is usually boot-, shoe-, or cone-shaped and was introduced in the 18th century in

Album quilt
Pieced and appliquéd cotton album quilt. c. 1840.

Alcock, Samuel & Co.
One of a pair of Alcock and Co. Staffordshire spaniels. c. 1840.

Alcock, Samuel & Co.
Staffordshire Warwick Castle pastille burner with detachable top. c1840.

England. Reproductions from the 19th and 20th centuries are more common today.

Alençon A town in Normandy, France, known since the mid-17th century for the production of needle lace, typified by the use of horsehair around motifs and an hexagonal mesh of twisted linen threads. From the mid- to late 17th century, desirable and expensive Venetian lace was imitated and perfected with assistance from immigrant Venetian lacemakers, and the town became part of the Royal French lace workshops under Jean-Baptiste Colbert, the finance minister for Louis XIV. The demand for lace declined after the French Revolution, but production continued, with demand rising again under Napoleon and styles growing in complexity during the late 19th century. A school was founded in 1903 to preserve lacemaking traditions, and the town continues to produce lace today.

Alentour Literally meaning "surrounding." A style of tapestry weaving first introduced at the GOBELINS factory in the early 18th century, becoming popular by the mid-18th century. Typically, a central figurative scene, characteristically feathery in style and appearing like a painting, is surrounded by a wide, elaborately scrolling border imitating a gilded wood frame, with floral swags and architectural elements.

Alexandrite A variety of the hardstone chrysoberyl, alexandrite is a rare and valuable gemstone because it changes color from bluish green in daylight to raspberry red in artificial light. Principal sources include Russia, Brazil, Sri Lanka, and Tanzania. Synthetic corundum is frequently mistaken for it.

Alexandrite glass ■ 1. Late 19th- and early 20th-century decorative glass with a multicolored surface, shading from amber to deep pink and purple. Each area is successively reheated to create the effect, in much the same way as AMBERINA glass. It was named after the hardstone ALEXANDRITE. It was first made around 1900 in Britain by Thomas WEBB & Son. 2. A dichroic material—it changes color from mauve to green, depending on the light. It was formulated by Josef Riedel c. 1930 in Czechoslovakia.

Alhambresque An adjective from the name of the palace in Granada, southern Spain, built for the Moorish kings during the 13th and 14th centuries. It refers to large vases with pear-shaped bodies and double wing handles, decorated in blue and gold luster in the Arab style that was known at the Alhambra.

Alia certosina A geometric mosaic inlay, named after the Certosa di Pavia monastery in Italy, and incorporating polygonal pieces of wood, ivory, bone, metal, and MOTHER-OF-PEARL. Popular in northern Italy in the 15th century, it was revived in Italy in the mid-19th century

when it was often used on furniture in the Moorish or North African style.

Allen, Robert (1745–1835) An English porcelain painter who started work at the LOWESTOFT porcelain factory as a painter in underglaze blue when he was only 12 years old. He later became foreman of the factory, and eventually, manager of the works.

Allison, Michael (c. 1785–1855) An American cabinet-maker of the FEDERAL period, active in New York City from around 1800 to 1847. His work combines the elegance of French taste with the grace of English Regency and is often compared with that of his better-known rival, Duncan PHYFE. Examples of his work are rare and highly prized.

Alloa glassworks A Scottish factory established in 1750 in Alloa and known for its production of bottles for ale and other beverages. It was one of several glassworks at the time to produce luxury goods using lower-quality materials to avoid duties on fine glass. In 1955 it became part of United Glass, and it continues to produce today.

Alloy ■ Two or more different metals combined chemically through melting to produce a "new" metal with more suitable or tailored physical properties. Alloys are intended to have properties that are more desirable than those of their

Ale glass
Drawn trumpet hops and barley ale glass. c. 1780.

Alexandrite glass
Alexandrite compote with blue to amber shading.

Alloy
Trifari tulip pin of lightweight silver-colored alloy. 1950s.

A

components. Almost all metals found in the decorative arts are alloys, including various gold alloys, STERLING SILVER, BRASS, BRONZE, and PEWTER.

Altenburg pottery ■ A type of STONEWARE made at Altenburg, Saxony, from the early 17th to the mid-18th century. Typical wares included tankards and jugs decorated with allegorical reliefs and coats of arms, sometimes with a characteristic pale brown glaze and applied BEAD decoration.

Aluminum A silvery white metal that is extracted from bauxite. Lightweight, malleable, and resistant to corrosion, aluminum was first discovered in 1825 and introduced generally in 1855, being used industrially first. In the 1920s it was used for such items as ART DECO cocktail equipment, ashtrays, and, occasionally, jewelry, and in the 1930s for Modernist furniture (for example, by Donald DESKEY).

Amatory jewelry ■ Rings, brooches, and other jewelry symbolizing sentiment and love, often with personal inscriptions. These were commonly given as love tokens from the 17th to the late 19th century. Early examples included the true lovers' knot, the POSY RING, and the "fede" ring, where two hands are clasped together symbolizing betrothal or friendship. Amatory jewelry became especially popular during the Victorian period, when figures such as Cupid were produced alongside less obvious symbolism such as combinations of certain gems that indicated hidden messages.

Amber ■ A hard fossilized resin exuded from coniferous trees that grew in the Oligocene age (30–50 million years ago). The more common variety is Baltic, ranging in color from a cloudy yellow to a rich orange-red, and from opaque to translucent in clarity. Other examples include Burmese, Sicilian, and Romanian. Amber is prized for its beauty, and since antiquity has been used variously for jewelry, *objets d'art*, and the decoration of furniture. It declined in popularity in the 18th century but was revived in the Victorian period. Amber may contain embedded insects or plants, although these can be introduced artificially.

Amberg ■ A town in Bavaria, Germany, where a FAIENCE factory was founded in 1759 by Simon Hetzendorfer, producing cream-colored EARTHENWARE and HARDPASTE PORCELAIN from 1790. In around 1850 it acquired molds from LUDWIGSBURG porcelain works, from which reproductions were made. It closed in 1910.

Amberg, Adolf (1874–1913) A German sculptor and metalworker, now remembered mainly for his work as a designer of sculptural porcelain figures. Between 1894 and 1904 he worked at Bruckmann & Sohn of Heilbronn, Germany, where he designed decorative ornaments and silver tableware. At the International Exhibition in Paris in 1900, a large silver fountain designed by Amberg in association with the architect Otto Rieth was displayed. In 1904 he designed 16 exotic figures for the "marriage procession" themed table centerpiece made for the wedding of the German crown prince. The designs were later made by the BERLIN Porcelain Factory and exhibited to acclaim at the 1911 Berlin Art Exhibition.

Amberina ■ Colored glass tableware and decorative pieces, made from a heat-sensitive glass mixture containing colloidal gold. The primary color is amber, but when the top area is reheated in the furnace, the gold turns the amber to a graduated ruby red. Patented by Joseph LOCKE in the US in 1883, the majority of American Amberina glass was made by the LIBBEY GLASS CO. Red bases indicate Reverse Amberina and opaque, white CASED GLASS examples indicate rare Plated Amberina. It was also produced under license in England by SOWERBY, and by Blenko in the US, in the 20th century.

Amberoid A material used to imitate AMBER, made up of small fragments of amber, sometimes in combination with other materials, that have been fused together using heat and pressure. It can be differentiated from amber by the appearance of a flow structure.

Amboyna ■ A decorative hardwood, varying in color from a pale reddish brown to orange, with mottled figuring and a

Altenburg pottery
Brown salt glaze stoneware humpen with polychrome painted decoration in relief.

Faux ruby, emerald, garnet, amethyst, ruby, and diamond
Amatory jewelry
Victorian love knot "regard" pin with faux stones. c. 1860.

Amber
Amber necklace. 20th century.

Amberg
Amberg jug. c. 1770.

tightly curled grain. It was imported from the Moluccas in the Malaysian archipelago and used for BANDING, INLAY, and VENEERS on high-quality 18th- and early 19th-century furniture. From the mid-19th century it was in more common use and also employed on lesser-quality pieces.

Amelung, Johann Frederick (1741–98)
A German glassmaker who emigrated to the US and founded the Amelung Glassworks, also known as the Etna Glassworks, the New Bremen Glassworks, and the American Glass Manufactory, near Frederick, Maryland, in 1784. The small works produced mostly window glass, bottles, and from around 1785 tableware, including rare engraved and colored examples comparable to contemporary BOHEMIAN glass. The works were sold in 1795, and closed during the 1810s due to commercial failure.

Amen glass
A mid-18th-century wine glass commemorating the Scottish Jacobite royal cause. The bowl has DIAMOND-POINT ENGRAVED decoration of a crown, verses from a Jacobite anthem, and the word "Amen." Only 35 genuine Amen glasses from the period are known to exist. Numerous copies have since been produced. See JACOBITE GLASS.

American Belleek
See BELLEEK, AMERICAN.

American China Manufactory
See BONNIN AND MORRIS.

American Chippendale ■
A style of formal furniture with certain features unique to North America, with makers active from around 1750 to Revolutionary War. The name derives from Thomas CHIPPENDALE, who achieved renown through the publication of his design ideas in the *Gentleman and Cabinet-maker's Director*, first circulated in 1754 and widely read in the US. Many American makers interpreted the style, ignoring most of Chippendale's Gothic details such as blind-fret carving and cluster column legs, and CHINOISERIES such as pagodas and "Chinamen." The result was a genre that compares to contemporary George III mahogany furniture, but is slightly larger, with carved Rococo elements that are bolder and more pronounced than on English furniture.

Standards of manufacture are generally high but vary widely according to region and individual maker, as do the wood species employed and the treatment of decorative forms such as BALL-AND-CLAW. Such variations are the subject of considerable documentation. The introduction of the BLOCK-FRONT form by the school of John GODDARD in Newport, Rhode Island, exemplifies the early development of this style, which was fully developed by cabinet-makers in New England, particularly Boston and Salem in Massachusetts, New York City, and Philadelphia. By the 1760s Philadelphia had over 100 cabinet-makers, notably Thomas AFFLECK, Benjamin

RANDOLPH, and William SAVERY, and produced some of the finest American Chippendale furniture, particularly chairs. However, many individual makers are now lost to anonymity. The name is used less today than in the past and many scholars prefer more precise terms, including American Rococo.

American Colonial
See COLONIAL STYLE.

American Federal
See FEDERAL STYLE.

American Flint Glassworks
An American glassworks established in 1769 by Henry William Stiegel, a German ironmaster and glassmaker who emigrated to the US in 1750. He set up three glassworks producing tableware in Pennsylvania in the 1760s, including the Manheim Glassworks, established in 1763. All his factories closed in 1774 due to financial problems and competition. Examples of Stiegel glass are difficult to authenticate and widely faked. Forms are comparable to period Bohemian vessels, made in low-lead, greenish gray glass, often with engraved or wheel-cut decoration.

American football memorabilia
See FOOTBALL, AMERICAN.

American Pottery Co.
A small factory established in Jersey City, New Jersey, by the Scottish immigrant David Henderson and his brothers in 1828,

Amberina
An American Blenko amberina glass vase, model 6223. c. 1962.

Amboyna
Amboyna wood showing characteristic swirling figuring.

Thumb molded rectangular top

American Chippendale
Chester County, Pennsylvania Chippendale walnut dressing table. c. 1770.

American Chippendale
Chippendale cherrywood chest-on-chest, North Shore, MA. c. 1775.

A

and active until 1854. The main products (usually unmarked) were utility wares in robust EARTHENWARE with yellow or ROCKINGHAM (streaky brown) glaze, and some printed ware.

Amorino From the Italian *amorino* (little cupid). Winged CHERUB, used in Italian RENAISSANCE ornament and BAROQUE work, commonly on porcelain, bronze, and wood-carving. Sometimes only the winged head is used. Derived from Classical sources, a well-known series appears on a Pompeii wall-painting.

Amphora ■ From the Greek *amphoreus* (pitcher). A two-handled jar with a narrow neck, used in Classical times to carry oil, wine, and water. Jars of amphora shape were made in the Rhineland from 720 CE to 1190 CE, to export Rhenish wine. With the rediscovery of Classical sites in the early 18th century, the shape appears as a decorative motif, for instance, in NEOCLASSICAL silverware and on furniture.

Amphora pottery ■ A Bohemian pottery and porcelain factory founded in 1892 in Turn-Teplitz as Riessner, Stellmacher & Kessel (R.S.K.). The factory made porcelain figures but was chiefly known for earthenware Art Nouveau vases. The factory stopped production some time during World War II.

Ampulla The Latin name for a type of small vessel made throughout the Roman Empire and used for storing oils and perfumes. Typically, it has a flat base, a round or ovoid body, and an elongated neck with one or two handles.

Amstel porcelain factory In 1771 Johannes de Mol bought a porcelain factory in WEESP and moved it to Oude Loosdrecht in the Netherlands in 1771. When he died in 1782, the factory became a limited company, and it was moved to Amstel in 1784, where it continued until 1820. Sometimes called Oude Amstel, it made fine porcelain in the style of MEISSEN and SÈVRES and used "Amstel" as a mark.

An hua ■ A term used in Chinese ceramics meaning secret or veiled decoration, the designs being visible through transmitted light. Produced either by incising the design into the porcelain before GLAZING and FIRING or by painting in white SLIP on the porcelain body, the technique was used in the early MING DYNASTY (1368–1644) and revived in the QING DYNASTY (1644–1912), particularly during the reign of the YONGZHENG emperor (1723–35).

Anchor escapement An ESCAPEMENT mechanism of a CLOCK incorporating an arm shaped like an anchor, with two pallets (catches). Developed in the mid-17th century, it was used in combination with the PENDULUM in most clocks by around 1800, as a more accurate form of regulation than the VERGE ESCAPEMENT.

Anchor motif An ornamental motif associated with a marine or commercial activity. Also seen as a repeating dart or arrowhead device frequently used in the enrichment of OVOLO or ASTRAGAL moldings. With a rope, it is called a "fouled anchor." See EGG AND DART.

Andirons ■ The forerunners of the fire basket and also known as fire-dogs, they comprise a pair of iron rests that stand in a hearth to contain logs. When ornamental, their front edges are often fashioned from brass, polished steel, or, more rarely, PAKTONG or silver. Examples of the latter date back to the mid-17th century.

Anemometer An instrument used to measure the velocity or the force of wind or air currents. A number of blades arranged in a fan, or a circlet of cups mounted on arms, are placed in the wind with the result being displayed on a dial. Portable anemometers were developed in the mid-19th century.

Aneroid barometer A type of BAROMETER that does not use fluid but has a small metal vacuumed capsule or bellows that expands or contracts with changes in atmospheric pressure. Invented by the French engineer Lucien Vidie in 1843, this barometer became more popular than the earlier mercury barometer from the late 19th century.

Amphora
Wedgwood black basalt amphora, painted with "Etruscan" enamels. c. 1800.

Amphora pottery
Amphora vase, model no. 15069. c. 1920.

An hua
An 18th-century an hua (veiled decoration) stem cup.

Andirons
Pair of brass and wrought iron andirons. Late 18th century.

Angarano pottery A group of factories active in the 18th century, up until the 1780s, near Bassano in northern Italy, producing CREAMWARE groups and figures. Family names involved in Angarano pottery include Manardi and Moretti. See NOVE.

Angell family An English 19th-century firm of silversmiths. Joseph II was made a freeman of the Goldsmiths' Company in 1804 and entered his first mark in London in 1804. His best-known work is the Battle of Issus Shield (1828), richly embossed and chased with a scene representing the battle between Alexander the Great and Darius of Persia in 333 BCE. Joseph III, his son, took over the family firm in 1849. He specialized in richly chased and enameled table centerpieces, tea and coffee sets, claret jugs, and other domestic pieces, typically decorated with motifs such as scrolls and strapwork.

Angle barometer A type of barometer made in the 18th century, in which the upper part of the mercury-filled tube is set horizontally at an angle. A modified form of the STICK BAROMETER, the angle barometer gives a more accurate reading as the mercury has to move over a greater distance for the same change in atmospheric pressure. Surviving items are rare as this barometer was never very popular because of its awkward shape.

Angling memorabilia ▣ Fishing with rod and line has been practiced from earliest times, but surviving items tend to date from the 19th century at the earliest. This covers a great variety of items, including reels, artificial spinning baits, flies, trade catalogs, art (paintings and prints from the 17th century to the present day), carved wooden trophies, stuffed fish in cases, rods, and accessories.

Anglo-Indian furniture ▣ A collective term for European furniture forms—chairs, tables, and CARCASS furniture—made in India from the mid-18th century, and throughout the 19th century, for both wealthy Indian and European clients. Although English in shape, the furniture was made from local hardwoods such as EBONY, and often extensively carved with Indian motifs such as elephants and elaborate foliage, and decorated with ivory inlays. See VIZAGAPATNAM.

Anglo-Japanese furniture ▣ A collective term for furniture made from around 1870 in Europe and North America, following Japan's reopening o the West, and reflecting the ensuing contemporary fashion for Japanese prints and artifacts. It contributed to the style of the AESTHETIC MOVEMENT and was often made of BAMBOO or EBONIZED wood, with MOTHER-OF-PEARL INLAY and painted panels incorporating Japanese motifs such as birds and flowers. One of its best-known exponents was E. W. GODWIN, who made exclusive ebonized furniture. At the other end of the market were inexpensive bedroom suites, writing tables, and chairs incorporating Japanese motifs.

Anglo-Moorish furniture ▣ A collective term for furniture produced in Britain in the late 19th century in response to the fashion for smoking rooms and exotic Moorish interiors, as exemplified at Leighton House, London. It was pioneered in Britain by H. & J. Cooper, who produced chairs with elaborately carved paneled backs, and by 1884 LIBERTY was retailing Anglo-Moorish chairs, tables, and hat stands.

Angoulême porcelain factory A factory started in 1780 in the Rue de Bondi in Paris under the protection of the Duc d' Angoulême. Porcelain with simple decoration was made as well as some more elaborate pieces, with JASPERED decoration simulating AGATE and TORTOISESHELL with gilt borders. The factory closed in 1828.

Angoulême sprig A name given to a simple pattern of cornflowers, often found on Parisian Angoulême but also used in other factories, especially at the English DERBY factory. While most porcelain factories were not permitted to copy the rich SÈVRES style, the Paris factory of the Duc d'Angoulême was one of nine Parisian studios exempted, and combined several colors and gilding.

Aniline dyes The first synthetic dyes, accidentally discovered by British chemist William H. Perkin in 1856, produced from

Angling memorabilia
Hardy turntable centerpin reel. 1937–39.

Anglo-Indian furniture
William IV Anglo-Indian rosewood work table.

Anglo-Japanese furniture
Ebonized mantel clock, in the Anglo-Japanese style, inset with satsuma tiles. c. 1885.

Anglo-Moorish furniture
Arts & Crafts Liberty & Co. walnut plant stand, in Anglo-Moorish style. c. 1890.

A

20

the oxidization of aniline, a by-product of coal tar, and used to color carpets and other fabrics. Early colors ranged from violets through to deep pinks, including Perkin's mauve. A tendency to run and fade saw them supplanted by color-fast CHROME DYES in the early 20th century.

Animal furniture A form of furniture made in the late 19th century, in which taxidermists and furniture-makers collaborated to create pieces from dead animals and birds. Typical examples included hollowed-out elephants' feet as wastepaper baskets, hall lamps fashioned from stuffed bears and monkeys, and lamp bases made from stuffed birds.

Animaliers, Les ■ A group of mid-19th-century French sculptors, led by Antoine-Louis BARYE, who specialized in naturalistic representations of animals. Produced in cast-bronze limited editions, these works were conceived in reaction to the Classical themes then dominating French sculpture. One of the most prolific and successful Animalier sculptors was Pierre-Jules Mêne. The term may now describe any sculptor making small animal bronzes.

Annaberg potteries A group of factories in Saxony, Germany, known for a dark brown SALT-GLAZED STONEWARE enameled in colors over relief-molded decoration, produced from around 1630 until the early 18th century. Typical shapes are HUMPEN and APOSTLE JUGS, often

with ARMORIAL motifs. Wares are often confused with those of the earlier factory of Kreussen, near Bayreuth.

Annagrun See URANIUM GLASS.

Annamese ware See VIETNAMESE POTTERY.

Annealing A technique for stabilizing glass or metal. Objects are heated in an annealing oven and allowed to cool at a slow and uniform rate. This alters the arrangement of molecules in the material and makes it more resistant to cracking.

Annealing oven See LEHR.

Annulet An architectural term for a narrow flat FILLET or band encircling a column. It is also used in heraldry for a small ring in a coat of arms.

Ansbach Both faience and porcelain were produced in Ansbach, Bavaria, south of Nuremberg (its 18th-century name was Onolzback). Faience of fine quality had een made here since 1710, but in 1757 the Margrave Karl Alexander opened a porcelain factory, bringing in the expertise of some MEISSEN workers. It was soon successful and in 1762 moved into the princely hunting lodge, Bruckberg. Johann Friedrich Kändler, a cousin of the famous Meissen modeler Johann Joachim KÄNDLER, was the artistic director, and the factory flourished between 1758 and 1777. The porcelain body has a

brilliant whiteness and the painting, by such artists as Scholhammer and Stenglein, is particularly good. Flower painters included such artists as Kahl and Schreimuller. Ansbach also sold large amounts of porcelain to the factory at The Hague from 1777 to 1790, where it was marked with their signatory stork. The business was in private ownership from about 1807, and finally closed in 1860.

Anthemion ■ A Classical ornament based on the ACANTHUS flower, but similar to a type of PALMETTE resembling the honeysuckle flower and leaf. The anthemion was commonly used in Greek and Roman architecture for ornamental banding on friezes, architraves, cornices, and the necks of Ionic capitals. Frequently combined with other motifs, it enjoyed renewed popularity in the 18th century and was fashionable for the decorative arts during the NEOCLASSICAL period.

Antimacassar ■ A decorative covering cloth thrown over the backs of upholstered sofas and chairs to protect the fabric from stains from the sitter's hair. It takes its name from macassar oil, a hair treatment for men during the 19th century. Victorian examples tended to be crocheted, while earlier 18th-century examples tended to be in silk.

Antimagnetic watch A watch made of nonmagnetic metal or in which the MOVEMENT is protected from magnetic flux, which can be particularly strong in industrial or military environments, by a

Typically lustrous bronze patina

Les Animaliers
"Elephant de cochine" bronze figure by Antoine-Louis Barye. c. 1860.

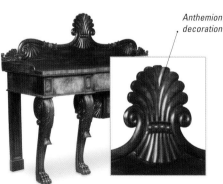

Anthemion decoration

Anthemion
Irish Regency mahogany sideboard with a scrolling back board and anthemion motif.

Made in Italy

Antimacassar
New York World's Fair woven and printed antimacassar. 1939.

soft inner case. Many parts of a movement are made from steel and are therefore subject to being magnetized or affected by magnetism. This can have an adverse effect on the accuracy of a watch. Swiss maker Tissot introduced the first antimagnetic watch around 1930.

Antiquities ■ The term used to describe an object or monument that dates from ancient times and has a historical, cultural, social, or decorative value. It is specifically applied to items from ancient Greece, Rome, the Middle East, East Asia, and South America.

Antwerp lace See FLEMISH LACE.

Aogai A Japanese LACQUERWORK technique, introduced to Japan from China in the 14th century, in which small pieces of MOTHER-OF-PEARL from the *Haliotis* mollusk are inlaid into a LACQUER surface.

Apostle jug A jug molded in relief with figures of the Twelve Apostles in niches around the body, found especially in 17th-century German earthenware (for example, Kreussen) and in the 19th century during the RENAISSANCE REVIVAL.

Apostle spoon ■ A silver spoon (pewter and brass examples also exist) whose stem ends in the small cast figure of one of the Twelve Apostles or the "Master" (Christ). Rare complete sets of 13 exist but individual spoons are far more commonly available

today. Each saint holds an emblem or symbol of his martyrdom (for example, St. Peter with a key), but these are often damaged or missing. Size and poor-quality casting can also make identification difficult. They were made throughout Europe from 1500 to about 1700. However, many apostle coffee spoons were mass-produced in Britain in the 19th and 20th centuries.

Apothecary jar ■ A glass or earthenware jar used in an apothecary's or druggist's shop, or in the apothecary of a monastery. Globular jars with a handle and a spout were for "wet" drugs, while those of cylindrical shape were for "dry" drugs. The name of the drug was given on an attached label. See ALBARELLI.

Apple wood See FRUITWOOD.

Appliqué ■ From the French *appliquer* (applied). A technique in which decorative pieces of one material are stitched onto a foundation of another material. The seams of appliquéd motifs are often in the form of decorative stitching or enhanced with braids.

Aprey pottery A faience factory in the Haute Marne region of France, founded in 1744 by Jacques Lallemont, Baron d'Aprey, and Joseph Lallemont de Villehaut (who is said to have also produced porcelain, but this has not been authenticated). The painter Protais Pidoux from MENNECY was responsible for lively floral decoration. The best wares date from about 1770 to

1790 with the work of François Olliver from NEVERS and the decorators Jacques Jarry and Antoine Mege. In the mid- to late 19th century, earlier molds were reused. Marks are "Ap," "APR," "AP," and, rarely, "APREY." The factory closed in the late 19th century.

Apron ■ Also known as a skirt, it is a shaped (often carved, pierced, or decorated) section of wood located beneath the seat rail of a chair or settee, the FRIEZE rail of a table, or the base of the framework of a piece of CASE FURNITURE.

Apt pottery A French faience and earthenware factory founded in 1728 by César Moulin at Le Castelet, making wares in the English style, including figures and yellow and brown marbled and AGATEWARE. It remained in the Moulin family until its closure in 1852. Products were of fine quality, with shapes often inspired by silver wares. Other potteries opened in the region, the best known being those of Elzéar Bennet and La Veuve Arnoux. The area is still a pottery-making center today.

Aquamanile A medieval bronze or brass EWER, to hold water for washing the hands during meals or religious ceremonies. Derived from earlier Middle Eastern pieces, the finest European examples were produced from the 12th to the 15th century in the Meuse valley, northern France, and are in the form of lions, stags, mythical beasts such as dragons and GRIFFINS, or mounted knights.

A
21

Antiquities
Roman marble head of a female. 3rd century CE.

Gilt figure with sacred dove

Apostle spoon
James I apostle spoon, St James the Greater, by John Saunders, London. 1615.

Apothecary jar
An Italian polychrome albarello apothecary jar, with oak leaf decoration. c. 1600.

Appliqué
Bruges lace table cloth, with appliquéd silk. Early 20th century.

Pendant finials

Apron
Queen Anne walnut-veneered dressing table with a shaped apron. Early 18th century.

Aquamarine A variety of the gemstone beryl, ranging in color from pale green to the valuable deep sea blue or bright sky blue, the latter frequently obtained or accentuated by heating. Aquamarine is highly transparent, with blue tending to supersede green in desirability. Crystals are mined primarily in Brazil, but are also found in Russia, Madagascar, and some parts of the US. Imitations include synthetic blue spinel, blue topaz, and glass.

Aquatint A popular printing technique from the 1770s onward, particularly for landscapes, so named because the overall effect is of watercolor wash. Finely speckled gradations of tone are achieved by evenly coating the printing plate with powdered resin before immersion in acid. Lighter areas are created by stopping the acid attack on the plate with varnish, and darker areas by greater exposure to or biting of the acid.

Arab Hall, The See ARABIAN STYLE.

Arabesque A pattern of stylized interlaced foliage using fanciful and intricate combinations of flowing lines, flowers, tendrils, spirals, knots, and zigzags. Contemporary with STRAPWORK, developed at Fontainebleau, France, in the mid-16th century, the arabesque originates from the Middle East and features strongly in European decorative ornament until the early 17th century. Craftsmen came from all over the Middle East and settled in Venice, producing densely decorated, engraved, and inlaid metalwork. Known as Venetian Saracenic, the style spread through published engravings and was used to decorate metalwork, pottery, marquetry furniture, jewelry, and lace.

Arabian style ■ Ornament fashionable in 19th-century Europe, featuring motifs drawn from North African and Middle Eastern cultures. Decorative patterns such as ARABESQUES from Islamic metalwork, textiles, and ceramics had been used in Europe since the Renaissance, but interest was renewed in the mid-19th century following the visits of such leading painters as Frederick, Lord Leighton to Arab countries. The best-known Western interpretation of an Islamic interior is the Arab Hall at Leighton House, London, featuring vividly colored and patterned tiles and richly carved wooden screens.

Arad, Ron ■ (born 1951) An Israeli-born British architect and designer. After studying architecture in London, he founded his own practice, One Off, in 1981 with Caroline Thorman. His highly individualistic early designs such as the Rover Chair of 1981, combined existing objects with a Post-Industrialist feel, creating "art" furniture. His later designs, which are more suitable for mass production and are more sculptural in feel, include the Well Tempered Chair of 1986 and the Tom Vac stacking chair of 1997. Both are manufactured by Vitra. Arad is also currently head of product design at the Royal College of Art, London, and has undertaken architectural commissions such as the Tel Aviv Opera House (1994) through his current company Ron Arad Associates.

Arbor A small revolving shaft or axle, usually made of steel, in a CLOCK or watch mechanism and on which a wheel, PINION, or lever is mounted.

Arcade Manufacturing Co. ■ A prolific American manufacturer in Freeport, Illinois, producing CAST-IRON toys from 1885 until 1943. From the early 1920s Arcade specialized in highly detailed, accurate road vehicles, including the famous Yellow Cab. Over 250 different toys, usually single or two-piece castings (riveted together), were each made in a variety of sizes, fitted with turning wheels, and finished in a single or dual color paint scheme and decorated with their name on a transfer.

Arcadian pottery ■ The trade name used on souvenir made by the firm Arkinstall & Sons Ltd. of Trent Bridge Pottery, Stoke on Trent, Staffordshire, from 1904 to 1924. They made inexpensive wares in the style of W. H. Goss, were taken over by Robinson & Leadbeater in 1908, then by A. J. Robinson & Sons, and later by Cauldon Ltd. in 1925. The Arcadian mark disappeared in 1937.

Arcading A series of linked arches, pointed or round-headed, and occasionally interlaced, supported on columns or piers. The arcade may be freestanding, as in covered walks and

Arabian style
De Morgan tile panel made for the "Arabia Companion frieze." c. 1890.

Arad, Ron
Rod Arad/One Off Ltd. car seat with headrest in black leather, mounted on a steel frame.

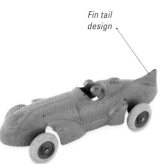

Fin tail design

Arcade Manufacturing Co.
Arcade cast-iron racer. 1936.

Arcadian pottery
Arcadian model of a fireplace, with the arms of Clacton-on-Sea.

cloisters, serving a decorative and structural purpose. Blind arcades, which are attached to a wall, are purely decorative, and are also a popular ornament on chair backs and the panels of chests.

Arcanist In alchemy, a general term meaning an initiate into a secret sought by alchemists, originally the search for a method of synthesizing gold. After the discovery of PORCELAIN in Europe by BÖTTGER in the early 18th century, it was used particularly in reference to the formula for making porcelain.

Archambo, Peter A HUGUENOT of unknown birthplace and date who became a Free Goldsmith (silversmith) in London in 1720. He produced a range of high-quality domestic silverware, first in a simple style and later in a French Rococo style, until about 1750, when his son Peter entered his first mark after his apprenticeship with Paul De LAMERIE.

Architect's table ■ A form of table, most commonly made in walnut or mahogany, introduced in the early 18th century for artists and draftsmen. They have hinged leaves or retractable slides, and feature either an adjustable—often double-hinged— top, an easel top, or an adjustable rising top. They also often incorporate adjustable brass candle stands to provide additional light on the work surface.

Architrave A term that describes the lowest section of the upper part, or entablature, of an architectural order. It can also refer to the MOLDING around a window, door, or other opening in a building or piece of furniture.

Arequipa pottery ■ Following the San Francisco earthquake of 1906 and a related tuberculosis epidemic, Dr. Philip King Brown founded a sanatorium in Marin County, California, as a country retreat for urban young women needing to recuperate from the disease. Inspired by one of the tenets of the ARTS AND CRAFTS Movement, that handicrafts had a life-affirming, curative role, patients were encouraged to take up pottery decoration. To maximize the possibilities of commercial success, the Arequipa Sanatorium (*Arequipa* is Peruvian for "place of peace") employed a succession of eminent ceramicists, including Frederick Hürten Rhead, Albert Solon, and Fred Wilde, as directors of the project. A high turnover of patients resulted in decoration of variable quality. However, some of the work—applied to tiles as well as pots and vases—was outstanding, and included luster glazes, carving, and slip-trailing (also known as squeezebag ornament). Production of what is now recognized as a substantial contribution to American Arts and Crafts pottery ceased in 1918.

Argand lamp ■ A type of oil lamp invented in Switzerland in 1784 by Aimé Argand and subsequently manufactured in France, Britain, and the US. The tubular hollow wick, covered with a chimney and fed with oil by a tube from the reservoir, ensured a plentiful air supply, which in turn ensured that the oil burned quickly, producing a bright light.

Argentan lace FRENCH NEEDLE LACE from Argentan in Normandy, similar to ALENÇON lace and also initially produced as part of Colbert's Royal French lace workshops. This fine 17th- and 18th-century lace has delicate floral designs on a hexagonal ground. It was used for the fashion and boudoir flounces popular before the French Revolution and underwent a revival in the 1870s.

Argyll, Argyle ■ Any small lidded jug or container for gravy, often made in silver or Old Sheffield plate, with some means of retaining or producing heat such as hot iron, burner, or hotwater jacket. Named after one of the Dukes of Argyll who had an aversion to cold gravy, these vessels are first recorded around 1760 and enjoyed great favor during the reign of King George III.

Argy-Rousseau, Joseph-Gabriel ■ (1885–1953) A French ceramicist-turned-glassmaker particularly renowned for his colored PÂTE-DE-VERRE and pâte-de-cristal designs, produced in comparatively small numbers from 1914. Such pieces are usually signed "G. Argy-Rousseau." However, he also produced vessels in clear glass decorated with colored enamels, which are signed "G.A.R." He is best known for his ART DECO vases.

A
23

Architect's table
Louis XVI mahogany architect's table stamped "A. Weisweiler." c. 1790.

Arequipa pottery
Arequipa vase embossed with branches of fruits and leaves on a mottled indigo ground.

Argand lamp
One of a pair of gilt, cast-bronze, and cut-glass Argand lamps. c. 1825.

Argyll, Argyle
George III vase-shaped Argyle, by Peter & William Bateman, London. 1806.

Argy-Rousseau, Joseph-Gabriel
Gabriel Argy-Rousseau *pâte-de-verre* vase.

A

Ariel glass ■ A technique developed in 1937 by Edvin Ohrstrom, Gustav Bergqvist, and Vicke LINDSTRAND at the Swedish glass firm ORREFORS. A clear or colored glass body is sandblasted to create INTAGLIO relief patterns of abstract, figurative, or animal subjects. This core is then reheated and encased in another layer of transparent glass, trapping air bubbles in the pattern of the design. This technique was widely adopted by later 20th century studio glassworks. See GRAAL glass.

Arita porcelain factories ■ In the early 17th century, Korean potters settled in and around Arita, in the Hizen province of Japan. Finding abundant local CHINA CLAY and fuel, they established kilns for producing STONEWARE and PORCELAIN.

The earliest Arita porcelain produced between 1620 and 1640 imitates contemporary Chinese wares of the late MING DYNASTY (1368–1644) as well as Korean stoneware. The wares produced before exports began were known as *Shoki-Imari*. In the late 17th century Arita became increasingly important, producing BLUE AND WHITE, IMARI, and KAKIEMON porcelain for export to Europe. These were transported to the port of Imari, shipped to the Dutch trading center at Nagasaki, and then to Europe. Wares included GARNITURES of large vases, dishes, bowls, plates, EWERS, and human and animal figures. The trade reached its zenith around 1700. With increasing competition from the Chinese kilns at JINGDEZHEN and changing tastes in Europe, Japan's export trade declined in importance, although pieces continued to reach the West throughout the 19th century, including wares from other important centers in the Arita region such as HIRADO and NABESHIMA.

Ark A form of English storage furniture, first made in the 13th century and used until the 19th, in the form of a wooden bin or chest. It was constructed usually from pegged split boards of oak or elm, with a canted or roof-shaped lid, and was traditionally used for storing meal or flour.

Armada chest A 19th-century term for a heavy iron-bound strongbox, often with complicated locks and hidden keyholes, which was made in Germany, Austria, and Flanders in the 16th and 17th centuries.

Armadio An Italian term for a cupboard, originally derived from a CASSONE or chest, with two doors instead of a lid. From the 16th century, the armadio developed into a two-tier cupboard with PILASTERS.

Armet A type of helmet that completely enclosed the head, used during the 15th and 16th centuries, along with plate armor. It comprised a skull cap, pivoting visor, opening cheekpieces, and sometimes a circular guard at the back called a rondel.

Armillary sphere A skeletal globe in which circles or hoops represent the horizon, poles, equator, ecliptic, and tropics of Cancer and Capricorn, with a central sphere representing Earth or the Sun. Used for teaching and demonstrating astronomy, globes were often made from pasteboard (stiff cardboard made by masting together layers of paper) or brass. Models vary in size from floor-standing to small portable examples.

Armoire ■ A French term, dating back to the 13th century, for a storage cupboard. Since the 17th century, it has been used more specifically to describe a large, upright LINEN PRESS or CUPBOARD, either with or without shelves, enclosed by a large door or two doors, and often with an internal drawer. Armoires remained in common use until the 20th century and were made in various qualities, from simple provincial examples in FRUITWOOD to more elaborate armoires with decorative INLAY.

Armoire à deux corps A French term for a type of CASE FURNITURE made in two sections for ease of transport, and comprising two cupboards—a larger cupboard beneath a narrower, recessed one. Both have two doors.

Armorial ware ■ Ceramics decorated with a coat of arms, armorials have been popular on European pottery from the RENAISSANCE, with examples seen on Italian

Ariel glass
Ariel vase by Ingeborg Lundin, for Orrefors. 1964.

Arita porcelain
Arita Imari saucer dish. Late 17th century.

Armoire
Provincial French armoire. Late 18th century.

Armorial ware
Chinese Qianlong Lung export enameled porcelain armorial charger. c. 1755.

ART DECO

The best Art Deco is characterized by a clarity of form that is angular and clean, with stylized, striking decoration and of stunning quality. Furniture manufacturers at the upper end of the market concentrated on high-quality pieces veneered in exotic woods such as AMBOYNA and EBONY, combined with IVORY, SHAGREEN, ENAMEL, and LACQUER. After around 1925 they also used new materials such as tubular steel.

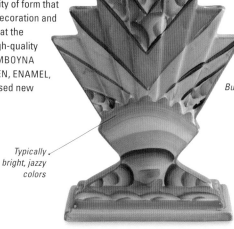

Typically bright, jazzy colors

"Fan" vase
Myott "fan" vase. 1930s.

Butterfly wing costume

Goldscheider figure
Model by Lorenzl, Goldscheider figure of a young woman adopting a stylish pose.

Art Deco poster
Poster depicting the actress Josephine Baker, by Jean Chassaing. 1931.

Boch vases
Pair of Boch Frères Charles Catteau vases.

Platinum brooch
French Art Deco platinum brooch, signed "Paul Billon."

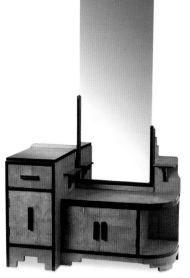

Skyscraper vanity
An American Art Deco "Skyscraper" dressing table in burr maple with ebonized pulls and banding. 1930s.

Side cabinet
Art Deco coromandel veneered side cabinet, by Whytock and Reid, Edinburgh.

MAIOLICA, SLIPWARE, English and Dutch DELFT, and on porcelain from the 18th century. The term is most often associated, however, with CHINESE EXPORT PORCELAIN, often decorated with the arms and crests of Europeans and Americans from the late 17th to the 19th century.

A

26

Armor ■

Equipment and clothing made to protect the body during combat, originally from natural materials such as wood, hide, horn, bone, and textiles. Metals were used from the Bronze Age, and fall into two main categories: "mail" made from interlinked metal rings, and "plate" made from rigid, shaped pieces of metal. The use of armor declined with increasing use of firearms and artillery from the 1650s and the need for the swift deployment of forces.

Arnhem pottery

Founded by Johannes van Kerckhoff in 1755, this factory at Arnhem in Holland was taken over by J. Hanau in 1756. Arnhem pottery made a type of TIN-GLAZED EARTHENWARE, usually decorated in blue and formerly attributed to Amsterdam. Active until 1773, it produced wares in the manner of DELFT, using a deep blue and a good-quality manganese, as well as pottery similar to those of STRASBOURG painted with ENAMEL COLORS. Scenes after Rococo prints were decorated in HIGH TEMPERATURE COLORS. The mark is a cockerel—not to be confused with a similar mark used by CANTAGALLI.

Arnold, John

(1736–99) An eminent English clock- and watchmaker. In 1764 he presented to King George III a watch with repeating work mounted onto a finger ring. His career was dedicated to the advancement of accurate horology and he invented a form of spring detent ESCAPEMENT used in CHRONOMETERS. He was succeeded by his son, John Roger Arnold, also a clock- and watchmaker.

Arnoux, Joseph-Léon F.

See MINTON.

Arraiolos

A Portuguese carpet-making center for the production of woolen embroidered carpets in the Alentejo. The earliest and rarest examples are from the 17th century. Production declined in the 19th century but revived in the 20th century and continues today. Carpets display a range of floral and folkloric motifs, birds, and animals, with early examples being inspired by Persian motifs and later examples by Portuguese folk art.

Arras porcelain factory

A factory in the Pas de Calais, France. It was founded in 1770 by Joseph François Boussomaert of Lille who made SOFT-PASTE PORCELAIN intended to compete with TOURNAI, but produced only medium-quality tableware, mostly decorated in UNDERGLAZE blue. The factory closed in 1790.

Arras tapestry factories

Arras, an ancient tapestry-weaving town in northern France, was once capital of the province of Artois in Burgundy. The term "thread of arras" came to mean the finest quality thread from which tapestries were made. The town was producing HIGH-WARP tapestries as early as the 11th century. The first written reference appeared in 1311 when a Countess of Burgundy ordered "figured cloth" in Arras. In 1394 Arras came into the possession of Burgundian Dukes, who became patrons of the tapestry-weaving industry. The term Arras has become synonymous with Gothic wall hangings; so valuable were they that in 1396 Arras tapestries were traded with Bajazet, Sultan of Turkey, for the lives of captured Burgundian and French nobles. Arras workshops went into decline after the town was ransacked by the French in 1477 and finally closed in the early 16th century.

Art Deco

The Art Deco style was first widely seen at the landmark *Exposition Internationale des Arts Décoratifs et Industriels Modernes* in Paris in 1925, although the term itself was not used until the 1960s. The origins of Art Deco were diverse: art movements such as post-Impressionism, Cubism, Fauvism, and Futurism all had an impact, as did the BALLETS RUSSES, the new jazz music, the excavation of the tomb of Tutankhamen, Tribal Art, and the innovative machines of the time, in particular, new forms of transport such as the automobile and the airplane.

The style evolved from around 1908, and many items accepted as pure Art Deco today, such as objects by Jacques-Emile

Armor
Reproduction suit of armor with fully articulated steel plates. c. 1880.

Art furniture
Ash dressing table with hinged extensions, designed by E. W. Godwin.

Art glass
An unsigned iridescent art glass vase with red heart and vine decoration.

Art glass
Iridescent art glass vase.

RUHLMANN and Paul IRIBE, were of prewar design. The Paris exhibition saw works by leading French designers such as Ruhlmann, René LALIQUE, and André GROULT shown to acclaim, as was silver by Jean PUIFORCAT and Charles CHRISTOFLE, and glass by BACCARAT. Touring exhibitions and immigrant architects and designers introduced the new style to the US, where by the late 1920s it was seen as a more purely American idiom in furniture by such influential designers as Donald DESKEY and Eero SAARINEN. It was ultimately all in the architectural triumph of the "skyscraper" that Art Deco style was assimilated. Exterior shapes were echoed on doors, light fixtures, and murals, and also on furniture such as Paul Frankl's Skyscraper line of the 1930s. A further phase of Art Deco in the US was exemplified by the "streamlining" designs of Norman BEL GEDDES. The World Fair Exposition of 1939 became a public affirmation of this development.

Art furniture ■ A term coined by Charles EASTLAKE, and introduced in the 1860s in Britain and the US to describe simple architect-designed furniture, usually in walnut or oak, made in reaction to various historical revival styles. Depending on form rather than decoration for aesthetic appeal, it anticipated the ARTS AND CRAFTS Movement, and had strong links with the AESTHETIC MOVEMENT. Early pieces often used ebonized or blackwoods, and major exponents were E. W. GODWIN and COLLINSON & LOCK.

Art glass ■ A term used from the mid-19th century for glass that has a strong decorative aspect, with an emphasis on high-quality materials, design, and craftsmanship. It is also not usually mass-produced, being made in limited quantities or as unique pieces. The term can also be applied to fashionable, colored glass such as AMBERINA,

ALEXANDRITE, and BURMESE, and the production of the numerous MURANO GLASSHOUSES. The name Art glass is also sometimes applied to STUDIO GLASS.

Art Nouveau ■ Fashionable from about 1890 to 1914, the Art Nouveau style strove to be consciously radical. The major sources of inspiration came from nature, Symbolist painting, literature, the ARTS AND CRAFTS movement, Japanese art, the Rococo period, and the GOTHIC REVIVAL. However, for all the varying differences, nature was the one unifying factor, often displaying an erotic or sensual quality combining fantasy, the beast and human, or human and plant forms. It could be represented in a literal way such as in a Wisteria lamp by Louis Comfort TIFFANY, or the effects of the natural world could be copied for decorative effect as in the IRIDESCENT glass created by both Tiffany and LOETZ-WITWE. Furniture used natural forms in elaborate inlays, although

A
27

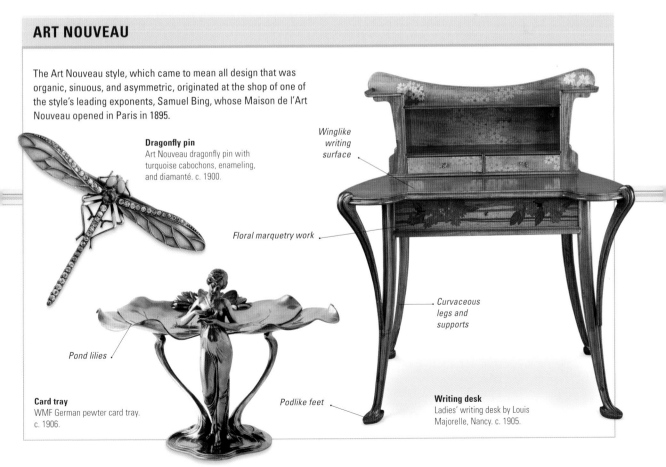

ART NOUVEAU

The Art Nouveau style, which came to mean all design that was organic, sinuous, and asymmetric, originated at the shop of one of the style's leading exponents, Samuel Bing, whose Maison de l'Art Nouveau opened in Paris in 1895.

Dragonfly pin
Art Nouveau dragonfly pin with turquoise cabochons, enameling, and diamanté. c. 1900.

Winglike writing surface

Floral marquetry work

Curvaceous legs and supports

Pond lilies

Card tray
WMF German pewter card tray. c. 1906.

Podlike feet

Writing desk
Ladies' writing desk by Louis Majorelle, Nancy. c. 1905.

ARTS AND CRAFTS

The Arts and Crafts Movement began in Britain in the second half of the 19th century. Based on aesthetic and moral principles, it had a deep impact on the applied arts in Europe and the US. Inspired by John Ruskin and William Morris, British artists and social reformers lamented the diminishing role of the artist-craftsman and the increasing dependence on the machine to meet the demands of a burgeoning middle class. The movement aimed to strengthen the balance between art and craftsmanship.

The term "Arts and Crafts" comes from the Exhibition Society of the same name that held its first show in 1888. The idea of such an exhibition was said to stem from a letter that the art and social critic John Ruskin (1819–1900) wrote to William MORRIS. The ART WORKERS' GUILD sponsored the Society.

Architects rose to the challenge first. Most of the important designers of the movement—Philip WEBB, C. R. ASHBEE, C. F. A. VOYSEY, W. R. LETHABY, Ernest GIMSON, Sidney and Ernest BARNSLEY, and William BENSON—had architectural training. William Morris began his career articled to architects G.E. Street.

One of the design cornerstones of the movement was "fitness for purpose." This meant that the purpose or function dictated the design. There was no point, for example, in making a chair with an elaborately carved SPLAT if it was uncomfortable. The movement was not against decoration, but insisted that it should be appropriate. In the case of furniture, they often used the construction methods of MORTISE AND TENON or butterfly joints as decoration.

Arts and Crafts was championed in the US by GUSTAV STICKLEY and ELBERT HUBBARD. The use of machinery, while not unknown among Arts and Crafts practitioners in Britain, carried less of a stigma in the US. Consequently the American vision of Arts and Crafts was able to reach a far wider audience than in Britain. Workshops large and small for furniture, metalware, glass, and ceramics grew up, prompted by the success of Gustav Stickley, Dirk Van Erp, and the ROYCROFTERS, or with a dedication to handcraftsmanship and truth to materials, championed by the eccentric potter GEORGE OHR.

Printed cotton
Morris & Co. "Strawberry Thief" pattern printed cotton.

Corbel arm supports

Square-section legs

Fixed-back armchair
American Arts and Crafts fixed-back armchair by Gustav Stickley. c. 1880–1920.

Grueby vase
Green Grueby vase, with mottled matt glaze.

Rookwood vase
Bulbous wax matt vase, painted by Olga G. Reed, with cherry blossoms on a shaded ground. 1904.

the best used the organic form in its structure rather than as mere decoration. Jewelers such as René LALIQUE created designs inspired by nature.

ÉMILE GALLÉ and DAUM FRÈRES are among the best known of the virtuoso glassmakers. Gallé also designed furniture, particularly excelling in MARQUETRY. Hector GUIMARD (who designed the entrances to the Paris Metro) and Louis MAJORELLE are two of the greatest names of Art Nouveau design. Elsewhere, Belgian architects Victor Horta and Henry VAN DE VELDE, Charles Rennie MACKINTOSH and the MACDONALD sisters in Scotland, Josef HOFFMANN and the WEINER WERKSTÄTTE in Austria, the Germans Richard REIMERSCHIMD and August ENDELL, Louis SULLIVAN in the US, Archibald KNOX and J. S. HENRY in England, and Antoni GAUDI in Spain, all brought their own unique artistry to the style.

Art pottery ■ The term for handmade and/or hand-decorated ceramics. It is often used for late 19th-century and also 20th-century pieces such as POOLE. The Victorian era saw the increased mechanization of the STAFFORDSHIRE POTTERIES and articles were mass-produced, molded, and printed. A premium was therefore placed on handcrafted pieces. The work of small potteries such as MARTIN BROTHERS and William DE MORGAN became sought after. The larger factories, noting their success, introduced their own handmade ranges. DOULTON

and MINTON proved particularly successful. In the US, companies such as ROOKWOOD and FULPER produced art pottery from the start of the 20th century.

Art Union, The Art Unions were societies established in Britain to promote fine and applied art. The Art Union of London was founded in 1836. Artists were rewarded and subscribers received their works via lottery.

Art Workers' Guild A group established in 1884 in London by like-minded architects, artists, and craftsmen. Nearly all the major figures of the ARTS AND CRAFTS Movement, including William MORRIS, were members. The Guild still exists.

Art Workers' Guild of America Modeled on the English ART WORKERS' GUILD, the US guild was established in Providence, Rhode Island, in 1885 by industrialist John Aldrich, artist and designer S. Burleigh, and painter C. W. Stetson.

Articulated ■ 1. A term used to describe the eyes in Classical sculpture when the pupils are clearly delineated rather than being blank and smooth. 2. A doll or figure with jointed limbs. 3. A type of jewelry held together by armor jointing.

Artificers' Guild ■ A guild founded in London in 1901 by Nelson Dawson that produced jewelry and domestic metalwork such as boxes, vases, goblets, lamps, and wall

sconces in an ARTS AND CRAFTS style. Silver, copper, and brass were typical materials, and forms were simple, being embellished with animal, foliate, and floral designs. Styles of the past were a strong inspiration and the handmade origins of pieces were emphasized. In 1903 the Guild was sold to Montague Fordham, who displayed the range in his London gallery. Edward Spencer was appointed Chief Designer after 1903, but other designers remained anonymous. The Guild was successful until its closure in 1942.

Artificial porcelain See SOFT-PASTE PORCELAIN.

Aryballos ■ A small vase, originally made and used in ancient Greece. It was designed to hold oil or perfume, and had a globular body and short narrow neck with a disk-shaped top and a flat vertical handle.

Arzberg porcelain factories There were four factories at the industrial center of Arzberg in Bavaria, Germany. The first was founded in 1839, but it was nearly a century later that the area came into prominence. In December 1928 the Arzberg Porcelain Factory began making simple, timeless tableware and vases. The Arzberg 1382 service, designed by Hermann Gretsch in 1931, is still produced today.

Ash A wood varying in color from a pale honey to mid-brown, it bends well when steamed and has been used for inexpensive

Art pottery
William De Morgan Persian-style vase painted with carnation sprays. 1888–98.

Art pottery
Martin Brothers stoneware bird. 1900.

Articulated
British silver metal articulated fish charm. c. 1900.

Artificers' Guild
Silver bookmark with green enamel ladybug, by Nelson Dawson.

Aryballos
Inca aryballos with trumpet rim, loop handles, and polychrome decoration. c. 1400–1532.

country furniture, especially chairs. Many WINDSOR chairs, for example, have ash members. However, few ash pieces made before the 18th century have survived, as the wood is particularly susceptible to worms.

Ash, Gilbert (1717–85) A cabinet-maker in New York City, specializing in WINDSOR and other chairs, including MAHOGANY-framed examples in the ROCOCO style. Some have survived, bearing the maker's label. Gilbert Ash was succeeded by his son, Thomas Ash.

Ashbee, Charles Robert ■ (1863–1942) An English architect, designer, Romantic socialist, teacher, and writer. He was a major figure in the ARTS AND CRAFTS Movement. He taught in the East End of London and founded the Guild and School of Handicrafts (1888–1902), which was reformed in Chipping Campden, Gloucestershire, as a community (1902–08). Ashbee believed in the integrity of the craftsman, and all pieces were handmade to a high standard. He was the principal designer and excelled in silver and jewelry, which influenced LIBERTY & CO.'s designs and the ART NOUVEAU style. After the closure of the Guild, Ashbee focused more on architecture and published books. He also traveled, undertaking restoration projects in Jerusalem.

Ashbury metal A hard ALLOY comprised of TIN combined with antimony and zinc, resembling PEWTER. It was

used in the late 18th and early 19th century for spoons, small boxes, buttons, and buckles.

Ashtead Potteries Ltd. ■ A factory founded in Surrey, England after World War I to provide employment for disabled servicemen. Professional potters tutored them in the production of tableware and smaller decorative EARTHENWARE pieces. It made Winnie the Pooh nursery wares and figurative subjects from around 1920 and 1930, respectively. The factory closed in 1935.

Ashworth & Bros., George L. A ceramic company based at Broad Street, Hanley, Staffordshire (1862–1968), which made EARTHENWARE and ironstone. The firm succeeded Morley & Ashworth (1858–60), which had acquired the rights to the MASON patent for ironstone, the Mason molds, and other materials on the formation of G. L. Ashworth & Bros. In 1860 it mostly produced Mason-type earthenware decorated with colored and TRANSFER PRINTS, although the firm is listed in some 19th-century directories as making porcelain. In March 1968 the old mark was replaced by "Mason's Ironstone China Ltd." and since 1973 the company has been part of the WEDGWOOD group.

Asparagus tongs ■ A silver or silver-plated 18th- and early 19th-century utensil, either scissorlike or of U-section, with narrow, corrugated grips to hold on to slippery asparagus spears.

Aspidistra stand A flowerpot stand raised on three or four legs, fashioned from wood, bamboo, wickerwork, or ceramic, and designed to display an aspidistra (or similar) plant. Mostly made in the late 19th and early 20th centuries, they are also sometimes called pedestal stands.

Asprey ■ A firm of jewelers, silversmiths, and retailers of luxury goods, established in 1781 by William Asprey and moving to its current New Bond Street, London, premises in 1847. The company began by producing and selling luggage and leather goods, expanding into silverware in the mid-19th century and jewelry in the late 19th century. It received Royal Warrants and its importance grew from the 1920s, with the company focusing more on high-end, luxury goods from the 1970s. The firm merged with the Crown jewelers Garrards in 1999 for three years and now have premises in New York and Hong Kong, among other cities.

Assay ■ The testing of gold or silver to determine the standard of purity and safeguard against adulteration. As pure silver or gold is too soft for general use, it must be mixed with other metals. Testing assesses the alloy for accepted or legal minimum fineness, body of known weight, and properties. Sophisticated chemical analysis is carried out today, but traditional methods used comparisons with control samples of known physical properties such as weight. The removal of a tiny piece of silver for

Ashbee, Charles Robert
Silver and turquoise brooch in the shape of a butterfly, by C. R. Ashbee. c. 1900.

Ashtead pottery
Art Deco Ashtead Pottery figure of "The Corn Girl."

Asparagus tongs
Tiffany & Co. silver asparagus tongs. Late 19th century.

Flame finial

Asprey
Asprey table cigar lighter, hallmark of A & Co. Ltd., Birmingham. 1933.

Assay
Marks on the underside of a silver teapot, by Robert Hennel of London. 1790.

assaying may leave a wriggly groove known as the assay groove. This is where the term "up to scratch" comes from. See HALLMARK.

Assyrian motifs ■ Originating in Assyrian architecture of the period 721 BCE to 633 BCE, and playing a key role in Classical Greek ornament, these motifs include the lotus, ROSETTE, winged bull, lion, eagle, the Tree of Life, and the DIAPER. Filtered through Greek prototypes, they indirectly influenced decoration in the NEOCLASSICAL period. Popular interest followed archaeological discoveries published in the mid-19th century and Assyrian motifs were used in jewelry, metalwork, furniture, and architecture.

Astbury, John (1686–1743) A potter from Staffordshire who, with his son Thomas, applied colored "sprigging" (separately made relief ornament, such as trailing vines) onto a red or brown body, which was then covered with a traditional lead glaze. "Astbury" is occasionally found incised or impressed on red earthenware manufactured between 1760 and 1780. The term "Astbury ware" describes earthenware models of horses, figure jugs, and utility wares covered with the same lead glaze of yellowish tone, made from about 1730 to 1780. Other potters of this name also worked in Staffordshire; most pieces are unmarked.

Astbury-Whieldon A generic term for 18th-century Staffordshire figures associated with John ASTBURY and

Thomas WHIELDON, decorated in relief and lead-glazed.

Astragal ■ A small MOLDING with a semicircular section used on furniture and metalwork, often enriched with BEAD AND REEL ornament. The shaped profile is used to underscore a difference in planes, or to provide decorative bands of light and shade as an accent or embellishment. Bead moldings side by side evolve into REEDING. The glazing bars of bookcases are often of this shape. Astragal is also known as bead molding.

Astrolabe A flat, circular, usually brass, time-telling, surveying, or navigational instrument used to measure the position of the sun and stars with reference to the horizion and the meridian, and introduced to Europe by Islamic peoples in the 10th century. There are two types: spherical (only one complete example is known to exist) and planispheric. The outer edge has a scale with an "alidade" or rule fixed to the center with a pair of sighting vanes. It also has a rotating fretted disk, containing a number of star pointers.

Astronomical dial See EQUINOCTIAL DIAL.

Asuka period A period of Japan's history from 538 to 645 CE. It is noted for the cultural advances that took place, championed by the Buddhist scholar and statesman Prince Shotoku.

Athénienne A lidded urn or basin raised on an ornamental tripod stand, and used as either an incense-burner, a JARDINIÈRE, a TORCHÈRE, or a washstand. Inspired by Classical Greco-Roman prototypes, it was adapted in the late 18th century as a NEOCLASSICAL ornament, and remained popular well into the early 19th century. Many examples were painted faux bronze or marble. See CASSOLETTE.

Atlas ■ A collection of MAPS or charts bound together and named after a Titan in Greek mythology who was forced to bear the world on his shoulders. Although manuscript sea charts (*portolans*) had been bound together from the 14th century, the earliest printed atlas was the 1477 Bologna edition of PTOLEMY'S *Geographia*. In the mid-16th century, various Italian publishers issued collections of maps, but the first truly modern atlas, with up-to-date and uniformly scaled maps, was ORTELIUS's *Theatrum Orbis Terrarum* (Theater of the World), which first appeared in 1570. MERCATOR'S 1585 atlas was the first book to use the

A

31

Assyrian motif
Kamseh "Tree of Life" rug.
c. 1900.

Molded dentil cornice

Elaborate astragals

Astragal
Edwardian mahogany corner display cabinet, the glazed door with elaborate astragals.

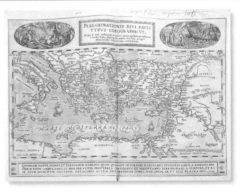

Atlas
Map showing the Mediterranean from an atlas by Gerard Mercator. 1589.

word "atlas." A high point of atlas production was the BLAEU *Atlas Maior* (Grand Atlas) of 1662.

A

32

Atmos clock  A type of clock designed by Jean Leon Reutter in 1926 and patented in 1928 and 1930 in Switzerland, in which the MOVEMENT is powered by slight variations in atmospheric pressure or temperature. Made from 1928 by the Swiss firm Jaeger LeCoultre, it was developed primarily as an extremely accurate timekeeper.

Atterbury & Co. An American glassworks founded in 1859 in Pittsburgh, making FLINT glass and colored PRESSED and blown glass tableware. Also known as the White House Works, it had closed by 1894.

Attick A supplementary architectural order used on the highest story, supported with columns, PILASTERS, or sculpted figures. It often features as the open loggia of Renaissance palazzi.

Atwell, Mabel Lucie ■ (1879–1964) An English illustrator of annuals, gift books, and advertisements. From 1911 to 1964 she designed postcards for Valentines of Dundee, with her widespread popularity peaking from the 1920s to the 1940s. She developed a genre of appealing, colorful, chubby children, inspired by her daughter Peggy, in various situations, with light humor and adult overtones. Her designs for ceramics were made by SHELLEY.

Aubusson carpets Carpet-weaving began in around 1743 in the French town of Aubusson, with SAVONNERIE-style piled carpets, but these were of inferior quality. In 1771 Aubusson began to weave the *tapis ras* (FLATWEAVE carpets) for which it became famous. During the First Empire (1804–1815), motifs from Classical antiquity, BEES, and military TROPHIES were used. Under Louis Philippe (1830–1848), designs were more intricate and used stronger colors: brown, dark red, olive green, and gold. The Second Empire (1852–70) heralded softer colors. Late 19th-century examples have pink and beige floral designs, often within a red surround. Aubusson, in the Massif Central, continues to produce fine carpets, often for specific commissions.

Audran, Claude III (1658–1734) A French designer, draftsman, and decorator. From 1696 he designed and painted elegant and exuberant decorations that included SINGERIE and ARABESQUES, for the royal palaces of Louis XIV. From 1699 he was a designer at the GOBELINS factory, where he produced many tapestry designs, including those for the *Portières des Dieux* (1699–1711) and the *Douze Mois* grotesques (1708). His work was popular in the Swedish court, and also influenced his pupil, the painter Jean-Antoine Watteau.

Audubon, Jean Jacques F. ■ (1785–1851) A French ornithologist, artist, and naturalist

who went to the US in 1803 to enter business, but also began to study and sketch North American birds. After bankruptcy in 1819, his studies intensified and he produced many accurate, colorful depictions of American birds. In 1826 he took his collection to Britain to seek patrons and publishers, gaining success in Edinburgh and London for his renowned illustrated volumes of *The Birds of America*. His reputation established, he settled in New York and worked on further ornithological and mammal print books until his death.

Auffenwerth, Johann (died 1728) A German enameler in Augsburg, Auffenwerth was a HAUSMALER artist, painting in his own workshop, decorating both MEISSEN and ORIENTAL porcelain and faience, predominantly in gold but sometimes silver, with CHINOISERIE subjects. His daughters Sabina and Anna Elisabeth Auffenwerth (later Wald) also painted in their own workshops.

Augarten factory Formerly the State Porcelain Works in Vienna (closed 1864), the Wiener Porzellanfabrik Augarten was set up in 1922 as the successor to the former Imperial company. It makes figures and porcelain, mostly reproductions of earlier VIENNA porcelain, and uses the banded shield or beehive mark with a crown and the words "Augarten Wien."

Augsburg ■ A city in southern Germany, superseding Nuremberg in the mid-16th

Chapter ring with Arabic numerals

Atmos clock
Atmos mantel timepiece by Jaeger le Coultre. 1952.

Atwell Mabel Lucie
Shelley "Boo Boo" nursery figure, designed by Mabel Lucie Atwell.

Audubon, Jean Jacques F.
Hand-colored etching and engraving by J. J. Audubon. 1836.

Augsburg
Silver cruet set by Johann Jakob Adam, Augsburg. 1753.

century as the most important German center for gold, silver, and brass production and a major influence on the rest of Europe during the 17th and early 18th centuries. Guilds of artists and craftsmen were established at an early period in Augsburg, and BAROQUE and ROCOCO pieces with fine engraving were much in demand. The workshops of Augsburg artisans supplied the courts and royal households of Europe with mirrors, *guéridons*, reliquaries, and statues, as well as fine tableware.

Auguste, Robert-Joseph (c. 1723–1805)
A French goldsmith and jeweler. Apprenticed to François-Thomas GERMAIN, Auguste became a master goldsmith in 1757 and was appointed goldsmith to the court of Louis XVI. He is best known for grand dinner services commissioned by European royalty, including Gustav III of Sweden, Catherine the Great of Russia, and Joseph I of Portugal. The earliest are in the Rococo style, but pieces from the 1770s are more elegant and restrained, decorated with Neoclassical FESTOONS, SWAGS, and BEADING. Auguste also made gold boxes and the gold crown, chalice, and other regalia (destroyed during the Revolution) for the coronation of Louis XVI in 1774. His workshop was taken over in about 1785 by his son Henri, who continued to make dinner services, including one for George III of England in 1787.

Augustus the Strong See FRIEDRICH AUGUSTUS I.

Auliczek, Dominicus (1734–1804)
A sculptor and porcelain-modeler born in Bohemia (Czech Republic), who died in Munich. In 1763 he succeeded BUSTELLI as master modeler at the NYMPHENBURG factory in Munich. He modeled many animal and bird figures and groups, often with a hunting theme, and several series of mythological figures. As court sculptor, he modeled statues for the park of Nymphenburg Castle. Auliczek became factory inspector in 1773, and retired in 1797.

Ault, William (born 1841) An English potter who worked in the Staffordshire Potteries from the age of 15 and became manager at T. G. Green's Church Gresley Pottery. In partnership with Henry Tooth, he founded BRETBY ART POTTERY

A

33

AUBUSSON TAPESTRIES

Small workshops grouped into guilds wove tapestries in Aubusson from the early 16th century. In 1665 the town was granted the title of royal manufactory, but unlike GOBELINS or BEAUVAIS, it catered to a local clientele, producing less expensive low-warp tapestries. Made in coarser yarns, the tapestries were known as *rustique*, more in tune with middle-class taste, depicting verdures and biblical and mythological subjects. Tapestries are still made and restored by hand in Aubusson.

Verdure tapestry
Royal Aubusson verdure tapestry. 17th century.

> Wooded landscapes are a feature of verdures

Verdure tapestry
Royal Aubusson verdure tapestry. Late 18th century.

> Attached bamboo border

> Scene depicting Piramus and Thisbe

Aubusson tapestry
Aubusson tapestry. Early 18th century.

A

(1883–1920), and in 1887 established Ault Pottery in Derbyshire, which he ran until the early 20th century. Between 1892 and 1895 the output of Ault Pottery included pieces designed by Christopher DRESSER.

Aumbry Originally a MEDIEVAL term for a built-in wall cupboard with shelving and wooden door, it gradually also came to mean a free-standing food cupboard, usually with pierced doors for ventilation, and popular until the late 16th century.

Aurene glass ■ From the Latin *aurum* (gold) and *schene* (sheen) 1. A type of ART GLASS with an IRIDESCENT metallic surface effect produced by spraying the surface with a metallic oxide, followed by stannous chloride, to produce Gold Aurene. Cobalt oxide is added to the BATCH to produce Blue Aurene. It was developed by Frederick CARDER at the STEUBEN GLASSWORKS, and was registered in 1904. 2. The name of a range of blue, ocher, and green mottled STUDIO GLASS designed by MICHAEL HARRIS and produced at the Isle of Wight Studio Glass from about 1975 to 1982.

Auricular style Ornament in a rippling, undulating style (also known as lobate style), supposedly based originally on the shape of the human ear. It is found in 17th-century silver and furniture. It as inspired by contemporary scientific interest in anatomical dissection and was developed by the VAN VIANEN family of silversmiths, of Utrecht in the Netherlands. The most characteristic example is a silver-gilt ewer of 1614, made by Adam van Vianen, now in the Rijksmuseum, Amsterdam. It is formed as a crouching monkey supporting fleshy scrolls and shells.

Automaton ■ A usually figure-shaped mechanical device that mimics the movement of humans or animals. Once it has been set in motion, it will operate itself. From the earliest times, humans have tried to add movement to images of themselves and their surroundings. Egyptians and Greeks created articulated statuettes, which could be animated by strings. The earliest surviving treatise on the automaton was written by Hero of Alexandria, in the second century BCE. Hero used animated models to illustrate physical properties such as the laws of hydraulics and mechanics. The invention of the spring-driven clock movement in the 15th century provided a portable source of motion, with differently shaped cams determining the type of movement. Elaborate animated displays were often connected to public clocks or were created for the amusement of royal patrons. From the 18th century onward, automata became increasingly popular throughout Europe, either as circus attractions or as exhibits in highly individualistic museums. Whereas the automata of the 18th century were usually one-of-a-kind, the 19th century introduced workshop- or factory-made automata. One of the first mass-produced automata

was the AUTOPERIPATETIKOS. Nowadays, automata are usually associated with the various artists working in the Marais district of Paris around 1900. The figures often reflected Parisian life and entertainment of that time, with characters such as pierrots, clairvoyants, musicians, magicians, and performing circus animals. They moved to popular tunes generated by one or more cylinders and combs. These automata usually had papier-mâché or BISQUE heads supplied by companies such as JUMEAU, and were dressed in either imitations of contemporary clothes or romantic interpretations of period costumes. Jean Roullet was one of the most prolific makers of the period. He founded a company in 1865 and was later joined by his son-in-law, Ernest Decamps. Roullet & Descamps continued to produce automata until 1972. Other well-known makers were Gustave Vichy, Blaise Bontems, Leopold Lambert, and the company Phalibois.

Automaton clock ■ A clock featuring automata or mechanical figures or devices

Mahogany case

Aurene glass
Steuben Aurene blown glass vase.

Auricular style
Victorian cast silver cream jug, its form and decoration inspired by the auricular style. 1861.

Automaton
"Oriental gentleman in ewer" automaton.

Automaton clock
Automaton "ship" white dial eight-day longcase clock.

such as rocking ships or windmills, often in combination with complex striking or musical mechanisms. Automaton clocks were produced from the 16th century, especially in Germany, but most examples found today date from the 19th century.

Automobile mascot See CAR MASCOT.

Autoperipatetikos The earliest form of walking doll, invented by Enoch Rice Morrison and patented in 1862. The autoperipatetikos (meaning "walking about by itself" in Greek) is a china or papier-mâché SHOULDER-HEADED doll, with an integral conical-shaped cardboard skirt housing a clockwork mechanism that causes the metal boots under the skirt to move alternately, thus simulating a walking movement.

Aventurine ■ A translucent glass incorporating golden specks of metal that give it the sparkling appearance of a type of quartz known in Italian as *avventurina*, and made at the MURANO glassworks in the early 17th century. The other possible source of the name is from the Italian *per avventura* (by chance), either due to the accidental nature of its discovery or the difficulty in producing it successfully. Minute metallic flecks are formed when copper oxide is added to the molten glass. Aventurine can be used as a glaze, and in some lacquerwork a similar effect is achieved by sprinkling metal particles onto the wet lacquer, an effect known as NASHIJI.

Avisseau, Charles-Jean (1796–1861) A French potter who founded a pottery at Tours, France, in 1842. He successfully imitated the pottery of Bernard PALISSY and also copied Henri Deux and SAINT-PORCHAIRE wares. His tradition was carried on by his descendants until the early 20th century.

Axminster carpet factory Established in Devon, England, in 1755 by Thomas Whitty to rival French SAVONNERIE carpets. Its wool-pile carpets were hand-knotted using a TURKISH KNOT, with linen or cotton warps and wefts. Motifs were similar to those on contemporary French carpets—fans, floral garlands, roundels, PATERAE—but English features such as strawberry plants and TUDOR-STYLE rose medallions were often included. Some 18th-century examples have a dark brown background. By the early 19th century the factory was the main center of British carpet-weaving, with most of its fashionable products based on French and Oriental designs. In 1835 production ceased due to a fire. The looms were transferred to WILTON, where production has continued to this day.

Aynsley, H. & Co. A pottery making stoneware, lusterware, and painted ware at the Commerce Works, Longton, Staffordshire, from 1873 to the present day.

Aynsley, J. & Sons A pottery making printed and colored china table services from 1864 to the present day at the Portland Works in Longton, Staffordshire. Founded by John Aynsley, a lusterware maker, it was later run by his grandson, John Aynsley.

Aynsley, John ■ An engraver of prints for ceramics and a maker of creamware from 1780 to 1809 at Lane End, Staffordshire. His mark was "J.Aynsley/Lane End."

Ayrshire work ■ Fine early 19th-century WHITEWORK made in Scotland, with small flowers and NEEDLELACE detail. It was used to decorate ladies' muslin collars during the mid-19th century and was also used for christening gowns.

Azmalyk A pentagonal camel trapping, often made in pairs to adorn each side of a bride's camel, woven by the Hekke and Yomut tribal groups of West Turkestan.

Azulejos From the Arabic *az-zulayj* (little stone). Spanish and later principally Portuguese tiles produced from the 14th century onward, used as wall decoration and for facing doorways.

Aventurine
Tortoiseshell and colored glass vase by Dino Martens, with aventurine highlights.

Aventurine
Black glass vase with bands of amber aventurine, by Ercole Barovier. c. 1925.

Aynsley, John
Engraving print by J. Aynsley on a creamware mug. 18th century.

Ayrshire work
Ayrshire lace bonnet. Mid-19th century.

B

Baby house A term used for all DOLLHOUSES up to the early 19th century. They were mainly commissioned from a carpenter or joiner and were often intended for adult amusement.

Baccarat, Cristallerie de ■ A French glasshouse founded at Saint Anne, Baccarat, Lorraine (in what is now Belgium), in 1764. From the early 19th century, it was a leading producer of high-quality CUT GLASS tableware. From the mid-19th century it also produced a range of OPALINE GLASS and outstanding PAPERWEIGHTS with MILLEFIORI designs, the latter produced from 1846.

Bacchus motif A decorative motif associated with Bacchus, the Roman god of wine and fertility, and his Greek counterpart, Dionysus. A popular subject for Classical and RENAISSANCE decoration, the theme of Bacchus and his companions—the wildly dancing Maenads and a drunken Silenus—was taken up again by decorators in the late 18th century. The myth of the god's discovery of wine was used in dining-room furniture, ceramics, and silver tableware. Bacchus's attributes are depicted by the GRAPEVINE, IVY, LAUREL, DOLPHIN, and panther. In the 19th century the motif was taken up by hotels and drinking establishments, and Bacchus was shown accompanied by PUTTI, trailing vine garlands, and bunches of grapes on drinking vessels and serving accessories.

Bacchus, George & Sons An English glass manufacturer established in Birmingham in 1818 and known by this name from 1840. In the 1830s the company made pressed glass. It showed CASED GLASS at the 1851 GREAT EXHIBITION in London, was one of the first to use transfer-printing, made engraved glass, and for a brief period from around 1848 made high-quality paperweights. The company was taken over by Stone, Fawdrey & Stone in 1860, but the Bacchus name was still used until the 1890s.

Bachelor's chest ■ A chest-of-drawers, typically of walnut or mahogany, that evolved from the beginning of the 18th century. Its small size and narrow proportions, combined with a versatile drawer arrangement and foldover top or BRUSHING SLIDE, made it suitable for bachelors' apartments.

Back screen A detachable screen introduced in the early 19th century, which was clipped onto the top rail of a dining-room chair to protect the sitter from the heat of the fire. They were usually made of woven cane or WICKERWORK.

Back stool A small, armless, three- or four-legged stool, sometimes fully upholstered, and constructed with a back, introduced in the late 16th century. In the early 18th century it became known as a SIDE CHAIR.

Backboards The unpolished wooden boards at the back of a piece of CASE FURNITURE or a framed mirror. They were often made from a soft wood such as PINE and simply nailed on, although they were also paneled on good-quality furniture from the late 18th and the 19th centuries. From the 20th century onward, they were often made of PLYWOOD.

Backplate ■ 1. The rear of the pair of metal plates encasing the MOVEMENT in a clock or watch. Backplates are generally made of brass and are often engraved with the name of the clock- or watchmaker, along with motifs such as SCROLLWORK or flowers. 2. The circular disk or shaped panel that is behind the swan-neck handle.

Backstaff A navigational instrument composed of two scaled arcs—one arc of 30°, the other of 60°—generally set at the opposite ends of a straight staff and supported by smaller staffs, forming two triangles. Invented by the English sea captain John Davis in 1594, they are usually constructed from ebony or rosewood with boxwood

---

Additional motifs include butterflies, birds, and deer

Baccarat
Scattered *millefiori* in blue carpet ground Baccarat paperweight. 1848.

Bachelor's chest
George II mahogany bachelor's chest.

Backplate
Herren-Savonette West End Watch Co. Swiss backplate in 14-ct. gold. c. 1910.

Brass handle mounted on birch veneer

Bail handle
Original brass bail handle on a New England Chippendale birch chest-of-drawers.

Baillie Scott
Oak and checker inlaid sideboard by H. M. Baillie Scott.

arcs, a movable shadow vane, and a pinhole sighting piece. The user stood with his back to the sun and aligned one scale with the horizon and the other with the shadow cast by the sighting piece. The two readings added together gave the solar altitude. The advantage was that the sun could be observed without looking directly at it. The backstaff was superseded by the OCTANT.

Bacon cupboard A piece of farmhouse furniture, known from the Middle Ages until the middle to late 18th century. It consisted of a SETTLE with drawers beneath and a tall closed cupboard forming a high back to the seat, which could be used for hanging up joints of bacon.

Badlam, Stephen (1751–1815) An American cabinetmaker of the FEDERAL period, active in Dorchester, Massachusetts. Badlam produced high-quality NEOCLASSICAL mahogany furniture in high style, some featuring detail by the Boston carver Simeon Skillin. He was succeeded by his son of the same name, who moved the business to Boston.

Baff The Persian word for "knot," often combined with a further description of a rug's origin. Thus, *bibi-baff* are very fine rugs knotted by a Persian princess (*bibi*).

Bail handle ■ A metal drawer handle in the form of a loop, shaped like a horizontal capital "C" between two small knobs and sometimes mounted on a backplate. It was first used around 1690.

Baillie Scott, Mackay Hugh ■ (1865–1945) An English architect and designer, Baillie Scott designed furniture for the palace of the Grand Duke of Hesse in Darmstadt, Germany, in 1898 and also worked with the Dresdener Werkstätte für Handwerkkunst. He used ART NOUVEAU motifs to decorate his furniture designs, which were otherwise in a simple and solid version of the ARTS AND CRAFTS style.

Bain, Alexander (c. 1811–77) A Scottish inventor and clockmaker who, with a clockmaker called Barwise, patented one of the first ELECTRIC CLOCKS in the 1840s. Powered by an earth battery, this clock had a magnetized PENDULUM, the swing of which was maintained by electrically charged coils on either side of the case. Some of his grandfather

clocks are still in existence. In 1846 he installed electric clocks in Edinburgh and Glasgow train stations, synchronized by a cable between the two buildings. He also developed the "ticker tape" telegraphic transmission and laid down the basics of the facsimile (fax) process.

Baize A coarse woolen or cotton fabric with a characteristic long nap. It is used chiefly for coverings and linings and is commonly used to cover billiard, snooker, and bridge tables, where it is sometimes called felt. In some countries, it is also used for clothes such as ponchos, cloaks, and skirts.

Bakalowits, E. & Söhne An Austrian glass decorator and retailer established in Vienna in 1845, known particularly for its chandeliers. Bakalowits himself is famed mainly for his connection with LOETZ.

Bakewell Glassworks An American glassworks in Pittsburgh founded by Benjamin Bakewell in 1808. Bakewell is known as the "father" of American FLINT GLASS and until about 1810, his was the only factory producing such CUT GLASS in the US. It was renowned for its elaborate decoration, brilliance, and its use of

BAKELITE

A revolutionary synthetic early PLASTIC, patented by the Belgian Dr. Leo Baekeland in 1907 from a phenolic resin and formaldehyde, Bakelite is a hard, opaque, nonflammable plastic that cannot be remolded once set. It has a limited color range, principally mottled brown or black, but also green and blue. When rubbed, Bakelite gives off a benzene-like smell. Bakelite became popular in the 1920s and 1930s when it was used for domestic items, jewelry, and electrical fixtures.

Plastalite desk lamp
Art Deco desk lamp designed by Wells Coates for E. K. Cole Ltd., of EKCO radio fame.1930s.

Bangle
Sculptural bangle carved with leaves and flowers. c. 1930.

Carved hanging pin
American orange Bakelite hanging pin carved with flowers. 1930s–40s.

Art Deco Fada Bullet radio
Model no. 189 with a blue, red, and cream Bakelite case. Early 1940s.

Regency designs and cutting patterns. In 1825 a very early patent for PRESSED GLASS was granted and manufacture continued until its closure in 1882.

B

Bakhtiari carpets ◼ Carpets made up to the present day by a formerly nomadic tribal group in southern Persia (today's Iran). Fine-quality carpets, rugs, flatweaves, saddlebags, and saltbags are made in strong and typically darker-toned polychrome colors. A rectangular compartmented field enclosing flora is a favorite design. Warps and wefts are normally of cotton.

Balance spring Developed either by Dutch astronomer and physicist Christiaan Huygens or English physicist and instrument-maker Robert Hooke, this flat spiral spring enabled portable timepieces to gain an accuracy only previously seen in PENDULUM CLOCKS, from the mid-1670s onward. The spring sits above the oscillating balance wheel and is usually connected to a balance cock (the wheel's support) and the balance itself. Ideally, it takes the same amount of time for a small oscillation of the balance as for a large one, which makes the watch very accurate.

Baldric A strap or belt, usually leather, worn from one shoulder diagonally across the chest and around the waist, to support a sword, shield, or musical instrument.

Ball foot A turned, spherical foot used on CASE FURNITURE and chairs from the late 17th to the early 18th century. After a revival in the early 19th century, it had generally faded from fashion by the 1850s.

Ball turning Rows of equal-sized, turned, wooden balls or spheres applied as decoration on the legs and stretchers of chair and table legs, and often employed from the mid-17th to the mid-18th century.

Ball, Tompkins and Black A New York City silversmith and jeweler, founded in 1839 as the successor to Marquand & Co. Heavily chased sterling silver hollowware in Neo-Rococo taste is typical and may bear a stamped mark. In 1876 the firm became BLACK, STARR & FROST.

Ball-and-claw foot ◼ A termination for furniture legs that became popular in the early 18th century, and was derived from Chinese bronzes in which a dragon holds a flaming pearl of wisdom in one of its claws. In Europe the claw of an eagle was often substituted for the dragon's claw.

Ballets Russes A ballet company established in Paris by the Russian Serge Diaghilev in 1909. Its exotic and colorful sets and costume designs by artists such as Picasso, Leon Bakst, and Coco Chanel had an impact on ART DECO style and on French art. The company was dissolved in 1929 after Diaghilev's death.

Ball-jointed doll A doll with a turned wooden sphere at each shoulder, elbow, hip, and knee, and sometimes also at the ankles and wrists. These are held in place by elasticated strings between two concave surfaces, allowing natural movements.

Balloon back ◼ A type of chair with a round or oval-shaped back. Associated with ROCOCO and ROCOCO REVIVAL, and with mid-19th-century Victorian styles.

Balloon clock ◼ A BRACKET CLOCK with a waisted or balloon-shaped case, popular in England from the late 18th to the early 20th century. Probably derived from French styles, it is usually made of satinwood or mahogany, with a convex or flat dial.

Baluch A Sunni Muslim, partly nomadic tribal group who still weave rugs in the Pakistan province of Baluchistan and on the Afghan-Persian (Iranian) border. Products include carpets, rugs, flatweaves, and artifacts. Wool is mostly used for the pile and foundation. Designs are geometric in form and the colors used tend to be somber.

Baluster A small turned or carved upright vase- or pear-shaped column, pillar, or post that was often imitated in chair legs and used as a central support for a table or as a SPINDLE for a gallery.

Baluster shape Describes various wares shaped like turned balusters, such as drinking glasses made in England from 1700 to 1730, and coffeepots.

Bakhtiari carpet
Bakhtiari rug from west Persia. c. 1920.

Ball-and-claw foot
George II mahogany ball-and-claw foot.

Balloon back
Victorian chair with a rosewood balloon back.

Balloon clock
Edwardian Adam eight-day mahogany-cased balloon clock. Early 20th century.

Balustroid  A lighter, slimmer form of the BALUSTER SHAPE glass, developed in England in the mid- to late 18th century. It often had a tall, thin stem with several knops, separated by sections of plain stem. Also known as light balusters.

Bamboo furniture Furniture made either from bamboo, or from turned, carved, and painted imitations of it. Popular in the CHINOISERIE styles of the late 18th and early 19th centuries, it enjoyed a notable revival in the US and Britain in the late 19th and early 20th centuries.

Band See FILLET.

Bandai  A Japanese toy manufacturer founded in 1950. The company originally made TINPLATE vehicles, in particular models of American cars, but also exported large numbers of tinplate mechanical robots in the 1950s and 60s, and plastic ones from the 1960s onward. Bandai are still producing toys, marking them with a gothic "B."

Bandelwerk See LAUB-UND-BANDELWERK.

Banding A narrow band of INLAY of contrasting colored and/or figured wood, around the edges of drawer fronts, table tops, and panels. The three major forms are: CROSSBANDING, HERRINGBONE BANDING, and straight banding, which is cut along the length of the grain.

Banister  A term derived from BALUSTER, used from the 18th century to describe both the upright elements that make up a balustrade and the vertical bars in seat furniture, as found in the mid-18th-century banister-back chair.

Banjo barometer  A type of WHEEL BAROMETER with a banjo-shaped wooden case. Introduced in Britain in the late 18th century by Italian craftsmen, the banjo barometer features a silvered brass DIAL, and sometimes also a level, a thermometer, a clock, a convex mirror, and/or a HYGROMETER, in which case it is also known as a "five-dial" barometer. Some ANEROID BAROMETERS have been made with banjo-shaped cases.

Banjo clock An American WALL CLOCK with a banjo-shaped case, invented in 1802 by Simon Willard of Massachusetts. The long trunk, with a rectangular base, usually has VERRE ÉGLOMISÉ panels and curved brass frets. Only 4,000 authentic Willard clocks were made, but the style was widely copied.

Bank See SAVINGS BANK.

Banko ware Japanese pottery made from the mid-18th century, originally inspired by the work of Numanami Shigenaga who used the seals *banko* (everlasting) and *fujiki* (changeless) for his wares. Pieces are typically decorated with human figures, monkeys, and other animals, picked out in enamels or glazes. Banko ware was revived in the 19th and early 20th centuries, when it was made of gray stoneware often in the form of a lotus or flowers. Also known as Sumida ware.

Banquette A French term for a long, low rectangular bench, supported on six or more legs, the seat of which is often upholstered with tapestries. It was developed in France in the late 17th century, when banquettes were used in state rooms and state bedrooms. Throughout its history it remained largely a French form of furniture, although some four-legged English versions are known.

Bantam work See LACQUER.

Barbeau The French term for cornflower. A blue, pink, or green cornflower sprig that was a popular decorative motif on French ceramics in the 18th and 19th centuries. It was reputedly introduced for Queen Marie-Antoinette of France at SÈVRES and is also found on the wares of the PARIS, CHANTILLY, and NIDERVILLER porcelain factories. The motif was adopted by English porcelain decorators who named it the ANGOULÊME SPRIG, as it was a recurring design at the Paris manufactory established in 1781 by the Duc d'Angoulême.

Balustroid
Balustroid wine glass, the stem with an annulated shoulder knop. c. 1720.

Bandai
Japanese Bandai Space Bus tinplate toy, operated with remote control. 1950s.

Banister
American heart and crown banister-back cherrywood armchair. c. 1730.

Banjo barometer
Mahogany cased banjo barometer by Galletti, Glasgow. Mid-19th century.

Barbedienne, Ferdinand ■ (1810–92)
The leading 19th-century French bronze-founder, working for BARYE and other sculptors; also a furniture manufacturer. In 1839 he went into business with Achille Collas, and by 1850 Collas & Barbedienne was one of the principal foundries in Paris, producing bronzes for leading sculptors and manufacturing high-quality furniture in various styles—GOTHIC, LOUIS XVI, and RENAISSANCE REVIVAL. In the 1880s he made JAPONAISERIE furniture and bronzes in imitation of Chinese and Japanese work.

Barber's basin or bowl ■ A round bowl used by barbers from the 16th to the 19th century, with a semicircular segment removed to fit around a customer's neck. They are found especially in English DELFTWARE and French and Spanish FAIENCE. Large numbers of porcelain examples were imported from China and Japan in the early 18th century.

Barbie doll ■ Probably the most successful doll ever produced, with sales of several million since she was first launched in 1959 in the US. Barbie was developed by Ruth Handler, cofounder of the California company Mattel Inc., from the Lilli doll, which was inspired by a mid-1950s cartoon character in a leading German newspaper. She was named after Handler's daughter, Barbara. Pre-1972 Barbie dolls are considered vintage examples and tend to be the most prized.

Barcelona chair See Ludwig MIES VAN DER ROHE.

Barge ware Brown-glazed EARTHENWARE pottery produced in Derbyshire from 1860 to 1910 for the barge-owners who transported ceramics from Staffordshire by canal. It was usually applied with white panels inscribed with the names of purchasers, dates, mottos, and verses, and brightly decorated with green, blue, and pink bird and flower motifs. The most common wares are highly utilitarian teapots, jugs, and CHAMBER POTS.

Bargello A simple needlework technique (also called flame stitch, Florentine stitch, and Hungarian stitch) in which stitches are worked vertically in parallel with the canvas weave and in a zigzag or flame pattern using a range of shaded colors to create an all-over design in silk or wool. Introduced from Hungary during the Middle Ages, the technique later spread throughout Europe and was used particularly for wall hangings, upholstery, and curtains.

Barley-sugar twist ■ A term used to describe spiral TURNING in furniture-making, named from the shape of a barley-sugar stick. It was used from the late 17th century.

Barlow, Arthur (1845–1909)**, Florence** (1839–1913)**, and Hannah** (DIED 1909) ■ Leading British ceramics artists, a brother and two sisters, who worked for DOULTON Lambeth making ART POTTERY stoneware. Arthur is known for his incised foliage, Hannah for her incised depiction of animals, and Florence for her PÂTE-SUR-PÂTE decoration, often depicting birds. Their works were marked with their respective initials; "ABB," "HBB," and "FEB."

Barnsley, Sydney (1865–1926) A leading light, together with his brother, Ernest, of the ARTS AND CRAFTS Movement. Sydney founded Kenton & Co. in 1890 with W. R. LETHABY, Ernest GIMSON, and others. After it closed in 1892, the brothers established a workshop, that later became the COTSWOLD SCHOOL, in Gloucestershire. They later moved to Froxfield, Hampshire, where their furniture design was continued by Sydney's son, Edward.

Barograph ■ An instrument that records the changes in atmospheric pressure over a period of time. Usually fitted into a glass-fronted wooden case, it typically features an ANEROID mechanism comprised of a set of bellows that expands and contracts. The bellows are attached to a pen or stylus, which records barometer readings on successive days on a paper chart mounted onto a metal drum that slowly revolves by clockwork. The earliest barographs, developed in the 19th century, were of the mercury type, but those with ANEROID mechanisms are more common.

Characteristically muscular modeling

Barbedienne
Bronze figure of a bull, with the Barbedienne foundry stamp. c. 1880.

Barber's bowl
Glasgow delft barber's bowl. Mid-18th century.

Barbie doll
Rare, dressed Barbie No.1. 1959.

Barley-sugar twist
Italian satin mahogany center table, with four barley twist supports. Late 19th century.

Barometer ■ An instrument for measuring atmospheric pressure and therefore forecasting changes in the weather. Invented in 1643 by the Italian philosopher and mathematician Evangelista Torricelli, it uses a glass tube containing a vacuum and mercury, the level of which rises and falls depending on atmospheric pressure. The earliest form was the STICK BAROMETER. The WHEEL BAROMETER was the most popular type during the 18th century—and the ANEROID BAROMETER the following century. Pocket aneroid barometers, used by travelers and climbers, were produced from about 1860 by the London firm NEGRETTI & ZAMBRA, among others. The first barometers for household use were introduced in the late 17th century, and were set in cases made by cabinet-makers or clockmakers. These were either wall-hung or free-standing, and reflected the style of period furniture and clock cases.

Baroque pearl ■ An irregularly shaped natural pearl that is less valuable than a round pearl, but which has been used in jewelry for centuries. Its appearance frequently suggests natural or organic forms. In modern times imitation Baroque pearls are widely used in COSTUME JEWELRY.

Baroque Revival A style of decoration reviving motifs and forms of the BAROQUE style and fashionable in Europe and the US in the second half of the 19th century. While incorporating Baroque elements—for example, scrolling foliage, figural sculpture, and luxurious materials—forms and ornament are larger, more exaggerated, and curvaceous.

Baroque style Named after the Portuguese *barroco*, meaning an irregularly shaped pearl, the Baroque style dominated European decorative arts from the 1620s for nearly 100 years. Baroque style originated in Italian art and architecture. In furniture it is evident in the use of such Classical architectural and sculptural elements as pediments, PUTTI, scrolls and VOLUTES, ACANTHUS, SWAGS, vases, and TROPHIES. The overall effect of grandeur is enhanced by monumental forms and elaborate moldings and carving. Luxurious materials were preferred, including velvet, BROCADE, and DAMASK upholstery, SEMIPRECIOUS STONES, and IVORY.

The style spread during the mid-17th century from Italy to France, where it reached its height during the reign of Louis XIV, particularly at the palace of Versailles, near Paris, where the unified scheme of decoration symbolized the power of the monarchy. Classical architecture and sculpture were the dominant influences, mingled with exotic elements, in particular CHINOISERIE, resulting in a fashion for imported LACQUERWORK panels and furniture, motifs such as pagodas and Chinese figures, and especially blue and white porcelain. The distinctive French Baroque style was disseminated throughout Europe in the late 17th and early 18th centuries. Books of engraved ornament by leading French designers such as Jean Le Pautre, and later, Jean BERAIN, circulated the style. HUGUENOT craftsmen, fleeing France after the Revocation of the Edict of Nantes in 1685, spread Baroque form and ornament further. Many Huguenots settled in the Protestant Netherlands and later in England, where the style was also made fashionable by King William III and Queen Mary II.

In the early 18th century Baroque was gradually replaced by a lighter style that prefigured ROCOCO. During the 19th century enthusiasm for historical styles led to its revival, particularly in France during the SECOND EMPIRE (1852–70). See LOUIS XIV STYLE, WILLIAM AND MARY STYLE.

Barovier ■ A leading manufacturer of Venetian glass, based on the island of Murano, near Venice. First established as Fratelli Barovier in 1878 by four members of the Barovier family, a dynasty associated with glass production since the early 15th century. In 1936 the firm merged with another glassmaking family to become Barovier & Toso, which went on to specialize in brightly colored and innovative ART GLASS, a development largely due to the efforts of the talented designer Ercole Barovier. Continuing the innovation that is associated with

Barlow, Hannah
Royal Doulton stoneware vase, with an incised band of cows and donkeys.

Bevel-glazed mahogany frame case

Barograph
Barograph with label for Chadburn's Ltd., 47 Castle Street, Liverpool.

Barometer
Walnut Admiral Fitzroy stick barometer, with Gothic cresting.

Baroque pearls
Miriam Haskell pin and earrings, with silvered faux "black" Baroque and seed pearls. 1950s.

Barovier
Barovier & Toso vase "Athena Cattedrale," designed by Ercole Barovier. 1967.

BAROQUE

The Baroque style was characterized by rich ornamentation, often based on plant forms such as acanthus, and intertwined animal, human, or mythical forms.

Angel
An Austrian Baroque angel carved from limewood, painted and selectively gilded. Early 18th century.

Fruit basket
Delft basket pierced with motifs, and painted with angels, shepherds, and landscapes. Mid- to late 17th century.

Chair
Queen Anne walnut chair, attributed to Thomas and Richard Roberts. c. 1710.

Tankard
Ivory body tankard made in Koblenz with figural carving in deep relief, and elaborate silver and gilt mounts. 1660.

Engraved ivory panels

Valuables cabinet
Early continental Baroque ebonized and ivory inlaid valuables cabinet.

Chest-of-drawers
Rare Charles II oak, walnut, and snakewood chest-of-drawers.

the name, the firm remains one of the most notable producers of Venetian glass today.

Barr, Flight & Barr See WORCESTER PORCELAIN FACTORY.

Barrel A hollow, drum-shaped device in a CLOCK or watch mechanism, typically made from brass. In weight-driven clocks, the cord to which the weights are attached is wound around the barrel; in watches and spring-driven clocks, the barrel contains the coiled spring, the force of which is often equalized by the FUSÉE in high-quality movements. A "going" barrel is a type of barrel in spring-driven clocks with teeth around the edge transmitting the power of the spring to the TRAIN, without a fusée.

Barry, Joseph B. (1757–1838) An Irish-born American cabinet-maker of the FEDERAL period, active in Philadelphia, from 1810 to 1822. Barry's work shows NEOCLASSICAL and Egyptian influences. Examples are highly prized and rank with the work of his American contemporaries Charles-Honoré LANNUIER and Antoine-Gabrielle QUERVELLE.

Barum ware ■ A type of ART POTTERY made from around 1879 at Barnstaple, Devon, under the direction of C. H. BRANNAM, typically made of red clay with a rich, shiny blue and green glaze. Production continues today under the name of Candy & Co., who took over the firm in 1979.

Barye, Antoine-Louis ■ (1796–1875) The finest sculptor of the French ANIMALIER school, working in the spirit of the Romantic Movement. Barye's bronze animal figures are characterized by their attention to anatomical detail and dynamic, often violent, tension. He also excelled in equestrian and mythological subjects. A collection of his work can be seen in the Louvre Museum, Paris.

Bas d'armoire A type of low cupboard originating in 18th-century provincial France as a substitute for the more elaborate COMMODE, and comprising cupboards and drawers enclosed by double doors.

Basal rim A slightly projecting ring on the bottom of a vessel, utensil, or plate made of silver, ceramic, or glass, which raises the object above the surface on which it stands. It is also called a chime or foot rim.

Basalt ware ■ A stoneware body colored black and unglazed in imitation of basalt, which, in its natural state, is a fine-grained volcanic rock. The term was used by Josiah WEDGWOOD in the 1760s when he was experimenting with different earthenware substances and was influenced by the discoveries in Italy at Herculaneum and Pompeii. Widely copied by other manufacturers, a another name for it was "Egyptian black."

Base metal Any of the common metals such as copper, tin, and lead, or an alloy of

them, as opposed to precious metals like gold, silver, and platinum. The term is often used of plated articles when it is not obvious which metal has been plated over, as in "a silver-plated base metal teapot."

Baseplate The term used to describe the removable metal plate on Leica and similar 35mm cameras that allows film to be loaded.

Basket-top clock ■ An early BRACKET CLOCK with an elaborate REPOUSSÉ or pierced metal or wood top, often with a carrying handle, fashionable in England from the 1670s to the 1720s.

Basketweave ■ A decorative pattern imitating interwoven rushes, cane, willow, or straw. With the fashion for pastoral decoration, basketweave patterns were popular for ceramics and metalwork from the early 18th century. The MEISSEN factory introduced porcelain plates decorated with wickerwork borders in relief, and silver baskets made of woven metal wire became fashionable. Basketweave patterns remained popular in metalwork, ceramics, and pressed glass throughout the 19th century. The pattern is also known as *ozier*, from the German for "willow."

Bas-relief Low relief, that is, carved or built-up work not raised very high above the ground. A decorative technique derived from sculpture but also widely

B

43

Barum ware
Brannam pottery vase, by James Dewdney, with the initials "JD." 1901.

Barye, Antoine-Louis
Bronze sculpture by Antoine-Louis Barye. c. 1855.

Basalt ware
Wedgwood black basalt Bacchus ewer, impressed "Wedgwood." 19th century.

Basket-top clock
Ebonized bracket clock by Richard Colston, with repoussé basket top. c. 1690.

Basketweave
Meissen plate, with a pierced basketweave border. 19th century.

used in panels on furniture and metalwork to give definition to design, producing effects of light and shadow.

Basse taille Originating in the Middle Ages, it is a method of enameling in which a gold or silver field is ENGRAVED or ENGINE-TURNED with imagery and the resulting cavities are filled with translucent enamel. The deeper the engraving, the greater the sense of three-dimensionality.

Bassett-Lowke Company ■ Founded in 1899 by Wenman Joseph Bassett-Lowke in Northampton, primarily as a mail-order company selling German tinplate model trains, designed specifically for the English market, but also producing their own examples later on. Bassett-Lowke recognized the superior detail, accuracy, and quality of German trains early on, and his company sold examples produced by primarily Gebrüder BING of Nuremberg, CARETTE, and, in smaller numbers, MARKLIN. Products ranged across all gauges from "00" to "IV," and used steam, electric, or CLOCKWORK power.

The company concentrated on 0-gauge from the 1930s, and production ceased in 1971 when a 45-year run of their most well-known steam-driven 0-gauge Mogul ended. They were responsible for the introduction of the first H0/00-gauge electric trains in 1935, made by Trix, first in Germany, and from 1938 in England.

Bassinet A type of cradle for a newborn baby consisting of a long wickerwork basket with a hood. It can be mounted on wheels to form a baby carriage.

Bat printing ■ A method of TRANSFER-PRINTED decoration in English ceramics, in which the impression of the STIPPLE ENGRAVING was taken onto soft, flexible glue sheets or "bats." The bats were used to transfer tiny drops of oil onto the porcelain, and the design was dusted with powdered pigment and then fired. It was commonly used in Staffordshire in the 19th century.

Batavian ware ■ A class of CHINESE EXPORT PORCELAIN decorated using a brown or "cafe-au-lait" glaze in conjunction with underglaze blue or FAMILLE ROSE enamels. Named after Batavia (modern Jakarta), the Dutch East India Company trading center in southeast Asia, the ware was produced for export throughout the first half of the 18th century and included vases, teapots, tea bowls, and saucers. The style was also copied by MEISSEN and other European factories.

Batch The mixture of raw materials such as sand, fluxing agents, and coloring agents, melted in a pot or tank furnace to make glass. CULLET is also added to aid the melting process.

Bateman & Co. ■ An English silver-smithing family. Hester continued her husband John's business in London after

his death in 1760, together with her sons, Peter and Jonathan. Her first mark was registered in 1761 and she retired in 1790. The family produced tableware, flatware, and tea and coffee sets in a simple yet elegant Neoclassical style. William Bateman, the son of Jonathan, continued the business into the late 19th century.

Bates, Elliott & Co. A factory at Dale Hall Works in Burslem, Staffordshire, from 1870 to 1875, then Bates, Walker (1875–78), Bates, Gildea & Walker (1878–81), Gildea & Walker (1881–85), and finally James Gildea until 1888. They made domestic earthenware, STONEWARE tea urns, and some JASPER WARE vases in John TURNER's old molds, and marked pieces "Turner Jasper Ware."

Bath metal An inexpensive bronzelike alloy of copper and zinc similar to PINCHBECK that was used from the late 18th century to make small boxes and buttons. It had also been used earlier in the century to make unofficial coinage.

Batik ■ The ancient art of decorating fabric using a wax-resist technique, known since Roman times but more closely associated with Java and Malaysia. Wax is applied in patterns to undyed fabric, and the exposed fabric is then dyed and the wax removed, revealing the pattern. The process could be repeated, depending on the number of colors and complexity of design required. First introduced in Europe by the

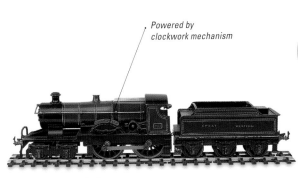

Powered by clockwork mechanism

Bassett-Lowke Company
A "City of Bath" locomotive and tender No.3433, made by Bing in Germany for Bassett-Lowke. Early 20th century.

Bat printing
Rare Spode pearlware bat-printed jug of Dutch shape. c. 1805–15.

Batavian ware
Nanking Cargo Batavian Bamboo and Peony pattern teabowl and saucer. 1750.

Dutch East India Company, by the 17th century batik patterns were produced in Europe from 1842 by the Swiss textile company P. Blumer & Jenny, among others.

Battam, Thomas (died 1864) Battam & Sons of Gough Square, London, were ceramic decorators from 1830 to 1870. Thomas Battam was at one time art director at Copelands, the ceramics manufacturer, and he also formed the Ceramic & Crystal Palace Art Union in 1858. His son continued the trade and his paintings in the style of LIMOGES ENAMELS were included in international exhibitions, notably in 1862 and 1871.

Battersea Enamel Factory ■ Founded by Stephen Theodore Janssen in London in 1753, the factory produced enameled items with the first TRANSFER-PRINTED designs, often in puce on white enamel over a copper base, a technique invented by John BROOKS, the manager. The colors are painted onto an engraved metal plate, printed onto paper and transferred to the object. The factory mainly produced small items, many decorated with landscapes or flowers, or imitating designs on MEISSEN porcelain. It only lasted until 1756 but influenced factories in Birmingham and Staffordshire.

Baudouine, Charles A. (1808–95) An American cabinet-maker of French origin, active in New York City in 1830. Baudouine produced large quantities of rosewood parlor furniture using a variation of the laminating process patented by his rival, John Henry BELTER. In the 1840s he was associated with Anthony Kimbel, best known through his partnership with Joseph Cabus as KIMBEL AND CABUS. Baudouine furniture is typically in elaborate ROCOCO REVIVAL style. Chairs and sofas have pierced, richly carved backs of laminated rosewood, which, unlike Belter's work, may be composed of two elements joined in the center. His attributed pieces are of less value than those of Belter.

Baudry, François (1791–1859) A French cabinet-maker born in Nantes, who by 1822 was making furniture in Paris, where he became *Ébéniste du Roi* (furniture-maker to the king) to Louis-Philippe.

Bauer, Johann Adam ■ (born 1743) A German porcelain modeler and a pupil of François Lejeune, whom he succeeded as sculptor to the Duke of Württemberg in southwest Germany from about 1770 to 1775. Bauer worked at the LUDWIGSBURG porcelain factory (owned by the Duke), producing groups and figures until 1771. He then became master modeler in the FRANKENTHAL factory from 1777 to 1779, and later worked in VIENNA and Sterzing-an-Brenner.

Bauhaus ■ Founded in Weimar, Germany, in 1919 by the Modernist architect Walter GROPIUS, the Bauhaus trained artists and craftsmen to design quality goods for industrial production. Its functional, geometric styles are still a source of inspiration for today's designers.

The Bauhaus, which can be loosely translated as "Architecture House" or "Construction House," is one of the most influential design schools of the 20th century. It was founded by Gropius, when he succeeded Henry VAN DE VELDE as director of the Art School and the School of Arts and Crafts in Weimar. Bauhaus courses focused on experimentation with materials, color, and form, rather than academic theory.

The architect and designer Marcel BREUER used chromium-plated tubular steel to create lightweight frames for furniture, exemplified by his 1925 Wassily armchair, produced by Standard-Möbel Lengyel & Co. and THONET. Among the most successful Bauhaus designs put into commercial production were the lamps designed by Marianne Brandt and Wilhelm Wagenfeld, manufactured by Korting and Mathiesen from the late 1920s. Innovative textiles were developed under Gunta Stolzl, while typefaces by Herbert Bayer heavily influenced typographic design. In 1925 the school moved to Dessau and the Bauhaus style became more defined under modernist designer Laszlo Moholy-Nagy. Gropius resigned as director in 1928, and one of his successors was Ludwig MIES VAN DER ROHE. The Bauhaus moved to Berlin in 1932, but was closed by the German National Socialists in 1933. The school had limited success in

B
45

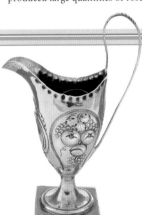
Bateman & Co.
George III vase-shaped cream jug, by Hester Bateman, London. 1789.

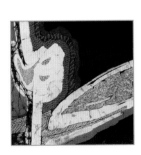
Batik
Batik picture on fabric. 1974.

Floral sprig decoration
Battersea enamel factory
Battersea enamel on copper patch box. Late 18th century.

Bauer
Miniature Ludwigsburg figure modeled by Johann Adam Bauer. c. 1765–70.

B

46

making quality design available to everyone. Many products were still handmade, although their geometric forms suggested machine production. As a result, original pieces from the 1920s or early 1930s are rare. Since the 1960s many furniture pieces have been reissued by Knoll (US) and Cassina (Italy), and from the 1980s Alessi (Italy) has manufactured some of Brandt's designs.

Baumgarten tapestry factory Set up in New York City in 1893 by William Baumgarten, a successful interior decorator, under the directorship of Jean Foussadier, previously head weaver at the English Royal Windsor Tapestry Manufactory. Baumgarten initially concentrated on seat-covers worked in simple floral patterns, and later also produced tapestries in the French taste. The factory closed in 1912.

Baxter print ■ A type of color print patented in 1835 by George Baxter, who combined the use of an INTAGLIO or engraved steel plate, which gave the basic black outline, shading, and color, with

each color being applied by a single, different block of wood or metal plate. They represent some of the earliest color prints and were commercially successful. In 1837 Baxter's book *The Picture Album* or *Cabinet of Painting* illustrated the merits of his process, which was soon licensed to other printers and widely used into the 1870s. It was replaced by other printing methods such as LITHOGRAPHY during the 1890s.

Baxter, Thomas ■ (1782–1821) A fine ceramics painter who worked at his father's studios in London, on French, Chinese, and COALPORT blank wares. He attended art classes at the Royal Academy under Henry Fuseli and was influenced by Greek and Roman vase painting. He returned to WORCESTER to work for FLIGHT, BARR

& BARR in 1814, and founded an art school there. In 1816 he moved to SWANSEA, then back to Worcester in 1819. He is especially known for his figure subjects and atmospheric landscapes.

Bay leaf motif See LAUREL.

Bayeux porcelain factory Founded in 1812 by Joachim Longlois in Bayeux in Normandy, France, the factory produced industrial and decorated wares. These included porcelain figures and tableware in the most popular 19th-century styles, particularly EMPIRE and JAPONAISERIE. The ownership changed frequently, as did the marks, but most incorporated the name of the town. Operations ceased at the factory in 1951.

Bayonet ■ A knife or DAGGER attached to the barrel of a firearm for close-range fighting, introduced in the second quarter of the 17th century and still used today. It is believed to have originated in the French city of Bayonne, where *bayonette* meant a large knife.

BAUHAUS

The main principles of the Bauhaus school were the unification of art, architecture, and the applied arts and cooperation between art and industry.

Armchair
Foldable armchair by Marcel Breuer, Bauhaus Dessau,1927 patent. Reissue, Tecta 2004.

Table lamp
Bauhaus table lamp, by Christian Dell. 1920s.

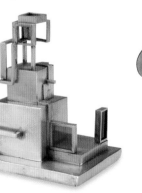

Form study of a cube
Cubic and rectangular forms by Naum Slytzky in brass, copper, ebony, and red and blue glass.

Wine cooler
Gray-blue wine cooler of rounded rectangular form with integral handles. c. 1938.

Bayreuth pottery and porcelain ■ A German faience factory founded in 1714 near Bayreuth in northwest Bavaria, allegedly with the help of a MEISSEN worker, Samuel Kempe. Stoneware in the style of J. F. BÖTTGER was made before 1726. The finest wares date from 1728 to 1744, when the factory was owned by a merchant, Johan Georg Knöller, and the pottery produced outstanding blue-painted ARMORIAL WARE. HARD-PASTE porcelain was produced from 1760, maybe earlier, and from 1788 to 1806 cream-colored earthenware faience were made. The high standards were not maintained after 1744. The factory closed in 1852. It was followed by the porcelain factories of Siegmund Paul Meyer, founded in 1900, and Anton Weide, founded in 1920.

Baywood See MAHOGANY.

Bead and reel A decorative motif, originating in Classical antiquity, of round bead forms alternating with small, oblong shapes resembling reels. It is frequently used as a form of decoration on furniture, and was popular for engraved ornament on 18th-century silver. It was also adopted by cabinet-makers and particularly favored for architectural moldings in the NEOCLASSICAL period.

Bead and spindle A decorative motif of round bead and long spindle forms, used in a variety of combinations for woodwork and moldings. It was especially popular in the 17th century. It enjoyed a revival in the 19th century, when it commonly featured on furniture, especially on chair-backs.

Bead edge A type of border work, characterized by small round beads of the same or graduated size, arranged in a single row. A Classical decoration used particularly on silver FLATWARE and CUTLERY in the late 18th century and second half of the 19th century, it is still widely used.

Bead molding See ASTRAGAL.

Beading A type of ornament comprised of a line of tiny cylindrical beads, resembling a necklace. Originating in ROMANESQUE decoration, beading was commonly used for MOLDINGS, and in the 18th century was a popular decorative motif for silver, furniture, and ceramics.

Beadwork ■ A form of embroidery in which small multicolored glass beads are threaded onto silk and stitched to a fabric ground, or threaded onto wire, which is then shaped. It was fashionable in the 17th century for pictures, mirror frames, and small cabinets, and later in the 19th and 20th centuries, for ladies' handbags. Many American Indian nations, including the Apache, Crow, Cheyenne, Sioux, Arapaho, and Iroquois, had a tradition of beadwork.

Beaker A cylindrical drinking vessel, made since prehistoric times, of pottery, porcelain, glass, wood, or silver. It is usually tapering, with no handle or stem, with or without a cover, and decorated in various ways.

Beatty & Sons An American glasshouse founded in Steubenville, Ohio, by glassmakers Kilgore and Hanna in 1830. After various changes in ownership, it was acquired by Alexander J. Beatty in 1852. The company produced clear and colored table glass, specializing in goblets. In 1900 it became part of the US Glass Company.

Beauvais carpet A pile- or flat-woven carpet made from the late 18th to the early 19th century at the BEAUVAIS TAPESTRY FACTORY. The designs and coloration are similar to those of the AUBUSSON and SAVONNERIE factories.

Beauvais (Beauvaisis) potteries

A group of potteries around Beauvais in Normandy, France, whose best-known wares were produced from the late 14th to the mid-16th century. Objects were made for both domestic and religious use, the latter including 16th-century Passion dishes, glazed in a typical color palette of yellow and green.

Beauvais tapestries ■ The town of Beauvais in Normandy, France, was a weaving center from the 16th century onward. Initial production centered around LOW-WARP verdures (hangings worked with designs of leafy plants). In 1664 it was established as a royal factory by Flemish weavers Louis Hinart and Philippe Behagle

Baxter print
The Departure of the Camden
Baxter print, on a lettered mount. 1838.

Classical scene of lovers in a woodland

Baxter, Thomas
Coalport vase, painted by Thomas Baxter. c. 1810.

Bayonet
Mauser bayonet, SS II Panzer Division.

Bayreuth
Bayreuth faience lidded tankard. c. 1800.

Beadwork
Pair of Sioux tanned buffalo hide moccasins, with beadwork. c. 1880.

B

under the patronage of Louis XIV's chief minister, Jean-Baptiste Colbert. It produced tapestries of outstanding quality, and a series designed after Jean BÉRAIN, featuring mythological figures known as Grotesques, was particularly popular. In 1726 the animal painter Jean-Baptiste Oudry joined the factory, becoming director in 1734 and employing François BOUCHER, whose bucolic ROCOCO designs helped Beauvais to acquire a reputation throughout Europe. Soft furnishings made en suite with tapestries became a specialty. Toward the end of the 18th century the increasing popularity of wallpaper, together with the upheavals of the French Revolution, led to a decline in the factory's fortunes. It was amalgamated with the GOBELINS factory in 1940.

Beaux Arts style Found in late 19th- and early 20th-century French and American architecture and decorative arts, this style is characterized by an academic interpretation of ancient Greek and Roman architecture. It was named after the École des Beaux Arts in Paris, the French national school of architecture, painting, and sculpture, which promoted the Classical ideal.

Bébé ■ A French BISQUE-headed child doll popular between 1860 and 1920, distinguished from the FASHION DOLL by its childlike torso with protruding belly and shorter, stubbier limbs. Pierre François JUMEAU claimed to have invented the bébé in 1855.

Bedstead A framework, mostly made of wood or metal, that supports a mattress.

Bee motif ■ In ancient Greek, Chinese, and occasionally Christian art, a device representing industry and order, and, less frequently, rebirth and immortality. It was adopted as an emblem by the powerful Barberini family in Rome, ornamenting the buildings commissioned by the Barberini Pope Urban VIII in the 17th century. It was also adopted by Napoleon in the lavish decoration of textiles, furniture, and architecture glorifying his reign. Bees appeared on ceramics and silver from the mid-18th century, and until the 1920s were a popular motif on tableware designed to contain honey.

Beech A tree native to Northern Europe, producing a pale straw-colored hardwood with a close, fine, straight grain that is easy to carve. It features in furniture-making in the 18th century in Britain, and particularly in France, where it was elaborately carved and gilded. It was used extensively in England in the early 19th century, when it was often painted to resemble more expensive lumber such as ROSEWOOD.

Behrens, Peter (1868–1940) A German architect, designer, and teacher known for his early and influential role in the development of both INDUSTRIAL DESIGN and modern German architecture. From around 1899, his early ART NOUVEAU style gave way to clean-lined,

modern forms. Walter GROPIUS, Ludwig MIES VAN DER ROHE, and LE CORBUSIER all worked for him at the start of their careers in 1910. His designs for the giant German industrial concern AEG, produced from 1903, are considered particularly influential, most notably the company's turbine factory of 1909, with its glass walls. In 1907 he became a founder member of the avant-garde Deutscher Werkbund (an organization set up to bring together the arts and industry for mutual benefit).

Beilby, William (1740–1819) **and Mary** ■ (1749–97) An English brother-and-sister team of glass decorators and the leading British exponents of enameling in the second half of the 18th century. They worked in Gateshead, decorating wine glasses, goblets, and decanters with white and bluish white enamel ornamentation and polychrome enamel and occasionally gilding in Rococo style.

Beinglas From the German *Bein* (bone). A type of semi-opaque white glass, often decorated with enameling, also known as MILK GLASS and Water Glass. It derives its name from the bone ash added to the ingredients. Produced mainly in Bohemia and Thuringia, in Germany, from the mid-18th to the mid-19th century.

Bel Geddes, Norman (1893–1958) An American industrial designer, who worked as a commercial illustrator before moving

Beauvais tapestry
Beauvais mythological tapestry panel. 18th century.

Bébé
French *Jumeau triste* or "Long Face" Jumeau bébé. c. 1885.

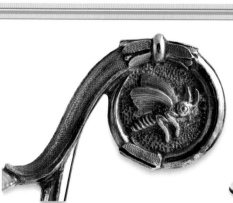

Bee motif
Handle of a silver confiturier with bee motif, by Jean Naptiste Claude Odiot. c. 1820.

Beilby
Beilby wine glass. c. 1765.

into theatrical set design in the mid-1910s, and INDUSTRIAL DESIGN during the late 1920s, when his work became internationally recognized. He was a leading exponent of STREAMLINING, a particularly American emphasis in 1930s and 1940s design, and the teardrop shape, which he believed was a perfect example of it. His work included designs for buildings, interiors, furniture, textiles, and other objects such as cocktail shakers.

Belfast Glassworks An Irish glasshouse founded by Bristol glass manufacturer Benjamin Edwards, operating from 1776 to 1812, and one of several established between 1784 and 1825 in Ireland to avoid the heavy glass tax imposed by British Excise Acts. It made jugs, bowls, decanters, and vases in the grayish lead crystal associated with Anglo-Irish glass.

Bell A small metal dome on a clock emitting a note when struck. Bells have been used on mechanical clocks since the early Middle Ages, when, because early clocks had no dials, they indicated the hours of prayer in churches and monasteries. They are generally made of a specific alloy of copper and tin known as bell metal, which produces a clearer sound than other metal, though many modern clock bells are made of steel. Tubular bells, which have a purer pitch, are hollow metal tubes struck with leather mallets. See STRIKING systems.

Bell and baluster A turned bell shape above a slender BALUSTER. The bell and baluster form was generally applied to the legs of English and Dutch furniture from the late 17th and 18th centuries.

Bell, John ■ (c.1811–95) A leading English Victorian sculptor, born in Suffolk. In 1829 he attended the Royal Academy Schools. He exhibited marble statues and busts in the Royal Academy Exhibition from 1833 to 1877. He made models for Sir Henry COLE's Summerly's Art Manufacturers and also for MINTON's Parian body from 1847, including the figures of Dorothea, Clorinda, and Una and the Lion. Some bear his name as part of the mark.

Bell metal A form of bronze. Alloys of copper and tin in different proportions yield, progressively, bronze, gun metal, bell metal, and brass. Bell metal is pale yellowish because of the relatively high proportion of tin (about 25 percent). When struck, bell metal resonates sonorously and is therefore ideally suited to the casting of bells.

Bell toy ■ A more or less elaborate young child's toy, popular in the US and made in TINPLATE from the late 19th century, CAST IRON in the early 20th, and pressed steel and plastic in the late 20th century. The toys consist of a simple mechanism in which a bell is operated by a cam and chimes as the toy is pulled—or pushed—along on its wheels.

Bellangé, Pierre-Antoine (1758–1827) ■ A French cabinet-maker and founder of a dynasty of furniture-makers. By 1788 he was a maître ÉBÉNISTE and was employed by royal households, primarily that of Louis XVIII, for whom he produced imposing EMPIRE STYLE furniture. He also executed furniture commissions for the White House in Washington, DC.

Bellarmine ■ A type of German salt-glazed STONEWARE wine or beer flagon, molded below the rim with a bearded face of a man said to be Cardinal Bellarmine, who was intensely disliked in Protestant countries. The shape originated in Cologne in the mid-16th century and was made in the Rhineland, Flanders, and London until the end of the 17th century.

Belle époque A French term for the period of comparative peace and prosperity from the end of the 19th century until the outbreak of World War I in 1914. The style was epitomized by the paintings and posters of the French artist Henri de TOULOUSE-LAUTREC.

Belle Vue Pottery Established in 1869 by Frederick Mitchell in Rye, Sussex, England. It lasted under family ownership until World War II in 1939. The Sussex pig, hops, and sprigs were popular motifs. Glaze colors were usually brown or green, the latter obtained from powdered brass left over from pin-making. It was reopened as the Rye Pottery by John C. Cole in 1947

B

49

Felt covering over wire frame

Bell toy
Pull-stroke bell toy, with felt dove and wire-spoke wheels.

Bell, John
Minton Parian model of Una and the Lion, modeled by John Bell. c. 1847.

Bellangé, Pierre-Antoine
Empire-style Pierre-Antoine Bellangé fauteuil. c. 1815.

Bellarmine
Rhenish stoneware bellarmine. Late 17th century.

B

and is still active, renowned for its hand-painted figures.

Belleek, American A term given in the US to late-19th- and early-20th-century porcelain of American manufacture that was inspired by Irish BELLEEK PORCELAIN, or more commonly, bellarmine and the Royal WORCESTER art porcelain. The name "Belleek" was used as a trademark and may be printed on the wares of the OTT & BREWER PORCELAIN FACTORY of Trenton, New Jersey, its successor, the LENOX PORCELAIN CO., and the Willets factory, also of Trenton.

Belleek porcelain factory Founded in County Fermanagh, Northern Ireland, in 1863 by David McBirney and Robert Armstrong. The delicate porcelain of PARIAN type with an iridescent glaze manufactured by Belleek was used for vases (often shell-shaped) and dishes. Other typical products are baskets with openwork lattice sides applied with roses, shamrocks, and daisies. The history of the factory has been divided into periods and the marks change accordingly. The factory also made earthenware for domestic use. The Belleek factory is still operating today.

Bellflower A term used mainly in American decorative arts to describe the pendant flower, commonly termed a HUSK in England, and used in the European NEOCLASSICAL period from

about 1775. Bellflower images are derived from Greco-Roman fresco painting and appear mainly as inlay in American furniture of the FEDERAL period, particularly examples made in Baltimore and chased on silver.

Bellin, Jacques Nicolas (1703–72) A French cartographer and publisher, and the French Navy's first hydrographic engineer. He carried out major coastal surveys of France and other parts of the world. Bellin is known for his many large-scale, high-quality sea charts. He also produced the decorative maps in Prévost's 1746 book of travel narratives, *Histoire Générale des Voyages*.

Bell-top case ■ A type of wooden case found on English BRACKET CLOCKS made from the 1760s to the 1810s, in which the top is shaped like the profile of a bell, with convex moldings above and concave moldings below. Inverted bell-top styles, with concave curves above convex curves, were popular from 1720 to the 1770s.

Belper pottery A producer of STONEWARE in Belper, Derbyshire, from 1809 to 1834. The name "Belper" is usually impressed into the body. It was owned by the BOURNE family of Denby and was transferred there in 1834. The Bournes also acquired the Codnor Park pottery, and the "Codnor Park" mark was used from 1833 until 1861, when the workmen were moved to the DENBY POTTERY.

Benares brasswork A term for domestic pale yellow brassware such as large trays and salvers, made by hand in Benares (Varanasi), India, and exported to the West in large quantities in the 19th century. Imitations were manufactured in Birmingham, England, sent to India, and reimported, but authentic Indian pieces can be identified by their engravings depicting scenes and deities from Hindu mythology.

Bendigo pottery An Australian pottery founded in 1857 at Bendigo in Victoria, Australia, by a Scot, George Guthrie. It made domestic ware until 1914, then developed a line of portrait jugs of military personnel. It is still in production today.

Bends ■ The curved pieces of wood, also called runners, that join the front and back legs of a rocking chair and allow it to rock.

Beneman (or Benneman), Guillaume (died 1811) A French cabinet-maker, probably born in Germany, who was working in Paris in around 1784. By 1785 he was a maître ÉBÉNISTE, making furniture for the royal household of Louis XVI, including a writing desk for the king, based on the famous *Bureau du Roi* made for Louis XIV by Jean-Henri RIESENER and Jean-François OEBEN. Beneman succeeded Riesener as court cabinet-maker and became responsible for all the furniture made for the royal palaces. However, he went on to become better known for his furniture in the DIRECTOIRE and EMPIRE

Bell-top case
George II bracket clock, in an ebonized inverted bell-top case. c. 1740.

Bends
Beechwood rocking chair with bowed bends, by Thonet. c. 1880.

Bennett, John
John Bennett vase, painted with hibiscus on an indigo ground. 1889.

Bennington pottery
Bennington flint-enamel standing lion.

styles, some after designs by Charles PERCIER, that he made for Napoleon I.

Bennett Pottery An American pottery founded by English-born James Bennet in East Liverpool, Ohio (now part of Pittsburgh), in 1839, to make inexpensive, utility pottery. In 1841 he was joined by his three brothers, Daniel, Edwin, and William, and the range later expanded to include PARIAN porcelain. Edwin went on to found a successful pottery in his own name in Baltimore in 1846, which made a wide range of wares, including majolica and art pottery, until 1936.

Bennett, John ■ (1840–1907) A Staffordshire ceramics decorator who worked for the DOULTON pottery and porcelain factory before emigrating to the US in 1877. In New York he sold MORRIS- and ISLAMIC-style pieces, decorated with colorful UNDERGLAZE painting, to TIFFANY & CO., among others.

Bennington pottery ■ The largest manufacturer of ceramics in the US during the 19th century was founded by John Norton as a brickworks in Bennington, Vermont, in 1793. It remained largely in the control of the Norton family until closure in 1894. Early production at Bennington was mostly crude redware and salt-glazed stoneware vessels of a type known in the US as "crocks," which include large storage vessels for water, maple syrup, and liquor. Crocks are typically of pale gray or buff color with impressed manufacturers' marks, and may be decorated with cobalt blue folk art designs. In 1842 the Norton family took Christopher Webber Fenton as a partner who, together with English immigrant workers from the COPELAND AND GARRETT factory, began the production of PARIAN porcelain, including statuary, pitchers, and mantelpiece vases. They also used a colorful mottled variety of ROCKINGHAM GLAZE termed "flint enamel" or, when it was brown, "treacle

glaze." This porcelain was known as Rockingham ware in the US. From 1849 to 1858, the works was known as the UNITED STATES POTTERY COMPANY.

Benson, William Arthur Smith (1854–1924) An architect by profession, Benson became a renowned late-19th-century English ARTS AND CRAFTS metalwork designer and also designed furniture. In 1880 he opened his own workshops, followed by a factory in 1883 (closed in 1923). Benson was a friend of William MORRIS, a director of furniture at Morris & Co. from 1896, and a founder member of the ART WORKERS' GUILD. His showroom in Bond Street was well regarded for his useful but aesthetic electric lamps and other domestic metalware.

Bent limbs As the name suggests, a baby doll's COMPOSITION or PLASTIC limbs molded at a slight angle at the elbows and knees, used to assemble the so-called five-piece baby body.

BELTER, JOHN HENRY

German-born John Belter (1804–63) emigrated to the US in 1840 and produced furniture in New York from 1844, where he focused on the production of parlor suites. In 1847 Belter patented a process of laminating rosewood sheets into a ply that could be bent into sturdy, curved forms. Belter furniture is of parlor type, in dark laminated rosewood, influenced by Rococo Revival. It was widely copied, notably by Anthony BAUDOUINE and Joseph MEEKS, leaving a legacy of American furniture still referred to as Belter.

Side chair
John Belter side chair. c. 1855.

Cabriole leg

Overstuffed upholstered seat

Sofa
Belter rosewood sofa, laminated rosewood construction with Rosalie pattern.

Love seat
Love seat, framed in ornately carved rosewood, by John Henry Belter. c. 1855.

B

52

Bentwood furniture A type of furniture constructed from solid or laminated wood, mostly BIRCH, that has been steamed or soaked in hot water to make it pliable and therefore easily worked into curved shapes. Although some 18th-century WINDSOR chairs incorporated this technique, it wasn't properly exploited until the 1840s, when Michael Thonet, an Austrian furniture-maker, produced strong but lightweight and elegant pieces, notably chairs, from steamed solid lumber. After Thonet's patent expired in 1869, many other firms began producing similar pieces. For example, J. & J. Kohn commissioned the influential designer Josef HOFFMANN of the WIENER WERKSTATTE to produce pieces. In the 20th century, designers such as Alvar AALTO and Marcel BREUER further exploited the technique by producing a range of bentwood pieces made by steaming laminated wood.

Bérain, Jean ■ (1637–1711) A leading and prolific French designer at the court of Louis XIV. The son of a gunsmith, he was employed as an engraver by the French court from 1670 and progressed to become chief designer to Louis XIV by 1690. He is best known today for his important contribution to the LOUIS XIV STYLE, including his engraved designs, published as a collection in 1711, for furniture, chimney pieces, objects, and other interior decoration, featuring light and elegant grotesques, incorporating figures of satyrs, bandwork, acanthus, festoons, birds, and

sometimes Chinese figures and monkeys. Such ornament is found on BOULLE marquetry furniture, BEAUVAIS TAPESTRIES, goldsmiths' work, and French FAIENCE of the time. See SINGERIE.

Bergama An important Turkish carpet-weaving area (formerly Pergamon), where village workshops have been producing rugs since the 13th century. Quality varies from coarse to fine wool pile on wool warps. The weft is usually reddish brown. Designs are geometric and strongly influenced by the Caucasus and Turkoman products. Harmonic shades of terra-cotta, blues, and apricot are typical. See TURKISH CARPETS.

Bergère ■ The French name for an upholstered armchair, introduced in the 18th century and often reproduced thereafter, and comprising an upholstered or cane back and sides and a deep seat with a SQUAB cushion. In Britain the term is often only applied to examples with a caned back and sides.

Berlin ironwork ■ Cast-iron jewelry and other small objects made in and around Berlin and popular from the early to the mid-19th century. It was first made in around 1800, and during the war with France, wealthy Prussian women were given iron jewelry in exchange for gold and silver pieces, to help the war effort. Such items as brooches, necklaces, rings, and fans had delicate OPENWORK designs,

often with NEOCLASSICAL, and, later, GOTHIC motifs.

Berlin potteries or faience From the late 17th century to the end of the 18th century, there were several faience factories in Berlin and northwest Germany, producing good faience decorated in both underglaze blue and colors. The earlier styles copied Chinese porcelain both in shape and in decoration. By the 18th century it had a more German flavor and beer tankards were produced in large quantities. Among known factories were those of Gerhard Wolbeer, Cornelius Funcke, and Karl Friedrich Lüdicke.

Berlin tapestry factory Set up in 1685 by Pierre Mercier, a Huguenot weaver from AUBUSSON. Most notable among early production was a series of histories of the Great Elector, Frederick William of Brandenburg, produced around 1693. In 1714 Jean Barraband took over; he was joined in 1720 by Charles Vigne. Under their influence, production changed to incorporate the fashionable CHINOISERIES, COMMEDIA DELL' ARTE, and hunting and genre scenes, many copied from French designs such as the GROTESQUES produced at BEAUVAIS. The factory closed in 1769.

Berlin woolwork ■ Embroidery worked in colored wools on a canvas background, either in plain TENT STITCH or CROSS STITCH with designs and wools originally imported from Berlin. It was a popular

Bérain, Jean
Louis XIV red Boulle commode, the top inlaid with Berainesque designs.

Bergère
Regency mahogany *bergère* armchair.

Berlin ironwork
Pair of Berlin ironwork floral motif earrings. c. 1820s.

Berlin woolwork
Berlin woolwork sampler by Sarah Harris. Sept. 14, 1869.

home craft in 19th-century England. The often religious, figurative, or floral designs were available on squared paper to be transferred to the canvas by the embroiderer or worked from a kit. Patterns available included slippers, bags, and fire screens. Pictures and sampler motifs were fashionable from the 1830s to the 1880s.

Bernberg pottery A pottery started by Johann David Kratzenberg in the town of Bernberg in northwest Germany in 1725. It produced faience decorated in Chinese blue and white style, often with LAUB-UND-BANDELWERK and coats of arms. The factory probably closed in 1774.

Bertoia, Harry (1915–78) An Italian-born metal sculptor and furniture designer. His family settled in the US in 1930 and he studied at the CRANBROOK ACADEMY from 1937 to 1939, thereafter teaching metalwork till 1943. An associate of Charles EAMES and Eero SAARINEN, he is best known for his wire mesh and tubular steel Diamond chair, designed from 1950 to 1952 for KNOLL International. Sculptures were commissioned by numerous companies and institutions as well as private individuals, some producing sounds if touched or moved by the wind.

Bessarabia An area in the borders of Moldavia and Romania known for weaving rugs, carpets, and KILIMS from the 18th century onward. Loose piled weavings were based on French SAVONNERIE designs, double-wefted with a TURKISH KNOT. Piled weaving ceased at the outbreak of the Crimean War in 1854. Kilims were made throughout the 19th century, and designs were simple and uncrowded, with a mixture of naturalistic floral forms in pastel shades on an ivory or black background.

Bevel A sloped or slanting edge of a flat surface, generally referring to glass or wood. Beveled glass has a CHAMFERED corner, made by cutting away the edge where the two flat surfaces meet at a right angle. This is seen, for example, on the edges of mirrors, which are usually beveled to protect against chipping. In furniture the term may also refer to an applied MOLDING.

B

53

Berlin vase
Berlin "crater shape" vase, with a blue underglaze scepter mark with a brown eagle and KPM. c. 1828.

BERLIN PORCELAIN FACTORY

Wilhelm Kaspar Wegely set up the first porcelain factory in around 1751. He recruited workers from MEISSEN and HÖCHST and produced both figures and utility wares, inspired by Meissen and VIENNA. However, Wegely went bankrupt in 1757. A merchant, Johann Ernst Gotzkowsky, set up a new factory, having bought the "secret" of porcelain-making from one of Wegely's workers.

Gotzkowsky, in turn, went bankrupt and the company was sold to Frederick the Great in 1763 and became the Royal Porcelain Manufactory, with the king taking an active interest. The style of the wares was strongly influenced by Meissen. The porcelain produced in the BIEDERMEIER period was often to the designs of Karl Friedrich Schinkel (1781–1841). Large vases with fine landscape painting are particularly noteworthy, as well as richly decorated "cabinet" wares. The painter Alexander Kips became artistic director in 1886 and exerted a great influence over the next 22 years.

In the late 19th century, Berlin produced large porcelain plaques, often finely painted with copies of famous paintings. At the turn of the century the sculptor and modeler Paul Scheurich worked at the factory for a short time, producing Rococo-style figures in contemporary dress. The factory was destroyed in World War II (in 1943) but the porcelain collection and library had been moved to Selb. The Berlin and Selb works were reunited between 1955 and 1957. Since 1918, it has been styled Staatliche Porzellan Manufaktur Berlin.

Berlin plaque
Solitude, a Berlin plaque, painted by Greiner, impressed with the KPM and scepter mark.

"KPM Berlin" mark
Art Deco "KPM Berlin" brown scepter mark with a partial crosshatch cross to the orb.

B

54

Beyer, Johann Christian Wilhelm ▪ (1725–1806) One of the leading German porcelain modelers of the 18th century. Born in Thuringia, Germany, Beyer trained as an architect, painter, and sculptor in Dresden, Paris, and Rome. From 1759 he worked for Duke Karl of Württemberg at the LUDWIGSBURG porcelain factory, where he produced a series of outstanding figures, with elements of both Rococo and NEOCLASSICAL styles. In 1768 he was appointed court painter and sculptor in Vienna, where he spent the rest of his working life.

Bi (or pi) A Chinese term for a flat disk of jade of various colors, with a hole in the center, used for ritualistic or emblematic purposes until the abdication of the last Manchu emperor in 1912. The earliest examples are undecorated and date from the Neolithic age (9000–2000 BCE), while later examples are more highly decorated. They represent the sun or heaven.

Bianchetto A buff pottery covered with a coating of fine white clay or SLIP, which is fired and then decorated with painted designs and covered with a soft lead glaze. It preceded MAIOLICA at FAENZA and other Italian potteries.

Bianco (or bianchi) di Faenza A type of white MAIOLICA introduced at FAENZA from around 1550, sometimes elaborately modeled and lightly decorated with colored motifs. Instantly popular, it replaced

ISTORIATO ware and was adopted by other Italian and European potteries, until the 19th century.

Bianco-sopra-bianco ▪ A technique originating in Italian MAIOLICA ware from the early 16th century, denoting painting in opaque white over a grayish white ground. From the mid-18th century the technique was adopted by other European potteries such as RÖRSTRAND, LAMBETH, and BRISTOL.

Bibelot From the French *beubelet* (trinket, or small jewel). A small, usually richly embellished object, often also described as an OBJET DE VERTU, which is either carried on the person or displayed on chimneypieces and/or furniture. Although it may have a function, its primary purpose is decorative.

Bible box ▪ A box, usually made of oak, used in Britain from the late 16th century and through the 17th century, to hold a Bible and important family documents. These had simple, sometimes sloping, hinged lids and were often set on a stand.

Bidet ▪ A small bath, basin, or bowl supported on a wooden stand, first made in the early 18th century in France and designed to allow women in particular to wash the lower parts of their body. The basin could be SILVER, METAL, or PORCELAIN, while the stand was often of WALNUT or some other hardwood. Although unusual outside France, 18th-century English designs by SHERATON do exist.

Bidri ▪ A type of Indian metalwork, originating in Bidar in the 17th century

BIANCONI, FULVIO

Italian draftsman, painter, and designer Fulvio Bianconi (1915–96) is known widely for his innovative glass designs produced from 1946, primarily at the Venini glassworks. Notable works include the Pezzato vase designed in 1950 and the Fazzoletto (handkerchief) vase designed with Paolo Venini around 1949.

Venini vase
Venini & Co. vase, marked "venini murano ITALIA." 1951.

Beyer, Johann Christian Wilhelm
Ludwigsburg figure, modeled by Johann Christian Wilhelm Beyer. c. 1765–66.

Fazzoletto vase
Venini & C. Fazzoletto vase, designed by Fulvio Bianconi. c. 1950.

Pezzato vase
Venini Pezzato vase with "tessere" pattern. 1950.

but now made throughout northern India. SPICE BOXES, hookah bases, jars, and other wares are cast from an alloy of zinc, blackened by immersion in a mixture of sal ammoniac and saltpeter, then inlaid with DIAPER, FLORAL, or LEAF patterns in silver, brass, or gold. Goods made in this way were imported to Europe during the 19th century.

Biedermeier A style of decorative arts popular in Germany, Austria, and Scandinavia from about 1815 to the 1840s. Its development was associated with the revival of the German furniture trade after the defeat of Napoleon and the increasing prosperity of the middle classes. The style was named after Gottlieb Biedermeier, a 19th-century German author of comic poems, and derives from *bieder* (plain) and *Meier*, a German surname.

In furniture-making, the style is characterized by simple and symmetrical classical forms derived from EMPIRE and REGENCY furniture. It used the traditional ornamentation of 18th-century furniture in simplified form, particularly urns, shells, lyres, and geometric shapes. The overall effect of the pieces is one of solidity and comfort. Cabinet-makers favored the use of large areas of VENEER, in light woods, especially MAPLE, CHERRY, and BIRCH, showcasing the wood grain, and often contrasted with EBONY inlay. Motifs are NEOCLASSICAL, such as columns, PILASTERS, and LYRES, and geometric. Much Biedermeier furniture was made

anonymously, although leading makers such as Josef Danhauser of Vienna designed in this style.

The Biedermeier style also influenced German and Austrian glass and ceramics. Glassmakers such as Dominik Biemann produced finely engraved pieces, decorated with Classical busts or religious scenes. New techniques of colored glassmaking, such as LITHYALIN, were used to embellish tumblers and beakers. These also appeared with topographical views, as souvenirs. Decorative pieces or small services, decorated with portraits or scenes and framed by gilt borders, were produced at the porcelain factories of BERLIN and VIENNA for the middle-class market, replacing the table services previously made for the aristocracy. Ceramic forms were based on Classical prototypes such as urns and KRATERS for vases, but shapes are heavier, more rounded, or flaring, than in the Neoclassical period. From the 1840s the Biedermeier style declined, as ornament became richer, incorporating elements of the ROCOCO REVIVAL style. Its simplicity and restraint, however, inspired avant-garde designers in the late 19th and early 20th centuries and copies continued to be made.

Biennais, Martin-Guillaume (1764–1843) A leading French silversmith and cabinet-maker. By 1789 he had set up business as a cabinet-maker and dealer in Paris, but after the dissolution of the guild system in 1797, he began manufacturing and dealing

in silver and jewelry. He produced large quantities of silver, in particular NECESSAIRES for Napoleon and his family, and Greek Revival dinner services for the Russian, Austrian, and Bavarian courts, as well as the regalia for Napoleon's coronation.

Biggin A coffeepot or hot-water jug in silver or SHEFFIELD PLATE with a stand and spirit burner, attributed to the 18th-century silversmith George Biggin. Introduced in 1790 and made throughout the 19th century, they were designed for portability—for example, while conducting parliamentary campaigns. They have minimal decoration and are often cylindrical with a lip spout, strainer, and a detachable cover.

Bigot, Alexandre (1862–1927) A French artist potter, important in the growth of ART POTTERY in Paris. Bigot experimented with FLAMBÉ GLAZES and was interested in incorporating ceramics as a decorative feature in architecture.

Bilbao mirror A type of mirror, framed with marble or marble and wood, popular in the late 18th century. They were named after the port of Bilbao in Spain, from where they were exported.

Billet A molding ornament of rounded or squared blocks. In ROMANESQUE STYLE architecture, the billet was typically spaced in a regular pattern along a molding.

B

55

Bianco-sopra-bianco
Bristol bianco-sopra-bianco delft plate. c. 1760.

Now leather, but originally wire

Bible box
American carved pine Bible box from New England. 18th century.

Bidet
Mahogany bidet with Chinese blue and white porcelain liner. 19th century.

Bidri
Bidri lid from Deccan. c. 1700.

A series of billets used together is sometimes known as a "billet frieze."

Billingsley, William ■ (1758–1828) An important English porcelain decorator, son of a decorator at the Chelsea factory. He was apprenticed as a painter at DERBY when he was 16 years old. From Derby he went to PINXTON. He was at Mansfield from 1799 to 1802 and at WORCESTER in 1808. In 1813 he went to Wales and worked at SWANSEA and NANTGARW, being largely responsible for the success of these factories. In 1819 he went to John ROSE's factory in COALPORT. His flower painting is in a soft, naturalistic style with the highlights added by brushing out the enamel colors; the Billingsley rose is a famous motif. He also painted landscapes and was a talented gilder on porcelain.

Bilsted A species of wood used as an alternative to mahogany in 18th-century North American furniture-making.

Bilston enamel factories ■ A group of factories in Bilston and Wednesbury, Staffordshire, producing enameled snuffboxes, scent bottles, small decorative plaques for jewelry, and other OBJETS DE VERTU, from the mid-18th century to the early 19th century. The largest firm was established by Benjamin Bickley in 1749. The enamel-on-copper wares, imitating MEISSEN and CHELSEA, feature typically Rococo-style painted decoration such as landscapes, floral bouquets, and exotic birds in pale colors, often embellished with gilding. Great quantities were exported to Europe and the US. The last factory closed in 1831.

Bilston japanning factories A group of factories at Bilston, Staffordshire, manufacturing JAPANNED wares such as trays and snuffboxes made from tin-plated sheet iron and decorated with CHINOISERIE patterns or flowers. The earliest pieces date from the 1690s, but production continued until it began to decline in the late 19th century. Japanned metalware tends to be generically called PONTYPOOL WARE or tôle. See TÔLEWARE.

Bing & Grøndahl ■ A porcelain factory in Copenhagen, Denmark, founded in 1853 by Harold Bing, whose products rivaled the COPENHAGEN PORCELAIN FACTORY. In 1885 Pietro Krohn took over as art director, and in 1888 he designed the Heron service. The company exhibited at the Paris Exhibition of 1900, in particular models by Kai Nielsen and Jean Gauguin, son of the artist Paul Gauguin. At the end of the 19th century the company began the tradition of annual Christmas and Easter plates, which continues to this day. Later designers for the factory included Henning KOPPEL.

Bing, Gebrüder ■ A German metalware company founded in 1863 by the brothers (*Gebrüder* in German) Ignaz and Adolf Bing in Nuremberg, using the trademark GBN from 1902. They began making tinplate toys in the early 1880s, prospering particularly in the lead-up to World War I and during the 1920s, but foundering after the world slump in 1929. Their vast catalog of STEAM, CLOCKWORK, and ELECTRICALLY-powered toys and models included trains and railroads, stationary steam engines, ships, and MAGIC LANTERNS. They exported their toys to Germany, France, England, and the US, tailoring their designs to each market. Bing produced teddy bears from 1907, with early examples resembling those produced by STEIFF, and using a similar metal identifying tag. Many bears made after 1910 had mechanical abilities—for example, some could even turn somersaults. The company closed in 1932.

Bing, Samuel (Siegfried) (1838–1905) An influential dealer, collector, publisher, and promoter of ART NOUVEAU and Japanese art in Paris. He opened his famous shop, the Maison de L'Art Nouveau, in 1895 and sold pieces by leading designers of the style—Émile GALLÉ, Louis Comfort TIFFANY, and René LALIQUE. He also commissioned work directly from designers such as Edward Colonna, Georges de Feure, Leon Jallot, and Eugene Gaillard.

Binns, Charles Fergus (1857–1934) An English-born American educator, technologist, and potter, and the most

Billingsley, William
Porcelain campana vase by William Billingsley, marked "Nantgarw." c. 1813–23.

Bilston enamel factories
Oval, blue and white enamel, Bilston patch box with Nelson imagery.

Bing & Grøndahl
"Hans Christian Andersen" porcelain model No. 2037, by Henning Seidelin.

Hand-painted body

Bing, Gebrüder
Clockwork sedan with driver and passenger, by Gebrüder Bing.

influential figure in American ceramics in the first quarter of the 20th century. In 1900 he became the first director of the New York School of Clay Working at Alfred University, which later became the New York State College of Ceramics, and remained director for 35 years. It was the leading institution for ceramic education and research in the US. Binns worked in high-fired stoneware of simple design, inspired by Chinese porcelain.

Birch ■ A tree native to Northern Europe that produces a golden wood with a reddish tinge, often used as a substitute for SATINWOOD veneer. From the late 18th century, furniture-makers—especially Russian and Eastern European—used solid birch for chairs and other furniture.

Birdcage support ■ A structure used from 1740 to 1765 on high-quality English and American TILT-TOP TABLES, consisting of four small pillars between a small square top and base. This "cage" is hinged to the top of the table and allows the top to be tilted vertically for storage. It provides a solid support for the table when it is in use as well as sufficient depth, so that the table top can be held rigidly to its central support by a wooden wedge or a brass catch.

Bird's-eye maple ■ A variant of MAPLE wood and native to Northern Europe, the US, and Canada. It has a figuring of light brown rings that resemble birds' eyes. It became fashionable as a VENEER in the late 18th century and in the REGENCY period,

and was used from the mid- to late 19th century onward for bedroom furniture.

Biscuit porcelain ■ A term used to denote the porcelain BODY after its first firing, when it is white and has a matte appearance before being glazed. It was used for making small sculptures at the end of the 18th century and the beginning of the 19th, at SÈVRES, especially MEISSEN, and also at DERBY.

Biscuit tin The famous British biscuit makers Huntley & Palmer first used tins, made from tin-plated steel, to store biscuits in around 1832. Early handmade tins were soon replaced by machine-made tins, and the development of offset LITHOGRAPHY, which the company acquired exclusive rights to in 1877, introduced a riot of bright colors and designs to biscuit tins. During the early 20th century they were produced in a wide range of novel and attractive shapes, including cars, trains, and books, sometimes in honor of events such as royal jubilees or Christmas.

Bisque ■ An unglazed porcelain mainly used between 1860 and 1925 to make DOLLS' heads. Bisque is fired twice, initially at a high temperature, before the surface is painted, and refired at a lower temperature.

Bizarre silk A style of European woven silk produced in the late 17th and early 18th centuries. Asymmetrical designs often incorporated elements from Chinese,

Japanese, and Indian floral patterns with architectural devices. The fashion for "bizarre" elements virtually disappeared by 1725 but was revived by Clarice CLIFF in her Bizarre pottery range of 1928.

Bizen potteries Located at Imbe in the Bizen province and one of the "Six Old Kilns" of Japan where many of the technical advances in Japanese ceramics were made in the 12th to 14th centuries. Bizen ware was one of the first types of Japanese pottery used for TEA CEREMONY articles. The main characteristics are a high-fired body, unglazed coarse texture, and a warm, reddish brown color, which varies with "chance" effects produced when oxygen is allowed into the kiln. In the 17th and 18th centuries a smooth ware imitating Chinese YIXING stoneware was made. Production continued throughout the 19th and 20th centuries.

Black basalt See BASALT WARE.

Black Forest clock A type of weight-driven WALL CLOCK made in the Black Forest region of Germany since the mid-17th century. Early examples were made almost entirely of wood by local craftsmen, but from the mid-19th century mass-produced clocks usually had steel or brass movements. CUCKOO CLOCKS and TRUMPETER CLOCKS were also made. They are often decorated with heavily carved motifs, including birds, leaves, and animal heads. Many are shaped like log cabins.

B
57

Turned center and corner columns

Birch
Detail of an Art Deco birch table. 1920s.

Birdcage support
Philadephia mahogany tilt-top tea table, with birdcage support. 18th century.

Bird's-eye maple
Detail of a Sue et Mare Bird's-eye maple and mahogany demi-lune side table. c. 1925.

Biscuit porcelain
Sèvres white biscuit porcelain bust of the Duchesse de Berri. c. 1816.

Bisque
French *Tete Jumeau*, size 16 pale bisque-head doll.

B

Black jack A sturdy drinking tankard or flask of stout or tapering form made from plain or decoratively tooled rigid leather, often with silver or pewter mounts or linings. Some black jacks are large, holding a gallon of beer. They are known since the 17th century, but were almost certainly used much earlier.

Black marble clock A type of mass-produced 19th-century French MANTEL CLOCK with a case made in or faced with black marble. Inexpensive versions feature polished black slate instead of marble.

Black, Starr & Frost ■ Silversmiths, jewelers, and retailers active in New York City from 1876, succeeding BALL, TOMPKINS & BLACK and operating mainly as a retailer, rivaling TIFFANY & CO. From 1920 to 1962 the company was in partnership with the GORHAM MANUFACTURING CO. Stamped marks appear on silver and metal mounts.

Blackamoor ■ A decorative device, originally imported from Italy, in the form of a carved figure of a black slave dressed in an exotic polychrome costume. Blackamoors were in popular use as a pedestal support for such pieces as TORCHÈRES from the early 18th century through to the early 20th century.

Blackwork Also known as Spanishwork, blackwork is a monochrome embroidery technique, usually using black thread on a white ground and sometimes embellished with metal thread. Blackwork was introduced into Europe by the Moors via Spain, becoming particularly fashionable on costumes during the 16th century.

Blaeu, Willem Janszoon (1571–1638) **and Joan** ■ (1596–1673) Willem Blaeu was the founder of one of the leading Dutch map-making firms of the 17th century. He produced important individual maps as well as a sea ATLAS and a series of world atlases that culminated in the publication, by his son, Joan, of the *Atlas Maior* (Grand Atlas) in 1662. Issued in various languages and editions between 1662 and 1672 (when a disastrous fire destroyed the plates and ruined the firm), the *Atlas Maior* is a masterpiece of Dutch Golden Age cartography and arguably the most magnificent atlas ever published. A work of art, it is prized for its superbly engraved maps, enriched by decorative CARTOUCHES and flowing calligraphy.

Blanc-de-chine A type of Chinese porcelain, usually white, made at DEHUA in the Fujian province, from the MING DYNASTY (1368–1644) to the present day. Wares include crisply modeled figures, cups, bowls, and incense holders. *Blanc-de-chine* was exported to Europe and copied in the 17th and 18th centuries.

Blank An undecorated object, usually in glass or ceramic, that is intended to be

decorated using techniques such as painting, enameling, cutting, engraving, or the application of transfer designs.

Blanket chest ■ A wooden chest, coffer, coffre, or joined chest, used as storage furniture since the Middle Ages. Early simple constructions comprised wooden boards (usually oak) simply nailed together. More sophisticated PANELED construction began in the 15th century. Some have inlaid or LINENFOLD panels or carvings, and display painted decoration.

Bleeding bowl A shallow bowl in silver, pewter, or ceramic, with a flat pierced handle. Made in the 17th and early 18th centuries, they were used by surgeon barbers when bleeding patients. Some had a semicircular segment removed. In the US a bleeding bowl is known as a PORRINGER. See BARBER'S BASIN.

Bleu celeste ■ A turquoise glaze used at the SÈVRES porcelain factory as a ground color. Introduced in 1752, it was developed by Jean Hellot, decorator and chemist at Sèvres from 1745 to 1766. It was also used on 19th-century copies of Sèvres.

Bleu de roi A blue (royal blue) glaze first used at VINCENNES in around 1749, then at SÈVRES. It was also employed on at CHELSEA, WORCESTER, and DERBY.

Bleu persan A dark blue glaze on a pottery body, copying Chinese and Persian

Black, Starr & Frost
American silver youth cup, made by Frank Smith Silver Co. of Gardner, MA. 1897.

Blackamoor
One of a pair of Continental Blackamoor figures. Late 19th century.

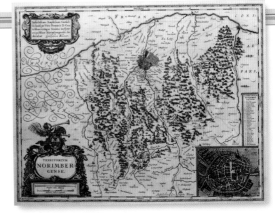

Blaeu, Willem Janszoon
Colored copperplate map by Willem Janszoon Blaeu. 1640.

styles. Designs of foliage, lace, or ironwork in opaque white enamel contrast with the solid blue background. A technique much used at the French faience factory at NEVERS and copied on early English DELFTWARE in the late 17th and early 18th centuries.

Blind tooling A technique for impressing leather, especially leather book covers, with imagery or numerals. Before the late Middle Ages, the impressions—which were neither gilded nor colored, but left plain—were worked by hand with a heated brass tool on dampened leather. Thereafter, however, they were more usually applied with a wooden-handled brass stamp, preconfigured to the desired pattern.

Blind tracery Ornamental decoration with flowing lines derived from GOTHIC architecture and applied as carved wood to furniture from the 14th century onward. Unlike PIERCED DECORATION, blind tracery has a solid backing.

Block-front An 18th-century American furniture form, used primarily on chests and desks, in which the front of the piece is divided vertically into three segments: the center being shallow concave in profile, and the two flanking outer segments being a shallow convex profile.

Bloom Clouding of interior of glassware, most usually vases and decanters, caused by calcium in hard water entering the surface of the glass. This can only be removed by mechanical cleaning. Also the powdery residue left on furniture stripped in a tank.

Blowing A method of making glass in which a blob of molten glass (often known as a gob) is gathered on the end of a hollow metal rod. The glassmaker then blows through the rod, forcing the glass into either a free-blown or a mold-blown shape.

Blue-dash charger ■ From the Middle English *chargeour* (a large flat dish for carrying things). Made of pottery, it was also a dish to hang on a wall or place on a DRESSER or BUFFET as decoration. The term was applied to English dishes made of TIN-GLAZED EARTHENWARE with blue dashes on the rim, and coined by A. E. Downman in his book of 1919.

Blue John ■ From the French *Bleu-Jaune* (blue-yellow). A variety of fluorspar, blue John is a purple to violet-blue to yellow banded HARDSTONE, which has been used in ornamentation for centuries. Indigenous to the Castleton area of Derbyshire, it is frequently called Derbyshire spar and reached the height of its popularity from the 1760s.

Blue mazarin See MAZARIN BLUE.

Blunderbuss From the German *Donnerbuchse* (thunder-gun). A short, large-caliber gun with a flared muzzle, used from around 1640 to the 1850s. Loaded with a heavy charge of lead pellets, it was devastating at close range and was favored by mailcoach guards and on board ships.

Boarded chest A simply constructed form of chest in which the front and back are made of planks of wood attached with nails to the vertical end pieces rather than by MORTISE AND TENON joints, as in a joined chest.

Bob pendulum A type of PENDULUM consisting of a brass or steel rod with a disk-shaped metal weight (bob) at the end, used in LONGCASE CLOCKS from about 1660. The timekeeping of a clock can be accelerated or slowed by altering the height of the bob so that the pendulum swings at a different rate.

Bobbin A slender, TURNED, wooden or bone spool or reel to hold thread for making BOBBIN LACE. Some are inscribed or weighted with glass beads. See LACE.

Bobbin lace This lace-making method required the aid of a parchment pattern marked with pins on a hard pillow. Threads wound on BOBBINS were passed around the pins. A ribbon of lace emerged as the pins were moved, resulting in "straightlace." Alternative lace motifs called "part lace" were made separately and then assembled. Italy led the way, but centers for making bobbin lace were formed throughout Europe in the 17th and 18th centuries, notably in FLANDERS.

Blanket chest
Montgomery County Pennsylvania painted blanket chest.

Gilt leaf scroll handle

Bleu celeste
Sèvres Seaux-a-Liquer, with decorators' marks for Jean-Jacques-Piere. 1768.

Blue-dash charger
English delft dish, depicting King William III, with blue-dash rim. Late 17th century.

Blue John
Piece of Blue John. 19th century.

Bobble head ■ A molded and painted hollow ceramic figurine where the head (usually oversized) is attached to the body by a spring. Movement or tapping the head causes it to bobble around, hence the name. Although characters from popular culture and real life personalities are commonplace, most examples are made to represent sports players, particularly from American football and baseball. They began to grow in popularity during the 1950s and 60s. Some early examples are made from papier-mâché.

Bocage ■ A mass of trees or shrubs from a 14th-century French word *bose*, or in literary English, "bosky," meaning bushes or a wood. When used in ceramics, it denotes bushes and/or branches around a figure, springing from supporting tree-trunks.

Body The composite material from which ceramics—POTTERY, PORCELAIN, EARTHENWARE, and STONEWARE—are made. The term refers both to the fired or unfired material. Porcelain body is also known as PASTE.

Boehm, Edward Marshall (1913–69) An American porcelain-maker, and founder of Edward Marshall Boehm Inc. in Trenton, New Jersey, in 1950. The firm specialized in realistic animal and bird sculptures in naturalistic BISCUIT porcelain, comparable to the work of Dorothy Doughty at ROYAL WORCESTER, modeled by Boehm. The firm continues, owned by Helen Boehm, wife of the founder.

Boelen, Jacob (1657–1729) A Dutch-born American silversmith active in New York City from around 1680. His pieces, which may bear the maker's mark "IB" within a shield, include rare tankards and cups.

Bohemian glass ■ This area of Eastern Europe had a flourishing glass industry from the 15th century, owing to its wealth of lumber for furnaces and variety of minerals. This was aided by the patronage of Rudolf II, who became Holy Roman Emperor in 1576 and established his court at Prague. Numerous factories began by producing Waldglas but were quick to learn new techniques. By the mid 18th century, Bohemian glass dominated world production. In the 19th century, Bohemia became a center for the production of new types of colored glass. Jirt, Count von Buquoy, produced an opaque black glass in imitation of Wedgwood's BASALT WARE in 1817, and in 1819 HYALITH, an opaque glass in red or black, often gilded. In 1818 Friedrich EGERMANN invented a yellow glass STAIN. In the 1820s and 1830s exhibitions at Prague inspired further experimentation: Bohemian glassmakers produced an ultramarine in 1826; in 1829 Egermann developed the opaque glass LITHYALIN, and in the 1830s a rich red ruby stain. Josef Riedel produced Annagrün (greenish yellow) and Annagelb (yellowish green) clear glass.

Many new glassworks were opened, including the Loetz factory that was to become the LOETZ, glassworks. In the 20th century, while designers such as Koloman MOSER established an ART GLASS studio, many Bohemian glassmakers concentrated on producing copies of other European glass such as IRIDESCENT GLASS, as well as a range of now rare heavy cut lead glass vases, bowls, and decanters in ART DECO styles. Glass is still produced in the area today and is known as Czech glass.

Bohm, August (1812–90) A Bohemian glass-engraver born in Meistersdorf, Bohm was one of the leading engravers of the BIEDERMEIER period (1820s–40s). He traveled widely, working in London, Manchester, and STOURBRIDGE in Britain, in Hamburg, and in the US, engraving goblets and plaques with portraits, as well as religious subjects and historic scenes.

Bois de rapport French term used for wood cut across, rather than along, the grain in order to create a distinctive figuring used for VENEERING or INLAY decoration.

Bois durci A form of simulated EBONY, patented in 1856 by François Charles Lepage, and popular in England and France during the second half of the 19th century. Made from sawdust bound with albumen from egg or blood, it was die-stamped into decorative moldings such as rosettes and medallions, and applied to furniture and trays.

Boiserie A French term for a type of carved wood paneling used on the walls of

Bobble head
German painted plaster Aviator Duck bobble head candy container. 1920s.

Bocage
Staffordshire pearlware depicting the "Flight from Egypt," with bocage. c. 1825.

Bohemian glass
Bohemian glass beaker with cover. c. 1700.

Bohemian glass
Bohemian amber glass goblet, with scenes of the city of Aachen. c. 1840.

BOCH FRÈRES

A ceramic firm founded by Pierre-Joseph Boch (died 1818) in Luxembourg in 1767, and continued by subsequent generations of the same family. It merged to become VILLEROY AND BOCH in 1836. When Belgium and Luxembourg were partitioned in 1839, the Belgian branch of the family set up a factory at Keramis in 1841 and traded as Boch Frères, making Art Deco pottery in the 1920s and 30s. The factory is still producing today.

Boch Frères Vase
Vase designed by Charles Catteau, marked "KERAMIS/ Made in Belgium/D943/Ch. Catteau."

the rooms of substantial buildings and houses. Often elaborately decorated with carved foliage and painted with gold ornament, it was used particularly in 17th- and 18th-century France and reflected the fashions for ROCOCO and NEOCLASSICISM.

Bokhara ■ A town (also known as Bukhara) in central Asia that was a major exporting center for Afghan and Turkoman carpets, rugs, and textiles in the 19th century. Many Turkoman tribal carpets are wrongly described as Bokhara, but this term should refer only to carpets made by the TEKKE tribe and should be called Tekke Bokhara.

Bole ■ A soft red variety of clay, found in eastern Mediterranean countries and used as a pigment. It was used by J. F. BÖTTGER in the stoneware he developed in 1707 at MEISSEN. It is employed in the compounding of ENAMEL COLORS and as a ground for gilding on furniture. It is a relatively pure clay consisting of kaolinite plus iron oxide.

Bolection molding A MOLDING, usually with an S-shaped section, used to cover the joint between two elements whose surfaces are not level and are often in the form of a framework around panels.

Bologna potteries Bologna was the center in Italy for LEAD-GLAZED earthenware from the 15th to the 18th century. The usual decorative technique was SGRAFFITO: incising the white slip coating to expose the buff or red clay body underneath and filling

in the grooves with metallic pigments. Kiln-wasters from 1450 to 1480 have been found at Bologna, some pieces bearing heraldic coats of arms of Bolognese families.

Bombé ■ The French term for "puffed out," employed in the early 18th century to describe the swelling convex shape on two or more axes used on the front of chests-of-drawers, made in France from the RÉGENCE period until the fashion for Classical furniture in the reign of Louis XVI; the equivalent American term is "kettle shape."

Bonbon dish ■ An open sweetmeat dish on a base for small sugared dessert items, made in glass or porcelain from the mid-18th century to the 19th century.

Bonbonnière From the French *bonbon* (a sweet). A box with a lid to hold small sweets or sugar-coated seeds or nuts used to freshen breath. Enamel bonbonnières in animal forms were made in imitation of MEISSEN porcelain in the 1770s and 1780s—for example, in BILSTON.

Bone ash The product of ground calcined bones, usually cattle bones, this pure white substance is sometimes used in porcelain and glass production. Bone china, which contains 45–50 percent bone ash, was first patented by Thomas Frye of the BOW factory in England in 1748.

Bone china A British PORCELAIN in which calcined ox bone is added to the

Bokhara
Bokhara Tekke Turkoman carpet, West Turkestan. c. 1900.

Bole
Meissen Bottgersteinzeug plaque depicting Judith with the head of Holofernes. c. 1711.

Bombé
Mid-late 18th century ormolu and marquetry bombé commode by Pierre Langlois.

Bonbon dish
English delftware heart-shaped bonbon dish. c. 1750.

BODY, which gives a very white color. First used by Thomas Frye of Bow in 1748 to make a type of SOFT-PASTE PORCELAIN. In the late 18th century, Josiah SPODE adopted it mixed with china clay and stone to make a harder version to compete with the import of Oriental porcelain. It is first fired to a translucent state without a glaze at 2,336°F (1,280°C) and then glaze-fired at a temperature below 1,976°F (1,080°C).

Bonheur, Isidore-Jules ■ (1827–1901) The sculptor brother of Rosa BONHEUR, known for his lifelike bronzes of sheep, cattle, horses, and wild animals. Many bronzes complemented his sister's works. Along with Antoine Louis BARYE, he was one of the leading French ANIMALIERS, with his first important work being shown at the Paris Salon in 1848.

Bonheur-du-jour ■ A type of ladies' small writing desk with a flat writing surface at the front, an arrangement of small drawers, cupboards, or shelves at the back, and a drawer below. An established form by the late 1760s, it was interpreted in different styles and with a variety of decoration—notably MARQUETRY and LACQUERWORK—throughout Europe during the 19th and early 20th centuries.

Bonheur, Rosa (1822–99) A leading 19th-century French animal painter and sculptor who is known for her anatomically accurate and lifelike lions, tigers, and horses. She exhibited at the Paris Salon from 1841, and

her most famous work is the Horse Pair of 1853. In 1865 she became the first woman to receive the French *Légion d'Honneur*.

Bonnet top ■ A term used in American furniture from the early 18th century to describe a domed or "broken" arched top PEDIMENT found mainly on early and better examples of the HIGHBOY. The form is derived from the WILLIAM AND MARY STYLE, and can also be in the form of a double arch, or "double bonnet" top. Some styles are also sometimes referred to as SWAN'S-NECK PEDIMENTS.

Bonnin and Morris porcelain factory
A partnership of Gouse Bonnin from England and George Anthony Morris of Philadelphia, who in 1770 established the American China Manufactory in Southwark, Philadelphia. The experiment was unsuccessful, closing in November 1772 when the works and contents were sold at a public auction. Products, which are very rare, are limited to blue and white painted or (rarely) printed wares of utility type, comparable to some BOW pottery. Marks include a blue painted "P" (for Philadelphia) or "S" (for Southwark).

Bontemps, Georges (1799–1884) A French glassmaker. From 1823 to 1848, he was director at the Choisy-le-Roi glassworks in Paris, where he initiated several important technical developments, including OPALINE GLASS. He perfected a method of molding glass called *moulé en plein*

around 1830, which characterized Baccarat's most distinctive form of glassware. In 1848 he moved to England to work at the Chance Brothers' Spon Lane glassworks in Smethwick, Birmingham, and wrote a technical treatise, *Guide du Verrier*, in 1868.

Boote, T. & R. Of Waterloo Pottery (and other addresses) in Burslem, Staffordshire, from 1842 to the present day. It made utility wares in earthenware, and also figures in PARIAN WARE and tiles, frequently printed in brown. Pieces from 1890 to 1906 have printed marks, including the firm's name and often the name of the pattern. Waterloo Pottery closed in 1906 and the firm concentrated on making tiles, being famous, among other things, for tiling the Blackwall Tunnel in London.

Booze bottles Initially, the bottles designed to hold whiskey made for Edmund G. Booz of Philadelphia by the Whitney Glassworks; thereafter, a general term used for spirit bottles not of flask form, mostly made during the second half of the 19th century. The bottles are shaped like a two-story house with a pitched roof.

Bordeaux potteries A group of FAIENCE factories in southwest France from the early 18th century. The first one known was founded by Jacques Hustin and made domestic ware and larger pieces from 1729 until 1783. Eight faience or porcelain factories were listed in 1790. There are still active potteries in the Bordeaux area.

Bonheur, Isidore-Jules
Bronze of a mounted polo player by Isidore Bonheur; signed. c. 1875.

Bonheur-du-jour
Bonheur-du-jour by Émile Gallé, frieze signed "Émile Gallé fecit Nancy." c. 1898.

Bonnet top
Chippendale cherrywood bonnet-top chest-on-chest, Massachusetts. c. 1775.

Boreman, Zachariah
Derby plate, with a landscape panel by Zachariah Boreman. Late 18th century.

Boreman, Zachariah ■ (1738–1810) A good painter of landscapes at the CHELSEA porcelain factory until 1783, and at the DERBY porcelain factory from 1784 to 1794, when he left to become an OUTSIDE DECORATOR in London. Boreman specialized in monochrome (black or brown) landscapes, often of Derbyshire scenes.

Borne, La Stoneware was produced in this center in the Loire, France, from the mid-16th century. Later, a series of studio potters settled in the area, including Henri-Paul-Auguste Beyer, Vassili Ivanoff, and the sculptor and potter Elisabeth Jouli.

Borussia-Glas A type of clear lead glass, CASED with opaque white and colored glass, often blue, red, or black, with cut and engraved CAMEO decoration, made at Haida in the Czech Republic in the early 20th century.

Boselli, Giacomo (1744–1808) Also known as Jacques Borelly or Boselly, an Italian manufacturer of FAIENCE at Marseilles until 1779, when he moved to the Italian town of Savona near Genoa. He made tin-glazed and cream-colored

Brass collar

earthenware pieces decorated with enamel colors, and figures in soft-paste porcelain.

Boston & Sandwich Glass Company ■ One of the largest commercial glassworks in North America, founded in 1826 in Sandwich, Cape Cod, Massachusetts, by Deming Jarves, who had previously founded the NEW ENGLAND GLASS COMPANY. Until its closure in 1888, the company produced an enormous variety of utility and ornamental ware, including cut and blown pieces and, later, pressed, three-part molded, and flashed (CASED) glass in colorful artistic designs of the "fancy" type, which is often generically referred to in the US as "Sandwich glass."

Boston rocker ■ An American form of rocking chair popular in Boston, Massachusetts, and throughout New England from about 1820. It resembles a conventional WINDSOR CHAIR with spool-turned elements, a seat that turns up at the back, and a scrolling back. The term is used commonly in the US for rocking chairs of this form.

Botanical flowers ■ A type of porcelain decoration, in which true-to-life flowers were painted from the scientific floras of the 18th century. It was used on the famous Flora Danica service, made in 1800 by the COPENHAGEN PORCELAIN FACTORY, after the studies of plants by the Danish botanist Linnaeus. The English factory of CHELSEA produced a series from Sir Hans

Soane's designs in the mid-18th century, and DERBY also favored this form of decoration, copying the designs from books of engravings.

Boteh A tear drop or leaf-shaped motif frequently seen in Oriental rugs, carpets, and textiles. Curvilinear and geometric versions exist in nomadic and urban pieces, often arranged in infinitely repeating patterns in the main field, and also seen as secondary ornaments.

Bott, Thomas (1829–70) An English painter and designer working at the WORCESTER porcelain factory, where he was responsible for the so-called LIMOGES ENAMEL style, inspired by the medieval enamels made in Limoges, France. The style was revived in the 19th century, predominantly with figures in white enamel against a dark, usually blue, background. His son, Thomas John Bott, was also employed at the Worcester porcelain factory for some years, painting in the same style as his father, before moving to COALPORT.

Böttger luster ■ A delicate pink-lilac lustrous glaze for ceramics invented by J. F. BÖTTGER, often used in the gilt-edged surrounds of CHINOISERIE subjects.

Böttger, Johann Friedrich ■ (1682–1719) The German ceramicist and ARCANIST responsible for the invention of European HARD-PASTE PORCELAIN. He boasted that he could turn base metal into gold and

Boston & Sandwich Glass Double-overlay, "frosted" and red glass lamp with brass hardware and marble base. c. 1860–80.

Boston rocker Boston rocking chair, probably Lancaster county, Philadelphia. c. 1830.

Botanical flowers Derby botanical plate by Quaker Pegg, "Orange lily and Morandia." c. 1813–15.

Böttger luster Meissen teacups, with Böttger luster and gilt Laub-und-Bandelwerk surrounds. c. 1730.

Böttger, Johann Friedrich Meissen coffeepot, made from white Böttger porcelain. c. 1730.

B

persuaded the King of Prussia to employ him to do so. But sensing failure, he fled to Dresden in Saxony. There he was imprisoned by Augustus the Strong, who was an obsessive collector of Oriental porcelain. Böttger worked with the scientist Von Tschirnhaus, and they finally made porcelain in 1708. Tschirnhaus died in that year. Böttger continued alone, making fine red stoneware, white porcelain, and luster. The Royal Saxon Porcelain Manufactory at MEISSEN was established in 1710 with Böttger as director, but by then his health had started failing. He died in 1719.

Bottle glass ■ An unrefined, commonly found glass, known also as "green glass" because of its dark green or dark brown coloring, which results from the addition of iron compounds to sand. It was used in England from the mid-17th century for bottles, and with the addition of colored flecks, for NAILSEA-type glass from the early 19th century.

Bottle ticket See WINE LABEL.

Bottle vase A shape with a globular or ovoid body and tall "bottle" neck, so combining the characteristics of both a bottle and a vase. The shape originated in China, possibly in the late TANG dynasty.

Boucher, François ■ (1703–70) A French painter and designer who studied in Rome. Elected to the French academy in 1734, he became court painter in 1765. His painting was enormously influential on 18th-century European tapestry and ceramics. In 1736 he designed a series of cartoons, *Les Fêtes Italiennes*, the first of over 40 he was to produce for BEAUVAIS. In 1755 he became artistic director of GOBELINS. His interest in Chinese porcelain inspired him to design groups of Chinese figures for CHELSEA and MEISSEN, and his pastoral scenes were to greatly influence decoration at SÈVRES. He became factory designer at Sèvres in 1754.

Boudeuse From the French *bouder* (to sulk). A type of French 19th-century SOFA also known as a "conversation piece," with a central backrest that separates the two occupants.

Boudoir doll ■ Made in France and Spain from about 1920 to 1930 to adorn beds and boudoirs, boudoir dolls represent seductive, long-limbed ladies. Their bodies are covered in silk, cotton, or a knitted fabric called stockinette, with painted facial features, including languishing eyes and bobbed silk hair. Heads are usually made of COMPOSITION and clothing is often elaborate and was fashionable at the time.

Bough pot ■ A European ceramic pot or vase, usually semicircular, with a flat back and removable top pierced with holes to hold cut flowers or bulbs. Delft TULIPIÈRES are specialized examples. Josiah WEDGWOOD referred to his examples as "rootpots."

Bouillotte lamp ■ A type of brass or gilt-bronze table-lamp made in France from the 18th century. Named after a card game (and probably developed to illuminate the small tables on which the game was played), it has a wide, dish-shaped base and a stem with candle brackets and a metal shade.

Boulle ■ A marquetry technique employing matching sheets of tortoiseshell and metal (mostly brass), also known as BUHL work, and named after the French *maître ébéniste* André-Charles BOULLE, who perfected the process in the late 17th century.

Boulle, André-Charles (1642–1732) A French cabinet-maker, who in 1672 was appointed *Ébéniste du Roi* and designed furniture and superb clockcases for the court of Louis XIV and other European rulers and rich patrons. Although his furniture is unstamped, pieces can usually be identified by provenance, the use of superb gilt-bronze ornaments, the eponymous elaborate, showy tortoiseshell, and brass marquetry. Earlier pieces by Boulle were decorated with wood marquetry.

Boulton, Matthew (1728–1809) An English metalworker and silversmith, born in Birmingham. He began in his father's business making buckles and buttons. In 1762 he built a manufactory in Soho, Birmingham, and went into partnership with John Fothergill, producing buttons, buckles, and a wide range of domestic ware

Bottle glass
A Nailsea-style sealed wine bottle, dark olive green with white enamelled flecks. 1830.

Boucher, François
Young lovers in a pastoral scene, attributed to François Boucher.

Boudoir doll
Boudoir doll smoking a cigarette. 1920.

Painted decoration in relief

Bough pot
Derby demi-lune bough pot and pierced liner, with painted pattern. c. 1800.

in fine-quality SHEFFIELD PLATE. He later made silver and fine ormolu in the ADAM style. He was a major campaigner in establishing the Birmingham Assay office in 1773. With James Watt he developed a steam engine to aid mass production and expanded the business to produce coins and medals. After he died the company was continued by his son until around 1846.

Bourdalou(e) An oval-shaped ladies' chamber pot, made from both porcelain and pottery by leading Continental and English factories, and even in China for export back to Europe. WEDGWOOD made them in creamware and referred to them as "coach pots"; other sources say that ladies carried them concealed in their muff. The name is derived from Louis Bourdaloue, a French preacher at the court of Louis XIV at Versailles, who was so popular that ladies had to line up for hours to be admitted to the church where he was to preach. Their use survived into the 19th century for long coach journeys.

Bourne & Son ◼ A family firm owning potteries at BELPER from 1812 to 1834, and at DENBY from 1834 to the present day. Earlier products included salt-glazed stoneware jugs with hunting scenes in relief and with greyhound handles. Most of their products were utilitarian. The factory now specializes in simply designed but well-made fireproof kitchen wares.

Boutet, Nicholas Noel (1761–1833) A French gunmaker, appointed artistic director of the Versailles Arsenal in 1793. Boutet concentrated on luxury arms for presentation to foreign dignitaries. His guns showed little technical innovation, but were made and decorated to the highest standards. He is the only gunmaker ever to have signed his work "Directeur Artiste."

Bovey Tracey Pottery See WEMYSS WARE.

Bow front A convex curving front on a CHEST-OF-DRAWERS, CABINET, SIDEBOARD, COMMODE, and other pieces of CASE FURNITURE. In the US it is sometimes referred to as a "swell front."

Bow porcelain factory A manufactory founded in 1744 in Stratford, east London (at that time in the parish of Bow). A patent, dated December 1744, was granted to a merchant, Edward Heylyn, and a portrait painter, Thomas Frye, for a new method of manufacturing, whereby a ware might be made of the same nature as china or porcelain. In November 1749 another patent was granted in the name of Frye alone. The new method referred to the inclusion of a substantial amount of BONE ASH in the body of the porcelain, making it very heavy. The factory was called New Canton, and a printed advertisement appeared in August 1748 stating that "useful and ornamental china" was for sale. Initially, Bow made blue and white wares in

a vibrant blue; documentary pieces are inkwells inscribed "Made at New Canton 1750." It also made tea sets, plates, jugs, mugs, and cutlery handles, which were produced throughout the history of the factory. Its white wares with prunus decoration in relief were inspired by the so-called BLANC-DE-CHINE, made at Dehua in China. Inspiration also came from the FAMILLE ROSE ware of China, as well as Japanese KAKIEMON porcelain—the "Two Quail pattern" was particularly popular. European-style subjects included botanic drawings and painted flowers and birds in the style of MEISSEN and SÈVRES. The Bow enamel blue is especially distinctive. The factory also made many figures, which often reflected a strong local interest, or topical subjects such as the actors Kitty Clive and Henry Woodward. Some of the earliest figures have a distinctive style with small heads. These are attributed to the Muses Modeler, after a set of the Classical Muses. Bow also copied MEISSEN figures. Its models of animals are naive but charming. In 1775 the factory closed and the molds and tools were transferred to DERBY.

Bowie knife ◼ A large hunting knife, said to take its name from the American frontiersman James Bowie. They normally have broad, single-edged blades, with sharply angled, curved points. The top half of the blade near the point may also be sharpened. Although they originated in the US in around 1830, many were made later in Sheffield, England.

Bouillotte lamp
French gilt bronze bouillotte lamp with tole painted shade. 20th century.

Boulle
Louis XIV red boulle commode. The top has a tortoiseshell and brass panel.

Bourne & Son pottery
Ginger beer bottle, with Bourne Denby pottery mark.

Bowie knife
An American Bowie knife with clipped back blade and sheaf. Early 20th century.

Box back A commercially made English DOLLHOUSE from the late 18th century to the 1930s, based on the style of a typical town house, with a flat facade projecting from a rectangular box.

Box bedstead A type of Northern European bed, built into the corner of a room and enclosed by a wooden canopy and curtains or sliding wooden panels that matched the wall paneling. They were popular in Scandinavia, Germany, and the Low Countries in the 17th century, where they were known as closets or cupboard beds. They were used in rural areas until the 19th century.

Box stool A 17th-century oak stool with a storage box underneath a hinged square or rectangular seat.

Boxlock ■ A type of FLINTLOCK or PERCUSSION LOCK where the moving parts were centrally mounted in a box-shaped housing (as opposed to sidelocks, where the housing was to one side). The

mechanism was in use from about 1710 until the second half of the 19th century.

Boxwood A tree native to Northern Europe and Asia, the lumber from which is pale yellow, sometimes brown or orange, with a close, even grain. Boxwood was used from the late 17th century onward for decorative inlay, turned members, TREEN, tool handles, carving, and blocks for engraving.

Bracket A small projecting element, often decorated with carved or modeled motifs and supporting another feature.

Bracket clock ■ A spring-driven clock, originally designed to stand on a wall bracket but later on a shelf or table; also known as a MANTEL or TABLE CLOCK. Such clocks were introduced after the invention of the PENDULUM in the mid-17th century. Bracket clocks usually have rectangular wooden cases with shaped tops and bases,

with French and later American examples featuring a more diverse range of materials.

Bracquemond, (Joseph-Auguste) Felix (1833–1914) A French ceramic designer, painter, and engraver. His designs are among the first to show Japanese influence, after he saw a book of Hokusai's work in 1856. He worked for Criel-Montereau, J. T. Deck, SÈVRES, and C. F. Haviland before opening his own studio.

Bradbury & Sons, Thomas A firm originally founded in 1769 in Sheffield, England, trading as Matthew Fenton & Co. and making Old Sheffield plate and silver, especially FLATWARE. It opened its first showroom in London around 1820 and by 1900 had become one of the best-known manufacturers of silver and plate. Thomas Bradbury was also known for his pocket-book of date letters on English silver. The company finally closed in 1943.

Braganza foot A rectangular ribbed and scrolled foot used on chairs and tables.

BOW PORCELAIN FACTORY

During its existence, from 1744 to 1775, the Bow porcelain factory in Stratford, East London, became the largest factory in England. The vast majority of its porcelain was inspired by East Asian designs, and in terms of palette initially took the form of *blanc-de-chine* and underglaze blue wares; later, polychromed enameled wares were produced, usually based on *famille rose* or Kakiemon designs.

Plate
Bow blue-gound Chinoiserie plate, painted with a mythical dragon and flaming pearl; painter's No.13. c. 1755.

Egg-yolk yellow and puce were popular Bow colors

Mug
Bow mug, painted in polychrome enamels with chinoiserie decoration. c. 1764–65.

Figure
Bow figure. c. 1765.

Sauceboat
Bow silver shaped sauceboat, decorated with gilt flowers and leaves. c. 1750–55.

Originating in England in the 17th century and named after Catherine of Braganza, Charles II's Spanish queen, it often replaced the bun foot during William and Mary's reign.

Brameld family See ROCKINGHAM.

Brampton potteries A small group of Derbyshire factories from the early 18th to the early 20th century, which made brown domestic stoneware. The main factories were those of S. & H. Briddon and J. Oldfield, who also made toffee-colored ware with relief decoration and Toby jugs in salt-glazed stoneware. See DERBYSHIRE POTTERIES.

Brandt, Edgar (1880–1960) A French ART DECO designer and metalworker, noted for his wrought iron designs. He exhibited at the 1900 Paris Exhibition, provided work for the ocean liner *Normandie*, and showed his work at the 1925 Paris Exposition. He opened showrooms in London and New York under the name of Ferrobrandt.

Brandy bowl or pan A one- or two-handled silver bowl, usually on a foot of oval or polygonal outline, often with a silver-gilt or gilded interior. It was used to warm drinks, including brandy, in the embers of a fire. Brandy bowls were made in large numbers in Europe, particularly in Holland, in the 17th and 18th centuries.

Brangwyn, Sir Frank (1867–1956) A Belgian-born painter and designer brought up in England, where he worked with William MORRIS. He also worked in Paris with Samuel BING, and designed textiles, carpets, stained glass, and furniture, as well as dinnerware for Royal Doulton.

BRACKET FOOT

A support for CASE FURNITURE, in use from the late 17th century and especially popular in the 18th century, in the form of two brackets mitered and joined at the corner. The early form was usually straight-sided; from around 1730 to 1740 the OGEE bracket foot was also used, together with, at the end of the 18th century, the splayed bracket foot.

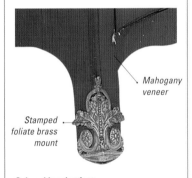

Mahogany veneer

Stamped foliate brass mount

Splayed bracket feet
Dutch mahogany serpentine *bombé* commode, with splayed bracket feet. 19th century.

Brannam, Charles Hubert ■ (1855–1937)
The Brannam family were potters in Devon from the late 18th century. Thomas Brannam exhibited jugs at the GREAT EXHIBITION of 1851. In 1879 C. H. Brannam took over his father's pottery in Barnstaple, North Devon, having studied art. He continued to produce traditional slip and SGRAFFITO-decorated pottery. He introduced more fashionable designs under the name BARUM WARE, sold through Howell & James, LIBERTY & CO., and HEAL & SON. His sons continued in the pottery, which is still in business today, although it moved to a new site in Barnstaple in the 1980s.

Brass An alloy of copper and zinc, first known in the 2nd millennium BCE. The ratio of the two metals alters the characteristics of the alloy—it becomes progressively whiter as more zinc is added. Ductile and easily cast, brass has been used since medieval times for household wares such as bowls, candlesticks, cooking pots, and fireplace furnishings. In the Middle Ages, the main production centers were the Low Countries and Germany, but from the 18th century Birmingham, England, was dominant, mass-producing buttons, buckles, door-knockers, and furniture mounts.

Braun, Georg 1541–1622) **and Hogenberg, Frans** (1536–1588) A German topographer and an engraver who published the first ATLAS of town plans and views, the six-volume *Civitates Orbis Terrarum* (Cities of

Boxlock
Three-barreled, 160-bore flintlock boxlock pocket pistol, by Whalley, Macclesfield. c. 1800.

Bracket clock
George III mahogany bracket clock with anchor escapement, by Eardley Norton.

Brannam, Charles Hubert
Pottery vase, by Beauchamp Wimple; incised "C.H. Brannam, Barum, 1899."

B

the World), in various editions from 1572 to 1617. It eventually included more than 500 detailed plans and bird's-eye views, many with portraits of local inhabitants.

Bread basket ■ A silver basket designed to hold bread, often oval and pierced to imitate wicker. 17th-century examples are rare and tend to have two handles. Those from the 1730s have a central swing handle, mounted on either side. Their weights vary, but average size is 12 inches (30 cm) long. Bread baskets were also made in plate and other materials.

Breakfront ■ A term for CASE FURNITURE (also broken front), most notably bookcases and wardrobes, with a projecting or protruding center section.

Breech The rear end of the barrel of a firearm, that contains the chamber where the gunpowder charge or the cartridge is ignited. As it has to withstand great pressure on firing, it is always of heavier construction than the rest of the barrel. Breech-loading firearms are easier to load than muzzle-loading versions. Although the type was introduced in the 15th century, it was not perfected until the 19th century, with the development of the metallic cartridge.

Bréguet, Abraham-Louis ■ (1747–1823) An eminent French clock- and watchmaker, credited with many inventions, including, in 1795, a modification to the LEVER ESCAPEMENT known as the tourbillon,

which rendered a watch immune to errors caused by its changing position as it was being carried. Bréguet also developed a form of BALANCE SPRING that was fitted to most precision watches that still holds his name.

Breloque A French term for a small decorative object in gold or enamel such as a figurine, locket, or seal, with a small ring for suspending from a watch chain or CHATELAINE.

Bretby Art Pottery An English pottery founded in Woodville, Derbyshire, by Henry Tooth and William AULT in 1883. Ault left in 1887 the pottery and became known as Tooth & Co. Two of its most popular ranges were East Asian subjects in relief and simulated copper and metal wares with jeweled ornament in the ART NOUVEAU style. It closed in 1920.

Breuer, Marcel Lajos ■ (1902–81) A Hungarian architect-designer who studied in Vienna and at the BAUHAUS, and worked in Germany, England (1935), and the US (from 1937). He was head of carpentry at the Bauhaus (1925–28), where he produced his first tubular steel chair designs (Wassily, 1925). In England he designed in plywood for Isokon, producing his now-iconic chaise longue. In the US he practiced as an architect while also designing furniture.

Brewster chair An American open armchair form of Elizabethan inspiration,

first made in Massachusetts in the mid-17th century. Brewsters are typically made of ash, maple, or hickory with woven rush seats and are a distinctive, large, early version of the more familiar PILGRIM CHAIR of COLONIAL America. Few original Brewsters exist but some excellent fakes are recorded. See CARVER CHAIR.

Brewster, Elisha ■ An American clockmaker. From around 1844, Brewster worked in partnership with Elias and Andrew Ingrahams at Bristol, Connecticut, producing inexpensive SHELF, MANTEL, and WALL CLOCKS with veneered wooden cases in a variety of designs, including the "steeple" clock with a pointed gable.

Brezová The more recent Czech name for the porcelain manufacturing town of Pirkenhammer, in what was formerly Bohemia. The factory was set up in 1802 by Friedrich Holke and J. G. List and had many changes of owners, including Fischer & Mieg in 1857. It is still in existence. Its mark is two crossed hammers, with or without the name of the town.

Bright cut decoration ■ A form of engraving on silver, primarily from 1770 to 1820. The engraver's tool removes V-shaped chips or facets of metal in simple patterns, often from around the borders of a piece. The result is a glistening or sparkling effect, as these facets reflect light at different angles.

Bread basket
German silver basket for fruit or bread. c. 1880.

Urn finials

Breakfront
George III mahogany library breakfront bookcase, with a writing table. c. 1770.

Bréguet, A. L.
Bréguet quarter repeating full hunter pocket watch in 18-ct. rose gold. c. 1900.

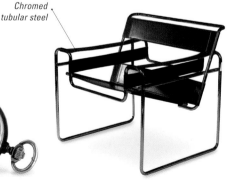

Chromed tubular steel

Breuer, Marcel Lajos
Wassily B3 chromium armchair, designed by Marcel Breuer. c.1925.

Briglin ■ A studio pottery founded in London in 1948 by potters Brigitte Appleby and Eileen Lewenstein. They were known for their glazed tableware and vases decorated with natural motifs using WAX-RESIST and SGRAFFITO techniques. Although commercially successful, a decline in sales led the company closing in 1990.

Brilliant cut The ideal form of cutting for diamonds, taking best advantage of the optical properties and brilliance of the stone. A brilliant consists of 58 facets; 33 above the girdle of the stone and 25 below on the pavilion. 19th-century brilliants tended toward a cushion-shape and were often ill-proportioned; modern stones are perfectly symmetrical and thus display maximum brilliance. Brilliant cutting is also the most distinctive form of American cut glass. First seen at the Philadelphia Centennial Exhibition in 1876, it was widely produced in the US and copied abroad.

Briqueté A term used to denote a form of decoration simulating a brick wall.

Brisé fan ■ A folding fan made from ivory, metal, or wood where the leaf of the fan is formed by the tapering sticks themselves, rather than by a paper or silk panel applied to the sticks.

Bristol glasshouses From the 17th century, the numerous glasshouses in Bristol were known for the production of window and BOTTLE GLASS. They later became famous for decorative enameling and gilding, opaque white glass, and finally high-quality colored glass. These late 18th- and early 19th-century Bristol blue glasses and decanters were colored with COBALT imported from Saxony via Bristol.

Bristol porcelain factories The earliest porcelain made here was a soft-paste porcelain by Benjamin Lund and William Miller of Redcliff Backs. Lund had taken out a license to mine SOAPSTONE in 1748 for a year. Figures of a Chinese man and some sauceboats are known, molded with "Bristol" or "Bristoll" as a mark, and some are dated 1750. In 1752 the Lund-Miller concern was bought by the WORCESTER Porcelain Company. In its short life this factory made some attractive products, now rare and much in demand. The second factory in Bristol, from 1770 to 1781, was moved there from Plymouth, where it had been founded by William COOKWORTHY in 1768, and made HARD-PASTE PORCELAIN. Richard Champion became manager and bought the business in 1773. The patent expired in 1775 and Champion sold his right to the Society of Staffordshire Potteries in 1781. The Champion factory made simply decorated wares for utilitarian use, but it also made some finer examples in the style of SÈVRES and DERBY. Champion also made some armorial services. They used a simple "X" mark and later copied the mark of MEISSEN. Wreathing, or low spiral ridges in the paste, is a characteristic of the BODY.

Bristol potteries A number of potteries were known in the area from the late 17th century, producing TIN-GLAZED EARTHENWARE (DELFT) and BLUE-DASH CHARGERS. The 19th-century factory of Pountney & Co. was originally known as the Bristol Pottery. It made tableware for domestic use and, later, for hotels, and WEMYSS WARE from 1904.

Britain Ltd., William ■ William Britain set up a family mechanical toy business at his home in London in 1847. William's eldest son (also William) developed the HOLLOW CAST method for producing lead figures in 1893 that weighed less and were cheaper to produce and ship. This revolutionized the toy figure market, and many companies copied them. Model soldiers, mostly in boxed sets, dominated their production but they also made farm figures, gardens, and zoos after World War II. Figures were also made for other companies, such as BASSETT-LOWKE. Horse-drawn army units followed, as did vehicles and some planes. Lead in toys was outlawed in 1966, and the company currently uses plastic and mazak DIE CAST alloys for their reproduction sets. In 1954 plastic soldier manufacturer Herald Miniatures was acquired by the company. Early figures are unmarked, but are recognizable by their oval bases and the excellent quality of the casting and painting, with strict attention to accuracy in

Brewster, Elisha
Transitional Brewster carver armchair, from Connecticut. c. 1750.

Bright cut decoration
George III teapot, with marks for Newcastle, with floral bright cut border. c. 1800.

Briglin
Glazed Briglin pottery vase, with thistle pattern. 1970s.

Brisé fan
Chinese export ivory brisé fan. Early 18th century.

the soldiers' uniforms and weapons. From 1900 paper labels were stuck to the base; cast lettering was used from 1905. After 1907 the toy figures had square bases. The firm was purchased by Ertl Co. in 1997 and by First Gear in 2005.

Britannia metal A soft alloy of 93% tin, 2% copper, and 5% antimony, similar to, but harder than, pewter, which will temporarily take a high polish. Made in Britain from 1770, it served as a cheaper alternative to silver and Old Sheffield plate, but was softer, less durable, and prone to perishing. From the mid-19th century it was widely used as a base for electroplated articles. One of the best-known makers was J. Dixon & Sons of Sheffield, England, who also exported large quantities to the US. Notable American makers include I. Babbitt and W. Crossman of Taunton, Massachusetts.

Broad glass A type of flat window or pane glass, also known as "cylinder" or "muff" glass because it was made from a large cylindrical-shaped piece of blown glass cut down the length, reheated, and flattened. The technique was first used in France in the 12th century. It was adapted by Venetian glassmakers in the 16th century, and further refined in 19th-century Britain. Production of broad glass is now fully mechanized.

Broadside ■ An early form of poster, printed on one side with an announcement, typically of an event such as a fair,

performance, or auction. Classed as EPHEMERA, broadsides favor text over imagery and were pasted to walls and trees. They were used from the late 19th century until the early 20th century, and were replaced by the poster as it is known today, when eye-catching graphics began to be used.

Broadsword A general term that originated during the 17th century for a heavy double-edged sword designed as a cutting weapon, principally for cavalry soldiers. Similar single-edged swords are known as backswords.

Brocade ■ A woven textile ornamented with a raised floral or foliate design formed by additional weft threads. Weaving was slow and expensive, hence many early brocades use silver and gold thread.

Brocard, Philippe-Joseph (died 1896) A French enameler, gilder, and glass artist inspired by Islamic mosque lamps, Islamic floral, geometric motifs, and calligraphy, which he copied. He first exhibited his work at the 1867 Paris Exhibition.

Brocart A French term for BROCADE.

Brocatelle 1. A type of variegated marble, sometimes called *brocatello*, often used for table tops in the 18th century.
2. A woven fabric, usually in silk and wool with a relief pattern, the background having a satinlike appearance, widely used in 18th-century upholstery.

Brocot (or pin-pallet) escapement ■ A type of DEADBEAT ESCAPEMENT invented in 1860 by French clock-maker Achille Brocot. Used mainly in late 19th-century French clocks, it features pallets consisting of cylindrical hardstone or steel pins. Brocot was also responsible for the Brocot suspension, a method of regulating a clock by inserting a key through the front of the dial to adjust the length of the PENDULUM spring.

Broderie anglaise A WHITEWORK embroidery with bold, punched, stylized patterns worked around with white stitched thread to decorate ladies' underwear and children's clothes. Used from the late 18th century until the present day.

Brogden, John (active 1842–85) An English goldsmith whose designs were inspired by RENAISSANCE, Moorish, and ASSYRIAN themes, and who used GRANULATION and FILIGREE motifs. He incorporated CAMEOS, enamel, and bold GEMSTONES such as garnet and turquoise.

Bronze ■ An alloy of copper and tin, with small amounts of other elements such as silver, zinc, aluminum, or lead. Developed in western Asia in the 4th millennium BCE, it has been used throughout the world for weapons, coins, and utilitarian household items, owing to its strength, hardness, and durability. Its fluidity when molten makes it one of the most suitable mediums for CASTING sculpture and decorative objects.

Britain Ltd. William
Britains Set 2069 Union Cavalry and Infantry, in "Regiments of all Nations" box.

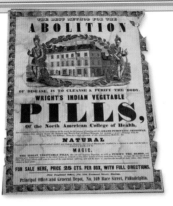

Broadside
Medical broadside of the North American College for Health. 19th century.

Brocade
Length of exotic French polychrome brocade. 19th century.

Bronze d'ameublement From the French *ameublement* (furniture). A small domestic item such as a clock case, ANDIRON, or light fixture cast in bronze and usually gilded.

Bronzitt (or Broncit) Glassware with a matte black, enameled, geometric decoration on clear or matte glass, designed by Josef HOFFMANN in about 1910 and made in Vienna by J. & L. LOBMEYR.

Brooks, John (c. 1710–60) The manager of the BATTERSEA ENAMEL FACTORY who tried to take out three patents in England in the 1750s, claiming to have "discovered the art of printing on Enamel, Glass, China, and other ware." He lived in Birmingham, the center of the enamel trade, and later in London.

Brouwer, Theophilus ■ (died 1932) An American potter and founder of the Middle Lane Pottery in East Hampton, Long Island, New York, in 1894. He produced vessels of simple form, decorated with iridescent and other experimental glazes. Marks may feature a whale jawbone centring an "M," and incised "Brouwer."

Brown & Co., George W. An American tin toy manufacturer who founded a factory in Forestville, Connecticut, in 1856. Credited as one of the earliest producers of clockwork toys in the US,

Brown made handpainted tin horse-drawn toys, trains, and boats. The company merged with J. & E. Stevens in 1868 to establish Stevens & Brown.

Brown Bess A late 18th-century nickname for the British FLINTLOCK MUSKET, used from 1710 to 1840. It probably derived from the German *Buchse*, meaning gun, and the browned finish of the barrel was designed to prevent rust.

Brownie (or Box Brownie) In 1898 the American inventor George Eastman and the camera designer and manufacturer Frank Brownell designed the Box Brownie as a low-cost, easy-to-use camera aimed primarily at young people. It was launched in 1900 and for 80 years was linked with modern popular photography. The camera was given its name after the popular pixie-like characters, drawn by Canadian illustrator and author Palmer Cox, that decorated the packaging.

Brown ware A term used to describe both Chinese brown-glazed STONEWARE of the Song Dynasty (960–1279 CE) and English brown salt-glazed stoneware made at Brampton, Derbyshire, from the early 18th century and throughout the 19th century. The main Brampton potter was William Bromley, who was succeeded by Robert Bambrigge & Co. Other 19th-century factories include Mrs. Blake's, formerly worked by her husband, and subsequently part of the Luke Knowles works (later

Matthew Knowles & Son), which made stoneware bottles, kegs, and barrels. William Briddon founded a factory in 1790, which was continued by his family. Thomas Oldfield went into business in 1810 and formed Oldfield & Co. in 1826, making jugs, figures, twisted pipes, PUZZLE JUGS, and TOBY JUGS. John Wright's factory near St. Thomas's Church was still in the family in 1878. Brown EARTHENWARE with yellow or orange TRANSFER-PRINTED designs of pseudo-Chinese scenes was made from 1800 to the 1850s in STAFFORDSHIRE and possibly SWANSEA and LIVERPOOL, but the factories are unidentified.

Brown-Westhead, Moore & Co. ■ A British maker of dinner services and MAJOLICA ornamental ware, based from 1862 at Cauldon Place, Staffordshire. It was previously known as RIDGWAY Bates & Co. (1856–58) and Bates, Brown-Westhead & Moore (1859–61). The company became Cauldon Ltd. in 1905, and Cauldon Potteries Ltd. from 1920 to 1962.

Bru Jeune et Cie ■ One of the most important Parisian manufacturers of bisque-headed FASHION DOLLS and BÉBÉS. The firm was established by Léon Casimir Bru in 1866 and sold to Henri Chevrot in 1883. Bru dolls are of very fine quality, with delicate lifelike molding and painting, and are marked with "Bru (Jeune)" or a circle and dot. Bru was one of the founding members of the SOCIÉTÉ

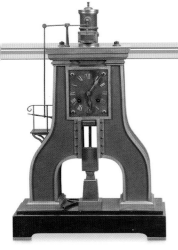

Brocot escapement
French Steam Hammer clock, with brocot escapement.
c. 1885.

Bronze
French Pointer bronze, after Jules Moignez (1853–94).

Brouwer, Theophilus
Brouwer vase, flame painted in lustered gold and amber glaze, and incised "M."

Brown-Westhead
Brown-Westhead, Moore & Co. parian bust of Albert Edward, Prince of Wales. c. 1864.

FRANÇAISE DE FABRICATION DE BÉBÉS ET JOUETS in 1899, which produced Bru dolls from the original molds until the 1950s.

B

Bruges tapestry factory Situated in Western Flanders (modern-day Belgium) on the Reie River, Bruges was not one of the largest centers of Flemish tapestry-weaving, but it flourished from about 1300 until the 17th century. Outdated cartoons discarded by the more important centers were often used. Verdures, GROTESQUES, and historical and religious tapestries were made in monastic and private workshops.

Bruin An early name given to the stuffed toy that came to be known as the teddy bear. The term "teddy bear" entered the dictionary in 1907, and although early bears made from 1902 by American maker Morris Michtom were dubbed "Teddy's Bear" after Theodore Roosevelt, the term Bruin was more commonly used.

Bruise A small area of surface damage on materials such as ceramics, glass, or metalware, which has been caused by knocking the object against something hard. This may manifest itself in a patch of scratches, an area of light roughness, or a shallow dent. In glassware it is seen in the form of cracks, or powdering.

Brunswick pottery A German FAIENCE factory, founded in 1707 by Duke Anton Ulrich, with Johann Philipp Franz as director. Heinrich C. von Horn rented it and in 1711 went into partnership with J. G. von Hantelmann until 1744. Thereafter, it changed hands frequently. Its earliest products were in blue and white, but it soon used polychrome colors and shapes such as fruit on plates and tureens in the form of birds, fish, and bunches of grapes. The factory closed in 1807.

Brush pot ■ A cylindrical container for calligraphers' or artists' brushes, from China and Japan. It can be made from a section of bamboo or from porcelain and decorated with calligraphy or blue and white scenes. Earliest known examples date from the 16th century, and these pots are still made today.

Brushing slide ■ A retractable shelf, often covered in green baize, fitted to the top of a CHEST-OF-DRAWERS. It can be pulled out and used for brushing or folding clothes, or as a writing surface.

Brussels lace ■ Flemish fine BOBBIN LACE with bold, detailed, and curving floral, foliate, and fruiting patterns, produced from the mid-17th century onward. During the late 17th century and early 18th century, figures began to appear in the design. After the 17th century it was set on a characteristic hexagonal mesh net ground. After 1820 the net was machine-made, rather than BOBBIN-made. Often of

very fine quality, it was exported around Europe, including Britain, and is sometimes known as *point d'Angleterre*. NEEDLE LACE was produced from 1720 and reached a high point in the mid-19th century, when it was known as *point de gaze* and often had three-dimensional designs. Sometimes the two different techniques were combined on one piece. Heavier BOBBIN LACE designs from this period are known as Duchesse lace.

Brussels pottery and porcelain Faience was made here in several factories from the mid-17th century. In 1705 a factory was started by Corneille Mombaers and Thierry Witsenburg that made tureens in bird, fish, and fruit shapes. A second factory was founded in 1802 by the brothers Van Bellinghen and closed in 1866. Porcelain was also produced in several factories in the late 18th century, but these appear to have all closed by 1803.

Brussels tapestry factories ■ Under the patronage of the Dukes of Burgundy, Brussels became an important tapestry-weaving center in the late 15th century. Pieter Coecke van Aelst undertook a commission from Pope Leo X for a series of tapestries, *The Acts of the Apostles*, from cartoons by Raphael. Hung in the Sistine Chapel, they gave Brussels an excellent reputation and marked a major change of creative control from the weaver to the artist. Peter Paul Rubens provided cartoons in the early 17th century, and despite some periods of decline, many fine works were

Bru Jeune et Cie
Bru Jeune Breveté doll,
c. 1870.

Brush pot
Kangxi *famille verte*
cylindrical brush pot.

Brushing slide
George III mahogany
serpentine dressing chest, the
top drawer with brushing slide
revealing various hidden boxes.

Brussels lace
Needlepoint appliqué Brussels
lace flounce. c. 1870.

produced in the late 17th century and into the 18th century. The last workshop closed in 1794.

Budai A Buddhist monk and god of contentment, usually represented seated and grinning, exposing his fat belly, sometimes with a sack. He was a popular subject in Chinese art, modeled in BLANC-DE-CHINE, or decorated in FAMILLE ROSE enamels. In Japan he is known as Hotei.

Buddy L ■ Fred Lundahl ran the Moline Pressed Steel Co. in Illinois, which made automotive parts. In 1921 he started to make pressed-steel toy vehicles. The large-scale range, strong enough to sit on, was named after his son, Buddy. The firm now makes steel and plastic vehicles, some with action and sound.

Buen Retiro porcelain factory When King Carlos IV of Naples and Sicily inherited the Spanish throne in 1759, he moved his royal porcelain factory from CAPODIMONTE (Naples) to the garden of the royal palace in Madrid. He took the artists and workmen, and even some of the clay, with him, so that the early wares are indistinguishable from those of Capodimonte. In 1804 KAOLIN was discovered in Madrid and so hard-paste porcelain—quite different from the soft paste of Capodimonte—was introduced. The factory closed in 1808.

Buen Retiro workshop A Spanish PIETRE DURE and MOSAIC workshop from about 1760 to 1808, specializing in elaborately decorated tabletops. It was founded in the park at the Palace of Buen

B

73

BUGATTI, CARLO

Italian furniture designer and maker Carlo Bugatti (1856–1940) is known for his unique style: some pieces are inlaid with ebony, copper, and pewter, and copper may be wrapped around uprights. He also used handpainted vellum. Inspired by nature and Moorish, Egyptian, and Japanese art, the use of asymmetry and tassels are features of his work. He was the father of Rembrandt Bugatti, the sculptor, and Ettore, the car designer.

Side chair
Carlo Bugatti side chair, of wood, copper, parchment, rope, pewter, and bone.

BUCKLE

Shoes and breeches commonly used buckles as a fastening in the 17th and 18th centuries, with simple examples made from steel or PINCHBECK set with paste or simply engraved; more richly ornamented examples were set with gems. Belt buckles have been used since Greek and Roman times and became highly ornamented during the second half of the 14th century. Waist buckles were popular at the start of the 19th century, and the ARTS AND CRAFTS Movement inspired colorful naturalistic themes.

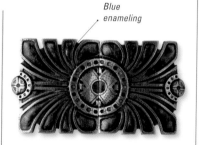

Blue enameling

Buckle
Liberty & Co. silver buckle, with blue and green enamel, Birmingham. 1911.

Brussels tapestry factories
Brussels tapestry, woven with Classical figures. Early 18th century.

Budai
Rose quartz seated Budai. 19th century.

Buddy L
Buddy L Long Distance Moving Van, in painted wood with bright original decals.

B

Retiro in Madrid by Charles III of Spain, when he came to the throne. The first craftsmen in the workshop came from the Naples Royal Pietre Dure factory.

Buffet A type of heavy, 16th-century doorless cupboard with tiers of shelves for displaying plate. The buffet went out of fashion from the end of the 17th century to the mid-19th century. It reemerged during the GOTHIC REVIVAL, also as a two- or three-shelf food cart.

Buhl See BOULLE.

Bulle clock A type of ELECTRIC CLOCK invented and patented by the French clockmaker Maurice Favre-Bulle in 1922. The MOVEMENT is usually skeletonized and set on a mahogany base, covered by a glass dome. The battery is concealed within a vertical brass pillar or in the base.

Bullet mold A metal accessory into which molten lead was poured to manufacture bullets. Molds were in use as early as 1375, but the development of the CARTRIDGE in the 19th century rendered them obsolete.

Bullet teapot ■ A style that first appeared during the 1730s, and was revived in the 19th century. Made from silver and porcelain and named for its spherical shape, resembling the round lead musket ball of the period.

Bullock, George (c. 1738–1819) An English furniture-maker, born in Liverpool.

By 1814 he was working as a sculptor and furniture-maker in London, where he became one of the leading names during the Regency period and designed furniture for Napoleon when he was imprisoned on St. Helena. The massive size and quality of his oak furniture was made even more impressive by decoration in the form of marquetry, often in EBONY or native woods such as HOLLY, ELM, and LARCH, and brass inlay in a variety of Classical motifs.

Bun foot A round, turned foot, flattened at the top and bottom, introduced in furniture of the late 17th century, and intermittently fashionable until the 19th century.

Bunzlau potteries ■ Gray STONEWARE (*grès*) was made here in Silesia, Germany, in the 16th and 17th centuries, but it is difficult to attribute accurately. In the 19th century there was a resurgence of gray stoneware, used to make coffee- and chocolate pots. A 15-foot- (4.5-m-) high, 19th-century coffeepot is preserved in Bunzlau town hall. Various factories operated into the early 20th century, including Lepper & Kuttner, Julius Paul & Son, and Reinhold & Co.

Burano See LACE.

Burato A coarse, woven fabric with a single warp thread and double-twisted weft. It was produced to form the base for embroidered LACE in Italy from the 15th century.

Bureau The French term for a form of desk introduced in the 17th century, and comprising a hinged sloping top set on a chest-of-drawers. The top drops down to produce a flat writing surface, behind which are variously configured small drawers and pigeonholes.

Bureau plat The French term for a writing desk with a flat top, usually with a tooled leather writing surface, and with drawers set in the FRIEZE.

Burgau porcelain ■ Founded at Burgau-Goschwitz in Thuringia, Germany, in 1900 by Ferdinand Solle, this porcelain factory produced utility, luxury, and ART NOUVEAU items.

Burges, William ■ (1827–81) An English architect and designer working in the GOTHIC REVIVAL style. Both Cardiff Castle and Castell Coch, in Wales, were built for his patron, the Marquis of Bute, and show a medieval influence. His work is rich in imagery, color, and texture. He also designed elaborately painted furniture and metalwork encrusted with precious stones.

Burgonet ■ A light steel HELMET worn by infantry and light cavalry in Europe from c. 1520 to c. 1650. They are generally open-faced with a peak, and have hinged cheekpieces (usually pierced with ventilation holes) and a high comb. "Closed" burgonets covered the entire

Bullet teapot
George I small bullet teapot with a molded spout and foot. c. 1720.

Bunzlau potteries
Bunzlau pewter-lidded tankard. 19th century.

Burgau porcelain
Burgau 27-piece coffee service, designed by Albin Muller. 1908.

Burges, William
Pine and walnut center table, with gold and black medieval motifs in the frame. 1867.

head, the front being protected with a detachable or hinged-shaped panel known as a buffe.

Burl A form of growth on a tree trunk, also known as a burr, which when cut reveals elaborate figuring that makes it useful for decorative veneering, as seen on burr walnut pieces.

Burmantoft pottery ■ An English pottery established in 1858 in Yorkshire by Wilcock & Co. to make architectural ceramics and bricks. In 1889 it was taken over by the Leeds Fireclay Company and the range was extended to include decorative EARTHENWARE fired at high temperatures. The company also produced single-glazed pieces in yellow, red, and turquoise, and colorful Isnik pieces inspired by William DE MORGAN. The factory closed in the 1950s.

Burmese glass ■ A type of opaque colored ART GLASS, shading from yellow to pink with a satin finish, which was designed by Frederick Shirley in 1881, patented in 1885, and made by the US MOUNT WASHINGTON GLASS CO. for producing table glass and small ornamental vases and dressing table articles. Similar to AMBERINA, the yellow glass takes on pink tones due to the addition of gold oxide and the heat of a furnace. The satin finish is created using acid. It found favor with Queen Victoria, and from 1886 the British company of Thomas WEBB & Sons was licensed to produce their own version known as Queen's Burmese, which was used for tableware and decorative glass, often with enameled decoration.

Burne-Jones, Sir Edward Coley (1833–98) An influential pre-Raphaelite painter and designer, who also became a partner in the leading ARTS AND CRAFTS firm of MORRIS & CO., for whom he designed stained glass, embroideries, tapestries, and furniture. Besides his paintings, his best-known and most successful designs are those for the tapestry-weaving workshops at Merton Abbey in London. His style continued to influence decorative arts after his death.

Burr See BURL and DRYPOINT.

Burse A stiffened square pocket or bag that has two common usages. The first is to carry the Lord Chancellor's great seal. In this case it is heavily embroidered with the monarch's coat of arms in metallic threads on a red velvet ground. A burse is also used to carry ecclesiastical vestments, in particular the corporal (linen cloth) used at Holy Communion.

Burt, John (1690–1745) An American colonial silversmith active in Boston from around 1715. Burt's products, which are rare and highly prized, include simple HOLLOWWARE and CANDLESTICKS that were made by very few early American silversmiths. He was succeeded by his sons, Benjamin, Samuel, and William.

Busby ■ A tall fur hat used as part of British military uniform, sometimes with a plume. The name originated from the military supplier W. Busby of the Strand, London, and originally only applied to the fur caps of the Hussars and Horse Artillery in the 18th century. It is applied to the full ceremonial headgear worn by Royal Engineers and the Corps of Signals in the British Army.

Bustelli, Franz Anton (1723–63) A fine and distinctive porcelain modeler who was born in Locarno, Switzerland, and died in Munich, Germany. Bustelli began his career as a sculptor at the NYMPHENBURG PORCELAIN factory, from 1754 to 1763. Although little is known of his early life, it is thought that he moved to Munich from Vienna. His numerous figures and groups, especially his COMMEDIA DELL' ARTE FIGURES, exhibit great sophistication and sensitivity. They represent the pinnacle of modeling of the ROCOCO period, and are rivalled only by the work of J. J. KÄNDLER at MEISSEN.

Butler's tray A portable table, developed in Britain in the 18th century and popular throughout the 19th, consisting of a wooden or silver tray, often with a solid GALLERY and pierced handles, mounted on a folding stand or legs.

B

75

Burgonet
German black and white peaked burgonet. Late 16th century.

Burmantoft pottery
Burmantoft faience vase, painted in the Anglo-Persian style. Late 1880s.

Burmese glass
Mount Washington Crown Milano biscuit jar, with enameled decoration.

Busby
Other Rank's busby, of The King's Royal Rifle Corps.

Butterfly table ■ An American 18th-century DROP-LEAF TABLE with supports resembling a butterfly with outspread wings (or the rudder of a rowboat). These tables usually have outward-slanting legs and one drawer. The term can also refer to a PEMBROKE table.

Button blanket ■ A ceremonial woven blanket decorated with animals or other figurative designs representing family crests or spirits, and embellished with cut abalone shells sewn to the eyes and other areas. Glass beads and pearl buttons were also used. It was worn by British Columbian, Alaskan, and other tribal dancers on the northwest coast of Canada at important feasts and ceremonies, with the light reflecting in the shells or buttons. It is typically made from a blue or black blanket traded from fur or other Western traders from the early 19th century onward, with the pattern marked out with red and white cut and shaped sections of blanket. The blankets are still made today, primarily for sale to tourists.

Buttoning ■ An upholstery technique in which buttons are used to secure the layers of padding inside the covering. It produces a decorative pattern on sofas and chairs.

Byzantine style ■ A term used to describe a style of art and architecture that flourished in the Byzantine Empire from the founding of Constantinople (Istanbul) as the capital of the eastern Roman Empire in 330 CE until its fall in 1453.

The term "Byzantine" is employed in a more general sense to refer to works produced in this period in parts of Western Europe, especially Italy, Spain, and France, as well as those made before and after the 15th century in Eastern Europe and Russia, where the Orthodox Church was the dominant form of Christianity.

Art of the Byzantine Empire is characterized by an overall effect of rich decoration, combining elements of late imperial Roman Classicism with ornament from Islamic art—for example, in the silks woven in Constantinople from the 8th century decorated with lions, elephants, and other motifs derived from Persian art. Silver dishes, chalices, and other ecclesiastical objects such as IVORY carvings, CLOISONNÉ enamels, and MOSAICS were also produced. Typical motifs include geometric patterns, vines, peacocks, PALMETTES, and stylized figures of emperors, saints, and angels. In the 19th century the style was revived but was not as widely adopted as the GOTHIC or RENAISSANCE REVIVAL. Byzantine influence is found mainly in jewelry, particularly in the use of CLOISONNÉ enamel, and GILDING, and in some furniture by the Italian ART NOUVEAU designer Carlo BUGATTI.

Butterfly table
A George III mahogany Pembroke table with butterfly molded square section.

Button blanket
Northwest coast button blanket, with mother-of-pearl buttons. 20th century.

Buttoning
Victorian mahogany open armchair, with scrolled button back.

Byzantine style
Late Roman-Byzantine gold pendant earrings with large sapphires and low-grade pearls. c. 400–500 CE.

C

Cabaret 1. A two-seater sofa configured to an S-shape, so that two people can be seated nearly face-to-face. 2. A small tray, often made of PORCELAIN, with a matching tea or coffee set. If designed for one person, it is referred to as a "solitaire"; if for two people, then it is a "tête-à-tête."

Cabinet A form of CASE FURNITURE with drawers, pigeonholes, and shelves used for storing and/or displaying valuable or small decorative objects.

Cabinet ware Richly decorated small pieces such as plates, cups, and saucers that were intended not for use but to be shown off in a display cabinet. This was a 19th-century concept, popular throughout Europe and the US.

Cable molding Carved ornament resembling twisted rope, sometimes called ropework and ropetwist. A ROMANESQUE form used on arches and ARCADING, it was used in the 18th century as an edging on silver and ceramics and also as imitation ropework legs and stretchers on furniture.

The motif was favored for ironwork in the 19th and 20th centuries, as it was well suited to being cast and for decanter handles.

Cabochon decoration ■ A French term for a smooth, domed gem that is not cut with facets. As a raised oval or circular ornament, the cabochon was a popular motif for carving and stonework in GOTHIC and GOTHIC REVIVAL architecture. It was also favored for jeweled STRAPWORK on ELIZABETHAN and JACOBEAN woodwork and metalwork, occasionally alternating with the LOZENGE. In ROCOCO furniture it may also refer to a small convex CARTOUCHE form with a carved surround on the knee of a cabriole leg. It was revived during the ARTS AND CRAFTS period as a decoration on metalware.

Caboose The rear car carrying the guard and workers on North American freight trains. Known as the guard's van in Britain.

Cabriole leg A leg used on chairs and CASE FURNITURE that consists of two curves, convex above blending into concave below to form an attenuated S-shape. It was introduced from France into English and American furniture in the first half of the 18th century. The cabriole underwent several stylistic evolutions, ranging from simple carving on the knee to elaborate carved decoration down its length, which was often gilded during the ROCOCO period.

Cachepot From the French *cacher* (to hide). A decorative receptacle to contain a flowerpot, a smaller form of JARDINIÈRE. The term was coined in the 19th century, although the items were made by many factories, including in STONEWARE by WEDGWOOD from the late 18th century, and are still made today.

Cachou box ■ A small box of gold or silver, often with enamel or lacquerwork and a close-fitting cover, made to contain breath-freshening tablets or cachous. They were usually circular and found favor in 18th-century continental Europe. Plain silver examples were common in Holland and were known as peppermint boxes. Some were hung on chains from CHATELAINES.

Caddy See TEA CADDY.

Caddy spoon ■ A small spoon, often fancifully shaped, for transferring tea from a caddy to a teapot, made from the 1770s. They are usually stamped from a thin sheet of silver, making them light and fragile. Handles are sometimes made from bone, ivory, or mother-of-pearl. Silver spoons, popular in the 19th century, are often DIE-STAMPED.

Cadogan teapot ■ A teapot in the peach shape of a Chinese wine pot, named after an earl of Cadogan. It was filled through a hole in the base. The tea was poured when the pot was held upside down. They were

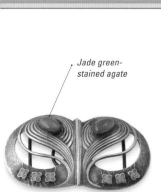

Jade green-stained agate

Cabochon decoration
Arts and Crafts silver buckle, with two oval stained agate cabochons. c. 1900s.

Cachou box
Bilston enamel cachou box in the form of a bird, on a sgraffito ground. c. 1770.

Caddy spoon
William IV fiddle caddy spoon, by Joseph Wilmore of Birmingham. c. 1831.

Cadogan teapot
Copeland and Garrett brown glazed cadogan teapot.

made by the ROCKINGHAM factory in the early 19th century. The molds were bought by SPODE after Rockingham closed in 1842.

Caduceus See AARON'S ROD.

Caen porcelain A porcelain factory in operation from 1793 at Calvados, Normandy, run by d'Aigmont-Desmares and Ducheval. The name of the town was used as the mark. It made tableware with landscapes in black in panels suspended from green and gold wreaths, until its closure in 1806.

Cafaggiolo In 1506 Piero and Stefano Cafaggiolo started to make MAIOLICA near Florence, Italy. For nearly 100 years the same family (later known as Fattorini) ran the workshop. From 1506 to 1526 they made maiolica of great distinction, boldly painted against a bright blue background and bearing the arms of the Medici family. The best examples are influenced by the work of Florentine artists such as Botticelli, and the factory's most outstanding painter was Jacopo Fattorini. From around 1535 the workshop made simpler wares decorated with ARABESQUES and PUTTI. It seems to have closed in the mid-18th century but later pieces are undated.

Caffiéri, Jacques (c. 1673–1755) A French metalworker and sculptor, who became a master metalworker of gilt-bronze in 1715. From 1736 he worked at Versailles and other royal palaces of Louis XV of France, producing elaborate gilt-bronze ROCOCO clock cases, chandeliers, and other furnishings, often in collaboration with his son Philippe Caffiéri.

Cagework A highly decorative silver mount, either pierced or chased, enclosing a plain inner section (or liner) of an object such as a cup, beaker, or tankard. In some cases, the liner might be in contrasting-colored gold.

Cailloute From the French *caillou* (pebble). A type of ceramic decoration, usually in gilding, of oval pebble shapes on a dark ground, especially popular at SÈVRES. It was also copied by some English factories.

Cairngorm A variety of Scottish quartz ranging from gray and pale yellow (citrine) to brown and with a smoky appearance. Found in and named after the Cairngorm Mountains of northeast Scotland, it has been used from the 19th century for mounting in decorative jewelry and silver—for example, in QUAICHS and plaid brooches, particularly for the Scottish market—but was also exported.

Cake basket ■ A receptacle for cakes, usually in openwork silver with a handle that could swing to one side. Similar items were also made in porcelain. These first appeared in the mid-18th century and continued to be used throughout the 19th century.

Calamander See EBONY.

Calcite glass ■ An opaque creamy colored glass simulating ivory, used at the US STEUBEN GLASSWORKS on ART GLASS ware and lampshades, from 1915. It was made by adding calcium phosphate (BONE ASH) to the BATCH. Different layers were built up to form the piece, and the exterior surface was sprayed with metal oxides to give it an iridescent effect, or sometimes acid-etched or engraved with a pattern.

Caldwell, J. E. & Co. ■ An American jeweler, silversmith, and retailer, founded in Philadelphia in 1839. Throughout the later 19th century Caldwell specialized in high-quality, elaborately CHASED or REPOUSSÉ silver HOLLOWWARE in revivalist style, which is clearly marked. Caldwell also produced elaborate French-influenced clocks, mantel GARNITURES, and other bronze work. The most highly regarded examples feature enamel decoration.

Calendar aperture ■ A small window on a clock or watch dial displaying the day, month, or year, or all of these. Calendar apertures are found on domestic clocks from the 16th century onward.

Calico Also known as Calicut, after the Indian city on the Malabar Coast from where it was exported in the 16th century. In the 17th century calico became a

Cake basket
George III silver cake basket, by William Plummer, London; marked "Desprez." c. 1786.

Pierced foliate and geometric forms

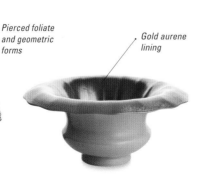

Calcite glass
Steuben gold Aurene on calcite bowl. c. 1925.

Gold aurene lining

Caldwell, J.E. & Co.
Silver cup, by Whiting Mfg Co., New York NY.

Calender aperture
Double fusée verge bracket clock, with false bob pendulum and calendar apertures.

general name for cotton cloths of all kinds imported from Asia, and subsequently also for various cotton fabrics made in Europe. Originally the cloth was printed, painted, or stenciled with (generally MUGHAL) patterns, but now the name is chiefly applied to plain, white unprinted cotton cloth, either bleached or unbleached.

Calotype The first practical photographic process to produce a negative from which identical positives could be printed. Patented in 1841 by the English pioneer of photography, William Henry Fox Talbot, calotypes were developed on paper and used gallic acid to reduce the exposure time from approximately one hour to around a minute. Sometimes known as a talbotype, it was never as popular as the DAGUERREOTYPE, despite being able to yield numerous paper positives. Both processes were used until about 1851, when they were superseded by the collodion wet-plate process.

Caltagirone potteries See SICILIAN POTTERIES.

Camaïeu, en A French term used to describe painting in different tones of the same color.

Cameo A gem, hardstone, or shell carved in relief to depict various subjects, including Classical groups, landscapes, and mythological deities. The color of the subject may contrast with the background where the original carved material has two differently colored layers. Purely decorative, cameos first appeared in Classical jewelry and furniture and were revived in the RENAISSANCE and in 18th-century NEOCLASSICAL ornament. Cameos were also popular in 19th- and 20th-century jewelry.

Camera obscura An optical device used since antiquity in which light entering a room via a pinhole casts an inverted image of the scene outside on the back wall of the room. These were constructed as panoramas in gardens or parks and to view eclipses, but were also used in box form by artists. The image is upside down but can be righted with a mirror and then traced or sketched. The camera obscura was mainly used from the 16th century to make enlarged drawings of small objects and portraits, and is the direct ancestor of the camera.

Campana vase From the Italian *campana* (bell). A Classical vessel, of silver or bronze, in the form of an inverted stylized bell.

Canabas The name by which the cabinet-maker Joseph Gegenbach was known. He was born in Baden, Germany, but by 1745 had settled in Paris, where he produced austere but practical multifunctional furniture, specializing in pieces such as CAMPAIGN FURNITURE that could be easily dismantled and reassembled for traveling.

CAMEO GLASS

A type of ART GLASS made from two or more layers of different colored glass, where the top layer(s) is cut or etched away to reveal a contrasting colored background. The pattern is thus in RELIEF. It was used by Roman glassmakers and revived in the 19th century. Notable practitioners include John Northwood, Thomas and George Woodall who worked for Thomas Webb & Sons of Stourbridge, England, and the Frenchmen Émile GALLÉ and DAUM FRÈRES.

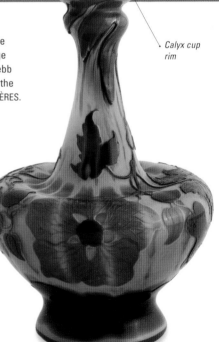

Calyx cup rim

Green over red loop handles

Acid-etched lilies

D'Argental vase
D'Argental cameo glass vase, with smoky glass blossoms on a yellow ground.

Daum vase
Daum cameo glass vase, with trailing vine decoration on a pink ground. c. 1905.

Gallé vase
Signed Gallé cameo glass vase with lavender-blue blossoms, buds, and stems. 1900.

CAMPAIGN FURNITURE

Furniture of the 18th, 19th, and early 20th century that could be easily assembled, and dismantled (or partly dismantled and occasionally packed flat) for military campaigns or traveling. Usually made of hardwoods such as teak or mahogany, with brass hardware. Typical pieces included chairs, writing chests, chests-of-drawers, washstands, and beds.

Campaign
William IV campaign sofa bed. 19th century.

C
80

Canapé ■ The French term for a SOFA or settee, a type of upholstered seat furniture with a back and arms and designed to seat two or more people. The term was first used in the late 17th century, and by the 18th century variations on the *canapé* proliferated, including the CONFIDANTE.

Canary glass ■ An American term used for glass of a yellow color, generally based on silver chloride, such as VASELINE GLASS, and mostly of 19th-century origin.

Cancellation mark One or more lines scratched across the sword mark on MEISSEN porcelain to indicate that the piece sold was below the usual standard. These pieces were probably decorated outside the factory.

Candelabrum A multibranched candlestick for use on a table. A candelabrum commonly has three to nine lights. Although it was known throughout history, silver examples do not predate the mid-17th century. They were also made in porcelain in the 18th century. They are similar in style to contemporary candlesticks.

Candle snuffer ■ A small scissorlike tool with a "box" section on the blades allowing a candle wick to be simultaneously extinguished, trimmed, and safely retained. The better quality examples were made of silver and had a small tray on which they were kept. The earliest surviving pair dates from 1512. They were common throughout the 18th century but were later superseded by the cone-shaped snuffer of the type found on CHAMBERSTICKS.

Candle stand See TORCHÈRE.

Candleslide A small wooden support for a candlestick found on desks, work tables, and similar pieces of furniture primarily from the 18th and 19th centuries. When not in use, it slides out of sight into a built-in recess.

Candlestick A stable column for holding a candle vertically in a socket at a given height for the purpose intended—for example, library, altar, hand-, or taper-candlestick. Although made from a variety of materials, silver is particularly suitable as it reflects light, with less expensive BRASS being the most common material. Surviving examples from before 1660 are extremely rare.

Cane 1. Woven fibrous strips obtained from rattan palms and used in the manufacture of furniture. Cane was imported into Europe from what is now Malaysia by the Dutch East India Company, and from around 1664 was used to make the backs and seats of chairs that were light, easy to clean, and durable. Cane chairs remained popular until the early 18th century, and then enjoyed a revival in the late 18th and early 19th centuries, and again in the early 20th century. 2. A bundle of monochrome or polychrome glass casing RODS, fused together by heating, melting, and marvering (rolling). When cool, the cane can be cut crosswise into sections for MILLEFIORE or MOSAIC glass, or twisted with other canes for the stems of drinking glasses. 3. Walking cane. A stick used to aid

Canapé
Louis XVI style giltwood *canapé*, on turned and fluted legs.

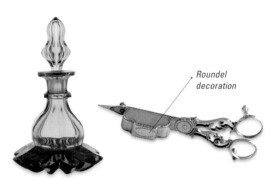

Canary glass
Sandwich Glass Factory paneled paperweight perfume bottle. c. 1840.

Roundel decoration

Candle snuffer
Silver candlesnuffer, by IB, London. 1778.

Caneware
Wedgwood caneware game pie tureen and cover. 1874.

walking, often with a decorative pommel in ceramic, silver, gold, or ivory. The pommel is sometimes called a TOY.

Canephorus An architectural MOTIF, often used on bronze furniture mounts, in the form of a female figure carrying a basket on her head. See also CARYATID.

Caneware ■ A buff or cane-colored stoneware made by Wedgwood and other contemporary Staffordshire potters, sometimes enriched with enamel decoration. It was a refinement of the ordinary buff body, which Wedgwood made in a lighter weight in 1770 and called "cane."

Cannelé From the French *cannelure* (flute). A fabric displaying a textured horizontally ribbed effect, created when an additional warp thread, often gold or silver, is fixed at intervals to the surface of a woven fabric, usually silk.

Cannetille A method of working gold, usually gold wire, into elaborate scrolls, spirals, coils, beads, and flowers. Notable uses were made in early 19th-century French and English jewelry, in which it was often combined with gemstones or cameos.

Canopic vase ■ An earthenware and alabaster vase used in the ancient Egyptian mummifying process. The liver, lungs, spleen, and stomach were entrusted to the gods in four canopic vases and painted with or molded in the form of heads of people,

baboons, falcons, and jackals, representing either the deceased or Egyptian deities. Named by archaeologists after the discovery of a jar-shaped representation of the deity Osiris, who was worshipped in Canopus, their use declined after about 1075 BCE.

Canova, Antonio (1757–1822) An Italian NEOCLASSICAL sculptor who became famous in his day and was patronized by Englishmen on the GRAND TOUR. He opened his studio in 1775, designed papal tombs, and his celebrated marble group of The Three Graces is now in the Victoria & Albert Museum in London. Many of his works were copied in PARIAN WARE.

Cantagalli, Ulisse ■ (1839–1901) An Italian potter who established a factory in Florence in 1877, making imitations of 16th-century Italian maiolica. His mark is a rooster, a rebus on his name. He also copied products of other potteries, including Iznik.

Cántaro The Spanish term (also *cantir* or *cantaro*) for a jug, made in CATALAN GLASSHOUSES, southern France, and Venice in the 17th and 18th centuries. It had a fixed ring-shaped vertical handle and two spouts: a short one for filling and pouring and a longer one to drink from. Another type resembles a CARAFE with a long, tapering spout.

Canted The surface produced by beveling off a corner. Also known as a chamfered corner, it was common on Gothic and 18th-century furniture and spirit decanters.

Canteen A service of matching silver or, later, plated FLATWARE fitted in a piece of furniture such as a side table or box. The term can also apply to these fitted boxes or to a set of flatware and cutlery with 12 place settings or more. Late 17th-century canteens exist but most are of a later date.

Canterbury A small stand, made from the late 18th century, with slatted racks or divisions, perhaps originally for an archbishop of Canterbury, and produced in two versions. The music canterbury was generally rectangular, with racks to hold sheet music. The supper canterbury was a round tray set above racks to hold cutlery and stood beside a dining table.

Cantilever chair ■ A chair without back legs, supported by a cantilevered frame in which the front legs curve around and under to form the base. It was particularly popular with 20th-century Modernist designers who explored the technique in tubular steel (see Marcel BREUER) and molded plywood. See ALVAR AALTO.

Canton enamel ■ A style of enamel painting on copper, developed in the late 17th century by the Chinese from European enameling techniques, and produced mainly at Canton and in south China for export. Painted wares included dishes, tea kettles, boxes, and, in the 20th century, matchboxes and ashtrays. Decoration was mostly figures, flowers, and insects in the FAMILLE ROSE or FAMILLE VERTE palettes.

Canopic vase
Egyptian limestone canopic jar; lid shaped as a son of Horus. c. 664–525 BCE.

Cantagalli, Ulisse
Cantagalli blue and white flask. Late 19th century.

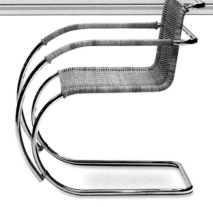

Cantilever chair
MR20 cantilever armchair, designed by Mies van der Rohe. 1927.

Canton enamel
Canton polychrome enamel circular footed plate. 18th century.

C

Canton porcelain ■ These wares, made in the 18th to 20th centuries, were exported from Canton in China. Mainly produced at JINGDEZHEN, they might have been decorated at Canton. 19th-century Canton FAMILLE ROSE was decorated with alternate panels of figures and birds, flowers and insects, mainly in pink and green. See MANDARIN PALETTE, CHINESE EXPORT PORCELAIN, and CANTON ENAMEL.

Cap and ball A slang term for a PERCUSSION LOCK—particularly when used to describe a REVOLVER—derived from a combination of the cap or primer and the spherical lead bullet or ball.

Cape Cod This peninsula off the eastern coast of Massachusetts was an important center of the American glass industry in the 19th century, owing to the availability of silica-rich sand and reeds (used for packing). Cape Cod is known for the early PRESSED GLASS in the mid-19th century and the manufacture of inexpensive pattern glass and lamps for whale oil until the early 20th century. The Cape Cod Glass Company was founded in 1858 in Sandwich by Deming Jarves and James D. Lloyd, with Jarves running the firm until his death in 1869. The company continued under new ownership, making some ART GLASS as well as tableware, until its final closure in 1882.

Capital The top or crown of an architectural column or pillar supporting the entablature. Although usually based on flowers and foliage, the carved decoration of a capital may include animals, wicker patterns, and cube and bell shapes.

Capitonné From the French *capiton* (padding). A form of upholstery in which a padded surface is drawn inward at intervals to produce an organized pattern. These indentations, held in place by decorative tufts stitched through the fabric and pulled tight, were fashionable in the 19th century.

Capodimonte porcelain factory Founded in 1743 in Naples when the "Porcelain Princess," Princess Marie Amalia of Saxony, married King Charles III of Naples and Sicily. The factory copied the styles of Meissen. Giovanni Caselli was a fine painter working there, and Guiseppe Gricci was a modeler from 1744. When King Charles succeeded to the Spanish throne in 1759, he moved his court and his factory to Madrid, and the factory was set up on the grounds of the BUEN RETIRO palace. The factory returned to Naples in the late 18th century and reproductions of the true soft-paste Capodimonte figures have been made in the area ever since.

Cappiello, Leonetto ■ (1875–1942) An Italian poster designer who settled in Paris. He made his name during the poster boom era, around 1900. His designs were similar to those of Jules CHÉRET, but the *fin-de-siècle* images were redesigned and adapted to new styles in design that were more relevant to the faster pace of the 20th century.

Capstan table See DRUM TABLE.

Car mascot ■ (US hood ornament) A cast metal or glass ornament attached to the top of a car radiator. Often a human or animal form, and sometimes in the form of a company logo or mascot, designs include Rolls Royce's Spirit of Ecstasy and the many beautiful glass forms created by René LALIQUE.

Carafe ■ A container for wine or water, shaped like a shaft and globe decanter but with no stopper. Decanters without stoppers were made in the early to mid-18th century but only became known as carafes from about 1775. A carafe with an inverted tumbler was also used as a bedroom water jug.

Carat The standard unit of weight for diamonds, gems, and pearls. Since 1913, when weights were standardized, one carat is equivalent to one-fifth of a gram (0.2g). The related term "karat" is used as a unit of fineness for gold, where the pure metal is divided into 24 parts, thus "9 karat" is 9 parts pure gold and 15 parts metal.

Carbine A short, light RIFLE or MUSKET for cavalry, artillery, or other specially trained troops. The term was first used in the 16th century for French horsemen called *carabins*, who were armed with short, light guns. Carbines were still in use in World War II.

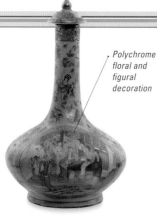

Polychrome floral and figural decoration

Canton porcelain
Canton celadon ground bottle and stopper. 19th century.

Cappiello, Leonetto
Mossant poster designed by Leonetto Cappiello, printed by Edimo, Paris. 1938.

Car mascot (hood ornament)
Rolls Royce Silver Cloud Spirit of Ecstasy.

Carafe
Opaque white carafe, with pink pull-up decoration and everted rim. c. 1860.

Carboy A large glass bottle or flagon, used to transport or store dangerous liquids such as ammonia, or for display in pharmacies. Practical examples have a basketwork cover or string to provide grip or some protection. More decorative 19th-century examples, used for display in drug stores, have long, elongated stoppers and a foot, the exterior cut or engraved with a pattern or facets. The term is derived from the Persian word *qarabah*, a large storage bottle.

Carcass The structure or body of a piece of CASE FURNITURE before elements such as drawers, doors, shelves, or feet are added. It serves as a foundation for VENEERS or other applied decoration.

Card table ■ A type of table introduced at the end of the 17th century, specifically designed for playing card games. It usually had a folding top covered in needlework or, later, west of England cloth, often green, that opened out.

Card-cut ornament A latticelike, unpierced, FRETWORK ornament for wood, cut in low relief. A popular motif for furniture in CHINOISERIE and GOTHIC taste, it was mainly applied in horizontal sections, such as along the top of a tallboy.

Carder, Frederick ■ (1864–1963) An influential and important English-born American glassmaker and designer who began his career at STEVENS & WILLIAMS in 1881. He ran the newly created STEUBEN GLASSWORKS in Corning, New York, from 1903 to 1918, when he was "demoted" to artistic director. During this period he introduced several successful ART GLASS lines, notably AURENE, which was designed to rival the popular FAVRILE glass of TIFFANY. In 1918 Steuben became a division of the Corning Glass Works, and although Carder continued as art director, he was increasingly distanced from production. He set up a small glassmaking studio in his office in 1932, which he continued to operate until his retirement in 1959. In later life Carder worked independently in Corning, making advanced art glass, including replicas of ancient vessels and CIRE-PERDUE work, most of which has an engraved signature.

Cardew, Michael ■ (1901–83) An English studio potter who learned his craft at Fishley Holland, Devon, and with Bernard LEACH at St. Ives, Cornwall. In 1926 he opened his own pottery, Winchcombe at Greet in Gloucestershire, making slip- and SGRAFFITO- decorated domestic pottery. Leaving Winchcombe under the direction of Ray Finch, he opened a new pottery at Wenford Bridge, Cornwall (joined by his son, Seth, in 1971). His enthusiasm for functional studio-made pottery led him to help set up potteries in several West African countries and in the Northern Territories in Australia.

Carette et Cie, Georges ■ (1886–1917) A toy-making company founded in 1886 in Nuremberg by Frenchman Georges Carette, concentrating on painted tin-plated toys. From 1900 to 1917 it made high-quality hand-painted and lithographed tin-plate trains, cars, steam engines, boats, and children's MAGIC LANTERNS. Some items were made specifically for BASSETT-LOWKE. Carette had to flee Germany in 1917 and his tools and patterns were disseminated into other parts of the German toy industry.

Carillon 1. A set of bells, or a tune played on a series of bells by manual or mechanical means, usually contained in a clock or MUSICAL BOX. 2. A large musical instrument made of at least 24 brass bells with different tones, struck in sequence using a baton keyboard to produce a harmony. Originating in the Low Countries in the 15th century, most are located in towers or municipal buildings.

Carlin, Martin ■ (died 1785) A French furniture-maker of German birth. By 1759 he had settled in Paris, where he may have worked in the workshop of Jean-François OEBEN, whose sister he married. He is known for his elegant small-scale furniture, in the LOUIS XVI style, often decorated with plaques by the SÈVRES porcelain factory.

Carlton House desk A type of writing table or desk that was first referred to in a cost book of GILLOWS in 1796, and is probably named after the residence of the then Prince of Wales. It has a superstructure with a pierced brass GALLERY and drawers

Carder, Frederick
Steuben double acid-cut back plum jade vase, in the Peking pattern. c. 1928.

Cardew, Michael
Michael Cardew kingwood slipware jug.

Chrome lithographic and hand-varnished decoration

Carette et Cie, Georges
Clockwork mechanism tin-plate sedan. Early 20th century.

Carlin, Martin
Transitional ormolu, amaranth and marquetry commode, marked "M. Carlin." c. 1770.

surrounding a leather or polished wood writing surface, with drawers in the frieze below. Desks of this type are still made as "reproduction" pieces.

C

Carlton ware ■ A trade name used from the mid-1890s by Wiltshaw & Robinson Ltd. of the Carlton Works, Stoke. It produced china and earthenware and crested souvenir type pieces, on which the name "Crown China" may occur. The name became Carlton Ware Ltd. in 1958, and various manufacturers now make limited edition pieces under license.

Carnival glass ■ Inexpensive, mass-produced, decorative pressed glass, with an IRIDESCENT surface finish, made to imitate the more expensive ART GLASS produced by STEUBEN and TIFFANY. A pressed, colored glass body was sprayed with metallic salts to give the iridescent effect. Typical colors were marigold orange or amethyst purple. Produced primarily in the US from around 1900, but reaching a high point during the 1920s and 1930s, notable makers included Northwood, Fenton, and Dugan Diamond. It was later also produced in at least 30 countries, including Britain and Germany, and is still being made today. Apparently, carnival glass got its name during the 1950s, when it was given away as prizes at fairs and carnivals.

Carolean style ■ The decorative style popular in England during the reign of Charles II from 1660 to 1685, also known as the RESTORATION STYLE. It is characterized by a reaction against the austerity of the CROMWELLIAN STYLE and by the introduction of Dutch and, to some extent, French artistic influences brought back by the court on its return from exile on the Continent. New types of furniture appeared in this period: cabinets-on-stands, chests-of-drawers, armchairs, wing chairs, day beds, and settees. Walnut veneer replaced oak as the most fashionable wood, while the use of JAPANNING, imported LACQUER, and cane for chair seats and backs reflected the craze for CHINOISERIE. Dutch influence appeared in the use of MARQUETRY and parquetry, while ornate carved and gilded supports were decorated with naturalistic fruits, foliage, and arabesques. The overall effect of magnificence and opulence was enhanced by CREWELWORK bed hangings and tapestries, and velvets and brocades for upholstery. Silver is characterized by embossing, especially of fruit and flowers, and flat-chased Chinoiserie scenes of Oriental-style figures and landscapes.

Innovations included toilet sets for wealthy patrons and tea- and coffeepots, arising from the popularity of these new drinks. This period is also marked by the development of the English glass industry, especially after the invention of lead glass by George RAVENSCROFT, around 1676. The fashion for collecting Oriental blue and white porcelain is also evident in the production of BLUE-DASH CHARGERS. After the 1688 Revolution and the accession of William III and Mary II, the Carolean style was superseded by the WILLIAM AND MARY STYLE.

Carpet toy Originally of wood or CAST IRON but now of plastic, they include pull-along trains (without tracks), large buses, and trucks suitable for a small child. Also known as a floor toy.

Carrara marble A fine white marble quarried near the town of Carrara in Italy, and prized since ancient Roman times for building construction and, especially, sculpture. Notable uses include Michelangelo's sculpture of David. In English ceramics the word has been used to denote a dense white stoneware with a slight glaze that gives its surface a texture suggestive of marble.

Carriage clock ■ A small, spring-driven clock, developed around 1796 by Abraham-Louis BREGUET, but most popular in France and England from the mid- to late 19th century. The case, usually plain or gilt-brass, is rectangular with a carrying handle and often set with glass or, more rarely, enamel or porcelain panels. An accompanying case allowed it to be carried on travels. A feature of carriage clocks is the PLATFORM ESCAPEMENT, sometimes visible through a glazed aperture on the top of the case.

Luster finish

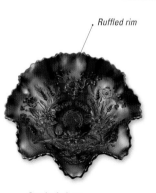

Ruffled rim

Carlton ware
Trumpet-shaped Carlton ware vase with stepped neck and foot and "Bell" pattern. c. 1933.

Carnival glass
Northwood "Good Luck" pattern amethyst Carnival glass bowl.

Carolean style
Walnut-framed Carolean style armchair.

Carriage clock
Twin chain fusée gilded carriage clock, by John Carter of London. c. 1850.

Carrickmacross A center for Irish lace that was first produced in the early 1820s and was subsequently promoted for employment after the potato famine of 1846. Although production declined dramatically with the outbreak of World War I, the lace is still made today. It is typified by delicate muslin floral motifs hand-stitched to machine net then cut out, and was used for collars, veils, and other clothing. A type known as guipure has no net, with the shaped muslin elements being held together by stitched bars known as "brides."

Carrier-Belleuse, Albert-Ernest ■ (1824–87) A French modeler and sculptor who worked in terra-cotta, marble, and bronze. He also made models for LIMOGES porcelain factories and worked in England as a modeler at MINTON and other STAFFORDSHIRE factories. He went back to France in 1876 and worked at SÈVRES as artistic director until his death. His pieces may be signed "A. Carrier."

Carriés, Jean (1855–94) A French sculptor and potter with kilns at Montriveau, near Nevers. He made stoneware influenced by Japanese pottery, including figures, masks, and animal models.

Carron ironworks A foundry started in 1759 near Falkirk, Scotland. It was one of the most successful British firms, producing cast-iron fire-backs, stoves, grates, and other furnishings, often using the NEOCLASSICAL designs of Robert ADAM. Such pieces were reproduced by the foundry in the early 20th century. The firm also gave its name to a short, barreled artillery piece called a "carronade."

Cartel clock ■ An ornate spring-driven WALL CLOCK made mainly in France during the 18th and 19th centuries, also in Germany and Italy. It features a white enameled dial set in a carved and gilded wood or gilt-bronze frame. Early ROCOCO frames are characterized by exuberant scrollwork, flowers, and shells, while later NEOCLASSICAL pieces feature laurel leaves, urns, and masks.

Carter, Stabler & Adams See POOLE.

Cartier ■ A jewelry company founded in 1847 in Paris by Louis-Francois Cartier, moving in 1899 to the prestigious Rue de la Paix. Louis's grandsons, Jacques and Pierre, opened shops in London in 1902 and New York in 1909, respectively. The company is famous for its jewelry created for the royal families of Europe and its early, innovative use of platinum in lavish designs. From the early 1900s they were among the first to make WRISTWATCHES and also sold the famous Hope diamond. Their Panthere brand, based on the skin of the panther, was developed from 1914.

Cartonnier ■ A piece of furniture, popular in France in the mid-18th century, with pigeonholes or other types of compartments designed to hold paper. An early type of filing cabinet, small versions were designed to sit on a writing table such as a BUREAU PLAT; larger versions stood independently next to a desk.

Cartoon 1. A full-size design for a painting, fresco, mural, or tapestry, sometimes colored, sometimes monochrome. Many famous painters produced cartoons for tapestry-weaving. Two notable examples are Raphael's cartoons for the BRUSSELS TAPESTRY workshop during the early 16th century and Boucher's design for BEAUVAIS during the 18th century. 2. Since the 1840s, a humorous drawing, with an element of caricature and often commenting on current affairs, usually first published in magazines such as the 19th-century French *Charivari* or the English *Punch*. Famous cartoonists include George du Maurier and Honoré Daumier.

Cartouche The French term for a scroll or an ESCUTCHEON. A framed ornamental panel in the form of a sheet of paper or a scroll with curling edges. Widely used in RENAISSANCE decoration and promoted by pattern-book engravers, the device frequently appears in 16th- and 17th-century ornament, but enjoyed its greatest popularity during the ROCOCO period, when it was seen on carved BOISERIES, ceramics, and silver and engraved on labeled decanters.

Cartridge From the Italian *carta* (paper). A round of ammunition, or a container

Carrier-Belluese
Albert-Ernest Carrier-Belleuse
Nymph bronze.

Cartel clock
French cartel clock,
signed "Hry Dasson a Paris."
Late 19th century.

Cartier
Platinum case Cartier Paris
watch, with original diamond-
set buckle. 1920s.

Cartonnier
French kingwood *bureau plat*
and cartonnier, of Louis XV
style. Early 20th century.

of ink for a fountain pen. Originally, ammunition cartridges were made of paper, but from the mid-19th century they were mostly made of metal and contained their own means of ignition. The first cartridge filling for fountain pens were glass cartridges, patented by the Eagle Pencil Company of New York, but Waterman's had more success with their model, released in 1936. Waterman's C/F pen, released in 1953, was the first pen to popularize the new plastic cartridges.

Carver chair 1. An American open armchair first made in New England in the mid-17th century. Carvers differ from BREWSTER CHAIRS in having no spindles beneath the rush-woven seat. 2. In the UK the term generally refers to the chair or chairs with arms in a dining suite.

Cary, John ■ (1754–1835) A pioneering English cartographer who produced many finely designed and engraved MAPS based on the latest available geographical data. Cary's output included clear and highly accurate English county maps, town plans, world and regional maps, GLOBES, and canal and road maps.

Caryatid ■ A Greek term for an architectural column in the form of a full-length male or female figure. The same motif was also used on 18th- and early 19th-century NEOCLASSICAL and EMPIRE-style furniture cast in bronze as brackets,

furniture legs, or small items such as desk handles. See also CANEPHORUS.

Case furniture A type of furniture designed to act as a receptacle or storage space. It generally consists of a boxlike structure or CARCASS into which drawers or shelves are fitted. The earliest example of case furniture, based on a hollowed-out log (hence the term "trunk" for a traveling case), is the medieval CHEST or COFFER, usually made of oak in northern Europe and walnut in Southern Europe. As furniture-making grew more sophisticated, the chest evolved into the CHEST-OF-DRAWERS in the 17th century. It was usually made with joints secured by iron nails, later with DOVETAILING. Drawers were a 16th-century development, initially called "tills" or "drawing boxes" in Britain.

The chest-of-drawers branched out into its many forms such as the COMMODE, LINEN PRESS, WARDROBE, CUPBOARD or DRESSER, the DRESSING TABLE, the many different types of BUREAU, and bookshelves. Each of these in turn developed more specialized forms.

Cased glass ■ A type of glass that consists of two or more layers of different colors. It is used for decorative effect and to lighten the principal color, such as in the case of CRANBERRY GLASS. The layers can be applied in a number of different ways—a gob of glass can be rolled in glass powder of a different color, which forms a glass layer when melted in the furnace; a separate gob

of glass can be applied to the main gob and smoothed over, thus forming a new layer; the main gob can be used to "gather" another layer of glass from the furnace; or a gob can be blown into a mold and have a separate gob of differently colored glass blown into it, thus forming layers. Layers are fused when the piece is heated. Common techniques include blowing opaque white glass into a colored, transparent glass within a mold, or "casing" colored glass in a thick layer of colorless glass, or glass of a different color. In the MURANO GLASSHOUSES the latter is known as SOMMERSO.

Cash pattern An Oriental ceramic pattern based on a design of small, circular Chinese coins with a square central hole for stringing. Occasionally the beribboned coins are painted as decoration on porcelain, and as a symbol of the Chinese Immortal Liu Hai.

Cassandre ■ (1901–68) The pseudonym of Adolphe Mouron, a Ukrainian-born graphic artist, stage designer, typographer, and painter, who is best known for his ART DECO poster designs, produced in France from the mid-1920s to 1939. His use of sharply angled perspective suggested speed, and he developed the idea of a series of posters for Dubonnet designed to be seen from a moving car. One of his most famous designs was for the Normandie cruise liner. After 1939 he concentrated on stage design and typography.

Cassapanca The Italian term for a wooden

Cary, John
English New Celestial Globe on mahogany stand by John Cary. c. 1800.

Caryatid
George II carved gesso console table, the top supported by angled caryatids.

Cased glass
Mdina glass double-cased fish vase, designed and made by Michael Harris. c. 1970.

Cassandre
Nord Express poster, designed by Cassandre. 1927.

bench, often with an upright back, in which the seat lifts up to reveal a storage chest.

Cassolette ◼ A vase with a reversible lid on which a candle could be placed. The candle-holder was concealed when the lid was in the "normal" position. A cassolette could also be a vase or urn in metal, earthenware, or porphyry, with a pierced cover in which scented charcoal or perfume was heated to create aromatic fumes. See ATHÉNIENNE.

Cassone ◼ The Italian name for a type of free-standing low chest, made in Italy from the 15th century, often with elaborate decoration in the form of carving, applied GESSO decoration, or painting. Cassoni were often wedding chests and so made in pairs, and decorated with heraldic devices and symbols associated with the two families as well as apt scenes from Classical mythology such as the marriage of Peleus and Thetis.

Castel Durante MAIOLICA was made here, near URBINO in central Italy, especially during the first 30 years of the 16th century. The town was renamed Urbania in 1635 after Pope Urban. The two great artists, Giovanni Maria and Nicola Pellipario, gave the decoration preeminence. Dishes with inner borders in BIANCO-SOPRA-BIANCO were a special feature, as were portraits of ladies and helmeted warriors. The workshops flourished in the 16th century, but declined in the next century.

Cast iron One of the two main types of iron for items such as grilles, fireplace furnishings, furniture, and railings (the other being wrought iron). It is produced by casting iron with a high carbon content in molds of compressed sand. In the 19th century, cast iron was popular for garden furniture, coat stands, and plant stands. It is more brittle than wrought iron.

Castellani, Fortunato Pio (1794–1865) An Italian goldsmith who pioneered the fashion for Classical, and particularly Etruscan, revivalist gold jewelry inspired by the recent archaeological discoveries. Frequently incorporating authentic ancient objects, including semiprecious stones and coins, Castellani rediscovered and mastered the technique of applying complex decoration such as granular filigree, which had been practiced by the Etruscans.

Castelli potteries ◼ A group of MAIOLICA factories in the 17th and 18th centuries, near Teramo in the former kingdom of Naples. Earliest wares included BIANCO DI FAENZA, but they were known for ISTORIATO ware from around 1650 to the late 18th century. The Grue and Gentili families were the best-known exponents. Their distinctly local style used cooler and lighter colors than other Italian makers of maiolica, including a pale gray-blue, buffs, browns, and olive green. The scenes were usually inspired by prints of BAROQUE artists depicting religious and mythological scenes as well as picturesque landscapes.

The scenes were often "pounced" on to the ceramic surface—the design was drawn on paper and holes were made along the lines; when a fine powder was rubbed over the paper, it went through the holes, transferring the design, which was then ready to be painted over. Small dishes were popular, and the wide rims were usually decorated with figures of PUTTI and garlands of fruit and flowers, highlighted with gilding. The Castelli potteries also manufactured large numbers of plaques, as well as ALBARELLI, double-handed bottles, and dragon-spouted syrup pots.

Caster, castor ◼ 1. From around 1600 these silver vessels were used for sprinkling powders, and more typically, sugar and spices to flavor food and drink. They are usually cylindrical (lighthouse), vase-, or baluster-shaped, with domed, pierced covers. 2. From the 16th century, small wheels known as casters were used on the ends of furniture legs, particularly dining tables and heavy chairs, to make moving them easier.

Castiglioni, Achille, Pier Giacomo, and Livio ◼ The eldest of the three brothers, Livio founded a design studio with Pier Giacomo in 1938, designing or contributing to designs for cutlery, lighting, and the Phonola radio. In 1944 Achille joined the studio after graduating, and the three produced architectural and product designs and founded exhibitions such as the Milan Triennale. Livio left the

Cassolette
Russian Fabergé-style silver gilt mounted hardstone cassolette and cover.

Marquetry decoration

Cassone
Italian walnut and marquetry *cassone*. Late 17th century.

Caster
George III vase-shaped sugar caster by Hester Bateman. 1788.

Castelli potteries
Italian Castelli maiolica socketed saucer, signed by Carmine Gentile. 1725–50.

studio in 1952 and Pier Giacomo and Achille went on to produce celebrated furniture designs, including the Mezzadro tractor stool of 1955, and lighting, including the famous marble and steel Arco lamp of 1962, the cone-shaped Taccia and Toio lights, and the Snoopy lamp in 1967, based on the famous cartoon character. Clients included Kartell, Zanotta, Knoll, and Siemens. After Pier Giacomo's death, Achille continued to design furniture and architecture for clients, including Alessi and Flos. All three brothers were highly influential on Italian, as well as global, product design, with Achille and Pier Giacomo also holding important teaching positions during their lifetimes.

Casting Forming a solid article from a liquid such as molten glass, silver, or bronze, or from a semiliquid such as wet clay or damp sand, by pouring or forcing it into a mold. After the liquid material has set or dried, the mold is either broken or dismantled. See LOST WAX.

Cast-iron toys Typically American, peak production was between the 1880s and 1930s. Toys may be single- or multipiece and are usually transport-related, such as cars, fire engines, and trucks. Money (piggy) banks were also made, some

with a mechanism triggered by the coin. Castings are riveted, bolted, or held together by interlocking springs and then painted. Notable makers include HUBLEY, ARCADE, and Kilgore. Fakes of cast-iron toys are common.

Castleford pottery ■ A Yorkshire factory founded in 1790 by David Dunderdale that produced CREAMWARE, PEARLWARE, WHITEWARE, BASALT WARE, and a white semitranslucent body of porcelain appearance. The mark combined Dunderdale's initials with the word CASTLEFORD. Dunderdale published a pattern book in 1796 depicting many creamware pieces. He died in 1799, and was succeeded by his son, also David. The factory closed in 1821.

Castleford ware The word Castleford covers a range of SLIP-CAST teaware that often has added relief decoration, usually semitranslucent, and looks similar to the wares of the LEEDS POTTERIES in the 19th century. Typical products are teapots with sliding and hinged lids, often with blue borders, which is usually the only glaze on the exterior. Some were made by David Dunderdale in Castleford, Yorkshire, from around 1790, but many are from Staffordshire.

Castle-top ■ Embossed or engraved decoration on silver card cases, snuff boxes, and vinaigrettes, depicting a castle, historic house, or landscape. Made from the 1830s, largely in Birmingham, UK, some were

CASTLE, WENDELL

A highly original American furniture-maker maintaining the craft tradition but with MODERN, and later, POSTMODERN forms and interpretations, Wendell Castle has worked with molded plastic and fiberglass and also with stacked and laminated, often exotic, woods. From the 1980s many of his designs were inspired by the ART DECO style and were frequently decorated with expressionistic, and often symbolic, surface patterns in bright colors. He established a workshop in 1980, and many of his pieces are unique commissions.

Ebonized uprights

Shelf with six blind drawers

Castiglioni
Mezzadro Tractor stool with chromium-plated steel stem and beech footrest. 1957.

Bookshelf
Wall-hanging bookshelf and counter, by Wendell Castle, with six blind drawers; from the Estate of Peter Joseph.

produced as souvenirs for tourists, as their popularity coincided with the opening of passenger railroads in Britain. The most prestigious maker was Nathaniel Mills.

Castwork Usually decorative sections on silver items, which have been cast and then soldered or applied to the main body of the article—for example, a CARTOUCHE or a FINIAL.

Cat A stand comprising three wooden or metal rods joined in the center, used in the 18th and 19th centuries for keeping plates warm in front of an open fire.

Catalan glasshouses The term used to denote the numerous glasshouses active from the Middle Ages in Catalonia, a region in northeast Spain famous for its long glassmaking tradition and distinctive 17th- and 18th-century regional forms such as the CÁNTARO, often with elaborate trailed and combed decoration. Barcelona, the Catalan capital, was known in the 16th and 17th centuries for its transparent glass with an unusually "white" body. By the 20th century, Catalan glasshouses were the main suppliers of glass for the home market.

Caucasian carpet ■ A carpet made in the region between the Caspian and Black seas. Carpets made here are woven by nomadic, seminomadic, and village weavers. Little is known about the carpets that may have been made here before the mid-17th century. The oldest identifiable group is the so-called KUBA dragon carpets. The name is, however, misleading, as it is now thought they were woven in the KARABAGH district of the southeast Caucasus. These rugs display a naively geometrical rendering of Persian animal carpet designs from Tabriz, Kashan, and Kerman during the Safavid period (1501–1732). Sometimes the design is so stylized that its origins are barely recognizable.

The nomadic tradition of weaving, inspired from earlier examples and carpets from Turkey, produced items with formal designs, displaying intensive geometric stylized plant and animal forms in vibrant jewel colors. Some districts and villages produce finer, woven carpets with greater detail. Kuba, Shirvan, and Dagestan represent this finer weaving tradition; Dagestan is particularly known for the production of PRAYER RUGS. They often have white MIHRAB and the design format is formal. In rugs from Karabagh and KAZAK, the designs are based on earlier Classical forms, both Persian and Anatolian. Designs from these two regions are considerably bolder, with more sparing decoration, although the color combinations remain powerful and jewel-like. Rugs are mainly woven and carpets rare and infrequently seen. Rugs made after 1880 often display one or several harsh chemical dyes—bright orange and purple are common. These colors tend to ruin the artistic quality of the rug. Earlier examples are considerably more attractive and highly individual.

Caudle cup ■ A vessel in silver or pottery with a lift-off cover to take caudle—a hot, spiced wine drink made with gruel or porridge, thought to be medicinal. These two-handled cups were usually of baluster form with a flat base or low feet and often with a matching broad-rimmed stand. They were produced from around 1650 to 1700. See PORRINGER.

Caughley porcelain factory ■ In 1772 Thomas Turner moved from WORCESTER to the Caughley pottery, near Broseley, Shropshire. He began to make transfer-printed porcelain called SALOPIAN ware, which was similar to Worcester, although Salopian ware footrims are square-shaped and Worcester triangular.

Early wares—mainly tea services—were painted or printed in UNDERGLAZE BLUE in Chinese style. The CHAMBERLAIN factory of Worcester bought large quantities of Caughley porcelain from 1780 to 1795 and much of the finest decorating was added by them. The blue printed patterns are generally marked with a "C" or with an "S" for Salopian. The early porcelain also included many shapes made at Worcester, including leaf-molded jugs with mask-molded spouts. Other shapes were openwork baskets, salad bowls, and butter dishes. When Thomas Turner sold off the Caughley works in 1799, he also sold the stock of unglazed goods, molds, and copper-plates. The factory continued for 15 years under Edward Blakeway and John ROSE of COALPORT.

Castleford pottery
Castleford creamware (Dunderdale and Co.) ink stand and cover. c. 1800.

Castle-top
Victorian silver castle-top card case, with a view of St. Paul's Cathedral. 1842.

Caucasian carpet
Caucasian Shirvan rug. c. 1890.

Caudle cup
A George I silver cup with ropework girdle and swirl fluting around the lower body. c. 1718.

C

Cauliflower ware ■ English pottery tea- and coffeepots, and wares molded to simulate cauliflowers (and pineapples), colored with fine semitranslucent glazes of green and yellow, and made from the mid-18th to the 19th century.

Cauling A furniture technique in which a heated "caul"—usually a panel of wood, but sometimes a sheet of zinc or aluminum—is clamped over a VENEER in order to attach it securely to a CARCASS. The pressure applied by the caul ensures that the adhesive binding the veneer to the carcass is evenly distributed, and also expels any air bubbles trapped within it.

Cavetto molding A quarter-round hollow molding, used in furniture-making from the 17th century, primarily for CORNICES on CABINETS that were faced with VENEER.

Cedar ■ The common name for several species of trees, mainly softwoods. The aromatic red cedar used from around 1750 as a moth-resistant lining for drawers, wardrobe trays, boxes, and chests was from the *Juniperus virginiana* or *Cedrela odorata* species.

Celadon A glaze derived from iron with a distinctive gray-green or blue-green color, used to imitate nephrite jade in China for over 2,000 years and almost as long in South Korea and Japan. Decoration is often molded or carved in low relief. Wares include bowls, vases, EWERS, CENSERS, and large dishes. Much celadon ware was exported from the 12th century, finding particular favor in the Middle East. The technique was revived and regained popularity in the 19th century.

Cellaret (or Cellarette) A free-standing square, round, or octagonal wooden chest for holding wine bottles or decanters, and often lead-lined to protect the wood from the ice. Most are mounted on casters so that they can be moved. The term can also refer to a drawer in a sideboard equipped for the same purpose.

Cellini, Benvenuto (1500–71) A renowned Italian sculptor and goldsmith. From 1519 he worked as a medallist and goldsmith in Rome under the patronage of Pope Clement VI, but from 1540 to 1545 was employed at the court of Francis I of France, where he produced his only surviving definitely attributed work: an ornate gold and enamel salt cellar (1540) with MANNERIST figures, seahorses, and dolphins. His autobiography, published in 1558, describes his workshop methods.

Celluloid ■ An early form of PLASTIC, invented in the US in the 1860s. The trade name for pyroxylin, its primary uses have been for dolls' heads and bodies, but also for combs, cutlery handles, and costume jewelry. Brittle and highly flammable, it had been largely superseded by other plastics before the 1950s.

Celtic Revival The late 19th- and early 20th-century revival of ancient Celtic ornament, particularly in Britain and Ireland. It is found in silverwork and jewelry produced by members of the ARTS AND CRAFTS Movement and in CYMRIC and TUDRIC wares produced by LIBERTY & CO. It is characterized by interlaced designs, colored enamels, and CABOCHON semiprecious stones.

Celtic style ■ The arts and crafts of the Celts, a race who originally inhabited an area comprising eastern France, Holland, West Germany, and Austria. In around 250 BCE they invaded the British Isles. They

CAUGHLEY

The Caughley porcelain factory is known for its printed underglaze blue and white ware in the Chinese style. Other pieces with painted floral decoration show a contemporary French influence, often augmented with gilding. Most of its polychrome pieces were decorated by the Chamberlain factory in Worcester.

Saucer
"The fisherman and Cormorant" pattern porcelain saucer. c. 1785.

Floral decoration

Teapot
Caughley porcelain teapot and cover, painted with Chantilly flower garlands. c. 1785.

Plate
Caughley lobed round plate, printed in underglaze with full napkin pattern. c. 1780–85.

Cauliflower pattern in relief

Cauliflower ware
Staffordshire cauliflower teapot. c. 1765.

were renowned for fine GOLD and BRONZE metalwork, including mirrors, weaponry, ARMOR, and jewelry, buried in the graves of chiefs and intended for their use in the afterlife. With the arrival of Christianity in Ireland in 435 CE, and in Britain in 635 CE, Celtic art also included CHALICES and other ecclesiastical SILVER, sculptural stone crosses, and illuminated manuscripts. Celtic art is characterized by decoration of stylized, curvilinear ornament, especially INTERLACING, knot work, LOZENGES and spirals, and sinuous animals and figures. Metalwork is often embellished with CLOISONNÉ and CHAMPLEVÉ enamels, and SEMIPRECIOUS or PRECIOUS STONES.

Among the most notable works of Celtic art are the bronze Battersea Shield (1st century CE), gold jewelry found at Sutton Hoo (mid-7th century CE), and in Ireland, the Tara Brooch and the Book of Kells (both 8th century CE). Celtic art had died out in England by the late 9th century, but survived until the 12th century in Ireland. Interest in Celtic art was revived following excavations in the late 19th century and the emergence of nationalist movements in Ireland and Scotland. Like all medieval art, it had a particular influence on British ARTS AND CRAFTS and ART NOUVEAU designers, manifested especially in designs for silver and jewelry with interlacing motifs and ENAMEL decoration.

Censer ■ A Chinese incense burner, generally made in BRONZE, JADE,

POTTERY, or PORCELAIN. They are usually shaped like a cauldron on three feet, often with three hanging chains, but can also be formed as a fabulous animal or bird. The Japanese equivalent is a KORO.

Centennial ■ A term used in the US when Americans celebrated the 100th anniversary of signing the Declaration of Independence (July 4, 1776). Centennial furniture is typically an authentic reproduction of high-quality COLONIAL or AMERICAN CHIPPENDALE furniture. Colonial Revival pieces tend to be in oak. American Chippendale reproductions, which were more popular and have remained in production, are in mahogany.

By the year of the Centennial, furniture-makers were well established in several American cities, notably New York, Chicago, and Philadelphia. The style was popularized by American furniture-makers at the Centennial Exposition, an international trade show in Philadelphia in the summer of 1876, modeled on London's GREAT EXHIBITION of 1851. Here, historical furniture of high quality, representing America's colonial past, was shown to a wide public and proved appealing to a newly unified US infused with patriotism. The term may also describe items made specifically for the 1876 Centennial celebrations, including historical documents that were reproduced in large editions. It is also applied to American folk art of around 1876, featuring patriotic imagery, particularly the Stars and Stripes, EAGLES,

and images of historic and notable former presidents, including George Washington and Abraham Lincoln.

Ceramics The word is used to describe a hard, brittle material made by firing clay or an object made from it. It includes POTTERY, PORCELAIN, STONEWARE, and EARTHENWARE.

Ch'ing dynasty See QING DYNASTY.

Chad Valley A leading British toy manufacturer, formed in 1820 at Harborne, Birmingham. The company has its origins in a printing and stationery business founded in the mid-19th century. During the 1890s, it began to produce board games and cardboard toys, which grew in number after the outbreak of war saw the end of German imports. In 1915 it began to produce TEDDY BEARS, noted for their large, golden, MOHAIR PLUSH bodies, large ears, and small feet, inspiring other teddy bear makers such as MERRYTHOUGHT LTD. Typical Chad Valley lines include the novelty stuffed toy Bonzo (a bull terrier based on a newspaper cartoon) and his girlfriend, Oolo (1930s), and the Great Western Railway series of jigsaw puzzles (1930s). In 1938 the company was awarded the Royal Warrant. After World War II Chad Valley continued to expand and acquired a number of companies, producing a range of tinplate "toy" biscuit tins, tinplate toys such as humming tops, money boxes, train sets, vehicles, plastic DOLLS, and dolls' tea sets.

C

91

Cedar
Carved cedar plaque.

Celluloid
Celluloid hand mirror. c. 1930.

Celtic style
Scottish School Arts and Crafts repoussé brass wall clock, with Celtic knotwork.

Censer
Chinese bronze censer. Late 19th century.

Centennial
Centennial-style mahogany highboy. 19th century.

In 1967 Chad Valley took over CHILTERN, and after a subsequent period of decline, it became part of Palitoy in 1978. In 1988 Woolworth's acquired the rights to the name.

C

92

Chaffers ■ One of a number of factories in Liverpool, England, producing porcelain in the 18th century. It was founded by Richard Chaffer in 1754, and was in business until 1765. Chaffers used a soaprock porcelain with a grayish blue body similar to most Liverpool porcelain. Other characteristics include a dark cobalt blue on blue and white CHINOISERIE ware, and FAMILLE ROSE colors on naively painted polychrome equivalents.

Chafing dish From the French *chauffer* (to heat). A serving dish with a heating apparatus below, either used for cooking or keeping food warm at the table, made from SILVER or PLATED wares in various forms during the 18th, 19th, and early 20th centuries. Heated by burning charcoal, the chafing dish is the forerunner of the electric hotplate.

Chain stitch A series of looped stitches that are interlinked. Worked either with a needle or a hook and sometimes referred to as TAMBOUR stitch, it was a comparatively simple stitch and therefore suited to large-scale furnishings such as curtains, wall-hangings and bed-hangings.

Chair A type of free-standing seat furniture with a back and with or without arms, designed for one person. With evidence of examples in ancient Egypt from the third millennium BCE, the chair is one of the earliest types of furniture. Early forms such as the Greek KLISMOS, the portable Roman folding X-CHAIR, and the medieval post seat, with posts at each corner of the seat, evolved over the centuries into a huge variety of armless SIDE CHAIRS and dining chairs, armchairs (see CARVER CHAIR), upholstered armchairs (see BERGÈRE and CONFIDANTE), and other styles such as the CANTILEVER CHAIR.

Chaise longue ■ From the French *chaise longue* (long chair). A day-bed with an upholstered back, allowing the occupant to recline on it. Introduced in France around 1625, it came to Britain with the restoration of Charles II (1660). Jacques-Louis David's portrait of Madame Récamier on a chaise longue (1800) made it fashionable again and it was often known as a *récamier* in France. Extravagant versions were popular during the late 19th century in Britain and the US, and it was popular with Modernist designers.

Chalice A wine cup or goblet used by the Catholic Church during Mass, made in SILVER, SILVER GILT, or GOLD, usually with a paten (a matching plate) to hold the offering of bread. It is also known as a Communion Cup. The term has also been more recently applied to any goblet too large for standard drinking use.

Chalkware ■ Decorative ornaments made from plaster of Paris and decorated with bright colors, popular from the 18th to the mid-20th century in the US and Britain. Made to imitate pottery and porcelain, forms were taken from STAFFORDSHIRE ceramic molds and porcelain figures and sold as considerably less expensive examples of authentic pieces.

Chamber pot ■ A toilet receptacle for use in the bedchamber. Made in metal, pottery, and porcelain, both simple and luxurious, in sizes for children as well as adults, and from early times until the 20th century. In late Victorian times chamber pots were included in bedroom sets with a jug and basin.

Chamberlain family A family of English ceramicists connected with the WORCESTER PORCELAIN FACTORY. Robert Chamberlain was apprenticed as a porcelain decorator at Worcester, but left in 1786 to set up independently. By 1791 his establishment was producing its own porcelain, a hybrid HARD-PASTE type, used for high-quality tea, dessert, and ornamental wares. After his death, his two sons and his nephew, Walter, carried on the business, which continued to operate successfully in competition with Worcester. In 1840 Walter Chamberlain and his brother-in-law, John Lilly, guided the company to a merger with FLIGHT, BARR & BARR, after which it became Chamberlain & Co. until 1852.

Chaffers
A Chaffers coffee can with chinoiserie landscape decoration. c. 1760.

Ivory silk damask upholstery

Chaise longue
Regency simulated rosewood and gilt-metal mounted chaise longue.

Ivory and black antlers

Chalkware
Pennsylvanian chalkware deer. 1820–40.

Chamber pot
Blue and white transfer-printed child's chamber pot. Mid-19th century.

Chambers, Sir William (1723–96)
An English architect born in Sweden of Scottish parents. He traveled widely and trained as an architect in Paris and Rome before settling in London in 1755, where he tutored George, Prince of Wales, later George III, in architecture. He became a highly distinguished architect and was responsible for Somerset House in London, among other buildings. He also designed some furniture in a sober NEOCLASSICAL style for Blenheim Palace (made by INCE & MAYHEW) and seat furniture for the Royal Society of Arts in London.

Chamberstick ■ A saucerlike dish with a central candleholder and a detachable conical snuffer or a slot to take scissor snuffers. A handle enabled the bearer to carry the lighted candle around safely. Chambersticks are generally made from noncombustible materials, particularly silver and plate. Although 17th-century silver examples are scarce, this type of candlestick is known to have predated the Reformation.

Chamfer The surface produced by planing or cutting an edge at an angle. Mostly applied to wood and stone, the technique can be used to protect an edge from damage, or be purely decorative.

Champagne glass ■ There are two styles: a FLUTE, with a deep, tapering cylindrical bowl that was intended to retain the bubbles, and from around 1830, the "coupe" glass, with a wide, shallow bowl, supposedly modeled on the breasts of Madame de Pompadour, Louis XV's mistress, though the form predates her birth by three centuries.

Champion, Richard (1743–91) A shareholder in the PLYMOUTH factory making HARD PASTE PORCELAIN. Champion took part in the management of the works and the original patent was transferred to him when William COOKWORTHY retired in 1774. Champion tried to extend the patent, due to expire in 1782, for 14 years, but the Staffordshire potters opposed it. Champion carried on but the factory closed in 1781 and the remaining stock was sold in 1782.

Champlevé ■ An ENAMELING technique in which colored enamels are poured into engraved channels on the surface of a silver, bronze, or copper object, and when set, are polished down to lie flush with the surrounding metal. See CLOISONNÉ.

Chandelier Although originally a French term for a candlestick, and sometimes also used in France to describe a wall-light, by the 17th century "chandelier" was generally used in Europe and North America to describe a light fixture, often with multiple branches and candleholders, suspended from a ceiling.

Chanel, Gabrielle "Coco" ■ (1883–1971) French fashion designer active in Paris in the 1930s and 1940s, remembered for the "little black dress," formal yet simple suits, handbags, perfume, and, most important to collectors, costume jewelry, especially pearls. The fashion house survives today.

Chang ware ■ Produced at ROYAL DOULTON from the early 20th century, after experiments by C. J. Noke with transmutation glazes. Inspired by the Chinese ceramics of the Sung dynasty, thick, brightly colored, and crackled glazes creep down the side of the ceramic articles. No two pieces of Chang are alike because of the random nature of the glaze. Production ended in the 1940s.

Chantilly A French center for BOBBIN LACE, producing a high-quality heavier black lace made with grenadine silk, and also blonde lace in the 19th century. Examples from the 18th century are scarce. Black Chantilly lace was exported to Spain for mantillas.

Chantilly porcelain factory ■ Founded by Louis Henri de Bourbon, Prince de Condé, in Chantilly, Oise, France, in 1725. The factory started making SOFT-PASTE PORCELAIN in the 1730s. At first the porcelain had a white TIN GLAZE, and later, a LEAD GLAZE. Ciquaire Cirou was the first director, from around 1725 to 1751, and worked with the modeler Louis Fournier. Many of the workers either came from SÈVRES or went there from Chantilly, including the painter Charles Buteux, who went to work at the Sèvres factory in 1756.

Chamberstick
George III silver chamberstick, by George Eadon and Co., Sheffield. c. 1806.

Champagne glass
Slice-cut hollow stem champagne glass. c. 1890.

Champlevé
French gilt metal and champlevé enamel cased mantel clock. 19th century.

Chanel
Chanel peacock pin with poured glass feathers and clear rhinestones. 1930s.

Chang ware
Royal Doulton Chang vase, by Charles Noke and Harry Nixon.

The Prince de Condé was a great collector of Oriental porcelain and much Chantilly ware was in the style of the KAKIEMON potters of Japan, who were also copied at MEISSEN on hard paste. Most wares are under 10 inches (25 cm) tall. The painting at Chantilly was done with great care, although much of the wares were for modest households. Chantilly produced table services, CACHE-POTS, jugs, bowls, and wine bottle coolers. It also made charming SNUFF BOXES, ÉTUIS, cane handles, and figures. In 1792 it was bought by an Englishman, Christopher Potter, who also owned the Paris factory. The mark was a hunting horn (usually in red), sometimes with the word "Chantilly." The factory closed around 1800. Chantilly ware was copied by SAMSON, the great French faker.

Chantilly sprig ■ Sprays of flowers, twigs, grasses, or ears of corn, usually in blue on CHANTILLY porcelain, but sometimes in crimson, manganese, or purple. It became popular at MENNECY, ARRAS, and TOURNAI, and was copied in England at DERBY and CAUGHLEY.

Chapter ring The ring on a clock dial on which the hour and/or minute numbers are painted, engraved, or attached. Roman numerals are used on most chapter rings, although Arabic numerals were popular in the late 19th and early 20th centuries.

Character doll ■ A doll, typically made from BISQUE, resembling a real child with strong facial expressions. KÄMMER &

REINHARDT was the first company to popularize the type when it introduced its range at the 1909 Munich Exhibition. Further examples followed, with character dolls from makers such as HEUBACH, Armand MARSEILLE, and the SOCIÉTÉ FRANÇAISE DE FABRICATION DE BÉBÉS ET JOUETS. They were produced in smaller numbers and for a shorter period of time than other dolls, as their strong expressions made them less popular with children. They tend to be scarce today.

Character jug A pottery drinking vessel caricaturing a fictional or real-life character. They were based on 18th-century TOBY JUGS, but portrayed just the head or head and shoulders. Character jugs were the brainchild of Charles Noke, a modeler at ROYAL DOULTON, who produced his first character jug John Barleycorn in 1934, although Doulton had produced a Lord Nelson jug back in the 1820s. Other manufacturers include Beswick, SylvaC, Kevin Francis, and ROYAL WORCESTER.

Charcoal blue A technique whereby polished steel is heated in a bed of burning charcoal to give it a decorative, brilliant blue finish, which also prevents corrosion.

Chareau, Pierre (1883–1950) A French designer and architect of ART DECO and the MODERN MOVEMENT. He began as a draftsman in the furniture department of WARING & GILLOW in their Paris office, but in 1919 set up his own practice. He designed the famous Maison de Verre in Paris, built between 1928 and 1931. He also designed for private commissions, and his work is clean and sophisticated, sometimes incorporating some form of movement.

Charger ■ A large, often ornate, dish or platter, principally for display but also for serving at the table. The term was used for 16th- and 17th-century ceramic, enamel, silver, and gold dishes.

Chantilly porcelain factory
The hunting horn mark of the Chantilly factory. c. 1740.

CHATELAINE

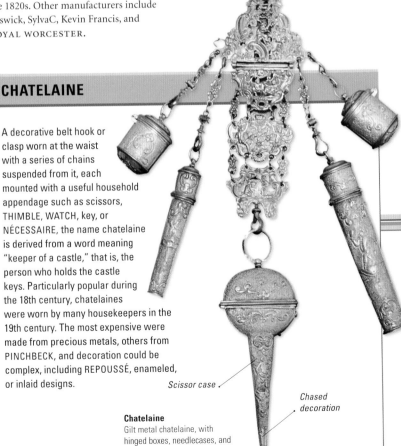

A decorative belt hook or clasp worn at the waist with a series of chains suspended from it, each mounted with a useful household appendage such as scissors, THIMBLE, WATCH, key, or NÉCESSAIRE, the name chatelaine is derived from a word meaning "keeper of a castle," that is, the person who holds the castle keys. Particularly popular during the 18th century, chatelaines were worn by many housekeepers in the 19th century. The most expensive were made from precious metals, others from PINCHBECK, and decoration could be complex, including REPOUSSÉ, enameled, or inlaid designs.

Scissor case

Chased decoration

Chatelaine
Gilt metal chatelaine, with hinged boxes, needlecases, and a scissor case. 19th century.

Chase Brass & Cooper Co. ■ An American metalware company. Founded in Connecticut in 1876 as the Waterbury Manufacturing Company, it initially produced domestic and industrial products such as copper pipes, screening, and novelties. By 1930 it was producing tableware such as coffee sets, salt and pepper shakers, candlesticks, lamps, and cocktail shakers in a MODERN style. Produced mainly in chrome and copper, many of the successful ranges were designed by Walter von Nessen and RUSSEL WRIGHT. When the US went to war in 1941, the company produced war-related materials and the domestic line was not restarted after the war.

Chase, Martha Jenks An American doll-maker who set up the Chase Hospital Doll Company in Pawtucket, Rhode Island, in around 1889. Her stockinet dolls have oil-painted hair and facial features and cotton-fiber-stuffed white sateen, or later, cotton bodies. Her company ceased trading in 1938.

Chasing A metalware technique, mostly associated with silverware, in which patterns are raised in relief with a punch or hammer by manipulating the metal without removing any of it.

Chassis The main frame of a vehicle carrying all the mechanical components, surmounted by the coachwork. In toy vehicles, it is used to indicate the base unit carrying the wheels, fender, and bumpers.

Chasuble An ecclesiastical vestment worn by a priest. Originally almost circular in shape, the shape changed in the 16th century and became elongated, allowing the arms to hang freely. These vestments are normally elaborately embroidered, frequently using gold and silver threads.

Chatônes A type of decorative nailhead used on Spanish furniture.

Checkerwork A pattern of alternating squares or LOZENGES of contrasting colors or textures, similar to the pattern on a chess board. A favorite motif in the 16th and 17th centuries for textiles and tiled floors, checkerwork was also favored by cabinet-makers for inlay decoration. A checker pattern was frequently adopted as a decorative motif on metal and ceramics, following the introduction of engine-turned decoration in the late 18th century.

Chelsea Keramic Art Works An American factory producing ART POTTERY glazed wares in Massachusetts in the late 19th century. Its Scottish owner, Hugh Robertson, wanted to replicate Oriental, high-fired CRACKLE glazes on original designs to make pieces look older. This was achieved by exposing twice-fired pieces quickly to cold air while still hot. Black coloring was then often added to accentuate the CRAZING. The factory moved to Massachusetts in 1896, and pieces from then until they closed in 1943 are known as DEDHAM POTTERY. Hallmarks of the style include crackle glazes, blue and white color schemes, and decorative borders. Rabbits were the company's most popular motif.

Chelsea porcelain factory The Chelsea Porcelain factory, thought to be the first in England, made SOFT-PASTE PORCELAIN with a glassy glaze. In 1749 the first director, Charles Gouyn, was replaced by Nicholas Sprimont, a young Huguenot silversmith from Liege. The factory's history can be divided according to the four marks that it used on its wares.

Early products from about 1744 to 1749 bore an incised triangle mark. Most were white and strongly influenced by silver designs. From 1749 to 1752—the raised anchor mark period—the paste and glaze were modified to produce a white, slightly opaque surface on which to paint. The influence of MEISSEN is evident in Classical figures among Italianate ruins and harbor scenes. Chelsea also made figures, birds, and animals inspired by Meissen originals. Flowers and landscapes were copied from VINCENNES. In the red anchor mark period (1752–56), KAKIEMON subjects were popular. Some English-inspired tableware decorated with botanically accurate plants was produced. The influence of SÈVRES was strong in the gold anchor mark period (1756–69), which saw rich colored grounds and lavish gilding in the ROCOCO style. In the 1750s and 1760s Chelsea was also famous for its BONBONNIÈRES, scent bottles, ÉTUIS,

C

95

Chantilly sprig
Worcester dish, painted in underglaze blue, stamped "Chantilly Sprig." c. 1780.

Character doll
French lady character doll, marked "favorite," made by Limoges. c. 1925.

Charger
Delftware oak leaf charger. c. 1700.

Chase Brass & Copper Co.
Chase copper and brass water pitcher, designed by Walter von Nessen.

C
96

THIMBLES, and small SEALS. The failing factory was bought in 1769 by William DUESBURY of Derby, who ran it until 1784.

Chenet The French term for an ANDIRON or FIREDOG.

Chenghua porcelain CHINESE PORCELAIN made during the reign of the MING DYNASTY emperor, Chenghua (1465–87). The wares tend to be small, decorated in UNDERGLAZE blue, a monochrome glaze, or in the DOUCAI palette. The Chenghua reign mark was extensively copied in the 19th and 20th centuries.

Chenille The French word for caterpillar. A velvety cord, usually silk but sometimes wool or cotton. Chenille has the appearance of being "hairy" and having short fibers that stick out from the central thread. Introduced during the 17th century as a decorative embroidery thread, it was particularly popular in the 19th century and is still used today, frequently in fringing.

Chequerwork See CHECKERWORK.

Chéret, Jules ■ (1836–1933) A French artist and poster designer. In 1867 he produced the first color LITHOGRAPHIC posters in Paris, designing over 1,000 posters during his lifetime. Recognized as the "father" of the modern poster, his colorful, figurative designs captured the

air and style of the period and were hugely popular, particularly for the theater and circus, and influenced TOULOUSE-LAUTREC and other artists.

Cherry A tree found in Europe, North America, and East Asia that provides a FRUITWOOD varying in color from pinkish yellow to brown. It was used for INLAY and small pieces of furniture in the 17th century, and for French provincial furniture in the 18th century. Also employed in ARTS AND CRAFTS furniture of the late 19th to early 20th century.

Cherub The first hierarchy of angels in Christian iconography. Later it came to designate a beautiful winged child. Often indistinguishable from the CUPIDS and PUTTI in secular schemes. The motif appears from the 15th century on architectural ornament, spoons, and clock faces.

Chesapeake Pottery Founded by Henry & Isaac Broughman in Baltimore, MD, in 1880. The pottery was sold to David E. Haynes in 1882, and then to Edwin Bennett in 1887. The factory made PARIAN WARE, MAJOLICA, and Calvert ware (a blue or green-glazed ware with bands of decoration). It closed in 1924.

Chest (chest-of-drawers, chest-on-chest, chest-on-stand) The chest, in the form of a wooden box with a lid,

was one of the earliest types of furniture and is found in almost all cultures. Primitive examples were simply hollowed-out logs, fitted with a lid, and known as "dugouts." The BOARDED CHEST developed in the 13th century and was gradually superseded by paneled chests (see CASSONE). Various types of CASE FURNITURE developed from the chest: from the mid-16th century the bases of traveling chests or coffers were sometimes fitted with small drawers, and by the mid-17th century an early form of the chest-of-drawers had evolved. Subsequently, it was to undergo several refinements and different styles and names such as the BACHELOR'S CHEST, the CHIFFONIER, the COMMODE, the tallboy and its US variant the HIGHBOY, and the LOWBOY.

Chesterfield A term used from the late 19th century to designate a large, overstuffed sofa with a straight back and often with buttoned leather upholstery.

Chestnut There are two species of chestnut tree in Europe—the horse chestnut (*Aesculus hippocastanum*) and the Spanish or sweet chestnut (*Castanea vesca*). *Castanea dentata* was native to the eastern US but has largely succumbed to disease. The wood from these trees is often confused, and they were all used as substitutes for SATINWOOD in the 18th century. Horse chestnut wood is soft, yellowish, and not very durable, but was used for some turned work and inlay; Spanish or sweet chestnut is light brown, more durable, and was used to make furniture.

Cherét, Jules
Art Nouveau poster by Jules Cherét, advertising the Eldorado music hall. c. 1894.

Cheveret
Sheraton period mahogany cheveret.

Child & Child
Child & Child aquamarine and citrine pendant.

"Quack quack" frieze
Children's ware
Wade Quack-Quacks pattern nursery mug, by Robert Barlow.

Chevalier de Béthune   The term for an ESCAPEMENT invented in 1727 and used by some French clockmakers throughout the 18th century. It is distinguished by having a double ARBOR. The Chevalier may have been an amateur horologist.

Cheveret ■   A small writing or work table, often with a detachable top for carrying books and usually made in SATINWOOD, ROSEWOOD, or MAHOGANY. It was common in the late 18th century. It is supported on long, tapering legs, has a drawer in the frieze, and shelves or pigeonholes to the rear of the work surface.

Chevron   One of the simplest geometric forms, composed of a linked zigzag motif or used singly in a vertical arrangement. An early symbol used on woven textiles and incised ceramics, the chevron was an important feature of the 19th-century neo-Norman style. In furniture chevrons appear in chip-carved ornament, and GOTHIC REVIVAL pieces frequently incorporate inlaid chevron bands. The chevron motif was one of the most popular geometric patterns adopted for ART DECO ornament in the 1930s.

Chiffonier ■   An anglicized term for a CHIFFONIÉRE. Introduced in the mid-18th century, it took the form of a small dining room cupboard with internal shelving enclosed by doors, sometimes beneath a row of drawers, and with a flat top.

Chiffoniére   The French term for the CHIFFONIER. Also a term used in the 18th century for a small set of shallow drawers for storing fabrics and sewing accessories.

Child & Child ■   A firm of London silversmiths and goldsmiths, active at the end of the 19th century and specializing in distinctive enamel, silver, and gold gem-set jewelry such as buckles and naturalistic brooches. Often lodged in green leather cases, its jewelry was invariably signed with a sunflower motif between the initials "CC."

Children's ware ■   Ceramic items produced specifically for children, including plates, cups, and saucers, and later, figures of animals. Originating in the late 19th century and often produced by the Staffordshire factories, these wares were made especially for the nursery and bore TRANSFER-PRINTED moral and educational MOTTOES and images. The child could thus be educated even while eating. Scenes of nature were also popular and the first half of the 20th century saw the start of a more relaxed and whimsical choice of subjects based around children's stories and popular culture, including the characters of Beatrix Potter and ROYAL DOULTON's Bunnykins figures.

Chiltern ■   (1908–67) A toy works in Chesham, Buckinghamshire, founded in 1908 by Joseph Eisenmann, and named after the hills in the surrounding area. The company also had factories at Tottenham, London, from 1921 until World War II, in Amersham, Buckinghamshire, from World War II until 1960, and at Pontypool, Wales, from 1947. It began by producing dolls, before making bears. Chiltern's first bear, the Master Teddy, with a flat face and googly eyes, was produced from 1915. The well-known Hugmee range of bears was introduced in 1923 and continued to be made until the company's takeover by CHAD VALLEY in 1967.

Chiltern
British Chiltern golden mohair teddy bear. 1920s–30s.

CHEVAL GLASS

A type of standing mirror in which the mirror glass is suspended between a four-legged frame, cheval glass derives its name from *cheval*, which in French means "horse." The frame allows the mirror to be tilted to facilitate a full-length reflection.

Turned stretchers

Splayed feet with paw terminals

Cheval glass
George IV mahogany cheval mirror.

C

Chimera ■ A fire-breathing beast of Classical mythology, with the head, mane, and legs of a lion, the tail of a dragon, body of a goat, and frequently the wings of an eagle. The RENAISSANCE borrowed it from Classical sources such as Pompeian wall paintings and grotesque ornament. Popular on 18th-century NEOCLASSICAL ornament, it was employed in the EMPIRE and REGENCY periods as supports for console tables or as the sides of armchairs.

Chiming See STRIKING SYSTEMS.

Chimney board See DUMMY BOARD.

China See BONE CHINA. A word used to denote porcelain, from the name of the country of origin of "real" porcelain. It was exported by the Chinese along the Silk Route to Istanbul (Constantinople) and from there to Europe. It was later shipped by the various East India companies in their ships bringing tea and silk to Europe in the 17th and 18th centuries, and was termed "china ware."

China cabinet ■ A type of cabinet, also known as a china case, introduced in the late 17th century to display the newly fashionable Oriental ceramics, with inside shelves and either glazed or solid doors.

China clay See KAOLIN.

China head doll ■ A doll with a glazed porcelain head. "China" (HARD-PASTE PORCELAIN) was commonly used to produce dolls from around 1840 until 1940, the molds reflecting the rapidly changing hairstyles and accessories of the 19th and 20th centuries. Once molded, the heads were fired at a high temperature, painted with facial details, glazed, and fired again. China SHOULDER HEADS were attached to commercial or homemade fabric bodies by means of two, and later three, pierced holes in the SHOULDER PLATE.

China stone The English name for PETUNTSE, the essential ingredient for making HARD-PASTE PORCELAIN. It is also known as Cornish stone. China stone refers to the feldspar (a silicate of potassium and aluminum) with which KAOLIN is mixed. The BODY is fired at a high temperature and the feldspar fuses to form

CHINESE CARPETS

First produced in the 17th century and associated until the mid-19th century with Ninghsia, on the Silk Route in northwest China, the symbols on Chinese carpets include DOGS OF FO, dragons, bats, cranes, peony blossoms, and lotus, woven in a harmonious mix of geometric and curvilinear designs. Colors are generally yellow, ivory, and blue. Carpets made in the 1920s are usually called "Nichols" after the company they were made for, using nontraditional colors often in 19th-century French SAVONNERIE styles.

Figural and floral carpet
Chinese carpet with a blue field and figural floral motifs set in an overall geometric pattern. Late 19th century.

Dragons and flowers carpet
Chinese carpet with red field, dragon, and flower pattern, and yellow border. c. 1930.

Bird and plant form pattern
Chinese carpet with a pale blue field and scattered bird and plant form motifs, within geometric motif borders. c. 1900.

a kind of natural glass, which gives the porcelain its hardness and TRANSLUCENCY. The Chinese meaning of petuntse is "little white bricks" (*pai tun tzu*), which reflects the process in China whereby the stone was pulverized and sent to the porcelain-makers in the form of small bricks.

Chinese Chippendale ■ A modern term for mid-18th-century furniture with any CHINOISERIE decoration, as illustrated in the *Gentleman and Cabinet-Makers Director* by Thomas CHIPPENDALE, and made by his workshop and other contemporary furniture-makers.

Chinese dynasty Chinese history is divided into dynasties of ruling families, and within these, reigns of emperors. Artistically, the most important dynasties are SHANG (c. 1500–1028 BCE), Han (206 BCE–220 CE), TANG (618–906), SONG (960–1279), YUAN (1260–1368), MING (1368–1644), and QING (1644–1912).

Chinese export porcelain ■ From the 16th century a wide range of porcelain was made and decorated in China exclusively for export to the West. Chinese export porcelain is generally decorative, but without the symbolic significance of wares produced for the home market. With the exception of the rare *huashi* (Chinese SOFT-PASTE) wares, Chinese porcelain is hard paste. In the 16th century Portuguese traders began importing late MING DYNASTY blue and white porcelain to Europe, resulting in the

growth of the KRAAK PORCELAIN trade. In 1602 and 1604, two Portuguese ships were captured by the Dutch and their contents auctioned, igniting a European mania for porcelain. Many European nations then established trading companies in the East, the most important being the Dutch East India Company or VOC.

Knowledge of Chinese export porcelain has been greatly enhanced by the recovery of the cargoes of several shipwrecked trading vessels. For example, the Nanking Cargo was the contents of the *Geldermalsen*, a huge Dutch East Indiaman (sank January 3, 1752), from which over 100,000 pieces of porcelain were salvaged in 1986.

Chinese export porcelain from the late 17th century includes blue and white and FAMILLE VERTE wares (and occasionally FAMILLE NOIRE and JAUNE) as well as BLANC-DE-CHINE porcelain and YIXING stoneware. Although European crests on Chinese porcelain can be found as early as the 16th century, around 1700 the demand for ARMORIAL porcelain dramatically increased. Chinese potters also copied the popular Japanese IMARI porcelain. From around 1720 the new FAMILLE ROSE palette was adopted and quickly supplanted the earlier *famille verte* porcelain of the KANGXI period. Specific patterns such as Tobacco Leaf and Faux Tobacco Leaf were popular, as were CANTON (decorated porcelain with figures, birds, flowers, and insects), from around 1800. As trade developed, finer quality items were shipped by private traders who rented space on the

East India Company ships. They were sometimes CLOBBERED in Holland and England to enhance their decorative appeal.

By the late 18th century, imports of Chinese porcelain were going down. Tastes were changing and competition from new European factories with mass production brought about by industrialization took its toll. Highly decorative Canton porcelain was produced throughout the 19th century but the quality of wares was on the decline. By the end of the century, blue and white wares in the KANGXI style (often with Kangxi and CHENGHUA reign marks) were produced in large quantities, and almost every earlier style and type of porcelain as copied into the 20th century.

Chinese furniture ■ Although Chinese furniture was made as early as the 14th century BCE, most of the earliest surviving wooden pieces were made in the MING dynasty (1368–1644), several hundred years after the fundamental change to chair-level living from around the 10th century CE.

The practice of sitting on chairs rather than on mats or low platforms encouraged the development of new furniture types to supplement the previously narrow range of the screen (*ping*), altar or ritual tables, and the *kang* (originally a heated brick platform used in northern China). In the Golden Age of Chinese furniture during the Ming and early QING dynasties (1368–1735), the *kang* developed into associated furniture types such as a low platform on legs used for sleeping, *kang* tables, and the X-frame chair

Chimera
French chimera brooch in gilt holding a diamond in its mouth. c. 1900.

China cabinet
An Edwardian china cabinet fashioned in mahogany in Georgian, Chinese Chippendale style. c. 1910.

China head doll
German "Grape Lady" china head doll. c. 1860.

Chinese Chippendale
Chinese Chippendale style chair. c. 1880.

C

from the SONG dynasty. During the late Qing period a flourishing export trade developed. Chinese furniture-makers adopted European forms and motifs. They cut down the legs of tables and chairs and produced 19th-century furniture that imitated older styles but lacked the high-quality joinery and subtle decoration of the originals. There were two basic types of furniture: waisted and waistless. In waisted furniture a recessed panel was inserted between the top and the apron of tables, legs were set at the corners of the piece and were often square, with *mati* (horsehoof) upturned feet that faced inward or outward. By contrast, on waistless furniture the top rested directly on the legs, which were usually round, set back with high stretchers, and splayed slightly outward.

Chinese furniture is constructed using joinery alone, partly to accommodate extremes of temperature, usually in the pure MORTISE AND TENON system without the use of DOWELS or nails, and with only the occasional use of glue. In China hardwood was not necessarily prized above softwood. Many of the finest pieces destined for the royal households were made of softwood covered with LACQUER, which was decorated and also served as protection against insects. Wooden furniture was rarely marked or dated and basic furniture forms were often made for centuries with few changes. By contrast, the bamboo furniture made in the south of China was essentially expendable and could be used outdoors.

Chinese glass ■ Made from around 300 BCE, but most pieces date from after 1680, when the Peking (Beijing) Imperial Glassworks was set up. It usually imitated precious materials such as blue and white, Imperial yellow porcelain, and lapis lazuli. Snuff bottles, often decorated like period porcelain, were also made and are widely reproduced today.

Chinese Imari An 18th-century CHINESE EXPORT PORCELAIN decorated in underglaze blue and overglaze red enamel to imitate Japanese IMARI PORCELAIN. The decorative motifs are Chinese and Japanese and are arranged over the whole surface.

Chinese pottery and porcelain
Dominating world ceramics, China has influenced nearby Korea and Japan, the Islamic world, and from the 16th century, Europe. Neolithic Chinese pottery (around 5000–2000 BCE) includes coiled pots and funerary urns. The use of FELDSPATHIC GLAZE was developed during the SHANG DYNASTY (around 1500–1028 BCE). Soft absorbent pottery became important for burial ware. The famous terra-cotta army of over 7,000 life-size warriors and horses was made to guard the burial site of Qin Shihuang, the First Emperor in the Qin dynasty (221–206 BCE). Pottery burial ware flourished in the Han dynasty (206 BCE–220 CE) and includes figures, horses, houses, tables, chairs, and fruit. Green and brown lustrous lead glazes were then developed. While

many examples are painted with flaky earth pigments, some fine large horses, camels, figures, and earth spirits are partially glazed, usually in green, yellow, brown, and sometimes blue from the TANG DYNASTY. The pure forms and subtle naturalistic decoration of SONG DYNASTY ceramics include DING WARE, RU WARE, JUN WARE, GUAN WARE, GE WARE, and slip-decorated Chizou ware. Ceramics were exported to the Middle East from the YUAN DYNASTY, using Islamic shapes and designs, and often with CELADON glazes. In the early MING DYNASTY the use of Imperial REIGN MARKS became widespread and BLUE AND WHITE wares became mainstream, including bowls, cups, dishes, and ewers. Monochrome, Celadon, or polychrome wares were also produced. Popular subjects included chrysanthemums, peony, and lotus; pine, prunus, and bamboo; dragons and phoenix. The most important early Ming reigns are Yonglo, XUANDE, and CHENGHUA.

The CHINESE EXPORT trade with Europe began around 1570, first with the Portuguese, then the Dutch, English, and other countries. The most important reigns of the QING DYNASTY are KANGXI, YONGZHENG, and QIANLONG. Enameled porcelain replaced blue and white as the technically most advanced ware of the time and the FAMILLE VERTE colors were introduced in the late 17th century. The imperial wares of the time were in extremely fine quality monochrome. CANTON PORCELAIN of the 19th and 20th

Chinese furniture
Stained wood elbow chair, with carved dragons, stylized cloud seat rail, and cabriole legs. 20th century.

Chinese glass
Chinese Beijing overlaid glass bottle vase, with Qianlong mark of the period.

Chintzware
Royal Winton Hazel milk jug. 1930s.

Typically dynamic modeling

Chiparus, Demêtre
Gilt and patinated bronze figure, Vedette, cast from a model by Demêtre Chiparus.

centuries tended to revive shapes, glazes, and styles of earlier centuries. See DOUCAI and WUCAI.

Chinkin-bori A Japanese term describing a type of decoration used on LACQUER, where lines are carved into the lacquer surface and filled with gold foil or powder. Associated with MAKI-E techniques.

Chintz Chintz was originally the name given to high-quality, floral-patterned glazed cottons imported from India. Chintz is described in early Greek literature, but it only appeared in the West during the late 16th and early 17th centuries. Used primarily for household furnishings such as curtains and bed covers, the term now describes both floral and plain glazed cloths.

Chintzware ■ The name given to an all-over floral pattern, mostly on tea services, and now much collected. It was used frequently by ROYAL WINTON.

Chip carving A simple form of geometric-pattern decoration applied to furniture, usually made of oak, during the Middle Ages up until the 16th century, and executed with a gouge or chisel. The decorative patterns are often set in roundels.

Chiparus, Demêtre ■ (1888–1950) A Romanian-born sculptor who worked in Paris from around 1914 and was renowned for his dramatic, yet elegant, ART DECO figures in BRONZE and IVORY. He also produced theatrical, religious, and sentimental sculptural subjects and ceramic

busts and figures. These are not as sought-after as his Art Deco female dancers in elegant poses and exotic costumes that were inspired by the BALLET RUSSES and other dancers of the time.

Chippendale, Thomas ■ This English cabinet-maker and furniture designer set up a cabinet-making workshop in St. Martin's Lane, London in around 1747. Chippendale first attracted national attention with the publication in 1754 of *The Gentleman and Cabinet-Maker's Director*. It was the first book of furniture designs to be published in England and became the most influential Rococo pattern book.

The third edition, published in 1762, reflected Chippendale's interest in the new

CHINOISERIE

European fascination with East Asian culture dates back to the 13th century but reached its heyday in the 18th century. Its motifs and forms, adapted to Western taste, translated well into the decorative arts.

When trade burgeoned between China and the West in the 17th century, so did the popularity of Oriental wares. Thanks to the foundation of the EAST INDIA COMPANIES and increased imports of luxury goods into Europe and North America, Chinese blue and white export porcelain was hugely influential. It was avidly collected by the wealthy in the late 17th century and displayed on furniture and mantelpieces. It was imitated in TIN-GLAZED earthenware at DELFT and NEVERS; typical products included tiles, dishes, ewers, and tulip vases, decorated with Chinese motifs and also with landscapes in the Netherlands. At Delft the fashion for blue and white was replaced in the early 1680s by the polychrome palette, influenced by Chinese FAMILLE ROSE and FAMILLE VERTE export porcelain, and Japanese IMARI and KAKIEMON porcelain.

During the early 18th century CHINOISERIE was popular as a variant on the Rococo style, often combined with

French commode
A Louis XV commode with marble top, ormulu mounts, and chinoiserie decoration on a black lacquer ground. Mid-18th century.

Rococo and Gothic motifs in fanciful designs. The 18th-century evolution of chinoiserie began in France, in the paintings of Antoine Watteau and François BOUCHER, but soon spread throughout Europe and North America. In European porcelain, there was continuing taste for decoration inspired by Japanese and Chinese originals—for example, in figures of Chinese men in flowing robes and paintings of Chinese-style landscapes in pieces made at MEISSEN, FRANKENTHAL, HÖHST, NYMPHENBURG, and many English factories. Tapestries and silks, mirror frames, ORMOLU mounts,

and silver were also vehicles for chinoiserie. Silver épergnes and centerpieces featured pagoda-like frames and Thomas Chippendale's *The Gentleman and Cabinet-Maker's Director*, first published in 1754, inspired a vogue for chinoiserie designs in furniture. The fashion continued throughout the Regency period—for example, at the Royal Pavilion in Brighton, England, and at the Palacio Real de Aranjuez in southern Spain, where the Porcelain Room was decorated in chinoiserie style in 1763. Its popularity declined in the late 19th century.

C

NEOCLASSICAL style. This interest was realized in some of his finest furniture—a series of elegant designs for the country houses of his native Yorkshire, with interiors designed by Robert ADAM. Sixty of the 161 plates in the book were devoted to Chinese-style furniture, which became known as Chinese Chippendale. For some of his most prestigious commissions, he supplied wallpapers and fabrics hand-painted in the Chinese taste to complement his furniture. The book became the bible for English furniture-makers in Britain and North America. By the mid-1760s copies had arrived in Philadelphia and gave impetus to the AMERICAN CHIPPENDALE style. Copies of the French version were held in the libraries of royal patrons such as Catherine the Great and Louis XVI of France. The Chippendale style became a worldwide phenomenon, and MAHOGANY chairs in particular were produced in hundreds of designs that focused on intricately carved SPLATS and serpentine TOP RAILS. The Chippendale style saw a revival from the mid-1800s into the early 20th century.

Chocolate pot ◼ A rare pot for preparing drinking chocolate, made of heavy-gauge silver with handles of FRUITWOOD or IVORY. They resemble COFFEEPOTS of the 1700s, but have two important differences: an aperture in the cover of the pot has a cover of its own through which a molinet or stirring stick can be inserted to stir up the chocolate sediment; and the handle is set at right angles to the spout to facilitate pouring. Chocolate was introduced to Britain as a drink around 1657 and was highly fashionable until around 1740. The earliest hallmarked chocolate pot dates from 1685. Some examples were converted from coffeepots.

Choreutoscope A wood- or metal-framed MAGIC LANTERN slide invented by L. S. Beale in 1866 and popular during the mid-19th century. Choreutoscopes carry six images on a single glass disk or strip, which can be moved along intermittently by turning a handle, thereby projecting the six images in turn. Based on the phenomenon of persistence of vision, these images can be shown in such rapid succession that they appear to be moving, the changeover being hidden by a shutter. It was the first device

CHIPPENDALE, THOMAS

Thomas Chippendale's *The Gentleman and Cabinet Maker's Director* proved one of the most influential and enduring furniture pattern books of all time and on both sides of the Atlantic. Of the three editions, the first two (published, respectively, in 1754 and 1755), promoted designs in the Gothick, Chinese, and anglicized French Rococo styles. The third edition, published between 1759 and 1762 in weekly sets of engravings, dropped the Chinese and Gothick to promote more Rococo designs. However, the incorporation in these of motifs such as masks, putti, trophies of arms, and fluted and tapering legs did reflect Chippendale's move toward classicism. The latter came to full fruition in the Neo-Classical pieces of furniture Chippendale made for Robert Adam. However, the designs for these were never published.

Chair
English Chippendale carved mahogany side chair. The shell-carved crest above a pierced and carved backsplat, and the slip seat raised on cabriole legs with shell-carved knees and ending in ball-and-claw feet.

Tallboy
An American Chippendale-style mahogany tallboy. Late 19th century.

to present the illusion of true moving pictures and embodied the basic principles of modern cinema.

Christmas tree lights See FAIRY LAMPS.

Christofle, Charles ■ (1805–63) A Parisian jeweler who began making domestic silverware in the 1830s. He pioneered ELECTROPLATING in France, acquiring French market patents for it from ELKINGTON & CO. in 1842. This effectively ended the far more labor-intensive and costly fused plate industry in France as Elkington had done with SHEFFIELD PLATE in England.

As Christofle's business grew, he concentrated increasingly on plating, and then late in the 1850s, began manufacturing silver articles. A second factory was opened and noted sculptors and designers such as Mathurin Moreau were employed. They began producing articles in a variety of styles, including RENAISSANCE REVIVAL, Greco-Roman, and Classical architectural styles. On Christofle's death, his sons, nephew, and grandson continued the business. In the 1860s and 70s, they experimented with Oriental and JAPANESQUE forms, possibly in response to market trends and competition, particularly from TIFFANY & CO., who employed Japanese metalworkers. In the 1880s the business changed direction stylistically, moving toward ROCOCO REVIVAL and the flowing forms and

sculpture of ART NOUVEAU. During the late 20th century the company employed notable designers such as TAPIO WIRKKALA, GIO PONTI, and Lino Sabbatini, and is still in operation today.

Chrome dyes Synthetic dyes made from around 1887 that use chromic salts as their mordant (color fixative). Used on fabrics, they display excellent fastness to light and washing, but do not subtly mellow with age as vegetable and insect mordant dyes do.

Chromium ■ A silvery metal obtained by smelting lead chromates and usually plated on a base metal over nickel. Although discovered around 1797 in France, it was not introduced commercially until the 1920s, when it was favored by progressive designers—for example, Marcel BREUER—for tubular steel furniture because of its high resistance to corrosion and brilliant sheen.

Chronograph ■ Any watch that tells the time and has a facility to measure elapsed time in seconds or fractions of a second, used particularly to record timed events and speed records in sport. The most familiar type of chronograph is the stopwatch, with a small knob for starting and stopping a seconds mechanism, which was first patented in 1869.

Chronometer ■ A portable precision timekeeper developed by John HARRISON in the 18th century to enable mariners to calculate longitude, so as to determine their

position at sea. It usually incorporates an extremely accurate spring DETENT ESCAPEMENT beneath a glazed cover in a square mahogany case, and is mounted on brass gimbals to keep the mechanism level at sea. Most chronometers are of one-, two-, or eight-day duration, with a subsidiary up/down dial to indicate the length of time before the instrument needs rewinding. The word was initially used to describe any timekeeping device.

Chryselephantine From the Greek *chrysos* (gold) and *elephantinos* (ivory). The term used to describe items made from ivory and gold, first produced in ancient Egpyt, Greece, and Mesopotamia. Today it is also frequently applied to the combination of bronze and ivory seen in the sculptures of Ferdinand PREISS and others. The metal is typically used on clothed areas and the ivory for areas of exposed skin.

Chrysoberyl A precious gemstone with three varieties, all visually distinct from one another. These include cat's-eye (a valuable honey yellow to greenish gem polished on CABOCHON to display a singular iridescent optical effect known as chatoyancy), alexandrite (green), and chrysoberyl (a yellowish green gem used extensively in the 19th century and commercially known as chrysolite).

Cigar case From the 1830s cases were made from various materials, including silver and leather, in rounded oblong form,

Chocolate pot
Turin silver chocolate pot with ebonized handle. 18th century.

Christofle, Charles
One of a pair of French Gio Ponti two flame silver-plated candlesticks. 1920s.

Blue-painted wooden top

Chromium
Chromium-plated tubular steel Marcel Breuer B-10 table. c. 1927.

Chronograph
Rolex chronograph, in Oyster case face. 1950s.

Chronometer
Rosewood and brass-bound cased two-day marine chronometer. Late 19th century.

curved to fit the pocket and large enough to take a small number of cigars, or tubular to take one cigar. Early, small versions were known as cheroot cases.

Cigar-store Indians Near life-size carved and painted wooden models of American Indians holding tobacco leaves and standing on a plinth advertising the merits of a brand of cigar. Popular in the late 19th century, they often stood outside cigar retailers.

Cinquefoil The five-lobed form of Gothic tracery. The cinquefoil was occasionally used in an arch where the central foil might be pointed. It was widely adopted as a motif, as its leaflike shape was a stylized version of the natural foliage favored in GOTHIC ornament. The cinquefoil was also a common device in heraldry, where it was known as a fraise, frase, frasier, quint, or quintfoil.

Circumferentor A surveying instrument with a central magnetic compass and a scale divided 0–360°, fitted with fixed and movable sights for taking horizontal angles

in the field. It was adapted in the 19th century to the miner's dial.

Ciré The French term for "waxed," used to describe a smooth surface that has the appearance of having been polished. It is normally applied to silk.

Cire-perdue The French term for "lost wax." A highly accurate casting technique for metal and glass objects, used since ancient times. It involves making a plaster cast of the object to be reproduced, which is coated with a layer of wax. A perforated layer of clay or plaster is then added and heat applied to melt the wax. The space left by the wax is then filled with molten metal or glass. After cooling, the outer mold is removed, and the clay core is removed, leaving a metal or glass mold, which can be filed or polished. Some cire-perdue molds were simply broken away from the objects cast inside them, resulting in unique pieces. The method has the advantage of allowing curves to be accurately reproduced.

Cistern barometer See STICK BAROMETER.

Cizhou ware Heavily potted Chinese stoneware produced from the SONG DYNASTY (960–1279) to the present day, with a coarse buff or grayish white body. It is often decorated with a coating of slip and painted or glazed in black or brown. Carved decoration and SGRAFFITO techniques were popular, where the designs were incised through layers of different colored SLIP. Another type of decoration uses slip in conjunction with enamel colors. Bold designs of flowers and foliage or bamboo were used. Wares included ceramic pillows, brush pots, MEIPING vases, and wine jars.

Clair de lune The French word for "moonlight." A term used to describe a glaze of a soft, pale lavender blue color used on Chinese porcelain from the KANGXI period (1662–1722). It was produced by adding tiny amounts of COBALT to the clear FELDSPATHIC GLAZE. The term is seldom used today, as the glaze is usually just referred to as "pale blue."

Claret jug An egg-shaped or spherical silver or glass jug with a long, narrow, decanter-like neck and pouring lip for serving claret wine. Before the 1850s, most claret jugs were made entirely of silver. After the 1850s they were usually made of glass, with silver mounts forming the neckpiece, lid, and handle. Early glass versions with neither a stopper nor a cover do occur from the late 18th century. Many Georgian and Victorian claret jugs have

CIGARETTE CARDS

A device to boost brand loyalty, cigarette cards were developed from the cardboard stiffener placed inside every paper pack of cigarettes produced from the 19th century. Cards were issued in sets, which a smoker would aim to collect and complete.

Among the earliest known is a set of American Presidential Candidates from 1880. Tobacco companies Allen & Ginter in the US and Wills in Britain made the largest number of cards by chromolithography, the peak period being between the world wars. In the 1930s penny albums were produced for collectors to stick in their ready-gummed cards. Since 1945 the fashion has moved toward tea and bubble-gum card issues, and more recently specially produced "trading" cards, many of which are also games.

Typical dynamic 1930s travel imagery

Cigarette card
"Ships That Have Made History" cigarette card, issued by Godfrey Philips Ltd. 1938.

Hugely popular prewar cricket imagery

Cigarette card
"Cricketers" cigarette card, issued by W. D. & H. O. Willis. 1928.

Clichy glassworks
Clichy checker paperweight. Mid-19th century.

distinctive looped handles that are taller than the pouring lip.

Clark & Co., David P. Based in Ohio in 1897, Clark patented a rotating flywheel system, the first American mechanism to challenge the European CLOCKWORK used to power toy vehicles. The Dayton Friction Toy Works produced Hill Climber FRICTION Power Toys with TINPLATE bodywork and CAST-IRON CHASSIS and mechanism until the early 1930s.

Classicism See NEOCLASSICAL STYLE.

Claw setting A method of mounting a gemstone whereby metal prongs extend from the base of the setting and are bent around the girdle of the stone, securing it firmly. A circular arrangement of claws is often called a coronet.

Claw-and-ball foot See BALL-AND-CLAW FOOT.

Claymore Originally a large Scottish cross-hilted, double-handed BROADSWORD, used from the 15th to the 17th century,

particularly by Scottish mercenaries in Ireland and on the Continent. From the mid-18th century onward it was used to describe the characteristic Scottish basket-hilted broadsword that is still carried by officers in Highland Regiments today.

Clichy glassworks ■ One of the great French glassworks. The early history of the factory is unclear, but it was founded in 1837 and had relocated to Clichy-la-Garenne in Paris, by 1846. In the same year, it probably began its production of the PAPERWEIGHTS for which it remains best known today. Although usually unsigned and undated, Clichy paperweights have several distinctive characteristic, such as the Clichy rose, a usually pink glass CANE cut across to resemble an open rose. This may be a central motif or may be found in the concentric rings or garland patterns used in the company's MILLEFIORI weights. A glass cane with the letter "C" may be included in the pattern. Bouquet weights by Clichy are scarcer than those by other makers as fewer were made. Miniature weights and those with moss green background are also sought after.

OVERLAY weights were also made, with several layers of colored glass, typically a soft turquoise or dark pink. Clichy weights are usually almost completely globular, with only a small flat base. Unlike most French paperweights, they are not made of lead glass and are therefore lighter. In spite of their success at the GREAT EXHIBITION in 1851, by the end of the 1850s few paperweights were being produced, and the glassworks closed down in 1885.

Cliff, Clarice ■ (1899–1972) An English ceramic designer and decorator renowned for her colorful ART DECO designs. She left school at 13 and became an apprentice painter at the Lingard Webster Pottery in Tunstall, Staffordshire. In 1916 she went to work at the factory of A. J. WILKINSON, near Burslem, and in 1922 she was apprenticed as a modeler. She later married the factory owner, Colley Shorter. Cliff excelled both as a painter and a modeler. She visited the Paris Exposition in 1925 and was influenced by Art Deco and Cubism. Her Bizarre decorated pieces, inspired by her idea of using discarded stock at the firm's Newport factory, went on sale from

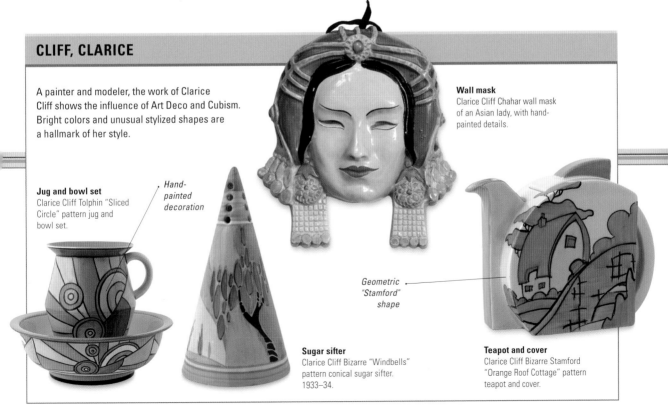

CLIFF, CLARICE

A painter and modeler, the work of Clarice Cliff shows the influence of Art Deco and Cubism. Bright colors and unusual stylized shapes are a hallmark of her style.

Wall mask
Clarice Cliff Chahar wall mask of an Asian lady, with hand-painted details.

Jug and bowl set
Clarice Cliff Tolphin "Sliced Circle" pattern jug and bowl set.

Hand-painted decoration

Geometric "Stamford" shape

Sugar sifter
Clarice Cliff Bizarre "Windbells" pattern conical sugar sifter. 1933–34.

Teapot and cover
Clarice Cliff Bizarre Stamford "Orange Roof Cottage" pattern teapot and cover.

C

1928 to 1929. With the help of Gladys Scarlett, also from the Wilkinson factory, the original Bizarre ware was created with triangular shapes and patterns outlined and filled with colored enamels. It was so successful that new designs were created and a new product range, Fantasque, was brought out in September 1928. These pieces were marked under the Newport pottery for tax reasons. From then on, more brightly colored, stylized landscape designs were produced. Clarice Cliff became art director of Wilkinson's in 1931. World War II made a break in the production of art pottery, and although Cliff continued to design in the 1940s and 1950s, the main period of innovative designs was prewar.

Clobbered ware ■ Pottery or porcelain with OVERGLAZE and ENAMEL COLORS added at a later date to enhance the decorative appeal. It is typically seen on 18th-century blue and white CHINESE EXPORT PORCELAIN, which was clobbered in Holland or England in the 19th century. Clobbering reduces the value of a piece.

Clockwork mechanism A key-wound spiral spring motor that provides power for an object with self-moving parts, such as a toy, MUSICAL BOX, or an AUTOMATON. The key may be fixed or removable. The spring may be of round or flat section.

Cloisonné ■ A method of enameling in which thin strips of metal are soldered onto the surface of an object to form individual decorative cells. These are filled with powdered enamel and then fired in a kiln. See CHAMPLEVÉ.

Close stool A movable latrine consisting of an enclosed box or trunk, usually richly upholstered and decorated, holding a metal or earthenware receptacle. They were used from the 15th until the early 18th century, by which time they were often incorporated in a chair. Close stools were superseded by night tables and pot cupboards.

Closed-back setting Commonly used in 17th- and 18th-century jewelry, these settings involve securing a gem against a solid metal background so that only the crown of the stone is visible. An open-back setting secures the gem in a sleeve without a back, enabling all the available light to pass through. See COLLET and FOILING.

Close-plating A method of plating steel or iron with silver leaf, and heating it to fuse the materials, patented in 1779 by the London goldsmith Richard Ellis. Much stronger than plated copper or nickel, it was used for such implements as knives and scissors. It was adopted largely by the Sheffield cutlery industry from the late 18th to the mid-19th century and was the precursor of plating methods such as SHEFFIELD PLATE.

Cloth doll See RAG DOLL.

Club foot In furniture, a type of foot shaped like a club, often resting on a turned, circular PAD FOOT, that was used throughout the 18th century in conjunction with straight or CABRIOLE legs.

Clutha glass ■ A type of glass in pale green, amber, and yellow with cloudy streaks, bubbles, and sometimes AVENTURINE inclusions, made by the firm of James Couper & Sons in Glasgow from around 1885 to 1905. Much of it was designed by Dr. Christopher DRESSER, with a few pieces by George Walton. It was used to line pewter ware designed by Archibald KNOX and sold by LIBERTY & CO. Vessels often reflect ART NOUVEAU plant forms.

Cluthra glass A type of colored ART GLASS developed by Frederick CARDER at the STEUBEN GLASSWORKS in Corning, New York, during the 1920s. It is typified by its mottled appearance, comprising several random, internal bubbles of different sizes, many being large. The term is now used to describe similar glass by other maker, such as the Kimble Glass Company.

Coach watch A large watch (also called a chaise watch) made in the 1770s for traveling and use in coaches. They were similar to contemporary pocket watches but about double the size to accommodate alarms or STRIKING or REPEATING mechanisms.

Clobbered ware
Clobbered Kangxi vase, with raised prunus bird and landscape decoration.

Cloisonné
Chinese cloisonné vase from the Ming dynasty. 16th century.

Clutha glass
Liberty & Co. pewter and Clutha glass bowl, designed by Archibald Knox.

Coade stone
Head of a young woman in cast coade stone; marked "Coade, London, 1793."

Coal scuttle
Brass helmet-shaped coal scuttle. Late 19th century.

Coade stone ■ A type of molded artificial stone used for decorative architectural features, monuments, and statues. It was made of prefired clay (to prevent shrinkage), sand, crushed flint, crushed glass, and clay, which was fired at a precise temperature to make it hard. It was produced by the Coade family in a factory in Lambeth, London, from 1769 to 1840. From 1771 to 1821 it was run by Coade's widow, Eleanor, and from then until 1840 by her relatives. Used by notable sculptors such as Flaxman; the lion at the south end of Westminster Bridge, London, made in 1832, is a fine example of a Coade stone statue.

Coal scuttle ■ A receptacle for coal kept by a fireplace. Introduced in the early 18th century when coal was first used for domestic heating, they are made of copper, brass, japanned tin, or wood, and generally painted. Most pieces date from the mid-19th century, when helmet, vase, or box shapes were especially popular.

Coalbrookdale Co. ■ An iron foundry in Shropshire, England, founded in 1708. A maker of CAST-IRON furniture in the 19th century, producing decorative grates, railings, stoves, wall plaques, and garden furniture. Some were exported to the US and Europe. It produced some designs by Christopher DRESSER. The firm is still in existence.

Coalport and Coalbrookdale porcelain factory ■ Founded around 1796, at Coalport in Shropshire, beside the Severn River, by John ROSE, believed to have been apprenticed to Thomas Turner at CAUGHLEY. Rose and his partners bought the Caughley factory in 1799 and made mainly blue-printed teaware. Some Caughley ware was decorated at Coalport. Another factory at Coalport (1800–14) belonged to John Rose's brother, Thomas, and his partners, Robert Anstice and Robert Horton. It produced similar wares with patterns like those of John Rose.

In 1814 John Rose bought his brother's factory, dismantled the Caughley works, and put all his efforts into Coalport. Early Coalport porcelain was unmarked and often confused with that of Chamberlain WORCESTER. Distinguishing features of the early pieces are the six slight indentations around the rim on the plates. Inexpensive enameled copies of Chinese patterns on teaware sold well, and from 1801 the much-imitated Indian Tree pattern was used. The use of independent decorators such as Thomas BAXTER accounts for much of the great variety of decoration. After 1810 Coalport achieved the soft white translucency and smooth surface for which it is celebrated. In 1820 John Rose was awarded the Society of Arts Gold Medal for his innovation of a leadless FELDSPATHIC GLAZE. After 1820 wares with this glaze had large circular printed marks.

Coalport's influences were varied. From Neoclassical and brightly colored "Japan" patterns, they turned to French-style floral wares, and from around 1820 to 1850 the factory specialized in painted flowers as well as ROCOCO REVIVAL applied flowers in high relief. These encrusted wares were known as English Dresden and gave rise to the term "Coalbrookdale" (the name of the neighboring area), which also describes similar productions by other factories. Marks include "C.D.," "C. Dale," "Coalport," and "Coalbrookdale" in underglaze blue.

Coalport ware after 1835 became more sophisticated—rich ground colors were introduced in imitation of CHELSEA and SÈVRES, and marks too were often copied. Coalport also copied SWANSEA bone china with fake marks. Much Victorian Coalport was unmarked until 1881. The Coalport

Coalbrookdale Co.
Coalbrookdale wrought-iron garden bench. 19th century.

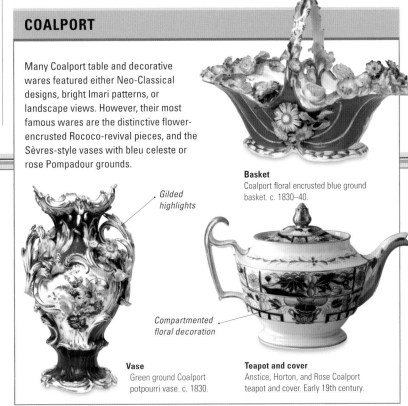

COALPORT

Many Coalport table and decorative wares featured either Neo-Classical designs, bright Imari patterns, or landscape views. However, their most famous wares are the distinctive flower-encrusted Rococo-revival pieces, and the Sèvres-style vases with bleu celeste or rose Pompadour grounds.

Gilded highlights

Basket
Coalport floral encrusted blue ground basket. c. 1830–40.

Compartmented floral decoration

Vase
Green ground Coalport potpourri vase. c. 1830.

Teapot and cover
Anstice, Horton, and Rose Coalport teapot and cover. Early 19th century.

factory changed hands several times. In 1924 it was sold to the Staffordshire firm of Cauldon Potteries Ltd., and in 1926 the works were transferred to the Cauldon Works at Shelton. In 1936 they moved to the Crescent Pottery at Stoke, formerly the works of George JONES & CO. In 1951 the name of Coalport China Ltd. was adopted. The works closed in 1958 when E. Brain & Co. (makers of FOLEY china) took it over and moved it to Fenton, Stoke on Trent, where production continues today. In 1967 Coalport joined the WEDGWOOD group; the main production is high-quality bone china tableware.

Coaster ■ A term originally used to describe a circular stand with a wooden base and pierced, engraved, or embossed silver GALLERY. They were used from around 1760 for passing wine bottles or decanters around the dining-table, the undersides covered with baize to protect the table. The term later came to include stands made in a variety of materials and used under drinking glasses.

Cobalt The black pigment cobalt oxide, which turns blue on firing. See CHINESE POTTERY AND PORCELAIN, BLUE AND WHITE.

Cobb, John ■ (c. 1715–78) An English furniture-maker. His partnership with William Vile (see VILE & COBB) was one of the most successful in London. He supplied upholstery to George III, and after Vile's retirement in 1765, took on furniture production, notably fine pieces with marquetry in Robert ADAM style.

Coburg pottery and porcelain A German factory producing TIN-GLAZED EARTHENWARE from 1738, marked "CB" and often painted by BAYREUTH decorators. It closed in 1789. In 1860 Albert Riemann founded a factory in Upper Franconia, making porcelain figures. The mark was "AR" and "Coburg."

Cock beading A small, curved strip of semicircular BEAD MOLDING used on furniture. It was applied as a finish to the edges of drawer fronts from the mid-18th to the early 19th century. Several strips of cock beading applied together create the effect of REEDING.

Cock motif A motif in Christian, Oriental, Scandinavian, and Celtic art. In Classical ornament, the cock is occasionally depicted pulling the chariot of the god Mercury and may also symbolize lust. Associated with the dawn and the rising sun, it often figures in designs featuring Apollo and in timepiece decorations as a symbol of day. For long a national symbol of France, the cock was embraced as an emblem of the Revolution.

Coconut cup ■ A goblet formed from the shell of a coconut, sometimes plain and polished or carved in low RELIEF, often mounted in silver. These exotic nuts were brought into Britain during the 15th and 16th centuries, and were also suspected to have mystical properties. The cups enjoyed a revival in the late 18th century, but early examples are extremely scarce.

Coffee can ■ A coffee cup of cylindrical shape, made from the end of the 18th century and early 19th century. Previously the form had been a tall, narrow U-shape.

Coffeepot After the spread of coffee-drinking in Europe in the early 18th century, pots of silver, ceramic, and other metals were produced. The earliest extant HALLMARKED silver example dates from 1681. Although they changed with fashion, their simple form is usually a tapering cylinder or baluster with a hinged, domed cover and a scroll handle. With the advent of the fashion for drinking chocolate, some were converted into CHOCOLATE POTS.

Coffer A portable storage box, or trunk, the simplest form of CHEST, and known from ancient times until superseded by the chest-of-drawers. Often made of wood and covered with leather and banding.

Cogswell, John (active 1769–82) An American cabinet-maker working in Boston, making fashionable carved mahogany furniture in the AMERICAN CHIPPENDALE style. Cogswell's work can be compared to that of Benjamin FROTHINGHAM, and includes chests-of-drawers of the BLOCK-FRONT type.

Coaster
One of a pair of George IV wine coasters, by John & Thomas Settle of Sheffield. c. 1828.

Cobb, John
George III mahogany window bench with a saddle seat, by Vile and Cobb. c. 1762.

Coconut cup
George III coconut cup, the interior silver bowl by Matthew Boulton. 1795.

Coffee can
Barr Worcester coffee can. c. 1800.

Coiffeuse From the French *coiffer* (to dress the hair). A 19th-century French term for a DRESSING TABLE.

Coiling A term denoting a pot hand-formed by "snakes" of clay coiled to the desired shape. The snake may vary from a thin strip to a large "sausage." Pre-Columbian American and West African pottery are examples of this method. Neolithic and Bronze Age people used the technique, which is still employed today for decorative effect.

Coin glass A term used for glassware displaying an encased coin (or coins). It usually refers to stemmed drinking glasses, or jugs, where a coin has been embedded in the KNOP or foot. Examples date back to the 18th century and they are still made today.

Coin molding See EYE-AND-SCALE MOTIF.

Cold painting Painting in colored enamels on ceramics, glass, and bronze, but without firing in a kiln, so the colors and gilding are not permanent. The technique was used on some early MEISSEN pieces.

Cold working Decorative techniques applied to a glass piece when the body is cold. Most cold working techniques are applied after the final form is nearly complete and include polishing, cutting, DIAMOND-POINT ENGRAVING, sand blasting, ACID ETCHING, and the application of ENAMEL patterns.

Cole, James Ferguson (1798–1880) **and Thomas** (1800–64) Notable English clock- and watchmaker brothers and business partners until 1829. In 1825 they made one of the earliest CARRIAGE CLOCKS in England. From 1829 Thomas worked independently as a maker of watches and extremely high-quality mantel and other ornamental clocks. In 1861 he was elected to the Royal Society of Arts, as well as being admitted to the British Horological Institute.

Cole, Sir Henry (1808–82) An English designer and arts administrator who also recognized the importance of INDUSTRIAL DESIGN. Under the pseudonym "Felix Summerly," he opened Summerly's Art Manufacturers (1847) in an attempt to produce good designs for household ware, particularly in ceramics. He was the driving force behind the GREAT EXHIBITION of 1851, using the profits to reorganize the South Kensington Museum, which became the Victoria and Albert Museum. He was the museum's first director.

Collar ■ Ring of glass applied to a wine glass stem, to disguise the joints between the bowl and the stem, the foot and the stem, and sometimes in between the KNOPS. It also refers to the thick rim of a bottle.

Collet setting ■ A sleeve or "dish" of metal holding a gemstone in signet rings and necklaces. Associated with diamonds, a collet necklace has a line of stones in settings of enclosing bands. A mille grain collet is a band decorated with tiny beads.

Collinson & Lock ■ English furniture-makers established in London in 1870 and known for their ART FURNITURE. They were taken over by GILLOWS in 1897. Designers who were associated with them include E. W. GODWIN, John Moyr Smith, and Bruce Talbert.

Cologne potteries ■ There were three main 16th-century stoneware factories in Cologne, in Germany's Rhineland: Maximinenstrasse flourished from 1520 to 1540 making religious figures, antique busts, and designs after engravings; Komödiengasse made "Graybeards," also called BELLARMINES, with leaf decoration and inscribed bands; and Eigelstein made ornamental tankards (schnellen) with religious and allegorical subjects. Though production of Rhenish stoneware was disrupted by the outbreak of the Thirty Years War in 1618, it was produced throughout the 17th century.

Colombo, Cesare "Joe" (1930–71) An Italian designer who studied painting and architecture before moving into product and furniture design in 1958. Best known for his chair and lighting designs, he was a pioneer of using injection-molded ABS plastic. The "Boby" cart, the "KD27" lamp, and "861 Universale" chair are among his most successful designs.

C
109

Collar
Georgian champagne flute, with collar and blade knop stem. c. 1820.

9ct gold collets

Collet setting
Gold and turquoise bracelet, each collet set with a turquoise cabouchon. Early 20th century.

Collinson & Lock
Collinson & Lock rosewood and calamander cabinet, designed by T. E. Collcutt.

Cologne potteries
German Cologne salt-glazed stoneware Bellamine jug. c. 1580.

COLONIAL STYLE

The period, the decorative arts, and the architecture of the North American colonies under Dutch and (mainly) English rule, from about 1600 to 1780 are what describes Colonial style. Few decorative pieces were produced before the third quarter of the 17th century, as the population was low and demand was limited due to a largely puritanical, self-sufficient lifestyle. Early settlers also tended to bring articles with them. Such pieces may be described as "Colonial," but the ones made in the US are of greatest value to collectors and museums.

The oldest surviving items include furniture made in New England coastal communities. Most is of jointed and paneled construction, held together with MORTISE AND TENON joints and pegging. Indigenous woods were plentiful in New England and BLANKET CHESTS were made from wide boards, particularly in Connecticut, where many were carved and even painted. "Presses," from the Dutch word for linen cupboard, were also made by the mid-17th century. They are normally of simple, paneled construction.

The diverse population included significant Dutch and French communities, all of whom produced their own distinctive pieces. Most of the ceramics and glass used by early colonists was imported, but by the late 17th century artisans were making silver, pewter, and other metalwork. Surviving examples are rare, and are typically plain and unmarked.

HUGUENOTS from France and the Netherlands, who sought political and religious freedom in the New World from about 1675, pursued the silver trade in particular. Among the best known was second-generation Paul REVERE. Most Dutch decorative arts of the 17th century are comparable to those made by English colonists, mirroring the cross-fertilization between the two cultures in Europe. However, one distinctively Dutch colonial furniture form is the *kas* (storage cupboard), made mainly in the Dutch settlements of northern New York, New Jersey, and Connecticut in the first half of the 18th century.

German Lutheran immigrants, many of whom settled in Pennsylvania,

continued the colonial lifestyle well into the 20th century. Their particular style and culture is generically referred to as PENNSYLVANIA DUTCH. American decorative arts and architecture produced mainly in the western and southern states under Spanish influence are referred to as SPANISH COLONIAL.

Chest
Pilgrim carved oak two-drawer blanket chest.

Burr walnut veneer

Chest-of-drawers
William and Mary walnut chest-of-drawers. 1700–20.

Armchair
Connecticut banister back armchair. c. 1720.

Maple chair
Portsmouth Queen Anne maple chair, by the Giles workshop.

Colonial revival See CENTENNIAL.

Color hardening A technique in which a steel item is heated in an iron box with high-carbon material. This makes the surface of the steel hard and durable. It also produces a decorative finish of swirling browns, blues, and grays.

Colt, Samuel (1814–62) An American firearms designer and entrepreneur, who popularized the REVOLVER, for which he obtained his first patent in 1835. His factory at Hartford, Connecticut, was among the first to use machinery to make firearms with interchangeable parts. Despite a slow start in the 1840s, orders grew from 1847 and Colt firearms were widely used in the American Civil War (1861–65) and in both world wars. The factory is still in production today.

Combed decoration A pattern of feathered lines, also called "feathering" or "combing," used in ceramic- and glassmaking. One color is trailed across a ground slip of contrasting color and a bristle, bulrush, or feather is then "combed" across the lines, to give the feathering pattern. John DWIGHT developed the technique in the 17th century, which then spread to the STAFFORDSHIRE POTTERIES.

Comedy and tragedy masks Traditional symbols of drama, MASKS are among the attributes of the Muses of Comedy and Tragedy and appear in Classical Greek drama to express the spirit or type of character being performed. From the Renaissance, the motif has been frequently linked with ancient instruments, such as pipes and cymbals, and widely applied to decorative ornament of a theatrical nature.

Commedia dell' Arte figures A genre of lively and ribald improvised comedy from 16th-century Italy. Characters were Harlequin; Brighella; Pantalone and the Doctor; the Captain, who had a huge nose; Pulcinella, with a humpback (the Punch of "Punch and Judy"); and Columbine and Pierrot, the lovers. Italian actors played in Germany in the 18th century and were the inspiration for MEISSEN figures. These were then copied in the 18th century by factories such as BOW and CHELSEA and made into the 19th century.

Commemorative ware ■ Articles in pottery, porcelain, and many other materials commemorating incidents of royal, historical, sociological, political, theatrical, and topographical interest. The event being commemorated could be painted or occasionally printed or molded in the body of ceramic ware. It is also found as figures or busts of people or animals and even models of infamous houses. Commemorative ware was made over a wide geographical area and over long periods of time.

Commode A French term for a low chest-of-drawers with deep drawers, first used in France in the late 17th century. The term was then adopted in Britain in the mid-18th century, when French furniture became fashionable, to describe highly decorative, low chests-of-drawers with SERPENTINE fronts and other curving forms that evolved in the ROCOCO style. In 19th-century England, the word was also adopted to describe a CLOSE STOOL.

C

111

Compass ■ A case, usually made of brass, holding a magnetized wire or needle that

COMFORTER DOG

A large earthenware figure of a spaniel made in the 19th century in Staffordshire, used as a fireplace ornament and also purchased by errant husbands to comfort their irate wives. Also referred to as Staffordshire dogs.

Comforter dogs
Pair of Staffordshire spaniels on cobalt blue bases. c. 1850.

Commemorative jug
Wedgwood jug commemorating the death of Benjamin Disraeli. May 16, 1881.

Commemorative rummer
Commemorative rummer, engraved with the London-to-York mail coach. c. 1825.

Commemorative brooch
Georgian commemorative brooch, with the J.W. woven hair cypher in seed pearl. c. 1850.

Commemorative plate
Aero Plate" commemorating the Hudson-Fulton Centennial Exhibition. 1909.

C

indicates the direction of magnetic north. The needle may be placed over a "rose" or "card" marked with compass points or a scale of degrees to ascertain the direction of north, and therefore of any other bearing or direction. An essential instrument for navigation at sea, as well as for surveying, compasses were developed in the 12th century by mariners in Europe and China.

Compendium A rectangular box, often made of mahogany or oak, used to store games such as chess and cards. Many have a hinged top and an upright front with small drawers. Most were made from the late 19th to the early 20th century.

Compensation The term used for treatment of a PENDULUM to ensure that it maintains a constant length in spite of temperature changes, so that the timekeeping of the clock remains accurate. Various types of compensated pendulum were developed in the 18th century, especially the gridiron and mercury types, though some simply incorporated a wooden rather than a metal rod (as wood hardly expands or contracts when heated or cooled) or sometimes a combination of metals, alloys, or silica. Compensated pendulums were used principally in precision clocks, for example, REGULATORS and CHRONOMETERS.

Comport ■ A dish, usually on a stem, to hold fruit for the dessert course. It is part of a service with a centerpiece, sauce tureens, covers and stands, ice pails, and plates.

Composition A mixture of whiting (chalk), resin, and glue used to make relief moldings for furniture, during the late 18th century. From the early 19th to the mid-20th century a version containing wood pulp and ingredients such as eggs and crushed bones was used to make doll's bodies, and sometimes doll's heads, before being generally superseded by PLASTIC.

Compound twist stems ■ A rare type of mid-18th-century wine glass stem in which several types of twists—air, colored, and opaque—are combined.

Comtoise clocks A type of LONGCASE CLOCK produced in the French Franche-Comté region, especially at Morbier and Morez, from the 18th century. It has a bulbous-shaped wooden case, sometimes inlaid or painted, and a glazed aperture and pressed-brass pendulum.

Comyns, William & Sons ■ English silversmiths, founded in 1848 in London by William Comyns to make handcrafted silver. They made good-quality Victorian pieces and also worked in the ARTS AND CRAFTS style. Comyns produced large quantities of small silver pieces and continues to trade today.

Concertina action A method for extending hinged-top tables, using a sliding device hinged to movable legs that straightens when the legs are pulled out and folds back when they are pushed back in.

Confidante A French term for a type of chair or sofa, known also as a "companion," "conversation," or "tête à tête." It was popular in France and Britain in the mid- and late 19th century, and consisted of two or three seats joined by a common S-shaped rail, a configuration in which seated occupants half faced each other.

Congreve clock A type of SKELETON CLOCK, also known as a rolling ball clock, in which the ESCAPEMENT is impulsed by a ball rolling back and forth across a pivoted plate. Such clocks were first developed in the 17th century, but the best-known version was invented by the English scientist and clockmaker Sir William Congreve in the early 19th century. The top of the clock is pediment shaped and set with three dials. Original 19th-century pieces are rare and most examples found today are 20th-century reproductions.

Connecticut chest ■ A generic term given to blanket chests made in the Connecticut River valley area in North America, from around 1680 to 1770. Most specimens are of oak and resemble contemporary English forms, including MULE CHESTS. Distinctive varieties include those carved with panels of stylized tulips or florettes and applied with ebonized stiles, identified with the area of Hartford or Wethersfield, and plainer chests with extensive shallow carving, which are termed "Hadley" chests after an area of the upper Connecticut River valley.

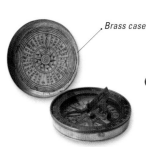

Compass
Folding sundial gnomon and paper card background compass. c. 1780.

Brass case

Comport
Spode "Greek" pattern footed comport. c. 1815.

Compound twist stems
Wine glass stem with a red corkscrew core entwined by a broad opaque spiral. c. 1765.

Comyns, William & Sons
Heart-shaped scent bottle by William Comyns, London. 1898.

Connecticut chest
Connecticut William and Mary maple and pine tall blanket chest.

Conran, Sir Terence (Born 1931) Initially a textile designer, Conran founded the Conran Design Group in 1956, producing designs for furniture and textiles. In 1964 he opened the first Habitat store in London, retailing domestic products in modern designs. He now owns the flagship Conran Shop and has built up a chain of restaurants.

Console table ■ A side table fixed or joined to a wall and supported at the front by either two legs or a decorative central bracket.

Cookworthy, William An English apothecary who used KAOLIN found in Cornwall in 1745 to try to make porcelain, first in PLYMOUTH, Devon, and later in Bristol. He had great difficulty in mixing and firing the BODY and made a rather poor HARD-PASTE PORCELAIN. In the 1760s he patented several formulas, which he assigned to Richard CHAMPION.

Cope An ecclesiastical cloak worn on important occasions by Christian priests. It is frequently heavily embroidered and made of fine materials, for example, brocade.

Copeland and Garrett The SPODE factory was taken over by W. T. Copeland and T. Garrett in 1833 and used various marks incorporating their names until 1847.

Copenhagen porcelain factory Although FAIENCE was produced in Copenhagen from the early 18th century, the production of PORCELAIN proved elusive. Between 1759 and 1766 the Frenchman Louis Fournier produced a limited amount of soft-paste porcelain, but discontinued owing to its prohibitive cost. In 1774 chemist Franz Heinrich Müller began to produce hard-paste porcelain, using KAOLIN from the island of Bornholm, which had been discovered in 1755. In 1779 the factory was taken over by King Christian VII and renamed the Royal Danish Porcelain Factory.

The earliest Copenhagen porcelain was grayish in color, decorated in UNDERGLAZE blue, notably the Immortell pattern, inspired by MEISSEN designs. Various other products included severe NEOCLASSICAL products influenced by other European factories such as Berlin, Vienna, and SÈVRES, and flower patterns, including the famous Flora Danica service, created as a gift for Catherine the Great of Russia. The service of 1,602 items was intended to display every wild plant in the kingdom, and was painted by the flower-painter Johann Christoph Bayer, who worked in Copenhagen from 1776. In 1801 the King pensioned off Müller and production declined. In 1824 Gustav Hetsch became director and the factory produced some richly decorated wares. From 1835 it began production of figures after the sculptor Bertel Thorvaldsen. The factory was sold in 1868 and became the Royal Copenhagen. The architect and painter Arnold Krog, director from 1885 to 1916, revived the factory's fortunes with underglaze blue decoration and products decorated with Japanese and ART NOUVEAU motifs. The factory retains its artistic reputation, still making figures and the Immortell and Flora Danica patterns.

Coper, Hans (1920–81) A German studio potter who worked in England. Coper first trained as an engineer before becoming a studio potter. He came to England in 1939 and became an assistant to Lucie RIE after his war service. He established a studio in 1956. Coper's work is often characterized by strong sculptural shapes.

COOPER, SUSIE

A ceramic and textile designer, Susie Cooper (1902–95) studied and worked in the STAFFORDSHIRE POTTERIES. A prolific designer from the mid-1920s to the 1970s, she started as a decorator and later as a designer for A. E. Gray & Co. Ltd. She opened her own decorating firm, Crown Works, and bought blanks from local firms before having her own shapes made. One of her most popular streamlined shapes was Kestrel-shape teaware. In 1940 she became a "Royal Designer for Industry." She bought the Bone China factory in London and exhibited at the Festival of Britain (1951). In the 1960s the factory merged first with R. H. & S. L. Plant, and later was taken over by the WEDGWOOD Group.

Coffee can and saucer
Gray's Pottery coffee can and saucer designed by Susie Cooper, pattern 8330.

Pale cream ground

Teapot
Stamford shape, Orange Roof Cottage pattern teapot, signed "Bizarre by Clarice Cliff."

Console table
Italian Rococo giltwood marble-top console table. 18th century.

C

Copland, Henry (1720–c. 1753) An English engraver who, in spite of the important role he played in introducing and developing the ROCCOCO STYLE in England, is little known, except for his involvement in two important PATTERN BOOKS for the new style: his own, *A New Book of Ornaments* (1746), and another book with the same title, in collaboration with Matthias Lock, which was published in 1752.

Copper A dense and soft red metallic element. Known since prehistoric times, copper is one of the most widely used metals both in its pure state, and alloyed with tin and zinc, as BRONZE and BRASS. Owing to its high conductivity of heat and electricity, its ductility, and resistance to corrosion, it has been used variously, including cooking vessels, jewelry, wire, and coins. Copper is also plated with silver to produce SHEFFIELD PLATE. Inexpensive and easily worked, hand-hammered sheet copper was popular with ARTS AND CRAFTS designers for small items such as vases, bowls, and frames, especially in the US in the late 19th century.

Coquillage The French word for shell. The shell form was one of the most prevalent motifs in ROCOCO ornament.

Coral Hard, and tree- or bushlike in appearance, coral is formed from the skeletons of marine polyps and has been used in jewelry and for decorating artifacts since ancient Egyptian times. The principal centers of manufacture in the 19th century were Naples and Genoa, and popular colors included Pelle d'Angelo (angel's skin), Rosso (red), and Carbonetto (ox blood). Red coral was believed to be a powerful talisman when used against the evil eye.

Coralene ■ A type of applied glass decoration named after the sprays of coral that it imitated. First patented by Schierholz in Germany in 1883, it was subsequently used by the MOUNT WASHINGTON GLASS CO. and other American and European factories. The technique involved thickly painting an enamel design onto a body and then sprinkling small glass beads onto it. These adhered to the enamel, but were further fused in place by heating the decorated body. The technique was used into the 1920s, but damage was common as the beads would wear off with heavy use.

Corbel A bracket or block of stone or wood projecting from a vertical member, used to support a beam or horizontal feature from below.

Cordial glass ■ A drinking glass with a small round bowl and disproportionately long stem, made and used from the second half of the 17th century to the last quarter of the 19th century. It was used for liqueurs and cordials.

Core forming One of the earliest glass-making processes, used from around 1500 to 1200 BCE in ancient Egypt and Mesopotamia, in which molten trails of glass were wound around a core of mud, clay, or straw in the form of the final object on a metal rod to make small bottles and flasks. The glass-covered body was then rolled on the MARVER table to give a flat surface and the core was removed when the body was cool and hard.

Corgi toys ■ Introduced in 1956 by METTOY under the slogan "The Ones with Windows," these mainly 1:43 scale DIECAST toy vehicles were in direct competition with DINKY TOYS. Corgis had windows, independent suspension, and hoods that could be opened. Celebrated for their TV and film tie-ins, the famous 1965 James Bond Aston Martin sold approximately four million in four years. Since the 1980s, after a few changes of ownership, the company has been producing collector's models.

Cork Glass Company ■ An Irish glasshouse founded in Cork in 1783 (and known until 1818). The company produced decanters, jugs, and other tableware in a generally poor-quality glass, often with engraved or shallow-cut decoration and sometimes marked on the base with the factory name.

Cork pictures Carving cork in relief was a popular hobby in the middle years of the 19th century. Subjects range from Classical scenes, particularly ruins, to castles and landscapes. Most pictures were sold as kits

Coralene
Satin glass vase, decorated with gold highlights and coralene.

Cordial glass
Opaque-twist cordial glass. c. 1770.

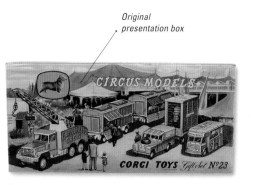

Original presentation box

Corgi toy
Corgi No. GS23 "Chipperfields Circus" Gift Set.

Cork Glass Company
Cork Irish mallet-shaped decanter with a stopper. c. 1810.

with black velvet backgrounds and maple frames. The material does not wear well and fine examples in good condition are rare.

Corncob motif A popular decorative motif in 19th-century American ornament for ironwork, ceramics, furniture details, and wallpaper, the corncob was first used with tobacco leaves for the Corinthian-style capitals devised by Benjamin Latrobe for the rebuilding of the Capitol in Washington, DC. In England, bread knives with corncob handles were first made by Summerly's Art Manufactures (an experiment by Henry COLE) in the 1850s, and remained a popular design well into the 20th century.

Cornelius & Co. ■ A metalworks in Philadelphia, founded by Christian Cornelius in 1812 for the manufacture of silver and cast bronze work. The company specialized throughout the American EMPIRE PERIOD in making elements for and assembling ARGAND LAMPS, which were extremely popular decorations in American homes throughout the 19th century. By 1845 it was the main producer of argand lamps in the US. From 1856 to 1874 the company was known as Cornelius & Baker.

Corner chair ■ A chair designed to stand in the corner of a room. Developed in England in the first half of the 18th century, it typically has a bowed top rail and backsplats on two sides.

Cornice A projecting molding or a horizontal member at the top of a piece of furniture, typically a tall cupboard.

Corning, New York An important American glassmaking center. Since the mid-19th century, Corning—about 250 miles (315 km) north of New York City—has been home to many glassworks. These include the Corning Glass Works, established in 1868 by Amory Houghton and known for its production of lead crystal blanks that were decorated with cut designs by the many surrounding cutting factories. The shock and heat resistant borosilicate glass known as Pyrex was developed in 1912, and from the 1920s to the 1950s the company went on to make important developments in optical and other types of specialty glass. Since 1903 the main firm has been STEUBEN, which still operates in Corning from a large complex also housing the Corning Museum of Glass.

Cornucopia ■ A symbol of fertility and abundance since Classical times. A goat's horn overflowing with ears of wheat and fruit, the cornucopia was popular from the RENAISSANCE for architectural ornament, including VOLUTES and BRACKETS. On French EMPIRE and American FEDERAL furniture, it was an emblem of peace and fortune; with Cupid's arrows and quivers it is a symbol of fecundity. In ceramic, cornucopias were popular from around 1750 to 1870, and were hung on walls with ribbons to hold flowers.

Coromandel lacquer A LACQUER technique, often used on folding screens. It involves coating a surface with white chalk before applying lacquer. When dry, the latter is selectively cut away to the desired pattern, revealing the underlying chalk, which is then painted. The screens were popular in Europe from the 17th century, when they were imported from India's Coromandel coast. They are still produced today.

Coromandel wood ■ A tree native to the Coromandel coast of India, which produces a timber known also as Bombay EBONY. The fine-grained, black hardwood has distinctive hazel brown or yellow stripes and was used on high-quality furniture, especially during the REGENCY period, for BANDING, STRINGING, and VENEERING.

Corona A type of 19th-century metal lighting fixture, similar to a chandelier, of one or more hoops with sockets for lamps or candles.

Corsage Worn extensively in the 18th and 19th centuries, a corsage (meaning bodice or blouse) jewel was usually a bold and imposing BROOCH set with diamonds and gems, and with clasps, chains, and tassels. It takes its name from the small bouquet of flowers worn at the waist or lapel, originating in the 18th century.

Costume jewelry Essentially a 20th-century term for jewelry made from nonprecious materials such as imitation

C

115

Cornelius & Co.
Five-light cast-brass chandelier, by Cornelius and Baker. Late 19th century.

Corner chair
Queen Anne corner chair, North Shore Massachusetts. c. 1770–1800.

Cornucopia
First Period Worcester cornucopia-shaped wall pocket. c. 1756–58.

Hazel brown figuring

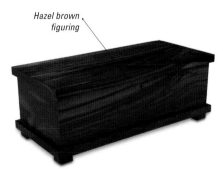

Coromandel wood
Scottish Art Deco coromandel wood box made by R&J Price. c. 1925.

gem stones and faux pearls set in silver or inexpensive base metals. However, many pieces date back to ancient times and incorporate semiprecious stones. In the 18th and 19th centuries PASTE, glass, CUT STEEL, base metals, and alloys such as PINCHBECK were used to imitate precious jewelry. However, in the 20th century costume jewelry saw a new wave of design with radically different criteria. It became associated with innovative creations comprising inexpensive materials, and in many cases, high-quality craftsmanship. Pieces were often inspired by events such as the discovery of Tutankhamen's tomb in 1922 or movements such as ART NOUVEAU. Paris in the 1920s and 30s was the center of world fashion, and costume jewelry developed rapidly into incredible flights of fancy, with designers such as René LALIQUE and Jean DUNAND. Americans, too, developed an insatiable appetite for affordable costume jewelry. It was this period that saw the rise of the best-known designers and manufacturers such as Marcel Boucher, Hattie Carnegie, Coro, Inc. (Corocraft), Miriam Haskell, Hobé, Mazer & Co., and Trifari. Hollywood jewelers such as Joseff designed for the most spectacular movies as well as ranges for mass production.

During World War II the manufacture of costume jewelry continued on a large scale in the US, while in the UK, austerity jewelry in the form of Bakelite Scottie dogs and patriotic symbols was more characteristic. Postwar prosperity increased demand for costume jewelry. Through the 1940s to the 1960s, CHANEL, Schiaparelli, Christian Dior, Kenneth Jay Lane, and Stanley Hagler produced an ever more diverse selection of designs. Trifari retained its popularity, aided by Mamie Eisenhower, who commissioned parures from them for the presidential inaugurations of the 1950s.

Cotswold School A term used for furniture that cannot be ascribed to a known maker, but that is handmade and in keeping with ARTS AND CRAFTS principles, in particular the work of Ernest GIMSON and Sydney and Ernest BARNSLEY, who originally had workshops in the Cotswolds in Gloucestershire, England. The term can also be applied to second-generation makers of the style.

Cottage A pottery or porcelain model, mostly English, made in large quantities in the 19th and 20th centuries. They may be in two sections for use as a PASTILLE BURNER, or in one with a slit in the roof, for use as a money box. Some were models of notorious houses.

Cottage clock A inexpensive MANTEL CLOCK, usually with a wooden case, produced in Britain during the 19th century. The term is also used for American SHELF CLOCKS.

Couch An alternative term for an upholstered DAY BED or CHAISE LONGUE.

Couched work An embroidery technique, common from the 16th century, in which a decorative thread is sewn onto a ground fabric by another thread.

Count wheel A metal wheel with a segmented edge or with pins on one side, used to control and regulate the striking TRAIN in early clocks. It was replaced from the late 17th century by the "rack and snail" device.

Counter box A 17th-century silver box, sometimes pierced, made to hold a set of gaming counters. In the late 18th century they were also made of turned ivory.

Coup perdu The French term for "lost stroke." A type of clock, usually French, that has a pendulum beating half-seconds but which registers full seconds with its second hand. The ESCAPEMENT allows the escape wheel to advance once for each alternate, rather than full, swing of the pendulum.

Court cupboard From the French *court* (short). A low or short cupboard, consisting initially of open tiers used to display plates. Such cupboards were first made in England in the late 16th century, usually in oak, and in Britain and North America in the 17th century. They were widely imitated in the 19th century.

Courtauld, Augustus (c. 1686–1751) An English silversmith who learned his trade in a HUGUENOT workshop. His best-known work is the Swordbearer's Salt in London's

Cotswold School
Cotswold School teak cabinet on a stand.

Cottage
Staffordshire lavender ground pastille burner, in the form of a cottage. Mid-19th century.

Court cupboard
Carved oak court cupboard. 17th century.

Courting mirror
American courting mirror, with original red paint. 18th century.

Cow creamer
Pearlware cow creamer, with seated milkmaid. c. 1815–20.

Mansion House. His son, Samuel, worked in the Rococo style.

Courting mirror ■ A pre-19th-century type of North American mirror glass, distinguished by a molded metal frame set with strips of painted glass.

Cow creamer ■ A milk or cream jug in the form of a cow, with the mouth as the spout and the tail looped over the back as a handle, made from the mid-18th century. One of the most famous makers of creamers in silver was John Schuppe. Numerous Staffordshire potters created them in ceramics.

Cozzi porcelain factory ■ Established in 1764 by Geminiano Cozzi in the San Giobbe district of Venice, with support from the Venetian Senate. Cozzi learned the art of porcelain-making from the German Nathaniel Hewelke (who had a factory in Udine) and from some workers from the Le NOVE porcelain factory. He made HARD-PASTE PORCELAIN and produced tableware, snuff boxes, cane handles, and figures. The mark was a large red anchor. The factory closed in 1812.

Crabstock ■ The handle of a tea- or coffeepot modeled as a branch of a crab apple tree, usually on pottery with the body of the pot in the form of the fruit.

Crace, John Gregory (1809–89) An English designer of interiors and furniture.

His grandfather, John Crace, worked for the Prince Regent from 1788, supplying furniture and porcelain for the Royal Pavilion in Brighton. His father, Frederick Crace, continued his work, being responsible for the interior of the Royal Pavilion. John Gregory joined the family firm in 1826, and was associated with A. W. N. PUGIN and the GOTHIC REVIVAL furniture and the interiors of the new Palace of Westminster, and with the Medieval Court at the GREAT EXHIBITION. His son, John Diblee Crace, specialized in interiors in Italian Renaissance style.

Cracked ice ■ A term used when referring to Chinese porcelain to describe a blue ground that represents the frozen water of rivers, with white lines indicating cracking ice. This decoration symbolizes the end of winter and the coming of spring. Also the name of a particular cut-glass pattern created by Stevens & Williams of Stourbridge around 1890.

Crackle ■ The deliberate crazing of ceramics for decorative effect. First discovered in the SONG DYNASTY (960–1279) in Guan ware, it was exploited by later Chinese potters and imitated in Western ceramics from the late 19th century onward, especially in STUDIO POTTERY. The similar term, "craquelure," describes age cracks in the varnish of oil paintings.

Crackled glass See ICE GLASS.

Crafts Revival This 20th-century movement in applied arts advocated a return to high-quality handcraftsmanship, the use of natural materials, and the production of unique objects or limited series. It began in the US in the late 1950s, mainly as a reaction against the standardization and poor quality of many mass-produced goods and the perceived austerity of the MODERN MOVEMENT. Influenced by the organic forms and materials of Scandinavian design, it is a survival rather than a revival of craft traditions, following on from the CRAFTSMAN STYLE of the early 20th century.

The development of the movement in the US was reinforced by the influx of refugee artists from Europe, some of whom had trained at the BAUHAUS, and the STUDIO GLASS and STUDIO POTTERY movements, which emphasized form, color, and technique rather than applied ornament.

Studio potters such as Gertrud and Otto Natzler, who emigrated from Austria to the US in 1938, produced earthenware with rough-textured glazes. From the mid-1950s the studio pottery movement was also influenced by current fine art movements, particularly in the work of Peter Voulkos, who produced sculptural, wheel-thrown, and modeled ware assembled from apparently disparate pieces of clay and with random coloring. Studio glassmakers such as Dale Chihuly also experimented with various techniques, especially hot glass. Crafts Revival furniture, for example, by Wendell CASTLE,

C

117

Cozzi porcelain factory
Small Cozzi figure of a young man. c. 1770.

Crabstock
Staffordshire creamware teapot and cover, with a crabstock handle. c. 1755–65.

Cracked ice
Chinese Kangxi blue and white jar, with a cracked ice ground.

Crackle
Dedham crackleware center bowl with indented rim.

continued to be influenced by ARTS AND CRAFTS traditions.

In Britain the craft tradition was strengthened by the emergence of the new profession of the designer-maker and the establishment of the Crafts Council in 1975. The furniture-maker Gordon RUSSELL combined traditional construction with a limited use of luxury materials. HEAL & SON produced limed oak furniture in limited editions, featuring rectilinear designs with minimal ornament. The studio ceramics movement flourished from the 1920s, under the influence of Bernard LEACH and Michael CARDEW. As in the US, significant artist-potters included refugees from mainland Europe, notably Lucie RIE and Hans COPER. In furniture-making, John MAKEPEACE and his followers created pieces in organic shapes, showing great respect for the nature and figure of the wood itself.

Craftsman style A term used to describe American ARTS AND CRAFTS architecture, interior decoration, furniture, and ceramics, from the 1890s until the end of World War I. The term is taken from Gustav STICKLEY's trademark "Craftsman Furniture" introduced from around 1900. In 1901 Stickley founded a periodical called *The Craftsman*, published until 1916, which helped spread his concepts of "simplicity, honesty, and integrity" in design. The style was taken up at the same time by potters such as Adelaide ROBINEAU and tilemakers such as Ernest Batchelder, who had been in touch with the ARTS AND CRAFTS Movement in Europe.

Cranberry glass A type of red-pink glass, also known as RUBY GLASS. The coloring comes from the addition of copper oxide or gold chloride, which turns the glass to a cranberry red when reheated. The technique was known to the ancient Romans but was at its most popular in the 19th century. Most was made at STOURBRIDGE in England. American cranberry glass was made at various glassworks, including SANDWICH.

Cranbrook Academy An American school of design founded in Bloomfield Hills, Michigan, by the newspaper magnate George G. Booth in 1925, under the directorship of the Finnish architect Eliel Saarinen, who also designed the campus buildings. Cranbrook was at the hub of American MODERNISM, particularly the

CREAMWARE

A refined cream-colored EARTHENWARE, creamware was the potter's answer to the rival PORCELAIN. Early in the 18th century Staffordshire potters had created a white ware of light weight and thin gauge with a smooth LEAD GLAZE, which had ousted tin-glazed DELFTWARE. When the white body was fired to a high temperature, it produced a STONEWARE. But when it was fired to a medium temperature and combined with a lead glaze, a new cream-colored ware evolved. Introduced around 1740, this became popular with Staffordshire, Yorkshire, and other potters. WEDGWOOD called it QUEENSWARE in 1767, but the usual term was "cream color," abbreviated to "cc." Creamware soon superseded other bodies and Wedgwood and others built up a flourishing export trade. It was decorated with RELIEF molding, painting, and OVERGLAZE printing. Apart from creamware made at Wedgwood, LEEDS, and a few other potteries, it is mostly unmarked, and therefore difficult to attribute.

Ewer and basin
Leeds creamware ewer and basin pattern No. 188; c. 1780.

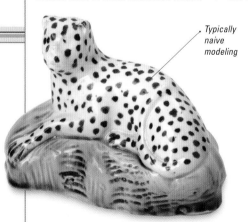

Typically naive modeling

Model of leopard
Staffordshire creamware model of a leopard. Early 19th century.

Popular satirical imagery

Mug
Creamware political satire mug, printed and painted with a scene titled "Narrow Escape of Boney through a Window." Early 19th century.

Coffeepot
Enameled creamware coffeepot, probably Staffordshire. c. 1770.

Organic style. Graduates include Harry BERTOIA, Charles EAMES, Florence Knoll, and Eero SAARINEN.

Crane motif ■ A motif appearing in both Roman ornament and medieval church decoration as a symbol of vigilance. The crane also features in Oriental art as a messenger of the gods in China, and as an emblem of happiness and prosperity in Japan. In the 18th century the crane played a leading role in CHINOISERIE decorative schemes, frequently paired with the HO HO BIRD. Common on engraved glassware.

Crane, Walter (1845–1915) An influential British painter and designer in the ARTS AND CRAFTS Movement. Crane was the ART WORKERS GUILD'S first president and became principal of the Royal College of Art (1898–99). Influenced by Japanese prints, he was well known for his paintings, book illustrations, textiles and wallpapers, and he also designed furniture and ceramics.

Crazing A fine network of cracks in a ceramic GLAZE, caused by the accidental unequal shrinkage of the body and the glaze during the cooling after firing.

Credenza ■ The Italian term for a serving table, credence table, or sideboard. It was used in the 19th century as a low side cabinet with a central door and display shelves.

Creil et Montereau ■ A French FAIENCE factory founded around 1796. It also attempted to produce porcelain but without success. The factory united with Montereau in the early 19th century and continued until 1895, producing cream-colored and white EARTHENWARE, much of which was purchased and TRANSFER-PRINTED by Stone, Coquerel & Le Gros. The views of Paris, French châteaux, and English country houses were very popular. Montereau continued using the name until 1955.

Cressent, Charles (1685–1768) A French furniture-maker who trained as a sculptor in Amiens, then became a furniture-maker and one of the leading exponents of the RÉGENCE and ROCOCO styles. His superb COMMODES and clock cases, decorated with ORMOLU mounts, which he cast and gilded himself, were produced for many royal and aristocratic European clients.

Cresson, Louis ■ (1706–71) An important French furniture-maker born into a respected family of Parisian MENUISIERS. In 1738 he became a master joiner and built his reputation as the most talented of the Cresson family, with a range of chairs and other elegant upholstered furniture for an aristocratic clientele that included the royal household of Louis XV. Other family members who worked as *menuisiers* included Michel and Jean-Baptiste.

Crested ware Ceramic souvenirs decorated with the coats of arms of various seaside resorts. Crested china was popular in the late 19th and early 20th centuries, when vast quantities were made in England and Germany. See also GOSS PORCELAIN FACTORY.

Cresting Carved wooden decoration along the top of a horizontal member, typically found on CASE FURNITURE, mirrors, picture frames, and the TOP RAILS of chairs.

Crewelwork A technique in embroidery using a wool thread on a linen or linen-mix ground, usually worked in chain stitch to create free-flowing designs, often depicting foliage, but sometimes also incorporating animals and birds. Fashionable during the 17th and 18th centuries, it is most commonly found on large-scale bed- and wall-hangings, curtains, and coverlets. Crewelwork was revived in the mid-19th century and early 20th century.

Cricket gourd A vessel traditionally used in China to house singing crickets kept for gambling games. Made from a hard-rinded fleshy fruit of the cucumber family, and often embellished with *Huo Hui* (fire painting), a decorative technique in which lines are scorched on the surface with a hot metal needle. The lids are made from a diverse range of materials such as sandalwood, jade, ivory, mother-of-pearl, tortoiseshell, and coconut shell.

Cricket table A type of small, plain table with three legs. It was made from the 17th

C

119

Crane motif
Detail of turquoise and gilt *pâte-sur-pâte* vase showing cranes among foliage.

Elaborate mounted, inlaid, and painted decoration

Credenza
Victorian ebony and tortoiseshell boulle credenza, with gilt brass mounts.

Creil et Montereau
Ceramic plate, "Aircraft," by Creil et Montereau. c. 1900.

Cresson, Louis
Louis XV carved giltwood fauteuil, in Beauvais tapestry. c. 1745.

C

century until the 19th century, and generally has a circular top with a triangular frieze below and a triangular shelf joining the three legs.

Cristallo The Italian name for a colorless SODA GLASS, developed in Venice in the mid-15th century, reputedly by Angelo BAROVIER. It remained malleable for a long time after heating and so was particularly suited to elaborate shapes. Too thin and brittle for cut or carved decoration, *cristallo* glass was instead often embellished with DIAMOND POINT ENGRAVING, enameled or gilded decoration, or trailing.

Crizzling A defect in the body of glass caused by an imbalance in the BATCH, which produces a network of fine internal cracks (also called criseling). Eventually, these may cause the "diseased" glass to degrade and even disintegrate. George RAVENSCROFT prevented this in lead glass with the addition of lead oxide.

Crock ■ A SALT-GLAZED stoneware utilitarian or commercial vessel, made throughout the eastern states of the US during most of the 19th and early 20th centuries. The most valuable crocks are early and attributable to, for example, Hubbell & Chesebro, New York, or William E. Warner, New York, with unusual folk art decoration in cobalt blue.

Cromwellian style The decorative arts, particularly relating to furniture and silver, produced during the English Commonwealth (1649–60), the government established by Oliver Cromwell. Owing to the influence of the Puritans and the absence of royal patronage, production of the decorative arts decreased dramatically, and those items that were made during this period are distinguished by austere forms with little or no applied ornament.

Cros, Henri (1840–1907) French sculptor, glass and ceramic artist, who redeveloped PÂTE-DE-VERRE (a process long favored by the ancient Mesoptamians and Egyptians) after many years of research. In 1884 he used the technique to make reproductions of antique cameo gems, and from 1889 he used the material in plaques and sculptural forms. From 1893 he worked for SÈVRES.

Crossbanding A line of decorative VENEER in which the veneer runs at right angles to the main veneer or timber on the drawer, panel, door, or table top of which it forms the edge.

Crossbow A projectile weapon consisting of a bow mounted crosswise on a wooden shaft, called a tiller. Crossbows were used in China from 400 BCE onward. Their first use in European warfare dates from around 1000 CE, but they were obsolete by the mid-16th century. They continue to be used for hunting and sport shooting today.

Cross-stitch A simple stitch in which two diagonal stitches are placed across a ground thread at right angles to each other forming an X. It became so popular in 19th-century sampler-making that it is occasionally referred to as "sampler stitch."

Crouch ware English stoneware made of common clay and sand, glazed with salt—usually of a greenish tint. Most crouch ware was made in Staffordshire in the late 17th and 18th centuries.

Crown Derby ■ A porcelain factory established in 1876 in Derby, England, by William Litherland and Edward Phillips and called Derby Crown Porcelain Co. until 1890, when it became Royal Crown Derby Porcelain, following the award of a Royal Warrant. Crown Derby still makes richly decorated pieces of a very thin porcelain, painted by excellent artists such as Albert Gregory and Cuthbert Gresley. The finest all-around decorator was Désiré Leroy, who used painting, jeweling, gilding, and burnishing. He died in 1908 and his work, which is now avidly collected, is very expensive and almost always signed.

Crown Devon ■ Pottery made by the Staffordshire firm of S. Fielding & Co., founded in 1870. It was originally called Railway Pottery, then Devon Pottery from 1911. The printed mark of "Crown Devon" was used from 1930 onward. It produced a wide range of good-quality majolica ware and earthenware, including figurines, TOBY JUGS, wall plaques, and novelty ware. The pottery closed in 1982.

Crock
American stoneware crock, by A. K. Ballard of Burlington, Vermont. c. 1855.

Crown Derby
Royal Crown Derby painted and gilt tray. 1911.

Crown Devon
Crown Devon "Fairy Castle" tube-lined vase.

Crown Ducal
Crown Ducal vase, designed by Charlotte Rhead.

Crown Ducal ■ A trade name used by A. G. Richardson & Co., of the Gordon Pottery in Tunstall, Staffordshire. The pottery was founded in 1915, then at the Britannia Pottery in Cobridge (1924–74). The company specialized in decal-decorated ware. Their most famous designer was Charlotte RHEAD.

Crown glass Sheet-glass made in a large, flat disk, obtained by cutting a glass bubble, and opening and spinning it at high speed to flatten it using centrifugal forces. The thickest part of the glass was at the center of the disk, the thinnest at the extremities. The disk was laid flat and allowed to cool before being cut up into panes, usually used for windows. Occasionally, concentric wavy lines can be seen, producing a slight rippling effect.

Cruet ■ A small glass bottle or jug with a stopper, to hold condiments such as oil or vinegar. They were made in various shapes and types of glass, as single items or in sets, and were also made in ceramic.

Crystal See LEAD CRYSTAL.

Crystalline glaze A glaze with crystals of zinc or calcium suspended in it, creating patches of color. The effect is produced by cooling the kiln in which the ware has been fired extremely slowly.

C-scroll A variation on Classical scrolled ornament developed in the ROCOCO period when the curved forms of c- and s-SCROLLS were used to create a fancy framework for other motifs.

Cubism A highly influential early 20th-century artistic movement created principally by the painters Georges Braque and Pablo Picasso in Paris between 1907 and 1914. Cubism is characterized by the use of two-dimensional geometric and angular forms rather than naturalistic representation. It was further developed by other artists and designers and inspired the abstract and geometric forms of ART DECO design.

Cuckoo clock A type of BLACK FOREST CLOCK with an elaborate carved wooden case (sometimes in the form of a chalet) from which a wooden cuckoo emerges when activated by the striking mechanism. Some also include two small organ pipes emitting simulated birdsong. Cuckoo clocks were mass-produced from the mid-19th century onward, and are still made today, mainly as souvenirs of the Black Forest region.

Cuerda seca ■ A decorative ceramic technique that originated in Persia (modern-day Iran) and much used in Spain by the 15th century. Applied to both tiles and pottery, it involves drawing lines around a design using a mixture of manganese and grease. The latter creates a barrier that stops different colored glazes from coalescing during firing, and in the process, also lends greater definition to the various areas and components of the design.

Cuir bouilli The French term for boiled leather. A technique, known in Europe from the 14th century, in which leather is soaked or boiled in liquid to make it soft, after which it can be molded into a shape such as a cup, flask, or casket, before it dries and turns rigid.

Cuirass The French term for breastplate. Properly, ARMOR to protect the torso. Comprises breast- and back-plates that could be worn with other armor or on their own.

Cullet Fragments of scrap or waste glass, or broken glass objects, added to the ingredients of a new glass BATCH to reduce its melting point.

Cup and cover column ■ Turned decoration, frequently used on furniture legs, bed posts, and BALUSTERS in the mid-16th and 17th centuries. Its bulbous form resembles a deep-bowled cup topped with a domed lid.

Cupboard A term used to describe a piece of closed storage furniture with a door on the front. The first cupboards were open sets of shelves. The earliest type of small closed cupboard or AUMBRY with one door was soon adapted into new forms with two doors, and two stories with four doors, and became increasingly elaborate, with carved columns and CORNICES.
See COURT CUPBOARD, ARMOIRE, LIVERY CUPBOARD.

Cruet
Late George II cruet stand, designed by Jabez Daniell and James Mince. 1759.

Cuerda Seca
A Grueby tile decorated in *cuenca* and *cuerda seca*. Early 20th century.

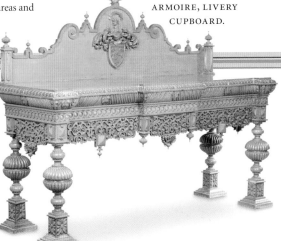

Cup and cover column
Early Victorian Jacobethan oak sideboard raised on carved cup and cover legs with pedestal feet.

C

Cupid motif From the Latin *cupido* (desire). The Roman god of love (Eros in Greece) was a favorite subject for Classical ornament. A popular theme in RENAISSANCE decoration and emblem books, Cupid frequently appears in the company of his mother, Venus, with a bow, quiver, and arrows. The Cupid motif became ubiquitous as an emblem of love during the 18th century, adorning bedroom furniture, decorative paneling, and marriage gifts. Cupid also appears with a personification of Time symbolizing the popular theme of Love's triumph over Time, a favorite subject on 18th-century French clocks.

Cushion drawer A drawer with a front that is convex from top to bottom and runs the full width of the piece. Such drawers were usually found on walnut or oak secretaire cabinets in the late 17th and early 18th centuries and may have been VENEERED or BANDED.

Cut glass A term used for glassware decorated with grooves and facets and usually cut by a rotating wheel. The technique was developed in ancient Egypt in around 1500 BCE and is one of the earliest forms of glass decoration. It was widely used in BOHEMIA in the 16th and 17th centuries and in English and Irish LEAD CRYSTAL in the 18th century. The development of lead glass around 1676 was a major breakthrough, as the thick, soft glass was ideally suited to cut decoration and allowed for deeper and more elaborate cutting. This started a fashion for cut glass in a wide range of styles, which reached its peak in the late 19th century with the highly polished American "brilliant" style cut glass. The high point dwindled in the early 20th century, although the technique saw much smaller, brief peaks again in the 1930s and 1950s in STOURBRIDGE.

Cut steel Jewelry made by riveting faceted steel studs onto plates to imitate gems, used extensively in 18th- and 19th-century England. The best-known maker was Matthew BOULTON, who produced jewelry and accessories such as shoe buckles and CHATELAINES. The main areas of manufacture were Woodstock in Oxfordshire, London, and Birmingham.

Cut-card work Relief decoration on silver articles of HUGUENOT origin that was popular in England and France in the late 17th and early 18th centuries. A pattern of swirls, leaves, or flames, for example, is cut from a thin sheet of silver, and is then overlaid and soldered to the body or cover of a piece.

Cutlass A sword with a short, broad single-edged blade, sometimes slightly curved, in use from the 15th century. During the 18th and 19th centuries its size made the cutlass ideal for use on a ship, and the name was then usually confined to naval swords.

Cutlery Traditionally, articles made by a cutler, who was responsible for edged weapons such as swords as well as some eating utensils, namely knives. The term is now, often incorrectly, used to include

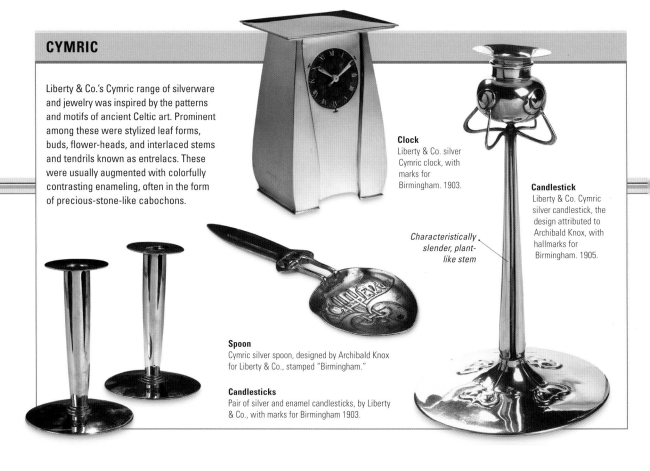

CYMRIC

Liberty & Co.'s Cymric range of silverware and jewelry was inspired by the patterns and motifs of ancient Celtic art. Prominent among these were stylized leaf forms, buds, flower-heads, and interlaced stems and tendrils known as entrelacs. These were usually augmented with colorfully contrasting enameling, often in the form of precious-stone-like cabochons.

Clock
Liberty & Co. silver Cymric clock, with marks for Birmingham. 1903.

Candlestick
Liberty & Co. Cymric silver candlestick, the design attributed to Archibald Knox, with hallmarks for Birmingham. 1905.

Characteristically slender, plant-like stem

Spoon
Cymric silver spoon, designed by Archibald Knox for Liberty & Co., stamped "Birmingham."

Candlesticks
Pair of silver and enamel candlesticks, by Liberty & Co., with marks for Birmingham 1903.

spoons and forks and services of FLATWARE, but really only applies to pieces with a cutting edge.

Cutlery urn ■ A KNIFE BOX in the form of a lidded urn, usually in mahogany or satinwood. The vase-shaped form was introduced in the 1780s and made in pairs to stand at either end of a sideboard. It remained popular until the early 19th century, when the cutlery drawer superseded the knife box.

Cut steel ■ Jewelry made by riveting faceted steel studs onto plate to imitate gems, used extensively in 18th- and 19th-century England. The best-known maker was Matthew BOULTON, who produced jewelry and accessories such as shoe buckles. The main areas of manufacture were Woodstock in Oxfordshire, London, and Birmingham.

Cylinder escapement Perfected by the 1720s by the clock- and watchmaker George Graham after Thomas TOMPION's design of 1695, the cylinder escapement was a vast improvement in timekeeping over its predecessor the VERGE ESCAPEMENT. The escape wheel comes into direct contact with the balance wheel and is also known as a frictional rest escapement.

Cylinder fall ■ A type of BUREAU or DESK with a curving or TAMBOUR roll top made up of horizontal slats or a single curved section of wood, sometimes elaborately inlaid, that slides up and back to reveal the writing surface. It was introduced in the 18th century, possibly by one of its most famous exponents, Jean-François OEBEN.

Cymric style ■ A range of ARTS AND CRAFTS-style silver jewelry and other small silver wares, and glassware, machine made by LIBERTY & CO. together with W. H. Haseler, silversmiths in Birmingham. Designers such as Archibald KNOX and Oliver Baker were commissioned by Liberty. The name reflects the fact that the style was heavily influenced by CELTIC motifs.

Cyphers A method of secret writing using substitution or transposition of letters, or a design consisting of interwoven letters used as a monogram, on a seal, or on porcelain forming part of the decoration.

Cypress A conifer native to Iran and the Middle East. Its wood is aromatic, with a close reddish grain that is highly resistant to worms and moths. Cypress was widely used for small storage boxes and linen chests from the end of the 16th century.

Cut steel
Regency butterfly pin of cut steel riveted to brass.
c. 1820–30.

Cutlery urn
One of a pair of mahogany cutlery urns or knife boxes.
19th century.

Cylinder fall
Late Victorian Sheraton Revival satinwood and marquetry cylinder desk.

D

Dagger A general term for a short-bladed stabbing weapon. Daggers have been made from a variety of materials—flint, bone, wood, copper, bronze, iron, and even plastic. Major types of dagger include the Baselard, DIRK, stiletto, eared dagger, rondel, and Swiss dagger. The main-gauche dagger was carried in the left hand, as its French name suggests, and used in conjunction with the RAPIER.

Daguerreotype ■ The first practical photographic process, invented by L. J. M. Daguerre in 1839. The daguerreotype is a direct positive image on a polished, reflective metal plate coated with light-sensitive silver halide and was the main means of processing until the 1850s. After exposure, the image was revealed by fuming with mercury. Daguerreotype images are sometimes hand-tinted and slotted into special cases, or fitted in lockets or other jewelry. Since a daguerreotype cannot be duplicated, each image is unique.

Daisho The long and short swords carried by Japanese samurai (warriors). The *katana*, or *daito*, is the longer of the two, and the *wakizashi*, or *shoto*, is the shorter of the two types. Used for close combat, both swords had identical guards, hilt-mounts, and scabbard decoration.

Dali, Salvador A Spanish artist (1904–89) who was a leading figure of the Surrealist movement. From the late 1920s to the late 1930s he created dreamlike images from the subconscious in a meticulous style. After World War II he continued to paint, but his style changed. He also designed theater sets, jewelry, and ceramics.

Damascening A method of decorating metal, usually steel, in which silver or gold or copper wire is inlaid into a pattern of fine grooves and hammered flush with the surface. Developed by metalworkers in the Middle East, the technique was first used in Europe in Italy in the late 16th century on swords and armor. It was popular in the mid-19th century for presentation pieces.

Damascus twist A technique for making gun barrels in which iron and steel wire is beaten into a ribbon, wound around a mandrel, and then hammer-welded in white heat to form the barrel tube.

Damask ■ A rich, woven fabric usually of silk, linen, or cotton, based on a satin weave. Damask relies for its effect on the different ways in which light is reflected from the warp and weft threads. Deriving its name from Damascus, in Syria, damask was imported into Europe from the 15th century. From the 16th century, heavy damask was used for furnishing fabric, and linen damask started to appear in household table inventories. Arabesques and complex, curving foliate or floral patterns are typical.

Darning sampler Popular from the late 18th century until around 1830, darning samplers were usually worked at school or under the instruction of a governess. They demonstrated a girl's ability to work darns that simulated a variety of woven cloths, and they often included floral motifs made by darning techniques.

Date aperture A small opening on a clock or watch dial displaying the date. See CALENDAR APERTURE.

Date letter First instituted in France in 1427 and in the UK in 1478, a date letter is a letter of the alphabet stamped with a punch in conjunction with HALLMARKS on British silver. Each letter represents a specific year, recording officially the exact date of manufacture of an article.

Daum Frères A French glassworks in Nancy, France, taken over by Jean Daum as a bad debt in 1875. His son, Jean-Louis Auguste, joined the firm in 1879, and his other son, Jean-Antonin, joined in 1885. The two brothers transformed the factory into a world-famous producer of ART GLASS. Inspired by the work of GALLÉ and others, they produced colored CAMEO GLASS in

Daguerreotype
An American daguerreotype, showing an elder in the Oddfellows association.

Cartouche-like frame

Damask
Crimson silk damask with a formalized floral and foliate pattern. 18th century.

Davenport pottery
Davenport potpourri vase and cover decorated in Imari style. c. 1830–c. 1840.

Davenport writing desk
Victorian burr-walnut davenport writing desk.

Yellow silk damask top cover

Day bed
Mahogany Biedermeier day bed. Early 19th century.

the ART NOUVEAU style from about 1900, using natural motifs and landscapes. One of their most famous forms was the Berluze, a vase with an ovoid body and an attenuated neck over twice the height of the body. In the 1930s and after World War II, Antonin's son, Michel Daum, perfected the manufacture of crystal and experimented with colorless crystal designs. Wheel-carved glass was also made, as was PÂTE-DE-VERRE and, later, ART DECO and sculptural pieces. Salvador DALI designed for them in the 1970s. The glassworks still exists today, producing luxury, decorative glass.

Daumenglas The German term for a cylindrical or barrel-shaped beaker made in Germany and the Low Countries in the 16th and 17th centuries.

Davenport pottery and porcelain factory ■ A large firm trading from 1795 for around 90 years. After working in Dublin and Liverpool, John Davenport took over a pottery in Longport in Staffordshire, England, at first producing EARTHENWARE, but in about 1800 he started to make PORCELAIN tableware and well-decorated REGENCY vases. The firm also made plaques (impressed "Davenport"). It closed in 1887.

Davenport writing desk ■ 1. A small desk first made in the early 19th century, purportedly for a Captain Davenport. Comprising a hinged sloping top above a CHEST-OF-DRAWERS, in which the drawers were set at right angles to, rather than aligned with, the top, davenports remained popular until the late 19th century. 2. In the US, a davenport also refers to a large parlor SOFA, fashionable in the mid–late 19th century, and often convertible into a bed.

Dawes library chair A type of chair with a back that reclined at the press of a lever. It often also incorporated a retractable GOUT STOOL. Such chairs were made from 1825 to 1840 by Dawes, an English furniture manufacturing company.

Day bed ■ A term used virtually interchangeably with CHAISE LONGUE and COUCH to describe an elongated chair, usually without side-supports, sometimes in two parts with a separate footstool.

Day, Lucienne (born 1917) A textile designer well known in postwar British design, who studied at the Royal College of Art in London from 1937 to 1940, and married eminent British furniture designer ROBIN DAY in 1942. Her designs for HEAL'S and Edinburgh Weavers embody simplicity of form, fitness for function, and appropriate ornament. In 1951 her ground-breaking and most famous Calyx design for screen-printed linen won a gold medal at the Milan Triennale. She has also designed carpets, wallpaper, and ceramics.

Day, Robin (born 1915) An English furniture designer. In 1948 he opened a design studio in London with his wife, the textile designer LUCIENNE DAY, and became particularly well known for an

D
125

DAUM FRÈRES

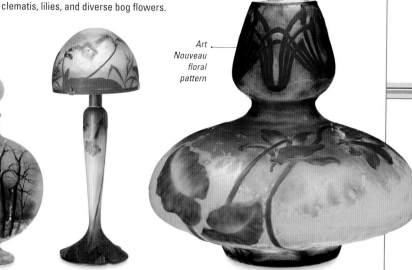

The primary source of decorative inspiration for Daum Frères was the Lorraine countryside surrounding their glass factory in Nancy. Thus riverbank, marshland, forest-walk, and summer meadow landscapes recur, as do more specific indigenous flora and fauna.

Particulary notable among the latter are dragonflies, daisies, wild roses, sweet peas, clematis, lilies, and diverse bog flowers.

Art Nouveau floral pattern

Cameo vase
Applied and wheel-carved Daum cameo glass vase marked "Daum, Nancy."

Perfume bottle
Daum etched and enameled scenic perfume bottle and stopper.

Table lamp
Art Nouveau Daum cameo slender table lamp with Majorelle label.

Overlay glass vase
Rare Daum clear glass vase, overlaid in dark purple and etched, cut, and martelé cut. c. 1898.

D

innovative range of furniture designs for Hille Ltd., in particular the Hillestak chair (1950) and the molded plastic Polyprop chair (Mark I, 1962; Mark II, 1963), which were all designed to be stacked and enjoyed a revival in the 1990s.

De Lamerie See LAMERIE, PAUL DE.

De Morgan, William Frend ■ (1839–1917) An English ceramicist, designer of stained glass windows, and novelist, married to the artist Evelyn De Morgan. One of the finest 19th-century art potters, his designs, use of color, and glazes were outstanding. He is known for his LUSTER glazes based on HISPANO-MORESQUE ceramics and those showing a Persian influence in turquoise, green, blue, yellow, and red. He made a variety of decorative items and tiles, some featuring in William MORRIS and Philip WEBB interiors. He established various potteries: CHELSEA (1872), Merton Abbey (1882), and Sands End in Fulham (1889). He stopped working as a potter in 1906 and became a successful novelist instead.

Deadbeat escapement A type of ANCHOR ESCAPEMENT used in precision timekeepers such as REGULATORS and first developed by the British clockmaker Thomas TOMPION in 1675 and put into widespread use by George GRAHAM in the early 18th century. It is more accurate than the ordinary anchor escapement because of the curved design of its pallets that prevent recoil, and thus, wear.

Deal A collective term for various softwoods, including species of pine, spruce, and hemlock. Mostly pale yellow or off-white in color, deal is traditionally used either to construct the CARCASSES of furniture VENEERED with more expensive hardwoods, or stained and grained in imitation of hardwood, or enhanced with painted decoration, or, for cheap country pieces, simply waxed or varnished.

Dean's Rag Book Co. ■ One of Britain's oldest surviving toy manufacturers, founded in 1903 by Henry Samuel Dean. Already well known for its children's printed fabric "rag" books, Dean's started selling bears in 1915. Also known for its dolls, the company was based in Merton in London until 1955, when it moved to Rye in Sussex, and finally to Pontypool in Wales in 1972. A new company was founded in 1988 which produces bears to this day.

Decanter ■ A decorative, typically handle-less, glass container with a matching stopper, used for serving wine, sherry, and spirits that have been emptied from the bottle (decanted). First made in the mid-17th century, the shapes and designs are plainer than those of the 19th century, which are more elaborate. Sizes and shapes were dependent upon which type of drink they held and also upon contemporary fashions.

Deck, Theodore ■ (1823–91) A French ceramicist who began by making ceramic stoves before establishing his own pottery in Paris, producing ceramics in the Persian style and later Chinese- and Japanese-influenced designs. He commissioned talented artists to decorate wall plaques for him, including Felix BRACQUEMOND. The rich turquoise glaze that he often used became known as *bleu de Deck*. In later years he was head of the SÈVRES factory and then director of HAVILAND at Auteuil.

Décor bois A decoration simulating wood, painted on porcelain, sometimes with panels of pictures for a TROMPE L'OEIL effect. It is usually European, in particular originating from the French factory of NIDERVILLER.

Décorchemont, François-Emile ■ (1880–1971) A French glassmaker who trained as a painter and potter, but in 1902 set up a glass workshop in Conches, where he produced thick-walled PÂTE-DE-VERRE vases and bowls with textured exteriors, smooth interiors, and veined, streaky colored decoration made using metallic oxides and pâte-de-cristal pieces. ART DECO and NEOCLASSICAL designs are typical.

Découpage ■ The art of decorating household objects and furniture with a montage of images made from colorful paper cutouts. Originating in 12th-century China, it flourished in Europe from the 18th century to the Victorian era, when collages were created with a notably sentimental feel.

De Morgan, William Frend
William de Morgan charger, painted red, with fantastical fish on a foliate background.

Dean's Rag Book Co.
"Child's Play" fabric glove puppet with heart badge, by the Dean's Rag Book Co.

Decanter
Decanter with prism cut neck, diamond and flute cut body, and mushroom stopper. c. 1830.

"Bleu-de-Deck" glaze

Deck, Theodore
Polychrome-painted earthenware model of a duck, by Theodore Deck.

Décorchemont
Art Deco vase in smoky brown glass with geometric and figural pattern. 1920s.

Dedham Pottery (1896–1943) See CHELSEA KERAMIC ART WORKS.

Dehua porcelain factories ■ These factories at Dehua, near Foochow in the Fujian province of southeast China, have produced BLANC-DE-CHINE from the MING DYNASTY (1368–1644) to the present day. Large quantities arrived in Europe as CHINESE EXPORT PORCELAIN in the early 18th century and it was copied at MEISSEN and elsewhere. Crisply modeled figures with a smooth white glaze were popular as were incense holders, brush pots, DOGS OF FO, libation cups, and boxes.

Delaherche, Auguste ■ (1857–1940) A French art potter who opened his own studio in 1887 making stoneware inspired by East Asia, using the thick, running glazes of Japan with floral or figured decoration. In the 1890s he increasingly used porcelain with various experimental oxidized, reduced copper FLAMBÉ, and crystalline glazes. From 1904, one-of-a-kind white pieces featured stylized flowers.

Delft ware ■ The town of Delft in Holland became important in the 17th century for the manufacture of tin-enameled earthenware. Delft ware was originally inspired by the BLUE AND WHITE porcelain brought to Europe from East Asia by the ships of the Dutch East India Company. In 1659 there were 23 workshops in the area; by 1680 there were about 30. During the 18th century, manufacturing steadily declined—first due to competition from porcelain and later from the creamware producers. By 1850, almost all the Delft manufactories had gone out of business, but the industry was revived and Dutch Delft is still made as reproductions. Among the many factories in Delft were: De Drie Klokken (Three Bells), 1671–1845, first owned by Barbara Rottewel, followed by her son, and finally by Van Putten & Co. (1830–40); De Drie Porseleyne Plessies (Three Porcelain Bottles), 1679–1764, owned until 1720 by the Kam family, then bought by Zacharias Dextra, who introduced enamel colors; De Dubbele Schenkken (Double Jug), 1648–second half of the 18th century; De Grieksche A (The Greek A), 1658–1820, making excellent products such as tulip vases, milk pans, and pagoda urns—some for Hampton Court and Chatsworth in England; De Paeuw (The Peacock), 1651–1779; and De Porseleyne Klaeuw (The Porcelain Claw), 1662–1840.

Delftware A term used to describe a British-made TIN-GLAZED EARTHENWARE that emulates the ware from Delft in the Netherlands. This delftware is usually more thinly potted and has a shiny, slightly blue glaze. Rarely marked, it was made in many places, including London, Norwich, Bristol, Liverpool, Wincanton, and Glasgow. The early pieces were inspired by Chinese patterns in blue, sometimes with the addition of yellow and manganese. Wares included large dishes (chargers), smaller plates, tankards, mugs, and more unusual objects such as bulb bowls, puzzle jugs, punchbowls, barber's bowls, jugs, and commemorative ware. Some early figures were made, but these are rare. British delftware was challenged and superseded in the second half of the 18th century by CREAMWARE and porcelain.

Della Robbia Pottery An English ART POTTERY company begun in 1893 by H. B. Rathbone and Conrad Dressler at Birkenhead, Cheshire. Mostly made in red clay decorated with colored slips and SGRAFFITO decoration, pieces are marked with a galleon and "DR," sgraffito, and painters' monograms. Decorators included Cassandia Annie Walker and Carlo Manzoni The firm closed in 1906.

Della Robbia, Lucca See ROBBIA, DELLA LUCCA.

Demi-lune A form of occasional or side table with a semicircular (half-moon-shaped) top. Often raised on four legs, and sometimes with an undershelf, it was designed to stand with the straight edge of the top aligned against a wall.

Denby Pottery ■ Based in Denby, Derbyshire, this pottery began producing Staffordshire-type STONEWARE in 1809 and is still working today. In its early days it specialized in GIN FLASKS, later in kitchen ware, notably the fireproof ranges and utilitarian wares such as the

D

127

Découpage
A Victorian découpage picture of the British royal family, including Queen Victoria. 1843.

Dehua porcelain factories
Dehua *blanc-de-chine* figure of Guanyin. 1630–50.

Delaherche, Auguste
Vase by Auguste Delaherche, Paris. 1890.

Delft ware
One from a garniture of three Delft vases. c. 1800.

Denby pottery
Denby Arabesque pattern handpainted coffeepot. 1964–70s.

D

128

Nevva-drip teapot in the 1920s. Ornamental pieces were also made, including Butterfly Ware vases in the early 20th century.

Dennis, Thomas (active c. 1660–1700) An English-born American carpenter and furniture-maker, active in Colonial Massachusetts and specializing in WAINSCOT CHAIRS. His style can be compared to that of his lesser-known mentor, William Searle, and follows the richly carved BAROQUE taste popular at the time in the English West Country, the birthplace of both men.

Dent Hardware Co. ■ A leading American hardware company founded in 1895 in Fullerton, Pennsylvania, which also produced CAST-IRON toys from 1898. Early examples included horse-drawn carriages, with cars, trucks, and planes coming later. The castings are particularly fine, with details such as running boards, but dating is hard due to a lack of catalogs. Toy production ceased by 1937 due to competition from less expensive diecast and steel toys, and the company closed in 1974.

Dent, Edward (1790–1853) A prominent English maker of carriage clocks, watches, and chronometers. Dent worked with the clockmaker John R. Arnold from 1830, but in 1840 he set up his own business. In 1851 he was awarded the commission to build the clock for the tower of the Houses of Parliament (Big Ben). After his death it was completed by his stepson, Frederick.

DEPRESSION GLASS

Mass-manufactured PRESSED GLASS made in the US during the 1920s–50s, Depression glass was so named because it became popular during the Great Depression. Inexpensive and colorful, this glass was made by automatic machines and was offered in a variety of different patterns and colors, from traditional floral or foliate patterns to ART DECO styles. Functional bowls, pitchers, drinking glasses, and plates were manufactured by the Jeanette Glass Company, Hazel Atlas Glass Company, and the Hocking Glass Company, among others.

Glass jug
Clear crystal Depression glass milk pitcher. 1930s.

Dentils, dentil rim From the Latin *dens* (tooth). An ornamental device from Classical architecture, dentils consist of a series of small rectangular blocks resembling teeth running beneath a CORNICE. In ceramics, a border painted with half scallops under a cornice is known as a dentil rim.

Derby ■ The factories at Derby produced what are considered to be some of the finest English porcelain figures. Derby already had a tradition of pottery manufacture by the time the HUGUENOT modeler Andrew Planché arrived in 1748. CHINOISERIE figure groups are among the first porcelain made there. Derby ware of 1750 to 1756 is sometimes known as "dry edge," as the creamy, glasslike glaze dribbled and had to be wiped before firing to prevent adhesion to the kiln shelves. Planché left Derby soon after 1756, when the factory was acquired by William DUESBURY and his business partner John Heath.

Duesbury and Heath's pieces included shepherds and shepherdesses, blackamoors, and leading actors of the day, all influenced by MEISSEN. TRANSFER-PRINTED wares included mugs with coronation portraits of George III and Queen Charlotte.

Duesbury died in 1786, and his son, also William, guided the factory through a particularly fine period in which display objects for a richer market were decorated by artists such as Zachariah BOREMAN and William BILLINGSLEY. William Duesbury II died in 1797. In 1811 Robert Bloor, the company clerk, bought the factory, remaining

Dent Hardware Co.
Dent cast-iron express truck.

Two-tone paintwork

Dentils
A mahogany and satinwood cheval mirror with a dentil cornice. Late 19th century.

Derringer
.41in RF Remington Derringer DB pocket pistol.

Desk
An Edwardian lady's writing desk in rosewood.

in control until 1825. In the 1830s the factory again copied Meissen and SÈVRES designs, but they could not compete with them or the Staffordshire factories. It closed in 1848, but other factories in the town carried on the name, including the Derby Crown Porcelain Co. in 1870, which in 1890 became Royal CROWN DERBY and continues today.

Derbyshire potteries A group of potteries in Derbyshire, England, including CHESTERFIELD and DENBY, producing wares similar to those of the STAFFORDSHIRE potteries, from medieval times to the present day.

Derringer The general name for a small pocket pistol. It takes its (misspelled) name from Henry Deringer of Philadelphia, who popularized small but powerful PERCUSSION pocket pistols in the 1840s. Most major American gun-making firms produced derringers, including COLT and REMINGTON.

Deruta An important pottery in Umbria, central Italy, from the Middle Ages. During the Renaissance, Deruta made MAIOLICA, reaching a peak of production after 1500 with wares that were technically accomplished and painted in a warm palette of yellow, ocher, and green. Some designs were influenced by the Umbrian school of painting, sometimes copying frescos by Perugino. Deruta was also known for the technique of LUSTER glazing, giving a subtle iridescent sheen to wares of softer coloring, typically decorated with overlapping scales and zigzag patterns. Deruta declined after 1530, but continued during the 17th century to produce much peasant-type maiolica. Today it makes popular reproductions of its traditional designs.

Desk ■ A piece of furniture that combines a flat writing surface and drawers or other

DERBY

Hand-painted botanical, exotic bird, and architectural landscape imagery are all characteristic of Derby porcelain. Chinoiserie scenes on blue and white wares are also used, but are less common. Favored subject matter includes pastoral, Classical, and mythological scenes.

Vase
Large Derby vase, painted in "Dodson" style with birds. c. 1820.
Stylized foliate gilding

Bocage decoration
Group of figures
Derby group of figures adorning a bust of Pan. c. 1780.

Dish
Derby heart-shaped dish with a bird pattern. c. 1820.

Coffee can
Derby coffee can with a "Near Lincoln" landscape vignette. c. 1815.

Serrated leaf-edge rim
Sauceboat
Derby leaf-molded sauceboat, painted in colors with sprays of flowers. c. 1758.

storage space for stationery. Before the late 16th century, the desk took the form of a small portable storage box, with a hinged sloping lid that acted as both a book support and a writing surface. By the end of the century, such boxes were supported on stands. Most of the different types of desks—BONHEUR-DU-JOUR, BUREAU, CARLTON HOUSE DESK, DAVENPORT, ESCRITOIRE, and FALL FRONT—are variations on this theme.

Deskey, Donald ■ (1894–1989) An American MODERN, INDUSTRIAL designer most widely known for the interior of Radio City Music Hall in New York (1932). He worked in many fields, including packaging, metal furniture, lighting, fabrics, wallpaper, and interiors, often using

modern materials such as CHROMIUM, BAKELITE, and aluminum. In 1925 he visited the Paris Exposition, and his work shows affinities to CUBISM and ART DECO and many of his designs exhibit early STREAMLINING. Donald Deskey Associates became one of the leading design practices in the US after World War II, designing interiors of houses, clubs, restaurants, and hotels throughout the country.

Dessert service Items used for the dessert course of a meal, which from the end of the 18th century was served after the main part of the meal (prior to that, all the food was put on the table at the same time). Sometimes dessert was served in a different room. The many confections such as ices, jellies, fruit, and nuts were

served on the dishes of the dessert service, which comprised ice pails, sauce tureens, COMPORTS, and plates.

Detent escapement A type of ESCAPEMENT used in precision clocks, especially CHRONOMETERS. It was developed in Britain in the 18th century, and incorporates a detent or steel catch, which controls the movement of the escape wheel.

Deutsche Blumen ■ Naturalistic flower motifs, fashionable from around 1740. They were first used at MEISSEN and then throughout Europe as porcelain became widely used. One of the principal sources was the eight-volume florilegium, *Phytanthiza Iconographia*, 1735–45,

DESIGN REGISTRATION

A mark printed, impressed, or incised on some British ceramics, glass, metalwork, and textiles from 1842 onward, indicating that the design of the object has been registered with the Patent Office. Until 1883 the mark— a form of copyright—consisted of a lozenge incorporating various numerals and letters indicating the day, month, and year of registration and the class of the article (e.g., Class I for metalwork). The "Rd" in the center of the diamond stands for registered design. This was replaced after 1883 by a serial number with the prefix "Rd No," "Regd.," or "Regd. No."

1842–67	1868–83
a = class	a = class
b = year	b = day
c = month	c = bundle
d = day	d = year
e = bundle	e = month

Registered number A post-1883 registered design number on the underside of a Royal Worcester porcelain jug.

The letters were not used in sequence but as follows:

1842–1867 (features a number in the right-hand corner of the diamond)

A	1845	E	1855	I	1846	M	1859	Q	1866	U	1848	Y	1853
B	1858	F	1847	J	1854	N	1864	R	1861	V	1850	Z	1860
C	1844	G	1863	K	1857	O	1862	S	1849	W	1865		
D	1852	H	1843	L	1856	P	1851	T	1867	X	1842		

1868–1883 (letter in the right-hand corner of the diamond)

A	1871	E	1881	I	1872	L	1882	U	1874	Y	1879
C	1870	F	1873	J	1880	P	1877	V	1876		
D	1878	H	1869	K	1883	S	1875	X	1868		

The months from both periods are shown as follows:

A	December	D	September	H	April	M	June
B	October	E	May	I	July	R	August
C/O	January	G	February	K	November	W	March

Classes

Class 1 Metal   **Class 4** Earthenware
Class 2 Wood   **Class 5** Paper
Class 3 Glass

Fabrics

Class 11 Furnitures (Printed Fabrics)
Class 12 (i) Other Fabrics
Class 12 (ii) Other Fabrics (Damasks)
Class 13 Lace

Hangings

Class 6 Carpets   **Class 9** Yarn
Class 7 Printed Shawls   **Class 10** Printed
Class 8 Other Shawls

compiled by J. W. Weinmann, which contained over 1,000 hand-colored engravings after drawings by G. D. Egret, J. E. Refiner, and B. Setter.

Devonshire potteries Several small factories in North Devon, England, notably at Barnstaple, Bideford, and Fremington, making SLIPWARE from the 17th century to the present day. The ware is similar to the products of other English slipware factories, apart from some large jugs decorated with nautical motifs such as mariners, compasses, and ships, which were made at Bideford.

Diagonal barometer See ANGLE BAROMETER.

Dial The part of a clock or watch that displays the time. The dial consists principally of a metal or wooden plate, the DIAL PLATE, with a CHAPTER RING and hour and minute hands. Minute hands were only introduced in the late 17th century when the invention of the PENDULUM increased the accuracy of timekeeping. Dials are also found on barometers and other scientific and surveying instruments, with the chapter ring being divided for atmospheric pressure or a compass reading. See CLOCKS.

Dial clock ■ A circular English WALL CLOCK comprising a large round dial in a simple wooden case, with a brass bezel and glass cover. It was used in stations, shops, and offices until the introduction of electric clocks in the early 20th century.

Dial plate A shaped metal or wooden plate attached to the front plate of a clock or watch movement. On clocks the dial plate is usually square, circular, or arched, with the latter sometimes incorporating a STRIKE/SILENT LEVER, calendar work, automata, or musical work in the arch.

Diamond Carbon in its crystalline state, which occurs naturally in many areas of the world in alluvial deposits and deep volcanic pipes. Diamonds are assessed according to the so-called "four Cs": 1. Color is the dominant factor. A D-color stone is completely colorless and letters of the alphabet from D to Z define an increasing intensity of yellow. 2. Clarity describes the presence or lack of inclusions and imperfections where "flawless" is the top grade. 3. Carat defines size. 4. Cut describes the faceting, shape, and finish of the polished stone.

Because of the complexity of diamond grading and the increasing number of convincing synthetics, many diamonds are routinely certified. Fancy-color diamonds, notably reds, greens, blues, and pinks, are among the most rare and costly of all gemstones. The diamond is the hardest material known.

Diamond-point engraving A form of glass decoration made by scratching the design onto the surface with a diamond-point stylus. This type of light decoration was mostly used on 17th-century Dutch and Italian glass, in particular wine glasses.

Diaper A decorative motif consisting of repeated diamonds, lozenges, squares, or other geometrical shapes. It was used on early Tudor brickwork and later was commonly used for woven textiles and in CHINOISERIE and JAPONAISERIE decoration. The pattern was particularly favored in the 19th century for furniture, floor tiles, ceramics, many types of textiles, and wall coverings.

Diecast The method of making an item by injecting molten metal, usually mazak (an alloy consisting mainly of zinc), under pressure into a closed metal die or mold. The casting is removed from the die after a short cooling period.

Die-stamping A method of forming the body or part of an article, developed in the late 18th century and used in the SHEFFIELD PLATE industry. Metal sheet was sandwiched under pressure between two shaped steel blocks or dies by machine, thus taking their form, and was consequently produced more economically than by traditional handmade methods.

Dimity A tough cotton fabric woven using a double warp thread for strength. It has a slightly ribbed pattern of stripes or checks and was used in household furnishings, from the 17th century.

Deskey, Donald
Donald Deskey Radio City Music Hall sofa, in vinyl, fabric, and rosewood. c. 1932.

Scattered floral motifs

Deutsche Blumen
Meissen ozier-molded tureen stand, painted with Deutsche Blumen. Mid-18th century.

Dial clock
English mahogany fusée dial clock. c. 1860.

Dinanderie Brassware such as candlesticks and drinking and cooking vessels, made in and around Dinant, in Belgium, in the early Middle Ages, until the town was sacked in 1466. The term is also used in a wider sense to describe any decorative or domestic brassware such as candlesticks and cooking utensils.

Ding (ting) ware 1. A type of Chinese porcelain made in the TANG DYNASTY (618–906) and throughout the SONG DYNASTY (960–1279). It has an ivory white glaze, orange translucency, and characteristic unglazed rims often bound with copper alloy or, more rarely, silver or gold. Conical bowls with carved, molded, or INCISED DECORATION are most common (formerly called *ting* ware). 2. Ding also refers to a small dent in metalware.

Dinky toys ■ This famous range of DIECAST toy vehicles was first made in December 1931. They were designed originally as accessories for the HORNBY O-gauge trains and sold as Modelled Miniatures. The first cars were released in late 1933 and the name Dinky was used from 1934. Early examples were cast in lead, but mazak (a zinc alloy) was used from 1934. Road vehicles form the majority of production, but planes and ships were also made, both pre- and postwar. Competition from the mid-1950s from CORGI and European factories caused Dinky to update their designs. A series of changes of ownership followed and the

brand ceased production in 1980. The most collectable Dinkies are prewar examples, which are now scarce and prone to fatigue (disintegration caused by impurities in the metal), and postwar reissues and new issues up to about 1964, particularly vans with advertising or examples with unusual color variations. Most of the later items were supplied in individual yellow boxes and are much more desirable when in the original box. From 1988 to 1992 MATCHBOX, who owned the name, produced a new range under the Dinky brand to sell to collectors.

Diorama ■ A scenic painting in which changes in color and direction are lit to simulate movement, originating from France in the 19th century, and later made in Germany and England. Many are three-dimensional with objects (sometimes moving) placed in front of the painting. Typically, they contain a small representation of a scene such as a garden or battle with correct perspective being a particularly important aspect. Their development is credited to L. J. M. Daguerre, inventor of the DAGUERROTYPE, who held an exhibition of them in Paris in 1822.

Dirk ■ A Scottish DAGGER carried by Highlanders from the mid-17th century onward. Its HILT was of dark wood—for example, ivy root—and carved with Celtic basketweave patterns. It was carried in a leather sheath, often with compartments for a small knife and fork.

Disbrowe, Nicholas (c. 1612–c. 1680) An English-born American Colonial "joiner" active in Hartford, Connecticut, from around 1639. Disbrowe is one of the earliest recorded furniture-makers in the US, associated with CONNECTICUT CHESTS of Hartford type, carved with formalized florette panels.

Disk joint A joint in soft toys made of two cardboard or metal disks connected by metal wire. It was first used by STEIFF in 1905, as an improvement on earlier rod jointing.

Dish ring ■ A spool-shaped stand made of pierced and/or chased silver and Old Sheffield plate, designed to support a dish of hot food but also serving as a decorative adjunct. Silver examples were produced largely in Ireland from 1740, but decorative reproductions were made in Victorian and Edwardian England.

Dished table top A wooden circular table top, with a slightly hollowed center to create a concave surface with raised edges.

Distressed A term used to describe either genuine furniture in a poor state, or furniture that has been deliberately treated to make it appear older or more worn. Among the techniques used are sanding, scratching, burning, scorching, acid-dipping, and various decorative finishes.

Dixon, James, & Son Ltd. ■ Originally founded by James Dixon and a Mr. Smith in

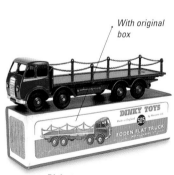

With original box

Dinky toys
Dinky Foden No.505 Flat Truck with chains, with 1st type maroon cab. 1952.

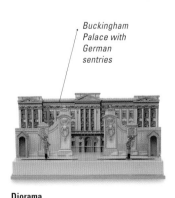

Buckingham Palace with German sentries

Diorama
Tinplate clockwork diorama called "Hitler's Palace," featuring Buckingham Palace.

Dirk
Scottish dirk with leather and gilt sheath. 1874.

Art Nouveau plant forms

Dish ring
Victorian Irish silver dish ring, by Gibson and Langman of Dublin. 1896.

Sheffield in 1806. The firm is best known for its high-quality silver and ELECTROPLATE wares, including FLATWARE, cutlery, and decorative functional HOLLOWARE, which was exported to countries around the world, including the US. It also produced designs by Dr. Christopher DRESSER during the 1880s. James Dixon retired in 1842, with the company opening its first London premises in 1873, and becoming a limited company in 1920. It went into decline when mass-produced stainless steel cutlery was introduced in the 1960s, but is still active today.

Doccia porcelain factory ■ Founded in 1737 by the Marchese Carlo Ginori on his estate in Florence. Johann Karl Wendelin Anreiter von Zirnfeld, a HAUSMALER from Vienna, arrived in 1737, and the early productions, around 1740, show strong links with Du Paquier's VIENNA PORCELAIN. Workers were also bribed to join from MEISSEN and this shows in the CHINOISERIE decorations. Doccia made figures in the style of Meissen but the modeling is heavier and clumsier. As renowned Italian artists were recruited, it created a character of its own. Doccia's *masso bastardo* body (a rather gray hard paste) was used for statues and vases in sizes not seen before. The figures were influenced by RENAISSANCE sculpture.

At the beginning of the 19th century Doccia bought molds and models from CAPODIMONTE and made copies of cups and saucers molded with battle scenes, on which they used the crowned "N" of

NAPLES. Essentially a family business, the firm still exists today, although in 1896 it was incorporated with the Richard factory of Milan to become Richard-Ginori. In 1897 the company was incorporated with the ceramic factory, and in 1906 it joined with the Rifredi factory in Florence to make electrical insulators. With eight factories in Lombardy, Piedmont, and Tuscany, Doccia now produces artistic porcelain and runs the Sesto Fiorentino, which deals with industrial production.

Dog of Fo A mythical animal used in Chinese art. The figures are made in pairs—the male usually has one paw on a brocade

ball, while the female is depicted with a pup. Originally used as temple guardians, they are also known as Buddhist lion dogs (*Fo* means Buddha). The Japanese equivalent is *Shi Shi*.

Dogtooth motif An early English ornament developed from the NAILHEAD pattern and consisting of a series of four-cornered stars diagonally arranged as a repeating embellishment for moldings. Carved in low relief, it remained popular for decorative brickwork and woodwork throughout the 15th and 16th centuries.

Doily A small napkin or mat, made of cotton, linen, lace, or paper, used to decorate

Doccia porcelain factory
"The Ball Gown," a painted and gilded porcelain figure by Doccia. Late 19th century.

DIRECTOIRE STYLE

A variant of the NEOCLASSICAL style found in French decorative arts, especially furniture, from around 1790 to c. 1804, the Directoire style reached its peak of popularity during the Directoire political period (1795–99). It is characterized by austere Classical forms such as tripods and X-framed stools and chairs, with minimal ornament. Some Directoire furniture, textiles, and ceramics are decorated with revolutionary symbols such as the cap of liberty. It was superseded by the EMPIRE style.

Cabinet
Directoire mahogany cabinet, with inset marble top. c. 1800.

Commode
French Directoire rosewood, kingwood, and tropical woods commode. c. 1800.

Clock
Directoire gilded bronze mantel clock "Le Bacchus Noir." c. 1810.

Carved and pierced backsplat

Chairs
Pair of Directoire mahogany chairs.

plates before food is added, or to protect the surface of the table from the ceramic or silver dish or pot.

Doll mark ■ Indicating the manufacturer, mold number, patent, or size of a doll, marks are usually impressed, incised, or stamped on the back of the doll's molded head. They sometimes appear as stamps or labels on kid leather, fabric, or composition bodies.

D

134

Doll ■ Toys in the shape of human figures have existed in most civilizations. Evidence of them has been found in Egyptian and Roman tombs, although the earliest surviving dolls tend to date from the late 17th century.

Some dolls of this date were made of wax, but most surviving English examples are of wood. In the first half of the 19th century, wax was commonly used to make dolls' heads. Initially carved from a solid block of wax, from around 1840 hollow poured wax heads took over, made by a technique perfected by two London-based Italian families, MONTANARI and PIEROTTI. Soon a cheaper alternative was developed, known as WAX OVER COMPOSITION. From about 1840 dolls made of china were produced by porcelain factories in Germany and the rest of Europe. The FROZEN CHARLOTTE china doll was made entirely of porcelain.

The charm and sophistication of the dolls of the last half of the 19th century are due to the development of bisque as a raw material. It dominated the doll market until the 1920s. The most important center of bisque doll manufacture was Thuringia, in central Germany. Till 1875 bisque FASHION DOLLS, showing the season's latest trends, were popular, made by such companies as the French BRU JEUNE ET CIE. By the 1880s these were supplanted by BÉBÉS, which were produced by French factories such as JUMEAU, STEINER, and Schmitt. Toward the end of the 19th century, competition from German imports forced French makers to found the SOCIÉTÉ FRANÇAISE DE FABRICATION DE BÉBÉS ET JOUETS (SFBJ).

The first quarter of the 20th century was dominated by German manufacturers of bisque-headed dolls such as Armand MARSEILLE, KESTNER, and SIMON & HALBIG. From 1890 these companies made cheaper dolls in direct competition with French makers, their most innovative designs being CHARACTER DOLLS. The beginning of the century also saw the emergence of commercially produced fabric dolls. In Germany Käthe KRUSE made fabric dolls, and in the US the fabric doll tradition, represented by Izannah Walker and Martha CHASE, was continued by companies such as Sheppard & Co. of Philadelphia. At the same time, LENCI produced felt dolls in Italy, as did Norah WELLINGS in England. Another popular material was celluloid. Composition, a substance made from wood or paper pulp mixed with various reinforcing ingredients, had been used for the manufacture of dolls' bodies since the mid-19th century and was a popular alternative to bisque for dolls' heads until 1950.

A huge variety of composition dolls was produced until first plastic, then vinyl, took over. Vinyl's most famous product is undoubtedly BARBIE, introduced in 1959 and still coveted by girls today. The early models are becoming an increasingly popular collector's item. See CHINA HEAD DOLL.

Dollhouse ■ Early forms of miniature "room settings" from Egyptian, Greek, and Roman civilizations still exist today and some may have been used as funerary offerings. In northern Europe, from the 15th century onward, the first dollhouses took the form of "dolls' cupboards," used by adults for storing and displaying collections of miniature porcelain and silver. In the late 17th century the first English dollhouses (baby houses) were made. Still in cabinet form, they were intended as playthings, rather than for an adult's amusement.

In the US, the first dollhouses date from the 18th century and show a Dutch influence. The Van Cortlandt Mansion of 1744 can be seen in the museum of that name in New York. Throughout the 18th century and the early part of the 19th century, dollhouses reflected the

Doll mark
A German "Handwerk" doll with an impressed mark to the back of the head. c. 1915.

Doll
German bisque-head character doll by Simon and Halbig. c. 1910.

Dollhouse
An English painted wooden dollhouse. c. 1870.

architectural styles of the period and were individually crafted. From the mid-19th century, the introduction of CHROMOLITHOGRAPHY meant that manufacturers could easily decorate wooden or cardboard houses, and dollhouses were produced in much greater numbers.

A dollhouse became part of the furnishings of the late 19th-century nursery, elaborately equipped with servants, dinner sets, and even tiny plaster food. From 1895 G. & J. LINES in London produced wooden houses with brick-printed paper, continuing to keep pace with fashion until the 1920s, when the company was renamed TRIANG. German firms such as Christian Hacker and Moritz Göttschalk continued to monopolize the international dollhouse market. The number of American dollhouses increased steadily after 1850. Later, around 1890, more decorative houses came into vogue, such as those produced by Rufus Bliss, which were quite small in size, with wooden structures, colorful chromo-lithographed exteriors, and miniature furniture to go inside.

From 1930 DINKY TOYS in Britain launched the Dolly Varden range for girls, including dollhouses with scaled-down furniture. Other well-known companies include CHAD VALLEY, who manufactured TINPLATE houses. From the 1950s, dollhouses were smaller than earlier versions and equipped with modern home appliances. This type of miniaturized appliance was manufactured by specialists such as MECCANO and BRITAINS LTD.

Dolphin motif A decorative motif with origins in Classical art and a powerful symbol in Christian iconography. Since the Renaissance, dolphins have featured in architectural ornament, as furniture and lamp supports, or adopted as GROTESQUES. It is a natural component of marine ornament, and remains popular for fountains, wellheads, and waterspouts.

Dominick and Haff ■ American silversmiths, established in New York City in 1872 by Blanchard Dominick and Leroy Haff. The firm made small items like VINAIGRETTES as well as high-quality silver-plated ware, including chased HOLLOWWARE in Japanese taste. It was sold in 1928 to become part of REED & BARTON.

Don Pottery ■ Founded in 1790, at Swinton, in Yorkshire, near the Rockingham factory, Don Pottery was acquired by John Green of the Leeds Pottery in 1800 and taken over by Samuel Baker of Mexborough in the late 1830s. The factory made CREAMWARE, EARTHENWARE, TRANSFER-PRINTED WARE, and also BLACK STONEWARE, using an impressed mark of DON POTTERY. It closed in 1893.

Dorflinger, Christian (1828–1915) A German-born (Alsace) American glassmaker, founder of the Greenpoint Glassworks in Brooklyn, New York, in 1860, and two other glassworks, including C. Dorflinger & Sons in White Mills, Pennsylvania. Dorflinger introduced advanced European techniques of cutting and making lead glass, mostly in a heavy style comparable to the best European work.

Doucai ■ A technique of painting (contrasting or dovetailing) on Chinese PORCELAIN where the design is first outlined in soft UNDERGLAZE blue, then filled in using OVERGLAZE enamels. It was introduced during the CHENGHUA reign (1465–87) for small, high-quality wares and revived from the early 18th century.

Doulton ■ A pottery bought in the early part of the 19th century by John Doulton in Lambeth, south London. It made stoneware chimney pots and products for the chemical industry, and was known as Doulton & Watts until the death of John's partner, John Watts, in 1858. Doulton's son Henry, then steered the company to success as Henry Doulton & Co.

Early stoneware products included hunting jugs, mugs, bowls, tobacco jars, and tea- and coffeepots. COMMEMORATIVE WARE featured strongly. Success with stoneware sanitation pipes enabled Henry Doulton to open a studio devoted to ART POTTERY. The project began with students from the Lambeth School of Art, including George Tinworth and the BARLOW family. By the 1880s it employed more than 200 workers. Doulton's art stoneware varied

Dominick and Haff
American silver bonbon dish, made by Dominick & Haff of New York, NY. 1889.

Don Pottery
Don Pottery meat dish, printed with a "Cascade at Isola" pattern. c. 1820–c. 1830.

Doucai
Chinese Doucai saucer dish with five dragons, and a Qianlong seal mark. 19th century.

Doulton
One of a pair of Doulton ovoid stoneware vases decorated by Hannah Barlow. 1880.

from stylized patterns in the Victorian taste to high-quality ART NOUVEAU designs. Doulton Faience was introduced for naturalistic hand-painted decoration, as were fine porcelain pieces.

In 1877 Henry Doulton bought a large stake in Pinder Bourne & Co., in Burslem, Staffordshire, which he later took over. Here he produced EARTHENWARE and later BONE CHINA. Charles Noke became art director, introducing decorative figures that developed into the "HN" series, followed by Series Ware in 1901. Then came Rembrandt and Holbein wares, Kingsware, and character and TOBY JUGS in 1934. Doulton figures such as the Old Balloon Seller were made throughout the 20th century. Decorative bone china figures designed by Lesley Harradine in the 1920s and 30s are avidly collected today. Highly individual ceramics resulted from transmutation glazes such as flambé, titanian, and crystalline. Production ended at Lambeth in 1956, but continues today at Burslem under the name of Royal Doulton Fine China.

Dovetail   A type of JOINT, first used in furniture-making at the end of the 17th century, in which two pieces of wood are joined at right angles by "dovetailed," triangular-shaped "teeth" at the end of one

piece that lock into corresponding recesses on the end of the other piece.

Dowel   A small headless wooden pin used in furniture construction to join two pieces of wood. It was first used in the 16th century as a peg to strengthen MORTISE AND TENON joints. Such pegged or joined construction was gradually abandoned by the mid-18th century when stronger glues were developed, but enjoyed a revival during the late 19th and early 20th centuries under the ARTS AND CRAFTS Movement.

Drabware   A line of earthenware introduced by WEDGWOOD in 1811, and reissued since then in various styles. Drabware is characterized by the enduring modernity of its monochromatic neutral hue, which has ranged from a pale coffee brown to a dark olive.

Dragon style   A style of late 19th- and early 20th-century Scandinavian, particularly Norwegian, silver, furniture, and TREEN, with forms and ornament inspired by Norse and Viking art. Silver vessels were made in the form of ships and drinking horns, often decorated with colorful ENAMELING and figures from medieval myths and sagas.

Dragon's blood   A red, resinous substance extracted from trees and traditionally used by painters and decorators to tint LACQUERS and VARNISHES. Notable sources include *Dracaena cinnabari* of Socrota (described in the writings of Pliny); *Dracaena draco* of the Canary Islands; and various *Daemonorhops* species of palm growing in the East Indies and Malaya. Depending on the source, colors range from bright red to a dark, reddish brown.

Dram glass   A small glass with a short stem, made with a variety of bowl shapes, some with thick bases, and used in 18th- and 19th-century taverns and clubs to serve spirits.

Drapery   A popular decorative device derived from antiquity. SWAGS of drapery sometimes appear in place of flower garlands in Classical and RENAISSANCE decorative schemes, and 16th-century STRAPWORK designs often feature MASKS swathed in drapery. A fitting accessory for the theatrical BAROQUE STYLE, drapery was enthusiastically embraced across Europe for painted and carved decoration, for mirrors, windows, and CHIMNEY PIECES. A favorite ornament on American FEDERAL and English NEOCLASSICAL furniture, lavish swags of real drapery decorated fashionable interiors in the early 19th century.

Draw-leaf table   A type of dining table with an extra leaf at either end beneath

DRESDEN PORCELAIN

A generic term for German porcelain wares and figures from in and around Dresden in Saxony, Dresden porcelain was made in the style of MEISSEN (not far away up the Elbe River) from the second half of the 19th century. It includes factories making porcelain, as well as decorating establishments, many of whom tried to copy the mark of Meissen. There were 40 decorating establishments at the end of the 19th century and some of the best-known factories are Dresden Porcelain Factory, Donath & Co., Helena WOLFSOHN, Carl THIEME of Potschappel, and the factory at Plaue on Havel in Thuringia. Dresden porcelain is still made. So-called Dresden ware was also made in English factories from the 19th century and continues to this day.

Dresden mirror   A late 19th-century wall mirror, mounted with putti and musical motifs, with a blue cross mark, and some small chips and repairs.

Dream baby
Armand Marseille "Dream Baby" character doll.

the main tabletop. The leaves could be pulled or drawn out to double the length of the table. The device, which was first introduced in Britain, Germany, and the Netherlands in the mid-16th century, is still used today.

Drawn stem A stem, also known as a drawn shank, formed by drawing glass from the bottom of the bowl of a drinking glass, rather than attaching the bowl to a separately formed stem.

Drawn thread work A decorative embroidery technique on linen produced by pulling threads apart and drawing them together using a variety of stitches in different combinations to form open patterns. Used for decorating clothing and household linen, it was particularly fashionable in the 16th and 17th centuries and was revived in the latter part of the 19th century.

Dream baby ■ A doll modeled on a newly born baby, with domed head, narrow eyes, chubby cheeks, bent limbs, and a fabric body. Dream babies are variations on Grace Putnam's Bye-Lo baby, designed in 1922. Overwhelming demand soon spawned imitations, the most common dream baby being mold number 341/351, first produced by Armand MARSEILLE in 1926.

Dredger A vessel, usually in cut glass or silver, with a perforated top, used for sprinkling powdery substances such as sugar, salt, and pepper on food, or for sprinkling fine sand, known as "pounce," on wet ink.

Dresden faience factory Founded by J. F. BÖTTGER in 1708, just before he discovered PORCELAIN. The best FAIENCE dates from 1710 to 1738, under the management of Peter Eggerbrecht from the BERLIN faience factory, and includes drug pots, COMMEDIA DELL' ARTE FIGURES, and large CHINOISERIE vases. The factory closed in 1784.

Dresser (US Hutch) ■ A piece of case furniture consisting of a rack of shelves to display or store pewter or ceramics on a base of drawers and a cupboard, or an open base with a pot board. Evolving from the side

DRESSER, CHRISTOPHER

The English designer Christopher Dresser was inspired by Japanese design. He visited cultural and manufacturing sites in Japan, being commissioned by Tiffany and Co. to bring back items. He also became involved in importing Japanese artifacts. His designs were used by Elkington (silversmiths), COALBROOKDALE (iron foundry), Hukin & Heath (silver and plate makers), J. Couper & Sons (glass, notably the Clutha range) and LINTHORPE (pottery), to name but a few.

Chamberstick
A Perry, Son & Co. brass chamberstick, designed by Christopher Dresser.

Bottle vase
Ault bottle vase by Christopher Dresser, glazed in a streaked green.

Cloisonné vase
A Minton cloisonné vase, mold No. 1384, designed by Christopher Dresser.

Garden bench
Arts and Crafts cast-iron garden bench, by Christopher Dresser for the Coalbrooke Dale Foundry. 1876.

D

table in the late 17th century, it is still popular as kitchen furniture. Many regional types were developed over the years. For example, BREAK-FRONT dressers with closed racks above drawers and cupboards are associated with North Wales, in contrast to the dressers with open racks and bases of South Wales.

Dresser, Christopher ■ A radical English designer, botanist, and teacher, Christopher Dresser (1834–1904) is considered one of the first practitioners of modern, industrial design. He could distill other cultures' design with his appreciation of form, based on studies of nature, while embracing machine and mass production. His designs of the 1870s and 1880s are still "modern" today. He wrote a much-acclaimed article, "Botany as Adapted to the Arts and Art Manufacturers," for the *Art Journal*. In 1862 he published his first book, *The Art of Decorative Design*. Dresser was impressed and influenced by Japanese design and spent four months in Japan in 1876–77. He visited cultural and manufacturing sites, being commissioned by TIFFANY & CO. to bring back items. He also became involved in importing Japanese artifacts. His designs were used by Elkington (silversmiths), COALBROOKDALE (iron foundry), Hukin & Heath (silver and plate makers), J. Couper & Sons (glass, notably the CLUTHA range), and

LINTHORPE (pottery), to name but a few. He won a prize for the design of a clothing fabric in 1854 as well as submitting botanical drawings to the Department of Science and Art. In 1861 he became a fellow of the Linnean Society, and in 1862 he published his first book, *The Art of Decorative Design*.

Dressing case A lockable, portable wooden box, often in MAHOGANY or COROMANDEL wood, with a fitted interior holding glass bottles and grooming accessories such as brushes and combs, as well as compartments for jewelry. Popular in the 18th and 19th centuries, it enabled gentlemen and ladies to safely transport vanity items together while traveling.

Dressing table A small table with drawers designed to hold the accessories for a lady's or gentleman's toilet. The term was in use from the 17th century. From the 18th century, such tables usually included a freestanding looking glass.

Dressoir The French term for a medieval multipurpose sideboard with storage cupboards, the top of which was used to display plate or serve food.

Dreyfuss, Henry ■ (1904–72) An American INDUSTRIAL designer, apprenticed to Norman Bel Geddes, and working on theatrical designs before founding his own practice in 1929. Much of his work is typified by clean-lined, curving

sculptural forms that exemplified STREAMLINING. His designs consider the consumer and user of the product as a major concern and include telephones, vacuum cleaners, and the interiors of aircraft.

Drinking glass See GLASS, DRINKING.

Drinking horn ■ A hollowed-out animal horn is one of the earliest known natural drinking vessels. From the first millennium CE, drinking horns have been mounted in gold or silver, often with a detachable cover, on a foot or feet, and decorated with enamel or jewels, perhaps for ceremonial use. They may be made in other materials such as rock crystal, ivory, wood, or silver. Drinking horns are still made as ceremonial items.

Drop handle A handle, also known as a tear or swing drop, shaped in the form of a single teardrop, and first used on good-quality CHESTS-OF-DRAWERS in the late 17th century.

Drop-in seat The term used for a removable chair seat, usually upholstered, that is made separately and then "dropped in," or inserted into the seat frame. Drop-in seats were introduced in the early 18th century.

Dropleaf table ■ The term used for a type of table introduced in the early 18th century, which has two hinged leaves that drop or fold down, supported by pivoting legs.

Dresser (hutch)
Georgian oak dresser with corniced and framed three-shelf plate rack.

Drinking horn
Silver drinking horn, with feet modeled as porpoises and the finial as a sea nymph. 1870.

Dreyfuss, Henry
"Sentinel Wafer" clock with copper surround, designed c. 1945.

Drug jar See APOTHECARY JAR.

Drum clock An early type of portable TABLE CLOCK with a cylindrical case on which the dial is mounted horizontally rather than vertically. Most drum clocks were made in Germany and Central Europe in the 16th century and often had finely decorated metal cases. A type of drum clock with a glass-fronted brass case was popular in the 19th century.

Drum stool A Chinese stool in the form of an up-ended barrel with pierced sides, known to have been made in hardwood during the MING period (1368–1644).

Drum table A table with a large circular top supported on a central PEDESTAL or tripod with drawers set into a deep FRIEZE. They were made in the late 18th and 19th centuries. Variants of this form included LIBRARY and RENT tables, the latter used for rent collection and incorporating a cash register in the top and, in the frieze, either four drawers (one for each quarter of the year) or seven (one for each day of the week).

Drypoint A technique in which a metal printing plate has an image directly scored into its surface with a sharp needlelike point. It produces a shallow groove, which is then filled with ink and gives a velvety black tone when printed on paper or canvas. The Dutch artist Rembrandt was a great exponent of the medium.

Du Paquier See VIENNA PORCELAIN FACTORY.

Dubreuil, André ■ (born 1951) A French designer particularly known for his sophisticated and imaginative furniture, some in the style known as New Baroque. His furniture is of good quality, often produced as limited editions and made in metal.

Dueling pistols A pair of FLINTLOCK or PERCUSSION pistols made for formalized personal combat. Pistols superseded swords for dueling from around 1780. English makers such as Robert Wogden and John Rigby excelled in making dueling pistols that were technically advanced, but usually without decoration. The pistols are invariably contained in a wooden case with accessories for loading and maintenance. Dueling was made illegal and eventually fell out of favor in different countries at different times during the 19th century.

Duesbury, William (1725–86) A great entrepreneur in English porcelain, starting out as a decorator of porcelain in London from 1751 to 1753. He went to DERBY and bought the factory there in 1756, then took over the failing factory of CHELSEA in 1770, running it for 14 years.

Dumbwaiter ■ A wooden stand with a tripod base and a central shaft supporting two or three revolving tiers, graduating in size. An English invention of the early 18th century, it was designed to stand by the dining table to let diners help themselves.

Dummer, Jeremiah (1645–1718) An English-born American silversmith. Dummer was one of the first silversmiths recorded in Boston, Massachusetts, where he was apprenticed to English silversmith John Hull. Examples, which may bear a maker's mark only, are plain and are typically of AMERICAN COLONIAL silver.

Dummy board A painted wooden cutout of a figure such as a butler, housemaid, cat, or a dog. Placed in a room, it either served as a firescreen (mostly in the 17th century), or was purely ornamental (mostly from the 18th century onward).

Dunand, Jean (1877–1942) A Swiss-born French designer and LACQUER artist. Traditional lacquer techniques in the ART DECO period were popularized by Dunand, although few could match him in ability. He is responsible for some of the best French Art Deco lacquerwork.

Dunhill, Alfred (1872–1959) An entrepreneur and marketer who developed his family's saddlery business during the early 20th century into a manufacturing and retailing empire that

D
139

Dropleaf table
Dutch mahogany and floral marquetry dropleaf table. Early 19th century.

Dubreuil, Andre
Andre Dubreuil "Spine" chair, in bent and welded steel. 1988.

Dumbwaiter
George III mahogany dumbwaiter. c. 1780.

D

offered high-quality items, including motoring accessories, luggage, wristwatches, and items associated with smoking.

Dunlap, John (1746–92) An American furniture-maker active in Goffstown, New Hampshire, from 1768. Dunlap and his brother, Samuel, made furniture of relatively plain type, mostly in local maple. Ambitious Dunlap pieces, including HIGHBOYS, are distinct from other contemporary examples by being embellished with exaggerated scrolls, cabriole legs, and carved aprons. New Hampshire furniture of this type is referred to as Dunlap School if it is otherwise unattributable.

Duplex escapement A type of ESCAPEMENT used principally in watches but also in some 19th-century clocks, in which there are two escape wheels rather than one.

Durand ■ Glass made at the Vineland Flint Glass Works, founded in Vineland, New Jersey, by Victor Durand Jr. in 1897. The first products were industrial and scientific glassware, but the range was expanded to include ART GLASS in 1924. A cofounder of QUEZAL and former employee of TIFFANY, Martin Bach Jr. was employed to design a range of mainly IRIDESCENT luster glass, of which the King Tut and Peacock Feather patterns are the most notable. From 1925 the company also produced CUT GLASS, CRACKLE GLASS, and lamp bases. In around 1931 the company merged with the Kimble Glass Company and the art glass

department was closed. J.G. Durand is one of Europe's biggest glassworks today.

Durlach pottery A faience factory started in 1723 near Baden, in southwest Germany, with a privilege granted by the Margrave Carl Wilhelm to Johann Heinrich Wachenfeld, who had previously been in STRASBOURG and ANSBACH. From 1723 to 1749 the blue-decorated ware was in the style of ROUEN. CREAMWARE was also made, impressed with "Durlach" after 1818. Many of the painters signed with their names, including Heim, Keirn, Lower, and Pfalzgraf. The factory closed in 1840.

Durra A tapestry-woven cotton carpet, rug, or wall hanging made in India. Traditionally they are of a rectangular shape with fringing.

DUTCH DELFT WARE

Dutch Delft wares are dominated by their original source of inspiration: the underglaze blue and white palette of Chinese export porcelain. However, from the early 18th century the basic blue and white was on many pieces augmented from a polychrome palette that included egg-yolk yellow, a greenish turquoise, a grayish green, a dry red, manganese-brown, and black. Whether blue and white, or polychrome, the recurring decorative imagery is either East Asian, European, or a fusion of both.

Posset pot
An 18th century Dutch Delft blue and white posset pot, painted with birds perched among foliage.

Tulip vase
A Dutch Delft blue and white heart-shaped tulip vase, painted mark "BN132." c. 1920.

Kraak-style dish
Dutch Delft ware dish decorated in Chinese kraak style in blue and white with floral borders. Early 18th century.

hand-painted polychrome floral decoration

Pair of cows
Dutch Delft ware recumbent and facing horned cows, polychrome painted with sprays of flowers. c. 1770s.

Dust jacket ■ The printed paper outer cover of a hardback book, the presence of which in excellent condition adds desirability and value to a collectible book. Most are printed with colorful graphics and the flaps usually hold information about the book and its author. It is also known as a "wrapper," "jacket," or "DJ."

Dutch colonial furniture ■ Furniture made in Dutch types and hybrid styles in the Dutch East Indies colonies (present-day Indonesia) from the early 17th until the mid-20th century. Case furniture, beds, chairs, tables, and other pieces were made in indigenous woods such as EBONY, CALAMANDER, SATINWOOD, and TEAK, both for officials of the Dutch East India Company and for export to Europe. CANE was often used in the early seating furniture as well as in the distinctive reclining veranda chairs developed in the 19th century.

Dutch Delft ware There were a few factories in towns in Holland other than DELFT that made both Delft ware and tiles. These include Amsterdam, Bolsward, Delftshaven, Dordrecht, Gorinchem, Gouda, Haarlem, Hoorn, Reiden, Makkum, and Middelburg.

Dutch peg doll See PENNY WOODEN.

Dutch strike A type of STRIKING SYSTEM in which the hours are sounded on a large, low-pitched bell and at the half-hour the succeeding hour is struck on a smaller, high-pitched bell. Dutch striking could be used only with the COUNT WHEEL and so is found mainly on clocks from before the late 17th century.

Dux See ROYAL DUX.

Dwight, John (1635–1703) An English potter who took out a patent for what he described as "Transparent Earthenware" in 1671. He founded a pottery at FULHAM and made BELLARMINES in Rhenish stone style. He also made REDWARE teapots similar to those of YIXING (China). These innovations paved the way for the development of English pottery in Staffordshire. Dwight made excellent salt-glazed stoneware figures, from small figures of ancient gods to a life-size bust of Prince Rupert.

Dye A compound that, when applied to textiles or other materials, will effect a permanent color change. The degree of permanence of the color is defined as its "fastness." A color-fast dye is capable of resisting washing, wear, and exposure to light without fading.

Dyes can be classified, according to the chemical process involved, into "direct," "mordant," and "vat" dyes. Direct dyes are frequently unstable, mordant dyes are more "fast," and vat dyes are firmly chemically attached to the fiber, although they tend to be weaker in shade. Until the 18th century, all dyes were derived from animal, mineral, or vegetable sources. The first reference to a synthetic dye, "essence of indigo," dates from 1740, but it was not until 1856 that the first fully synthetic dyes appeared. Although these first synthetic, or ANILINE, dyes were not very color-fast, by the end of the 19th century thousands of good synthetic dyes in all colors were widely available.

D

141

Dyottville Glassworks An American glassworks founded in 1771, in Kensington, Pennsylvania, and acquired fully by Dr. T. W. Dyott in 1831. Typical glassware included bottles, flasks molded with portraits or historical images, and inexpensive tableware of all types in clear and colored glass. It closed when Dyott went bankrupt in 1838, reopening under new ownership in 1844.

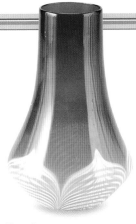

Durand
Durand Art glass vase with cranberry top and feather-pull base. 1907.

Dust jacket
First edition of J. R. R. Tolkien's *The Hobbit, or, There and Back Again*. 1937.

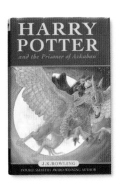

Dust jacket
First edition of J. K. Rowling's *Harry Potter and the Prisoner of Azkaban*. 1999.

Dutch colonial furniture
Open armchair with a rosewood frame and a leather-upholstered seat squab. 19th century.

142

Eagle An ancient symbol of power and victory. The eagle was associated with Jove, celestial king of the Olympian gods, and hence stood for preeminence and regality. The double-headed eagle symbolizes watchful power. The Roman army featured the noble bird on its standards and it has been used ever since by many kingdoms and nations, from the Hapsburgs to the American republic. The American eagle is often portrayed clutching a sheaf of thunderbolts. It was a key motif of the Napoleonic EMPIRE style and, more generally, tends to

appear wherever a heavy Classical style of ornament is being used—for example, on gateways, console supports, or mirrors.

Earnshaw, Thomas (1749–1829) An English clock- and watchmaker. He began his career as a finisher of verge and cylinder watches, but is best known for developing the spring DETENT ESCAPEMENT for marine CHRONOMETERS. Earnshaw was one of the first clockmakers to produce chronometers on a commercial basis, allowing them to become more affordable to the general public.

Earthenware Pottery made of a porous clay body that has to be waterproofed by a coating glaze. Pottery can be divided into two main types: earthenware and STONEWARE. A criterion for this division is the porosity of the BODY after firing. Earthenware has a porosity of more than five percent. See MAJOLICA, FAIENCE, and SLIPWARE.

East India Company A trading company formed to trade with southeast and east Asia and India, initially to break the spice trade monopoly held by Spain and Portugal. The British East India Company was formed by the Royal Charter of Elizabeth I in England in 1600 and granted a monopoly over trade in the East Indies. Later, similar companies were formed by the Netherlands, France, Sweden, and Denmark to import tea, spices, lumber, and porcelain.

The company helped expand British influence—for example, in China in the 19th century. Its commercial monopoly was broken in 1813, and from 1843 it became primarily an administrative body for the British government in India, until its final demise in 1858. See CHINESE EXPORT PORCELAIN.

Eastlake, Charles Locke ■ (1836–1906) An English writer, journalist, and designer who trained as an architect, Eastlake was at

EAMES, CHARLES

An American architect, furniture designer, and filmmaker, Charles Eames, together with his wife, Ray Kaiser, a painter, were the pioneers of the American Modern Movement. Their chair designs were particularly influential. Eames first started experimenting with PLYWOOD with Eero SAARINEN, making molded shells for chairs. Early examples show the influence of Finnish design. Later designs are of fiberglass or plastic shell type. In 1950, an Eames chair for Herman Miller had fiberglass-reinforced

plastic, the molded seat supported on metal rod legs. It was the first chair of its type to leave the plastic shell exposed. One of their most famous and popular designs is the lounge chair with ottoman, which won a gold medal in the 1960 Milan XII Triennale.

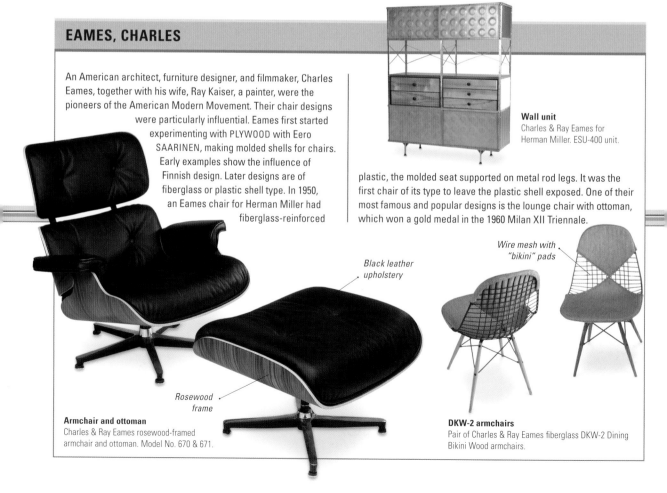

Wall unit
Charles & Ray Eames for Herman Miller. ESU-400 unit.

Armchair and ottoman
Charles & Ray Eames rosewood-framed armchair and ottoman. Model No. 670 & 671.

Black leather upholstery

Rosewood frame

Wire mesh with "bikini" pads

DKW-2 armchairs
Pair of Charles & Ray Eames fiberglass DKW-2 Dining Bikini Wood armchairs.

his most influential as a promoter and writer on design. In 1868 his book, *Hints on Household Taste*, was published. It was hugely popular and was responsible for taking the design debate beyond the realm of artists and architects to a wider audience. It was particularly popular in the US, where it was reprinted eight times. Charles Eastlake was an exponent of ART FURNITURE, rather than mass production, and he advocated discussion and dialogue between the buyer and the maker. He promoted the use of traditional methods of joinery, particularly pegged joints, which proved popular with the ARTS AND CRAFTS Movement.

Although he was in favor of MARQUETRY decoration, gilt highlights, and linear fluting, Eastlake was against FRENCH POLISH, preferring wood to have a natural finish, simply rubbed with boiled oil or stained black. The book included many of his own designs for furniture and wallpaper, inspiring copies and variations, which are referred to as the Eastlake style in the US.

Eastlake designed for various British firms: metalwork for Benham & Froud; wallpaper for Jeffrey & Co.; and fabrics for Cowlshaw and Nicol & Co. His jewelry was retailed through Howell, James & Co. and his furniture was made by the Art Furniture Company, Jackson & Graham, and Heaton, Butler & Bayne.

Eastman, George (1854–1932) An American industrialist, whose developments in photography led to its proliferation among the general public for the first time. In 1880, after three years of experimentation, he devised a "dry" photographic plate that no longer required photographers to mix complex chemicals to produce light-sensitive photographic "wet" plates just before they wished to take a photograph. After starting a company for their manufacture, from 1884 he began to use flexible paper rolls instead of hard plates, and conceived his first Kodak box camera, launched on the market in 1888. The camera was preloaded with a roll of paper film and, once used, was sent back to Kodak to be developed. In 1889 transparent film rolls replaced the paper rolls and the company became known as the Eastman Kodak Company. In 1900 he introduced the BROWNIE, which was sold for one dollar and aimed at children and amateur photographers.

By 1927 Eastman had a virtual monopoly on the photographic industry in the US, and this strength continued until the development and proliferation of digital photography in the early 21st century. Eastman was also a generous philanthropist, and gave away more than $75 million to educational institutions and also to his employees.

Easy chair Introduced in the late 17th century, it was originally a term for a comfortable, upholstered WING armchair designed primarily for the elderly and infirm, but has since been used to describe many types of upholstered armchairs.

E

143

Ébéniste A French term for a cabinet-maker, introduced in the 17th century. The contemporary fashion for EBONY in Europe demanded a revival of veneering that was largely the province of skilled cabinet-makers, and thus they became known by the name of the luxury hardwood with which they worked. See MENUISIER.

Eberlein, Johann Friedrich ■ (1696–1749) A German sculptor who worked at MEISSEN under KÄNDLER from 1735 to 1749. He assisted with the Monkey Band figures for the Japanese Palace, and in 1742 designed the ROCOCO decoration for the Swan Service. His work also includes figures of Classical deities and allegorical characters.

Ebonized Wood or furniture whose surface has been stained or polished to resemble EBONY. The decorative technique was in use by the late 17th century, with notable revivals during the 19th-century fashion for the AESTHETIC style and JAPONISME.

Ebony ■ A heavy black hardwood with a smooth, close grain from trees native to the Indian subcontinent and Sri Lanka. Used since ancient Egyptian times for carved

Eastlake, Charles Locke
Rosewood and marquetry side cabinet, in the Eastlake style. Late 19th century.

Eberlein, Johann Friedrich
Meissen harlequin figure, modeled by Johann Friedrich Eberlein. c. 1743.

Ebony
A Regency games table made from snakewood and, for the black squares and selective highlights, ebony. c. 1810.

E

144

artifacts, furniture (mostly as a VENEER or for moldings), and in more recent times, for black chess pieces. See COROMANDEL.

Eclecticism The combination of motifs and forms from different styles in a single object. Eclecticism was evident in the decorative arts in the 18th century, when the development of the Picturesque Movement encouraged the combination of ROCOCO, GOTHIC, and CHINOISERIE motifs for aesthetic effect. However, it became one of the distinguishing features of the VICTORIAN STYLE from the 1830s as a result of several factors: the widespread interest in historical styles; the emergence of the tourist industry leading to a fashion for exotic motifs and ornament derived from Byzantine, Indian, Egyptian, Persian, Turkish, and other non-European arts; the introduction of new methods of manufacturing that enabled exact reproductions of historical objects; the establishment of museums of the decorative arts and schools of design; and the display of products from around the world at the numerous 19th-century international exhibitions.

Pattern books such as the *Grammar of Ornament* (1856) by Owen JONES, featuring motifs from a great range of styles, allowed designers to appropriate a wide variety of ornament for every type of object. In high-quality pieces, decoration remained restrained and finely executed, but in less expensive items, motifs were often indiscriminately combined with little regard for scale or

proportion or for the form or function of the object. Eclectic attitudes toward design also led to the development of styles such as the JACOBETHAN, which combined Tudor, Elizabethan, Jacobean, and sometimes Gothic motifs. In the late 19th century the ARTS AND CRAFTS Movement challenged eclecticism, advocating a simpler, more purist approach in which ornament should be appropriate to function.

Ecuelle ■ A shallow, circular, silver or ceramic dish, used for individual soup servings. It had a flat handle on each side and a cover with a finial. Ecuelles were popular in France during the late 17th and 18th centuries. They were less common in the rest of Europe, although silver examples were made in England by refugee HUGUENOT craftsmen.

Edo period The Japanese period, named after Edo (the former name of Tokyo), extending from 1615 to the beginning of the MEIJI period in 1868. During this time, the production of PORCELAIN, LACQUER, and IVORY-carving flourished.

Edwards, John (1671–1746) An American silversmith active in Boston, Massachusetts, making domestic and church plate of simple design, similar to the work of Jeremiah DUMMER. Edward's pieces are extremely rare and may be marked with an "IE" or "IE and IA" in a QUATREFOIL (during his

association with the silversmith John Allen). Edwards began a dynasty of Boston silversmiths that included his sons, Samuel and Thomas, and grandson, Joseph.

Egermann, Friedrich ■ (1777–1864) A Bohemian glassmaker born in Blottendorf, Bohemia, who set up a glass factory in Haida (Novy Bor) and experimented with new types of colored glass from 1817. He successfully created a yellow STAIN in around 1820, a ruby red stain using copper oxide in 1832, as well as LITHYALIN glass in 1828. Ruby flash glassware bearing his name is still produced today in Novy Bor, in the Czech Republic.

Egg and dart An OVOLO molding, also called "egg and tongue," consisting of a repeating pattern of alternating egg and arrowhead shapes. One of the most commonly used Classical moldings, egg and dart featured on woodwork from the 16th century and was popular in the 18th century on NEOCLASSICAL furniture, and for moldings on Classical-style buildings.

Eggshell porcelain Thinly potted porcelain, first produced in the MING DYNASTY reign of Yongle (1403–24), sometimes with anhua decoration. Later produced in the QING DYNASTY (1644–1912), and from around 1900, mass-produced in Japan for export to the West. It was also made in Europe, notably at the BELLEEK PORCELAIN FACTORY, Ireland.

Pastoral decoration

Ecuelle
Dresden Empire style porcelain ecuelle, with cover and stand. Late 19th century.

Egermann, Frederich
Bohemian colored vase by Egermann. c. 1835.

Egyptian pottery
Egyptian terra-cotta, part of an anthropoid sarcophagus. c. 720–712 BCE.

Electroplate
Victorian electroplate on copper tea urn and cover.

Egyptian pottery ■ The Egyptian ceramics industry dates back some 8,000 years, when various regional wares were produced. Among these were the fine, burnished brown or red Badarian wares, from the late 5th millennium BCE, with simple ripple decoration and a black upper body. More lively decoration appeared soon after this period, including Amratian pottery, a red ware painted in white with trees and animals. From around 4000 BCE a light-colored ground stoneware known as Gerzean or Naqada II was produced. This was decorated in red and imitated pottery tomb vessels. These elegant ground stone vessels made of basalt, ALABASTER, or granite are unique to ancient Egypt. Highly polished red-brown Meydum bowls represent the best pottery of the Old Kingdom (2700–2200 BCE). In Roman Egypt the Egyptian faience technique was used for pottery known as "glazed quartz FRITWARE," colored with an intense turquoise blue. Fritware was revived by Islamic potters throughout the Middle East from the 12th century CE.

Elbow chair A 17th-century term initially used to identify the CARVER, armchair, or armchairs in a set of dining chairs, but which subsequently came to describe any type of chair with arms.

Electric clock A type of clock using electricity rather than a spring or weight to power the MOVEMENT. Pioneered by Alexander BAIN in the 1840s, electric clocks were originally developed as precision timekeepers, but in the early 20th century they were also produced for domestic use, one of the earliest being the BULLE CLOCK. Today the quartz-crystal clock is one of the most common electrically powered clocks.

Electroplate ■ A layer of metal (often gold or silver) chemically deposited by electrolysis onto any object (usually base metal) that will conduct electricity. For example, a copper pot can be placed in a solution of silver salts, and then a current passed through the pot and the liquid. The pot acts as the cathode and positively charged ions of silver in the solution migrate toward and adhere to it. The longer the process continues, the heavier the deposit of silver. Pioneered by George ELKINGTON, electroplating became commercially viable from 1840 and effectively put an end to the SHEFFIELD PLATE industry. One important advantage was that worn articles could be easily and inexpensively replated.

Electrotype A metal article, often copper (but can be other base metals or silver), reproduced from an original of which a mold is made. The mold is then used as a pattern, and by the action of prolonged electroplating, a replica metal object is built up or formed within the mold, faithfully reproducing the form and shape of the original article. The process was developed by several different people in

EGYPTIAN STYLE

Forms and motifs inspired by ancient Egyptian art and architecture informs the Egytian style. Typical motifs include hieroglyphs, winged GRIFFINS, PALMETTES, lotus leaves, SPHINXES, and OBELISKS. The vogue for Egyptian ornament reached its peak in the late 18th and early 19th centuries, as part of the REGENCY, EMPIRE, and FEDERAL styles.

Egyptian motifs

Fauteuil and stool
Empire fauteuil and stool by Jacob Freres, with front legs and arms carved like Egyptian sphinxes. c. 1800.

Vase
Unmarked lime green glass vase, in the style of Dr. Christopher Dresser, painted with Egyptian motif bands.

Polychrome and gilt decoration

Scarab pin
Egyptian Revival silver scarab pin with turquoise, purple, green, blue, and red enamel. 1920s.

Blue enamel

Egyptian cat
Royal Crown Derby porcelain Egyptian cat with original box. 1986.

the 1830s, and improved in the 1840s by George ELKINGTON.

Elephant motif ■ A motif that has been used as a symbol of sovereignty, wisdom, and moral and spiritual strength since ancient times. The elephant enjoyed an illustrious reputation in the cultures of Greece, India, Persia, and China, and is widely represented in the Hindu and Buddhist religions. The elephant features prominently in medieval decorative schemes and, along with other motifs with roots in the East, was adopted for Italian silk designs as early as the 13th century. The elephant's alternative role as a beast of burden is echoed in its decorative function as a support for furniture, clocks, and vases.

Elers Brothers, John and David Dutch potters who settled in Vauxhall, London, in 1688. They made red STONEWARE in London until 1693, then in Staffordshire, using a red clay that they sifted to make a fine body. SPRIGS of foliage and birds were made in engraved brass and copper molds and then applied to the body, in imitation of the Yi Hsing stoneware from China. Their workshop closed in 1698.

Elizabethan Revival ■ A style of architecture and decorative arts popular in England from the 1820s to the 1850s, reviving elements of the ELIZABETHAN style, often combined with TUDOR and JACOBEAN styles. Its popularity was reinforced by the association of Queen

Victoria's reign with that of Elizabeth I, due to economic prosperity and the expansion of maritime trade. Motifs such as STRAPWORK, GROTESQUES, and heraldry, as well as needlework upholstery and spiral TURNINGS, are characteristic of the Elizabethan style. A later revival took place in the 1920s and 30s, with furniture and fabrics made by LIBERTY & CO.

Elizabethan style The architecture and decorative arts dominant in England during the reign of Elizabeth I, from 1558 to 1603. It was essentially the last phase of the TUDOR style, although the Italian Renaissance style prevalent in the mid-16th century was to some extent supplanted by MANNERISM. Elizabethan style first appeared in the great country houses built during the late 16th century by the English nobility and gentry, featuring symmetrical facades and elaborate chimneys, friezes, and relief sculpture. In the decorative arts typical motifs included CHERUB heads, STRAPWORK, GROTESQUES, and ARABESQUES. Derived from French, Flemish, and German pattern books, including those by Virgil Solis, Hans Vredeman de Vries, Hans Brosamer, and Jacques Androuet du Cerceau, such motifs were also introduced by Protestant refugee craftsmen fleeing religious persecution on the Continent.

Elizabethan furniture is characterized by the use of oak and massive, heavy forms with ornate carving and large bulbous shapes modeled on silver cups and covers for bed posts, table legs, and supports

for cupboards. Some pieces feature MARQUETRY and INLAY of architectural perspectives and naturalistic ornament. All-over patterns of arabesques, fruits and flowers appear on needlework hangings, table covers, and other textiles. Similarly, silver, of which mainly ceremonial pieces such as ewers, cups, covers, and salt cellars have survived, was decorated with strapwork, animal heads and masks, naturalistic snails, fruits and flowers, arabesques, and grotesques. The Elizabethan style evolved into the JACOBEAN style at the start of the 17th century, during the reign of James I.

Elkington, George Richard ■ (1801–65) The founder of Elkington & Co. Ltd., a prominent English silversmithing and plating company. Elkington pioneered ELECTROPLATING in Britain and patented the process in 1840, also licensing it out to other manufacturers such as Charles CHRISTOFLE and James DIXON & Sons in 1848. After various partnerships, George Elkington built two large factories in Birmingham to handle the production of his silver and plated wares with the help and financial support of his partner, Josiah Mason. The firm adopted the name of Elkington, Mason & Co. in 1842. It had a London showroom and further expanded the business by making ornaments and perfecting its GILDING processes, with premises in London, Dublin, Liverpool, and Birmingham. The partnership with Mason ended in 1858, George died in 1865, and the firm continued as Elkington & Co.

Elephant motif
Doulton majolica jardiniere and stand, with elephant motifs. c. 1860.

Elizabethan revival
An Elizabethan style oak refectory table with anthemion frieze and bulbous cup and cover legs.

Foliate fret piercing

Elkington, George Richard
Edwardian inkstand, with two cut glass inkwells and pen depression. c. 1907.

with his partners and sons, Frederick, James Barclay, Alfred John, and Howard, at the helm.

The company was a great retailer, but also produced trade catalogs and vast quantities of silver and plated wares, from domestic flatware to ceremonial and display pieces, bronzes, enamels, and ornaments, and supplied to hotels and steamships as well as individuals. Elkington's employed numerous artists and designers, notably Léonard Morel-Ladeuil, Edward Welby PUGIN, and Christopher DRESSER. The firm was represented at most of the major exhibitions from 1840 to 1914, including the GREAT EXHIBITION of 1851 in London and that of 1855 in Paris. The company became limited in 1887 and continued until 1963, when it became a division of British Silverware Ltd.

Ellicott, John ■ (1706–72) Son of John Ellicott the elder, a maker of mirrors and clocks in London. Ellicott produced high-quality clocks and watches and became clockmaker to George III. He is best known today for his invention of a COMPENSATED PENDULUM in the mid-1750s, featuring a brass rod attached to an iron rod and

incorporating a system of levers. When the brass expands under heat, the levers are raised; when it contracts, they are lowered to compensate for the differing rate of expansion and contraction of iron. Expensive and complex to make, it was never as popular as the other types of pendulum.

Elm Various species of timber native to Europe and North America (now largely destroyed in the US and UK by Dutch elm disease) that provides a coarse-grained, light gingery brown hardwood. It was used for country furniture such as chairs and table tops. BURR elm was a popular veneer in the late 18th and early 19th centuries.

Elmslie, George Grant (1871–1952) A Scottish-born American architect and designer who studied with Frank Lloyd WRIGHT under the architect J. L. Silsbee, and later worked in partnership with the architects William Grey Purcell and George Feick Jr. It is thought that Elmslie was responsible for the decorative detail and interiors of their commissions, which included furniture, fixtures, and hardware.

Elton, Sir Edmund Harry ■ (1846–1920) An English ART POTTER who set up a pottery and kilns in Clevedon, Somerset. He is known for his vases decorated in relief, with

flowering branches covered with streaky gold, platinum, silver, and copper glazes.

Embossing ■ The decoration of metals (or leather) using hammers to bulge or force the material to one side. Popular from the late 1660s, embossing produces a raised (relief) or hollowed (incuse) three-dimensional pattern. The pattern is usually further enhanced by CHASING. As well as decoration, embossing adds strength and rigidity to what might otherwise be a plain, flimsy article. See REPOUSSÉ WORK.

Emerald ■ The green gem variety of beryl. It is found in several locations, but the most valuable deposits are the Muzo and Chivor mines of Colombia. The rarest stones are of a vibrant bluish green and the scarcity of INCLUSIONS increases the value considerably. Many modern emeralds are enhanced with artificial oils and resins.

Empire The Empire style spans Napoleon I's reign as consul (1799–1804) and emperor (1804–15) of France. It influenced the REGENCY style in England and dominated those countries of Europe where members of the Bonaparte family were the occupying rulers. It also spread to the US, where there was a strong sympathy with the French.

The Empire style can be seen as the last phase of NEOCLASSICISM, but it was more opulent and historically accurate. Napoleon modeled his vast empire on that of ancient Rome, and the style was inspired by

E

147

Ellicott, John
Longcase clock decorated with flora and fauna and mythological scenes. Signed Ellicott—London. c. 1745.

Elton, Sir Edmund Harry
Sunflower Pottery vase and cover, by Sir Edmund Elton, with gold craquelure glaze.

Embossing
An Arts and Crafts copper firescreen with embossed decoration of a masted ship. Late 19th century.

Emerald
Art Deco clips in white precious metal set with green emeralds and diamonds. c. 1930.

archaeological excavations in Greece, Italy, and Egypt. The architects Charles PERCIER and Pierre-Francois-Léonard FONTAINE established the style and Roman ornament was used in bronzework, carpets, furniture, silver, and ceramics. There was also a vogue for EGYPTIAN STYLE motifs inspired by Napoleon's campaigns in Egypt (1797–98). Furniture by François-Honoré-Georges JACOB-DESMALTER was based on Classical forms: X-CHAIRS, LITSEN-BÂTEAU, and TRIPOD TABLES with SABER LEGS, lion monopodia, and CARYATIDS as supports. Porcelain produced by SÈVRES was based on Neoclassical urns and vases but was heavier.

Despite Napoleon's fall from power in 1815, the Empire style persisted in Europe and was taken up by many Federal cabinet-makers, such as Duncan PHYFE in the US. In North America, from about 1800, the French Empire style became popular in the eastern states, due in part to the emigration of wealthy and fashionable French revolutionary exiles, including cabinet-makers and other craftspeople. New York City, Baltimore, and

especially, Philadelphia, were the main centers of French settlement, and Empire style furnishings remained popular into the early 1840s. The most ornate treatment appears on this type of furniture, which also saw an increase in gilding and the introduction of stenciled decoration. The French immigrant cabinet-maker Charles-Honore LANNUIER is considered the best exponent of this style.

American Empire style draws influence from contemporary French furniture, publications documenting archaeological discovery in the ancient world, and design journals, notably that of Thomas HOPE. New and popular forms included the KLISMOS chair. DOLPHINS, winged GRIFFINS, and SPHINXES adorn tables made by the best French immigrant and American furniture makers. Many are richly decorated with PARCEL GILDING, stenciling, and paint.

Enamel Often erroneously used to mean the opaque glaze applied to EARTHENWARE,

enamel correctly describes colored glass fused by heating in a furnace to create a design or decorative finish on a metallic surface. It can be produced in a broad spectrum of translucent or opaque colors and can be successfully used to imitate gemstones. There are many distinct enameling techniques: some, such as CLOISONNÉ, date back to 1400 BCE. GUILLOCHÉ ENAMEL was used extensively by FABERGÉ and CARTIER. PLIQUE À JOUR was much used by ART NOUVEAU goldsmiths. *En ronde bosse* (the opaque enameling of miniature objects or figures in high relief) was used in the Middle Ages. GRISAILLE enameling is executed in black and white, or shades of gray. *Enamel en resaille* is a rare type of enameling inlaid in glass. Painted enamel is a method of creating a picture similar to painting on canvas, but is usually executed on copper. In counter enamel, a coating of plain enamel on the reverse of a decorated enamel plaque was used to strengthen it during firing. This is often seen in Swiss enamel jewelry. See CHAMPLEVÉ and BASSE TAILLE.

EMPIRE

Characteristic forms and motifs of Empire style that identified Napoleon Bonaparte's France with Imperial Rome included wreaths, oak leaves, fasces, figures of Victory, eagles, and winged torches. Anthemion, palmettes, and stars were among other motifs also derived from Classical antiquity. Egyptian imagery such as scarabs, lotus flowers, and hieroglyphics, acknowledged Napoleon's North African campaign, while his personal emblem—the bee—signified a link with the early Frankish kings.

Candelabras
A pair of Empire gilt and patinated bronze candelabras, their stems winged and draped Classical maidens. Early 19th century.

Mantel clock
French Empire gilt bronze mantel clock with wheatsheaf, eagle, soldier, and weapon trophy motifs. Early 19th century.

Venus sculpture
A French gilt bronze figure, probably by Jacob Fréres of Paris. Early 19th century.

Enamel colors Vitreous onglaze ceramic pigments that fuse when fired at a relatively low temperature (700–900°C). They are also known as *petit feu* colors, as opposed to *grand feu*. The technique derives from China and the Middle East and was used in Europe by Venetian glassworkers in the 16th century. A full palette of colors was in use by the end of the 17th century. See HIGH-TEMPERATURE COLORS.

Enamel twist decoration Decoration used in wineglass stems, where threads of colored glass are incorporated in a twisted pattern within the colorless glass stem. The threads are usually white, but can include red or green, with blue and yellow being very rare; multicolored plaid twists are rarest.

Encaustic tile A tile with colored clay inlaid in a pattern within the body clay. The decoration is permanent even when the covering glaze has worn. The Cistercian monks produced them as paving tiles, but they are better known today from the mid-19th-century revival for use in fire-surrounds and floors.

Encoignure From the French *coin* (corner). A type of 18th-century corner cupboard on legs with graduated shelves. They evolved from triangular-shaped freestanding or hanging cupboards that fitted into the corner of a room. Probably first introduced in the early 17th century, encoignures were common by the late 17th century.

End board The solid board forming the end of a chest or the support (often shaped) for a bench or pre-17th-century stool made without legs.

End grain The grain that is revealed when a piece of wood is cut across rather than along the grain.

End support A general term used by furniture-makers to refer to an upright post or support.

End-of-the-day glass ■ An item made by a glassworker in his own time from the molten glass that was left in the pot at the end of the working day or week. Standard designs made by the glass factory can also be made under these circumstances, but usually differ in terms of color, proportions, or size. See FRIGGER.

Engine-turning A form of ENGRAVED decoration, notably geometric patterns such as circles, waves, or simple grooves, applied to metals and other materials by engraving while turning them on a lathe.

English cottage style A term used in the US to describe a style of interior design and architecture contemporary with Edwardian England (1901–10). It is a revival of the WILLIAM AND MARY style.

Engraving ■ 1. A technique for decorating glass and metal in which the design is cut with a sharp instrument such as a DIAMOND POINT or WHEEL to create an image in small dots or INTAGLIO or relief. See STIPPLE, HOCHSCHNITT. 2. A print made by cutting a picture into wood or metal (copper or steel), inking the plate, and pressing paper onto it. On wood, the print is in relief; on metal, in intaglio.

Entrée dish ■ A term now normally applied to silver and plated vegetable dishes with domed covers and handles. They were made in pairs or sets of four or more and could be square, circular, or oval. Late 18th-century dishes are far less common than 19th- and early 20th-century examples.

Entrelac ■ From the French *entrelacer* (to interlace). Interlaced tendril ornament of Celtic origin, primarily used in jewelry-making and revived by ARTS AND CRAFTS designers, including Walter CRANE and William MORRIS. *Entrelac* decoration also featured in ART NOUVEAU stone- and metalwork designs at the end of the 19th century, and in CELTIC REVIVAL designs.

Ephemera From the Greek *ephemeros* (lasting only a day). A term applied to all kinds of printed matter intended for immediate use and subsequent disposal. In packaging, the design and style can indicate the social attitudes, tastes, and style of design of a bygone age. Other ephemera includes tickets, matchbox labels, wine labels, trade cards, cigar labels, BROADSIDES, and shop

E

149

End-of-the-day glass
Czechoslovakian end-of-the-day glass flaring vase.

Engraving
Leather-lined Scottish drinking mug with engraved cartouche. 1767.

Entrée dish
Victorian sterling silver gilt covered entrée dish, by Paul Storr of London. 1838.

Entrelac
Enameled silver buckle, the ends with interwoven *entrelacs*. c. 1901.

window advertisements. Some collectors specialize in one area such as postage stamps, CIGARETTE CARDS, GREETINGS CARDS, and POSTCARDS. Some of the earliest wrappers and labels were fairly austere in design but soon became broadly pictorial with the advent of CHROMOLITHOGRAPHY. Collecting tends to be concentrated on items from the 19th and the 20th centuries.

EPNS An abbreviation for electroplated nickel silver and referring to any article made of a nickel base that is electroplated with silver. The initials "EPNS" are often stamped on such 20th-century articles. See ELECTROPLATING.

Equation dial See MEAN TIME.

Equinoctial dial ■ A horizontal SUNDIAL usable in all latitudes, made largely during the 18th century before being superseded by the CHRONOMETER. It is usually octagonal, with a central compass and a hinged, curved arm rising up on one

side marked with degrees of latitude. A hinged ring bearing the GNOMON is marked with the hours and slides up and down the curved arm, depending on the latitude of the user. The latitudes of certain cities are often inscribed on the back to help the user set the dial correctly.

Escapement A mechanical device regulating the motive power from the weights, spring, electric current, or other power source of the MOVEMENT in a clock or watch. The simplest form of escapement comprises a toothed wheel and an arm with a pallet (a catch) at either end; the wheel is positioned so that only one tooth "escapes" at a time. Early clocks were fitted with a VERGE escapement, but the introduction of the ANCHOR ESCAPEMENT in the late 17th century, used in conjunction with the PENDULUM, dramatically improved the accuracy of timekeeping.

Escritoire ■ A French term for a type of writing desk or SECRÉTAIRE made

from the 16th century. A vertical FALL FRONT writing surface is hinged at the bottom, so that it opens to provide the writing surface, and folds up when not in use. The earliest portable writing boxes were called escritoires, but the closest relative is the 16th-century Spanish VARGUEÑO.

Escutcheon 1. In heraldry, either a shield bearing a coat-of-arms or a similar shield-shaped ornament. 2. A metal plate (often brass, and sometimes elaborately shaped) surrounding and protecting the edges of a keyhole in a door or a piece of furniture.

Esherick, Wharton ■ (1887–1970) An American craftsman and sculptor, working in Paoli, Pennsylvania, who kept the craft tradition alive in postwar America. He began as a painter, but abandoned this in 1924 to make furniture. His MODERN style is typified by sinuous, organic lines with a sculptor's eye for space and form, using traditional techniques and skills.

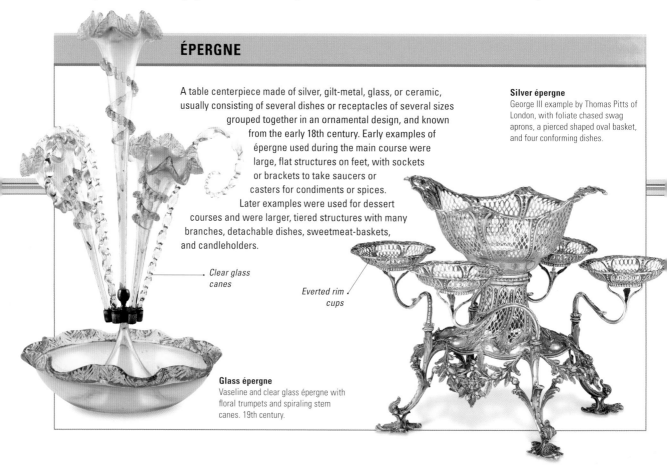

ÉPERGNE

A table centerpiece made of silver, gilt-metal, glass, or ceramic, usually consisting of several dishes or receptacles of several sizes grouped together in an ornamental design, and known from the early 18th century. Early examples of épergne used during the main course were large, flat structures on feet, with sockets or brackets to take saucers or casters for condiments or spices. Later examples were used for dessert courses and were larger, tiered structures with many branches, detachable dishes, sweetmeat-baskets, and candleholders.

Silver épergne
George III example by Thomas Pitts of London, with foliate chased swag aprons, a pierced shaped oval basket, and four conforming dishes.

Clear glass canes

Everted rim cups

Glass épergne
Vaseline and clear glass épergne with floral trumpets and spiraling stem canes. 19th century.

Espagnolette The term for a female mask surrounded by a large, stiff, lace collar, which may have been of Mexican origin. A popular French decorative motif in the 18th century, the espagnolette was widely used by furniture designers during the RÉGENCE and the Louis XV period, featuring in the designs of Daniel MAROT, Claude AUDRAN, Jean BÉRAIN, and Jean-Antoine Watteau, as well as in Boullework.

Estampille The French term for the mark struck with a cold iron stamp on French furniture. The intaglio impression carried the maker's name or monogram, and was compulsory on furniture made by Parisian MENUISIERS-ÉBÉNISTES from 1751 to 1791; pieces made for the Royal household were exempt.

Este pottery Founded in Este, near Venice, in around 1779 by a French modeler, Jean-Pierre Varion, who had worked at VINCENNES with Gerolamo Francini. The partnership was later dissolved. Varion began to manufacture porcelain, but he died in 1780 and the business was continued by his wife. No tableware has been identified, but the figures are of fine quality. These were modeled by Varion and made after his death. Francini went on to make CREAMWARE.

Étagère A 19th-century French term describing free-standing shelves in two

ETRUSCAN

Human figures and animal imagery, both real and mythological, recur in Etruscan ornament, and range from lions and birds, to chimeras, griffins, and sphinxes. Equally prevalent, however, are plant forms such as husks and festoons, as well as tripods, urns, and medallions.

Charger
An Elkington brass electroform charger. Late 19th century.

Spherical above spiraling and conical forms

Centerpiece
Royal Worcester potpourri centerpiece, of Etruscan shape. 1895.

Earrings
A pair of Victorian Etruscan-revival earrings fashioned in gold and gold wire. c. 1860.

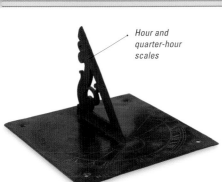

Hour and quarter-hour scales

Equinoctial dial
English Charles I bronze square equinoctial sundial, initialed "E.R." c. 1628.

Escritoire
French rosewood and kingwood escritoire. c. 1880.

Esherick, Wharton
Walnut console table by Wharton Esherick, with a carved cipher. 1952.

E

or three tiers, either square or rectangular, supported by corner posts or upright members. Similar to the English and American whatnot, the *étagère* was also used to serve food.

Etching See ACID ETCHING.

Etling ■ La Societé Anonyme Edmond Etling & Cie was founded in Paris by Edmond Etling shortly after World War I, selling OPALESCENT PRESSED glass made at the Choisy-Le-Roi glassworks outside Paris. A number of designers, including Lucille Sevin, Genevieve Grainger, George Beal, and the Hungarian sculptor Geza Hiecz produced designs that focused on dishes, bowl, vases, and figurines. All were in the ART DECO style and bear strong resemblances to glass made by René LALIQUE. Pieces are usually marked "Etling France" and production ceased with the outbreak of World War II.

Etruria pottery See WEDGWOOD.

Etruscan maiolica See MAIOLICA.

Etruscan style The decorative arts and interior decoration inspired by the discovery of ancient Etruscan and Greek artifacts in the late 18th century. Part of the NEOCLASSICAL STYLE, it is characterized by the use of a palette of terra-cotta and black and white, and motifs such as PALMETTES and ANTHEMIA found on late Classical Greek figure vases, which at the time were thought to be Etruscan. The most notable example of the style is the Etruscan Room (1775) at Osterley Park in Middlesex, designed by Robert ADAM. In the 1870s there was a vogue for historically accurate adaptations of Etruscan gold jewelry, featuring GRANULATION and WIREWORK decoration.

Étui ■ A pocket-sized case dating from the 18th to the 19th century, made of silver, gold, enamel, gilt metal, tortoiseshell, or lacquer. They were usually of tapering, rectangular form with a hinged cover and a button catch, equipped inside to contain various small useful articles such as lancets, writing sets, scent bottles, sewing accessories, or knife, fork, and spoon sets. They could be carried hung by a chain from a CHATELAINE.

Everted ■ A term designating an outwardly turned or flaring shape. It is most frequently used to describe the lip of a jug, pitcher, or sauceboat, or the rim of a vessel made from ceramic or glass.

Ewer ■ A large jug or pitcher with a wide mouth. The word originates from the 14th-century French word *évier*. They were made in many materials, including metal, glass, earthenware, and porcelain. Originally used for carrying water for washing hands, the occupation of "ewerer," a servant who supplied guests with water for that purpose, is derived from it.

Excelsior A material made of wood shavings, similar in appearance to straw, and used as a stuffing in TEDDY BEARS and some other stuffed toys.

Export porcelain See CHINESE EXPORT PORCELAIN.

Eye motif A decorative device (and a symbol of protection) originating in ancient Egypt. For the ancient Greeks the eye was a good luck charm. In Christian iconography it features in emblem books representing the eye of God and it is often depicted as the focus of a triangle symbolizing the Holy Trinity. In both American and French Revolutionary ornament, the eye symbolizes enlightenment. It was also an 18th-century term designating the center of a VOLUTE SCROLL in the Ionic Order.

Eye-and-scale motif An American term for coin molding, a repeating pattern of overlapping disck, used horizontally or vertically, primarily on massive Classical styles. Coin molding is known as "eye-and-scale" when used to describe mold-blown or pressed glass.

Etling
Editions Etling Marcell Guillard earthenware figure, modeled as a Gascony Duck.

Gilt sewing accessories

Étui
South Staffordshire enamel *étui*. c. 1770.

Everted
A George III silver mug, its straight tapering sides with everted rim and slightly spreading base. c. 1775.

Ewer
Italian majolica ewer. 20th century.

F

Facet A type of decoration used on glass and jewelry, consisting of a series of shallow cuts in the manner of a cut diamond, creating sharp edges that reflect the light. Facet-cut stems were first used on English wineglasses from around 1745–1750 and remained popular until the end of the century.

Façon de Venise ■ A French term for "in the Venetian style." It referred to glassware made in the Venetian manner in other parts of Europe, often by emigrant Venetian glassmakers, from the mid-16th century and throughout the 17th century. The overall appearance of this glass was lightweight and often flamboyant and it was the dominant style of glassmaking during this period.

Faenza potteries This influential Italian center of MAIOLICA production probably started in the 13th century with the manufacture of lead-glazed pottery and was well established by 1450. The early wares used green and purple colors, as seen in Orvieto ware, with human and animal figures and heraldic monsters against hatched backgrounds. This style was followed by one dominated by blue where many motifs of Middle Eastern origin were used. Gothic foliage characterized by bold leaves in manganese, orange, and a strong blue, and peacock feathers, were also used to form borders and all-over diapers. After 1500 the products became more distinctive: one workshop was called Casa Pirota and had a motif of a *pyros rota* (fire bomb), a rebus on the family name. Early in the 16th century pictorial painting was introduced and gave rise to the ISTORIATO style. Large dishes and ALBARELLI were made, the latter with borders of foliage and the labels in Gothic letters. Some wares directly copied Chinese MING porcelain and were called "alla porcellana." The Casa Pirota painted wares in opaque white on a pale blue ground were called *herettino*. The artists of early Faenza are mostly unknown, but from about 1530, when the istoriato style was copied from URBINO, the artists Baldassare Manara, Giovanni B. dale Falle, and Francisco Mezzarisa are known. From 1600 to 1675 the industry was in decline but revived in 1693 when Count Annibale Ferniani bought the main workshop. The Ferniani factory survived into the 20th century.

FABERGÉ, CARL

Son of Gustav Fabergé, a St. Petersburg goldsmith of HUGUENOT descent, Carl Fabergé (1846–1920) took over the family business in 1870 on returning to Russia, after serving an apprenticeship in Frankfurt, Germany. He won the Gold Medal at the Pan-Russian Exhibition of 1882 and swiftly gained a reputation for his jewelry and *objets d'art*, combining the very highest artistic flair with minute attention to detail. He came to the notice of the Imperial Court and

Nephrite elephant
Carved nephrite elephant by Fabergé, with rose-cut diamond eyes. c. 1910.

was commissioned to make the first Easter Egg by Czar Alexander III in 1884. Over the next 30 years he won the patronage of numerous royal houses and established shops in several Russian cities as well as in London. In 1917 the Revolution ended the Romanov dynasty and Fabergé's demise paralleled that of his patron, the czar. He fled Russia in 1918 and died in Lausanne, Switzerland. Fabergé's incomparable skill as a master craftsman was matched by the progressive methods he adopted to run his business. He had a team of workmasters, each with his or her own individual specialty and responsibility. Although best known for the 57 Imperial Eggs, they created hardstone carvings, flower studies, silver jewelry as well as functional boxes, bellpushes, and frames. Fabergé achieved a level of competence in enameling and goldsmithing unlikely ever to be surpassed.

Cigarette case
Gold case with a medallion decoration enclosing a diamond Czar Nicholas II monogram. 1903.

Façon de Venice
Southern Dutch *Façon de Venice* wine glass. Late 17th century.

Faience A French term for tin-glazed earthenware popular in Europe in the 16th and 17th centuries. Faience was used as a general term from around 1610 and probably derived its name from the town of Faenza in Italy. The German word for faience is *fayence*. Faience was lightly baked earthenware of a buff or pale red color, covered with white enamel or glaze, which gives it the appearance of porcelain. There are two kinds of faience: *faience blanche*, which was only lightly decorated, if at all, and *grand feu*, painted in high temperature colors from metallic oxides—blue, purple, yellow, orange-red, green, and sometimes red. *Grand feu* colors are painted onto the unfired glaze, the colors melting into the glaze in the firing. In around 1750 *petit feu* colors were developed in France. These were brighter and included pink, crimson, and vermilion. With *petit feu*, the glaze was fired and painted on, then fired again at a lower temperature. Faience was used for making table services but also for garden pots. The industry was widespread in France, the chief centers being Aprey, Lyons, Luneville, Marseilles, Montpellier, Moustiers, Nevers, Rouen, Sceaux, and Strasbourg. The industry reached its peak in France in the first three-quarters of the 18th century and then declined due to porcelain and CREAMWARE imports, although it has survived in many provincial areas, particularly QUIMPER.

Fairing ■ A small porcelain figure or, more often, a group, made in eastern Germany, mostly by Conta & Boehme of Possneck.

Fairings were given as prizes or bought cheaply at fairs. They are usually amusing and may have some sexual innuendo.

Fairy lamp A small 19th-century glass, porcelain, or colored glass night light holding a slow-burning candle. The term comes from the trademark of Samuel Clarke, the most prolific British maker. It also refers to the small electric Christmas tree lights descended from votive candles.

Fairyland Lustre The designs by Daisy Makeig Jones when she was working at WEDGWOOD in the 1920s. Painted and printed in gold, they portrayed fairies, goblins, and pixies in magical landscapes. The patterns are numbered and prefixed with a "Z." Rarely, they bear the initials of Miss Jones.

Falize, Alexis (1811–98) A Parisian jewelry-maker who, along with his son, Lucien, specialized in colorful CLOISONNÉ enameling with a strong Japanese influence. His designs were also inspired by historical styles, including medieval, Renaissance, and Rococo. Lucien Falize went into partnership with Germain Bapst from 1880 to 1892 and favored jewels of neo-Renaissance or Persian design.

Fall front ■ The straight front flap (also called drop front) of a bureau, cabinet, or desk that is hinged at the bottom and opens or falls toward the sitter to form a horizontal writing surface.

False plate A sheet or cast-iron plate set between the dial and MOVEMENT on some LONGCASE CLOCKS with painted iron dials. They were introduced with mass-produced painted iron dials in the 19th century and had holes for attaching the dial to the movement.

Famille jaune, noire, rose, verte ■ Terms used to classify Chinese porcelain by its color palette. *Famille verte*, adopted in the KANG XI reign (1662–1722), uses green and iron red with other overglaze colors. It developed from the WUCAI style. *Famille jaune* is a variation, using *famille verte* enamels on a yellow ground. *Famille noire* uses *famille verte* enamels on a black ground, although some CLOBBERED WARES had the black added in the 19th century. *Famille rose*, introduced around 1720, used mainly pink or purple and remained popular throughout the 18th and 19th centuries. See CHINESE EXPORT PORCELAIN, CANTON PORCELAIN.

Fans ■ Fans were used in China and Japan for centuries before they permeated Western culture through trade. By the 17th century fans were made in Europe as well as imported. They were status symbols and combined function (cooling) with aesthetics. The earliest fans were fixed open, usually with a central stick, made from luxury materials such as ivory and tortoiseshell, carved and decorated with precious metals or stones. Leaves were made of silk or paper, often printed or painted with pastoral or social scenes.

Fairing
"Long pull and a strong pull" dentist's chair fairing.

Fall front
Rosewood and mahogany secretaire with fall front from the 1925 Paris Exhibition.

Famille noir
Large Chinese Kangxi period *famille noir* vase, with six-character Chenghua mark.

Chinese figures in a rural landscape
Famille rose
Qianlong large Chinese *famille rose* bowl.

Farnell & Co. An English toy and doll manufacturer founded by John Farnell in Notting Hill, London, in 1840. Farnell was producing rabbitskin-covered soft toys by 1897 and claimed to be the first English firm to have made MOHAIR PLUSH TEDDY BEARS. In 1921 Farnell took up the Alpha trademark for its fine-quality bears. It is said that A. A. Milne's character, Winnie the Pooh, was based on a Farnell bear given to his son, Christopher Robin. Farnell bears had plump bodies and long, plump limbs, and are often referred to as the English Steiff due to their similarity in terms of form and quality. The factory closed in 1968.

Fasces A latin term for "bundles." A bound bundle of rods, often incorporating the head of an ax, the emblem of authority of the magistrates in ancient Rome. The *fasces* was an important motif in furniture decoration in the EMPIRE style and reappeared in the first decade of the 20th century.

Fashion doll A bisque or occasionally CHINA HEAD DOLL (also called Parisienne), mainly produced in France between 1860 and 1890, usually with kid leather bodies. They represent fashionably dressed young ladies rather than babies. Clothes are intricately made and elaborate, and an entire street in Paris was once devoted to selling the latest fashions for these dolls. Notable makers included Huret, Jumeau, Bru, and Gaultier.

Fauteuil ■ The French term for an upholstered open armchair.

Faux bois A French term for "fake wood." It is used to denote cheaper, plainer softwood, painted to look like a more expensive, attractively figured or colored hardwood.

Favrile glass A corruption of *fabrile*, the old English word for "handmade." A form of IRIDESCENT glass developed by Louis C. TIFFANY, patented in 1894, and used for a range of ART NOUVEAU glassware, most notably decorative vases in organic plant and flowerlike shapes. The level and tone of the iridescence, which was sprayed on, is determined by the choice, tone, and thickness of the underlying colored glass. Blue and gold tend to be the most common, with trailed or other applied or worked patterns being rarer.

Fazackerley A style of floral painting on English delft, the name was probably derived from two LIVERPOOL POTTERY ware mugs painted with the names of Thomas and Catherine Fazackerley that were destroyed during World War II. However, "Fazackerley colors" came to mean bright enamel colors that were used to decorate plates, punch bowls, flower bricks, and bowls with flowers and foliage.

Fazzoletto ■ An Italian term for a vase that looks like a handkerchief. They were designed by Fulvio BIANCONI and Paolo VENINI from 1948 to 1949 and were initially made at the Venini glassworks on MURANO. Since then, other Muranese glass factories have copied the design. Fazzoletto can be found in many bright colors and patterns typical of mid-20th-century Italian glass design. Authentic Venini examples are identified from an acid-etched mark on the base and a delicacy of form and design.

Feather banding See HERRINGBONE BANDING.

Feather-edge A silver and plated FLATWARE pattern (also used on porcelain knife handles). This variant of the Old English pattern is distinguished by an engraved narrow border of diagonal feather-like cuts. First made in England around 1765, this pattern is still produced today.

Feathery The name given to a golf ball made from the early 17th century from compressed, boiled feathers, tightly and densely packed inside a stitched leather orb. When the damp feathers dried the ball became hard and tight. Time-consuming and expensive to make, they were replaced by the GUTTIE in the 1840s.

Feathers motif The emblem adopted for the Prince of Wales in England from the 14th century. By the early 18th century it was widely used, without any heraldic significance, as an ornamental cresting on mirrors and featured in the designs of Daniel MAROT and Jean BERAIN. During the Adam period, feathers appeared on capitals in Classical-style interiors. In the 19th century the feather emblem was fashionable for chairs, tables, pediments, bookcases, and beds.

Famille verte
Kangxi large *famille verte* dish with dragon. c. 1690.

Fan
Ivory fan decorated with muses. c. 1750.

Fauteuil
One of a pair of Louis XVI fauteuils, signed "Nicolas-Quinibert Foliot, Paris." c. 1775.

Fazzoletto
Venini & Ci. Fazzoletto (handkerchief) vase by Fulvio Bianconi. c. 1950.

F

Featherwork ■ The use of colored feathers as decoration originated in Oceania and Pre-Columbian America where exotic bird feathers adorned clothes and textiles. It reached the height of its use in Aztec Mexico, and was later used in the 18th and 19th centuries in Europe for textiles and domestic pieces; some feathers were dyed to add color.

Federal style ■ This Neoclassical style from the US began in the 1780s and lasted until the dwindling of Neoclassical taste in the 1830s. The best Federal style captures the elements of confidence and prosperity felt in the newly formed United States.

This style emerged after independence from Great Britain and the establishment of the first Federal government under George Washington in 1789. The importance of the NEOCLASSICAL style to the dignity of the recently united country is seen in the government buildings of the day, notably the White House in Washington, DC.

The Federal style was heavily inspired by British taste, particularly in the realm of furniture design. The architectural concepts of Robert ADAM are the foundation of most Neoclassical design of this period. However, it was the popularizers of Adam who were widely read and interpreted in the US. The publications of the English designers George HEPPLEWHITE, Thomas Shearer, and Thomas SHERATON were the most influential works and some Federal cabinet-makers copied them closely. American designers were also inspired by

contemporary discoveries of the ancient world, particularly Pompeii. Culturally, the new American republic identified closely with ancient Rome and with post-revolutionary France.

Federal cabinet-makers developed new forms. Bookcases and desks were combined into one piece, called a SECRETARY, which replaced the earlier slant-front desk or bureau bookcase form. A classic Federal mirror form is the circular wall mirror with wide OGEE-molded frame, holding a convex "bull's-eye" glass. Such mirrors often have patriotic and heraldic eagle mounts.

Among the best-known and most sought-after Federal cabinet-makers in the British tradition are Benjamin Randolph of Philadelphia, John and Thomas Seymour of Boston, and Duncan PHYFE of New York, who later also adopted the French style.

Feilner, Simon (1726–98) A German porcelain modeler, born in Weiden. He worked as a stuccoist and painter at Schloss Saarbrucken and then as a flower painter, decorator, and modeler at HÖHST. In 1753 he went to FÜRSTENBERG and in 1770 to FRANKENTHAL as a modeler and ARCANIST, later becoming a director. He is known for his COMMEDIA DELL'ARTE and Classical figures and miners.

Feldspar A crystalline mineral derived from granite, used as one of the fusible ingredients of PORCELAIN or as a FLUX.

Feldspathic glaze A glaze containing a high (50–100) percentage of FELDSPAR. The term is also used for a glaze that, while containing less then 50 percent of feldspar, is compounded of minerals that create an artificial feldspar.

Fell, Isaac (1758–1818) An American furniture-maker, active in Savannah from about 1780. Fell worked mainly in mahogany, making furniture in the English taste, but his work is considered more provincial than contemporary pieces from the northeastern states.

Felt doll A type of doll mainly produced between 1920 and 1940 by manufacturers such as LENCI, STEIFF, CHAD VALLEY, and Norah WELLINGS. The felt used for the doll's face was usually molded over a buckram base to enhance longevity. Facial features were typically painted or sewn on and fingers could be delineated by stitching.

Fender ■ A low metal screen used since the 17th century to prevent coals from rolling from the hearth into the room.

Fern ■ A popular motif in the late 19th century when ferns were avidly collected and used to decorate cast-iron garden furniture and architectural features such as column capitals. In keeping with the contemporary taste for heavy and extravagant forms drawn from nature, fern patterns were also favored as decoration for glass, textiles, and ceramics.

Featherwork
Inca panel with blue, yellow, and orange feathers on a plain cotton. c. 550–590 CE.

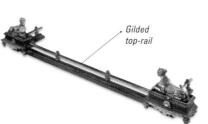

Gilded top-rail

Fender
Cast-iron and gilt-metal fender, each end with a figure of the sphinx. 19th century.

Fern
Coalbrookdale-style "fern and berry" pattern cast-iron garden bench.

FEDERAL STYLE

Federal furniture is distinguished from British furniture by its scale, which is usually a little grander, its regional stylistic variety, details such as carving or inlay, construction techniques (which are less uniform), and materials. MAPLE, a pale wood indigenous to North America, was used as an alternative to satinwood for inlay or contrast—on drawer-fronts, for example.

Vase-shaped backsplat

Painting
Scene of a woman seated in a Federal interior; oil on canvas.

Federal style furnishings

Armchair
Federal Portsmouth carved mahogany and flame-birch veneer armchair, attributed to Langley Boardman.

Andirons
Pair of Federal Philadelphia brass andirons. c. 1810.

Clock
Mahogany pillar and scroll clock, by Seth Thomas. c. 1810.

Cherrywood casing

Chest-of-drawers
Federal inlaid mahogany bow-front chest-of-drawers, from the Southern States. c. 1810.

Side chair
Federal Philadelphia carved mahogany side chair. c. 1790.

Case clock
Federal cherry tall case clock. c. 1805–1810.

F

Ferronnerie The French term for "wrought ironwork." Scrolling patterns of arabesques and volutes, derived from *ferronneries*, were used to decorate 16th-century tin-glazed ceramics from Antwerp. It was also used on faience from Moustiers, Strasbourg, and Rouen dating to the 17th and early 18th centuries. A number of designs by Jean BÉRAIN include *ferronneries*.

Festoon ◼ Ornament in the form of a garland of fruit and flowers, tied with ribbons and leaves and suspended in a loop from both ends. Originating in the temple decorations of Classical Rome, festoons spread during the Renaissance, sometimes embellished with rings, rosettes, lion masks, and putti. Festoons were frequently also enriched with vegetables and shells in the 16th and 17th centuries. The taste for lavishly chased and embossed SWAGS on silver vessels complemented the extravagant BAROQUE festoons carved for furniture and interiors in the 17th century. Although the festoon fell from favor early in the 18th century as the fashion for elaborate, heavily carved decoration waned, it reemerged in a lighter style in the NEOCLASSICAL period in the designs of Robert ADAM and remained a popular decorative motif well into the 19th century.

Fiddle pattern Silver and plated FLATWARE, so named because the stems of spoons and forks resemble the shape of a violin or fiddle. Popular in 18th-century France, this pattern appeared in England around 1740 and became one of the most well known, with a popular variant called the "fiddle, thread, and shell" pattern.

Fielded panel A framed or enclosed flat panel, usually wooden, that is raised above its surround, and can be decorated or left plain.

Figuring The natural markings and graining found on wood that make a decorative pattern.

Filigrana ◼ An Italian term for transparent glass decorated with embedded thin threads of opaque white or colored glass in a twisted or other pattern. The technique was first used in Murano, Italy, in the second quarter of the 16th century and flourished there until the 18th century. It was revived by MURANO glasshouses in the mid-20th century.

Filigree ◼ Ornamental work of twisted gold and silver wire, soldered into openwork forms or two-dimensional panels. It was used as decoration or in articles like small caskets, trays, frames, and *objets de vertu*. This extremely delicate art form was popular throughout Europe in the late 17th century and enjoyed sporadic comebacks during the 19th and 20th centuries.

Filigree glass The English term for FILIGRANA. A clear glass piece decorated with a fine network of white or colored threads in a variety of complex patterns.

Fillet A narrow band or strip of wood, found between moldings or used as an inlaid STRING.

Finial ◼ A decorative turned or carved ornament surmounting a prominent terminal, generally taking the form of an acorn, pine cone, or urn, although frequently much more elaborate. Finials appear on furniture from the 15th century on the uprights of chairs, bed testers, and cabinet cornices, and on the covers of silver, pottery, porcelain, or glass vessels, where they often double as handles to the tops. See KNOP.

Firangi A North Indian term for "foreigner" used to refer to an Indian sword with either an imported European blade or one made in the European style. These swords were principally used in the Maratha empire from the late 16th century.

Fire gilding See MERCURY GILDING.

Fire polishing Also known as flame polishing, it involves a process of reheating a finished glass object in the GLORY HOLE to give the surface a smooth, lustrous, and glossy finish. Marks left on the surface through the use of tools or molds may also be reduced this way.

Fire-back A heavy arched cast- or wrought-iron panel set at the back of a fireplace. It was used partly for decoration, partly as an aid to retain and radiate the heat of the fire and also to shield the wall

Oak garland festoon

Festoon
Detail of George II carved gesso console table.

Filigrana
Aureliano Toso vase, *"mezza filigrana bianca nera,"* by Dino Martens. c. 1954.

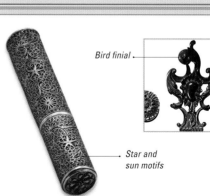

Star and sun motifs

Filigree
Tubular bodkin needle case, with floral filigree against a gilt ground. c. 1800–20.

Bird finial

Finial
Philadelphia Chippendale-style bonnet-top high chest-of-drawers. Late 19th century.

from excess heat damage. Made from the 16th century, fire-backs are often decorated with heraldic or religious devices, foliage, figures, or mythological scenes in low relief. Late 16th- and early 17th-century examples are particularly decorative, often cast in relief with figures, coats of arms, and dates. They were superseded in the early 18th century by one-piece fireplace grates.

Fire-dog See ANDIRON.

Fire screen ■ A portable device used to screen people from the excessive heat of an open fire. Used from the Middle Ages and until the demise of the open fire as the main form of heating, fire screens were made in a variety of forms, usually consisting of a portable wooden support and frame, sometimes carved or painted and gilded, with a fixed or adjustable panel made of needlework, tapestry, leather, or scrapwork. See POLE SCREEN.

Firing The process of heat treatment of ceramic ware and enamels on glass in a kiln or oven to develop a vitreous or crystalline bond. The temperature required ranges from about 1,470°F (800°C) for earthenware to about 2,640°F (1,450°C) for porcelain. The achievement of sufficiently high temperatures for firing was a major factor in the development of true porcelain.

Firing glass A short-stemmed sturdy DRAM glass with a thick foot, and sometimes engraved with Masonic symbols. Made from the mid-18th century onward, such glasses were traditionally rapped on the table after a toast and sounded like muskets firing, hence the name.

Fish slice ■ A silver or plated serving trowel or slice, usually with a single blade on one side. Designed during the 18th century for serving fish, it later became a common serving piece in most CANTEENS.

Fitzhugh pattern ■ An elaborate border pattern on CHINESE EXPORT PORCELAIN of butterflies, finger citron (a East Asian fruit resembling a hand), flowers, foliage, and cell DIAPER, usually in underglaze blue, but also in bright green, brown, and orange, popular with the American market from around 1790 to 1810. It was named after Thomas Fitzhugh, a director of the EAST INDIA COMPANY, who ordered a service in around 1780. The pattern was taken up by the CAUGHLEY and COALPORT factories.

Fitzroy barometer Designed by and named after Admiral Robert Fitzroy, a British meteorologist who introduced daily weather forecasts in *The Times* in 1860. Devised around 1860, they typically comprise a barometer, thermometer, and storm glass containing chemicals that change with atmospheric conditions. Readings are taken from a detailed paper

backing printed with Fitzroy's weather predictions. They are usually set in carved and glazed rectangular wooden cases.

Five-dial barometer See BANJO BAROMETER.

Fixed eyes Enameled or glass eyes set in a doll's head and held in a rigid position.

Flagg, James Montgomery ■ (1877–1960) An American illustrator, poster artist, and portrait painter, famous for his World War I recruitment poster of Uncle Sam with the caption "I Want You." He designed many film posters, including *Lost Horizon* (1937), and covers for magazines.

Flagon A tall, often narrow cylindrical vessel, similar to a tankard. It was used from the 16th century for serving beer, usually with a molded foot, flat or domed lid, a lip, a large curving handle, and thumbpiece. Flagons were generally made of pewter, stoneware, or ceramics, although silver examples, often former ecclesiastical ones, also survive.

Flambé glaze A high-fired glaze (2,190°F/1,200°C), which may flow in the kiln, giving rise to flamelike streaks of purple or blue in Chinese wares, for example, SANG DE BOEUF, and in some modern pottery.

Flamboyant Gothic A variant of the Gothic style in medieval architecture and the decorative arts, characterized by

Fire screen
Large Victorian rosewood fire screen.

Monogrammed handle

Fish slice
Silver fish slice, made in London by M. Chawmer. 1828.

Fitzhugh pattern
Chinese export porcelain orange Fitzhugh dish, with American eagle decoration.

Flagg, James Montgomery
"I Want You for US Army" recruitment poster, by James Montgomery Flagg. 1917.

F

160

elaborate flamelike branching tracery. It is found mainly in 15th-century metalwork, decorated with detailed naturalistic foliage, arches, crockets, frets, and bosses.

Flame stitch See BARGELLO.

Flame veneer A technique in which a veneer is cut at an angle to produce a swirling, flamelike FIGURING.

Flanders See FLEMISH LACE.

Flange A collar or rim that strengthens an object or is used to attach it to another object.

Flange neck See SOCKET HEAD.

Flashed glass or Flashing ■ A technique whereby a usually clear and colorless glass body is covered with a thin layer of colored glass or vitreous stain. This is different from CASED GLASS, as the layer is thinner and is created by dipping the body into molten colored glass to coat it lightly. The clear glass body may also be coated with powdered colored glass, which, when melted, creates the same effect. As the layer of colored glass is so thin, it can be easily cut, engraved, or etched away to reveal the underlying colorless glass, therefore creating a contrasting color pattern. Both flashing and subsequent cutting were commonly used in

BOHEMIAN GLASS,
particularly in the
19th century.

Flashed glass
Two-color Bohemian stained flashed goblet and cover. c. 1850.

Flat (toy) A thin, cast-lead figure with one or both sides molded in relief. Flats originated in Germany and became popular in the 19th century, particularly in the form of soldiers. Usually handpainted, flats continued to be produced until the 1920s and are still made today as souvenirs. The principal maker was Ernst Heinrichsen, and his figures are the most collectible today. Color-printed cardstock was also used from the mid-19th to the early 20th century, and plastic was used in the 1960s.

Flat chasing A form of CHASING on the flat surfaces of silver articles such as the center of a salver. It was in widespread use from the late 17th to the early 19th century.

Flatback ■ A Staffordshire pottery figure or group made by various potters in the 19th century. They were made flat so that they could stand against the wall on the mantelshelf, and were painted in bright colors on the front but left white on the back to cut costs.

Flatware The term for all flat articles of tableware such as plates, except those with a cutting edge (knives). Other tableware may be called HOLLOWWARE.

Flatweave A pile-less rug or carpet, like KILIMS, SOUMAKS, Verneh, SILEH, and Indian DHURRIES, woven with a tapestry technique. Their name depends on where and how they are made.

Flatback
Staffordshire flatback figural group of "Samson and the Lion." 19th century.

Flaxman, John (1755–1826) The leading English Neoclassical modeler and sculptor. His father worked for WEDGWOOD and John worked for them as a modeler from 1775. He modeled friezes of Classical scenes such as *The Muses* (1777) and *Hercules in the Garden of the Hesperides* (1787), as well as relief portraits of many contemporary notables. Wedgwood sponsored Flaxman to study fine art in Rome from 1787 to 1794, although, while there, he continued to supply Wedgwood with designs for JASPER WARE and BASALT WARE. Later he worked mostly as a marble sculptor and also made models in silver.

Flecked glass ■ Glass with flecks of opaque glass, bonded to or embedded in its surface. It is made by rolling a glass body over colored glass chips, which adhere to the hot surface. Made since Roman times, the best-known examples were made in England in the late 18th and early 19th centuries, when the technique was used to make a range of inexpensive novelties. Interesting variations were also made in Europe and the US. See NAILSEA.

Flemish lace A general term for needle and bobbin LACE made in Flanders, notably Antwerp, BINCHE, Brabant, Cluny, Bruges, BRUSSELS, and Mechelen. Flemish flax produced an exceptionally fine thread, ensuring the highest quality lace.

Flemish scroll A double scroll that was used on the front legs and stretchers of late

Flecked glass
Nailsea green window glass flagon, flecked with white. Late 19th century.

Flintlock
55-bore flintlock boxlock pocket pistol, the frame engraved with swags. c. 1800.

17th-century chairs in which the foot scrolled inward and the knee outward.

Fleur-de-lis (or lys) ■ A French term for "lily flower." A stylized lily, this heraldic flower with three petals appears in Christian iconography as an emblem reflecting the purity of the Virgin Mary. A central device in the royal arms of France from the 12th century, the *fleur-de-lis* was a popular motif in late Gothic tracery designs, and was taken up by the Gothic Revival style, featuring as an ornament for screens, tiles, and ironwork.

Flint glass An archaic term often used for English LEAD GLASS. It refers to glass made from around the mid-17th century in which ground flint, rather than sand, was the source of silica. The resulting glass was known as LEAD CRYSTAL. The name "flint" is also sometimes used to describe clear, colorless glass.

Flintlock ■ A mechanism for striking sparks from flint and steel. Its earliest form was the SNAPHAUNCE, which appeared in the mid-16th century. This was refined around 1600 by LeBourgeois. The flintlock was easy and cheap to make and remained in use until the middle of the 19th century.

Flirty eyes SLEEPING EYES in dolls, which can move from side to side.

Florence potteries A group of factories around Florence in the late 14th century until about 1475 when FAENZA took the lead. Maiolica was made in Florence from around 1300. Technical and decorative devices originated from Hispano-Moresque wares imported into Italy in large quantities. Their forms included jugs, ALBARELLI, and OAK LEAF JARS. Human and animals figures in stylized foliage appear before the end of the 15th century on tiles and large dishes, most of which seem to have been made for use rather than decoration. The pottery in Florence seems to have closed after 1530.

Florence Tapestry Factory ■ Founded in 1545 by Duke Cosimo de Medici, the Arrazzeria Medicea was intended to make Florence a major tapestry-weaving center. With cartoons by major Florentine artists and subsidies from the Medicis, the factory flourished. From 1554 all production was for the Medici household. The factory closed in 1737 when the last Medici died.

Florentine carving A general term for elaborate scroll and leaf carving used on picture and mirror frames from the 17th century. It may also refer to the carving used in Florence during the BAROQUE period of the late 17th and early 18th centuries, when sculptors created, carved, and often gilded armchairs and decorated them with putti, mythological figures, and masks.

Florentine mosaic An English term used to describe PIETRA DURA mosaic panels made in Florence from the mid-16th century and later variations in the technique in countries as far afield as England and India. Cut shapes of colored semiprecious stones were inlaid in marble in designs that included landscapes, flowers and fruit, and birds. The resulting panels were used to decorate interiors, and from the late 17th century into the 19th, the tops of tables.

Florentine stitch See BARGELLO.

Flow blue ■ A deep COBALT blue used for underglaze painting on ceramics. The color, which tends to flow into the glaze and gives a blurred effect, is obtained by placing volatile chlorides in the SAGGER containing the ware. Chlorine is given off and combines with the cobalt, making it slightly soluble in the glaze.

Flower brick ■ A ceramic holder for flowers, of 18th-century origin. Most were rectangular but some were square. The top was pierced with holes for the stems of the flowers and usually had a central square hole to fill the brick with water.

Flute ■ A drinking glass with a tall, tapering, cylindrical or octagonal bowl, often with a slightly inverted rim, upon a short stem. Early examples were used for wine in Germany and Holland in the 17th century. In the late 18th and early 19th centuries the flute spread to other countries. Long flutes were used as CHAMPAGNE GLASSES.

Florence Tapestry Factory
Flemish mythological tapestry, woven in wools and silks. 16th century.

Flow blue
Sylvia Flow blue pitcher, transfer-printed in deep flowering blue. Late 19th century.

Flower brick
London delftware flower brick, with a landscape scene. c. 1750.

Flute
German champagne flute. 19th century.

F

Fluting ■ A pattern of shallow, rounded, parallel channels running vertically along the shaft of a column, PILASTER, or other surface. A favorite ornament for furniture from the 16th century, fluting has been used to decorate ceramics and silver vessels as well as the bowls for centuries, most especially between 1770 and 1845. It is the opposite of REEDING or GADROONING.

Flux A material, commonly either soda, lead oxide, potash, or wood ash, added to the ingredients (the batch) in glassmaking to reduce the temperature at which they melt and fuse together.

Flywheel A heavy wheel designed to improve the smooth running of steam engines but also used to maintain balance in certain toys like tops, gyroscopes, and motor cycles. See FRICTION MOTOR MECHANISM.

Fob chain See ALBERT.

Foiling A technique of jewelry-making used since the Renaissance. Foiling is a way of enhancing the color and luster of a gemstone or paste imitation by inserting plain or colored tin foil behind the stone and securing it in a CLOSED-BACK SETTING. The practice of foiling has inevitably resulted in deliberate deception, for instance, colorless rock crystal being passed off as sapphire by the insertion of blue tin foil.

Folded foot A type of foot in which glass is folded over to strengthen it and prevent chipping. The method originated in 16th-century Venice.

Foley pottery See SHELLEY.

Fondporzellan See GROUND COLORS.

Fontaine, Pierre-François-Léonard (1762–1853) A French architect and designer of furniture, textiles, silver, and interiors. Born in Pontoise, he studied architecture at the Ecole des Beaux-Arts in Paris, where he met a fellow student, Charles PERCIER, in 1779. After studying Classical and Renaissance architecture in Rome, they set up a partnership. In 1799 they were commissioned to redecorate the interior of Malmaison, the residence just outside Paris of Josephine de Beauharnais, the consort of Napoleon I, and later the Tuileries Palace and the Louvre. They created the EMPIRE style, which was illustrated in their *Receuil des Décorations Intérieurs,* published in 1801. In keeping with the style, most of their furniture is elegant yet simple and heavily embellished with Classical and antique motifs.

Foot warmer ■ A portable metal or ceramic container for hot water or burning coals, used for keeping the feet warm. They were used by travelers in carriages from the 17th to the 19th centuries; earthenware examples were used into the 20th century.

Footman A four-legged TRIVET stand, made of iron or brass, that stood in front of the fire and was used as a stand for hot dishes. Known from the late 18th century.

Foot rim The projecting circular support on the bottom of a plate, utensil, or vessel, sometimes called a basal rim or foot ring.

Fornasetti, Piero ■ (1913–88) An Italian designer and painter known for his Classical, yet often witty, designs for ceramics, furniture, and textiles. He collaborated with Gio PONTI on furniture and also decorative work for interiors such as the casino at San Remo. His style commonly combines images from antique engravings and surrealistic and TROMPE L'OEIL effects, typically in black and white, sometimes highlighted with gold.

Fortuny, Mariano (1871–1949) Born in Granada, Spain, Fortuny settled in Venice in 1889. He had become a textile and fashion designer by 1906. In 1909 he patented a technique for undulating and pleating silk, as used for his famous Delphos dresses. In 1921 he opened a factory that recreated historic woven fabric designs on cotton, using an industrial printing process that he developed himself. The factory still operates today.

Foxing A term applied to antique books and prints, indicating spots or blotches of brownish discoloration on paper.

Franck, Kaj (1911–89). Finnish designer best-known for his innovative MID-

Fluting
George IV silver mustard pot of drum form with part fluting and a gadrooned border. c. 1825.

Foot warmer
Royal Winton chintz Mecca foot warmer.

Fornasetti, Piero
Bureau bookcase *Architettura,* by Piero Fornasetti and Gio Ponti. c. 1950.

Gilded rim and ball finial

Frankenthal Porcelain Factory
Frankenthal teapot and cover. c. 1770.

CENTURY MODERN designs for the Arabia porcelain factory from 1945 to 1961, and for the Nuutajärvi glassworks from 1950 to 1976. Highlights include the ergonomic, mix-and-match "Kilta" tableware for Arabia, and the simple, tapered, seascape-color-tinted "Kartio" collection of glassware for Nuutajärvi.

Frankenthal Porcelain Factory ■
One of the leading German 18th-century porcelain factories, known for its wares in high ROCOCO style. It was founded in 1755 at Frankenthal, in Germany, by Paul-Antoine Hannong with J. J. RINGLER. Hannong's two sons, Charles François Paul and Joseph-Anton, took over the factory in 1759. Their output was considerable but they were financially unsuccessful, and the factory was acquired by the Elector Palatine in 1762. Adam Bergdoll was director until 1775, followed by Simon FEILNER until 1797. The factory made tableware, vases, and clocks, sometimes finely painted by Jakob Osterspei with mythological scenes, which are highly prized today. But figure production (often BISCUIT porcelain) was predominant. The modelers were court sculptor Konrad Link, who made ambitious theatrical figures, J. W. Lanz, Johann F. Luck, and Karl G. Luck. In 1795 the factory was occupied by the French, and closed around 1800. Some molds went to NYMPHENBURG and were used to reproduce figures.

Free-blowing
Technique for making glass in which the glassmaker collects a GATHER of molten glass from the furnace on the end of a blowing rod and then inflates it with his breath, manipulating the glass with tools and moving the rod to create the desired shape. See STRASBOURG POTTERY AND PORCELAIN FACTORIES.

French needle lace
From the 1660s, France imported VENETIAN NEEDLE LACE until Louis XIV appointed Jean Baptiste Colbert as minister for French lace. The French then developed their own *point de France* lace for elaborate flounces. Lace-making centers were established in ALENÇON and ARGENTAN.

French polishing
A technique popular around 1820 that speeded up the lengthy traditional method of achieving a high gloss

FOLK ART

Description of a wide range of objects, including paintings, sculpture, and other decorative art forms, that are representative of the craft traditions and social values of primarily rural social groups, folk art varied widely from established tastes, practices, and formal academic education in cities and was representative of the region or culture in which it was made. Functional items such as household utensils or small items of furniture, often with decorative aspects, were also made in the folk art style.

Noah's Ark
German painted wooden Noah's ark and animals. Mid- to late 19th century.

Folk portrait
American folk oil portrait of a lady, by Charles Curtis. 1840.

Carved wooden dog
Folk art carved dog, by Aaron Mountz (1873–1949).

FRAKTUR

A form of American FOLK ART produced in Pennsylvania during the 18th and 19th centuries, Fraktur was brought to the US by German settlers. The word "Fraktur" is derived from the name of a type of German lettering used in 15th-century Germany. Frakturs are illustrated manuscript texts, usually recording births (*daafscheine*), baptisms (*taufscheine*), or a godparent's greetings to a new child (*taufwunsch*). The manuscripts contained hymns or other text derived from religious records. Printed examples were mass-manufactured and became commonplace by the 1780s, and are more attainable than handmade ones. Late 19th-century examples are also printed in different languages. Other, more secular, Fraktur include examples of penmanship, writing samplers, book plates (*vorschriften*), rewards of merit, presentation documents, and love letters (*liebesbriefe*). Besides the wording, ornate foliate or floral designs are also commonly found, as are human and animal figures, and other natural or religious motifs. See also PENNSYLVANIA DUTCH STYLE.

Fraktur
Pennsylvania watercolor and ink on paper fraktur, inscribed "Jacob Leith, 1818."

the GOTHIC and Chinese taste. In furniture, fretwork was used on bookcases, tables, cabinets, and chairs, frequently as a border or to form a GALLERY. Fanciful Rococo fretwork was toned down in the NEOCLASSICAL period, replaced by GREEK KEY patterns, and was confined to border decoration on furniture, silver, and ceramics. In the late 19th century the term was chiefly applied to ornamental openwork patterns carved from wood with a fretsaw.

Friction motor mechanism ■ Also known as "push and go," this method of driving toy vehicles uses a FLYWHEEL geared to an axle as an energy store to propel the toy. When the toy is pushed hard, the flywheel speeds up and absorbs the necessary power to drive it. This method is used mainly on tinplate vehicles, but also on some later DIECAST toy vehicles.

Friedrich Augustus I Elector of Saxony and King of Poland (1670–1733), popularly known as AUGUSTUS THE STRONG from the number of his amours and illegitimate children. He converted to Catholicism in order to claim the throne of Poland. Augustus had a considerable effect on the history of ceramics and was an obsessive collector of Oriental porcelain. He was the founder, patron, and eventual owner of the MEISSEN porcelain factory. He is notorious for having bartered an entire regiment of 600 dragoons for 48 Chinese blue and white vases from Frederick the Great of Prussia.

finish on furniture using SHELLAC dissolved in turpentine. The high gloss finish is achieved by a skilled process known as "spiriting out."

Fretwork ■ A carved geometric decoration of intersecting lines in which the spaces may or may not be pierced through (in the latter case, it is called "blind" fretwork). A common decoration of ancient origin, fretwork became popular in the mid-18th century in ROCOCO items, particularly in

Fretwork
Gothic Revival mahogany corner shelf, with fretwork borders and sides. Late 19th century.

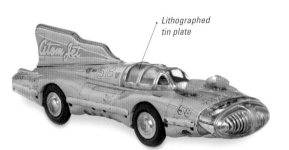

Lithographed tin plate

Friction motor mechanism
Japanese space lithographed friction-powered tin toy car Atom Jet, by Yonezawa. c. 1950.

Frigger
Colored and clear frigger of a seaside town. Late 19th century.

Frieze Originally an architectural term that describes the section between the ARCHITRAVE and CORNICE on the upper part of a Classical order. It is also used to describe a horizontal piece of wood that supports the top of a table, or a cornice on a piece of CASE FURNITURE.

Frigger ■ A method of using leftover colored glass to make small decorative or whimsical objects such as models of ships. LAMPWORK is often employed. See END-OF-THE-DAY GLASS.

Fringe The loose strands of wool, cotton, or silk at each end of a rug or carpet. In handmade examples, they are an integral part of the rug, formed by the warp threads. They often enhance the visual appearance of a piece and are sometimes plaited and braided.

Frit A mixture of powdered or ground ingredients added to the BATCH during the glassmaking process. The term also describes impurities found in old glass.

Fritware A low-fired artificial porcelain body of ground quartz, white clay, and glaze, introduced by 12th-century Islamic potters in imitation of Chinese Ding porcelain, which reached the Middle East from China. It is white and translucent when thinly potted, and covered with a translucent alkaline glaze, and resembles the later, more highly fired, European SOFT-PASTE PORCELAIN bodies.

Frosted glass ■ Glass with a translucent matte or "frosted" finish, obtained by immersing the object in acid. It was popular in the ART DECO period, when it was used on decorative glass by such masters as René LALIQUE and also on pressed decorative glass.

Frog mug ■ An English, mainly 19th-century, ceramic mug of cylindrical shape with a frog modeled and attached to the inside of the mug about two-thirds of the way down, which became visible to the drinker as the level fell.

Fromanteel family An English family of clock-makers of Dutch or Flemish origin. Ahasuerus Fromanteel I worked as a clock-maker in Smithfield, London, from about 1620 to 1690. He was the first maker of pendulum clocks in England, helped by his son, Johannes Fromanteel, who studied their manufacture in the Netherlands from 1657 to 1658. Father and son were responsible for the design of the basic pendulum mechanism used in British clocks during the 17th and 18th centuries. Other clock-makers with the Fromanteel name were recorded in the late 17th century as members of the Clockmakers' Company in London.

Frosted silver A textured or matt finish on the surface of silver giving the effect of a layer of frost. This surface finish is achieved either by hand with the use of fine chasing tools or by immersion in acid.

Frothingham, Benjamin (1734–1809) An American cabinet-maker, Frothingham was active in Charlestown, near Boston, Massachusetts. He made high-quality, fashionable case furniture in the American CHIPPENDALE style.

F

165

Frozen Charlotte ■ A porcelain doll with molded hair and painted features, stretched limbs and bent arms with clenched fists. Also known as Frozen Charlie and Bathing Baby, the dolls were made in the late 19th century by various German factories.

Fruitwood Country furniture was often constructed from the wood of fruit trees. For example, pearwood, strong and heavy with a fine, red-tinged grain, was stained black and polished or varnished to imitate ebony. It was used as an inlay on Elizabethan and Jacobean furniture. In the 17th and 18th centuries pearwood was used for picture frames and bracket clocks. Applewood, a light, warm-toned fruitwood, was also used for decorative veneer, inlay, carving, and small decorative boxes. Plum and cherry also provide a similar dense-grained wood.

Fubako A Japanese box made from wood or papier-mâché and used for storing letters and correspondence. The exterior of these boxes is often decorated with LACQUER.

Frosted glass
Baccarat "It's You" perfume bottle in clear and frosted crystal, for Elizabeth Arden. c. 1939.

Frog mug
Inside of creamware frog mug, printed on the outside with verses. c. 1790.

Frozen Charlotte
Three German china Frozen Charlotte dolls.

F

Fuddling cup ■ A tavern joke known from the 16th to the 18th century. Formed of three or more conjoined cups with an interconnecting pipe, the drinker was "befuddled" as to which to drink from without causing spillages. Examples in 17th- and 18th-century English DELFTWARE are particularly sought after.

Fulda Pottery and Porcelain Factory
Founded in Hesse, Germany, in 1741 by the Prince-Bishop of Fulda, Heinrich von Bibra, with Nikolaus Paul from Berlin and the painter J. P. Schick. The factory burned down in 1767, but was eventually rebuilt and continued production until 1790. They made tableware influenced by MEISSEN, painted with landscapes featuring ruins and shipping, blue and manganese wares, and well-modeled figures.

Fulham pottery John DWIGHT founded a pottery at Fulham in London in the 17th century, making BELLARMINE and brown stoneware. It carried on production through the 19th century.

Fuller A groove cut into the sides of a sword blade to reduce its weight without loss of strength. Often referred to (wrongly) as a "blood groove."

Fulper pottery ■ An American pottery established at Flemington, New Jersey, in 1805. Fulper produced simple, utilitarian wares in its early period, all of which are unmarked. From about 1910 Fulper made artistic wares under Martin Stangl and William H. Fulper II. It specialized in matte- or crystalline-glazed vessels in Japanese or ARTS AND CRAFTS form. Most were marked with a vertical printed or impressed FULPER. The most valuable examples are large table-lamps with shades that have inset glass panels and artist-signed lusterware. The pottery closed around 1935.

Fumed oak ■ A type of oak furniture, popular in the later ARTS AND CRAFTS and ART DECO periods, with a distinctive powdery gray surface. It was achieved either by painting the piece with ammonia or by exposing it to ammonia fumes in a fuming box until the desired color was reached.

Functionalism A movement in architecture and the applied arts, advocating the theory that the form of an object should be determined solely by its function. Its earliest proponent is considered to be the American architect Louis Sullivan, who contended in the late 19th century that "form follows function." In practice, the term refers to the international modernist style of the 1920s and 30s, characterized by austere, geometric forms devoid of ornament. It is associated particularly with designers of the BAUHAUS, for example Marcel BREUER, who aimed to create good-quality, efficient, and standardized design for all, particularly through new materials such as tubular steel.

Fürstenberg ■ One of the leading German manufacturers of HARD-PASTE PORCELAIN, producing high-quality wares from 1753 to about 1800. Founded in 1747 by Charles I, Duke of Brunswick, its attempts to manufacture porcelain were unsuccessful until the arrival of Johann Benckgraff from HÖCHST in 1753. Early wares suffered from defective colors and firing specks. Many figures produced at Fürstenberg imitated those produced at MEISSEN, HÖCHST, and BERLIN. The most important modeler was Simon Feilner from Höchst, who became chief modeler in 1754. His work included a fine series of characters from the COMMEDIA DELL'ARTE. WEDGWOOD became a dominant influence at the end of the 18th century. Crude copies of the earlier models were reproduced at the factory in the 19th century.

Fusée A grooved, cone-shaped device used in spring-driven clocks to offset the force of the spring as it runs down.

Fuddling cup
English delftware fuddling cup. c. 1640.

Fulper pottery
Geometrical form vase with a black-streaked "Flemington" green flambé glaze. 1909–14.

Fürstenberg
Oval porcelain snuff box. c. 1768.

G

Gabbeh A type of tribal rug made in Persia, with a thick wool pile and bold, abstract, colored designs. Originally for domestic use, the rugs are now produced for the export market. Examples from the 19th and 20th centuries are most common.

Gadrooning A decorative border of convex flutes or lobes, usually applied as an edging on a curved surface. It developed during the Renaissance from Classical reeding and was popular on furniture and woodwork from the 16th century, particularly for bulbous supports and moldings. It was also widely adopted for ornament around the bases of silver and ceramic vessels. Throughout the 18th century it was used on chests, HIGHBOYS, tables, and chairs, as well as on NEOCLASSICAL silver and ceramic urns, vases, and glassware.

Gainsborough chair An armchair made from the mid-18th century onward, so called because of its appearance in the portraits of Thomas Gainsborough. It has an upholstered seat and back and concave arm supports. The legs and arms are often carved with GOTHIC, CHINOISERIE, or ROCOCO motifs.

Gallé, Émile ■ (1846–1904) Gallé was the son of a glass and ceramics factory owner in Nancy, Lorraine, France. He studied botany, drawing, and landscape painting and visited London, studying the ancient glass collections in the British Museum, including the PORTLAND VASE. Gallé set up a glass workshop in Nancy before joining forces with his father. He went on to produce virtuoso pieces of French ART NOUVEAU glass, furniture, and ceramics. Initially, the factory produced clear colored glass with enameled decoration, drawing on Gallé's love of plants and animals. By 1890 Gallé's factory employed over 300 workmen,

GALLÉ, ÉMILE

Technical skill and artistic inspiration reached its height in the work of this supreme French glassmaker. Gallé produced a range of CAMEO GLASS wares. These had naturalistic relief decoration; subtle detailing with wheel-carving; applications of glass cabochons; and internal decoration ranging from mica and foil inclusions to crackle and bubbles. Gallé also made vases to simulate hardstones, sculpted pieces, and produced mold-blown pieces. Gallé gave his workers artistic freedom (except for his studio pieces), with the proviso that nature should be represented accurately.

Floriform vase
Verre Parlant floriform cameo vase, the base engraved with "Cristallerie de Gallé Nancy."

Vase (detail)
Gallé signature on a cameo glass vase.

Clematis vase
Blown-out cameo vase, with clematis and cameo signature.

Cabinet
Ash, oak, calamander, and marquetry signed cabinet.

producing a series of spectacular pieces similar in style. He opened several shops, and from 1896 his work was exhibited at La Maison de l'Art Nouveau, the Paris shop opened by Samuel (Siegfried) BING. Gallé was the first glassmaker to routinely sign his work. His studio work is the most rare and valuable today. Other work includes carved cameo, commercial acid cameo, and posthumous output, indicated by a cross beside the signature.

Gallé also opened a carpentry shop, employing cabinet-makers to produce furniture. His specialty was MARQUETRY. After his death, the factory's work was marked with a star beside the word "Gallé." The factory closed in 1914 but reopened after World War I, continuing until the early 1930s.

Galleon motif ■ A motif based on a traditional ship of war. It was adopted by the ARTS AND CRAFTS Movement as a decorative pattern for ironwork, tiles, ceramics, textiles, and glass.

Gallery An ornamental miniature railing of wood or metal, set around the edge of a tray, table, cabinet, or shelf.

Games compendium A wooden or cardboard box or case, containing a selection of games such as chess, checkers, backgammon, cards, cribbage, and roulette. A popular domestic item from the 1860s, some can be very decorative.

Gardner Porcelain Factory ■ The most successful private porcelain factory in pre-Revolutionary Russia, founded around 1765 by an Englishman, Francis Gardner, in Verbilki, near Moscow. Its most famous wares are the four services that were made at the imperial orders of St. George, St. Andrew, St. Alexander Nevsky, and St. Vladimir between 1777 and 1785. From the early 19th century until its closure in 1891, the factory made brightly colored pictures and models of tradesmen and craftworkers.

Garnet A gemstone occurring in various shades of red (almandine and pyrope), brown (spessartite), orange (hessonite), and the rarer and far more valuable green variety (demantoid, uvarovite, and radite). Garnet was used extensively throughout the 19th century, either faceted or as polished CABOCHON. Bohemian garnets are the pyrope variety, used in PAVÉ SETTINGS in decorative costume jewelry.

Garniture de cheminée A set of five or seven vases, comprising three baluster-shaped items with covers and two trumpet-shaped beakers, designed to stand on a mantelshelf. First produced in China in the 17th century for the European market, they were soon being made in Europe, especially in DELFT. Small sets of three would comprise one covered jar and two bottles.

Garrard, Robert (I) ■ (1760–1818) A respected London silversmith who became a freeman at the firm of Wakelin & Co., Panton Street, and went into partnership with John Wakelin in 1792, gaining a reputation for quality and workmanship.

He had three sons: Robert, James, and Sebastian. Robert (II) entered his first mark in 1818 after his father died and developed the business, gaining many commissions. He became Royal Goldsmith and Jeweler to King William IV in 1830. Garrards still retains the royal warrant. The company amalgamated with ASPREY in 1999.

Gasolier A lighting fixture, resembling a CHANDELIER, used for gas lighting in domestic and public buildings from the mid-19th century until the advent of electric lighting in 1880. Usually made of brass, with glass shades at the end of each branch, it comprises a central shaft through which gas is distributed to each burner.

Gastaldi, Giacomo (c. 1500–c. 1565) Cosmographer to the Venetian Republic and the foremost Italian cartographer of the 16th century. Works include the landmark 1548 Venetian edition of PTOLEMY'S *Geographia*, which was the first to be translated into Italian, the first pocket-sized ATLAS, and the first to contain regional maps of the New World, including the first of North America's east coast and South America.

Galleon motif
Arts and Crafts earthenware plate, painted with a galleon. Johnson Bros. plate mark.

Gardner Porcelain Factory
Russian Gardner two-handled porcelain urn. c. 1830.

Garrard, Robert (I)
William IV silver salver, by Robert Garrard, with London hallmarks. c. 1830.

Gateleg table ■ A table with a hinged folding top of one or two leaves that open out and are supported on pivoting legs joined at the top and bottom by stretchers. Introduced in the 16th century, they are still made today.

Gather The blob of molten glass on the end of the blowing iron, before it is blown and manipulated into shape with tools and molds. The blob is "gathered" by dipping and twisting the rod into the molten glass in the furnace.

Gaudí i Cornet, Antonio (1852–1926) A Spanish architect and one of the most original ART NOUVEAU designers. Floral embellishment and asymmetry typified his furniture, the majority of which was produced to accompany his eccentric buildings. His organic style was strongly influenced by his Catalonian heritage, the GOTHIC REVIVAL, John Ruskin, and HISPANO-MORESQUE art and architecture.

Gaudy Dutch or Gaudy Welsh Staffordshire (and other) pottery decorated for the American market, especially for the Pennsylvania Dutch (Deutsch), from around 1810 to 1830. They were usually "cottage" wares painted first in UNDERGLAZE blue and then in thick, bright overglaze enamels, often imitating IMARI-pattern wares.

Georgian style ■ The architecture and decorative arts in the period between 1720 and 1837 that reached an elegance that has remained unmatched and is still imitated.

The early Georgian period, from the accession of George I in 1714 to the 1730s, was dominated by the PALLADIAN style. Typical motifs included triumphal arcs or temple fronts. Interiors of this period were commonly adorned with heavily sculpted eagles and dolphins. On his return from the GRAND TOUR, Richard Boyle, 3rd Earl of Burlington, designed Chiswick House, London, and built it from around 1725 to hold his collection of Greek and Roman art and sculpture. The Classical theme was continued in furniture by William KENT, a protégé of Burlington's. Around 1740 the ROCOCO style reached Britain. Its impact on design was evident by the middle of the century, in the work of the HUGUENOT silversmiths, in CHIPPENDALE furniture, porcelain from CHELSEA and DERBY, and engraved glassware and mirrors.

When George III ascended the throne in 1760, the main source of inspiration in

G

169

GEORGIAN STYLE

The Georgian style includes varying elements but was inspired by the proportions and ornament of Classical architecture.

Silver candlesticks
A pair of Georgian silver candlesticks with scalloped design feet, hallmark for William Cafe. 1757.

Writing slope
A Georgian brass-bound writing slope.

Butler's tray
A late Georgian mahogany folding butler's tray with well figured timber, on a modern stand. c. 1820.

Open armchair
A mid-18th-century George III carved mahogany open armchair.

Champagne flute
A Georgian champagne flute, with high panel cutting, on collar and blade knop stem. c. 1820.

architecture and the decorative arts was still the Classical world. However, further discoveries at Herculaneum and Pompeii influenced the designers by the delicate decorative motifs they revealed, resulting in the NEOCLASSICAL style, led by Robert ADAM. Silverware, porcelain, and glass also reflected this style.

During the 1780s forms became even more refined, especially in furniture, where timbers imported from all over the world were used for sophisticated VENEERS and MARQUETRY. This style was associated particularly with Thomas SHERATON and George HEPPLEWHITE. Elegant Classical lines were still the basis of the REGENCY style from 1811, but were embellished with lavish French-inspired decoration, in accordance with the tastes of the Prince Regent. During the late Georgian and Regency period, the popularity of Turkish, Indian, Chinese Rococo, and Gothic motifs anticipated the eclectic VICTORIAN style.

Germain, Thomas (1673–1748) France's greatest ROCOCO gold- and silversmith. Born into a family of goldsmiths, he worked as an apprentice in Italy and returned to France in 1706. He became a master goldsmith in 1720 and Goldsmith to the King, Louis XV, in 1723. In contrast to earlier silver, his work is asymmetrical and naturalistic. His hunting table centerpiece of around 1730, for instance, is modeled and cast in high relief with game, shells, scrolls, and reptiles. He made many objects for the French royal family and European nobility, but most were lost in the Lisbon earthquake of 1755 or melted to finance the Seven Years War (1756–63).

German silver See NICKEL SILVER.

Gesso A pastelike mixture of chalk or plaster of Paris or gypsum with glue, used as a base for carved and gilded decoration on wooden picture frames and furniture from the Middle Ages onward. It was especially popular on carved and GILTWOOD furniture in the late 17th and 18th centuries.

Ghashghai ■ An important tribal group from the Fars district of southwest Iran who were weavers of fine and coarse rugs, KILIMS, and functional artifacts. Examples from the 19th century are particularly fine, with jewel colors employed in designs of stylized flora and fauna. Later pieces tend to be coarse and lack the individuality of earlier ones.

Ghiordes knot See TURKISH KNOT.

Ghom ■ An important center of rug and carpet production in central Iran, where weaving began around 1930. Wool and silk are used for the pile, while warps and wefts are of cotton or silk. Curvilinear designs in subtle colors are used on a white ground; the BOTEH motif appears frequently, as do geometric designs inspired from the Caucasus.

Gibbons, Grinling (1648–1721) The leading woodcarver and sculptor of the English BAROQUE style. He probably trained in Amsterdam but had returned to England by 1667. He attracted the attention of Sir Christopher Wren, and by 1693 was appointed Master Carver to the Crown, producing outstanding ornamental carved wood decoration for such royal residences as Kensington Palace, Hampton Court, and the Royal Apartments at Windsor Castle, as well as St. Paul's Cathedral.

Gien pottery ■ The produce of a FAIENCE factory recorded in the town of Gien on the Loire River, northwest France, from about 1822. It made cream-colored EARTHENWARE, which was plain or marbled, sponged, simply painted, or printed. After 1860 various decorative techniques were exploited such as LUSTER and FLAMBÉ, and large vessels, sometimes painted in the Renaissance style, became a specialty. The town still produces high-quality FAIENCE.

Gilding ■ A decorative finish in which gold (or silver) is applied to wood, leather, silver, ceramics, or glass. It was also applied to other metals such as iron, copper, and bronze. Known from ancient Egypt, the process involves laying gold leaf or powdered gold (or silver) onto a base—of GESSO, for example. Wood gilding may be water gilding, which takes a high burnish, or the cheaper and more durable oil gilding. In Europe gilding was extensively

Ghashghai
Ghashghai rug from southwest Persia. c. 1890.

Ghom
Silk Ghom rug from central Persia. 20th century.

Gien pottery
One of three Gien plates, each printed in black with a humorous aviation scene.

Gilding
Italian Rococo console table with painted and gilded frame and faux marble top. c. 1770.

used on furniture from the 17th century onward. Different types included HONEY GILDING, MERCURY GILDING, and WATER GILDING.

Giles, James ■ (1718–80) An English outside decorator of porcelain and glass. He is recorded from 1749 as a "Chinaman" (in other words, a vendor or importer of porcelain) and from 1763 as a painter. He decorated white porcelain from WORCESTER and probably also from BOW and LONGTON HALL. He seems to have gone bankrupt in 1776. His work is not signed.

Gillinder, William (1823–71) An English-born American glassmaker, who worked at Bacchus & Sons before emigrating to the US in 1853. In 1861 he moved to Philadelphia and acquired a glassworks, which he renamed the Franklin Flint Glass Works. In 1867 his sons, James and Frederick, joined the firm and it became Gillinder & Sons. Shortly afterward they acquired the Philadelphia Flint Glass Works, which made pressed glass tableware.

A favorite pattern, "Westward Ho," featuring images of buffalo, elk, and American Indians, was made until the company closed in the 1930s but continues to be reproduced by other companies today.

Gillows ■ An English family firm of furniture manufacturers founded by Robert Gillow in Lancaster in around 1727. By 1769 Robert Gillow II was managing a showroom in London's Oxford Street, and Richard Gillow was overseeing the Lancaster factory. Gillows became the leading furniture manufacturers outside the capital. Their success was largely due to good quality and workmanship, and a shrewd choice of middle-of-the-road designs that appealed to the provincial middle classes. From around 1780 some of the furniture was stamped "GILLOWS LANCASTER," and by the end of the century, Gillows launched several new furniture types, including the DAVENPORT. In 1900 Gillows merged with S. J. Waring & Sons to become WARING & GILLOW.

Gilt bronze See ORMOLU.

Giltwood Wood that has been gilded, usually with GOLD LEAF over GESSO.

Gimmal A type of flask (also called gemel) made from the 17th century, consisting of two separately blown bottles that are then fused together to form a double bottle with individual containers, each with a separate neck and mouth that sometimes face in opposite directions. Most often used for storing oil and vinegar.

Gimson, Ernest William ■ (1864–1919) An English architect and designer, renowned for his furniture designs and metalware. He was a leading figure of the ARTS AND CRAFTS Movement and what became known as the COTSWOLD SCHOOL. With Sydney and Ernest BARNSLEY, he revived the best traditions of English cabinet-making to produce beautifully handcrafted pieces. He employed the Dutch cabinet-maker Peter van der Waals to run his workshops.

Gin flask ■ A salt-glazed stoneware flask produced from the 1820s to the 1850s to commemorate important events, people, or royalty, particularly associated with the Reform Act in 1832. Main producers were Stephen Green, Lambeth, and Oldfield & Co., Chesterfield. Some have an impressed mark of the wine and spirit merchant or the public house for which they were made.

Ginger jar A small, squat, baluster-shaped jar with a cover, made in China but also copied by European factories in the 17th century, and usually decorated in UNDERGLAZE blue. It was originally used to hold Chinese stem ginger.

Girandole An Italian term that referred to an elaborate CANDELABRUM with cut crystal pendants in the late 17th century, but by the 18th century was used to describe all types of candelabra and CHANDELIERS. In 18th-century England, girandole was also used to describe ROCOCO-style carved GILTWOOD SCONCES as well as wall-brackets, sometimes with a MIRROR back.

Girl in a Swing ■ The name given to porcelain, previously attributed to CHELSEA, but now believed to be

G

171

Giles, James
Worcester plate, painted in colored enamels from James Giles's London atelier. c. 1770.

Gillows
George III mahogany rent table, stamped "Gillows, Lancaster." c. 1790.

Gimson, Ernest William
Brass chandelier in the Arts and Crafts style, by Ernest Gimson for Robert Weir Schultz.

Gin flask
Pair of salt-glazed stoneware gin flasks, modeled as Punch and Judy. 19th century.

G

produced in the house of Charles Gouyn, in Bennet Street, London, from 1749 to 1759. Gouyn was a jeweler and specialized in "toys"—porcelain scent bottles, bonbonnières, and seals, with gold mounts. The term "Girl in a Swing" is derived from a figure group attributed to Gouyn's factory, now in the Victoria and Albert Museum, London.

Giuliano, Carlo (c. 1831–95) A goldsmith from Naples, initially employed by CASTELLANI, who settled in London around 1860 and established an "art jewelry" business. Making technically superb enameled gold work, he chose gems for color rather than value as did his sons Carlo and Arthur. The business closed in 1914.

Glasgow Potteries ■ A factory at Delftfield (1748–1810) that made tin-glazed earthenware decorated with Chinese-style flowers in manganese, yellow, blue, blue-green, and dark violet. From 1770 it made cream-colored earthenware. John and Matthew P. Bell founded a second factory (1842–1940) at Glasgow, which made PARIAN and earthenware.

Glasgow School A Scottish group of designers active from the 1890s up to World War I. Central figures were Charles Rennie MACKINTOSH, his wife, Margaret Macdonald, her sister, Frances, and her husband, Herbert McNair. They developed their own version of ART NOUVEAU with some CELTIC influences.

Glass A hard, brittle material, usually translucent, made by fusing together ingredients by heat. The basic component is silica, found in sand and quartz, to which an alkaline FLUX and other components are added to form the desired type of glass BATCH.

Glastonbury chair A 19th-century term for a reproduction of a late 16th-century wooden folding chair, usually of oak, possibly based on a chair made for the last Abbot of Glastonbury, England. It was devised for use in churches before pews became commonplace.

Glaze A layer of glass fused into place on a ceramic body, which provides a hygienic covering (because it is nonporous) and also increases the strength of the ware. It is applied to the body in the form of a layer of powder, composed of fluxes, stabilizers, and glass-forming material, which fuse during firing and make a compact layer of molten material.

The fluxes are alkaline oxides, usually soda, potash, magnesia, or lead oxide. Alumina is the most commonly used stabilizer. Glazes may be either transparent, as in LEAD GLAZE, or opaque, as in TIN and CELADON glazes. Lead glaze was used in China as early as 200 BCE and celadon glaze was used from the time of the SONG DYNASTY. The practice of glazing spread slowly across Europe from the East, probably by the Moors, and was standard by the 18th century.

Glazing bars See ASTRAGAL.

Globe ■ A spherical map of the Earth (a terrestrial globe) or the heavens (a celestial or astronomical globe), ranging in size from novelty pocket globes to larger library globes on stands. First used to aid navigation, the oldest known terrestrial globe was made in 1492 by the German Martin Behaim, though globes were made in ancient times. Islamic globes were mostly constructed from copper, brass, or silver. In Europe they were made from a PAPIER MÂCHÉ and plaster sphere covered with printed elliptical strips of paper called "gores." In the 20th century cartographical images could be printed directly onto spheres without using gores. Important makers include John Moxon, Dudley Adams, Charles Schmalcalder, and John Senex. Globes were part of the furnishings of private libraries and are still universal schoolroom equipment. Pocket globes can be dated from the geographical knowledge of the time—for example, new tracks and coastlines were defined by the findings of Captain Cook's three voyages (1768–74).

Glory hole A small hole in the side of the main glass furnace, or a separate furnace altogether, into which the glass GATHER is inserted on a rod to reheat it, allowing it to be shaped and worked.

Glug jug ■ A ceramic jug (also called a gurgle jug), usually in the form of a fish, with the mouth forming the opening and

Girl in a Swing
Gilt-metal-mounted bonbonnière, with hinged cover. 1749–54.

Glasgow Potteries
Glasgow delft plate, painted in underglaze blue. c. 1760.

Globe
One of a pair of Wilson's New American globes. c. 1835.

Glug jug
Majolica glug jug probably made by Thomas Forester & Sons. 19th century.

the tail forming the handle. When liquid is poured from it, air is trapped in the tail, causing a glugging sound. The larger the jug, the deeper the sound. Many were made by Dartmouth Pottery in England during the 1950s.

Gnomon ■ Often of triangular form and cut out of pierced metal such as copper or brass, the gnomon is the part of the SUNDIAL that projects a shadow from the sun to give a reading from the dial.

Gob A lump of hot, molten glass that is drawn from a furnace.

Gobelins Tapestry Factory Set up in Paris in 1662–63 to make furnishings for Louis XIV, the factory at the Hotel des Gobelins was the brainchild of the minister of finance, Jean-Baptiste Colbert, and the court painter, Charles Le Burn, who became the art director. Colbert employed over 800 artists, weavers, dyers, and apprentices at the Gobelins factory. Most tapestries were commissioned by the crown, which supplied the materials including silk, gold, or silver threads.

After the deaths of Colbert and Le Brun and with royal spending curtailed because of the war with the Netherlands, artistic originality stagnated at the Gobelins factory. In April 1694 the factory almost closed completely, and some workers went to work at BEAUVAIS. One workshop remained active and in 1699 the workshops reopened. The tapestries gradually

began to reflect the evolution of a lighter style. By the early 18th century *tapestries à alentours* (simulating a panel with elaborate floral surrounds), became popular.

Production recovered during the Empire period, with tapestries commissioned for the Imperial palaces. After the fall of the SECOND EMPIRE, there was an unsettled period. The factory was renamed the Manufacture Nationale des Gobelins and produced large hangings for public buildings. In 1939 it moved to Aubusson, where artists like Gromaire, Picasso, and Miró produced cartoons for monumental hangings for state buildings. Today the factory continues its tradition of basing tapestries on paintings.

Goblet A drinking glass with a large bowl supported by a stemmed foot. Goblets can be made from metal, ceramics, or glass.

Goddard, John ■ (1723–85) An American cabinet-maker active in Newport, Rhode Island, from about 1745. He and his brother were apprenticed to Job Townsend. The Goddard Townsend school of furniture is considered the earliest and possibly finest exponent of AMERICAN CHIPPENDALE, a style John Goddard is credited with developing. Features include richly colored mahogany with bold shell carving, often centred within a BLOCK FRONT. Examples are rare and valuable. Goddard's sons carried on the firm until the mid-19th century.

Godwin, Edward William (1833–86) An English architect and designer whose first important commission was Northampton town hall, influenced by John Ruskin's studies of Venetian architecture. In Ireland he built Dromore and Glenbeigh Towers. Godwin was one of the first to study Japanese art and used it to produce original work in the context of Western culture. His furniture designs were made by William Watt, Art Furniture Company, and COLLINSON & LOCK, but he also designed wallpaper, metalwork, and dresses for LIBERTY & Co. Godwin patented his furniture designs because they were often copied.

Godwin, Thomas and Benjamin ■ The partnership made blue and white printed wares in Staffordshire from about 1809 to 1834. Thomas Godwin continued the company from 1834 to 1854, producing printed designs that included some American scenes. He also used green and brown.

Going barrel See BARREL.

Gold glass A glass object to which gold leaf has been applied on the surface or sandwiched between two layers. Also referred to as ZWISCHENGOLDGLAS. Known since ancient Greek and Roman times, patterns can be cut, engraved, or etched into the glass and gold layer. The term can also apply to glass to which colloidal gold has been added to give the glass a ruby red coloring when reheated. See GOLD RUBY.

Gnomon
Wood diptych sundial, with string gnomon, by Stockert of Bavaria. c. 1840.

Goddard, John
Newport Chippendale carved mahogany slant-lid desk. c. 1770.

Godwin, Thomas and Benjamin
"View of London" platter. c. 1820.

Gold tooling Decorative embossing or tooled work on leather, particularly book bindings, which is picked out or heightened by gold leaf. The term is also used for gold motifs or borderwork inset into channels or inlaid into another metal, and for the CHASING or tooled work on gold items. See DAMASCENING.

Gold-ruby glass ■ Glass with a deep red ruby color (also called *Goldrubinglas*) created by adding colloidal gold to the BATCH and reheating the object in the furnace. The technique was perfected by Johann KUNCKEL in about 1679, in Potsdam, Germany, and was then used in both Nuremberg and Augsburg to make luxury pieces, many of which were decorated with engraving and gilding. See AMBERINA.

Gong A coil of steel wire attached at one end to a clock's MOVEMENT, emitting a bell-like sound when struck. Smaller than a bell, it was popular in STRIKING SYSTEMS from the early 19th century.

Goode & Co., Thomas A famed retailer of fine china and glass, established in 1827 in central London. It moved to a custom-redesigned building in South Audley Street in 1845 and is still there to this day. Goode & Co. is a retailer of WEDGWOOD, Royal DOULTON, and Royal WORCESTER, among others, as well as glassware by the leading British and European makers. Two large MINTON elephants bought from the 1878 Paris Exhibition have become its trademark.

GOLDSCHEIDER EARTHENWARE AND PORCELAIN FACTORY

Founded by Friedrich Goldscheider in Vienna in 1885, the factory was continued by his widow and then his sons until it closed in 1954. At the turn of the 19th century the factory specialized in figurative subjects and ART NOUVEAU terra-cotta figures of maidens, and in the 1920s and 30s ART DECO figures and masks.

Wall mask
Goldscheider "tragedy" wall mask. c. 1925–28.

Figure
Art Deco Goldscheider pottery figure.

Googly eyes ■ A term used for the usually large, round, and sideward-glancing glass dolls' eyes, generally associated with CHARACTER DOLLS, which were first marketed in 1911.

Gorham Manufacturing Company ■ The largest American silversmiths and one of the biggest in the world. It was founded in 1818 in Providence, Rhode Island, by Jabez Gorham, and became the Gorham Manufacturing Company in 1865. From around 1841 Gorham's son, John, joined the firm and expanded the business dramatically. In 1848

Gold-ruby glass
German *Goldrubinglas* rummer. 19th century.

Sideways-glancing eyes

Googly eyes
Composition Googly doll.

Gorham Manufacturing Co.
American hammered silver water pitcher. Late 19th century.

Gorham Manufacturing Co.
Silver belt buckle, with Native American motif and a turquoise cabochon. c. 1900–05.

he introduced the impressed anchor trademark that is still used today. The firm converted to steam power in the 1850s and introduced electroplating techniques pioneered by ELKINGTON & Co. The sterling standard of silver, not previously required of American silversmiths, was adopted in 1868. For the next 30 years the firm produced high-quality silver and silver-plated wares, specializing in HOLLOWWARE in RENAISSANCE REVIVAL or NEOCLASSICAL taste, much of it by European craftsmen, including the Englishmen George Wilkinson, chief designer from 1854 to 1891, and Thomas J. Pairpoint, who joined in 1868. The firm also made mixed metal and enameled pieces in AESTHETIC or Japanese taste. The best examples of Gorham JAPANESQUE silver are comparable to TIFFANY & CO. A line of ARTS AND CRAFTS-style ecclesiastical ware—for example, chalices in silver, wood, stone, and bronze—was made from 1885. From 1894 the firm was run by Edward Holbrook who, with the English art director, William Christmas Codman, introduced the MARTELÉ range with its distinctive marks and French ART NOUVEAU forms. Only around 5,000 Martelé pieces were made.

During the early 20th century Gorham was a foundry for bronzes by modern American sculptors (including Harriet Whitney Frishmuth), rivaling the Roman Bronze Works of New York City. The firm was sold to Textron Inc. in 1967, to Dansk International in 1989, and then to Brown-Forman in 1991.

Goss, William Henry ■ (1833–1906) An English maker of glazed PARIAN ware, terra-cotta, and "ivory" and EGGSHELL porcelain at the Falcon Pottery, Stoke-on-Trent, from 1858. The factory used the impressed or printed mark of "W. H. Goss" from 1862 onward. From about 1880, Goss made vast quantities of cheap, mass-produced trinkets with the coats of arms or crests of nearly every town in the British Isles. These sold widely at the time. The firm even issued a Goss Collectors magazine, and by 1912 the League of Goss Collectors had over 1,000 members. Other firms tried to cash in on their success, but genuine examples have a printed mark of a goshawk. It was renamed Goss China Ltd. around 1931 when it was taken over by Cauldon Potteries Ltd. In the 1980s DOULTON, which possesses a number of the original Goss pattern books, restarted production of some Goss porcelain.

Gothic Revival ■ This style revival began in the 18th century but grew in the 19th century, promoted by designers such as A. W. N. PUGIN and W. Burges. It was a revival of the medieval Gothic style and employed arches, tracery, flying buttresses, quatrefoils and trefoils, carving, GROTESQUE imagery, heraldic motifs, cornices, and inlaid motifs. Used chiefly in Church architecture, it also influenced domestic furnishings. Gothic Revival furniture, for example, was heavy and decorated with architectural details.

Pugin was responsible for the furnishings of the new Houses of Parliament in London

and the design of the Medieval Court at the GREAT EXHIBITION of 1851, and his designs followed the forms and ornament of historical examples. The GOTHIC REVIVAL soon came to be considered the national style of British art and architecture and was emulated by later 19th-century designers such as William BURGES and Bruce TALBERT.

The Gothic Revival influenced the ARTS AND CRAFTS Movement. It was also popular in France, where its chief advocate was Eugène-Emmanuel Viollet-le-Duc, as well as in the US, where Alexander Jackson Davis designed Gothic-style furniture and buildings in the 1840s. See GOTHIC.

Gothic ■ Gothic was the dominant style in European ecclesiastical architecture from the 12th to the 15th centuries, replacing the ROMANESQUE style. It also inspired architecture and the decorative arts throughout the 18th and 19th centuries.

The characteristics of medieval Gothic architecture can also be seen in the furniture of the time, such as COFFERS and tables, and in metalwork, especially in ecclesiastical silver such as CHALICES, patens, monstrances, and reliquaries.

The manufacture of STAINED GLASS reached its peak, while IVORY carving, mainly of religious and courtly themes, was also of exceptional

Goss, William Henry
A London crested china model of the Cenotaph.

Gothic Revival
Two silver-gilt pedestal bowls, by Nathan & Hayes. c. 1903 and c. 1913.

Gothic Revival
Pitch pine King Carver dining chair, in the Gothic Revival style. c. 1880.

G

quality. The Gothic style was superseded by the RENAISSANCE style in Southern Europe in the 15th century, but it flourished in Northern Europe well into the 16th century, especially in metalwork.

Gothic style A style of 18th-century architecture and decorative arts inspired by medieval GOTHIC architecture. Unlike the more historically accurate 19th-century GOTHIC REVIVAL, it was essentially decorative and fanciful. Although first used for garden buildings, the style was employed for interior decoration and furnishings at the writer Horace Walpole's house at Strawberry Hill, Twickenham, Middlesex (1750s), and at Fonthill Abbey, Wiltshire (begun 1796), built for the collector William Beckford. However, Gothic architectural motifs were simply applied to 18th-century forms and sometimes fancifully combined with ROCOCO or CHINOISERIE motifs; little attempt was made to replicate authentic medieval furnishings. Arches, pinnacles, crockets, tracery, frets, quatrefoils, and other architectural motifs are characteristically added to standard 18th-century forms.

Gouda potteries ■ An early factory was set up in Gouda, Holland, in 1621, by Willem Jansz who made tin-enameled earthenware but was not successful. The later factory, Zuid Holland, was founded in 1898 and was one of the leading Dutch potteries until it closed in 1965. Gouda pottery was particularly important in the early 20th century, producing many pieces in ART NOUVEAU and ART DECO styles. There are three modern factories in Gouda.

Gouge carving Shallow, carved decoration, often fluted or architectural, scooped out with a gouging tool and most commonly found on late 16th- and 17th-century oak furniture.

Gout stool ■ A foot stool with an adjustable seat, the height and angle of which could be altered by a ratchet to suit the gout sufferer; alternatively, a fixed stool with generous upholstery. Gout stools were especially common in late-18th- and 19th-century England.

Gouthiere, Pierre (1732–1813) A French bronzeworker and gilder. He became a master gilder in 1758, and in the 1760s and 1770s was the preeminent gilder and bronzeworker at the court of Louis XVI. He produced a wide variety of furnishings in the NEOCLASSICAL style, including candlesticks, chandeliers, mirror frames, furniture mounts, and clock cases, characterized by high-quality CHASING and modeling. Gouthiere executed models by leading sculptors, including Louis-Simon Boizot, who designed his most famous work, the Avignon Clock (1771). His work is rare and fakes are common.

Graal ■ A complex decorative glass technique developed by designer Simon Gate and master glassblower Knut Bergqvist at the ORREFORS glass factory in Sweden from 1916. This was the first time that colored decorative motifs were encased internally within the walls of the vessel as opposed to being applied to its surface. A glass "blank" was made, sometimes comprising a number of layers of differently colored glass. It was then CAMEO cut to create a pattern and reveal underlying layers before being reheated in the furnace, allowing it to be blown and formed. These processes could cause the pattern to expand with the form and impart a fluidity to the design. After 1930 a thick layer of usually colorless clear glass was added, creating an optical effect and a heavy weight. The technique is still used today.

Graffito See SGRAFFITO.

Graham, George (c.1673–1751) A renowned English clock- and watchmaker. He began as assistant to Thomas TOMPION but set up his own business in London after Tompion's death. Graham made various types of clocks and instruments, but is best known for two mechanisms designed to improve the accuracy of clocks: the invention of the DEADBEAT escapement in 1715 and the development of TOMPION'S CYLINDER ESCAPEMENT in the early 1700s.

Graining The painting of woodwork or wooden furniture, almost invariably

Gothic
Regency Gothic oak bookcase cabinet.

Gouda potteries
Gouda pottery vase, with painted marks and a bird.

Gout stool
Gustav Stickley gout stool.

Multiple layers of glass

Graal
Wedgwood graal vase, designed by Ronald Stennett-Willson. 1970s.

constructed from softwood, with a counterfeit grain in imitation of a more expensive hardwood.

Gramophone A machine using recorded discs, a stylus, and a diaphragm to reproduce sound that is amplified through a horn. The American inventor Thomas Edison pioneered the use of wax cylinders to reproduce sound with his PHONOGRAPH in 1877, but the gramophone, using flat discs, was developed by Emile Berliner in 1888. It may have external or concealed horns or horns mounted on decorative cabinets. The gramophone evolved into the record player with an electric turntable.

Grand Rapids Furniture Grand Rapids was an American center for furniture production from the mid-19th century. The Grand Rapids Fair was a place for manufacturers to attract retailers. Gustav STICKLEY chose to launch his furniture at the 1900 show in an attempt to attract more support for his furniture among the middle classes. By 1908 there were 49 furniture factories here. Many closed in the Depression of the 1920s but revived in the late 1930s with mass-produced modern designs.

Grand Tour ■ The journey undertaken by young European gentlemen, especially British, to complete their education. In a tour lasting one or two years, they visited major cities in France, the Low Countries, and sometimes Germany and Eastern Europe. The tour always culminated in Italy, regarded as the center of art, architecture, and learning. The Grand Tour developed in the late 16th and early 17th centuries but was most popular during the 18th century, when visitors to Italy went to admire ancient Roman sculpture and architecture and RENAISSANCE and BAROQUE painting.

Collecting art and antiquities eventually became one of the main functions of the tour, and the formation of collections by British visitors had a powerful impact on the development of Classically inspired architecture and design in 18th-century Britain. One of the earliest travelers making the Grand Tour was Thomas Howard, 2nd Earl of Arundel, who made several tours, most notably one in 1613 in the company of architect Inigo Jones, and who formed the first collections of Classical sculpture and Old Master drawings in England.

In the following century the development of the PALLADIAN STYLE was largely a result of the enthusiasm of Richard Boyle, 3rd Earl of Burlington, for the work of the architect Andrea Palladio, which he saw on his second Grand Tour in 1719. Artists and architects also made the tour, in particular Robert ADAM, James Wyatt, and William CHAMBERS, renowned exponents of the NEOCLASSICAL style in Britain. The popularity of the Grand Tour reached a peak in the late 18th century, following the discovery of Herculaneum and Pompeii. It declined with the development of modern tourism.

Grande sonnerie A STRIKING SYSTEM in which the quarter hours strike one, two, and three times with a different tone from that of the hour bell. The preceding hour may also be struck at each quarter.

Grandfather clock See LONGCASE CLOCK.

Grand-feu See HIGH-TEMPERATURE COLORS.

Graniteware ■ The term used for several types of English and North American 18th- and 19th-century pottery. 1. Wares made by mingling segments of differently colored clays (solid AGATEWARE) or given a surface coating of differently colored slips or glazes. 2. Earthenware or stone china sprayed with lead glaze to give a speckled appearance, made by WEDGWOOD and several Staffordshire potteries in the 18th century. 3. Durable white ironstone-type services and functional ware produced by DAVENPORT and others from about 1850.

Granulation ■ The creation of decorative patterns or texture on gold or silver, usually by applying granules, beads, or particles of the metal to the surface of the piece.

Grapevine motif ■ A decorative motif with ancient origins, sacred to Bacchus and Apollo in Classical mythology. The grapevine also plays a symbolic role in Judaic and Christian iconography. An important element of Renaissance

Grand Tour
Italian micromosaic table top, with Doves of Pliny at the center. Late 19th century.

Faux granite finish

Graniteware
Enameled metal graniteware candlestick holder.

Granulation
George IV open-faced pocket watch with a granulated gold dial. 1820.

Grapevine motif
Ring with a lapis lazuli in a silver grapevine motif setting. c. 1900.

ornament, grapevines decorated vessels associated with the serving and drinking of wine and the handles of 19th-century flatware and glassware in the 17th and 18th centuries. The motif appears in decorative schemes as a symbol of fall.

Grate ■ A raised container in a fireplace, usually an iron or steel basket, introduced in the 16th century to hold coal, which required an updraft to burn. Grates became more elaborate and designs were included in cabinet-makers' pattern books.

Gravity clock A clock in which the power source is the weight of the clock itself. The clock mechanism slides slowly down two columns under the influence of gravity to provide the power. See RACK CLOCK.

Gravity escapement A type of ESCAPEMENT developed in the mid-19th century in TURRET CLOCKS—for example, Big Ben at the Houses of Parliament, London. The impulse from the escapement to the pendulum is independent of the power applied to the TRAIN and also of the action of wind and weather.

Gravyboat See SAUCEBOAT.

Gray, Eileen ■ (1878–1976) An Irish architect and furniture designer, born in Enniscorthy, County Wexford. She trained at the Slade School of Art, London, then moved to Paris in 1902 to train with a Japanese LACQUER master. Her early designs were largely for lacquer furniture: screens, tables, and some larger pieces. Her all-white lacquer bedroom suite shown at

the Salon des Artistes Decorateurs in Paris, in 1923, was equally admired and criticized. From 1925 she made increasing use of tubular steel, glass, and aluminum in her furniture designs.

Great Exhibition, The The "Great Exhibition of the Works of Industry of All Nations" was held in the Crystal Palace in Hyde Park, London, from May to October 1851. It featured manufactured objects from all over the world, with an emphasis on technological innovations. Profits were used to build the new South Kensington (later Victoria & Albert) Museum.

Greatbach, William (1735–1813) A modeler, potter, and maker of transfer-printed creamware at Lane Delph in Fenton, Staffordshire, and best known for teapots

GREEK REVIVAL

A style of architecture and decorative arts inspired by ancient Greek art, Greek Revival was popular in Europe and the US from around 1750 to 1850. Interest in Greek art emerged as part of the NEOCLASSICAL STYLE through the publication of Greek studies such as *The Antiquities of Athens* (1762) by James Stuart and Nicholas Revett. An early strand of this, known in France as the *goût grec* ("Greek taste"), was characterized by well-proportioned forms decorated with architectural motifs—Vitruvian scrolls, urns, Greek key pattern—and was much heavier than the later style popularized by Robert ADAM.

The Greek Revival reached its peak of popularity during the REGENCY period, perhaps stimulated by the arrival of the Parthenon (Elgin) Marbles in England in 1806. Dominated by austere, monumental forms, it was adopted by leading architects such as Sir John Soane and Benjamin Latrobe, while Thomas Hope pioneered a more archaeologically accurate approach to furniture, copying designs from ancient Greek pottery. Massive urn and krater forms, sparingly decorated with palmettes, ANTHEMIONS,

and BEADING, were popular in silver (for example, pieces by Benjamin Smith) and ceramics (WEDGWOOD vases). John Flaxman popularized flat, linear depictions of Greek mythology through his illustrations of Homer's works. The style declined from the 1850s, but Greek motifs were used throughout the 19th and into the 20th century.

Dish
Spode Greek series dish, depicting Artemis drawn by a griffin and a lynx. c. 1815–30.

Bergère
Louis XVI giltwood *bergère*, stamped "Jacob." c. 1785.

Console table
George II carved giltwood eagle console table, the marble top resting on a deep frieze carved with Greek key pattern.

depicting the Prodigal Son. An extant bill for modeling designs for WEDGWOOD (with whom he was closely associated) includes "a leaf candlestick, 1 pineapple teapot." Early wares are not normally marked, but waste pieces have been found with the impressed "W.G." monogram.

Greek key See KEY PATTERN.

Greek pottery ■ Greek civilization began around 1700 BCE, when Hellenic people from the north settled in the mainland and islands of what is now Greece, the first extensive civilization being the Mycenaean. Greek pottery is mostly utilitarian, wheel-made, painted, unglazed, and low-fired. Large vessels were made in sections and LUTED, then smoothed on the potter's wheel. Most became distorted in the firing process. Shapes used over the centuries include the AMPHORA (storage jar), KRATER (mixing bowl), *kyathos* (jug for wine), *kylix* (shallow stem cup), *hydria* (three-handled water pot), *oenochoe* (jug for wine), *kantharos* (small drinking goblet), *lekythos* (oil jug), ARYBALLOS (small vase for oil or ointment), *pyx* (toilet box), and the *psykter* (cooler for iced water).

Greek pottery is classified by style: 1. Geometric style (1000–700 BCE): Shapes include amphoras and *hydrias* decorated with bands of geometric motifs and human and animal figures in silhouette. Some were large, egg-shaped vases with trumpet necks and tall stems for tomb monuments, painted with funeral processions. 2. Oriental influence (750–550 BCE): The Geometric style declined and became simply narrow bands. Shapes were more interesting—lion-mouthed jugs, owl, perfume bottles, and later, human- and gorgon-head scent bottles. Silhouette painting was gradually reduced to outline, while animals, birds, and plants became naturalistic. 3. Black Figure style (600–530 BCE): Developed by Corinthian potters who painted human figures and built up an extensive export trade, it was improved by Athenian potters. Some wares are signed. Greeks traveled to many areas of the Mediterranean, and pottery has been found wherever they settled—for example, in Italy and Egypt. 4. Red Figure style (530–470 BCE): Figures were drawn in a fine line against a black ground, showing anatomical details and flowing draperies. 5. Mixed style (from 450 BCE): The defeat of Athens in the Peloponnesian war brought an end to painted pottery vases and metal (bronze) vases became more commonly used.

Green glazed wares ■ Green has been one of the most common colors used in pottery decoration and glazes from early times. Copper in a lead glaze gives a leaf or sea green; in an alkaline glaze, it is blue-green. Copper was used to produce the greens of early tin-enameled pottery and the overglaze pigments popular from the 18th century.

Greene & Greene An architectural practice of brothers Charles Sumner Greene and Henry Mather Greene in Pasadena, California. They designed the furniture and furnishings for their characteristically long and low bungalows. Their work shows the influence of Japan and the ARTS AND CRAFTS Movement. Pieces are jointed with screws concealed in slots, and pegs were used to decorative effect; the edges are rounded and softened. The Peter Hall Manufacturing Company made their designs to a high standard.

Greetings card Originating from 18th-century European visiting cards, greetings cards were popular in the mid-19th century. Sir Henry COLE hired artist John Calcott Horsley to design the first Christmas card in 1843 and this was followed by cards produced for all manner of occasions. Raphael Tuck & Sons and Thomas De La Rue were the principal makers of British Victorian cards. In the 19th century elaborate cards were made for Valentine's Day, Easter, and Christmas.

Grendey, Giles (1693–1780) An important mid-18th-century English cabinet-maker. Born in Wootton-under-Edge, Gloucestershire, he was apprenticed in London in 1709. By 1716 he was a freeman of the Joiners' Company. His clients included Spanish and English nobility, for whom he made high-quality walnut, MAHOGANY, and JAPANNED pieces.

Griffen, Smith & Hill A pottery founded in 1880 in Phoenixville, Pennsylvania, by

G

179

Grate
George III cast-iron and brass fire grate with a railed basket above a pierced frieze. 19th century.

Gray, Eileen
The non-lacquered version of Gray's Art Deco Transat chair. 1925–26.

Greek pottery
Plaque, representing the head of Demeter. 550–500 BCE.

Green glazed wares
A Yorkshire green-glazed creamware jug with ribbon and floral decoration. c. 1770.

a partnership headed by John Griffen, an ironmaker, as a successor to the Phoenix Pottery, established 1872. It is best known as the producer of Etruscan majolica, the most successful majolica glazed ware in the United States. Most Etruscan majolica, which resembles English majolica, is marked with a "GSH" monogram, sometimes including the word "Etruscan" or a design number with the prefix "E."

Griffin ■ A mythological creature (also called griffon, or gryphon) with the body of a lion and the head, claws, and wings of an EAGLE, with origins in the ancient East. It was a popular decorative motif for RENAISSANCE furniture. An emblem of courage and watchfulness, it often appears without wings in heraldry designs. Its association with Apollo, the sun god, rendered it appropriate for CANDLESTICKS, TORCHÈRES, CANDELABRA, perfume burners, and engraved glassware during the NEOCLASSICAL period. The motif was also used in the REGENCY and EMPIRE styles.

Grisaille ■ The French term for decorative patterns or imagery painted on wood, GLASS, CERAMICS, plaster, or stone in a palette of gray, black, and white. Favored during the RENAISSANCE period, it was adopted in the 16th century by LIMOGES enamelers. The technique was sometimes used to imitate CAMEO decoration and was used by NEOCLASSICAL designers in the late 18th century who wished to simulate original Classical sculpture and moldings.

Grödnertal ■ A valley in Tirol, Austria, that has become a generic term for early 19th-century wooden dolls. Grödnertals can be distinguished from ordinary PEG DOLLS by their finely painted features and hair, often with an accentuated comb on the crown and kiss-curls on the forehead. They are slender, usually with double-jointed limbs and gessoed hands and feet.

Gropius, Walter (1883–1969) A German architect and teacher who worked with Peter BEHRENS from 1908 to 1910, and in 1919 effectively founded the BAUHAUS, of which he was director until 1928. Gropius was a Modernist whose modular furniture greatly influenced postwar designers. He moved to London in 1934, where he practiced architecture and was head of design at Isokon. After staying in Britain, he emigrated to the US in 1937 and became a professor at Harvard.

Gros bleu ■ An intense UNDERGLAZE blue, introduced at VINCENNES in 1749. When copied by English porcelain factories, it was often called MAZARIN.

Gros point An embroidery stitch in which the embroidery thread usually crosses two threads of the coarse canvas foundation on which it is worked. Gros point was particularly fashionable for seat covers during the 18th and 19th centuries.

Grotesque Ornament consisting of linked motifs such as animal and human figures, masks, panels, SPHINXES, and flowers, often combined in fantastical compositions. Grotesques first appeared in European decorative arts during the RENAISSANCE of the early 16th century. They were derived from the discovery of painted and sculpted wall decoration with such motifs in the ruins of subterranean Roman buildings (known as "grotte")—for example, the Golden House of Nero, excavated around 1500. This Classical ornament was adapted for interior decoration by Raphael in his designs for the interiors of the Vatican Loggie, executed largely by his assistant, Giovanni di Udine. Thereafter, grotesque motifs were introduced throughout Europe in every medium of applied art, especially textiles, murals, tapestries, and ceramics.

The style of grotesques evolved over the centuries. Mannerist designers of the 16th century, including Jacques Androuet du Cerceau, Cornelis Floris, and Cornelis Bos, incorporated scrolls and broad bands of STRAPWORK. In the late 17th and early 18th centuries, the individual elements of grotesques became lighter and more attenuated, in keeping with the RÉGENCE and ROCOCO styles, such as in designs by Jean BÉRAIN. Grotesques remained a popular motif in the NEOCLASSICAL period and the 19th century, but fantastical elements were more restrained and the ornament was often arranged within panels rather than as loose structures.

Griffin
Regency giltwood and bronzed griffin stool. c. 1810.

Grisaille
Qianlong grisaille coffee cup, with the arms of Wilson. c. 1765.

Grödnertal
Wooden Grödnertal doll, with painted hair and a comb. c. 1830.

Gros bleu
Pattern "4051" Spode scent bottle and cover, with mazarin blue ground. c. 1805.

Grotto ornament Decorative ornament inspired by artificial grottoes, particularly irregular rockwork, exotic shells, and creatures such as frogs and snails. This type of ornament originated in the 16th century, particularly in ceramics by Bernard PALISSY, but was also a feature of the 18th-century ROCOCO style, especially in the silver of Juste-Aurele Meissonnier, Nicholas SPRIMONT, and Paul Crespin.

Groult, André (1884–1967) A French furniture designer and member of the Société des Artistes Décorateurs, who contributed to several pavilions at the Exposition des Arts Décoratifs et Industrielles Modernes in Paris in 1925. He is best known for his ART DECO furniture, often in oak, decorated luxuriously with SHAGREEN mosaic and rosewood inlaid with ivory.

Ground color The surface color of ceramics, onto which painted decoration is often applied. Originating in China during the MING DYNASTY, ground colors were used in Europe from the early 18th century, first at MEISSEN and later at almost all porcelain factories.

Growler A sound-producing mechanism (also called a "voice box") used in TEDDY BEARS from the early 20th century until the 1950s. It usually consisted of a weight in a cardboard tube with air holes.

Grueby, William Henry ■ (1867–1925) An American art potter and founder of the GRUEBY FAIENCE COMPANY in Boston. Grueby is thought to have been influenced by the work of French potters Chaplet and DELAHERCHE, who had exhibited in the US. He is best known for his hand-thrown vases, which have relief or carved decoration, particularly leaves and flowers, and distinctive matte glazes in browns, greens, and ochers. Today the most desirable examples of Grueby's work include large, signed vases with decoration in contrasting colors (usually yellow petals on a green background) and lamp bases that were made for TIFFANY. In the late 20th century inexpensive decorative Grueby copies became common in the US.

Guard chain A long gold, silver, or gilt metal chain usually composed of a series of small, uniform, repeated links. Guard chains were frequently used to suspend a fob watch, locket, keys, or accessories and were in common use from the early 19th to the early 20th century.

Gubbio potteries A center of MAIOLICA manufacture in Urbino, Italy, famous for LUSTER decoration. This was introduced by Giorgio Andreoli in 1490, and wares bearing his signature survive today. He produced a gold luster that is much finer than that made by the DERUTA potteries and a brilliant ruby luster. From around 1530 wares from Urbino and Faenza were sent to Gubbio to be enriched with luster. In the 19th century, luster decoration was revived in Gubbio by Giovannni Spinacci.

G

181

GRUEBY FAIENCE COMPANY

This American art pottery was founded in 1894 by William H. Grueby in Boston. Throughout its history, the company specialized in handmade tiles and slip-cast vessels with thick, matt glazes in organic Grueby vase tones, mostly shades of green, brown, yellow, and ocher. Although the pottery it produced was much admired, the company was never prosperous. In 1908 it went bankrupt, and in 1910 William opened the Grueby Faience and Tile Company, which made architectural wares. In 1920 this was bought out by the C. Pardee Works of Perth Amboy, New Jersey.

Tin-glazed vase
A Grueby vase with tooled and applied overlapping broad leaves, finished in a matt vegetal green tin glaze.

Maker's mark
Grueby vases are marked with a circular designation "Grueby Pottery—Boston, Mass" around a lotus blossom.

Tin-glazed tile
A Grueby yellow and vegetal green tin-glazed tile depicting a candlestick.

Guéridon A small ornamental wooden stand originally designed to hold a CANDELABRUM. Introduced in France in the mid-17th century, the pedestal base of Louis XIV *guéridons* often took the form of a carved figure of an African carrying a round tray. By the end of the 18th century the term *guéridon* was used for round tables with a splayed support and waisted legs.

Guglet ■ A ceramic or glass water bottle often with a hollow KNOP at the top of a tall neck, causing the water to make a gurgling sound as it is poured.

Guild of Handicraft Ltd. A guild founded by C. R. ASHBEE in London in 1888 as a School of Handicraft, which later became a guild of artist-craftsmen. Ashbee designed for them and some early work appears with his initials "CRA." When the guild was registered as a limited company in 1898, the marks became "G of H Ltd." The company moved to Chipping Campden, Gloucestershire, in 1902. Although it closed in 1908, it continued loosely as a guild, with the remaining silversmiths, metalworkers, and furniture-makers working as individuals until 1921. The silversmith George Hart continued to make silverware and the work continued through his son, Henry, grandson, David, and his great-grandsons. The Hart silversmiths have used the mark "G of H" since 1912.

Guilloché ■ A continuous scroll pattern of interlacing bands twisted to form a braid, the gaps occasionally filled with rosettes or other floral motifs. Originally a FRIEZE ornament in Classical architecture, it was revived in the RENAISSANCE. Adopted as a decorative motif for metalwork and carved, inlaid, and painted furniture from the middle of the 16th century, the pattern was popular during the NEOCLASSICAL period. Guilloché is often produced by mechanical methods for gold and silver items.

Guimard, Hector ■ (1867–1942) A principal French ART NOUVEAU architect, decorator, and designer, best known for his designs for the entrances to the Paris Metro. The creator of wonderfully fluid, organic and often asymmetric designs, Guimard was highly regarded for his furniture and metalware. He emigrated to the US in 1938.

Gul A Persian term for "flower." It refers to a stylized flowerhead motif seen particularly in Central Asian Turkoman rugs.

Gunmetal A bronzelike alloy used mainly in the manufacture of gun barrels, but also for some furnishings.

Gustavsberg Pottery ■ A factory founded near Bredsjö, Sweden, in 1786, initially producing FAIENCE in the style of MARIEBERG. From about 1820 the factory made STAFFORDSHIRE-type pottery and also copied Wedgwood's JASPER WARE. In the 1840s and 1860s, it used self-colored prints in UNDERGLAZE blue or black, with scenic centers and elaborate borders in the English manner of the period. A modern revival took place around 1900 when Gunnar Wennerberg was appointed as the art director, followed by Wilhelm Kåge in 1917, whose famous Argenta range was produced from 1929 to 1952. The factory is still in operation.

Guttae Small, droplike projections beneath the triglyph on the ARCHITRAVE of a Doric column. Decorative ornament resembling guttae, known in the 18th century as "bells," "drops," or "Doric drops," appears on NEOCLASSICAL furniture. Occasionally guttae formed the feet of tables and chairs, as seen in the designs of Thomas CHIPPENDALE.

Gutta-percha A rubberlike material made from the resin of the Malaysian *Palaquium* tree, and used from the mid-19th century for various items, including dolls, photograph frames, and golf balls.

Gutty The name given to a golf ball made of GUTTA-PERCHA, which replaced the FEATHERY ball.

Guglet
Worcester porcelain hand-painted blue and white guglet. c. 1758.

Guilloché
Detail of amaranth, and marquetry commode showing guilloché. c. 1770.

Guimard, Hector
French Art Nouveau bronze vase, by Hector Guimard.

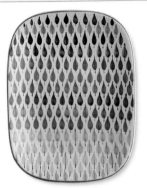

Gustavsberg Pottery
Gustavsberg plate with a polychrome trellis pattern. c. 1940–50.

H

Hagenauer, Carl (1872–1928) Goldsmith-trained Austrian designer who founded the Hagenauer Werkstätte in Vienna, in 1898. The workshop, which closed in 1956, is best known for its sculptural figures fashioned in metal and often combined with wood. Subjects range from sticklike African figures to Western athletes, sailors, and animals.

Haig, Thomas (died 1803) An English businessman, now better known as the partner and bookkeeper of Thomas CHIPPENDALE, with whom he worked following the death of Chippendale's first partner, James Rannie, in 1766. After Chippendale's death, Haig carried on the business with Chippendale's son, Thomas Chippendale the younger.

Haircloth A hard-wearing furniture covering made from a woven combination of hair from horses' manes and tails or camel hair and linen or cotton. Following its mention in George HEPPLEWHITE's pattern book, *The Cabinet-maker and Upholsterer's Guide*, it became a popular choice for upholstery for library and dining chairs from the last

quarter of the 18th century. Haircloth was also used for stiffening garments.

Hairwork picture ■ An embroidered picture worked in hair and occasionally with fine SILK onto a silk satin ground. They were fashionable in the late 18th and early 19th centuries, especially as mourning pictures.

Hairy paw foot ■ A foot, complete with hair, carved in the form of an animal's paw, usually a lion's. This type of foot originated in Classical Greece and was commonly used on 18th-century and REGENCY furniture.

Half-hour strike See STRIKING SYSTEMS.

Half hunter See HUNTER.

Half-tester See TESTER.

Hall chair ■ A formal high-backed wooden chair, with a hard seat and with or without arms. It was introduced in the 18th century and placed in the halls or corridors of grand houses, where it was used as a waiting chair. Usually made of OAK or MAHOGANY, the backs were often carved with Classical motifs, family crests, or coats of arms.

Hall stand ■ A stand with rows of hooks for hats above an open umbrella stand. Introduced in the early 19th century, these were made of wood or metal, usually in elaborate cast iron, and often included a shelf, drawers, and a mirror.

Hallmarking The practice of stamping on a GOLD or SILVER item to attest to its purity and also enable it to be traced to its source, in the event of its proving to be below standard. In most European countries hallmarking dates back to the Middle Ages. Usually, gold- and silversmiths belonged to guilds who administered their own standards.

From 1300 onward, silversmiths in Britain were required to have silver items ASSAYED. In 1327 Edward III granted a charter to the Worshipful Company of Goldsmiths to enforce the assaying system, and silversmiths had to take their wares to the Goldsmiths' Hall in London for testing. The Goldsmiths' Company ensured that a standard of purity for metals was maintained and kept records of all silversmiths and their maker's marks. If a piece passed the tests, the hallmark was stamped on it.

French silver was marked from around 1272 and a royal decree introduced a standard in 1378. French silver was stamped by the silversmiths' guild from the 16th century but the purity of the silver still varied. It was not until after the Revolution, in 1797, when control passed from the guilds to the state, that two standards were established: 95 percent and 80 percent purity, denoted by the numerals 1 and 2, respectively.

German silver standards were also

Inlaid whiplash plant-form motifs

Hairwork picture A 19th-century gold mourning brooch with a lock of hair.

Paw foot

Hairy paw foot
A Regency mahogany cellaret on hairy paw feet with brass casters. Early 19th century.

Hall chair
One of a pair of mahogany hall chairs, with carved back. Early 19th century.

Hall stand
English Art Nouveau mahogany hall stand, with inlay and tile work. c. 1890.

H

184

controlled by the guilds until Germany became a state at the end of the 19th century. Items were struck with the town and the maker's mark. Some larger towns also had a date letter system. A crown and crescent mark was introduced in 1888 to denote purity of at least 80 percent. From the 16th century, Spanish silver had the town and the maker's marks, with the assay master also adding his own mark. A number denotes the year of testing.

Assay offices were set up in Moscow and St. Petersburg in the 17th century. Russian silver was struck with a city mark, assay mark, and the maker's mark. In the US a standard for purity and marking was not established until 1869, when the sterling standard was adopted.

Hamada, Shoji ■ (1894–1978) A Japanese STUDIO POTTER, born in Tokyo, who was influential in Britain, Japan, and the US.

He was a lifelong friend and supporter of Bernard LEACH and helped him to establish a pottery in St. Ives, Cornwall. Hamada worked at ST. IVES from 1920 to 1923, and exhibited in London in 1923, 1929, and 1931. He established his own pottery in Mashiko, Japan, in 1930, and was declared "A National Living Treasure" in 1955.

Hamadan carpets Carpets made in Hamadan, a city in West Persia, and the surrounding villages in the 19th and 20th centuries. Hamadan carpets have a coarse, open weave and a geometric or stylized floral design in shades of pink and blue. Characteristically, pieces are woven with wool pile on a single-wefted cotton foundation.

Hammered A term used to describe metal that has been fashioned into shape over a wooden block or leather pad by repeated hammer blows. Although a hammered

finish is often polished smooth, during the ARTS AND CRAFTS period in particular, the numerous small hammer dents were often left or even added as surface decoration to give a textured, mottled effect.

Hanau Pottery ■ A German FAIENCE factory started by two Dutch potters, Daniel Behaghel and his son-in-law, Jacobus van der Walle, in 1661. It continued under several changes of ownership until 1806. The factory had Dutch owners and employed Dutch workers until it was taken over by Heinrich von Alpen in 1726. Although the early wares are imitative of Dutch blue and white ceramics, they did not use the lead OVERGLAZE (*kwaart*) that gave the Dutch ware its shiny surface. Dutch and Chinese influence lasted until the middle of the 18th century, when it gave way to DEUTSCHE BLUMEN and some use of enamel colors and gold. The quality

HALLMARKS

A hallmark usually consists of a collection of stamps on silver or gold items, which gives a brief history of the piece. Stamps may denote the purity, the maker's name, the place of origin, and the date of assay. In the UK assaying centers were first established in Birmingham, London, Sheffield, and Edinburgh. The hallmark on a silver item made in the British Isles after 1544 consists of five statutory items: the maker's mark; the sterling mark attesting

to the required standard of silver; the assay mark indicating the town in which the piece was tested; the date letter (which varies from town to town); and finally, special commemorative marks added by the maker. Pre-Revolution French silver had four stamped marks, which comprised the stamp of the silversmith, a town or city mark related to the *ferme générale*, a uniquely styled date mark guaranteeing the silver content, and a duty mark. After 1797

the marks were reduced to three: one showing a cockerel, an old man's head, or the head of Minerva guaranteeing the silver content; a duty mark; and the maker's mark. Later French marks show Minerva's head and the makers' mark. In the US there was no standard system of assaying and hallmarking until 1869, though some goods from the mid-1800s were marked from "standard" to "premium." In 1869 sterling silver was adopted throughout the US.

French hallmark
French hallmark for Pierre François Grandguillaume, Besançon. 1743.

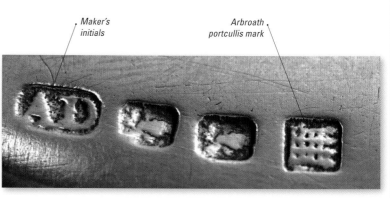

Maker's initials

Arbroath portcullis mark

Scottish hallmark
Scottish hallmark for Andrew Davidson, Arbroath. c. 1825.

of the wares declined from 1787 and the factory finally closed in 1806.

Hancock, Robert (1731–1817) An engraver who made prints for TRANSFER PRINTING onto porcelain. He worked at BOW from 1753, then at WORCESTER, CAUGHLEY, and other factories. His best-known subjects are The Tea Party, L'Amour, and The Fortune Teller. Some examples on Worcester porcelain are marked with the letters "RH," and an anchor, which is a rebus on the name of Holdship, a director of the factory.

Hancock, William (1794–c. 1860) An American furniture-maker active in Boston from 1820 to about 1850. Hancock's early designs in the fashionable English Regency style compare to Duncan PHYFE. After around 1830, Hancock made parlor furniture and is credited with introducing the spring-seated ROCKING CHAIR with buttoned upholstery, known generically as the "American rocker."

Hand cooler A solid, egg-shaped piece of glass, marble, or hardstone to cool the hands. Made in France and England in the 18th century.

Hand warmer A small receptacle containing hot water or charcoal embers for warming the hands in cold weather. Hand warmers were made from the late Middle Ages in COPPER, BRASS, or SILVER, often with a pierced, spherical outer cover, sometimes in the shape of a book.

Handcraft See L. & J.G. STICKLEY.

Handel Company ■ An American glass manufacturer founded in Meriden, Connecticut, in 1885, by Philip J. Handel and Adolph Eydam, and named The Handel Company in 1893. Handel specialized in decorating reverse-painted glass lampshades. These are typically hemispherical and painted or enameled, with scenic views or flora on the interior and with a FROSTED or "chipped ice" finish on the exterior. Most were signed on the shade border and metalwork, particularly from 1910. Rare designs rival many TIFFANY lamps in value. The company closed in 1936.

Handkerchief table A type of 18th-century American table, with a single drop leaf. Both the leaf and top are triangular in shape, and when the leaf is raised, the top forms a square. The table fits neatly in a corner when the leaf is closed.

Hanger A short SWORD often used for hunting. Sometimes called a "cuttoe," from the French *couteau de chasse* (hunting knife). The term also describes the device used to suspend a sword from a waist belt.

Hansen, Fritz Cutting-edge furniture manufacturer founded in Copenhagen in 1872, and still in production today. First known for it post–World War I steamed bentwood furniture, it went on to work with many of the 20th and early 21st century's leading furniture designers, the most notable

being Arne JACOBSEN, for whom Hansen produced the iconic laminated wooden "Ant" chair (1952), and the "Egg" chair (1958).

Hanoverian pattern A pattern of FLATWARE and cutlery that first appeared around 1710 just before the reign of George I (1714–27), the first Hanoverian King, and that has been in production ever since. The handles have a raised rib or ridge down the front and back and a rounded terminal or end; the forks generally have two or three prongs. The early spoons produced from around 1710 to 1730 have a decorative RAT TAIL running down the length of the back of the bowls.

Hardoy chair ■ A chair consisting of a leather seat suspended by corner pockets from a rigid frame made from a continuous strip of metal. A post–World War II design, it was inspired by a folding chair used by Italian forces in the North Africa campaign and was named after the Argentinian designer Jorge Ferrari-Hardoy.

Hard-paste porcelain A hard, dense ceramic made from a compound of the feldspathic rock PETUNTSE and KAOLIN fired at a very high temperature. First made in China around 800 CE, the secret of its manufacture was not known in Europe until 1709, when J. BÖTTGER of MEISSEN discovered the formula. Despite attempts to keep it secret, the process spread to other German factories and eventually became known throughout the West.

Hamada, Shoji
St. Ives slipware pottery jar, by Shoji Hamada. c. 1922.

Hanau Pottery
Faience jug, with hand-painted blue landscape scene. c. 1720.

Handel Company
Handel table lamp shade, with reverse-painted and etched peacock design.

Hardoy chair
A black leather and chromed steel Hardoy butterfly chair.

Hardstone A collective term for decorative opaque gemstones such as ONYX, cornelian, jasper, and AGATE, suitable for carving into urns, CAMEOS, INTAGLIOS, inlay work, and PIETRA DURA.

Harewood A term for SYCAMORE or MAPLE wood that has been dyed silvery gray or green with iron oxide. It was used for VENEERING and BANDING small items such as TEA CADDIES and high-quality furniture.

Harigaki The Japanese term for a decorative lacquerwork technique that involves scratching or incising imagery with a needle into the surface of the lacquer before it is dry.

Harlequin set A term used to describe a set of furniture or ceramics, popular in the 18th century, in which the pieces are similar rather than identical. Today the term is also used to describe items of the same pattern or design that have been put together to make a set.

Harlequin table A variation on the sofa or PEMBROKE table, introduced at the end of the 18th century. It included a set of small drawers and pigeonholes concealed within the body of the table, which rose up by means of a system of weights.

Harrach Glassworks ■ An important glassworks founded in Harrachov, North Bohemia (Czech Republic), in 1712. The first Bohemian glassworks to use coal-fired furnaces and famous for its façon d'Angleterre cutting. Known for its luxury tableware during the 18th and 19th centuries, the company focused on Bohemian and Venetian revival designs, including cut and engraved works, some by Dominik BIEMANN. By 1900 the company was producing glass for other companies such as J. & L. LOBMEYR and MOSER, and had also become a pioneer in ART NOUVEAU glass. MODERNIST designs were produced as early as 1903, by Jan Kotera, Julius Jelinek, and Alois Metalek. After being absorbed into the Communist national glass conglomerates from 1948, the company produced blown tableware and cut lead crystal. The Harrtil range, with an internal mesh of glass fibers, similar to Kaj FRANCK's effects, was designed in 1955 by Milos Pulpitel and Milan Metalek. The company continues today.

Harris, (William) Michael (1933–94) An English glassmaker and designer who studied and taught glass design at the Royal College of Art in London, before founding MDINA Glass in Malta in 1968, ISLE OF WIGHT STUDIO GLASS in England in 1972, and Gozo Glass in Malta in 1989.

Harrison, John (1693–1776) An English clockmaker who trained as a carpenter and land surveyor, but took up clockmaking in around 1715. He invented the gridiron pendulum, a form of temperature-compensated PENDULUM, in around 1725. However, he is best known for his lengthy but eventually successful experiments to develop a marine CHRONOMETER that would enable sailors to calculate longitude accurately and thus determine their position at sea. The British government offered a prize of £20,000 for anyone who could develop such a device. Harrison began in 1728 and completed his first attempt in 1735. He was belatedly awarded the full sum by 1773, after his fourth version successfully completed sea trials in 1762.

Hausmaler ■ A German term for "home painter," used for a freelance painter who decorated porcelain and glass bought "in the white" from a factory or sold as defective goods. *Hausmalerei* of the 18th century is not classed as forgery and the work of some artists is highly prized. These include pieces by Johann and Sabina AUFFENWERTH of Augsburg, Ignaz Bottengruber of Breslau, F. J. Ferner, and Bartholomäus Seuter of Augsburg.

Haviland & Co. ■ A French pottery and porcelain factory founded in 1842, in Limoges, by the American David Haviland. The factory made porcelain mainly for the American market and achieved great commercial success. It used industrial techniques and cheap methods of decoration such as CHROMOLITHOGRAPHY as well as overglaze and underglaze painting. In 1873 a design studio was established in Paris, directed by David Haviland's son, Charles, which made ART POTTERY. In 1890 David Haviland's son, Theodore built a new factory in Limoges, which is still in production as Haviland SA. Haviland's

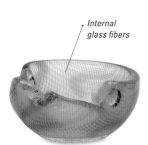

Harrach Glassworks
Harrach Harrtil glass bowl.
1950s.

Internal glass fibers

Hausmaler
Meissen tea cup and saucer, with hand-painted scene by a *hausmaler*. c. 1750.

Haviland & Co.
Haviland & Co. vase, decorated by Eugene Chaplet.

Heal & Son
Heal & Son oak Letchworth tallboy chest. 1920s.

grandson, Charles Field Haviland, took over the Alluaud porcelain factory in LIMOGES and also founded the company in New York that bears his name.

Heal & Son ■ A firm of furniture-makers and retailers founded in 1810 by John Harris Heal. Under his great grandson, Sir Ambrose Heal, the company established its place in 20th-century design history, with his own designs for furniture ranging from ARTS AND CRAFTS to ART DECO. New premises were built in 1913 in Tottenham Court Road, London. The top-floor gallery showed work by designers such as Alvar AALTO and Marcel Lajos BREUER in the 1920s and 30s. The shop still exists but the Heal family is no longer involved.

Heaped and piled effect ■ An accidental effect on Chinese blue and white porcelain of the early MING DYNASTY, where cobalt oxide was unevenly applied, producing dark spots. The effect was copied in the 18th century by painting in dark dots.

Heartwood The dense lumber from the inner core of the tree. It is usually harder and often darker in color than the SAPWOOD, the contrast between the two being used to decorative effect with such woods as YEW and LABURNUM.

Hellenistic The period of Greek civilization from the death of Alexander the Great in 323 BCE to the defeat of Antony and Cleopatra in 30 BCE.

Helmet ■ See ARMOR and MORION. An item of defensive armor for the head, used from the earliest times to the present. Helmets were made from various materials, including padded textiles, leather, horn, wickerwork, plastics, ceramics, and metals such as iron, steel, and bronze. In Europe helmets fell out of use from around 1650, although they were revived during World War I as a defense against shrapnel.

Helmet ewer ■ A EWER with either the whole or the upper body, rim, and spout resembling an inverted helmet. These ewers were made in silver and bronze, ceramics, glass, hardstone, and enamel from the early 16th to the early 18th century.

Henri Deux See SAINT-PORCHAIRE.

Hepplewhite, George ■ (died 1786) An English furniture-maker. Little is known of his life except for his PATTERN BOOK, *The Cabinet-maker and Upholsterer's Guide*, which was influential both in Europe and North America. It was published posthumously in 1788, with revised editions in 1789 and 1794. The book contains Hepplewhite's designs for slender, elegant furniture, with inlaid and painted rather than carved decoration of motifs such as SUNBURSTS, HUSKS, scrolls, and PATERAE, and for chairs with distinctive shield-shaped backs or square backs incorporating Prince of Wales feathers. His wife, Alice, continued the business after his death.

HEPPLEWHITE, GEORGE

Hepplewhite's designs are most admired for their lightness of touch and clarity of composition. Best known are his chairs with shield-shaped backs, often comprising interlaced hearts.

Hepplewhite chair
One of a set of four Hepplewhite-period, mahogany shield-back armchairs. c. 1780.

Heraldic decoration ■ A variety of emblems representing the bearer and his status in society. Developed during the 12th century, heraldic ornament was applied to architecture and on precious possessions such as silver and gold objects, porcelain, and books. From medieval times the arms of the wife's family were added to

Heaped and piled effect
Chinese vase showing heaped and piled effect on stems and tendrils. Mid-14th century.

Helmet
French cavalry trooper's steel helmet.

Helmet ewer
Transfer-printed pearlware helmet-shaped jug. c. 1820.

Heraldic decoration
Chinese armorial plate, painted with the arms of Count Tessin. 18th century.

H

187

H

those of her husband upon marriage and sometimes incorporated into the decoration of a house interior, on tapestries, or the marriage bed. In the 16th century, cities, towns, and guilds in Germany and in the Low Countries began incorporating heraldic motifs on stoneware. Coats of arms were used on dinner services in Europe and North America from the turn of the 18th century and also on CHINESE EXPORT PORCELAIN. They are still widely used on commemorative pieces of all kinds.

Herat An important carpet-producing town in the KHORASSAN district of northeast Persia during the 16th century. Carpets were very fine with floral, curvilinear patterns in jewel colors. Carpet production had effectively ended here by the mid-18th century.

Herati ▪ A frequently seen repeat design on Oriental carpets. The motif is created by a central diamond lozenge, with four serrated leaves, often resembling fish, forming the corners. It is seen in both urban and tribal rugs, carpets, and also in KILIMS from Kurdistan.

Hereke An important Turkish carpet-manufacturing town. Carpet-weaving started at the end of the 19th century and is still prolific today. The town is renowned for fine silk rugs, many of PRAYER design with delicate floral patterns, others with overall repeat designs. Woolen carpets are also made there today.

Herend Porcelain Factory ▪ Founded in Hungary in 1839 by Moritz Fischer, this factory made (and still makes, although nationalized in 1948) copies of all kinds of European and Oriental porcelain. They may be marked with the name "Herend" and the coat of arms of Hungary.

Heriz A town in northwest Persia producing carpets and some rugs during the 19th and 20th centuries. The designs have an overall repeat format or a central medallion. Earlier colors included ivory, terra-cotta, and pale blues; stronger colors were used in the 20th century. They were usually wool on cotton, although some were of silk in the late 19th century.

Herman Miller Inc. ▪ A firm of American furniture manufacturers founded by Herman Miller in Zeeland, Michigan, in 1905. In the 1930s, under Gilbert Rohde, the company became one of the most progressive makers of postwar furniture, a reputation that survives today. Designers who have worked for the firm include Charles and Ray EAMES, Isamu Noguchi, Poul Kajaerholm, and Verner Panton.

Herman, Samuel ▪ (born 1936) An American artist and glassmaker who studied at the University of Wisconsin from 1962 to 1963, after which he went to England, taking with him the STUDIO GLASS techniques he had learned from Dominick Labino and Harvey Littleton. He taught at

the Royal College of Art in London, from 1968, founded the influential Glass House in London in 1969, and worked as a consultant for Val St Lambert in France.

Hermann ▪ The Hermann dynasty of German toymakers was founded by Max Hermann in 1920 near Sonneberg, Thuringia. The first PLUSH bears were produced in 1913. Most can be distinguished by their inset snouts of shorter plush and three claws. Gebrüder Hermann introduced "Zotty" bears in the 1950s to compete with STEIFF. Hermann still produces toys today.

Herringbone banding A banding of veneer formed by two narrow strips laid together, with the grain of each running diagonally to produce a herringbone or feather effect. Herringbone banding was adopted for drawer fronts on walnut furniture of the late 17th and early 18th centuries, and was also used in early brickwork.

Herter Brothers German-born Gustav and his half-brother, Christian, were leading furniture-makers and interior decorators in New York. Gustav established his interior decorating firm in the 1850s, having previously designed silver for TIFFANY & CO. He was joined by Christian in 1860; when Gustav returned to Germany in 1870, Christian continued running the firm till around 1880. Until its

Herati
Northwest Persian carpet with a Herati border. c. 1900.

Herend Porcelain Factory
One of a pair of Herend porcelain owl bookends. 20th century.

Herman Miller Inc.
Plywood LCW chair, designed by Charles and Ray Eames. c. 1946.

Herman, Samuel
Freeform studio glass vase.

Hermann
Hermann open-mouthed teddy bear. 1930s.

closure in 1905, the firm produced some of the finest American Aesthetic and Renaissance Revival furniture, specializing in intricate inlaid work in exotic woods, and also embraced Japanese influences and the EASTLAKE style. Most examples are signed or well documented.

Heubach, Gebrüder A porcelain factory in Lichte, Thuringia, taken over in about 1820 by the Heubach brothers. After 1909 it specialized in CHARACTER DOLLS, often with INTAGLIO eyes and molded hair. Gebrüder Heubach dolls are distinguished by their facial expression, the "petulant boy" being the most sought-after. The factory also produced FAIRINGS and other biscuit porcelain and is known for its all-bisque PIANO BABIES. It closed in 1940. The company's mark was a square or a rising sun. Not to be confused with the unrelated dollmaker Ernst Heubach of Koppelsdorf.

Heyde, Georg One of the principal manufacturers of German toy soldiers, established in Dresden in 1872, producing metal solid-cast painted figures. By around 1900 he was the world's leading exporter of toy soldiers, producing armies of the world, figures of the Wild West and the ancient world, and knights. Heyde continued

production up to World War II. The factory was bombed during the war and production ceased in the late 1940s.

Highboy ■ A double CHEST-OF-DRAWERS or chest-on-chest, the American form of the English TALLBOY. Highboys were made throughout the northeastern states of the US from around 1710. The most valuable are formal, carved mahogany examples, with important family provenance and a known maker. Plain examples, typically of MAPLE, CHERRY, or WALNUT, are more common.

High-temperature colors These include colors such as shades of green (copper oxide), blue (cobalt), purple (manganese), yellow (antimony), and orange (iron), used to decorate tin-glazed earthenware until the 18th century (after which *petit feu*, or ENAMEL COLORS were more common). Known in French as *grand feu*, due to the high temperature used to unite them with a tin glaze.

High-warp A tapestry-weaving technique, used at the GOBELINS factory in Paris. The loom holds the warp threads vertically, tensioned between two horizontal rollers. The bulk of the warp is rolled onto the upper roller and the completed work is rolled at intervals onto the lower one.

Hille Company Ltd. Manufacturers of quality reproduction furniture, founded by Salomon Hille in London in 1906. It supplied

furniture to Waring & Gillow and Maples. In the 1920s and 30s Ray Hille, Salomon's daughter, created ART DECO designs and Chinese LACQUERWORK pieces after CHIPPENDALE. Robin DAY became Design Director at Hille in 1950.

Hilt The handle of a SWORD, BAYONET, DAGGER, or knife, composed of a grip, the pommel (a counterweight for the blade), and the guard, which protects the hand. Hilts, made from metal and a variety of materials, were often the most decorated part of the weapon.

Hinge A folding metal joint between two pieces of wood, such as a door and frame, or chest and lid, allowing them to open and close. In the early 17th century coffer lid hinges were made from wire loops; by the end of the century wrought-iron butterfly and strap hinges were used. Subsequently, hinges became more refined.

Hipped knee A type of CABRIOLE chair leg, which rises to the level of the seat, or in some cases above it, and which features carved decoration from its upper outward curve ("knee") upward. It was used in the early 19th century on the saber legs found on hipped knee CARD and PEMBROKE tables.

Hirado ware ■ Japanese porcelain made at Mikawachi near ARITA and exported from the port of Hirado. The main period of production was from around 1750 to about 1830.

Highboy
American North Shore, Queen Anne-style carved walnut bonnet-top highboy.

Hilt
Hilt of an Elizabeth II Wilkinson court sword.

Hirado ware
Japanese Hirado blue and white vase and cover. 19th century.

Hiramé
Three-case *hiramé* ground *inro*. Late 18th century.

H

Hiramé ■ A decorative technique in which pieces of gold or silver sheet are applied under a clear LACQUER. See NASHIJI.

Hispano-Moresque ware The Moors invaded Spain in 711CE and introduced two techniques of producing ceramics to Europe: glazing with an opaque white tin glaze and painting in metallic lusters. Malaga in southern Spain was particularly celebrated for its gold LUSTERWARE in the 14th century; Valencia and its suburbs, Manises and Paterna, also became important centers. ALBARELLI and luster dishes with coats of arms were made for rich Italian and Spanish families. The Moors were expelled from Spain in 1492, but the Hispano-Moresque style survived in the province of Valencia. Later wares usually have a coarse reddish buff body and dark blue decoration and luster.

Historicism The 19th-century revival of historical styles. While the 18th century saw revivals of the GOTHIC and classical styles, the 19th century was more concerned with accurate representations of Gothic and Classical art. There was also interest in RENAISSANCE, BYZANTINE, ISLAMIC, EGYPTIAN, ELIZABETHAN, and ORIENTAL art inspired by archaeological discoveries, scholarly publications, and the foundation of decorative arts museums. Technical advances and mechanized manufacture allowed exact replicas of historical pieces, although styles were often bizarrely combined. See ECLECTICISM.

Historismus glass ■ Largely German 19th-century glass made in styles from earlier centuries. It was popular following the reunification of Germany in 1871, when, in an attempt to create a national identity, traditional drinking glasses such as HUMPEN and RÖEMER were produced with enameled decoration of fictional coats of arms. The term is often applied to any glass in the style of earlier centuries.

Hitchcock, Lambert (1795–1856) An American chairmaker active from about 1818 in Hitchcockville (now Riverton), Connecticut. Introduced in the mid-1820s, the Hitchcock chair is still made in Riverton. Made in BIRCH or MAPLE, it is JAPANNED with a layer of black over red and decorated in gilt stenciling. Most have rush seats and a lightweight design showing the influence of SHERATON. Early Hitchcock chairs are often signed. Similar American chairs are described as "Hitchcock type."

Ho A Chinese bronze kettle with a cover and three or four legs, made from the SHANG (c. 1500–1028 BCE) to the Han dynasties (206 BCE–220 CE). The earliest form has a bulbous body, cylindrical spout, and loop handle. A later version has an oblong body, short cabriole legs, and animal mask spout.

Ho ho bird ■ The Japanese equivalent of THE PHOENIX, a mythical bird symbolizing fire, the Ho Ho bird appeared in Italian GROTESQUE ornament in the 16th century. With a long beak, curving neck, a flowing tail, claws, and crest, it was often part of 18th-century CHINOISERIE decoration for ceramics, woodwork, and plasterwork. It is frequently portrayed as an amalgam of several birds, including the PHOENIX, pheasant, stork, heron, and bird of paradise.

Hobbs, Brockunier & Co. An American glass manufacturer established in 1845 in Wheeling, West Virginia, on the site of a glassworks founded in 1818. It produced molded, cut, and plain colored and FLINT GLASS. By 1879 it was the largest glassworks in the US and was amalgamated into the US Glass Company in 1891. Before its closure in 1893, it specialized in PEACHBLOW and pressed AMBERINA glass, both introduced in 1886.

Hochschnitt A German term for "high cut." A form of relief decoration on glass where the background is cut away to leave the design standing proud on the surface. Used on early Roman glass, it is now most closely identified with superb pieces made by Bohemian and German glassmakers in the late 17th century.

Höchst pottery and porcelain factory A faience factory in Höchst run by Adam von LOWENFINCK, producing tureens and dishes modeled as turkeys, boar's heads, pheasants, fruit, and vegetables in ROCOCO form. After the arrival of Joseph RINGLER and Johann Benckgraff in 1750, the factory began to produce porcelain. It made charming Rococo

Historismus glass
Historismus beaker with the coat of arms of Prince Conty.
c. 1880.

Ho Ho Bird
Detail of Chelsea dish, with central Ho Ho bird motif.
c. 1750.

Hoffmann, Josef
Four J. & J. Kohn mahogany-stained beech tables, designed by Josef Hoffmann. 1905.

wares and figures with a creamy white paste. The modelers G. F. Riedel, Laurentius Russinger, J. P. MELCHIOR, and Simon FEILNER produced figures in MEISSEN style, including Italian conversation and comedy groups, often inspired by French engravings. Melchior modeled many groups of children. Late figures use an UNDERGLAZE blue wheel mark from around 1750 and are NEOCLASSICAL in style. Production ceased in 1796. The old Höchst molds were passed to Damm, established in around 1827, which produced the designs in FAIENCE. Other factories such as Dressel, Kister & Co. at Passau (from 1840), and Mehlem of Bonn (from 1836) also made copies.

Hoffmann, Josef ■ (1870–1956) An Austrian architect and a leading 20th-century designer. He was a founder of both the VIENNA SECESSION (1897) with Koloman MOSER, and the WIENER WERKSTÄTTE (1903), and also designed furniture (often for THONET), metalwork, jewelry, and glass (for J. & L. LOBMEYER). Hoffman favored a more geometric approach within the ART NOUVEAU style and was influenced by the work of Charles Rennie MACKINTOSH.

Hogarth chair A mid-19th-century term for a chair in the QUEEN ANNE style with cabriole legs and a splat back. It was named after the artist William Hogarth, in whose paintings such chairs are often depicted.

Hogenberg, Frans See BRAUN; Georg and HOGENBERG, Frans.

Hohlwein, Ludwig ■ (1874–1949) A German artist and poster designer. He was a pioneer in the use of large, flat areas of color and compositions of extreme simplicity. His work was evocative of the 1920s and 30s, and his designs are found on travel and other advertising posters.

Holbeinesque ■ The term given to 19th-century gold and enamel jewelry inspired by the designs of Hans Holbein, a 16th-century court artist to Henry VIII. Holbeinesque jewels are invariably enameled in several primary colors and are set with correspondingly vivid gemstones such as garnets cut in CABOCHON, chrysolites, and diamonds.

Hollow-cast figures A process invented by BRITAINS LTD. in 1893 to reduce the weight and production cost of their lead figures. The mold was filled with molten lead and left for a short while for the outside surface to cool, after which the liquid center of the figure was poured out. The method was soon copied by other makers.

Hollowware ■ A term used in relation to silver or plated wares, but also used for articles made in other metals and ceramics. It describes domestic articles such as jugs, coffeepots, and baskets that are hollow or hollowed as receptacles for food and drink. See FLATWARE.

Holly A tree (*Ilex aquifolium*) native to Britain and Europe with a hard, fine grain, and an ivory or greenish white color. It was used for inlay and MARQUETRY from the 16th century onward.

Holmegaard ■ A glassworks founded in 1825 in Zealand, Denmark, initially producing bottles and then tableware. Freelance designers were employed from about 1905 and worked in the ART DECO and MODERNIST styles, but it was with the arrival of full-time artistic director Jacob Bang in 1927 that the factory rose to prominence. Bang's designs tend to be modern, yet austere, with minimal surface decoration and an attention to function and form. His successor was Per Lütken, who joined in 1941 and produced organic, curving, budlike forms and the brightly colored Carnaby range in 1968. Bang's son, Michael, also carried on his work. Lütken designed for the factory until his death in 1998. A second glassworks connected to Holmegaard was built at Kastrup, Denmark, in 1847, changing hands many times until 1965, when it merged with Holmegaard. The company still produces glass today under the Royal Scandinavia group.

Holster A container, usually made of leather, for a pistol or REVOLVER worn on a belt or saddle.

Honey gilding A technique for gilding ceramics, and also glass. It involved mixing ground gold leaf with honey, brushing it on

Hohlwein, Ludwig
Poster advertising Munich Zoo, designed by Ludwig Hohlwein. 1911.

Holbeinesque
Holbeinesque brooch, with rubies and seed pearls. Late 19th century.

Molded and chased decoration

Hollowware
Two items of a silver hollowware tea service by Barraclough & Barraclough. 1939.

Holmegaard
Small red-cased vase of the Carnaby range, designed by Per Lütken.

H

the surface, then firing at a low temperature. The gilding could also be applied more thickly and chased and tooled. In widespread use until the end of the 18th century.

Honiton lace ■ BOBBIN LACE made in rural Devon in the 17th and 18th centuries was despatched to centers such as London from the town of Honiton and became known as Honiton lace. Designs used naturalistic motifs, including roses, birds, and wild flowers. In the 19th century the lace motifs were occasionally appliquéd onto machine-made net.

Hood ■ The part of the case on a LONGCASE CLOCK enclosing the dial and MOVEMENT, set above the trunk housing the pendulum and weights. The hoods on longcase clocks made before the 1700s were generally square and decorated with architectural-style pediments and twist columns. Later hoods were made in a variety of styles, for example, with PAGODA TOPS.

Hoof foot The hoof of the goat or ram employed as a terminal to the legs of furniture (also called cloven hoof foot). A motif first used by the ancient Egyptians, it was introduced in Europe in the late 17th century. Found on the legs of early CABRIOLE chairs, the hoof foot, also known by the French term *pied de biche*, remained a popular device throughout the 18th century.

Hooked rug ■ A type of piled rug where the pile tufts, which may be

lengths of wool or strips of material, are tied to the foundation of canvas or burlap using a hooked tool. This was a common domestic craft in Europe and the US in the 18th and 19th centuries and survives in rural areas today.

Hope chest ■ An American term for a carved or painted wooden blanket chest of a type also called a marriage or dowry chest. The most desirable hope chests are of PENNSYLVANIA DUTCH origin.

Hope, Thomas (1769–1831) An English collector and furniture designer who traveled widely in the Mediterranean and in the Middle East before settling in London, where he designed his house in Duchess Street around his collection of pictures, and furnished rooms in different styles. He collected Greek and Roman Classical sculpture and *objets d'art*, but he also took up the Egyptian style promoted by the French designer Dominique Denon. Hope's book, *Household Furniture and Decoration* (1807), was one of the most influential collections of archeologically accurate NEOCLASSICAL and REGENCY furniture designs, and included his well-known Grecian chairs.

Hornby, Frank ■ (1863–1936) The most significant figure in the British toy industry. Hornby invented the construction set called Mechanics Made Easy in 1901, renamed MECCANO in 1907. Hornby trains, in "0" gauge lithographed TINPLATE,

were introduced in 1920. The early examples up to 1925 were bolted together, as in Meccano. They were powered by CLOCKWORK until electric train sets were made in 1926. A short-lived, 240-volt set was sold from 1925. A safer 6-volt DC source was used from 1929. The range expanded into train types, rolling stock, stations, and lineside accessories like DINKY TOYS, mostly made of lithographed tinplate. When production restarted after World War II, only the small 4-wheel locomotives reappeared, and they ceased production in 1957. However, the Hornby-Dublo, the "00" gauge system produced from 1938 to compete with BASSETT-LOWKE'S Trix, was successful. Hornby was taken over by TRIANG in 1964 but became Hornby Railways again in 1971. The firm still produces today.

Höroldt (Herold), Johann Gregor (1696–1775) A German miniature and enamel painter, Höroldt went to MEISSEN in 1720, became court painter in 1723, and director in 1731. During his time, a new source of clay was discovered that produced a creamy white body. Höroldt was a color chemist and rediscovered the "secret" of the UNDERGLAZE blue used earlier by David Kohler and various other enamel colors, including those for KAKIEMON patterns. He produced a book of etchings of CHINOISERIES for use on porcelain and also a book of his color researches. He fled at the outbreak of the Seven Years War in 1756, returned to Meissen in 1763, and was pensioned off in 1765.

Honiton lace
Honiton lace handkerchief, with rose, shamrock, and thistle design. c. 1860.

Hood
Hood of an eight-day Edinburgh longcase clock, with a white dial in a mahogany case. c. 1785.

Hooked rug
American pictorial hooked rug. c. 1900.

Hope chest
Pennsylvanian painted pine dowry chest. Early 19th century.

Horse brass A decorative brass plaque attached to a horse's harness, probably of medieval origin. They were mainly produced in the 19th century in a range of often symbolic or commemorative designs such as trees, animals, flowers, diamonds, and stars. Early cast brasses are heavier than later machine-stamped ones.

Horse hair Curled horse hair has been used for upholstery since the 17th century because its springy nature retains its shape after constant use. Horse hair was also used to make a hard-wearing woven cloth for upholstering seat furniture in the 19th century.

Horseshoe table A small LIBRARY, WRITING, or WORK TABLE shaped like a horseshoe. The term also refers to a Hunt table associated with the drinking from STIRRUP CUPS prior to the start of a hunt. The shape was introduced in the 18th century and was extant throughout the 19th century.

Horta, Victor ■ (1861–1947) A leading Belgian architect and ART NOUVEAU designer. He designed integrated interiors for his buildings, including metalwork fixtures, door frames, and paneling. Horta's style was sinuous and organic and he was a catalyst in establishing the Art Nouveau style. From around 1905 he focused on teaching architecture.

Hot working The opposite of COLD WORKING, where glass is manipulated, decorated, and formed while it is still hot and molten, and thus, pliable.

Hot-water plate A dinner plate or dish popular in the REGENCY and VICTORIAN periods, made of silver, plated ware, pewter, tinned metals, or ceramics. It has a container underneath and an aperture through which it is filled with hot water to keep the plate and its contents warm.

Hour-striking A clock that strikes on every hour, invented in the 16th century. The hour-and-half-hour strike that sounds both on the hour and every half-hour is a derivative of the hour-striking.

Hourglass ■ An instrument for measuring time (also called sand glass), widely used since the Middle Ages. Early examples have two clear blown glass bulbs mounted one above the other and bound together at the necks; from the mid-18th century they were blown in one piece. Set in a metal, wood, or ivory frame with a quantity of sand flowing from the upper container into the lower at a known speed, its uses also included measuring a ship's speed.

Howard & Sons One of the best-known furniture manufacturers of its day, founded in London in 1820 by John Howard. From the 1860s the company made pieces by ARTS AND CRAFTS designers as well as its own range of high-quality upholstered furniture, notably armchairs.

Hu An ancient Chinese bronze vessel, originally used for storing wine for ritual use. The body of the vessel, often with two handles near the mouth, is usually pear-, gourd-, or flask-shaped.

Hubbard, Elbert Green (1856–1915) A leading exponent of the ARTS AND CRAFTS movement in the US. In 1895 he founded a community of craftsmen, the Roycrofters, in East Aurora, New York, based on the principles of William MORRIS, whom he had met on a visit to England in 1894. The Roycrofters produced metalwork, leatherwork, and simple MISSION furniture, marked with "R" and a cross with two horizontal bars in a circle. Hubbard's son, Elbert Hubbard Jr., took over the Roycrofters when Hubbard and his wife went down on the *Lusitania* in 1915. The Roycrofters workshops closed in 1938.

Hubley Manufacturing Company ■ One of the leading American manufacturers of early CAST-IRON toys, founded by John E. Hubley c. 1894 in Lancaster, Pennsylvania. Successful lines included horse-drawn wagons, fire-engines, and circus trains, and by the 1920s included cars and motorbikes. They were marked "Hubley" and noted for their complexity. Cast-iron production ceased in 1942 due to the war effort, with diecast and plastic being used after the war.

Huguenot The term for Protestant refugees who fled France and settled in

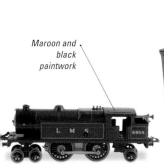
Hornby, Frank
Hornby "0" gauge clockwork 4-4-2 locomotive in LMS maroon livery.

Maroon and black paintwork

Horta, Victor
Mahogany double bed, designed by Victor Horta.

Hourglass
Turned whalebone and glass hourglass. 19th century.

Hubley Manufacturing Co.
Hubley cast-iron coupe, painted in blue.

England and other Protestant countries such as Germany, Holland, and Switzerland, following the revocation of the Edict of Nantes in 1685. After the accession of William III in England in 1688, many Huguenot craftsmen arrived in London, bringing with them the French BAROQUE style in the influential furniture designs of Daniel MAROT. Engraved decoration and new forms, including soup tureens, sauceboats, and wine coolers, were introduced by leading Huguenot silversmiths such as Paul de LAMERIE. Silk textiles were produced in SPITALFIELDS by Huguenot weavers. The silversmith and porcelain-maker Nicholas SPRIMONT was of Huguenot origin.

Hummel figure ■ A small porcelain figurine depicting a rural child, made from 1935 at William Goebel's factory in Bavaria from the designs of a Franciscan nun, Sister Maria Innocentia (Berta Hummel). Many of the original designs are still in production.

Humpen ■ A German drinking glass in the form of a tall, straight-sided beaker with a projecting foot and often a cover, used for drinking beer and wine. They were made in Germany and Bohemia from the mid-16th to the 18th century, usually of WALDGLAS, often with an enameled coat of arms. See HISTORISMUS GLASS.

Hunter ■ A watch made from around 1800 to the early 19th century with a protective hinged cover over the dial, often engraved or enameled. A half-hunter, used from about 1860, has a circular aperture in the cover through which the time can be read.

Hunting carpets A carpet design created by Persian artists of the early Safavid period (1501–1732) depicting huntsmen on horseback armed with lances and bows, tracking down their prey or fighting wild beasts. These motifs originate from Safavid manuscripts. Countless variations on this theme can be found on carpets produced since the 19th century in Persia, Turkey, and India.

Husk motif A stylized motif based on a husk of corn or the BELLFLOWER and composed of three short, flat leaves, typically in swags or bands, sometimes graduated in size or alternated with beads. It was a popular decoration on furniture, ceramics, engraved glass, and metalwork in the late 18th century, particularly in England and the US, where it replaced the heavy, florid FESTOON. Husk swags were also adopted for marble and STUCCO work.

Hutch An English term derived from the French *huche*, which denoted both a roughly constructed chest and a more sophisticated storage piece with legs, one or more doors, and carved decoration. Both were used for storing food and clothes from the Middle Ages and into the 16th century.

Hyalith glass An opaque sealing-wax-red or jet-black glass created around 1818 in Bohemia at the glasshouses of Jiri, Count van Buquoy. Hyalith glass was thought to have been inspired by the BASALT WARE and ROSSO ANTICO ware of Josiah WEDGWOOD, and was used to make similar wares, often with CHINOISERIE designs. See LITHYALIN GLASS.

Hybrid paste A porcelain formula developed around 1782 at the English factory of New Hall, Staffordshire. It combines ingredients of HARD-PASTE and SOFT-PASTE PORCELAIN in an attempt to produce a more workable body.

Hydrofluoric acid A colorless, corrosive acid that attacks silica and silicates, used by glassmakers. First discovered in 1771, from the mid-19th century it was used for ACID ETCHING, ACID POLISHING, and in the making of FROSTED GLASS, often in combination with sulfuric acid.

Hygrometer A device indicating the level of humidity, which is set on the cases of many 18th- and 19th-century WHEEL BAROMETERS. It usually consists of a single fine human or animal hair or bulbs covered with damp fabric that reflect variations in the moisture content of the air. Contraction and expansion of these organic substances move a spring linked to a needle on a dial. There are many different types of hygrometer—this describes a mechanical hygrometer.

Hummel figure
Goebel Hummel "Strolling Along" figurine.

Humpen
German Humpen with enameled armorial design.
c. 1720.

Hunter
Swiss 18 carat gold lever hunter pocket watch.

I

Icart, Louis (1888–1950). French artist and graphic designer, best-known for his Art Deco prints and posters. Most feature "modern" wealthy Parisian women of the 1920s and '30s, often depicted nude or semi-nude, erotic, and in luxurious surroundings, and sometimes interacting with sleek-looking animals, such as swans or lions. Compositions tend to be dominated by two or three soft, shaded colors.

Ice glass A type of glass with a rough surface resembling cracked ice, first made in Venice in the 16th century and revived in Europe in the 19th century. The effect is created by plunging partially blown molten glass into cold water to create fissures on the surface, which then expand when the glass is gently reheated. An alternative method is to roll the hot body in chips and canes, which are partially melted into the surface.

Ideal Novelty & Toy Company A toy company founded in 1903 in New York by Rose and Morris Michtom. They claimed to have made the first teddy bear in 1903 based on a cartoon depicting "Teddy" Roosevelt refusing to shoot a bear cub. Early Ideal bears are rarely marked but can be recognized by their long, triangular snouts and pointy toes. The company also made dolls during the 1930s, including the Shirley Temple doll, using composition, fabric, and hard plastic. Other toys were also produced. Ideal was taken over by CBS Inc. in 1982.

Iittala Finnish glassworks, established in 1881, that become internationally renowned after producing ALVAR AALTO'S iconic, undulating free-form "Savoy" vase, designed in 1936. In the 1950s and '60s Iittala became a major international design force, through the art glass and tableware designs of Tapio Wirkkala (1915–85) and Timo Sarpaneva (1926–), the most distinctive of which are have rough, ice- or barklike textures suggestive of the Finnish winter landscape.

Imari porcelain ■ A type of Japanese porcelain made at ARITA from the late 17th century and shipped from the port of Imari. It has a characteristic palette of underglaze blue, decorated with iron red and gilt. The style was adapted by Chinese craftsmen (CHINESE IMARI) and by many of Europe's major porcelain-making factories from the 18th century, including those at MEISSEN, DELFT, and DERBY. See JAPANESE POTTERY AND PORCELAIN.

Imperial yellow ■ A clear, strong yellow glaze based on iron or antimony, applied on Chinese monochrome porcelain from the mid-15th century. From the 16th century it was also applied on biscuit porcelain. Particularly fine examples with incised or molded decoration were made in the KANGXI period (1662–1722).

Incalmo ■ An Italian term for the creation of a type of glass made on the island of MURANO. Two separate gathers of different colors are formed and blown, with open ends of the same size. The two are then joined at their open ends while still hot, fusing them together. Difficult to achieve successfully, the technique allows a single piece to have two distinct areas of color.

Ince & Mayhew ■ An English cabinet-making and upholstery firm. William Ince and John Mayhew set up business in Soho, London, in 1759, and in 1762 they had a joint wedding to two sisters. They were also jointly responsible for *The Universal System of Household Furniture*, a collection of over 300 engraved furniture and metalwork ROCOCO designs issued between 1759 and 1762. Their later designs were NEOCLASSICAL and Grecian in inspiration. The firm closed around 1803.

Incised decoration Motifs cut into a surface with a sharp-pointed metal tool.

Inciso ■ The Italian term used to describe a glass technique called COLD WORKING where the surface

I

195

Imari porcelain
Rare Japanese Arita Imari porcelain wall-vase, in the shape of a standing bijin.

Incalmo
Murano *incalmo* glass vase, by Alfredo Barbini, signed "A. Barbini." 1968.

Ince & Mayhew
One of a set of eight George III giltwood armchairs, by Ince and Mayhew. c. 1770.

Teardrop sommerso center in cherry red

Inciso
Vetro pesante vase, with *inciso* decoration all over, signed "A. Barbini." c. 1962.

of the glass is incised, cut, or etched on a wheel or using a stilus, with a series of fine lines to create a linear textured surface.

Inclined plane clock See RACK CLOCK.

Inclusions A term used for all types of small particles of decorative material that are embedded in the body of a glass piece.

Indian style Architecture and decorative arts inspired by the culture of the Indian subcontinent. Indian artifacts had been imported into Europe from the 17th century, but it was only after the British consolidated their power in the subcontinent in the late 18th century that Indian influence emerged in British art. Features such as OGEE arches, pointed onion domes, and LATTICEWORK were used to create a picturesque, exotic style in such buildings as the Guildhall in London, by George Dance, and the remodeled Royal Pavilion in Brighton, by John Nash. As India became more significant within the British Empire, the popularity of the style grew. The Durbar Room at Osborne House, one of the Queen's residences, is one of the best examples of Indian-style interior decor, with elaborate projecting cornices and ornate plasterwork. Indian influence is also evident in the use of richly patterned fabrics, motifs such as elephants, and designs on ceramics.

Indianische Blumen ■ The German term for "Indian flowers," a decoration commonly used on MEISSEN and other porcelain from around 1720. Based on the Japanese KAKIEMON style, it was derived from Oriental porcelain brought to Europe in the ships of the East India companies.

Indo-Portuguese furniture ■ European furniture made from the early 16th to the mid-17th century in the Portuguese colonies of Cochin, Ceylon (now Sri Lanka), Goa, Malacca (west coast of the Malaysian peninsula), and also in Bombay and near Calcutta. Chairs, tables, bedsteads, and case furniture were made from indigenous TEAK and EBONY, first for the local European population and later for export. Dutch occupation from the mid-17th century resulted in the development of DUTCH COLONIAL FURNITURE in most previously Portuguese colonies, except Goa.

Inkstand ■ A tray or box made of silver, papier-mâché, wood, and other materials, with feet and a hinged cover or covers either fitted with or containing writing equipment. Early 17th-century examples usually had a compartment for quills, an INKWELL, and a CASTER for POUNCE. Inkstands of the 18th century often have a bell; 19th-century examples usually have two inkpots and a sealing wax container.

Inkwell A small container used to hold liquid writing ink. Glass inkwells had the advantage of being both acid-resistant and transparent. They were made in huge quantities throughout the 19th century, ranging from simple glass inserts to cylindrical bottles with inverted cone-shaped centers to square inkwells. Some had cut decoration and cut glass hinged lids.

Inlaid decoration ■ A technique applied to solid wooden furniture, in which contrasting colored materials such as colored wood, ivory, metals, or mother-of-pearl are set into cut-out recesses that form the outline of an image or pattern. Used throughout Europe in the 15th and 16th centuries, it was largely superseded by MARQUETRY and VENEERING techniques.

Inlay A type of furniture decoration, first used on OAK and WALNUT furniture in the 16th and 17th centuries. Patterns made up of different colored woods or other materials such as bone, horn, IVORY, and MOTHER-OF-PEARL are sunk into the solid wood surface, rather than covering the surface as in MARQUETRY.

Inro ■ A small rectangular box made up of sections, usually decorated with lacquer and used to hold herbs or tobacco. It hung from the OBI (sash) of a kimono (which had no pockets) and used a NETSUKE as a toggle. Used in Japan from the mid-16th century, *inros* are still made today.

Intaglio ■ The Italian term for a type of cut or engraved decoration on glass where the design is incised or cut into the glass, creating a sunken relief. The German for *intaglio* is *tiefschnitt*, meaning "deep cut."

Indianische Blumen
Meissen Kakiemon plate, painted with insects and sprays of Indianische Blumen. c. 1740.

Indo-Portuguese furniture
Teak and rosewood cabinet-on-stand, inlaid with ebony and ivory. Late 17th century.

Miniature taperstick cover

Inkstand
Edwardian silver two-bottle inkstand, by Charles Stewart Harris. 1903.

Inlaid decoration
Art Nouveau Majorelle cabinet, with inlaid decoration.

This type of decoration was a German and Bohemian specialty from the 17th century and was perfected in the 18th century. The term is also used to describe a method of PRINT-MAKING.

Intaglio eyes Molded and painted dolls' eyes with a raised white dot on the concave pupils. They are usually found on CHARACTER DOLLS.

Intarsia The Italian term for pictorial INLAY or MARQUETRY decoration applied to paneling and furniture, using a diverse range of colors and textured materials such as wood, ivory, tortoiseshell, and metal. The decoration is used to create highly realistic still life, landscape, or architectural imagery.

Interlacing See ENTRELAC.

Iribe, Paul (1883–1935) A French commercial artist and designer of wallpaper, furniture, jewelry, and textiles. Beginning in the ART NOUVEAU style, he was an early exponent of what later came to be called the ART DECO style. His work between 1910 and 1914, particularly for the couturier Jacques Doucet, was influential in setting the style. He lived in the US, designing film sets in Hollywood, before returning to France, where he designed jewelry for CHANEL.

Iridescent glass ■ Glass with a lustrous, rainbowlike surface that changes color depending on how light hits it. The natural iridescence found on excavated Roman glass as a result of burial in damp earth was imitated in the 19th century by exposing glass to metal oxide fumes or by spraying or painting it with metal oxides. See FAVRILE and TIFFANY.

Irish glass Name given to the glass made in Ireland from the late 18th century to the present day, initially in English styles but subsequently in distinctive Irish forms such as bowls with turn-over rims or canoe-shaped bowls with scalloped edges and heavy, square "lemon-squeezer" feet. Bowls, decanters, butter dishes, and salt cellars were made in colorless, heavily cut lead glass at glasshouses in BELFAST, Cork, Dublin, and Waterford. The heyday of Irish glass was from around 1785, when the ban on exporting glass was abolished, until around 1825, when excise duty was imposed on Irish glass. The Irish glass industry still continues today at Waterford.

Iron A durable and malleable metal, one of the most abundant and widely used around the world. It was used from around 3500 BCE for tools and weapons, but large-scale production of wrought and CAST IRON began only with technological advances in the late Middle Ages. Iron has been and is used for fireplace furnishings, candlesticks, jewelry, and cooking utensils.

Ironstone china See MASON'S PATENT IRONSTONE CHINA

Isfahan An important Persian city renowned for the production of fine carpets during the 16th and 17th centuries under the Safavid dynasty and also for carpet production in the 20th century. Fine wool and silk are used to create highly detailed, intense, curvilinear designs in subtle complementary colors. Rugs, carpets, and prayer rugs are also made. See PERSIAN CARPETS.

I

197

Islamic pottery ■ The Islamic era started in 622 CE, the date of Prophet Mohammed's journey to Mecca. From 633 CE Islamic armies moved rapidly, conquering first the Byzantine and Sassanian empires, then Syria, Palestine, Mesopotamia, Anatolia, Persia, Afghanistan, and Egypt. Spain was under their control by 711 CE. At the height of its power, the Empire comprised a great number of quite disparate traditions. As a result, little aesthetic or stylistic unity is evident in Islamic decorative arts from its early years. By the late 8th century, however, a style of pottery that became recognized as unmistakeably Islamic had emerged, as is evident in the continuity of motif styles employed across the Empire.

Ceramics from the Islamic era are often divided over three periods:
1. Early Medieval Era (622–1200): Trade links with China were well established by this time and the influence of ceramics from the Tang dynasty can be seen on LUSTERWARE, produced by Mesopotamian potters, and on some early white wares excavated at Samarra in the

Inro
Gold lacquer five-case *inro* and a pink hardstone *ojime*. Meiji Period (1868–1912).

Intaglio
Stevens & Williams *intaglio* thistle decanter. c. 1890.

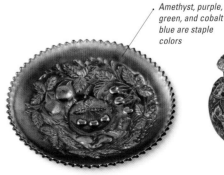

Amethyst, purple, green, and cobalt blue are staple colors

Iridescent glass
Northwood "Three Fruits" pattern amethyst Carnival glass bowl.

Islamic pottery
Persian polychrome pottery bowl, with domed cover and ovoid body. 19th century.

I

198

Persian Gulf. Ceramics from this period were excavated at Nishapur (in modern-day Iran) and Samarkand (Uzbekistan). The HISPANO-MORESQUE style emerged under the Fatimids in Spain in the 8th century. 2. Middle Era (1200–1400): Ceramic decoration from the period of the SONG dynasty in China, particularly white porcelain of Dingyao and Yingquin, and green CELADONS, notably of Zhejiang, all impacted the style of pottery of this era. Wares, however, were not merely imitative. In striving to perfect their craft, Islamic potters developed wares of their own, such as FRITWARE, as well as many techniques that are still used by modern potters. 3. Late and Post-medieval Era (1400 onward): The influence of blue and white porcelain of the Yuan and Ming dynasties is evident in ceramics made by Middle Eastern potters. Wares made in IZNJK and Kiitahya in Anatolia are particularly notable and had a major influence on European decorative arts—for example, on 19th-century MAJOLICA.

Islamic style ■ Some early writings of the Prophet forbid the depiction of humans and animals. Ornament on much Islamic art, therefore, including metalwork, glass, ceramics, and textiles is dominated by flat, dense, repeating abstract patterns, pierced FRETWORK, and interlacing and calligraphic KUFIC script. This style has influenced the arts of countries to which Islam spread in the Middle Ages, especially Spain

and Turkey. It was also popular in the 19th century as part of the European interest in non-Western arts—for example, on DAMASCENED metalwork and enameled glass. It also flourished in the 19th-century adoption of ARABIAN STYLE.

Isleworth Pottery and Porcelain ■ An English ceramics factory established around 1760 by Joseph Shore and Richard and William Goulding. Until around 1825 they made various utility wares of the Staffordshire type, including combed SLIPWARE, using the mark "S&G." German 19th-century wares made at Bodenbach in Bohemia and at Aschach in Bavaria have been erroneously attributed to Isleworth.

Istoriato ■ The Italian term for "story-painted." A painting telling a story and found on Italian MAJOLICA, especially at URBINO in the early 16th century. At first it was confined to the center of the plate but was later used across the entire surface. Copied from engravings by Marcantonio Raimondi among others, istoriato covered historical, mythological and biblical scenes.

Ivory ■ Mainly taken from the African elephant, there are two forms of elephant

ivory: soft ivory from the east of Africa, and harder darker ivory from the west. Before the introduction of mechanical carving machines at the turn of the 20th century, all ivory was worked by hand, using chisels and gouges.

Ivory-carving has a long history in China, with examples found in tombs dating from the SHANG DYNASTY (18th–12th century BCE). The Japanese came to ivory-carving relatively late, but were great exponents of the art by the early 17th century. Its major use was for carving NETSUKE but it was also used for other items, including boxes. As in China, the late 19th and early 20th centuries saw a decline in quality with the production of items for the export and tourist markets, for example, chess pieces, card cases, boxes, OKIMONO, and brooches.

Ivory has been used in the Middle East for centuries, primarily as an inlay or for carved panels on boxes, doors, and furniture. In the West, ivory was used for religious panels known as "ivories" until the 15th century; these were commissioned by pious laymen or the clergy. In the 18th century seamen and whale-hunters carved ivory into ship models and SCRIMSHAW. Perhaps its most widespread Western use, apart from chess pieces and inlay or

IVORY

Ivory is primarily obtained from elephant tusks, but it can also be obtained from walrus, sperm whale, and narwhal tusks, and to a lesser degree from wild boar tusks and hippopotamus teeth. It is durable and smooth, with a creamy luster when polished, and is ideal for carving. For these qualities, it has been considered a precious material since ancient times.

Islamic style
Silver-inlaid brass ewer, with calligraphy decoration. Late 19th to early 20th century.

Figurine
Chinese ivory carving of an immortal carrying a basket of flowers. 19th century.

Characteristically intricate carving

Netsuke
Japanese ivory *netsuke*, depicting a shishi dog. 18th century.

banding on furniture, was for piano keys.

The late 19th century saw an increase in awareness of the declining numbers of African elephants. Replacement materials were sought such as a plastic developed by Alexander Parkes in the late 19th century known as "ivorine" or Parkesine. This resembled ivory in color and surface texture, but the fine striations were more regular. Today, in some parts of Africa, elephants have been hunted almost to extinction in the quest for ivory. The production of ivory pieces is now strictly monitored and discouraged; worldwide trade in elephant ivory has been effectively banned since 1990. The illicit trade continues, however, and purchasers should check the origin of ivory articles offered as "antique."

Ivory glass Glass formulated to resemble old carved ivory. The technique, patented in Britain by Thomas WEBB & SONS in 1887, was used to produce opaque pale yellow/white glass with etched and engraved designs that were similar to CAMEO and heightened with colored stains. See IVRENE.

Ivrene Ivory-colored translucent ART GLASS with a slightly iridescent surface, often wrongly called "white Aurene." Developed at the STEUBEN GLASSWORKS by Frederick Carder in the 1920s, it was initially used for light fixtures and later for ornamental glass. The noniridescent variation is known as ivory glass.

Ivy motif ■ A popular motif in Greek and Roman ornament, particularly for ceramics. Sacred to Bacchus, ivy plays an integral role in the decoration of Classical objects such as drinking vessels. Because of its tenacious tendrils, it also symbolizes fidelity, friendship, marriage, and, being evergreen, immortality. It appears frequently in GOTHIC ornament with other TREFOIL-shaped leaves. In the 18th century it appealed to the GOTHIC taste for images of rustic decay associated with ruins. The 19th century favored ivy as a motif for jewelry as well as for cast-iron balconies and garden furniture, catering to the Victorian taste for lush evergreen foliage. In the US ivy was a favorite ornament of the GOTHIC REVIVAL.

Iznik potteries ■ Potteries existed since the 15th century in the town of Iznik, southwest of Istanbul, where the finest Ottoman Turkish ceramics were produced. The ancient Nicaea of biblical times, Iznik flourished due to its position on one of the main trade routes across Anatolia from the East and its wares show the influence of China and Central Asia.

Production at Iznik falls into three phases. The first phase from around 1490 to 1525 produced mostly blue and white wares, with shapes derived from metal prototypes and showing a strong Chinese influence. From around 1525 to 1535 more varied colors such as shades of turquoise and sage green and flower motifs such as tulips, carnations, and bluebells were

introduced. From the second quarter of the 16th century, coinciding with the reign of Süleyman the Magnificent (1520–66), there was a leap forward in artistic achievement, with the use of more brilliant blues and a characteristic "sealing-wax" red standing out in relief from the surface. A wide variety of wares was produced, including dishes, jugs, and mosque lamps.

Iznik also produced TILES for the mosques and palaces of Istanbul, including the mosque of Riistem Pasha (1550) and the Sultan's palace of Topkapi Saray (1571–72). The provision of over 20,000 tiles for the Blue Mosque, completed in 1617, marks the end of Iznik as a major supplier of tiles to the court. At the peak of production, over 300 workers were employed, but the weakening of Ottoman power and patronage meant that by around 1700 the industry was nearly extinct. Thereafter, the main center moved south to Kütahya.

Iznik pottery was exported to Europe in the 16th century, often acquiring European silver-gilt mounts. It influenced the design of Italian MAIOLICA. Interest faded until the mid-19th century, when the revival of interest in the Middle East led to imitations in France. William DE MORGAN and other art potters in Britain were also inspired to produce Iznik-style designs. Iznik also describes ceramic decoration characterized by long, curling, serrated saz leaves and flowers on thin, spiraling stems.

I

199

Isleworth Porcelain
Blue and white tea bowl, printed with figures in a riverbank scene. c. 1765–75.

Repeat bird motif around the inner rim

Istoriato
Urbino charger, decorated with an istoriato scene. Late 16th century.

Ivy motif
German earthenware beer mug, by R. Merkelbach, with ivy tendrils; signed "1729 D."

Iznik potteries
Brightly decorated dish, with tulips and carnations. Early 17th century.

200

Jack in the Pulpit

Jack in the Pulpit ■ A vase, usually made of glass, that resembles the poisonous flower of the same name. It can be recognized from its bulbous base, slim, attenuated neck, and wide, open rim that curves down at the front and up at the back. First used in the mid-19th century, the form was popularized by TIFFANY and was most popular from the late 19th to the early 20th century.

Jackfield pottery A type of English red earthenware with a glossy, black glaze, first made at the factory of Maurice Thursfield, in Jackfield, near Coalport in Shropshire, from around 1750 to 1775. The name "Jackfield" has since become a generic term used incorrectly to describe similar ware that was produced by many potters in Shropshire and Staffordshire in the mid- to late 19th century. Also known as "japanned ware," this type of pottery is often embellished with gilded decoration. Jackfield pottery includes well-made tea- and coffeepots as well as ornamental pieces such as vases, animal figures, and souvenir ware.

Jacob, Georges ■ (1739–1814) A French cabinet-maker whose career and designs spanned markedly different political and artistic styles—LOUIS XV, LOUIS XVI, and EMPIRE. Born in Cheny, Burgundy, he arrived in Paris in 1755, was a maître ÉBÉNISTE by 1765, and by the 1780s had established a reputation as one of the most important cabinet-makers in Paris. He produced COMMODES with EBONY, SATINWOOD, and PEWTER MARQUETRY and elaborate beds for aristocratic patrons. But he is probably best known as an innovative chair designer. He lightened and simplified chair design, introducing such features as the tapering fluted leg topped by a ROSETTE and SPLATS carved and PIERCED with NEOCLASSICAL motifs. He was the first French maker to use MAHOGANY, probably under the influence of Thomas CHIPPENDALE. An established cabinet-maker of the *Ancien Régime*, he survived the French Revolution, protected by the artist Jacques-Louis David, for whom he made the earliest examples of furniture directly based on Greek and Roman prototypes. This came to be known later as the EMPIRE style.

Jacob-Desmalter, François-Honoré-Georges (1770–1841) A French furniture-maker and son of Georges JACOB, under whom he trained. He ran the family business with his brother Georges Jacob II as Jacob Frères when his father retired in 1796. Following the death of Georges Jacob II, his father became his business partner. The company, now known as Jacob-Desmalter et Cie, produced mainly EMPIRE style furniture for both the imperial residences of Napoleon and the royal palaces of Europe.

Jacobean ■ A term applied to decorative arts produced in England during the reign of James I (1603–25) and generally from the first half of the 17th century. The style is characterized by the prevalence of OAK for furniture and the use of rich velvet, silk, and needlework UPHOLSTERY. New forms of furniture such as GATELEG tables, DAY BEDS, SETTEES, trestle benches, and WAINSCOT and X-FRAME chairs were developed at this time. The style is similar to the ELIZABETHAN but uses RENAISSANCE ornament such as STRAPWORK, geometric motifs, and GADROONING.

Jacobean Revival A style of 19th-century architecture and decorative arts in England, principally furniture, inspired by early-17th-century JACOBEAN originals. Characteristic elements are spiral-turned legs and STRETCHERS, tall, crested chair backs, and rich CHINTZ UPHOLSTERY.

Jacobethan A revivalist style popular in the late 19th and early 20th centuries, combining elements of the ELIZABETHAN and JACOBEAN REVIVALS such as bulbous legs on tables, carved FRIEZES, and spiral TURNINGS. Motifs such as PALMETTES

Engraved thistle motifs

Jack in the Pulpit
Quezal Jack in the Pulpit vase.

Jacob, Georges
Louis XVI giltwood large canapé, attributed to Georges Jacob. c. 1780.

Jacobean
English Jacobean yew wood chest-of-drawers.

Jacobite glass
Plain-stemmed, engraved goblet, with the remains of the gilding. c. 1745.

and PATERAE from other styles such as the NEOCLASSICAL were also incorporated.

Jacobite glass ■ Wineglasses made from 1688 engraved with Jacobite symbols such as the rose and the oak. See AMEN GLASS.

Jacobsen, Arne ■ (1902–71) A Danish architect and designer credited with introducing MODERNISM to Denmark. His two most famous buildings—for which he also designed the interior decoration and furnishings—were the SAS Air Terminal and the Royal Hotel in Copenhagen. He designed furniture for Fritz Hansen, including the iconic Ant (1951), Series 7 (1955), and Swan and Egg chairs (1957–58). He also designed the Cylinda Line of stainless steel tableware for Stelton (1967) and the AJ cutlery service (1957) for Georg Jensen, which was used in the movie *2001: A Space Odyssey*. His strongly Scandinavian designs are sculptural and elegant but also consider function and structure, giving them a timeless appeal.

Jacquard loom ■ A loom invented around 1805 by the French inventor Joseph-Marie Jacquard. It used an interchangeable, perforated card system rather than the manual lifting of the warp threads to produce complex, woven designs, so initiating MASS PRODUCTION, particularly from the 1820s.

Jade ■ A collective term for two exceptionally hard minerals, jadeite and nephrite, used in jewelry and for small figures and decorative artifacts. Jadeite is rarer and found in a range of colors, the most precious being a translucent emerald green known as Imperial Jade. Nephrite ranges in color from a highly prized "mutton fat" white to various shades of brown and green.

Jalousie From the French for "jealousy," this is the blind or shutter with an openwork pattern; it was perhaps so called because one could look through it without being seen.

Jambiyah ■ A type of knife found throughout the Arab world. Its blade is always curved and double-edged but there are regional distinctions in its HILT and scabbard.

Japanese pottery and porcelain Jomon ware, named after the rope impressions sometimes used as decoration, is the earliest Japanese pottery. It was made throughout the Neolithic period, using unrefined clays and coiling techniques. In the 4th to the 7th centuries CE, terra-cotta tomb figures called Haniwa figures, similar to those made in China, were produced. In the 12th to the 14th centuries the introduction of oxidation firing advanced the industry, while by the early 16th century the Buddhist tea ceremony or *cha no yu* became increasingly important, developing a complex protocol that required specific utensils that looked humble.

In the 16th century, Japan invaded Korea, and the returning Japanese forces were accompanied by Korean stoneware potters who settled around the town of ARITA in the southern province of Kyushu. The immigrants produced the first Japanese porcelain from around 1620 to 1640, with designs following Korean stoneware. In competition with the Chinese porcelain industry, the Arita potters continued to expand and supply the growing European demand for porcelain, producing IMARI, KAKIEMON, and blue and white wares. Both IMARI and KAKIEMON designs were extensively copied and adapted in Europe.

Apart from porcelain exports, Japan closed trading links with the West for fear of the corrupting influence of foreigners. However, in 1853 the US Navy entered Japanese territorial waters, opening up trading relations with the West after over 200 years of self-imposed Japanese isolation. The Japanese porcelain industry responded by increasing production and making brilliant showpieces for international exhibitions and trade fairs, held in London (1860s), Paris (1867), and Philadelphia (1876).

Vast quantities of Japanese ceramics flooded the markets of Europe and the US. The most sophisticated, with the finest decoration, enthralled the public and inspired the Impressionists, the designers of the AESTHETIC MOVEMENT, and porcelain factories such as ROYAL WORCESTER. Japanese ceramic marks, in the form of impressed seals or painted characters, are both numerous and inconsistent. In addition to the family name and sometimes the name of a place, articles

Jacobsen, Arne
Swan chair made of aluminum and steel with a foam and wool seat. 1957.

Jacquard loom
Pennsylvania woven jacquard coverlet, with floral design and tulip border.

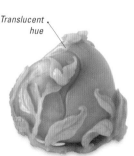

Translucent hue

Jade
Chinese jade carving of a peach, symbolic of long life and happiness. 18th century.

Jambiyah
Moroccan silver-mounted *jambiyah* and silver sheath. Late 19th century.

were often inscribed with an "art-name," granted to the potter by a patron or adopted as a workshop name. Cyclical dates and Japanese period names (*nengo*) occasionally appeared on porcelain made in the 18th century and earlier. Otherwise, wares from this period were seldom marked.

Japanesque It refers to 19th-century European interpretation of Japanese design, particularly popular from the 1860s to 1900. See JAPONAISERIE.

Japanning ■ The process of coating objects with layers of colored varnish in imitation of true Chinese and Japanese LACQUER. The varnish was made up of gum-lac, seed-lac, or SHELLAC dissolved in alcohol; the lac being a secretion of the lac beetle (*Coccus lacca*). Each layer was allowed to dry, then sanded down, before another layer was applied. Japanning, usually in black, scarlet, or green, was used on a wide variety of pieces, from small wooden boxes and trays to larger items of CASE furniture. Relief decoration was built up from sawdust and gum arabic and many pieces were also decorated with CHINOISERIE decoration. Japanning was first introduced in the mid-17th century and the first accurate account of the process can be found in *A Treatise of Japanning and Varnishing* by John STALKER and George Parker, published in 1688. A French patent for VERNIS MARTIN followed in 1730. Japanning was practiced extensively in Europe in the 18th and 19th centuries on wooden objects, including CHESTS-ON-STANDS, BUREAU CABINETS, and SECRETAIRE CABINETS. It was also used in North America, where it became known as TÔLEWARE, from around 1740 onward.

Japonaiserie A style of European and American decorative arts (also called Japonisme) inspired by Japanese art and design. Western interest in Japan was stimulated by the reopening of trade between Japan and West in the 1850s and subsequent displays of Japanese art in international exhibitions. Japanese design had a particular influence on designers of the AESTHETIC MOVEMENT, for example, E. W. GODWIN, who designed EBONIZED furniture in simple, rectilinear forms. Many European and

JAPANESE CERAMICS

While many Japanese ceramics are consciously simple in both form and decoration, others are immensely sophisticated. This is most evident in the highly detailed and naturalistic hand-painted decoration of human figural groups in landscapes, and indigenous flora and fauna.

Dish
Large Japanese dish. c. 1900.

Naturalistic decoration

Satsuma vase
Japanese Satsuma vase, decorated with five storks beneath flowers and foliage and bears a gilt signature. Meiji period (1868–1912).

Satsuma vase
Japanese Satsuma vase in Kinkozan style, with gilt signature. Meiji period (1868–1912).

Polychrome printed floral decoration

Arita tea bowl and saucer
Japanese Arita small tea bowl and saucer, printed in colored enamel and gilt. 17th century.

Nabeshima dish
Japanese Nabeshima small dish, painted with cloud scrolls, with a silver handle.

American potters also experimented with luster and IRIDESCENT glazes as found in Japanese ceramics. BACCARAT was an important maker of Japonaise glass. TIFFANY produced silverware, featuring mixed metal decoration of copper and brass. Popular motifs in Japonaiserie included birds, flowers (especially chrysanthemums), and stylized branches.

Japy Frères A firm of clock- and watchmakers, established around 1770 at Beaucourt in the Jura region of France, by Frederic Japy. The firm, later taken over by his three sons, specialized in the MASS PRODUCTION of brass movements and watches. But from the late 1880s it began to produce complete clocks such as MANTEL CLOCKS. The company ceased making clocks in 1936.

Jardinière ■ A large ornamental vessel, usually ceramic, for holding cut flowers or for growing plants. Popular in Europe from the 17th century onward.

Jasper ware ■ A fine-grained, unglazed, sometimes slightly translucent ware, introduced by Josiah WEDGWOOD in 1774. It was regarded by Wedgwood as a BISCUIT PORCELAIN and was sometimes fired to the point of vitrification. It contained a new ingredient, sulphate of barium, which was known as "cawk." The jasper ware BODY can be white or stained with metallic oxides, producing colored bodies, including the well-known blue. The colored ground was often decorated with Classical-style figures in white relief. Jasper dip refers to a piece with a surface layer of color over a white body.

Jaune jonquille The French term for "daffodil yellow." A pale yellow ground color, also known as *jaune clair*, used at SÈVRES in the 1750s, although rarely because the critical firing temperature resulted in many wasters in the kiln.

Jefferys, Thomas (c. 1695–1771) An English cartographer best known for his maps of North America and the West Indies. Many were published after his death by his successor, William Faden, or by the firm of Sayer and Bennet.

Jelly glass ■ A small glass vessel used to serve savory or sweet jellies, made in Britain in the 18th and 19th centuries. Sometimes of an inverted conical or bell-like shape, supported by a short stem.

Jennens & Bettridge ■ An English manufacturer who specialized in PAPIER-MÂCHÉ wares. Based in Birmingham and active between 1816 and 1864, the company made a wide range of JAPANNED papier-mâché items, many with an impressed signature, from small boxes and trays to larger pieces such as chairs, work tables, and cabinets, some inlaid with mother-of-pearl.

Jensen, Georg ■ (1866–1935) This leading Danish silversmith and designer founded a firm that developed a modern style, combining simple, elegant forms with ornamentation. During his apprenticeship to a goldsmith, he took art classes and studied modeling and engraving. He then worked as a goldsmith while attending the Royal Danish Academy of Fine Arts, his ambition being to become a sculptor. Having completed his studies, he briefly worked as a modeler for the BING & GRØNDAHL porcelain factory.

Eventually, Jensen decided to become an independent silversmith. He opened his first workshop in Copenhagen in 1904, producing a small selection of silver jewelry that was influenced by the ideals of the ARTS AND CRAFTS movement and was aimed at an artistically enlightened middle class.

The tradition of jewelry still continues with the firm today, although Jensen's international reputation is based on silverware, especially FLATWARE, teapots, coffeepots, and other domestic wares, with their characteristic clean outlines, sense of balance, and satiny finish. The firm commissions work from the best contemporary designers. One of the first was Johan Rohde, who in 1915 designed the "Acorn" pattern flatware, which is still popular today. Others who offered excellence in design were Harald Nielsen and Sigvard Bernadotte before World War II, and in the postwar period, HENNING KOPPEL and Jensen's son, Søren George Jensen, who was also chief designer from 1962 to 1974. Today the firm has branches worldwide and still produces many of Jensen's designs.

J
203

Japanning Red japanned cabinet on gilt stand. Late 17th century.

Jardinière Roseville green Baneda jardinière and pedestal set.

Jasper ware Wedgwood jasper ware vase, depicting Apollo and the nine Muses. c. 1785–95.

Jelly glass Jelly glass, with panel-molded bowl and domed foot. c. 1750.

Jennens & Bettridge Black papier-mâché tray, with mother-of-pearl border. 19th century.

Jersey City Porcelain and Earthenware Company An American ceramics factory founded in 1825 in Jersey City. The following year it won a silver medal at an exhibition of the Franklin Institute in Philadelphia for the quality of its china, none of which survives. It was sold in 1828 to David and James Henderson, who mechanized production to make molded stoneware. In 1833 the company name was changed to the AMERICAN POTTERY MANUFACTURING COMPANY. Production ceased in 1854.

Jesuit ware A type of 18th-century CHINESE EXPORT PORCELAIN, named after the French Jesuit missionaries in China from the 17th century. It was decorated with typical Christian subjects such as the Crucifixion, Resurrection, and Ascension from European prints, usually in black or sepia monochrome with gilding.

Jet A very hard form of fossilized wood (lignite). Black or blackish brown in color, it has been carved and polished to a glossy finish for jewelry and decorative artifacts since around 10,000 BCE and was particularly popular in Victorian MOURNING JEWELRY during the second half of the 19th century. Most of the jet during that time was mined around Whitby in England.

Jeweled decoration A form of decoration on ceramics and glass simulating precious and semiprecious stones and pearls set on the surface. For example, colored drops of enamel backed by gold foil were used at SÈVRES in the 1780s. It was also used in the 19th century in England, particularly at WORCESTER and COALPORT, and in the form of CABOCHONS on many Celtic-Revival pieces designed by Archibald KNOX for LIBERTY & CO.

Jeweling A term used to describe the presence of jewels in a watch MOVEMENT, in order to reduce friction and wear on the PIVOTS. In modern watches, synthetic jewels are used. Most modern watches are "fully jeweled," that is, fitted with a minimum of 15 jewels. The technique was the invention of the Swiss watchmaker, Nicholas Facio, who patented it in England in 1704. Jeweling was first used extensively by Abraham-Louis BRÉGUET.

Jiajing (Chia Ching) porcelain ■ Chinese porcelain made in the reign of the MING DYNASTY emperor, Jiajing (1522–66). BLUE AND WHITE wares were popular, often with Daoist themes such as children at play. Monochrome and polychrome wares were also produced. European export trade also began at this time.

Jingdezhen The main center of the Chinese ceramic industry, in the Jiangxi province, which produced much of the MING and QING dynasty porcelain (except BLANC-DE-CHINE and YIXING stoneware). The kilns

JENSEN, GEORG

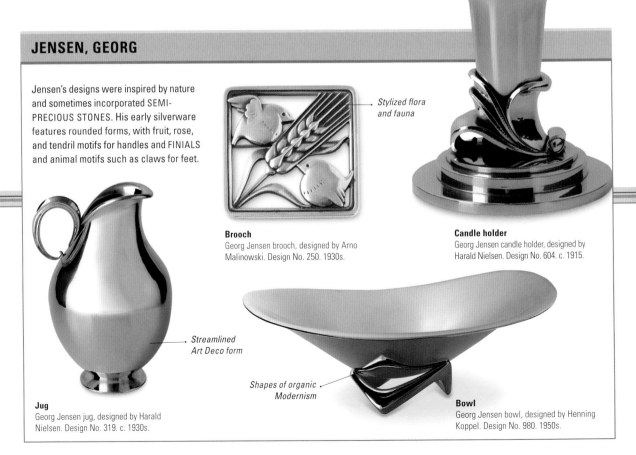

Jensen's designs were inspired by nature and sometimes incorporated SEMI-PRECIOUS STONES. His early silverware features rounded forms, with fruit, rose, and tendril motifs for handles and FINIALS and animal motifs such as claws for feet.

Stylized flora and fauna

Brooch
Georg Jensen brooch, designed by Arno Malinowski. Design No. 250. 1930s.

Candle holder
Georg Jensen candle holder, designed by Harald Nielsen. Design No. 604. c. 1915.

Streamlined Art Deco form

Shapes of organic Modernism

Jug
Georg Jensen jug, designed by Harald Nielsen. Design No. 319. c. 1930s.

Bowl
Georg Jensen bowl, designed by Henning Koppel. Design No. 980. 1950s.

gained Imperial patronage from the reign of Emperor Hongwu (1368–98). It was destroyed by fire in 1675 and rebuilt in 1683. Jingdezhen is still a major ceramics center.

Joel, Betty (1896–1984) A British furniture designer who was one of the relatively few British designers to produce ART DECO designs. She opened her own factory, Token Works, with the support of her husband, David Joel. She often used exotic woods and most pieces bear a label with the names of the designer and the cabinet-maker, and the date.

Joint (or joined) stool ■ A type of stool, made primarily in the 15th, 16th, and 17th centuries, using glueless, pegged MORTISE-AND-TENON joints.

Jones, George & Sons ■ An English pottery founded in 1861 at Trent Potteries, Stoke-on-Trent. It produced earthenware, including MAJOLICA and PÂTE-SUR-PÂTE, and tinted PARIAN. The firm started making BONE CHINA in 1872 and quality porcelain tableware in the 20th century. The first mark was a monogram of the initials "GJ," with "& Sons" added from December 1873 and a crescent shape from 1874. George Jones died in 1893 but the factory continued until 1951.

Jones, Owen (1809–74) An influential English architect and designer. His furniture is often inlaid with floral and foliate decoration, inspired by his travels in the Middle East and Spain, where he developed a love for Islamic and Hispano-Moresque designs. Owen designed some furniture for the 19th-century furniture-makers Jackson & Graham but is best known for his theories on decoration, published in his *Grammar of Ornament* in 1856.

Joubert, Gilles (1689–1775) A French furniture-maker employed by the Royal household of Louis XV, for whom he produced pieces with elaborate inlay and heavy ormolu mounts.

Ju ware See RU WARE.

Judaic decoration Decoration relating to Judaism, usually found on ritual objects of the religion such as the menorah, torah ornaments, wine cups, and Passover and Seder plates. It includes representations of these ritual objects as well as Hebrew inscriptions, naturalistic birds, fruit, flowers, and scenes from the Old Testament.

Jufti knot A type of Persian knot used in carpet-weaving, which instead of covering two warp threads, covers four, making the knot density 50 percent less than usual. The carpets produced tend to be less durable. The knot is frequently used in carpets from KHORASSAN.

Jugendstil ■ The German name for ART NOUVEAU, meaning literally "young style." It was derived from the name of the contemporary art magazine *Jugend* (first published in 1896). *Jugendstil* was, with one or two exceptions, more restrained than the French equivalent, as it was also influenced by the English ARTS AND CRAFTS movement. *Jugendstil* also influenced and was affected by the VIENNA SECESSION.

J

205

Jumeau ■ A French doll-making company established in 1842 and one of the largest doll-making companies of the 19th century. The Jumeau factory was founded in Paris in 1842 by Pierre François Jumeau and continued under the direction of his son, Emile, until it became one of the founding members of the SOCIÉTÉ FRANÇAISE DE FABRICATION DE BÉBÉS ET JOUETS in 1899. Jumeau made exquisite fashion dolls and BÉBÉS, including the Jumeau Triste with its wistful expression, modeled by Henri Carrier-Belleuse. The generally high quality of the BISQUE deteriorated in the company's last ten years. Jumeau dolls can be recognized by their typical facial expression, their bulging PAPERWEIGHT eyes, and their finely painted features. Many of the products are stamped or labeled.

Jun ware Chinese stoneware (also called Chun ware) made in the Henan province during the SONG DYNASTY (960–1279). The glaze can be green, lavender, blue, or blue splashed or streaked with purple. It is always thick, opaque, and suffused with tiny bubbles. Pieces include bulb pots, flower pots, and vases.

Joint stool
English joint stool, with saddle-shaped elm top, splayed legs, and stretcher base.

Bold, naturalistic majolica forms

Jones, George & Sons
Majolica game pie dish and cover, with a quail knop. c. 1870.

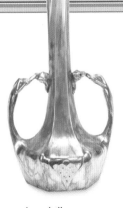

Jugendstil
Orivit *Jugendstil* pewter vase, stamped "Orivit" and numbered "2654."

Jumeau
Early Jumeau doll, size 15, with fixed wrists and blue mark on body. c. 1860–70.

K

206

Ka'aba An ancient cube-shaped stone building located in the Great Mosque at Mecca, which is considered the most sacred place on earth for Muslims. Wrapped in a black cloth, it contains columns and a black stone, which is said to have been given to Adam by God. As part of the holy pilgrimage, Muslims walk around the Ka'aba and kiss the stone.

Kaga ware Ceramics made in Kaga, on the Japanese island of Honshu. Large quantities of stoneware were produced here from early times, but porcelain began to be made only in the 19th century and is known as KUTANI ware.

Kakiemon  The Japanese potter Sakaida Kakiemon is credited with being the first in Japan to discover the secret of enamel decoration on porcelain and develop the distinctive palette of soft red, yellow, blue, and turquoise green. Kakiemon has become a generic term describing wares made in the ARITA factories since the mid-17th century, using the characteristic overglaze enamels and decorative styles. However, blue and white and celadon wares were also produced.

Kakiemon porcelain was imported into Europe and prized even above Chinese porcelain. It proved a major influence on the new porcelain factories of 18th-century Europe. Meissen copies could be extremely close to the originals. Alternatively, the factory painters simply borrowed designs and used them with other shapes and styles, MEISSEN'S INDIANISCHE BLUMEN being one such Kakiemon derivative.

The Kakiemon style was also adapted in Germany and Austria by the DU PAQUIER and VIENNA factories, in France at CHANTILLY, MENNECY, and SAINT-CLOUD, and in England by BOW, CHELSEA, and WORCESTER, and occasionally, LONGTON HALL. Kakiemon was also an

KAKIEMON

Kakiemon decoration is usually of high quality, delicate and with asymmetric well-balanced designs. These were sparsely applied to emphasize the fine white porcelain body known in Japan as NIGOSHIDE, which was used for the finest pieces. Wares include bowls, dishes, and plates, often hexagonal, octagonal, or fluted with scalloped edges. The *nigoshide* body was only used with open forms and not for closed shapes such as vases, bottles, and teapots, or for figures and animals.

Foliate molded form

Bowl
Molded bowl in Kakiemon style, with prunus and pomegranate. 19th century.

Dish
Japanese small dish. c. 1690–1710.

Dish
Japanese porcelain dish. 17th century.

Plate
Plate, with underglaze blue and overglazed enamels of rockwork and flowers. c. 1690–1710.

influence on DUTCH DELFT pottery and CHINESE EXPORT PORCELAIN.

Kakihan A Japanese term for a small personalized seal, often made up of *kanji* characters carved or written on objects to identify the artist, in association with the impressed seal or signature.

Kaleidoscope ■ An optical toy developed and patented by the Scottish physicist Sir David Brewster in 1816 and sold by many scientific instrument-makers in London in the 19th century. It usually consists of a tube made of tin or cardboard containing two mirrors running the length of the tube at 60 degrees to each other. The tube has a compartment at one end with a frosted glass cover, holding pieces of colored glass or other small objects. The viewer holds the instrument up to the light, and as he looks down the tube, multiple reflections in the mirrors are seen in symmetrical patterns, which change as the bottom compartment is rotated. The number of reflections and the complexity of patterns depend on the angle between the mirrors. Kaleidoscopes are still sold today.

Kalo Shop ■ Metalworking studio (*kalos* is Greek for "beautiful") founded in 1900 in Chicago, Illinois, by Clara Barck Welles.

A graduate of the Art Institute of Chicago, Welles aimed to teach arts and crafts to young women. Her all-female staff created a wide range of handmade jewelry in the ARTS & CRAFTS style, typically in silver, but sometimes in gold. Hammered, chased, or pierced effects are typical, as is the use of enamel or semiprecious stones. Silver and copper tableware in the same style was also made. The studio and shop closed in 1970 after a long period of success.

Kamakura period The Japanese period from 1185 to 1333, under the rule of the Minamoto and Hojo Shoguns, who were based in Kamakura. It was a period of great literary and artistic activity, when many Buddhist temples and gardens were created. The "Six Old Kilns" were the most important ceramic centers. See JAPANESE POTTERY AND PORCELAIN.

Kämmer & Reinhardt ■ A German doll factory founded in 1886 by Ernst Kämmer & Franz Reinhardt in Waltershausen. Their trademark "KR" is often found with "S&H," referring to SIMON & HALBIG, the factory that produced most of Kämmer & Reinhardt's BISQUE heads. The company's best-known product is its 100 series of bisque CHARACTER DOLLS, the first of which was the Kaiser Baby, mold 100, and first produced in 1909. Character children came in girl or boy forms with painted features and mohair hair. Another of Kämmer & Reinhardt's popular lines was the Mein Liebling ("My darling") doll,

which had a closed mouth and sleeping glass eyes. The factory closed in 1940.

Kändler, Charles An important early 18th-century gold- and silversmith of German descent, working in London in partnership with James Murray (their first piece of dated work was recorded in 1727). Though little is known about his life, the sculptural quality of his work has led scholars to speculate that he may have had some family connection with Johann Joachim KÄNDLER of the MEISSEN porcelain factory. His partnership with Murray dissolved and he entered several marks at Goldsmiths' Hall on his own. His work appears bearing date letters for up to 1751. His most famous surviving work is a massive silver wine-cooler of 1734, now in the Hermitage museum in St. Petersburg.

Kangxi porcelain ■ Chinese porcelain made in the reign of the QING dynasty Emperor Kangxi (1662–1722) at JINGDEZHEN in east China. During the Kangxi period the factory was reorganized and new colors and glazes were developed. Production increased for the domestic market, the Imperial court, and the European export market. Wares include BLUE AND WHITE, the new FAMILLE VERTE, JAUNE, AND NOIRE porcelains, fine monochromes, BLANC-DE-CHINE, YIXING stoneware, ARMORIAL ware, human and animal figures, and at the end of the period, CHINESE IMARI and FAMILLE ROSE wares.

K

207

Kaleidoscope
French kaleidoscope, with brown cloth-covered body and brass lens. c. 1890.

Kalo Shop
Sterling silver candlestick. c. 1920–25.

Kämmer & Reinhardt
Simon and Halbig, Kämmer & Reinhardt bisque doll.

Kangxi porcelain
Chinese blue and white cylindrical brush pot. c. 1680.

Kaolin White china clay, a pure aluminum silicate, is the main substance used to make porcelain. The name derives from the main place of discovery—the mountain Kao-Ling in Jiangxi, China in 1867. In Europe it is found at Aue and Passau in Germany; Bornholm in Denmark; Vicenza in Italy; Limoges in France; and St. Austell in Cornwall, England. Georgia is the largest producer in the US.

Kapok A cottonlike fiber derived from the seed pods of the kapok tree (*Ceiba pentandra*). Notable uses include filling in upholstery and, from the 1890s, stuffing for TEDDY BEARS and other soft toys.

Karabagh A carpet-producing area of the Caucasus that borders north Persia,

important for the production of rugs in the 17th to the 19th century. Rugs have long, thick piles and use bold, geometric designs with colors tending to be too bright or too somber. Sometimes European floral and Rococo-inspired designs are seen, although crudely interpreted. FLATWEAVE products are also made.

Karakusa An octopus scrollwork pattern, originating from Chinese vine scrolls, and a favorite on Japanese ARITA porcelain.

Karatsu potteries Japanese potteries established in and around the town of Karatsu, near ARITA in the Hizen province, by Korean immigrant potters from the late 16th century. About 200 kilns made coarse-textured wares for daily use and

occasionally for the TEA CEREMONY. Pottery may be plain or decorated, often in the Korean style. Dark TEMMOKU and opaque white glazes are typical. It declined in the mid-17th century in favor of porcelain. See JAPANESE POTTERY AND PORCELAIN.

Kas ■ A large Dutch provincial clothes cupboard or wardrobe (*kast* in Dutch) originating in 17th-century Holland. The form was introduced to the US by Dutch settlers, principally in New Jersey and New York in the 18th and early 19th centuries.

KÄNDLER, JOHANN JOACHIM

The chief modeler at the MEISSEN factory between 1733 and 1775, Johann Joachim Kändler (1706–75) was responsible for some of its finest individual figures and groups in the 1730s and 40s. He joined the factory in 1731, after an apprenticeship under Benjamin Thomas at Dresden, the leading sculptor at the Saxon Court. In spite of his lack of knowledge of porcelain, Kändler took to the new medium with ease, assisting KIRCHNER in a series of large, white porcelain animals for the "Japanese" palace of Augustus the Strong, Elector of Saxony. The difficulties and high cost of producing such works encouraged Kändler to experiment with small-scale figures. From 1735 he modeled over 1,000 figures, including COMMEDIA DELL'ARTE actors and actresses, Paris street vendors, people from distant lands, and crinoline groups. Collecting these figures became a great fashion. Many pieces were inspired by contemporary engravings and were copied by other European factories. Kändler and his modelers also created an extensive range of ARMORIAL dinner and tea and coffee services for members of the aristocracy. The Swan Service for Count von Brühl, Augustus the Strong's chief minister, comprised over 2,200 items, all exquisitely

modeled. The MONKEY BAND series of 1753, modeled by Kändler and Peter Reinicke after drawings by the French Rococo painter Huet, was widely imitated. Kändler stayed in Meissen during the Seven Years War (1756–63), when the occupation of Dresden by Frederick the Great halted porcelain production. When the factory was reorganized in 1763, fashions had changed and Kändler was pushed aside for new talent.

Typical slightly severe facial expression

Finely detailed feathers

Characteristically twisted stance

Hen pheasant
Meissen model of a small hen pheasant, modeled by Johann Joachim Kändler. Mid-18th century.

Baker
Meissen figure of a baker, after a model by Johann Joachim Kändler. c. 1745–50.

Kashan ■ An important Persian city, the center of silk carpet-making during Safavid rule (1501–1732). Carpet-weaving was revived at the end of the 19th century, and fine-wool rugs and carpets with curvilinear designs in jewel colors and a high knot count were produced. PRAYER RUGS are also a favored product.

Kashgai See GHASHGHAI.

Kashgar A carpet-producing region in the Xinjiang province of China, well known for rugs and carpets produced in the 18th and 19th centuries. A mixture of geometric motifs and naturalistic flowerheads is seen in a formal format, typical colors being shades of terra-cotta, light blue, yellow, and brown. Silk is sometimes used for weaving.

Kassel pottery and porcelain factories
Two factories made faience at Kassel in Germany from 1680 to 1788 and from 1771 to 1862. A porcelain factory operated from 1766 to 1788, although not to a high artistic level. The ARCANIST was Nikolaus Paul, the REPAIRER Franz Joachim Hess, and the modeler Pahland from FURSTENBERG. The mark was a lion rampant and the initials "H. C."

Katar A distinctive Indian DAGGER, used by Hindus. It features two crossbars, which are gripped by the fist. The *katar* is used with a punching action. The blade is straight, double edged, and its point is often reinforced to pierce chain mail armor.

Kayser & Söhne A German firm of pewterers founded in 1885 by Engelbert Kayser at Krefeld-Bochum, near Düsseldorf. From 1896 a range of pewter was mass-produced, including dishes, ashtrays, vases, and lamps in ART NOUVEAU style, featuring curvilinear shapes and sinuous flower and plant decoration. These are marked KAYSERZINN with a number above and below, or with a number in a circle or oval. The firm closed around 1904.

Kazak An important rug-producing district in the Caucasian republic of Armenia in the 18th and 19th centuries. The rugs display bold, geometric designs of stylized floral and animal forms in strong, harmonic jewel colors. The pile tends to be long and made of quality wool.

Kelsterbach Pottery and Porcelain Factory A German faience factory was founded near Kelsterbach in 1758 by Wilhelm Cron and Johann Christian Frede. In 1761 it was taken over by Landgrave Ludwig VIII von Hessen-Darmstadt and began to make porcelain. Christian D. Busch, a porcelain painter from MEISSEN was the director until 1764. In 1766 a new factory was built, but after the Landgrave's death in 1768, production of porcelain ceased. For the next 20 years the factory made only faience. In 1789 the director, J. J. Lay, began to make porcelain again, but production was discontinued in 1802. Until the factory closed in around 1823, it made cream-colored earthenware.

Kendi ■ A Persian drinking vessel with a bulbous body, a side spout, and a waisted, cylindrical neck, which acts as a handle, made for the Persian market in China, Korea, Japan, and the Middle East.

Kent, William ■ (1685–1748) An influential English architect, interior decorator, and designer of furniture and metalwork. Born in Bridlington, Yorkshire, a sponsored trip to Italy enabled him to absorb the ROMAN BAROQUE style and meet Richard Boyle, 3rd Earl of Burlington, under whose patronage he became a leading interior decorator through his designs for Burlington's Palladian villa, Chiswick House. His GILTWOOD, walnut, and mahogany furniture reflects the influence of his Italian studies and is made on a grand, massive scale, richly carved with PUTTI, MASKS, and other Classical motifs, such as shells, a favorite motif of Kent.

Kenzan, Ogata Shinsei A famous Japanese potter, working near Kyoto from around 1687 and later at Edo (Tokyo). He was the younger brother of Ogata Korin, a celebrated painter, with whom he sometimes worked, making brown-glazed stoneware. Well educated, he was also a poet, painter, lacquerer, and calligrapher. Kenzan took lessons from the master potter, Ninsei. His wares were usually made for the TEA CEREMONY in low-fired pottery, using bold, beautiful, and original designs in Japanese taste with flowers, pine, and

Kas
Early American Pennsylvania walnut kas.

Kashan
Mothtasham Kashan prayer rug from Central Persia. c. 1880.

Kendi
Chinese Hatcher Cargo Kraak porcelain *kendi*, decorated with panels. c. 1643.

Variegated marble top

Kent, William
George II carved gesso console table, attributed to William Kent.

notably snowy landscapes in white slip. His palette included grayish blue, green, brown, and black. A copy of his notebooks, the *Edo Densho*, was published in English by Bernard LEACH.

K

Kerman An important carpet-producing city in southeast Persia from the Safavid era (1501–1732) to the present day. Rugs and carpets are made with a curvilinear formal design repertoire. Examples from the 19th century are particularly finely woven with soft color combinations, often on an ivory-colored background. Kerman was also famous in the 19th century for the production of pictorial rugs and carpets. Post-1930 pieces tend to be of poor quality.

Kestner & Co. ■ A German manufacturer of dolls and doll parts in Waltershausen, Thuringia, founded by Johannes Daniel Kestner in 1805. Previously unsuccessful in the production of PAPIER-MÂCHÉ buttons and slates, he tried his luck with papier-mâché dolls clad in swaddling (baptism) clothes, sold as Täuflinge. From 1860 china and bisque heads were produced. Kestner's best-known products are the Gibson Girl of 1910, the KEWPIE produced from 1913 onward, and the Bye-Lo baby. Most of the company's products are marked "JDK" and examples made for export to the US may be marked "EXCELSIOR." Production stopped in 1930.

Kettle shape See BOMBÉ.

Kettle stand ■ A small stand or table designed to hold a hot-water urn or kettle. Introduced in the first half of the 18th century, following the fashion for specialized TEA TABLES, early examples usually took the form of small tripods supporting a round top, but later versions were made in a variety of shapes, with square, galleried tops and pull-out slides for the teapot or teacup.

Kew Blas The trademark used by the Union Glassworks of Somerville, Massachusetts, from around 1895 to 1915 on iridescent ART GLASS inspired by glass made by Louis Comfort TIFFANY glass. The glass is typically golden in color, often with "pulled feather" decoration in shades of tan, green, and brown.

Kewpie An all-bisque doll designed by Rose O'Neil in 1909, first produced by KESTNER in 1912. Kewpies have since been copied in various materials by a number of factories, particularly in Japan. They can be recognized by their molded blonde locks, sideward-glancing INTAGLIO EYES, jointed arms with spread fingers, and tiny blue wings. They can be found in a number of poses and designs.

Key pattern ■ An important Classical design of interlocking vertical and right-angled lines. Variations, including the well-known Greek key, were widely

used in Greek and Roman art and for much later Classically inspired ornament. Sometimes they included ROSETTES or PATERAE within the squares of the design. In the medieval period, the key pattern appealed to the taste for INTERLACING and labyrinth forms.

Keyless watch The keyless mechanism was invented and patented in 1820 by Thomas Prest, an apprentice to John ARNOLD. It allowed the watch to be wound by a winding crown instead of a separate key. Also known as "stem winder" in the US, it was initially used by many watchmakers but was not universally taken up. Keyless watches were cased in gold until the 1880s. See also WINDING MECHANISM.

Khilim See KILIM.

Khiva A marketing town for rugs and carpets on the Uzbekistan–Turkmenistan border in central Asia. While carpets woven by the nomadic Turkoman tribes are erroneously classified under this name, few, if any, rugs were ever produced here.

Khmer pottery ■ Wares made in Cambodia, at Phnom Kulen, from the 9th to the 15th century. Bowls, jars, and KENDI as well as architectural ceramics were produced from a poor-quality clay and usually had either a green or a mottled brown glaze. Decoration included zoomorphic forms and simple geometric designs.

Kestner & Co.
Kestner fashion doll on a kid body, with a blonde mohair wig and the original outfit. c. 1880s.

Kettle stand
Chippendale mahogany kettle stand. c. 1760–80.

Greek key border

Key pattern
Detail of a Louis XV ebony and ormolu center table, with stylized Greek key pattern. c. 1760.

Khmer pottery
Brown-glazed stoneware figure of an elephant from Angkor Wat. Late 12th century.

Khorassan A carpet-weaving province in the northeast of Persia that was prolific during the 16th and 17th centuries. The carpets have curvilinear floral designs in somber shades of deep red and blue. The quality ranges from coarse to fine. In the 19th century carpet-weaving was revived in the region, at Mashhad and neighboring villages. Some pieces made in the 20th century are extremely fine and bear the signatures of the master weavers, Amoghli and Sabir being the most famous.

Khotan A carpet-weaving town in east Turkestan that produced distinctive rugs and carpets in the 18th and 19th centuries. Wool and silk pile weavings, sometimes with metal thread BROCADE, were made with a repeating flowerhead design in a typical color palette of terra-cotta and shades of blue, yellow, and brown. A particularly famous design includes a repeating pomegranate and foliate pattern, often seen on a blue background.

Kick A shallow or deep indentation in the base of bottles and glassware made by pushing up the PUNTY at the base of the object to prevent a rough PONTIL MARK. It was also used to give stability to the object, to reduce its capacity, and as a decorative feature.

Kidderminster An English town that housed several carpet factories, believed to have started in the early 17th century,

although no examples of this date have been identified. The moquette carpet in the Brussels style, introduced in 1753, was popular through to the 19th century.

Kidney table ■ A table with a kidney-shaped top. First introduced in the mid-to late 18th century, the kidney shape was commonly used for WRITING TABLES, KNEEHOLE DESKS, DRESSING TABLES, and small WORK TABLES for ladies.

Kilim ■ A term used for a pileless, smooth-surfaced weaving. The pattern is formed by the different colored weft shoots that conceal the warp threads. Kilims were made of wool, cotton, and sometimes silk, by nomadic tribes and in villages.

Kimbel and Cabus An American furniture partnership of Anthony Kimbel and Joseph Cabus (a former employee of Alexandre Roux), active in New York City from 1863 to 1882. The firm made innovative, modern furniture, including neo-Gothic designs and aesthetic pieces influenced by Charles Locke EASTLAKE.

Kindjal A long knife commonly carried in the Caucasus. A dual-purpose artifact doubling as tool and weapon, it is characterized by a double-edged blade, often with multiple FULLERS. The HILT is usually of horn and is a simple "I" shape. The scabbard is often decorated with silver NIELLO work.

King's pattern ■ An ornate silver and silver-plated FLATWARE pattern, with a distinctive waisted or wavy stem decorated on the lower section with a thread border and two protruding "shoulders" and on the upper section with a stamped scallop, SHELL MOTIF, and a scroll border. King's is probably the most prolifically made pattern and dates from around 1810 to the present.

Kingsbury Manufacturing Co. ■ An American toy manufacturer established in 1894 by Harry T. Kingsbury in Keane, New Hampshire, upon his acquisition of the Wilkins Toy Company. It used cast iron and medium-grade pressed steel to produce good, solid toys, and was famed for the toys of land-speed record cars made in the 1920s and 30s. Versions of the Chrysler Airflow were painted in brilliant colors and equipped with sealed CLOCKWORK motors, which Kingsbury patented. The company began to make machinery from 1916, and although toy production ended in 1942, it continues to manufacture machinery and mechanical components today.

Kingwood A 19th-century name for a rich brownish purple timber (*Dalbergia cearensis*), known as "princewood" when first imported into Britain from Brazil in the late 17th century. Kingwood was particularly popular in France for MARQUETRY, BANDING, and INLAY.

Kidney table
Mid-Victorian walnut- and marquetry-inlaid kidney table.

Kilim
Turkish kilim wool rug. c. 1965.

King's pattern
Reverse of a King's pattern silver caddy spoon, by Paul Storr of London. 1820.

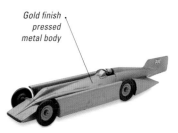

Gold finish pressed metal body

Kingsbury Manufacturing Co.
Clockwork model of the Golden Arrow record car, with Dunlop rubber tires.

K

Kinji A Japanese term for highly polished gold LACQUER. It is produced by sprinkling or brushing powdered gold over a lacquered ground, then covering it with numerous additional layers of clear lacquer. The opposite term, *fundame*, denotes dull or matt gold or silver lacquer finish.

Kinkozan ■ A Japanese kiln founded in the 17th century at Kyoto. In the 19th and early 20th centuries the family pottery made ornate, cream-colored pottery in SATSUMA style for Western markets. It became one of the largest manufactories of Satsuma pottery with over 1,000 workers. The kiln closed in 1927.

Kinrande The Japanese term for "gold brocade." Chinese porcelain with OVERGLAZE gold decoration, particularly popular in Japan. *Kinrande* was made in the 16th century, notably during the JIAJING reign (1522–66). The most common wares are bowls with *kirande* decoration scrolls on a blue overglaze and iron red, green, or white ground.

Kirchner, Johann Gottlob (born 1706) A German ceramics modeler, born in Merseburg. Kirchner worked in MEISSEN from 1730, becoming its first chief modeler in 1731. He produced the life-size porcelain figures for the Japanese Palace in Dresden and made several animal models, but these did not meet with the approval of the Elector, Augustus the Strong. With the arrival of J. J. KÄNDLER, Kirchner found himself out-

classed and resigned in 1733 to return to being a sculptor. He spent his last years in Berlin.

Kirchner, Raphael (1876–1917) A Viennese portrait painter and illustrator who worked in the US and moved to Paris in 1905, where he was greatly influenced by ART NOUVEAU. He designed many postcards in this style, often using his wife as a model. Some of these are similar in style to those of Alphonse MUCHA.

Kirk, Samuel & Son A firm of American silversmiths established in Baltimore by Samuel Kirk in 1815 and still active today. Throughout the late 19th century, Kirk specialized in FLATWARE and HOLLOWWARE, with heavy REPOUSSÉ work or CHASED decoration, often in neo-Rococo taste. Most products are signed.

Kirman carpet See KERMAN.

Kirman pottery A type of pottery made at Kirman in central southern Iran from the 12th to the 19th century. See PERSIAN POTTERY.

Kitsch ■ A word used as a noun or adjective to describe inexpensive, commercial objects of the mid-20th century, made in a style that reflects no understanding of traditional aesthetics or tastes. Pieces are designed purely to appeal to popular taste and are often of poor quality. Pop culture also plays a role, and although the term can be derogatory, this is not always the case.

Klismos The Greek term for a light, elegant chair with a broad curved TOP RAIL and distinctive concave SABER legs that splay outward, first developed in ancient Greece around the 6th century BCE. It strongly influenced GREEK REVIVAL furniture—often painted with motifs—that was designed in the late 18th and early 19th centuries by Thomas HOPE, among others.

Kloster Veilsdorf ■ A porcelain factory founded in 1760 in Thuringia, Germany, by Prince F. von Hildburghausen. After his death in 1795, it was owned by Duke Friedrich von Sachsen-Altenberg. He later sold the factory to the Greiner family, who ran it until 1822, making good-quality, early-Rococo-style products. Services in the MEISSEN style and Italian comedy figures modeled by Wenzel Neu are highly valued today.

Klösterle A ceramics factory founded by Ignaz Prosse in Bohemia in 1794, which made porcelain from 1819. Its earliest production was in the style of Thuringian ware. It was taken over by Count Mathias Thun and was known as Grafuch Thunsche Porzellan Fabrik Klösterle until the 20th century. Its best-quality porcelain, often in the MEISSEN style, was produced between 1830 and 1850. Five other factories in the region joined forces to create the Porcelain Union, but this dissolved in 1939. The factory at Klosterle (now Klasterac) ceased production in 1993.

Kinkozan
Japanese Satsuma square section, reticulated vase.

Kitsch
A clockwork cigarette dispenser, with devil's feet and angel finial.

Kloster Veilsdorf
Porcelain figure of Apollo, after a model by Wenzel Neu. c. 1765.

Solid mahogany top

Kneehole desk
Mahogany kneehole desk. Mid-18th century.

Kneehole desk ■ A table with one or two drawers along its length, a central recess for the user's legs (often with a cupboard), and drawers down each side, also called a dressing table. It was introduced in France and the Netherlands in the late 17th century and gave rise to the PEDESTAL DESK in the mid-18th century, and has been in use ever since.

Knibb family An English family of clock- and watchmakers, principally John Knibb and his brother, Joseph Knibb. The family was originally from Oxford but moved to London. Joseph Knibb became a member of the Clockmakers' Company in 1670 and was one of the leading clockmakers in late 17th-century London. He produced LANTERN clocks, BRACKET clocks, walnut-veneered LONGCASE clocks, and wall clocks. He also devised the Roman striking system for bracket clocks. See STRIKING SYSTEMS.

Knife box (or case) A case with a decorative exterior and an interior with slots for storing cutlery: knives and forks handle up, and spoons bowl up. Introduced in the 18th century, they were often made in pairs, in a box shape with a slanting top and a BOW- or SERPENTINE-front, often in SHAGREEN or mahogany with silver or brass mounts. See CUTLERY URN.

Knife rest A small, low piece of glass, (sometimes porcelain or metal), which was placed on a dinner table to keep the carving knife off the surface. They were made in various shapes from the 18th century.

Knole settee An upholstered, high-backed SETTEE with sides that can be lowered to form a DAY BED. The prototype was made for Knole, a palace in Kent, from around 1605 to 1620, and had sides that were lowered using a ratchet. It enjoyed a revival in the 1920s and 30s, when the sides were tied to the back with loops.

Knoll Associates A design group and maker of furniture founded in 1938 by Hans G. Knoll as Knoll Furniture Company, New York. Hans married Florence Schust, a designer with the company in 1946. The name changed to Knoll Associates as other designers joined them. From 1948 Knoll produced MIES VAN DER ROHE's Barcelona Chair and encouraged Harry BERTOIA to make

K

213

KNOX, ARCHIBALD

An internationally recognized designer from the Isle of Man, UK, Archibald Knox was an exponent of the Celtic interpretation of ARTS AND CRAFTS and ART NOUVEAU. He is principally known today for his designs on jewelry, clocks, vases, and carpets for LIBERTY & CO. He made use of the ENTRELAC motif, enamel, and cabochons of turquoise. His CYMRIC style jewelry was mostly in silver, sometimes enameled or set with precious or semiprecious stones.

Pewter butter or preserve dish
A Liberty Solkets English Pewter jam dish and cover, with clear glass liner, designed by Archibald Knox.

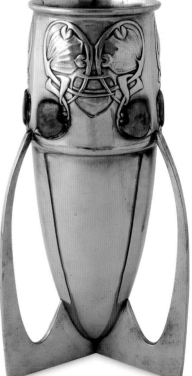

Tendril and leaf handles

Vase
Tudric pewter Liberty Art Nouveau vase attributed to Knox. c. 1903–05.

Tudric range pewter bowl

Clock
Liberty Tudric Arts and Crafts pewter clock, with enameled clock face. c. 1905.

Vase
Liberty Tudric pewter and enameled vase. c. 1905.

his wire chairs. Other designers included Pierre Jeanneret, Eero SAARINEN, and Isamu Naguchi. Hans died in 1955 and the company was subsequently sold in 1959 and again in 1965. In 1968 it took over Gavina and its stable of designers. It was known in Europe from 1951 and in the US in 1969 as Knoll International.

Knop ■ The decorative knob on lids and covers, or the cast finial at the end of a spoon handle. In metalwork and ceramics, knops frequently serve as handles on the lids of tureens, in forms suggesting the contents of the vessel, such as vegetables or fruit. A knop is also the decorative bulge on the stem of a drinking glass, goblet, or candlestick, usually halfway up the stem. A popular form of decoration in Britain after the development of lead glass in the late 17th century, the knop appears in many shapes, including a tire, egg, cylinder, acorn, mushroom, cone, drop, cushion, or ball.

Knotted lace One of the original forms of lacemaking, closely related to utilitarian products of knotting such as fishnets and hammocks. Its appearance depends on the weight of the thread and the precise technique, but designs are usually geometric.

Knowles, Taylor & Knowles ■ An American ceramic-maker founded in East Liverpool, Ohio, by John Taylor and Homer Knowles in 1870. The firm made ironstone, ROCKINGHAM ware, and from about 1889, American BELLEEK porcelain, sold under the trademark Lotus Ware. Products may be signed with a mark resembling that of Royal WORCESTER. The factory closed in 1929.

Knuckle joint A type of wooden, movable interlocking joint used in the 18th century for dropleaf tables. It was the hinge for the strut and leg, which swung out to support the raised leaf. It was cut by hand in the wood of the rail and strut, and a flat-topped iron pin was then inserted through the center.

Knulling A type of irregularly outlined GADROONING used to decorate silver ware. A popular technique in mid-18th-century England, it was favored mainly for the borders of trays and platters.

Knurling A series of fine ridges or serrations stamped or impressed on silver or metal articles, allowing the piece to be gripped more easily, like the twist cap on a flask. It is also used as a border decoration.

Kobako The Japanese term for "small box." Made for general use rather than a specific purpose, these boxes are usually rectangular, sometimes with lift-out compartments. Made from papier-mâché, pottery, or porcelain and often decorated with

LACQUER, they can be highly ornate, intricate works of art.

Kodansu Small Japanese lacquer cabinets that contain a chest-of-drawers. They often have engraved silver mounts, but the best examples are inlaid with mother-of-pearl and tortoiseshell. They were made for export in the 19th and 20th centuries.

Kogo The Japanese term for "incense." A small box and cover, usually circular, to hold incense. Made in LACQUER, pottery, or porcelain, they were used in the TEA CEREMONY. Lids may be modeled in relief and the box formed as a bird, animal, fruit, or flower.

Königsberg potteries Founded around 1772 to 1775 by J. E. L. Ehrenreich in Königsberg, near Hamburg, the potteries produced quality FAIENCE, making plates with pierced borders and painted flowers. Stoneware and earthenware were also made. See MARIEBERG POTTERY.

Koninklijke Nederlandse Glasfabrik See ROYAL DUTCH GLASSWORKS.

Koppel, Henning (1918–81) A prominent Scandinavian sculptor and designer who joined the Danish firm of silversmiths and retailers Georg JENSEN in the late 1940s. Koppel injected a fresh approach into postwar silver and jewelry design, which won him various medals. He used

Knop
Balustroid wine glass, with central and base ball knops on the stem. c. 1720.

Flared trumpet bowl

Knop

Knowles, Taylor & Knowles
Lotus ware potpourri vase and cover. c. 1892.

Koro
Japanese Satsuma earthenware lidded *koro*. Late 19th century.

Kosta Glasbruk
Kosta Boda glass vase, by Goran Wärff.

the curving "free form" and organic asymmetry in contrast to the more regimented, geometric style that typified Jensen's later designs. He also worked for ORREFORS, BING & GRØNDAHL, but perhaps his most famous form is the Model No. 992 pitcher (1952) produced by Jensen.

Korean porcelain and pottery Although inspired by and resembling Chinese styles, Korean ceramics have their own character. The oldest pieces date from around 100CE and are unglazed gray stoneware, with porcelain being used from the 11th century onward. There are three groups, named after dynasties: the Silla (57BCE–936CE), the Koryo (936–1392), and the Yi (1392–1910). The Koryo was the golden age of Korean ceramics, with fine-quality celadon glazes in Chinese style used on boxes, wine jars, and vases. Motifs include plants, flowers, dragons, stars, and lobed and reeded moldings.

Koro ■ A Japanese incense burner or CENSER, often used for the TEA CEREMONY. Examples are usually globular in form with three feet, made in pottery, IMARI PORCELAIN, KAKIEMON, SATSUMA, enamel, or bronze.

Kosta Glasbruk ■ Royal Swedish glassworks founded in the Småland region in 1742. Early production consisted of window glass, chandeliers, and drinking glasses, but the factory was later at the forefront of new trends and technical developments, producing PRESSED GLASS

from the 1840s and setting up a new glass-cutting workshop in the 1880s. From the 1920s onward, Kosta built on its reputation as one of the leading Swedish manufacturers with a range of fine art glass and tableware by such distinguished designers as Monica Morales-Schildt, Vicke Lindstrand (artistic director from 1950 to 1973), and Goran Wärff (designer from 1964 to 1974, and again from 1985). The company was eclipsed by ORREFORS from the 1920s. In 1964 Kosta and two other glass factories, Boda and Åfors, formed an alliance and the company is still active today.

Kothgasser, Anton ■ (1769–1851) An Austrian glass and porcelain decorator. A painter at the Imperial and Royal Porcelain Factory in VIENNA, he is best known today for the transparent enameled decoration of landscapes, cityscapes, and portraits that he applied to beakers and tumblers.

Kovsh ■ A drinking vessel or ladle peculiar to Russia, with a shallow boat-shaped body and a rising handle at one end. Examples from the 18th and 19th centuries were often made from silver and gold, possibly enameled, but in early times the *kovsh* was probably made from wood, sometimes in hardwood like MAZER BOWLS.

Kraak porcelain ■ A type of CHINESE EXPORT PORCELAIN produced from the WANLI reign (1573–1619) until around 1640 and named after the Portuguese ships (carracks) in which it was transported.

Kraak was the first Chinese export ware to arrive in Europe in large quantities. It is BLUE AND WHITE, decorated with stylized flowers such as peonies and chrysanthemums, and with wide border panels. Wares include large dishes, bowls, and vases. Pieces are often warped and fused and have tool "chatter marks" on the bases. Kraak was copied by ARITA and DELFT potters.

Krater The Greek term for "mixing bowl." It was used to mix wine and water before serving. A Greek krater could be VOLUTE, column, or bell shaped.

Kris ■ The distinctive knife of the Malay Archipelago. The blade incorporates meteoric iron and often has wavy edges. The HILT is sometimes made in the form of the Hindu god Vishnu.

Kruse, Käthe (1910–68) A German dollmaker whose dislike of mass-produced dolls inspired her to manufacture a virtually indestructible, realistic doll. After an unsuccessful joint venture with KÄMMER & REINHARDT in 1910, she set up her own workshop in Bad Kösen, Silesia. All Kruse dolls produced before 1950 are made of stockinet over buckram with oil-painted facial features. Käthe Kruse Doll Studio is still in production today.

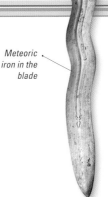

Meteoric iron in the blade

Stylized spread-winged eagle decoration

Kothgasser, Anton
Viennese beaker, decorated with Cupid, inscribed "Blühe immer." c. 1825.

Kovsh
Fabergé enameled silver *kovsh*, with gem setting.

Kraak porcelain
Chinese blue and white Kraak teapot. 17th century.

Kris
Unusual Moro *kris*, with broad, wavy blade. 18th century.

Kuba ■ A major rug-producing district in the eastern Caucasus. Village and nomadic rugs with geometric designs were made with a high density of knots and frequently with cotton for the foundation. Kubas have centralized designs, jewel colors, and a great variety of motifs. The pile tends to be clipped short and braided fringes are characteristic. Carpets survive from the 16th century and are still made today. See CAUCASIAN CARPETS.

Kufic script A type of Arabic calligraphy, frequently used in stylized form in early Islamic architecture, carpets, and pottery. Widely adopted as a decorative motif by European craftsmen who were ignorant of its original function, Kufic inscriptions appear in jumbled forms on Italian silk cloth, Hispano-Moresque architecture and pottery, and less frequently on French and English ornament. In the 19th century Kufic script was regarded as an integral part of the Turkish or Moorish ornamental styles.

Kulah A rug-weaving town between Izmir and Ushakin in Turkey, well known for its PRAYER RUGS with multiple borders. Rugs have red or white wool warps, with the weft of cotton or wool. Often they have a charcoal field with meandering vine borders. Rugs have been made here from the 16th century. See TURKISH CARPETS.

Kunckel, Johann F. (c. 1630–1703) A German chemist and glassmaker. He was employed as a chemist and alchemist by various royal patrons, including a period in the secret laboratory of the Elector of Saxony in the 1670s. In 1678 the Prussian Elector Friedrich Wilhelm invited him to Potsdam to be the director of the Potsdam Glasshouse, established in 1674. Here he developed a clear crystal glass and a new type of red glass—GOLD-RUBY GLASS or *goldrubinglas*—used for luxury pieces such as vases and drinking glasses. The leading glass technologist of his day, he published three treatises: *Chymische Anmerkung* (1677), *Ars Vitraria Experimentalis* (1679), and *Laboratorium Chymicum* (1716).

Kungsholm Glasbruk A Swedish glasshouse, founded in Stockholm by an Italian glassmaker, Giacomo Scapitti, in the late 17th century, and later run by Swedish noblemen. From the early 18th century it produced fine goblets incorporating Venetian and German elements and with intricately wrought stems. The factory closed in 1815.

Kunstschrank A type of German CABINET (also called *Kabinettschrank*) with drawers and recesses and used for storing precious objects, derived from the Spanish VARGUEÑO. Designed as works of art rather than furniture, they were the product of a collaboration between cabinet-makers, goldsmiths, and sculptors, and combined luxurious materials such as TORTOISESHELL, EBONY, hardstones, IVORY, and LACQUER. Most kuntschranks were made in Augsburg in the 16th and 17th centuries.

Kurdistan ■ One of the most prolific carpet-producing areas in Persia, including the city of Senneh, where pile carpets were made from the 19th century and from where the term SENNEH KNOT derives. Weaving existed in Kurdistan since the 16th century, but was most active in town workshops, villages, and among nomadic tribes in the 19th century. Today, production is more centralized. The *Souj-Bulak* is a compact, strong Kurdish carpet. See also PERSIAN CARPETS.

Kurk Very soft, lustrous wool, taken from the neck and belly area of sheep in winter, when it is most oily. It is especially associated with fine-quality KASHANS.

Kutani ■ The name of a Japanese village (meaning "nine valleys"), *Kutani* is also used as a catch-all term to refer to pottery and porcelain made at various potteries and factories at that location. The first porcelain was made there from around 1655 to around 1710. Known as *Ko-Kutani* (old *Kutani*), and now exceptionally rare, it is characterized by bold designs dominated by a green, yellow, red, purple, and deep blue palette. However, most *Kutani* porcelain

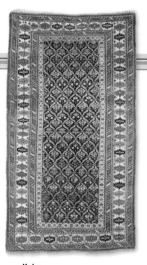

Kuba
The Kuba on the left from c. 1880 is from the northeast; the one on the right from c. 1900 is from the east.

Kurdistan
Persian Kurdish rug, with lozenge medallions and cruciform panels.

Shoza-*style* gilding

Kutani
Japanese *Kutani* cat.

found today dates from the mid-19th century onward, and has been produced in various styles, including blue-dominated *Yoshidaya*; detailed red *Lidaya*; saturated polychrome and gold *Eiraku*; and, best-known, gilt and brightly enameled *Shoza*.

Kuttrolf The German term for a decanter flask, with a neck made up of two or more thin tubes twisted together to ensure that the liquid inside the flask pours very slowly. Made in Germany in the Middle Ages, it probably evolved from a Roman precedent.

Kuznetzoff family A family that ran large porcelain factories in Russia in the 19th century. They made commercial wares, mainly imitating Western European styles, and figures of Russian peasants. The Kuznetzoff family started with a factory in Novocharitonova, which existed until 1870. In 1832 they opened a factory in Duljewo, and in 1842 a factory opened in Riga and another in Wolchow, employing over a thousand workers. In 1887 the family business was converted into a company with the assimilation of other porcelain factories such as the GARDNER

factory near Moscow. The family still runs the business today.

Kwaart A lead overglaze applied to DELFT WARE after the decoration and firing, giving it a shiny appearance.

Kyoto potteries ■ Japanese potteries in and around the imperial city of Kyoto. In the Edo period (1600–1868) many small potteries flourished, mainly in Awata, a suburb of Kyoto, producing wares for the home market. The most important were Ninsei and Ogata KENZAN. In the MEIJI PERIOD (1868–1912), as Japan reopened trade links with the West, commercial concerns around Kyoto began mass-producing pottery in the SATSUMA style for export. While most was of poor quality, a number of studios made Satsuma-style wares of exceptional quality such as KINKOZAN. See JAPANESE POTTERY AND PORCELAIN; RAKU WARE; and TEA CEREMONY WARE.

Kutani
Two-handled vases, with traditional iron red and gilt decoration. Late 19th century.

Composition dominated by iron-red with selective gilding

Kyoto potteries
Edo period Kyoto pottery bowl by Ogata Kenzan, decorated with grass sheaves and flower pods.

L

Laburnum ■ A tree native to Europe and the US with a hard, yellowish brown streaked wood with a strongly contrasting HEART. It was used for INLAY, PARQUETRY, and OYSTER VENEER from the late 17th century.

Lacloche Frères A firm of jewelry manufacturers based in Paris and London, founded in 1897. It quickly established a reputation for elegant diamond garland jewels and vivid ART DECO jewelry such as Egyptian revivalist bracelets and pendants depicting scenes from the fables of La Fontaine.

Lacca povera ■ An Italian term for an inexpensive substitute for LACQUER. Applied to Italian, especially Venetian, furniture since the 18th century, it comprises decorative paper scraps or cut-out prints stuck to the surface and sealed under layers of varnish.

Lace box A small square or rectangular box with a flat, hinged lid and interior compartments that were used for storing lace, gloves, or other items. Made in the late 17th and early 18th centuries, lace boxes were often decorated with MARQUETRY or paper cutouts and are sometimes accompanied by walnut stands of a later date.

Lacework An imitation of lace made in porcelain, achieved by dipping fabric lace into porcelain slip, which is then dried and fired so that the textile is burned away. The technique was introduced in MEISSEN around 1764 and was used on Continental porcelain in the 19th century, including that of DERBY and MINTON in England.

Lacquer ■ A resin produced from the sap of the *Rhus verniciflua* tree, originally native to China but also introduced in Japan. Once processed and dried in air, the resin forms a hard, impermeable, smooth, and lustrous surface. Used from the 6th century and often known as *urushi* lacquer, it was popular in Asia and particularly in Japan where lacquerwork rose to a fine art, with lacquered objects being expensive and highly prized. Lacquer not produced by the Japanese, the leading exponents, is sometimes known as bantam work (after a village in Java). Traditionally, lacquer has been applied to many items, including furniture, boxes, cases, and INROS. It is most commonly seen with naturalistic, figurative, or emblematic designs picked out in gold against a *roiro* (black) background, but it may also have a red or a gold background. Gold backgrounds can consist of specks of gold dust, giving a cloudy effect known as NASHIJI. Pieces can also be highlighted with *chinkin-bori* (engraved lacquer), crushed shell (known as *raden*), or small inset pieces of mother-of-pearl, known as *aogai*. Lacquerwork takes great skill on the part of the craftsperson. The lacquer is applied using a brush to a wood or COMPOSITION base in very thin layers that are each dried and polished to a lustrous finish. Techniques include MAKI-E where flat or raised designs are built up with gold or colored lacquering. Some 18th- and 19th-century pieces that appear lacquered are in fact JAPANNED.

Lacquer gilding A method of applying gilt decoration to ceramics (used on BÖTTGER wares) by grinding gold leaf with lacquer varnish and brushing it on. It was more permanent than the earlier method of SIZE-GILDING.

Lacroix, Roger Vandercruse (1728–99) A leading French furniture-maker. He was the brother-in-law of Jean-François OEBEN and became a maître in 1755. Lacroix supplied furniture to aristocratic patrons and Parisian dealers, specializing in small elegant pieces decorated with floral MARQUETRY, SÈVRES porcelain plaques, and VERNIS MARTIN.

Lacy glass A term used in the US for PRESSED GLASS produced from the 1830s onward and decorated with

Laburnum
Desk seal made of laburnum. Mid-19th century.

Lacca Povera
Venetian *lacca povera* bureau bookcase, decorated with découpage. Early 18th century.

Lacquer
Japanese lacquer five-case *inro*. 19th century.

Ladder back
American Bucks County ladder back armchair. c. 1770.

elaborate, symmetrical patterns and dots resembling lacework. Typical examples include SANDWICH GLASS bowls and plates with scalloped, ruffled rims.

Ladder back ■ A modern term for a chair, often with a rush seat, with a number of horizontal runglike rails linking the back uprights. Such chairs were first made as country furniture in ELM, OAK, and BEECH in the 17th century. In the 18th century they became part of the urban cabinet-makers' repertoire, and from around 1740 to 1790 were also made in MAHOGANY.

Ladik A town in western Turkey famous for the production of PRAYER RUGS in the 18th and 19th centuries. Colors are strong and jewel-like, with the MIHRAB bright red

with blue for the SPANDRELS. Stylized tulip motifs are often seen as decoration.

Lads A knotted net onto which patterns are embroidered with needle and thread for church and domestic linen. Also known as darned netting and FILET.

Lag and feather A popular banding pattern on English ceramics. Adopted as a decorative motif by a number of ceramic manufactories in the late 18th and early 19th centuries, particularly WEDGWOOD, lag and feather imitates in two dimensional form the FLUTING and HUSKS favored for metalwork in the ADAM STYLE.

Lalique, René ■ (1860–1945) A leading French jeweler and glassmaker who excelled at the highest level in two different periods, styles, and mediums. René Lalique was apprenticed to a Parisian jeweler and studied in London before returning to Paris in 1880, where he continued to study while working as a jewelry designer for firms including Boucheron and CARTIER. He opened a small workshop in 1886, creating innovative jewelry in the ART NOUVEAU style. His reputation soon grew and he designed for the actress Sarah Bernhardt and received the support of Samuel BING, followed by critical acclaim at the Paris Exposition Internationale in 1900.

In the mid-1890s Lalique began experimenting with glass, looking for sculptural effects and materials that would

L

219

LALIQUE GLASS

Lalique's use of demi-crystal glass, which needed little finishing after it came out of the mold, coupled with a restrained use of the molds, gave a high quality of definition. Using his knowledge of the chemistry of glass, he could produce OPALESCENT GLASS as well as glass with a range of vibrant colors.

Perigord vase
Lalique "Bacchantes" vase with high relief frieze of nudes, in opalescent glass with blue patina and original bronze base. c. 1927.

Symbol of strength and speed

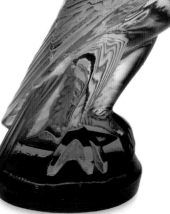

Wheel-cut decoration

Perfume bottle
A Lalique clear, frosted, and sepia-stained "Chypre" perfume bottle and stopper. 1920s.

Avalon vase
A Lalique "Avalon" vase with birds and fruit wheel cut in relief, in clear and frosted glass. c. 1930.

Hood ornament
A Lalique "Falcon" hood ornament in clear, frosted and amethyst-tinted glass. Late 1920s.

add a different dimension to his work. The turning point came with a commission from François Coty for scent bottles, which led to commissions from other perfume houses. His designs transformed an industrial process into a vehicle for creating beautiful objects, combining genius at design with an unrivaled understanding of creative glass molding. In 1918 he bought his own glassworks at Wingen-sur-Moder, making all manner of glass objects, from ashtrays to hood ornaments, and lampshades. He received critical acclaim for his glass at the Paris Exposition in 1925. The glass made in his lifetime is marked "R. Lalique"; after his death, only the word "Lalique" appears. The firm continues today.

Lalonde, Richard de (fl. 1780–90) A French furniture and metalwork designer, best known for his *Cahiers d'Ameublement* (furniture exercise books), which included detailed technical designs for a range of furniture, predominantly in the LOUIS XVI style, although some NEOCLASSICAL designs were also included. Some 30 of the exercise books were eventually published as *Oeuvres Diverses de Lalande* (c. 1780–85).

Lambeth potteries A group of potteries in Lambeth, London. TIN-GLAZED wares were made from the 1630s to the end of the 18th century. STONEWARE was made from the late 17th century and continued, with relief and incised decoration, into the 19th century. Despite differences in glazes and bodies, it is difficult to distinguish between the wares of Lambeth, SOUTHWARK, and BRISTOL. Stoneware continued to be made in Lambeth by DOULTON.

Lambrequin ■ Originally the decorative covering over armor and the hangings at jousting tournaments and in battle. The term is now used for the shaped, stiffened surround placed above a door or window. Often made of wood, lambrequins are set in front of any curtaining. The word is also used for decorative fringes on furniture, silver, and ceramics.

Lamé A woven fabric, often silk or a synthetic equivalent, interwoven with metallic threads, used extensively during the 20th century in the production of formal evening-gowns.

Lamellé A leatherwork technique in which thin slits are cut into the leather and strips of colored leather or foil are threaded through to make patterns.

Lamerie, Paul de ■ (1688–1751) The most important English silversmith of the 18th century. The son of French Protestants who fled France, Paul de Lamerie was brought to London as a boy and apprenticed with HUGUENOT silversmith Pierre Platel in 1703. Lamerie entered his first mark at Goldsmiths Hall in 1713 and became goldsmith to King George I in 1716, with his premises in Windmill Street, St. James's. He moved to Gerrard Street, Soho, in 1738. Although BRITANNIA STANDARD silver was not obligatory after 1720, Lamerie continued to work in this purer and costlier metal until 1739, when he entered his first STERLING maker's mark at Goldsmiths' Hall. Unusually, he made most of his own molds for casting handles, finials, feet, and other applied silver ornament. Lamerie saw the potential of the new decorative style, English Rococo, when it emerged in the late 1730s. With five or six other Huguenots, he raised the techniques and artistry of English silversmithing to new heights. As some of his original invoices and numerous pieces survive, it is known that he supplied great quantities of silver to many members of the English aristocracy and in spite of a prodigious output, he was able to maintain high standards in his work.

Lamination ■ A technique in which thin layers (laminates) of wood are sandwiched together, with their grain alternated at right angles for strength, and glued together. This technique eventually led to the production of PLYWOOD. The process was described by Thomas SHERATON and different types of lamination were used by furniture-makers such as John Henry BELTER. Designers such as Charles EAMES and Alvar AALTO revolutionized chair design by use of plywood.

Lampwork ■ A decorative glass technique whereby CANES or tubes of glass are heated

Filigree conical bowl

Lambrequin
Meissen plate, with lambrequin design border.

Lamerie, Paul de
Goldsmiths and Silversmiths Company silver shell dish, in Paul de Lamerie style. 1898.

Lamination
Lawo Design laminated birch lounge chair, designed by Hans Pieck. c. 1946.

Lampwork
Lampworked cockerel in the stem of a Bimini glass.

in a gas flame until soft and then manipulated into intricate shapes. It was known in 15th-century Venice and was used throughout Europe in the 17th century to produce intricate glass figures. In the 19th century, it was used to make PAPERWEIGHTS and novelties to be sold at fairs, and in the 20th century for MURANO tourist glass.

Lannuier, Charles-Honoré (1779–1819) A French-born cabinet-maker active in New York City from 1803. He applied the LOUIS XVI style of his native country to American furniture types to create a popular Franco-American style. His high-quality furniture uses extensive gilding and NEOCLASSICAL motifs and luxurious materials such as ROSEWOOD, marble, and ORMOLU. Lannuier became one of the US's most fashionable furniture suppliers and popularized the French style, in what came to be known as American Empire or New York Empire style.

Lantern clock ■ A type of weight-driven wall clock, shaped like a lantern. Introduced in Britain around 1620, it was made almost completely in brass and comprised a square case on ball or urn feet, a large circular dial (with a CHAPTER RING extending beyond the width of the case in early examples), a single hour hand, and a large bell and finial on top. It usually had ornate fretwork on top.

Lapis lazuli ■ A deep blue hardstone with distinctive flecks of gold-colored pyrites. Lesser-quality stones are paler blue with

veins or patches of white calcite. Deposits are found in Afghanistan, Chile, Siberia, and the US. It has been used since ancient times as a decorative hardstone and, when powdered, as an artist's pigment.

Lappet A rectangular band of high-quality lace used in pairs to hang from the back of ladies' fashionable lace caps around 1690 and throughout the 18th century, often pinned in loops. See ALENÇON; POINT DE NEIGE; VALENCIENNES.

Lapping A method of concealing exposed copper on the edge or rim of a SHEFFIELD PLATE object. From around 1758 it involved cutting the edge of the plated copper so that the silver layer extending over it could be turned under to cover it. In the 1770s this was replaced by soldering a U-shaped, flattened tube of silver along the exposed edge.

Larch A deciduous conifer native to northern Europe that provides a straight-grained timber ranging from yellowish white to reddish brown. It was used for country furniture and CARCASSES in the late 18th and 19th centuries.

Latticework ■ A network or pattern of repeating diamond shapes, which is fashioned in wood or metal, or painted on the surface. It was used notably on mid-18th-century CHINESE CHIPPENDALE furniture and on seat backs and brass grilles on the silk-lined doors of side cabinets of REGENCY furniture.

Latticino, latticinio From the Italian *latte* (milk). A term used to describe clear glass decorated with internal opaque colored threads in a variety of usually twisted patterns. It was first made in 16th-century MURANO and spread throughout Europe via FAÇON DE VENISE. Although the word latticino is used widely, the accepted Italian term is in fact FILIGRANA.

Lattimo See MILK GLASS.

Laub-und-bandelwerk A German term for "foliage and scrollwork." A late BAROQUE decorative motif depicting formalized interwoven leaves and intertwined bands. Originating in late-17th-century France, it was championed by Louis XIV's leading decorators, Charles Le Brun and Jean BÉRAIN. The foliate scrolls and foliage framed by flat bands resemble embroidery patterns and *parterre* garden designs. In 18th-century Germany it was used on room paneling, furniture, metalwork, glass, leather, and textiles. At Meissen it was applied to BÖTTGER stoneware and as a border for chinoiserie ornament during the J. G. HÖROLDT period.

Laurel ■ A Greek ornamental motif composed of forms resembling bay leaves (identified from Roman times as the European or "true" laurel). In Classical ornament the laurel was an emblem of renewal, glory, and honor, presented in the form of a wreath to herald achievements or military victories. The simple and

Lantern clock
Double fusée lantern clock. 17th century.

Lapis lazuli
Silver and carved lapis lazuli shell-shaped box. c. 1750.

Latticework
George III mahogany dining chair, with diamond latticework back.

Hand-gilded laurel

Laurel
Small Sèvres cup and saucer, painted with gilt laurel bands. c. 1770–80.

L

222

distinctive shape of the laurel leaf made it an appropriate choice for garlands and festoons. A band composed of laurel leaves often incorporates laurel berries, similar to the fashion of depicting ACORNS with oak leaves.

Lava cameos ■ The lava that spilled so dramatically from Mount Vesuvius became a popular curiosity after the excavation of Pompeii in 1748. Italian glasscutters used an ancient Roman technique to carve cameos from the lava in matt shades of brown, gray, white, and black for travelers doing the GRAND TOUR. Subjects included Classical heads in profile as well as Italian portraits of prominent national figures, both of which were popular souvenirs.

Lava glass Iridescent gold ART GLASS, known also as volcanic glass, developed and patented by Louis Comfort TIFFANY in the late 19th century. Pieces usually have an irregular form with a rough stonelike surface and "dripping" decoration that resembles the flow of molten lava.

Lava ware A hard and coarse form of durable stoneware used for inexpensive tableware from around 1850 to 1900. Made from a mix of slag from iron foundries and clay, it often had a blue or purplish color.

Lawn A fine, lightweight, white or cream-colored fabric, either linen or cotton, used for handkerchiefs, children's clothes, and blouses.

Lazy Susan ■ An American term from the 19th century, now used also in Britain, for a revolving serving tray. It may have developed from "dumbwaiter" tables from which guests helped themselves when servants were not available late at night.

Le Corbusier (■) (1887–1965) Charles Edouard Jeanneret, or Le Corbusier as he chose to be known, is the most important French architect-designer of his generation and a driving force in MODERNISM. After studying in Switzerland and under Peter BEHRENS, he designed his first house in 1905 and founded a practice with his brother, Pierre Jeanneret, in 1922. His approach to the house as a "machine for living" was represented in many of his designs, including those for high-rise apartment blocks and interiors. He began to design furniture, which tied in with this ethic, with Charlotte Perriand in 1927. Inspired by industrial shapes and materials such as chrome, his designs have an aesthetic purity. Model B306 CHAISE LONGUE and Model LC2 Grand Confort club chair, both designed in 1928 and originally produced by THONET, have become classics.

Leach, Bernard Howell ■ (1887–1979) An English studio potter, born in Hong Kong, who studied painting and etching in London. On a teaching visit to Japan, he became interested in ceramics and studied Japanese and Korean pottery from 1916 to 1919. In 1920 he returned to England and opened the ST. IVES POTTERY in

Cornwall with the help of his friend and potter, Shoji HAMADA. His work falls broadly into two areas: pieces showing an Oriental influence and those inspired by the English slipware tradition. In his work, teaching, and writing, Leach inspired his own generation and subsequent generations of studio potters.

Lead crystal Glass with a high (at least 20 percent) lead oxide content that produces a heavy, soft, brilliant METAL, ideally suited to CUT decoration. Perfected by George RAVENSCROFT around 1676, it is also popularly known as "crystal" or "quartz crystal" because of its brightness and light-reflecting quality.

Lead glaze A translucent glaze composed of silicaceous sand, salt, and an alkali such as potash and a mineral to color it, fused with the acid of natural sulfide of lead (galena) or lead oxide. It is applied to pottery that has already been fired and is united to the surface by a subsequent firing at a lower temperature. It was used in the Middle Ages when the general colors were brown or green. The lead fumes, however, proved injurious and lead glazes have seldom been used since the early 19th century, when a translucent FELDSPATHIC GLAZE was developed.

Leaf ornament ■ Foliate ornament widely used as a decorative motif, most frequently as a molding or DIAPER pattern. Since antiquity, leaf ornament (the Egyptian lotus

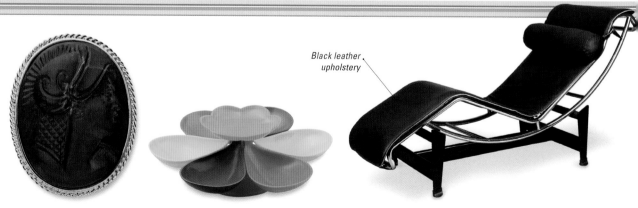

Lava cameos
Lava cameo pin, with silver gilt and rope-effect mount.

Lazy Susan
A Lazy Susan carousel in polychrome plastic. 1970s.

Black leather upholstery

Le Corbusier
Cassina Le Corbusier day bed, designed by Le Corbusier, Charlotte Perriand, and Pierre Jeanneret. 1928.

leaf or Greco-Roman ACANTHUS foliage) was used to embellish column capitals, which by the late Gothic period, were more naturalistic. Leaf decoration for MOLDINGS and FRIEZES generally features as repeating ornament interspersed with other motifs, or it takes the form of a densely packed Classical wreath or scrolling foliage. Leaves commonly adopted for ornament are the grapevine, oak, ivy, palm, LAUREL, and thistle. In the 19th century leaf shapes enjoyed popularity as ceramic or metalwork bowls and dishes. Leaf foliage played a key role in ART NOUVEAU and ART DECO ornament, frequently with flowers and fruit.

Leather The skins of animals, primarily cattle, horses, and pigs, that have been treated and preserved to allow them to be used decoratively and practically. Practiced for over 7,000 years, leather-making skills were developed by the Egyptians and Hebrews, and were improved on greatly by the Arabs during the Middle Ages, with Morocco and Cordovan leather being highly prized. Once treated and colored, principally with tannins from minerals or plants (hence the term tanning), leather can be worked, punched, gilded, and tooled, and used to great aesthetic and practical effect for binding books, covering boxes and cases, providing a writing surface on desks, and upholstering seating. Large skins have also been worked and impressed as decorative wall coverings, which are now scarce.

Leech jar A large pottery or glass jar used by pharmacists for storing medicinal leeches. English examples were either urn-shaped with handles or cylindrical with a pierced lid. It was made of glass or CREAMWARE in around 1780 by LEEDS POTTERY.

Leeds pottery ■ Founded at Hunslet near Leeds in around 1760 and run by Humble, Greens & Co., from 1770 to 1775. From 1775 to 1780 it was called Humble, Hartley Greens & Co. and Hartley Greens & Co. from 1781 to 1820. Soon after 1770 it made CREAMWARE, similar to that of WEDGWOOD but with a less even and yellow-tinged glaze. From the 1780s the factory made PEARLWARE and later added black BASALT to its range of tableware, which was decorated in ENAMEL COLORS or with TRANSFER PRINTING in red or black. It also made models of large horses for saddlers. In the 19th century BATAVIAN WARE was made. The firm went bankrupt in 1820, then had various owners until 1878. The works closed a few years later. From 1888 Slee's Modern Pottery reproduced 18th-century style wares.

Leerdam See ROYAL DUTCH GLASSWORKS.

Legras & Cie ■ Auguste-Jean-Francois Legras acquired the Verrieries & Cristalleries de Saint-Denis et des Quatre Chemins in Paris in 1864 and took over another glassworks in Pantin, France, in 1897, thereby forming Legras & Cie. The company produced much tableware and decorative glass, introduced in 1900 and inspired by the work of Émile GALLÉ, which brought great success to the company. It closed temporarily during World War I, opened again in 1919 under a different name, and used the "LeGras" trade name on some glass into the 1930s.

Lehmann, Ernst Paul (EPL) A German toymaker who established the Lehmann factory in 1881 in Brandenburg. The factory made vast numbers of lightweight, often inexpensive, TINPLATE TOYS, which were brightly and colorfully decorated with offset LITHO printing for the mass market. Their novelty toys took the form of human or animal figures, which moved by CLOCKWORK, sometimes in amusing ways. They exported to Europe and the US and the name lives on in Nuremberg today.

Lehr A warm oven used to gently cool and anneal glass immediately after it has been formed. If glass cools too quickly, it may crack or split due to differences in temperature through the body. Initially, a lehr was connected to the main furnace, but it is now usually separate. In 1780 George Ensell of Stourbridge developed a steel-lined tunnel

L

223

Wheel-carved in-relief

Leach, Bernard Howell
St. Ives pottery bowl, with "snail on a branch" design; signed "B.L."

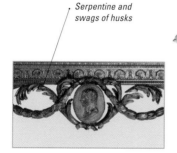

Serpentine and swags of husks

Leaf ornament
Detail of early George III giltwood rectangular side table, with leaf husk design. c. 1760.

Leeds pottery
Creamware teapot and cover, painted in the *famille verte* palette. c. 1770.

Legras & Cie
Cameo vase, with fruiting vine pattern. c. 1910.

lehr, through which glass was slowly moved on sliding iron pans, a principle still employed today at many glassworks.

Leica The world's first successful small-format camera, and the name of the company founded on its success, and of subsequent models that have been continuously developed from it. The first model—the "Ur-Leica"—was developed in 1914 by Oskar Barnack at the Leitz optical factory in Wetzlar, Germany, (and was named as a contraction of Leitz camera). Delayed by World War I, it didn't go into commercial production, as the Leica A, until 1925—at which point its portability, reduced negative format, and the ability to enlarge the (high-quality) photographs at a later stage, rendered restrictive traditional, heavy plate cameras obsolete.

Lenci ■ A Turin-based doll company, established in 1919 by Enrico and Elena di Scavini, which produced FELT DOLLS with expressive faces in colorful felt and muslin clothes. Many of Lenci's dolls were commissioned from leading Italian artists. The dolls were sophisticated and intended for display, more for adults than for children. They had hand-painted, pressed felt faces and wore detailed costumes. Lenci dolls are still made today. From 1928 they introduced EARTHENWARE and PORCELAIN figures and wall-hanging face masks that offered distinctive style, fashion, and their own brand of humor. Examples in ART DECO style are the most prized.

Lenox Porcelain Company ■ An American porcelain manufacturer established in 1889 in Trenton, New Jersey, by Walter Scott Lenox, a former employee of the OTT & BREWER PORCELAIN FACTORY. The firm specialized in American BELLEEK, using a thinly potted, ivory-colored porcelain with sparse decoration, which is still manufactured today.

Lenticle ■ A small, usually oval or round, glazed aperture on the trunk of a LONGCASE CLOCK, revealing the pendulum inside. Often fitted with a cast-metal surround.

Lesney Products ■ An English toy and metal component maker, set up in 1947 in London by Leslie and Rodney Smith, who combined their first names to form "Lesney." The first DIECAST toys, including vehicles, were made the following year. From 1950 to 1959 their increasingly popular toys were exclusively distributed by Moses Kohnstam Ltd., and their tradename, "Moko," appears on many toys. A Royal Coach was produced in two sizes in the early 1950s. Over a million of the smaller size were sold in 1953, the year of Queen Elizabeth II's Coronation. That year the MATCHBOX 1:75 Series of small toy vehicles was begun, followed in 1956 by Models of Yesteryear, initiated by employee John Odell. It was taken over in 1982 by Universal Holdings of Hong Kong and production moved to Macau.

Lethaby, William Richard ■ (1857–1913) An English architect and designer who founded a design group, Kenton & Co., in 1890. He designed furniture for it in the ARTS AND CRAFTS style, using carved and inlaid indigenous wood. The firm closed in 1920.

Lever escapement Invented by Thomas Mudge in 1754, lever escapement (also called detached escapement) was one of the first successful watch escapements to let the balance oscillate freely. A few early makers such as Josiah Emery and A. L. Breguet tried versions of the lever escapement, but it was only widely used from the 1880s, and was the basis of watch mechanisms from then on.

Libbey Glass Company ■ The largest modern American glassworks, founded in Toledo, Ohio, by William T. Libbey and his son, Edward, in 1888 as a successor to the NEW ENGLAND GLASS COMPANY. It became known as Libbey in 1892. Libbey concentrated on colorless, cut, and pressed lead glass and colored ART GLASS such as AMBERINA and PEACHBLOW. Libbey changed direction in the 1940s, away from art glass to machine-made tableware, which has remained their central product to this day.

Liberty & Co. ■ A department store founded on Regent Street, London, in 1875 by Arthur Lasenby Liberty, originally called East India House. Its fabrics attracted interest abroad and resulted in the Italians

Lenci
Lenci Mascotte doll, with original clothes. 1920s.

Lenox Porcelain Company
Gourd-shaped pitcher, decorated with two tall birds in the Asian style.

Lenticle
Lenticle on the case of a Brouncker Watts marquetry longcase clock. c. 1693.

Lesney Products
Lesney Matchbox No.56 London Trolley Bus, with box. 1960s.

LIBERTY STYLES

From the 1870s to the present day, London department store Liberty & Co. has promoted numerous styles in the decorative arts, as wide-ranging as Oriental, North African, Middle-Eastern, and Eastern European. However, the styles for which it is best known, and for which the wares were in many cases sold as Liberty-branded lines, are ART NOUVEAU and ARTS AND CRAFTS.

Wall cabinet
Softwood hanging wall cabinet, with overhanging top and side shelves.

Pre-Raphaelite-style center panel

Chair
Liberty & Co. oak chair, designed by C. F. A. Voysey. 1905.

Brooch
Murrle Bennett & Co. silver and enamel brooch for Liberty & Co. c. 1900.

Vase
Ceramic urn in pomegranate pattern, by Moorcroft for Liberty & Co.

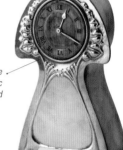

Shaped like a Celtic arrowhead

Mantle clock
Liberty & Co. Tudric pewter and enamel mantle clock.

referring to ART NOUVEAU as *Stile Liberty*. Liberty started selling shawls and silks but soon added ARTS AND CRAFTS products, Japanese porcelain, screens and fans, as well as imports from India, Persia, China, Morocco, and Turkey. In 1884 Liberty opened a costume department, directed by E. W. GODWIN, and then Maison Liberty, for clothing, in Paris in 1889. Later it commissioned from the British designers Christopher DRESSER, Walter CRANE, Rex Silver (who designed the "Peacock Feather" pattern), and C. F. A. VOYSEY. In 1885 a wallpaper department was added, selling both imported papers and Liberty's own patterns. Carpets were also commissioned and made in Donegal, Ireland, from 1902. The store introduced ART POTTERY from Britain and Europe in the 1880s, including ware from BRANNAM, MOORCROFT, DOULTON, and the German firm Max Lauger. It also sold

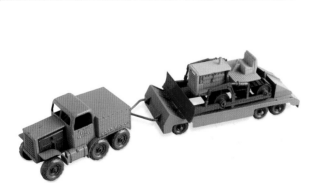

Lesney Moko
A rare Lesney Moko large-scale six-wheel prime mover and six-wheel trailer.

Lethaby, William Richard
Robert Weir Schultz oak high barrel-back chair, designed by William R. Lethaby.

Libbey Glass Company
Libbey amberina ribbed baluster vase.

L

226

glass by James POWELL & SON, CLUTHA, and LOETZ from Austria. In 1894 they registered a silver mark, "LY & CO," at Goldsmiths Hall, but it was not until 1899 that their own silver, marketed as Cymric, and jewelry appeared. Tudric pewter followed in 1901–02, designed by Archibald KNOX, Bernard Cuzner, Oliver Baker, the Silver Studio, and Jessie M. King, among others. The establishment of a Furnishing and Decoration Studio in 1883 saw a broad range of styles for sale. The Arts and Crafts pieces in oak designed by Leonard F. Wyburd and E. G. Punnett are the ones most usually recognized as Liberty designs. Liberty & Co. is still in business today.

Library steps ■ Folding or fixed ladders and steps for use in libraries. First introduced in the 17th century, they were in general use by around 1750 and took various forms, ranging from mobile in contemporary styles to ingenious folding steps that converted into stools or armchairs. See METAMORPHIC FURNITURE.

Library table A large DRUM TABLE designed to stand in the center of a library. Popular in the late 18th and 19th centuries, most examples incorporated drawers in the FRIEZE and often had one or more cupboards in the PEDESTAL.

Lignum vitae A hard, dark brown, black-veined, oily wood (*Guaiacum officinale*) exported from South America and the West Indies to Europe in the 17th, 18th, and 19th

centuries. It was used for OYSTER VENEERS, PARQUETRY, small veneered pieces, turned bowls, and other TREEN.

Lille pottery and porcelain factories Factories in the French town of Lille included a FAIENCE factory founded by Barthelemy Dorez in 1711. It also produced a SOFT-PASTE PORCELAIN similar to that of SAINT-CLOUD. It closed in around 1820. In 1784 a HARD-PASTE PORCELAIN factory called the Manufacture Royale de Monseigneur le Dauphin was established with royal support. Articles were marked with a dolphin. This factory closed in 1817.

Lily pad decoration A GATHER of glass applied to the lower part of a vessel and drawn up to resemble a lily pad. It is thought to have been introduced to the US by immigrant German glassworkers in the 18th century and was a popular American motif in the early 19th century.

Limbert, Charles P. (1854–1923) An American designer and furniture-maker who established the Limbert Furniture Company near Grand Rapids, Michigan, in 1894. The company's ARTS AND CRAFTS furniture, mostly made in OAK, but sometimes in MAHOGANY, displays European influences, notably that of Charles Rennie MACKINTOSH in Glasgow, Scotland, and the avant-garde SECCESSIONIST designers of Germany and Austria, including Josef HOFFMANN and Koloman MOSER. The confluence of

these two strands of Arts and Crafts style gave rise to the use of strong, rectilinear forms, complemented by highly stylized decorative details such as cut-out geometric shapes—squares, rectangle, hearts, and triangles. The Limbert factory closed in 1944.

Lime A linden tree (*Tilia vulgaris*) native to Northern Europe with soft, close-grained, pale white or yellow wood, well suited to carving. It was used for decorative picture and mirror frames and chimneypieces by Grinling GIBBONS and others of his era.

Limed oak ■ OAK that has been treated with lime, which remains in the grain to produce a decorative streaked surface with gray-white speckles.

Limehouse Porcelain Factory ■ A short-lived but important factory established by Joseph Wilson & Co. in 1746 in Limehouse, London. Its products were influenced by CHINESE EXPORT PORCELAIN Triangle period—the shapes were imitative of contemporary ROCOCO silver and decorated in blue and white. The factory went bankrupt and closed in 1748. The site was only discovered in 1989; before this date many of its wares had been attributed to William Reid's factory in Liverpool.

Limited edition An item, typically a modern collectible such as a toy, produced in a limited quantity and aimed specifically at collectors. The quantity can be as low as

Lathe-turned handrail

Library steps
Victorian set of oak and ash library steps.

Limed oak
North German limed oak armoire. 18th century.

Limehouse Porcelain Factory
The Old Vice-Roy (*sic*) of Kanton, blue and white porcelain figure. c. 1746.

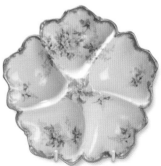

Limoges porcelain
Oyster plate, with hand-painted floral and gilt decoration. c. 1895.

two examples, but can easily exceed 10,000. Each example is usually numbered (against the total quantity produced), often on the item itself or on an accompanying certificate, for example, 250/5,000. The larger the edition number, the less appealing it is likely to be, unless the type of item appeals to an enormous number of people. Once the stated full quantity has been reached, no more examples are made.

Limited production An item, typically a modern collectible such as a toy, produced for a set period of time such as a year and aimed specifically at collectors. This differs from a LIMITED EDITION, as there is no maximum quantity that will be made. Instead, as many items as possible will be made during that time, or as many as the company is able to sell. Examples are not usually numbered, but may bear a special mark or be accompanied by a certificate stating that it is a Limited Production piece. Once the end of the period is reached, no more examples are made. The company may indicatate the number of items made.

Limoges enamel ware Enameled objects produced in Limoges, France, during the 16th and 17th centuries are considered the best in Europe during that period. The town had been known as a center for religious enamel ware since the 12th century, but moved over to secular production later. Produced primarily by a small number of families, designs included early Gothic-style religious

scenes, Mannerist motifs, and monochrome designs. Bright rather than harmonious colors dominated later production.

Limoges porcelain ■ Many factories sprang up in Limoges, France, in 1768, because of KAOLIN deposits at nearby St Yrieix. Limoges became a generic name for wares produced locally. There were nearly 90 factories and decorating shops in and around the town through the 19th and 20th centuries, including François Allaud and the Grellet Bros. Porcelain is still produced in the area today. See HAVILAND & CO.

Lindstrand, Vicke ■ (1904–83) A Swedish designer who designed primarily glass, but also ceramics and textiles. He worked for the notable ORREFORS glassworks from 1928 to 1940, designed ceramics for Karlskrona Porslinfabrik from 1935 to 1936, and Upsala Ekeby from 1942 to 1950, before moving to KOSTA in 1950. He is known for his simple, curving organic forms and heavily stylized, engraved, and cut designs executed on clear, colorless glass.

Line inlay See BANDING.

Linen-backed The term used to describe a poster that has been attached to a treated linen canvas. This is done by a professional as a means of preserving a poster's condition and lessening the chances of damage when it is displayed or stored. A poster may also be restored in the process, with creases, tears, or detached pieces being removed or repaired.

Linen press ■ 1. A device for pressing damp linen, consisting of two flat boards, the top one with a spiral screw that "pressed" the boards together, thereby flattening the linen. Known as early as the 16th century, they were often mounted on stands, clamped to the top of chests-of-drawers, or made as free-standing movable pieces. 2. The term also describes a cabinet or cupboard for storing linen or clothing. It usually comprises sliding trays enclosed by doors above a set of drawers.

Linenfold ■ A decoration of 15th-century Flemish origins, resembling a piece of linen cloth hanging in vertical folds. Evolved by Tudor woodcarvers for paneling and furniture—especially chests and the doors of wardrobes—linenfold decoration was also widely adopted with regional variations in France and Germany. However, its popularity waned in the Renaissance period.

Lines, G. & J. and Lines Bros. ■ A wooden toy and baby equipment manufacturing firm established by George and Joseph Lines in King's Cross, London, during the 1850s. In 1876 the company became G. & J. Lines, with many rocking-horses being supplied to the London department store Gamage's. G. & J. Lines continued until Joseph died in 1931, but in 1919 his three sons founded Lines Bros., which also produced toys, many made from wood. The trade name "Tri-ang" was registered in 1924, with "Minic" (miniature clockwork) being registered as a trade name

L

227

Lindstrand, Vicke
Kosta vase, designed by Vicke Lindstrand. c. 1955.

Linen press
Fruitwood linen press, with a single frieze drawer on square legs. 19th century.

Linenfold
Oak monk's bench, with foliate-carved and linenfold-paneled back. Late 19th century.

Lines, G. & J. and Lines Bros.
Edwardian G. & J. Lines nursery rocking-horse, with baskets.

L

in 1935. Soft toy production began in 1937, and in 1938 it registered the name "Pedigree" for its range of dolls. Other toys included pedal cars, trucks, planes, trains, doll buggies, scooters, large-scale pressed-steel toy vehicles, construction sets, wooden soldiers, forts, and theaters. The company made munitions during World War II, but continued to grow during the 1940s and 50s, launching Sindy as a competitor to BARBIE in 1962 and becoming one of the world's largest toy producers during the 1960s. The company failed and was split up in 1971 due to problematic overseas business and competition from inexpensive foreign imports.

Linke, François (1855–1946) A French cabinet-maker of Czech birth. Linke became a leading cabinet-maker in Paris in the late 19th century, producing few, but superb-quality COMMODES and CABINETS, mostly in the Louis XV revival style, with curving shapes and ORMOLU mounts.

Linthorpe Pottery Set up by local entrepreneur John Harrison in 1879, with the help of designer Christopher DRESSER until 1882, to make ART POTTERY and alleviate unemployment in Linthorpe, Middlesborough, in the UK. The factory was built on an old brickworks and red clay was used for the pottery. Dresser was the art director, and although he was not directly involved, he provided distinctive designs, often covered with streaky glazes. The pottery closed in 1889.

Lion mask A motif used from antiquity as an emblem of strength, courage, and majesty. The lion mask holding a ring in its mouth for a handle derives from ancient Roman furniture and it continues to be popular as a doorknocker. Both Venetian and FAÇON DE VENISE goblets feature decorative PRUNTS molded in the lion mask shape, alluding to the symbol of Venice, the lion of St. Mark. From the early to mid-18th century, the lion mask enjoyed popularity as a favored motif for furniture ornament, used as an arm rest support or to decorate a cabriole leg. Occasionally a lion's paw or pelt appears alongside the mask.

Lion's-paw foot ■ A foot carved to resemble the paw of a lion and a popular form for furniture legs, mostly of chairs, in RENAISSANCE, NEOCLASSICAL, REGENCY, EMPIRE, and various classical revival styles.

Lionel Manufacturing Corporation ■ Founded by Joshua Lionel Cowen in New York in 1900 as the Lionel Manufacturing Company, it was the most famous producer of electric toy trains in the US and was particularly noted for its working of lineside features such as loading ramps, bridges, and stations. All models were electrically powered and many had operating whistles and smoke units. The early sets were tinplate but it was using diecast locomotive bodies by 1949. Cowen developed his Standard or "S" gauge in 1906, which had three rail tracks. This was replaced in 1939

by the smaller "0" gauge, which the company had introduced in 1915 and is still in use today. The models are exclusively of American outline and design, with the 400E (introduced in 1931) and the 700E (introduced in 1937) rapidly becoming classics. The 2333 EMD F3 diesel in Santa Fe "warbonnet" livery, introduced in 1948, became the company's bestseller. In 1930 Lionel also gained control of their main rival, Ives. Cowen sold his interest in 1959, but the company continues to produce today after a number of different owners.

Lit-en-bateau A French term for "boat bed." A free-standing bed with deep curving open sides that rose and curled over at the head and foot to form a boat shape. Introduced in France in the early 19th century, such beds were often designed to be set against a wall, with luxurious decoration on the exposed side and elaborate canopies.

Lithography ■ From the Greek *lithos* (stone). A printing technique developed in Germany by Aloys Senefelder around 1798. It involves drawing an image or pattern on a stone or metal surface with a greasy crayon. When first water and then ink is poured over it, the crayoned areas repel the water but retain the ink. When applied under pressure to the surface to be decorated, the image or pattern is transferred (or printed).

Lithophane ■ A light screen of biscuit porcelain into which relief molds are

Lion's-paw foot
Carved lion's-paw foot on a French Empire mahogany chair.

Lionel Manufacturing Corporation
Lionel "0" gauge locomotive, "Santa Fe," No. 2333–20, in silver and red with yellow trim. In mint condition, with box. 1949.

Lithography
Color lithographed "Jane" poster, designed by Louis Rhead. c. 1897.

pressed, creating the "picture." The thicker parts make shadows and the thinner parts make the light. They can be framed and hung in windows or included in cup and plate bases. Some pictures were erotic. Lithophanes were first made in the 1820s by KPM BERLIN, then by MEISSEN, PARIS, and factories in Thuringia, Bohemia, Japan, and the UK.

Lithyalin glass ■ Opaque marbled glass designed to resemble hardstones. Invented by Friedrich EGERMANN and patented in 1828, it was widely imitated and used throughout the 19th century for beakers and scent bottles.

Littler, William (1724–84) An English potter who was apprenticed at the age of 14. At 21 he went into partnership with his brother-in-law, Aaron Wedgwood, making STONEWARE. In 1750 Littler became manager of the LONGTON HALL PORCELAIN factory, renowned for its brightly painted, molded porcelain, usually adorned with fruit and vegetable motifs. The variable quality of the factory's porcelain contributed to the firm's bankruptcy in 1760. Littler moved to Scotland in 1764 and opened a porcelain works near Musselburgh.

Littler's blue The deep cobalt glaze that William LITTLER is credited with having invented in around 1750. Littler applied the color to fine stoneware throughout his career.

Live steam mechanism ■ The use of steam, generated by an alcohol burner, to create power through a cylinder and crank linkage. It is mostly seen in toy or model steam-powered engines. Its popularity declined after 1939, as availability of electric power increased.

Liverpool pottery and porcelain factories Throughout the 18th and 19th centuries, Liverpool was one of the major centers of ceramics production, from tin-glazed earthenware, also known as English DELFTWARE, to porcelain. By 1760 there were 12 factories in Liverpool making blue and white delftware similar to that produced at BRISTOL and LAMBETH. From the early 19th century much of the Liverpool ware was exported to US. These were often adorned with transfer-prints of subjects to suit the American market or were decorated in an unusual range of ENAMEL COLORS, known as FAZACKERLEY. Notable pottery factories in Liverpool included SADLER & GREEN, Pennington's, which made cream-colored earthenware and delftware, and Herculaneum, which produced cream-colored earthenware. Among the porcelain factories that flourished from the mid-1750s were those of Samuel Gilbody and William Reid. The best known, however, was that of Richard Chaffers, founded in 1756. He used both steatitic (soapstone) and BONE ASH porcelain to produce teaware in underglaze colors based on those of the FAMILLE ROSE. Upon his death, he was succeeded by his partner, Philip Christian.

Livery cupboard A free-standing or hanging cupboard, usually with perforated doors for ventilation, used for storing "liveries" (servants' food for the night). First designed after 1625, the cupboards were made until the 18th century.

Lledo A DIECAST toy company founded in 1983 by John Odell (Lledo is Odell backwards), an employee and designer at LESNEY PRODUCTS, who designed the Models of Yesteryear range that was released in 1956. Odell acquired much of the diecast and tooling machinery from Lesney when the company went bankrupt in 1982, and produced his own range of largely historical vehicles, most of which he designed. The firm was bought by Corgi in 1999.

Lloyd Loom furniture ■ Invented by the American Marshall Burns Lloyd and patented in 1917, Lloyd Loom furniture is made from twisted paper strengthened with lengths of metal wire. The paper is then woven into a "fabric" and nailed onto a wooden frame. First made in Menominee, Michigan, it has the appearance of wicker because of the way it is woven, but no loom is involved in the process. The material was first marketed as Art Fiber because it was thought that no one would buy furniture advertised as being made of paper. In fact, it is incredibly durable, and unlike cane or real wicker, does not have sharp edges that catch at clothing. The furniture's popularity was helped by a shortage of cane and rattan after World War I. It first became available in

Lithophane
Lithophane of a naked lady on the base of a German ceramic puzzle jug.

Lithyalin glass
Egermann Lithyalin glass and gilt beaker. c. 1830.

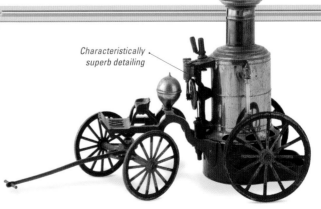

Characteristically superb detailing

Live steam mechanism
Weeden live steam fire pumper, with double-oscillating cylinder engine and a brass boiler.

LOETZ GLASS

A Bohemian glassworks founded by Johann B. Eisner von Eisenstein at Klostermuhle in 1836 and acquired by Johann Loetz in 1840. After his death in 1848, it was run by his wife, Susanna, and "Witwe" (German for "widow") was added to the company name. In 1870 Loetz's grandson, Max Ritter von Spaun, took charge, leading the company to greater artistic heights, particularly with its successful marbled glass and ranges that imitated semiprecious stones. In around 1895 Von Spaun patented a technique for IRIDESCENT GLASS, introducing organic-shaped, ART NOUVEAU–style vessels. Much was exported to the US. The glassworks closed in 1948.

Ovoid vase
Loetz dimpled, ovoid, iridescent glass vase.

Iridescent vase
Vase by Loetz in a characteristically innovative waisted and bulbous cylindrical shape. c. 1900.

Europe in 1922 and sold well on both sides of the Atlantic until World War II. Companies attempted to copy Lloyd Loom, but genuine items can be easily identified with the help of a magnet—only Lloyd Loom used metal wires. Marshall Lloyd sold the rights to make Lloyd Loom furniture in the US to Heywood-Wakefield in 1921; abroad, he sold the rights to several companies, including Lusty's in East London, which was the most successful. Lloyd Loom furniture is still produced today.

Loading The term for material, usually pitch, resin, or plaster, and weights such as lead or iron disks, used to fill hollow, lightly constructed

silver articles like candlesticks that are too delicate or unstable for practical use. Such materials were used, as silver was expensive as a filling.

Lobmeyer, J. & L. ■ A Viennese shop founded in 1823 by Josef Lobmeyer that commissioned high-quality pieces of glassware designed by freelancers. His sons, Josef and Ludwig, continued the business, adding their initials to the company name in 1856. In 1902 the firm became a public company and was run by Josef and Ludwig's nephew, Stefan Rath. Under his directorship, they entered the new century, commissioning designs by the VIENNA SECESSION artists Josef HOFFMANN,

Dagobert Peche, Otto Prutcher, and other members of the WIENER WERKSTÄTTE. The company is still in family hands.

Locke, Joseph (1846–1936) An English glassmaker, born in Worcester, who worked for several English glasshouses. In 1882 he emigrated to the US to work for the NEW ENGLAND GLASS COMPANY in Massachusetts. Locke became a leading designer and developed new types of colored ART GLASS such as AMBERINA, POMONA, and a type of PEACHBLOW. From 1891 he was the chief designer for the United States Glass Company, and in 1900 he set up his own company, the Locke Art Glass Company, for which he designed and made

Lloyd Loom furniture
Armchair, with chromed metal base and cushion. c. 1936.

Lobmeyer, J. & L.
Cobalt blue glass jug, with enamel design. c. 1870.

Locket
French silver Art Nouveau mirrored locket and silver chain. c. 1920.

Long Eliza
Worcester blue and white pattern mug, with a Long Eliza figure. c. 1760–65.

glass until his death. Many of these pieces have his mark Locke Art hidden in the pattern on the glass.

Locket ■ An oval, circular, or heart-shaped pendant that opens to reveal compartments suitable for keeping hair, miniature paintings, or photographs. Often very sentimental, many Georgian examples could only be opened with a tiny key and were inscribed with messages of affection. Larger silver and gold lockets, pinned on broad collars, were popular at the end of the 19th century.

Long Eliza ■ Also known as *lange lyzen*, a Dutch term describing tall Chinese women on Chinese porcelain. They were usually found in UNDERGLAZE blue and copied on DUTCH DELFT, and then on delft and English porcelain.

Longcase clock ■ A tall, narrow, free-standing, weight-driven clock, introduced around 1660. The longcase is composed of a HOOD, housing the dial and MOVEMENT, a trunk, encasing the weights and pendulum, and a plinth base. Cases were usually made by specialist cabinet-makers and thus reflect contemporary furniture styles. Ebony-veneered oak and walnut veneers were popular in the 17th and early 18th centuries, but these were later superseded by mahogany. Early styles are relatively plain, with square dials and pediment-shaped hoods, but later longcase clocks often feature elaborate scrolled ornament, marquetry, fluting, ball-and-spire finials, and arched dials (some featuring AUTOMATA) or painted or engraved decorative dials. The American equivalent of the longcase clock is the TALLCASE CLOCK. Longcase clocks are also known as GRANDFATHER CLOCKS. Smaller examples were called grandmother clocks.

Longton Hall Porcelain Factor ■ Founded in 1750, in Staffordshire, by William Jenkinson with William LITTLER as manager. Excavation of the site in 1955 revealed great quantities of kiln waste with signs of severe kiln failure, suggesting that it had initial problems with porcelain-making. However, a wide range of utility wares was made, notably strawberry leaf dishes, with delicate polychrome painting. It also made figures, first showing the influence of MEISSEN influence and later of Bow. The company went bankrupt in 1760.

Longwy ■ French industrial ceramics manufacturer, best known for its hand-finished ART DECO, stoneware, and earthenware pots and vases of the 1920s and 30s. Some of its wares had innovative crackled glazes and saturated colors that gave them the appearance of ancient artifacts found in archaeological digs, while others had stylized animal, floral, and human imagery derived from vocabularies of ornament that included African and ancient Egyptian, Greek, and Roman. Its main retailer was Primavera, the stylish homeware section of Le Printemps department store in Paris.

Loo table ■ A card table with a circular or oval top supported on a central pillar terminating in three or four feet. The name derives from a card game called lanterloo or 100, which was first played in the 18th century and became very popular in the mid-19th century when these tables were introduced.

Looking glass See MIRROR.

Looping A type of glass decoration in which looped threads are attached to stand vertically proud of the rim, instead of being applied to the surface as in TRAILING. Looping was popular for such pieces as sweetmeat dishes.

Loos, Adolf (1870–1933) An Austrian architect and designer. Born in Brunn, Moravia (now Brno in the Czech Republic), he trained as a bricklayer and then as an architect in Dresden. After a trip to the US (1893–96), Loos set up his own practice in Vienna and became influential in the development of industrial design. His opposition to the WIENER WERKSTÄTTE and the decorative excesses of ART NOUVEAU are evident in his writings, such as the 1908 article *Ornament und Verbrechen* (Ornament and Crime), and in his simple, unadorned, rectilinear designs for furniture, metalwork, and interiors. He created a range

L

231

Longcase clock
Oak eight-day, arched dial longcase clock, with cabinet. 18th century.

Longton Hall Porcelain
Strawberry leaf plate, painted and molded with strawberry leaves and exotic birds. c. 1755.

Longwy
Longwy ceramic glazed earthenware vase, designed by M. P. Chevallier.

Loo table
Early Victorian circular mahogany loo table.

L
232

of equally minimalist glasses for the Austrian glass manufacturer LOBMEYER.

Lopers The sliding rails or runners that are pulled forward to provide support for the opened flap of a BUREAU.

Lorenzl, Josef (1892–1950) A prolific Austrian sculptor, who worked in the ART DECO style in patinated bronze and ceramic. His figures usually depict slender dancing girls adopting stylish poses without great detail. Lorenzl bronzes are instantly recognizable, with their long-limbed, androgynous figures, acrobatic or athletic poses, and fluid props such as cymbals, tambourines, or scarves. They are generally COLD-PAINTED and some have additional colored decoration to the dresses, signed

"Crejo." Carved ivory was used for faces, heads, and hands. His work was issued through GOLDSCHEIDER, for whom he also designed ceramic figures, which are now avidly collected. Bronzes are signed in full or with shortened variations of "Lorenzl."

Lost wax casting See CIRE PERDUE.

Lotto carpets Referring to a specific design in some Ottoman TURKISH CARPETS of the 16th and 17th centuries, so named because it appears in paintings by the late Renaissance Italian artist Lorenzo Lotto. The pattern is a development of Chinese brocade designs and features stylized yellow vines, leaves, and palmettes on a bright red ground. Some may have *kufic* motifs. Portraits of Henry VIII (1491–1547) show him standing on Lotto

carpets. In the 17th century Spanish carpet-makers based their designs on Lotto carpets, featuring a grid of arabesques.

Louis Philippe style ■ The main style of decorative arts in France during the reign of Louis-Philippe (1830–48). It encompassed a variety of revival styles, in particular the RENAISSANCE, LOUIS XV, and LOUIS XVI. Its popularity was largely due to the King's restoration of the royal palaces of Fontainebleau and Versailles. The style is characterized by massive, solid forms with profuse ornament such as GROTESQUES, foliage, and mythological figures.

Louis Revivals ■ Revivals in the 19th century of the styles of the decorative arts current during the reigns of LOUIS XV and

LOUIS XIV STYLE

Louis XIV furniture was of a grand scale, with rich Italian velvet and brocaded upholstery, elaborately carved and gilded mounts and frames, and tall, rectangular padded backs on chairs. Luxury materials and gilt-bronze mounts abounded—in particular, hardstone MOSAICS on cabinets and tables, EBONY VENEER, and imported LACQUER panels.

S-scrolled arms

Side table
Louis XIV provincial walnut side table, with shaped marble top. c. 1710.

Giltwood table
A Louis XIV style giltwood table with acanthus carved frieze.

Table
A Louis XIV walnut fauteuil with tapestry cover. c. 1715.

LOUIS XVI in the 18th century. The Louis XV Revival, closely related to the Rococo style, reemerged during the reign of Louis-Philippe. Some pieces were copied directly from surviving 18th-century originals, but most were loosely imitated to suit the requirements of comfort and solidity, as determined by the growing middle classes. Forms are therefore heavier and larger than the originals, with deep-button upholstery on furniture and lavish use of gilding, piercing, and carving. The Louis XVI Revival was popular during the SECOND EMPIRE period and continued into the early 20th century. While the Louis Revivals began in France, they also became popular in other parts of Europe and in the US.

Louis XIV style ■ The style of decorative arts and architecture fashionable in France during the reign of Louis XIV (1643–1715) developed directly from the personal tastes and character of the King. Its emphasis on size, symmetry, formality, grandeur, and luxury reflected the autocratic nature of his government and the magnificence of his court.

From 1661, when Louis began his personal rule, he ordered sumptuous furnishings for the royal palaces in a unified decorative style from the Manufacture Royale des Meubles de la Couronne (Royal Manufactory of Furnishings) at GOBELINS. It was founded by the King's finance minister, Jean-Baptiste Colbert, and directed by the painter Charles Le Brun. Le Brun commissioned designs for furniture, silver, bronzework, HARDSTONES, and TAPESTRIES, all made to exceptionally high standards.

The palace of Versailles, near Paris, was furnished with luxurious silver furniture and mirrors. These furnishings, intended to display royal wealth and power, show the influence of the Italian BAROQUE STYLE with a distinctively French restrained classicism. The cabinet-maker André-Charles BOULLE developed BOULLE MARQUETRY in elegant, symmetrical ARABESQUES, influenced by the designs of Jean BÉRAIN. For propaganda, the King required that symbolic motifs such as the sunburst and head of Apollo (Louis styled himself as the Sun King), the FLEUR-DE-LIS, and the King's monogram of two interlaced "Ls" were liberally applied. East Asian imports inspired CHINOISERIE motifs.

The style spread through England, the Netherlands, Germany, Switzerland, and the English colonies in North America after the revocation of the Edict of Nantes in 1685 forced HUGUENOT craftsmen to emigrate to avoid religious persecution. With the patronage of Huguenot artists by William III and Mary II in England, Louis XIV style came to have a strong influence on WILLIAM AND MARY style. Toward the end of his reign a reaction against the stiff and somber formality of the style emerged, and the lighter and simpler RÉGENCE style became more popular.

Louis XV style ■ The style current in France during the RÉGENCE period (1715–23) when the King was a minor, and the years after he attained majority and ruled independently (1723–74). The ROCOCO style dominated the century, overlapping with the Régence at the beginning and the NEOCLASSICAL at the end.

New furniture types were developed such as the *bergère*, with a deep seat and enveloping padded back, the *causeuse* and *marquise*, which were seats for two people, and the *duchesse*, a form of chaise longue with a rounded back. Furniture by leading cabinet-makers such as Charles CRESSENT and Jean-François OEBEN is characterized by the use of decorative gilt-bronze mounts, featuring elaborate C- and S-SCROLLS, curling tendril forms, and boldly modeled PUTTI birds and dragons; high legs; elaborate geometric PARQUETRY and MARQUETRY of flowers and ribbonwork; exotic woods such as amaranth and tulipwood; and BOMBÉ fronts and SERPENTINE lines. Some luxury furniture was also embellished with polychrome imitation LACQUER or VERNIS MARTIN panels, often featuring designs of flowers, Chinese-style figures and landscapes, or porcelain plaques.

While porcelain was produced at MENNECY, CHANTILLY, and SAINT-CLOUD, the most important factory was VINCENNES (later SÈRVES). In 1745 the King granted Sèvres a 20-year exclusive privilege to produce SOFT-PASTE PORCELAIN, and it was the only French porcelain factory allowed to use gilding and yellow ground color. The popularity of

L

233

Louis Philippe style
Mahogany writing cabinet, with inlay and gilt-brass work.

Louis Revivals
Louis XV-style boullework mantel clock. 19th century.

Louis XVI style
Fine ormolu-mounted mahogany architect's table, attributed to David Roentgen. c. 1785.

Louis XVI style
Blue silk upholstered and carved giltwood fauteuil. c. 1775.

L

Sèvres porcelain among European aristocracy was partly the result of the patronage of Madame de Pompadour, the King's mistress. The factory's output included groups of lovers and children, which are favorite Rococo themes, and wares decorated with bouquets and sprigs of flowers. Flowers also feature on silks woven at Lyons, tapestries at BEAUVAIS and GOBELINS, and carpets at SAVONNERIE. The Rococo emphasis on naturalism is also found in silverware by leading silversmiths Thomas GERMAIN and Juste-Aurèle MEISSONNIER. In the 1750s and 60s a reaction against the frivolous Rococo emerged. The Neoclassical style was fully developed in France by the end of the King's reign, but it is now more associated with the LOUIS XVI period.

Louis XVI style ■ The style of French decorative arts associated with the reign of Louis XVI (1774–93). The period was dominated by the NEOCLASSICAL style, which had developed in the 1760s, toward the end of the reign of Louis XV. It was characterized by restraint and simplicity, as opposed to the ROCOCO flourishes of the LOUIS XV STYLE. Geometric forms were widely used—for example, ovals and squares for chair backs and octagons in the plates of the Arabesque service (1783–87) made by the SÈVRES porcelain factory. Classically inspired shapes such as urns and vases were also popular in silver and ceramics. In contrast to the all-over decoration of the Louis XV period, ornament was divided into panels, with motifs derived from Classical art and architecture—for example, FLUTING,

VITRUVIAN SCROLLS, PALMETTES, ANTHEMIONS, FRETS, HUSKS, and ARABESQUES. Colors became more subdued and GRISAILLE, inspired by ancient Roman frescoes and CAMEOS, was especially popular, while the light-hearted decorative themes of the Rococo were replaced by morally elevating Classical subjects. Nevertheless, the decorative arts of the Louis XVI period remained essentially luxury items, particularly furniture by Martin CARLIN, Jean-Henri RIESENER, and Adam WEISWEILER, featuring elaborate Neoclassical gilt-bronze mounts, porcelain panels, geometric MARQUETRY, and a revival of BOULLE marquetry and PIETRA DURA INLAY. A more austere version of the style developed in the 1770s and 80s, with simple wood VENEERS and

LOUIS XV STYLE

The fashions of the Louis XV period contrast strongly with the earlier Louis XIV style. The magnificence, gravitas, and grandeur were replaced with informality, spontaneity, and intimacy. These characteristics are evident in the use of smaller and lighter forms in furniture.

Console table
Carved giltwood console table, with clock, garniture, and torchères. c. 1730.

Center table
Ebony and ormolu center table, attributed to Joseph Baumhauer. c. 1760.

Bergère
Carved giltwood *bergère*, with dusky rose pink damask upholstery. c. 1745.

Commode
Louis XV ormolu, tulipwood, amaranth and marquetry commode. c. 1750.

refined forms. Louis XVI fashions continued even after the start of the French Revolution in 1789 and the execution of the King in 1793, but evolved into the much more severe DIRECTOIRE style.

Love seat ■ The modern term for a type of wide chair or narrow SETTEE, introduced in the 18th century. It could just accommodate two people sitting side by side. The French equivalent was the *causeuse*, which resembled a small CANAPÉ. The term can also describe S-shaped seats that accommodate two people.

Love spoon A wooden spoon with a decoratively carved handle. It originated in Wales in the 17th century as a gift from a young man to his beloved as a token of his affection. The handles are commonly carved with symbols or shapes in relief or may have PIERCED or FRETWORK ornament.

Low Art Tile Works An American decorative tile manufacturer established in Chelsea, Massachusetts, in 1879, by John Gardner Low. Low produced a wide range of high-quality, award-winning glazed tiles, specializing in dust-pressed, relief-molded portrait and scenic tiles with monochrome MAJOLICA glazes. Most are clearly marked. The firm operated until around 1902. W. H.

Grueby worked at the factory and set up the GRUEBY FAIENCE COMPANY in 1897.

Low temperature colors See ENAMEL COLORS.

Lowboy ■ A low DRESSING TABLE or WRITING TABLE, with tall legs and one to three drawers. Introduced in the early 18th century, it was perceived as ladies' furniture on which a freestanding mirror could be placed. They are mostly veneered with walnut, but later examples use mahogany and oak. In the US it was often made to match a HIGHBOY.

Lowenfinck, Adam Friedrich von ■ (1714–54) A much-traveled porcelain and faience painter who specialized in KAKIEMON-style figures and flowers in a distinctive style. He worked at MEISSEN from 1727–36, then in Ansbach for a short period, and from there moved to the BAYREUTH factory. In 1741 he was appointed court enamel painter in Fulda. From 1746 to 1749 he was technical director at HÖHST, where he may have made only faience. He then worked as director of the faience factory of Hannong in Hagenau from 1749 until his death. His wife and two brothers were all porcelain painters.

Lowestoft Porcelain Factory ■ Founded in Suffolk in 1757 by four partners, Philip Walker, Obed Aldred, John Richman, and Robert Browne. It made a BONE ASH body resembling that of BOW. At first, simple

underglaze blue wares in the style of Chinese porcelain were made; from around 1760 colored decoration was used. Its blue and white ware copied WORCESTER. It had a good trade with Holland as well locally for inscribed and dated pieces, including birth tablets, which are unique to Lowestoft. It also made a few figures of animals and children. The factory closed in 1802.

Low-warp A tapestry-weaving technique in which the loom is placed horizontally, with the tensioning rollers placed in the front and at the back. The warp thread is stored on the back roller and the finished tapestry is rolled onto the front roller. The cartoon is placed under the warp threads. This method was used at AUBUSSON and predominated in the Flemish workshops.

Lozenge A geometric motif often used in jeweled STRAPWORK as a DIAPER pattern or forming the ground for other patterns. In Romanesque ornament its role is similar to the CHEVRON or zigzag as a molding enrichment. Heraldry decoration often features the lozenge surrounding the arms of a spinster or widow.

Lucca silk factories Lucca is the capital of the Tuscan province of the same name. Although its exact origins are unknown, the silk industry was firmly established here by the 12th century. Facilitated by the free trade treaties with Genoa in 1153 and 1166, raw silk, dyes, and metal threads from the East were available to the Luccese silk

Love seat
George II mahogany framed love seat.

Lowboy
Country fruitwood lowboy, with two drawers. Late 18th century.

Lowenfinck, Adam Friedrich von
Meissen tea canister, hand-painted in the Lowenfinck style. 1740.

L

workshops. Controlled by merchants and sold through agents all over Europe, Luccese silks appear in the accounts of royal wardrobes, church, and papal inventories of 1295 and 1361. The area remained a center of silk production until the late 18th century.

Luce, Jean (1895–1964) A French designer of glass and ceramics in the ART DECO style. He exhibited ceramics at the 1925 Paris Exposition. His tableware for HAVILAND has stylized clouds and sunbursts in gold and platinum.

Luck (Lücke), Johann Christoph Ludwig von (c. 1703–80) He began as an ivory sculptor but worked as a modeling master at MEISSEN in 1728 (dismissed in 1729 because of unsatisfactory work). In 1751 he was in VIENNA as "first master modeler" but soon moved to FÜRTENBERG. Luck founded the SCHLESWIG faience factory in 1755. He is recorded in England (1760), Dresden, and Danzig.

Luckenbooth A heart-shaped brooch popular in 18th-century Scotland as a love token or protection against the evil eye. Usually made of silver and occasionally gold or metal, they were sold in the small shops or "luckenbooths" clustered around the High Kirk of St. Giles in Edinburgh.

Lucotte A Paris-based toy manufacturer that began making high-quality, hand-painted, solid-cast lead soldiers and figures in around 1790, mainly depicting First Empire and Revolutionary figures. In 1825 the firm was sold to the rival toy soldier company C.B.G. Taken over itself by Mignot a few years later, this company continues to make toy soldiers today.

Ludwigsburg Pottery and Porcelain Factory ■ Founded in Württemberg in 1758 as a "necessary attribute to splendor and dignity" by the decree of Duke Karl Eugen of Württemberg. The factory was first set up in a barracks but was later moved to a small castle in 1760. It was under the directorship of J. J. RINGLER until 1802 when he retired. The wares are in MEISSEN style, although the body is smoky and gray-brown in tint. The modelers Johann BEYER and Jean-Jacob Louis produced delightful figures, including a set of miniatures of the stalls and sideshows at the annual Württemberg Venetian Fair and figures of dancers of the Court Ballet and musicians. The business closed in 1824.

Lund's Bristol See BRISTOL PORCELAIN FACTORY.

Lunette In architecture, a semicircular or crescent-shaped decorative area that is left plain or occasionally ornamented. In 17th-century woodcarving, lunette-shaped ornament was applied in a series to form a band, occasionally filled with ACANTHUS foliage. This device reemerged in the JACOBEAN REVIVAL. Lunette windows typically feature in architecture of the late 18th and early 19th centuries.

Lunéville ■ A French faience factory founded by Jacques Chambrette in 1731, which produced faience similar to STRASBOURG, NIDERVILLER, and SCEAUX. Wares are ROCOCO in style but with less delicate painting and a less pure white tin glaze. They are indistinguishable from SAINT-CLÉMENT, which was also owned by Chambrette. Lunéville made large figures of lions and dogs to decorate doorways or gardens and smaller figures in white-bodied earthenware after models by P. L. Cyfflé, who founded his own factory in Lunéville around 1766. When Chambrette died, he left his factory to his son, Gabriel, and his son-in-law, who started producing cream-colored earthenware in the English style. They sold the molds in the 1780s to Sebastian Keller. Throughout the 19th century, earlier models such as the lions and dogs were repeated, with an impressed mark "Lunéville."

Luster ■ A shaped PRISMATIC cut-glass drop used in candelabra and candlesticks, both for decoration and to increase reflected light. It is also used as a general term for such types of CANDLESTICK and centerpieces.

Lusterware ■ Pottery with a shiny, metallic, iridescent surface, created by

Fine-quality hand-painting

Ludwigsburg Pottery and Porcelain Factory
"Print Seller" figure, modeled by J. J. Louis. c. 1766.

Lunéville
One of a pair of ice buckets, with handles and hand-painted designs. c. 1790.

Luster
Glass table luster, with a faceted stem and circular base. Late 19th century.

Lusterware
Sunderland pink luster jug, printed and painted with verses. Early 19th century.

painting on a mixture of pigments of metallic oxides and then firing the piece so that the metals form a thin film on the surface. The metal is deposited on the glazed surface by reduction of the metal from a compound to the pure metal. Some of the metals used are gold, silver, platinum, copper, bismuth, and tin. The temperature required is 1,380°F (750°C) and good ventilation of the kiln is essential, as the pigment is poisonous. Made in Mesopotamia and Persia as early as the 8th century, lusterware spread through the Middle East (Sultanabad, Rayy, Kashan) and then into Spain and Italy (see DERUTA and GUBBIO) in the 15th and 16th centuries. By the 19th century, lusterware was being made at numerous potteries in Staffordshire and Sunderland. Production continues today. See FAVRILE glass.

Luting The process of joining two parts of a large clay vessel when it is "leather hard" by wetting the seam. Slip or slurry is used for fine clays; coarse clays are more effectively softened with water.

Lynn glass ■ A mid-18th-century English drinking glass or decanter with distinctive bands of horizontal ribbing. The name was first used in the late 19th century and was derived from the town of King's Lynn in Norfolk, where such glassware was incorrectly presumed to have been made.

Lyons potteries ■ Factories in Lyons, France, where Italian workers made faience from around 1520. A group of late-16th-century dishes and ewers in ISTORIATO style in the manner of URBINO are attributed to the workers. Subjects were often derived from woodblock prints in books and bibles published in Lyons. Only one marked piece is known (in the British Museum, London), signed "GTVF/léon" and dated 1582. Known workers at Lyons include Jules Gambin, who went on to start the first faience factory in NEVERS with the Conrade brothers in 1588. In 1733 Joseph Combe revived the production of painted faience when he founded a factory with a royal privilege; his wares are similar to those of MOUSTIERS. Several other factories, the wares of which cannot easily be differentiated, were operating in the city in the 18th century. Their speciality was *faïences patronymiques*—in other words, wares painted with saints and inscriptions of names and birth dates.

Lyre clock ■ A SHELF or WALL CLOCK developed in late 18th-century France, the most distinctive element of which is a gridiron PENDULUM with metal rods like the strings of a lyre. The marble or bronze frame, based on the LYRE MOTIF, is often set with GILT-BRONZE mounts, ENAMEL decoration, or paste gemstones.

The term also refers to a variant of the BANJO CLOCK developed by Aaron Willard (brother of Simon Willard) in the US.

Lyre motif ■ This ancient musical instrument was adopted as a decorative motif for Grecian-style NEOCLASSICAL ornament. Although the invention of the lyre is usually credited to the god Mercury, the motif mainly appears in decoration as an attribute of Apollo. As the god of song and music, Apollo's lyre frequently features—occasionally with an Apolline mask—in the decorative schemes and furniture of music rooms, most notably on music stands. Decoration on French and American LYRE CLOCKS from the late 18th to the 19th century often reflects Apollo's role as the god of the sun. The lyre was a popular ornamental device for chair backs from around 1780 to 1820, and was also used on WRITING TABLES, where it alludes to Mercury as inventor of the alphabet.

Lynn glass
Lynn horizontally ribbed tumbler. Mid 18th century.

Chinoiserie scene

Lyons potteries
Lyons platter, decorated with a green and yellow floral and foliate pattern. 1740–70.

Lyre clock
Howell & James lyre-shaped clock. 19th century.

Lyre motif
Lyre motif on the back of a Regency mahogany chair. c. 1810.

238

Macdonald, Margaret (1865–1933) **and Frances** (1874–1921) Designers, sisters, and leading members of the GLASGOW SCHOOL. They studied at the Glasgow School of Art and worked separately and with their husbands, Charles Rennie MACKINTOSH and Herbert McNair. Both worked in various media and Frances taught at the Glasgow School of Art from 1908.

Machine knotting Carpet-making by machine, which started at the end of the 18th century with the advent of steam power. This saw the rise of companies such as WILTON and AXMINSTER in England and many comparable firms in other countries such as Belgium.

Macintyre, James & Co. (C. 1847–1913) A pottery at Burslem, Staffordshire, producing mainly utility ware and best known for its links with William MOORCROFT, who made ART POTTERY for the company until he set up his own factory in 1913.

Mackintosh, Charles Rennie ■ (1868–1928) A Scottish architect, furniture, graphic, and textile designer, and watercolor artist. He practiced architecture at

Honeyman and Keppie in Glasgow from 1889 to 1914, becoming a partner in 1901.

Mackintosh was a leader of the GLASGOW SCHOOL style that grew out of the need among some artists, designers, and architects, as they approached the new century, to be the masters of their own creations, rather than repeating historical precedents. In this sense, there is an allegiance to ART NOUVEAU. His two most famous architectural commissions were the Glasgow School of Art, which he won in an open competition in 1896–97, and Hill House in the town of Helensburgh, west of Glasgow. Mackintosh also designed detailed, integrated interiors for the buildings.

Another of his patrons was Kate Cranston, who commissioned him to design her chain of tea rooms in Glasgow. He provided

MACKINTOSH STYLE

Mackintosh developed his highly individual approach to design in his native Glasgow. This both embraced the ideals of the ARTS AND CRAFTS Movement whilst incorporating the organic elements associated with ART NOUVEAU. His buildings, interiors, and furniture manage to include Japanese and Scottish vernacular influences and pre-empt the geometry favored by ART DECO designers.

Stylized tree-form motif

Bedroom chair
Ebonized sycamore chair with drop-in seat pad, designed by Mackintosh for Hous'hill, in Nitshill, Glasgow. 1904.

Light fixtures
Set of four Mackintosh-designed pendant ceiling lights, their house-shaped tin bodies pierced with leaded and stained glass windows. 1900.

Adjustable horizontal support

Pine easel
Designed by Mackintosh for the Glasgow School of Art, this pine easel has been stained a darker brown. c. 1910.

Pine cabinet
Mackintosh stained pine cabinet with pierced, crescent-shaped handles. c. 1905.

Secretaire desk
A white-painted secretaire with a fitted interior and paneled fall above an arched apron. c. 1904.

furniture for her tea room in Argyle Street, and the first of his high-backed chairs with a distinctive oval top rail was designed for this interior. The finest and perhaps the most famous tea room was The Willow in Sauchiehall Street. For this, Mackintosh redesigned the facade of the mid-Victorian terrace as well as the interiors. It also showed the "light-feminine" and "dark-masculine" code that Charles and his wife, Margaret MACDONALD, had initiated in the design of their home. From 1905 Mackintosh's workload began to decline and he took up painting again. With the exception of remodeling 78 Derngate, Northampton, in 1916, from 1915 to 1923 he produced textile designs for various makers with his wife, thereafter concentrating mainly on painting.

Mackmurdo, Arthur Heygate (1851–1942) An English architect, designer, and cofounder of the Century Guild, which aimed to promote unity of design. He traveled to Italy with RUSKIN and is celebrated for a chair with a distinctive sinuous back and the title page to *Wren's City Churches*, both of which anticipate ART NOUVEAU.

Madrid tapestries The Real Fábrica de Tapices y Alfombras de S Bárbara, Madrid, was founded in 1720 by Philip V. The Spanish court had previously commissioned Flemish tapestries. Madrid tapestries were initially woven on LOW-WARP looms, but in 1727 a HIGH-WARP weaver was recruited from GOBELINS to improve standards. From copying earlier Flemish

tapestries, the factory went on to commission cartoons of contemporary life from Spanish court painters. The most notable ones were by Francesco de Goya. The factory continued into the 20th century, later copying earlier tapestries.

Magic lantern ■ Around 1660 the Dutch scientist Christian Huygens made what is regarded as the first magic lantern—an early projector. The source of illumination (either sunlight, candlelight, or oil burners) was placed in front of a concave mirror that served to concentrate and reflect the light onto the lenses. Handpainted or printed glass slides in wooden frames were then placed between the lens and the light, and the resulting large image was projected onto a wall or screen. Some slides had moving parts to give the effect of movement. Although lanterns were used for entertainment, they were also used for educational purposes in the 19th century, often illustrating ghoulish tales. The birth of moving pictures in 1896 signaled the end of the magic lantern for recreational purposes.

Magistretti, Vico (1920–2006) Commercially successful and multi-award-winning, post–World War II Italian architect and designer. His notable furniture designs include the butterfly-silhouette "Nihau" chair; colorful stacking "Maui" tables (and chairs); and the stainless steel and fabric- or leather-covered injection molded "Basket" armchair. Lighting fixtures include the painted aluminum "Atollo" table lamp.

Magot The French term for "dwarf." The name for a seated figure of a Chinese "buddha"—a Chinese man with a smiling face and long ear lobes, based on the Chinese figure of Pu-tai Ho-shang. Some were pierced so that the figure could be used as a PASTILLE BURNER; the smoke escaped through the eyes and ears. They were made in porcelain at MEISSEN, CHANTILLY, and MENNECY.

Mahal ■ An area of west Persia where loosely woven carpets were made in the 19th century and are still made today. Designs of various kinds are seen—bold, all-over designs in pastel colors are particularly popular. Shades of red, blue, and ivory are common background colors.

Mahogany ■ A tree (*Swietenia mahagom*) native to Central and South America and the West Indies that provides a hard-wearing, deep reddish brown timber with a close grain. From 1730 large quantities of mahogany were imported into Europe from Jamaica (Gamaica wood), and then from Cuba, San Domingo (Spanish mahogany), and Honduras (also known as BAYWOOD). When supplies of WALNUT declined, mahogany became the preferred wood of cabinet-makers, used both in the solid and as a veneer. Its popularity was due to its inherent strength and the width of the boards, which were ideally suited to table leaves made in one piece.

Maiolica ■ Tin-glazed earthenware was known as "maiolica" in Italy due to the

Magic lantern
Mahogany and brass magic lantern, labeled "J. H. Dallmeyer/ Optician/London."

Mahal
Room-sized rug, with garden design on a blue field and red border. 19th century.

Mahogany
Mahogany tilt-top tea table, Philadelphia, PA. c. 1765.

M

importance of the island of Majorca (Maiolica in medieval Italian) in the trading network. The term first applied to Hispano-Moresque LUSTERWARE from Spain, then to lusterware made in Italy in factories such as CASTEL DURANTE, FAENZA, FLORENCE, MONTELUPO, and VENICE, and eventually included all tin-glazed pottery. Wares can be dated by the colors and motifs used in the decoration. Maiolica has been made from the 13th century and is still produced today.

Majolica A corrupted form of the word MAIOLICA, used in the 19th century for a type of earthenware elaborately modeled and covered with thick lead blue, purple-pink, turquoise, and yellow glazes. It originated at MINTON in Staffordshire and was first shown at the GREAT EXHIBITION of 1851. The catalogue mentions "Messrs. Minton & Company and their excellent Flower Vases colored after the style of old majolica." It became popular especially for large objects such as JARDINIÈRES, umbrella stands, garden seats, large fountains, and human and bird figures. Novelties included large cheese "bells" with grazing cow finials, oyster plates in the form of shells, pie dishes, and tureens with quarries of the hunt modeled in relief. Majolica was occasionally termed DELLA ROBBIA ware, FAIENCE, or PALISSY ware.

From 1850 to 1855 models were designed by CARRIER-BELLEUSE, who later returned to Sèvres. It was made in England in factories such as

WEDGWOOD, George JONES, and Minton; in France by Massier Choisy-le-Roi, SAINT-CLÉMENT, Sarreguemines, LUNÉVILLE; and also in Germany, Czechoslovakia, Portugal (Caldas), Italy, Sweden, and Russia. The American public discovered both English and American majolica at the 1876 Philadelphia CENTENNIAL Exposition and it remains popular today. American majolica makers were GRIFFEN, SMITH & HILL of Phoenixville, Pennsylvania; there were eight other factories in the same town, which is an indication of the ware's high regard. Others making American majolica were James Carr of New York City, George Morley of East Liverpool, and Trenton Potteries.

Majorelle, Louis ■ (1859–1926) A French cabinet-maker who trained as a painter before taking over and industrializing his father's (Auguste Majorelle) cabinet-making business in Nancy in 1879. He was a master of ART NOUVEAU furniture and also designed metalware. His style is sinuous and fluid Rococo with a contemporary twist. He was associated with Émile GALLÉ in the Ecole de NANCY, a society aimed at promoting art in the Lorraine region of France.

Makepeace, John ■ (born 1939) An English furniture designer at the forefront of the British Craft Revival. He set up workshops at Parnham in Dorset, followed by a School for Furniture in 1977.

Maki-e ■ The Japanese word for "sprinkled picture." A form of Japanese lacquerwork with a naturalistic, figurative, or emblematic design in gold or colored LACQUER on a black, gold, or red background. The three main types are the raised *takamaki-e*, the flat *hiramaki-e*, and *togidashi maki-e* in which gold or silver dust is sprinkled onto the surface. They are most commonly found on boxes and INROS.

Malachite ■ An ornamental, bright green hardstone with distinctive concentric bands and circles of dark and pale green. Primarily sourced in Russia, malachite was widely used in the 19th century for candelabra and desk ornaments and for smaller objects such as cameos, beads, and jewelry.

Málaga potteries The Spanish center producing lustered Hispano-Moresque ware from the mid-13th century, when they had a flourishing export trade with Egypt, Italy, Sicily, and from 1303, with England. The large Alhambra vases may have been made in Granada. Málaga stopped making lusterware in the early 15th century, although it made tin-glazed earthenware until the mid-16th century.

Malling ware ■ Produced in Newcastle upon Tyne from 1762 to 1963, Malling was, during its heyday, the largest pottery in the world, with showrooms in Denmark, New Zealand, and Australia during the 1920s. Production was broad, ranging from everyday white ware such as kitchen ware, innovative

Maiolica
Pesaro maiolica dish, decorated with the "Triumph of Bacchus." 16th century.

Majorelle, Louis
Majorelle carved walnut and marquetry cabinet. c. 1900.

Makepeace, John
Mollusk desk of washed oak, by John Makepeace. c. 1980.

machine-made marmalade jars, and crockery for railroads and shipping lines to highly decorated LUSTERWARE. Early factory marks include "CTM," which was extended to create the trade name "Cetem ware" in the early 1900s. Black ground wares were introduced in 1910 and became the first truly distinctive Malling ware, followed by prolific designs from Lucien Emile Boullemier in the 1920s. With World War II, the company began to decline, and it finally closed in 1963. The pattern books showed that 16,500 designs had been produced.

Mallet vase A Chinese vase with a cylindrical body and narrower cylindrical neck, possibly with two handles.

Malling jugs The name given to early DELFTWARE jugs from one found in the church of West Malling in Kent. They have ovoid bodies, cylindrical necks, and speckled brown, blue, and turquoise glazes. Some have silver mounts. Malling jugs are the earliest tin-glazed earthenware thought to be made in England in the mid-16th century, but they may in fact have been made in the Netherlands.

Mamluk carpets Egyptian carpets made from 1250 to 1517, with dense overall geometric designs, usually in green, crimson, and white, with yellow detailing.

Mamluk pottery The Mamluks were a dynasty in Egypt from 1250 to 1382, originating from Turkish slaves taken to Egypt. Much of the so-called Mamluk pottery was in fact made in Syria and pottery in the style of Raqqa (Syria) was copied in Egypt. They made LUSTERWARE and used SGRAFFITO on a thick, heavy body. Some wares were decorated in UNDERGLAZE blue and black. Imitations of Chinese CELADON and BLUE AND WHITE ware were made in the 15th century.

Mandarin palette A decorative style on CHINESE EXPORT PORCELAIN in the second half of the 18th century, using FAMILLE ROSE enamels with iron red gilding and other colors. The designs include Asian figures in landscapes or gardens, usually set in panels on a Y-diaper, cell DIAPER, or UNDERGLAZE blue ground. Staffordshire makers imitated the style in the first half of the 19th century. See CANTON PORCELAIN.

Manganese ■ A mineral used since Egyptian times in the manufacture of STEEL and ALLOYS and also in ceramics as a stain for GLAZES and BODIES. In a lead glaze, manganese gives a rich purple-brown color; in an alkaline glaze, it gives purple or violet; and mixed with iron, it gives a rich near-black hue. Routinely used in glassmaking to neutralize iron (green) contamination in sand.

Manierblumen A term meaning "flowers in a mannered style," used to describe sharply defined 18th-century flower painting on MEISSEN porcelain.

Mannerist A style of painting, sculpture, architecture, and decorative arts developed in Rome and Florence from the 1520s. The style was introduced in painting, sculpture, and architecture—for example, in the work of Michelangelo and Giulio Romano. It spread throughout Europe during the 16th century, especially after the Italian artists Rosso Fiorentino and Francesco Primaticcio went to France to supervise the decoration of the chateau of Fontainebleau for Francis I. It was also disseminated through engraved ornament and pattern books.

STRAPWORK is the most distinctive ornamental motif, combined with sinuous, exaggerated, and twisted figures and three-dimensional representations of fantastical animals, birds, and sea creatures, often grouped in bizarre and illusionistic compositions. GROTESQUES and GROTTO ornament such as shells, animal masks, and realistic depictions of reptiles were also popular. Such ornament is found particularly in ceramics by Bernard PALISSY and in silverware by Benvenuto CELLINI and Wenzel Jamnitzer. It also features in designs for silver, furniture, and tapestries by Romano and other Italian artists, and by French and Flemish artists such as Jacques Androuet Du Cerceau and Hans Vredeman de Vries. Cups and ewers of semiprecious stones, NAUTILUS shells, and other exotic items were set in elaborate silver-gilt mounts. An original late version of the Mannerist style, known as the AURICULAR style, which originated with the VAN VIANEN family in the

M
241

Maki-e
Kajikawa School *inro*, with a pigeon perched in *takamaki-e*, with details in *hiramaki-e*.

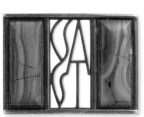

Malachite
Josef Hoffmann Wiener Werkstätte silver brooch set with malachite. c. 1905.

Malling ware
Earthenware vase, relief-molded and painted with flowers and leaves.

Manganese
Delft tile, with manganese decoration of a vase of flowers. 1750.

M

Netherlands in the early 17th century, continued the Mannerist preoccupation with fantastical forms derived from nature in the use of amorphous, fleshy, lobed shapes to decorate silver and furniture.

Mantel clock ■ A type of clock designed to stand on a shelf or mantelpiece. The term is used to refer to BRACKET CLOCKS, as well as to some late 18th- and early 19th-century French clocks that often featured gilt-bronze or marble cases embellished with figures, porcelain plaques, and NEOCLASSICAL motifs. From the 1830s the French mantel clock was usually part of a set, including matching urns and candelabra. Wooden and slate mantel clocks were favored in the late 19th century and reproductions remain popular today.

Manton Bros. (John: 1752–1834; Joseph: 1766–1835) Regarded as among the greatest English gunmakers. Born at Grantham in Lincolnshire, the brothers set up business in London in 1781 and became Gunmakers-in-Ordinary to George III and to the Honourable East India Company. They were known for the manufacture of all types of firearms, but especially fine-quality sporting guns. The development of the English shotgun, austerely decorated but beautifully proportioned and superbly made, owes much to the Manton brothers.

Maple ■ Trees in the genus *Acer*, of which one of the most common is the sycamore maple. Maple provides a hard, pale yellow-white wood used in furniture-making in Britain and Europe. It was also used in MARQUETRY, often stained black to imitate EBONY in the 17th and 18th centuries, and was occasionally used as a VENEER. Several species of maple are also indigenous to North America and were used in American furniture from the end of the 17th century.

Marbled glass Glass with a swirling multicolored surface that resembles marble. Such glass was made in Venice from the 15th to the 17th century, and was also part of the development of colored BOHEMIAN GLASS such as LITHYALIN. It is usually made by mixing a number of colors of molten glass together in the pot, but ensuring that they do not become homogenous. See AGATE GLASS.

Marblehead Pottery ■ An American ART POTTERY founded in 1905 in Marblehead, Massachusetts, by Dr. Herbert J. Hall, and owned by Arthur Eugene Baggs from 1915 until it closed in 1936. It specialized in matt-glazed ware, including tiles, garden ornaments, and bowls of simple form and decoration.

Marbling ■ A decorative technique in which marble or other variegated stones such as granite are simulated using paints and glazes. Usually applied to plaster or wood, the technique has been employed since Classical Roman times, but proved particularly popular in the various NEOCLASSICAL or Classical-Revival styles of the 18th and 19th centuries.

Marcotte, Leon (c. 1825–85) A French-born American furniture-maker, interior designer, and retailer, active in New York City from 1854. His company specialized in Renaissance and Louis XVI Revival styles manufactured in its New York workshops, but was known for its furniture imported from France. He returned to Paris in 1869.

Marieberg pottery A Swedish FAIENCE and PORCELAIN factory founded in 1758 on an island near Stockholm by Johann Ehrenreich. After initial difficulties with porcelain production, it made faience, producing fine wares, including *trompe l'oeil* pieces, in the prevailing ROCOCO style. The SOFT-PASTE PORCELAIN they made until 1777 shows strong French influence. The factory was bought by RÖRSTRAND in 1782 and closed in 1788. See KONIGSBERG.

Marinot, Maurice ■ (1882–1960) A French artist who turned to pioneering studio glassmaking in 1911, at the works of Viard Fils, near Troyes. His sculptural, thick-walled glass, often with relief decoration, acid etching, and bubble or colored enamel INCLUSIONS, dates primarily from around 1920 to 1937. Widely acknowledged as the world's first studio glassmaker.

Mark, porcelain ■ Marks—impressed, painted, modeled, or printed—are applied to ceramics for a number of purposes: 1. factory marks; 2. artists' signatures; 3. marks of ownership or dealer's marks; 4. to show date or quality; mold, and pattern numbers;

Mantel clock
Louis XV-style gilt-bronze mantel clock. Late 19th century.

Maple
New England Queen Anne maple highboy. c. 1775.

Marblehead Pottery
Vase by Hannah Tutt, with crouching panthers against stylized trees.

Marbling
Marbled beech and mahogany stool, after a design by C. H. Tatham. c. 1800.

243

5. workmen's signs. The drawing of the dome of Florence Cathedral by the MEDICI factory from 1575 to 1587 is the first use of a factory or maker's mark in modern times. The first regular use of a factory mark was at MEISSEN from 1723. Regular dating of wares was first used at SÈVRES. Adding the name of the country was made cumpulsory for imports into the US by the US McKinley Act of 1891. See HALLMARKS, REIGN MARKS, TOUCH MARKS.

Märklin ■ The most important German factory producing TINPLATE TOYS during the late 19th and early 20th centuries. Gebrüder Märklin (Märklin Brothers) was founded in 1859 by Theodor Friedrich Wilhelm Märklin in Goppingen. After Märklin's death in 1866, the company was managed by his widow, and then by one of his sons, Eugen, from 1888. In 1891 the company acquired the Ludwig Lutz tinplate toy factory and combined its handmade techniques with processes of mass production to enlarge the business and find a middle road between unique, handmade products and mass-produced, inexpensive toys using LITHOGRAPHY. In the same year, at the Leipzig Spring Fair, Märklin introduced simple clockwork trains that ran on rails of standardized sizes and was the first "system railway" to which pieces could be added one by one.

Over subsequent years, stations, engine sheds, and signals were added to the train sets. Many were accurate representations of actual buildings—for example, Stuttgart station. Trains were made in gauges from I to III, with clockwork and steam being used for the power. A great many were exported to the rest of Europe and to the UK and the US, and by 1900 the company had become a market leader. Foreign lettering was used on the export models. By 1910 the smaller "0" gauge had become more popular and by 1925, 20-volt electric trains had been introduced. Model cars, boats, and stationary steam engines were also produced, as were many smaller working toys designed to be driven by the steam engines.

With the build-up of naval power in the early 20th century, large battleships, torpedo boats, and submarines were popular, and are today some of the scarcest models due to their frequent submersion in water and subsequent rusting. The smaller "00" gauge "miniature railway" was introduced in 1935 and a wide range of DIECAST, trains, and military vehicles was on sale by 1939. Production ceased during the war but resumed afterward, with the company concentrating on a new range of diecast vehicles and extending their railroad models. Tinplate manufacture ceased completely in 1950. This has been the pattern since, and Märklin continues to be one of the largest toy manufacturers in Europe.

Marlborough leg ■ An English furniture term of uncertain derivation and used from the mid-18th century. It may have originated as a compliment to George Spencer, fourth Duke of Marlborough, the patron of INCE AND MAYHEW. It refers to a square, normally plain leg with CHAMFERED edge, usually terminating in a block (square) foot. The Marlborough leg was common on English formal furniture in Chinese taste in the third quarter of the 18th century. In the US, and Philadelphia in particular, it gained popularity over the CABRIOLE leg, especially in the work of Thomas AFFLECK.

Marot, Daniel (1663–1752) An influential French architect and designer who worked for most of his life in Holland and England. The son of a well-known French architect, in 1685 he fled to Holland as a HUGUENOT refugee. There he was appointed architect to William of Orange, for whom he designed interiors and furniture at Het Loo and Appeldorn. After William ascended the British throne in 1688, Marot also worked at Hampton Court Palace, near London. His style blended the European BAROQUE and WILLAM AND MARY styles. His engraved designs, published around 1700 in *Livres d'Appartements*, influenced furniture design in the first decades of the 18th century.

Marotte ■ A BISQUE doll's head mounted on a handheld stick, usually in a multi-colored clownlike outfit, housing a music box triggered by turning the stick quickly clockwise. The heads were made by Armand MARSEILLE and other leading 19th-century German manufacturers. Versions were also made in CELLULOID in the 1930s and 40s, often in Japan.

Marinot, Maurice
Bottle and stopper, with enameling around the rim. 1910–20.

Mark, porcelain
Meissen crossed swords mark, with gilder's numeral "26." 1739.

Märklin
Märklin 1-gauge B-spirit steam locomotive, with a 2-A tender No. 4001.

Serpentine back with canted scrolling arms

Marlborough leg
Philadelphia Chippendale mahogany sofa, with square Marlborough legs. c. 1785.

M

244

MARQUETRY

A type of decorative VENEER applied to furniture, made up of a sheet of small pieces of colored woods and often other materials such as ivory, mother-of-pearl, and bone, which were laid out in a pattern and then applied to the carcass. The technique was invented by Dutch cabinet-makers and was introduced into Britain in the 1660s. It took several forms, including floral marquetry (fashionable from around 1660 to 1690) and SEAWEED or ARABESQUE (fashionable around 1690). It fell out of fashion briefly in the early 18th century in England, but was revived in the 1760s and 1770s, and has been intermittently fashionable since then. See also PARQUETRY.

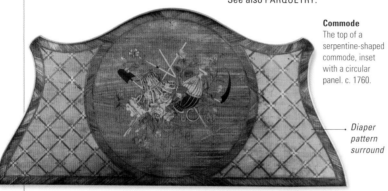

Commode
The top of a serpentine-shaped commode, inset with a circular panel. c. 1760.

Diaper pattern surround

Marriage A piece of furniture composed of parts that were not originally made together but have been combined at a later date. It is most common with two-piece cased furniture such as bureau-bookcases and dressers, where the upper part may have been lost or damaged and replaced with a contemporary or later equivalent. It is also common with replacement tops or bases for small tables.

Marrow scoop ■ A silver utensil used for extracting the marrow from cooked bones, first known from the 1690s, with a regular spoon bowl at one end and a channeled scoop at the other. This pattern was superseded by the scoop design, made from the early 18th to the 19th century, which had a scoop at each end of different sizes.

Marseille, Armand ■ (1885–1940) A famous and prolific maker of BISQUE dolls and dolls' heads, with his son, also Armand Marseille. Marseille was born in Russia in 1856 and acquired the Mathias Lambert toy factory and the Libdermann & Wegscher porcelain factory in Thuringia, Germany, in 1884. Most of Marseille's doll heads are marked with the factory's initials "AM" or its full name, in conjunction with a mold number. Vast numbers of both dolls and dolls' heads were made from 1890 to 1930, with mold numbers 390 and 370 being the most common. In 1924 the DREAM BABY, the most popular doll made by Marseille, went into production, marked with mold numbers 241 for the CLOSED MOUTH and 251 for the OPEN MOUTH. These came in many versions, including black and Asian. The factory also made CHARACTER DOLLS and remained in production until the late 1930s.

Marseilles potteries An important center of faience manufacture with many factories based around Bouches-du-Rhône, France. Production started at St Jean du Desert, which was worked from 1685 by Joseph Clerissy. The factory remained in Clerissy's control until 1733 and continued until 1743. In the following decades, with the expansion of trade and also export trade with the French colonies, the number of

Double scoop-design

Marrow scoop
Irish silver marrow scoop, made by Sam L. Neville. 1811.

Marseille, Armand
Schoolgirl, with bisque head and composition body, in original outfit. c. 1890s.

Martelé
French silver *sucrier* (sugar bowl), decorated with martelé work. Late 19th century.

Martin Brothers
Stoneware bird group, incised "R W Martin & Bros, Southall 1.10.1914."

factories multiplied. But by 1790 trade declined, and in 1809 only one factory survived. The most important factories were Joseph Fauchier (1711–95), Louis Leroy (1741–78), Claud Perrin (1740–48), continued by his widow until 1793, and then by her son until 1803, Honoré Savy (1764–82), Antoine Bonnefoy (1762–93), and Joseph Gaspart Robert (1750–95). Early products show the influence of NEVERS and MOUSTIERS and *style Bérain*.

Marshall, Mark Villars (died 1912) An English potter, renowned for his distinctive, bold work in stoneware for DOULTON, LAMBETH, and some ART NOUVEAU pieces.

Martelé ■ A textured, uneven surface produced on metal, especially copper and silver, by repetitive hammering. Strongly associated with ART NOUVEAU–style metalware, it is also used to describe a form of faceted glass that looks like hammered metal and was developed by DAUM FRÈRES. See PLANISHING.

Martin Brothers ■ An English family of STUDIO POTTERS. Robert Wallace Martin was the modeler, having originally trained as a stone carver. He opened a small pottery in Fulham in 1873 and moved to Southall in 1877, where he formed a partnership with his brothers. Walter Frazer Martin was responsible for the throwing, colored glazes, and some of the incised decoration. Edwin Martin was the chief decorator and was particularly good at aquatic subjects

and scenes. Charles Martin helped out part-time with the business affairs. They produced salt-glazed pottery. The vases had carved or incised decoration and the grotesque birds were modeled with separate heads and superb characterization. The pottery closed in 1914.

Martin, Fernand ■ France's biggest manufacturer of tin toys. Martin founded a factory in 1878 in Paris producing small novelty toys—mechanical human and animal figures—from TINPLATE. These amusing pieces were colorfully painted or dressed in fabric costume. Taken over by Victor Bonnet et Cie in 1919, many of the toys were reissued in the 1920s.

Marvering The process in which molten glass gathered on the end of an iron rod is rolled on a polished metal or marble table (a marver), either to smooth and shape it or to acquire or consolidate decoration.

Marx & Co., Louis ■ An important American toy company founded in 1919 in New York by Louis Marx (1896–1982), who had worked for Strauss, another toy manufacturer. He initially designed toys that were made and then sold elsewhere, but in 1922 he acquired the struggling Strauss company and modified many of its designs, most notably the "climbing monkey." Marx developed his company rapidly and successfully, and by the 1930s he owned three factories in the US. By 1955 Marx was the largest toy manufacturer in the world,

with over 5,000 designs and factories in ten countries. This success was based on well-priced TINPLATE with offset LITHO-printed (later plastic) vehicles and other toys, often with novelty action. Their trade mark was "MAR" on a large X in a circle. Marx retired in 1972, and after two changes of ownership, the company closed in 1980. The name and rights were revived in 1995 and a new company, the Marx Toy Corporation, continues today.

Mary Gregory glass ■ The generic name given to pieces of colored glass painted in vitreous opaque white enamels with white or pink-white figural designs of Victorian children, popularly made in the late 19th century in England, Bohemia, and the US. The name may derive from a glass decorator at the BOSTON AND SANDWICH GLASS CO. who was inspired by the book illustrations of Kate Greenaway.

Mask ■ A universal decorative motif originating in Classical antiquity, representing the heads of humans, gods, goddesses, animals, birds, or monsters. Masks were revived during the RENAISSANCE and feature as popular ornament on NEOCLASSICAL silver and furniture, frequently with monopodia. In architecture, masks are either decorative (for example, as ornament on capitals and KEYSTONES) or useful (as in a waterspout).

Mason, Miles and family See MASON'S PATENT IRONSTONE CHINA.

Martin, Fernand
Toy depicting an Asian figure pulling a woman in a rickshaw. c. 1889.

Marx & Co., Louis
Lithographed tin and clockwork Marx Merry Music Makers.

Kate Greenaway-inspired imagery

Mary Gregory glass
Bohemian vase decorated with scenes of a boy and a girl playing tennis, with gilt rim.

Mask
Lion's head mask from a Sicilian side table. Late 18th century.

Mason's Patent Ironstone China ■

Miles Mason was a dealer in Chinese export porcelain, but when the East India Company stopped importing Oriental china, he had to look for a new business. After a short but unsuccessful partnership with Thomas Wolfe in Liverpool, which ended in 1800, Mason moved to Staffordshire and in 1802 founded a major porcelain works making hybrid hard paste at Lane Delph. It used both Chinese and English designs and a neat impressed mark M. Mason as well as seal marks. In 1813 he passed the business on to his two sons, George and Charles James. It was Charles James who introduced in 1813 the famous Patent Ironstone China, which is a hard earthenware made by adding ironstone slag to the porcelain mix. It became popular for dinner services because it was strong and held heat well. It was usually decorated with bold Oriental patterns with flowers and birds. Production also included such items as fireplaces and large vases.

Charles James was declared bankrupt in 1848 and subsequent Mason patterns and shapes have been produced under many company banners, including George ASHWORTH & BROS., and most recently, since 1973 as Mason's Ironstone under the WEDGWOOD Group.

Masonic emblem ■

A motif that originates from the symbolism and myths of masonic ritual, used for decorating objects belonging to freemasons as well as to decorate their meeting places. Since the roots of freemasonry derived from the medieval craft guilds of the stonemasons, many emblems represent their working tools, such as the drawing board or compass. Masonic emblems are most commonly found on glass and ceramic objects from the late 18th to the early 19th century, including German enameled beakers, American flasks, and English transfer-printed pottery, as well as on furniture used at masonic gatherings. Masonic emblems were often used to symbolize justice and equality.

Mass production

The manufacture of identical items in large quantities by mechanical methods. The introduction of machine methods such as die-stamping in silver and press-molding in glass during the late 18th and early 19th centuries enabled manufacturers to meet a growing demand for standardized, inexpensive products, resulting from the increased prosperity of the urban middle classes. Mass production reached its high point with the introduction of the moving assembly line by Henry Ford for the Model T Ford in 1913. However, at the end of the 19th century, the subordination of aesthetics to technology, which had become a distinguishing feature of mass-produced items, was challenged by the ARTS AND CRAFTS MOVEMENT, advocating a return to handcraftsmanship, and continued in the 20th century by the CRAFTS REVIVAL Movement.

Massier, Delphin (1836–1907) and Clément ■ (1844–1917)

French potters working predominantly in the ART NOUVEAU style, who had factories in Golfe-Juan (Clément) and Vallauris (Delphin) in southern France. Delphin produced primarily high-fired MAJOLICA wares, and to a lesser extent, LUSTERWARE, whereas Clément specialized in highly complex and brilliantly iridescent metallic luster glazes.

Masudaya toy company

Founded in 1924 as the Masutoku Toy Factory, and eventually known as the Modern Toys Co., Masudaya was one of Japan's leading TINPLATE and mechanical and later battery operated TOY-MAKERS of the post–World War II era, and is still in operation today. Notable wares include cars, boats, robots, and space ships.

Match holder

The part of the MATCHLOCK that held the glowing cord, known as a slow match, which ignited the powder charge. Also known as a serpentine from its curving, sinuous form.

Matchbox toys ■

LESNEY registered their Matchbox 1:75 Series in 1953. The toys were small, accurate, sturdy, usually two-piece castings of road and construction vehicles and were brightly enameled and packed in boxes designed to look like matchboxes. The series was extremely successful and the range was kept at 75 models, with one toy being dropped as a new one was introduced. The Models of Yesteryear range was introduced for collectors in 1956. The quality of the

Mason's Patent Ironstone
Pair of Mason's Patent Ironstone China vases and covers. Early 19th century.

Masonic emblem
Silver Masonic pocket watch, the dial decorated with masonic emblems. c. 1880.

Massier, Delphin
Clément-Massier vase, covered with a luster glaze.

Matchbox toys
Matchbox Series No. 22 Vauxhall Cresta, in pale gray with lilac side panels.

models declined in the 1960s, and in 1982 Lesney was taken over by Universal Holdings.

Matchlock The earliest firearm mechanism that allowed a shooter to fire while taking an effective aim. It used a length of cord soaked in saltpeter (slow match), which burned at a steady rate. The cord was gripped in the MATCH HOLDER, which was attached to the trigger. When the trigger was pressed, the glowing end was lowered into a small pan filled with gunpowder, firing the gun. The matchlock was simple to use and cheap to make. It survived in European warfare from around 1470 to about 1700.

Matchsafe See VESTA CASE.

Mathews, Arthur Frank (1860–1945) An American painter, architect, interior decorator, and furniture designer in Oakland, California. Mathews is considered the founder of the California style of ARTS AND CRAFTS, characterized by a bold use of color and Californian flora on furniture and textiles. He founded The Furniture Shop (active 1906–20), making and selling integrated elements of interior decoration.

Matryoshka A set of Russian peasant dolls of decreasing sizes placed one inside the other, with a tiny solid doll at the center. A set usually contains seven dolls.

Matting A decorative technique, dating from the 16th century, for producing a textured matte surface on metal, notably silver and gold. It is achieved either by applying multiple, closely spaced blows with a punch or hammer or by the application of acid.

Mauchline ware ◾ Distinctive wooden SOUVENIR WARE, including boxes and small household goods, usually made from SYCAMORE MAPLE with printed transfers, most often showing a view. It takes its name from the location of the factory in Mauchline in Ayrshire, Scotland, and was made primarily by J. J. Smith from the 1820s. Production stopped in 1933 when the factory burned down.

Mazarin or mazareen blue An English name for an intense dark blue. Said to be inspired by Cardinal Mazarin, the term was first used to denote a deep blue in 1686 and a material of the same color in 1694. It was introduced at CHELSEA around 1755 and later at other factories to imitate the *gros bleu* of VINCENNES and SÈVRES. It also came to describe a blue garment worn by Common Councilmen in London.

Mazarine Generally refers to 18th-century pierced silver and Old SHEFFIELD stands. Oval in outline, mazarines sat within the border of silver serving dishes to support the fish or meat and allow the juices to strain through to the well below.

Mazer bowl ◾ A drinking bowl of turned hardwood, usually MAPLE, with gold, silver, or SILVER-GILT mounts around the rim and base or foot, and sometimes a decorative disk or boss in the center of the bowl. Mazers survive in fairly large numbers from the 14th century but HALLMARKED silver ones are rare.

McGill, Donald (1875–1962) An English watercolor artist who produced comic pictures for postcards from 1904 and has been called "the king of the saucy seaside postcard." They have been in use from Edwardian times to the present day. McGill produced around 12,000 designs, of which over 200 million cards were made, with popular subjects being drunken men, fat ladies, attractive young women, honeymooning couples, and the seaside.

McIntire, Samuel ◾ (1757–1811) An American architect, woodcarver, and sculptor, active in Salem, Massachusetts, from around 1782. He carved chair and sofa rails with baskets of fruit and other devices for Salem cabinet-makers such as William Lemon, Jacob SANDERSON, and Nehemiah Adams.

McLaughlin, Mary Louise ◾ (1847–1939) An American pioneer of ART POTTERY who began as an amateur china painter in Cincinnati in 1874. After seeing the CENTENNIAL Exposition in 1876, she developed a type of earthenware painted in Barbotine style (underglaze painting in colored slip). In 1898 she began to make porcelain comparable to LIMOGES. Her Losanti range is prized today. She also designed for the ROOKWOOD POTTERY.

Mauchline ware
Mauchline ware box, inscribed "When shall we three meet again." c. 1840.

Silver mounts

Mazer bowl
Omar Ramsden mounted fruitwood mazer bowl. 1937.

McIntire, Samuel
Federal carved mahogany four-drawer chest. c. 1800.

McLaughlin, Mary Louise
Losanti bulbous porcelain vessel, carved and modeled by Mary Louise McLaughlin.

Mdina Glass ■ A glassworks founded in Malta by glass designer and maker Michael HARRIS in 1968. Typical colors include green and blue, and designs are often thick-walled, heavy in weight, and cased in clear glass. The name was taken from the ancient capital of Malta. Although Harris left in 1972, the company continues to produce similar designs today.

Measham ware See BARGE WARE.

Meccano ■ Mechanics Made Easy, a constructional toy range invented by Frank HORNBY in 1901, which changed its name to Meccano and was launched in 1907. Sets consisted mainly of metal strips and plates held together by nuts and bolts. Various special parts were introduced to enable increasingly complicated models to be assembled. Clockwork, electric, and even steam engines could be added. The educational value of this toy was a strong marketing feature. Constructional sets for cars and airplanes were made in the 1930s. The company was acquired by LINES BROS. in 1964 and Airfix in 1972. Financial problems saw the closure of the British factory in 1980, although Meccano is still made by Nikko of Japan.

Mechanical bank An American SAVINGS BANK, popular in the late 19th century, with moving parts and springs triggered by a coin to perform humorous feats.

Medici glass Glassware made from the 16th to the 18th century at the various glasshouses established in and near Florence by the Medici family. In the 16th century Cosimo I de' Medici, a major patron of the arts, invited VENETIAN glassmakers and notable painters and engravers to develop glass designs. From the 17th century production included medical and scientific instruments as well as elaborate and ingenious drinking glasses, dishes, TAZZAS, and EWERS, often marked with the family or papal coat of arms.

Medici porcelain In the 16th century the Grand Duke Francesco Maria I of Florence was the wealthy patron of a porcelain factory in the city (the first in Europe from which examples still survive). Production probably continued from around 1575 to about 1587. It produced a form of SOFT-PASTE PORCELAIN in which the BODY resembled glass in texture with a white tin glaze painted in UNDERGLAZE blue in Chinese style. But the factory experienced heavy kiln failures, and although work continued during the reigns of the next two Medici grand dukes, only 30 or so pieces have survived. Most are in museums around the world. They have as a mark the dome of the Cathedral of Florence with the initial "F." One mark of six circles with the initials "FMMDE II" for Francisco Medici magnus Dux, Etruriae II is known.

Meeks, Joseph and Sons A large and important American furniture-maker established in New York City in 1797 and active until 1868. The firm began making formal furniture in the FEDERAL period, but is best known for the exuberant and large-scale furniture produced in the second quarter of the century in late American EMPIRE STYLE. After around 1850, it made parlor furniture comparable to the work of John Henry BELTER.

Meerschaum ■ The German term for "sea spray." A hard, white mineral from Asia Minor and North America used primarily for making pipes for smoking tobacco.

Meigh Pottery ■ A family-run Staffordshire pottery (also called Old Hall Works) based at Hanley, which made good-quality EARTHENWARE. It was founded around 1770 by Job Meigh and was later joined by his sons from 1805 to 1834. One son, Charles, ran the factory from 1835 to 1849, adding Gothic Revival stoneware to the factory's repertoire. The firm was variously called C. Meigh & Son & Pankhurst (1850–51); Charles Meigh & Son (1851–61); Old Hall Earthenware Co. Ltd. (1861–86); and the Old Hall Porcelain Works Ltd. (1886–1902), when it closed. Charles won a medal at the GREAT EXHIBITION for two stoneware gilt vases painted with royal portraits and views of Crystal Palace. Another branch, W. & R. Meigh, produced pottery at Stoke from 1894 to 1899.

Meiji period The Japanese term for "enlightened government," denoting the

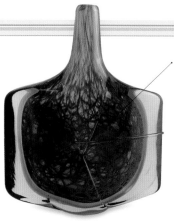

Distinctive blue-cream color combination

Mdina Glass
"Fish" vase, signed
"Mdina 1984."

Meccano
Meccano No.1 Constructor Car, a two-seater open tourer, made for the French market.

Meerschaum
English meerschaum pipe, carved with the head of Prince Albert. 19th century.

Meigh Pottery
Large Bacchanalian Dance jug, relief-molded in buff stoneware. c. 1850.

historical period from 1868 to 1912. After world isolation during the Edo period (1600–1868), the Meiji Emperor was restored to power and Japan opened up to the Western world. The arts and crafts were encouraged. LACQUER wares, metalware, ENAMELS, and CERAMICS were shown to great acclaim and influence at international exhibitions. See KINKOZAN, KUTANI, and SATSUMA POTTERIES.

Meiping A classic Chinese vase shape with a short, narrow neck and bulbous shoulders tapering toward the base. It was made from the SONG DYNASTY (960–1279 CE) onward, and was designed to hold prunus blossom.

Meissen ■ The first factory in Europe to make "real" or HARD-PASTE PORCELAIN.

Founded in Dresden, Saxony, in 1710 by royal decree, it was the result of the work of the alchemist Johann Friedrich BÖTTGER and the court chemist Count Ehrenfried Walther von Tschirnhaus. Three months later the factory was moved to Meissen, near Dresden. From 1710 to 1719 it made a high-fired red stoneware imitating Oriental stoneware.

By 1719, when Böttger died, a slightly yellowish porcelain was produced. In that year J. G. HÖROLDT was appointed as director. A new source of KAOLIN gave a pure white body and Höroldt developed wonderful ground colors. Augustus the Strong, Elector of Saxony, was an obsessive collector of Oriental

porcelain and was a knowledgeable and encouraging patron. In the early years, the main influence was Oriental and the senior painters included Adam Friedrich von LÖWENFINCK and Johann Gottfried Klinger. Figure production grew with the arrival of Johann Joachim KÄNDLER in 1731.

By 1756 the factory was beginning to experience competition. During the Seven Years War (1756–63), the factory fell into the hands of Frederick the Great, who took many of the best workmen to his own factory in BERLIN. When the war ended, the factory was reorganized and production resumed. To adapt to changing fashions, a French sculptor, Michel-Victor ACIER, joined in 1764 and an art school was set up,

MEISSEN PORCELAIN

Meissen's wares reflected the individual style of designers. Klinger's painting included the popular DEUTSCHE BLUMEN. Kändler modeled figures and groups of the most widely divergent styles—COMMEDIA DELL'ARTE and CHINOISERIE figures, satirical groups, saints, and the well-known MONKEY BAND. Smaller items included SNUFF BOXES, ÉTUIS, thimbles, and cane handles.

Horses emerging from waves

Jug
Porcelain water jug from the Elements series. 1818–60.

Domed lid with ball knop

Coffeepot
Pear-shaped coffeepot, decorated with red floral design. c. 1800.

Figure group
Figure group, modeled by J. J. Kändler in the Rococo style, of a seated lady with her pug and servant. c. 1740.

which is why it came to be known as the Academic Period (1764–74). In 1774 Count Camillo Marcolini became director, and the factory began its so-called Marcolini Period (1774–83). From 1814 to 1833 the factory produced wares in the NEOCLASSICAL style. From 1833 to 1870 the director of the factory was Heinrich Gottlob Kühn and Meissen produced porcelain copies of famous paintings in the Dresden galleries and copied earlier figures and styles.

Export to the US increased steadily in the late 19th century. ART NOUVEAU wares included plates by Henry VAN DE VELDE and figures of dancers and musicians. Since 1945 the factory has been styled VEB (Staatliche Porzellan-Manufaktur Meissen) but it continues to use the famous crossed-swords mark.

Melchior, Johann Peter ■ (1742–1825) A German porcelain modeler, born in Lintorf near Düsseldorf and apprenticed to sculptors in Düsseldorf and Aachen. He became master modeler at the HÖCHST porcelain factory in 1767, where he was also the court sculptor. He moved to the FRANKENTHAL factory in 1779 and stayed until 1793. From 1797 to 1822 Melchior was master modeler at the NYMPHENBURG porcelain factory.

Memento mori The Latin term for "remember you must die." Memento mori jewelry was a reminder to make the best of one's time on Earth and prepare oneself for the inevitability of death. From the 17th to the 19th century, gold rings, brooches, and lockets contained symbols of mortality such as skulls, urns, and coffins, possibly with an inscription.

Memorabilia ■ An item not necessarily of intrinsic value or interest itself, but which becomes more desirable and valuable due to its association with a famous person, event, place, or activity. ROCK AND POP memorabilia is one of the most recognized forms but SPORTING memorabilia is also highly regarded. Items of memorabilia can include paper EPHEMERA, photographs, personal items, COMMEMORATIVE WARE, and autographs.

Memphis ■ An Italian design group founded in 1981 by an international group of architects and designers led by Ettore SOTSASS, to design and make furniture, lighting, and other domestic wares of a highly decorative and colorful nature. Their work and aims were in complete contrast to the "sterility" of modernism (as they saw it), and are part of the POST-MODERN Movement.

Mennecy Porcelain Factory ■ François Barbin founded a factory in Paris in 1734 and was later given permission by the Duc de Villeroy to build a factory on his estate at Mennecy, around 1748. It made a creamy SOFT-PASTE PORCELAIN, painted in enamel colors with bright floral designs. The early figures include some charming groups of children and also some finely modeled biscuit porcelain COMMEDIA DELL'ARTE figures. The factory also produced domestic ware and small items such as knife-handles. They are marked "D.V.," sometimes with a ducal coronet. In 1773 the factory shifted to Bourg-la-Reine, and from 1780 it mainly made earthenware pieces. The factory closed in 1806.

Menu holder Sometimes known as place-card holders, these small stands of silver and allied materials were made in sets to sit on tables either to indicate where each diner was to sit or to hold a menu card. Popular from around 1890 to about 1920, they were often decorated with enamel or engraved scenes, depicting themes such as hunting or fishing.

Menuisier A French term for a joiner. Until the French Revolution in 1789, there was a distinction in status between the *menuisier* who specialized in small pieces of furniture constructed from plain wood and then carved, and the ÉBÉNISTE who specialized in veneered pieces. The distinction was introduced in the mid-17th century, formalized in the mid-18th, and lasted until the guild system was abolished during the Revolution.

Mercator, Gerard (1512–94) A major Flemish cartographer, second only to PTOLEMY, Mercator had a profound influence on both the art and science of map-making. Although he did not invent the projection (a way of representing a

Melchior, Johann Peter
Höchst figure group "Putti at the altar of Love." c. 1770.

Memorabilia
The Beatles, by Royal Command, souvenir concert program.

Memphis
Italian Memphis "Kristall" table, patterned and designed by Michele de Lucchi. 1981.

Mennecy Porcelain Factory
Porcelain custard cup and cover, with polychrome flowers. c. 1765.

sphere on a flat surface) that bears his name, he applied it in navigational charts and in his 18-sheet world map of 1569. Mercator also produced maps of Europe and Britain (now extremely rare) and the maps for the 1578 Cologne edition of Ptolemy's *Geographia*. His best-known work is his *Atlas* (the first compilation of maps to bear that title), published between 1585 and 1595, and revised and reissued many times by the Dutch cartographic firms of Hondius and later Jansson.

Mercury gilding Also known as "fire gilding," it is a technique for applying a gilt finish to metal, glass, and ceramics. An amalgam of ground gold and mercury is painted on the surface of the object and then fired at a low temperature. The mercury vaporizes and leaves behind a thin film of gold—a process that can be repeated if a greater thickness of gilt is required. The technique was known in ancient China (4th century BCE) but reached its apogee in late 17th-century France in the work of Parisian craftsmen such as André BOULLE and Jacques CAFFIERI.

Mercury twist stem ■ The stem of a type of mid-18th-century drinking glass made of two skillfully twisted, elongated, and flattened TEARS or threads of glass that refract light and therefore have a silvery, mercury-like appearance.

Merryman plates A set of six DELFT plates, inspired by the Dutch potter John

van Hamme, made in both England and Holland. Each was painted in blue with one line of a verse: "What is a Merry Man/Let him do what he can/To entertain his guests/With wine and merry jests/But when his wife do frown/ All merriment goes down." Made from the late 17th to the early 18th century, Merryman plates were copied in the 19th and 20th centuries.

Merrythought ■ An English toy company known for its teddy bears and soft toys. The origins of the company lay in a mohair spinning mill acquired by W. G. Holmes and G. H. Laxton in 1919. A weaving factory was acquired in 1920, and A. C. Janisch (sales director at J. K. FARNELL) and C. J. Rendle (production director at CHAD VALLEY) were hired. In 1930 the company moved to warehouses in Coalbrookdale, Shropshire, where teddy bear and soft toy production began. Its fine-quality products were made from MOHAIR and comprised jointed and unjointed bears and other animals. The company's best-known products are the Bingie bear and the Cheeky bear with bells in its ears.

Metal A term often used virtually interchangeably with glass to describe the molten or fused ingredients from which glass is made.

Metal fatigue The breaking or weakening of

any metal due to fluctuating stresses within it. For example, the repeated bending of a silver spoon may eventually cause it to break. Cast metals are particularly susceptible to fatigue. The term also applies to alloys where the combination begins to break down, causing the pieces to fall apart or sag. For example, prewar DINKY toys used a zinc alloy known as mazac, which tends to granulate over time, causing it to break.

Metal head dolls Popular from about 1880 to around 1920 as a lighter and stronger alternative to BISQUE, most of these dolls were made in Germany by companies such as Joseph Schön, Büschow and Beck, Minerva, and Juno.

Metamorphic furniture ■ Furniture that is designed to change in form and/or function, and which often incorporates space-saving features. Typical examples include chairs and tables that convert into LIBRARY STEPS. Introduced in the early 18th century, such pieces have remained popular ever since.

Mettlach pottery A German glazed-earthenware factory founded in 1809 by Jean-François Boch, notable for its images of rural life in medieval and Renaissance Germany and its ART DECO wares. Boch also owned a second factory at Septfontaines in Luxembourg. The Boch factories were united in 1836 with those of the Villeroy family. The joint firm, VILLEROY & BOCH, acquired a number

M

251

Mercury twist stem
Mercury air twist wine glass.
c. 1745.

Spiraling air twist stem

Merrythought
Merrythought teddy bear.
1930s–40s.

Metamorphic furniture
Oak metamorphic chair and library steps. c. 1870.

M

of other factories but lost those in East Germany after World War II. The factory at Mettlach is still in production.

Mettoy Co. Ltd. ■ An English toymaking company founded by Philip Ullmann in Northampton in 1933. The main products were lithographed TINPLATE vehicles. By 1941, dollhouses, stoves, and more general toys followed. DIECAST models first appeared in 1948, followed by a brief run of plastic vehicles. The company concentrated on their new CORGI range of diecast vehicles from 1956, with all other production ceasing in 1958. Mettoy closed in 1983 with its most popular brand, Corgi, being sold off.

Mezzotint An Italian term for "half-tint." A technique discovered around 1642 that enabled printmakers to achieve a greater tonal range. The metal printing plate is uniformly pitted with an implement called

a roulette or rocker so that the rough parts hold the ink. Lighter areas are produced by using a burnishing tool that smoothes parts of the plate.

Micromosaic See MOSAIC JEWELRY.

Microscope An instrument developed by Dutch spectacle-maker Zaccharias Janssen in 1608 who experimented with several lenses in a tube with which objects close by appeared greatly enlarged. Early examples were often constructed from wood, pasteboard, and vellum. Where a number of lenses are used to magnify the object, it is known as a compound microscope. In the 18th century ivory and brass were used, and in the 19th century was used alone. English makers included John Marshall, Edmund Culpeper, George ADAMS, and John Cuff.

Midwinter Midwinter was founded in Burslem, Staffordshire, in 1910, and became

known for its ART DECO–style tableware, which dominated production until after World War II. In 1940 the company began to modernize, and with the appointment of new designer Jessie Tait in 1946, new patterns and shapes started to emerge, including Stylecraft in 1953 and the lean lines of the Fashion range in 1955. These new lines were aimed at young home-makers and became very successful. Other famous designers included Hugh Casson and Terence CONRAN, whose designs are highly collectible.

Mies van der Rohe, Ludwig ■ (1886–1969) A German architect and designer of major importance to the MODERN MOVEMENT and the International Style of architecture. In his early years as an architect, he worked for Peter BEHRENS and took over the directorship of the BAUHAUS in 1930. He is known for his tubular-steel cantilevered furniture,

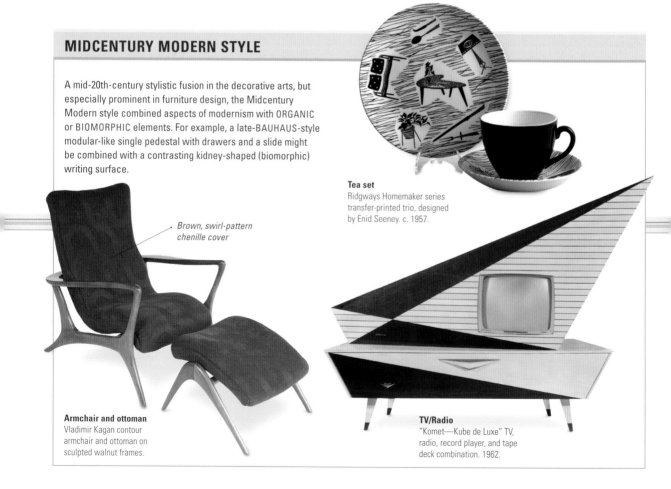

MIDCENTURY MODERN STYLE

A mid-20th-century stylistic fusion in the decorative arts, but especially prominent in furniture design, the Midcentury Modern style combined aspects of modernism with ORGANIC or BIOMORPHIC elements. For example, a late-BAUHAUS-style modular-like single pedestal with drawers and a slide might be combined with a contrasting kidney-shaped (biomorphic) writing surface.

Tea set
Ridgways Homemaker series transfer-printed trio, designed by Enid Seeney. c. 1957.

Brown, swirl-pattern chenille cover

Armchair and ottoman
Vladimir Kagan contour armchair and ottoman on sculpted walnut frames.

TV/Radio
"Komet—Kube de Luxe" TV, radio, record player, and tape deck combination. 1962.

especially chairs, made by the firm of Berliner Metallgewerbe from 1927 to 1931. These are considered modern classics, as are the BARCELONA CHAIR of 1929 and the Brno chair of 1930. He emigrated to the US in 1937 and became head of the Chicago School of Architecture in 1938.

Mihrab In Islamic architecture, a niche or an indication of a niche in the wall of a mosque facing Mecca; a stylized version is the central motif on Oriental PRAYER RUGS. The design is also used on Islamic TILE decoration.

Milan pottery and porcelain factories From the mid-18th century, three small potteries in Milan produced wares influenced by forms of silver, Chinese and Japanese porcelain, and French FAIENCE. The last of these closed around 1830. In 1833 a porcelain and faience factory was founded by Luigi Tinelli. Among other wares, they made copies of WEDGWOOD. In 1841 Luigi's brother, Carlo, who had taken over management of the factory, went into partnership with Giulio Richard from Turin. Under their management, wares with printed patterns as well as cream-colored EARTHENWARE were made. In 1870 Richard became the sole owner and renamed the factory Società Ceramica Richard in 1873. In 1896 his son, August, expanded the factory and absorbed the Ginori factory at DOCCIA, becoming Richard-Ginori. The firm continues to be a leading manufacturer of Italian ceramics today.

Milchglas See MILK GLASS.

Mildner glass Glass decorated with ZWISCHENGOLDGLAS medallion-shaped panels inserted into the sides and sometimes on the base. The name derives from Johann Joseph Mildner, the Austrian glassmaker who developed the technique and used it for beakers and tumblers from around 1787 until 1808.

Military furniture See CAMPAIGN FURNITURE.

Milk glass ■ An opaque white glass based on BONE ASH that resembles white porcelain. Developed in Venice in the late 15th century, it was popular during the 17th and 18th centuries. It was made in France (as *blanc-de-lait*), Germany (*Milchglas*), and Britain, and was often decorated with CHINOISERIE enameling and gilding. During the 19th century it was used for PRESSED GLASS, the BOSTON & SANDWICH GLASS COMPANY being a notable maker.

Millefiori ■ The Italian term for "thousand flowers." Glass decorated with slices of colored CANES embedded in clear glass. Although used in Roman glass, the technique is now largely associated with decorative pieces such as PERFUME BOTTLES, and since the mid-19th century, with PAPERWEIGHTS.

Ming dynasty The imperial dynasty that ruled China from 1368 to the beginning of the Qing Period, in 1644. In this period, trade between China and Western Asia and Europe expanded significantly, as did the production of CHINESE EXPORT PORCELAIN, textiles, JADE, IVORY, and lacquerware. The Ming dynasty is associated with the manufacture of porcelain of exceptional quality, particularly in JINGDEZHEN in the province of Jiangxi in southern China. The BLUE AND WHITE wares, characterized by a light, thin body and glassy glaze, produced during the CHENGHUA PERIOD (1465–87) are regarded as some of the finest ever made. Motifs such as dragons, PHOENIXES, and landscape scenes are typical. The DOUCAI and WUCAI polychrome OVERGLAZE enamel techniques were also introduced in this period as was KRAAK porcelain. These wares reached Europe in large quantities from the reign of the Ming Emperor Wanli (1573–1619).

Miniatures ■ 1. A painting up to a few inches across, developed from illuminated manuscript work and popular from the 16th century onward. Usually painted on a vellum, metal, or ivory support, these portraits, often of loved ones, were incorporated into jewelry, watches, or other items carried on the person, such as SNUFF BOXES, sometimes hidden underneath a false cover. 2. An item intended as a toy for children. Among these are the furnishings produced for DOLLHOUSES, mass-produced in Germany, Britain, and the US from

M
253

Original box enhances value

Mettoy Co. Ltd.
Mettoy for Coral Plastics, T17 London Transport Routemaster Bus.

Mies van der Rohe, Ludwig
"Barcelona" lounge chair, with chromium cross frame and brown leather cushions.

Milk glass
German milk glass perfume bottle, with brass mount and stopper. c. 1900.

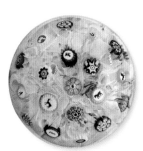

Millefiori
Baccarat scattered *millefiori* paperweight on a tossed muslin ground.

M

the mid-19th century. Other toys that can be classified as miniatures include TINPLATE figures, boats, TRAINS, racecars, and airships made by firms such as MÄRKLIN. 3. Miniature furniture that may have been made by apprentice cabinet-makers as part of their training. These "apprentice pieces," made from the 17th to the early 19th century, are now highly sought-after, as is miniature furniture made as samples for traveling salesmen to advertise their full-sized wares or to place in shop fronts to attract customers.

Other similar miniatures of note include musical instruments such as violins, and sets of pottery and porcelain, the latter made in considerable quantities from the 17th to the 19th century, by factories such as CAUGHLEY, MASON'S, and SPODE, as well as by Chinese potters for export to Europe. As small-scale, portable versions of larger designs, CARRIAGE CLOCKS can also be classified as miniatures.

Mint condition A term describing a piece in the condition it left the factory, being either unused or showing no signs of wear. A piece in mint condition is typically more valuable than a used one.

Minton ■ Thomas Minton trained as an engraver at CAUGHLEY. He founded a ceramic factory in Stoke-on-Trent in 1796, initially producing EARTHENWARE in UNDERGLAZE BLUE. From 1798 the factory also made SOFT-PASTE PORCELAIN tableware and elaborately decorated romantic figures, often copied directly from MEISSEN pieces. In the 1820s it started to produce utility wares and decorative pieces in BONE CHINA.

By the time Thomas Minton died, his firm had become one of the leading ceramics factories in England. Under the direction of his son, Herbert, Minton began to produce HARD-PASTE PORCELAIN of the very finest quality. No expense was spared to ensure that the porcelain was flawless, the glaze clear and smooth, and the decoration second to none. Its copies of fine pieces from the 18th century were particularly successful. In 1849 Leon Arnoux, a ceramicist from Sèvres, became art director, bringing other French artists with him. Among his innovations was the development of MAJOLICA in the RENAISSANCE style. Some of this was shown at the 1851 GREAT EXHIBITION in London,

alongside large Sèvres-style vases. Around this time Minton also made figures and busts in PARIAN. After Herbert's death in 1858, the firm continued as Herbert Minton & Co. until 1883 and thereafter as Mintons Ltd. From the 1860s the company was greatly influenced by Oriental decoration, producing CLOISONNÉ-style vases and other wares. In 1870 Marc-Louis SOLON introduced the PÂTE-SUR-PÂTE technique from Sèvres. The quality of Minton's output has remained consistently high and its products such as the ART NOUVEAU-style majolica vases have reflected contemporary fashions. Today Minton is still produced and the company is part of the DOULTON group.

Miquelet lock A variant of the FLINTLOCK, developed in Spain and also found in other parts of the Mediterranean and the Balkans. It differed from the true flintlock by having the mainspring mounted on the outside of the lockplate. This lock first appeared around 1650 and survived into the mid-19th century. It was also adapted to PERCUSSION.

MINTON CERAMICS

From its foundation at the end of the 18th century to the present day, Minton has been one of Britain's most innovative ceramics factories. Mediums and techniques have ranged from UNDERGLAZE- blue earthenware, and SOFT-PASTE PORCELAIN, to fine-quality HARD-PASTE PORCELAIN, Renaissance-style MAJOLICA, PARIAN WARE figures, and SÈVRES-style PÂTE-SUR-PÂTE. Forms and imagery have ranged from NEOCLASSICAL to ART NOUVEAU.

Modeled on a sculpture by Johann von Dannecker

Parian figure
Minton Parian figure of Ariadne reclining naked on the back of a panther. Mid–late 19th century.

Auricular handle

Pâte-sur-pâte moon flask
Children playing are set against a black ground on this flask. 19th century.

Monkey teapot
Majolica monkey teapot, in the form of a monkey clinging to a large coconut, with his head as cover. 1874.

Mirror A polished surface designed to reflect an image. Although mirrors made of polished metal or glass backed with metal were known in the Roman Empire, it was the development of BROAD GLASS in Venice in the 16th century and plate glass in Paris in the late 17th century that revolutionized mirror production. From this time onward, a huge variety of shapes and sizes of mirror was made, as well as decorative frames in a range of materials such as wood, silver, and GESSO. Mirror designs reflected contemporary styles, and ranged from architectural mirrors such as PIER GLASSES, to freestanding dressing and CHEVAL mirrors to mirrors mounted on furniture.

Mirror black A term used to describe a lustrous black glaze, occasionally with slight iridescence, used on Chinese porcelain from the KANGXI Period (1662–1722) onward. It is derived from iron oxide and manganese oxide and is known as *wu chin* in Chinese. Some of the best examples of mirror black porcelain are embellished with delicate gilt designs. It is distinct from the FAMILLE NOIRE palette.

Mirror painting Decoration painted in oils on the reverse of mirror glass. The technique, thought to have developed in England at the end of the 17th century, involved removing areas of silvering from the back of the glass and painting the decoration in reverse.

Mission style The term used in the US to describe architecture, furniture, and decorative arts of the ARTS AND CRAFTS period, made in a simple, honest style comparable to the plain and frugal designs of early American Mission churches and chapels. The term is used less frequently today; most collectors and professionals prefer the synonymous American Arts and Crafts. This preference is due in part to the lack of correspondence, beyond coincidental stylistic similarities, between the American Arts and Crafts designers and designers of Mission buildings and furnishings. Most so-called Mission style was designed in the eastern or midwestern states from about 1890 until the 1920s by artists who were chiefly influenced by contemporary movements in Europe as well as the US's COLONIAL past and native American culture. Mission buildings, which are mostly found in the southwestern states and may date from the 17th or 18th centuries, are of relatively insignificant influence on this movement. The term is most commonly applied to practical and robust oak furniture made in large quantities and in various standards of quality by scores of firms in numerous locations from around 1890 to the 1940s. The best-known makers are members of the STICKLEY family, who operated three separate firms, the first headed by Gustav Stickley. Mission furniture of generic type

is common in the US and is typically found in good condition.

Miter-cutting A type of cut decoration used on glass, made with a V-shaped grinding wheel to produce angled grooves.

Mixed stem ■ A decoration (also called mixed twist) within the stem of a glass that combines one or more clear spirals of air with opaque white and/or colored twisted CANES. The technique was invented in Venice in the early 17th century and was revived in Europe, especially in England and Holland from around 1750.

Mocha ware ■ A popular and inexpensive type of pottery, first produced in England in the 1780s and also made on the Continent and in the US throughout the 19th century. It is derived from "mocha stone," a variety of moss AGATE with feathery markings. The decoration was achieved by dripping an acid colorant onto an alkaline ground, the chemical reaction forming a tree or leaf motif. Mocha ware was made by a number of firms. Usually it is not marked, although some rare examples by SPODE are known.

Mock pendulum A term describing the secondary pendulum bob attached to the actual PENDULUM of a clock and visible through an aperture on the DIAL, especially on 18th-century BRACKET CLOCKS.

Modern movement ■ A term embracing diverse forms of decorative arts from around

M
255

Miniatures
Mahogany miniature bookcase chest, 32 in (81 cm) tall. 19th century.

Miniatures
American miniature on ivory, depicting a baby in a long dress. c. 1840.

Mixed stem
Wine glass, with fluted bowl, mixed air and enamel twist stem, and plain foot. c. 1765.

Mocha ware
Rare mocha covered bowl, with blue, black, and green bands and seaweed decoration.

1920 to the 1950s, which favored clean lines and no decorative adornment. The technological changes occurring after World War I spurred a mood of change characterized by geometry, abstraction, and mass production. In art, it manifested as Cubism, Fauvism, Futurism, De Stijl, and Constructivism, while in design, the machine was seen as a symbol of the new century and modern technology as the means to achieve good functional design. Teachers and students at the BAUHAUS came to dominate the style, advocating that form should follow function. New materials had a great impact on the movement's expression and facilitated mass production. There was, for example, no historical precedent for tubular-steel furniture. The CANTILEVER CHAIR took advantage of the metal's strength, while chromium plating provided a clean, hygienic finish.

Mohair   A fine, lustrous, silklike yarn, originally made solely from the hair of the Angora goat, but more often made from a mixture of Angora hair spun with cotton or silk. Used primarily for upholstery and hangings during the 17th, 18th, and 19th centuries, it was also used for dolls' hair in the 19th century. See MOHAIR PLUSH.

Mohair plush ▪ A fabric made from MOHAIR spun with cotton or silk yarn. Similar to velvet, but with a coarser, longer pile, it was used in the 19th century primarily for upholstery, curtains, and table coverings, and from the early 20th century for TEDDY BEAR fur.

Monart   An ART GLASS range produced by the MONCRIEFF GLASSWORKS from 1924 to 1961, as a result of a collaboration between Isobel, wife of John Moncrieff Jr., and Salvador YSART and his sons. Mold-blown and free-blown shapes were made using a technique in which colored glass was sandwiched between two layers of clear glass. After World War II, it was made by Salvador's son, Paul Ysart, who specialized in PAPERWEIGHTS.

Moncrieff Glassworks   A Scottish glassworks established in 1865 by John Moncrieff in Perth. The major production was industrial and laboratory glass, although the company is better known for its MONART range. It closed in 1996.

Money bank   See SAVINGS BANK.

Monkey Band ▪ An "orchestra" of porcelain monkeys dressed as humans in 18th-century court costume, modeled at MEISSEN by J. J. KÄNDLER. The full complement is 21 figures, including a singer, instrumentalists, and a conductor, with a music stand. They are still being made and have been copied by other factories.

Montanari, Augusta   (1818–64) Together with Henry PIEROTTI, the most important maker of WAX DOLLS in the 19th century. Her workshop was in London, from where her blue-eyed dolls with their rooted hair and chubby limbs were exported to the rest of Europe and the US.

Monteith ▪ A large bowl with notched or crennelated rims (sometimes detachable) made in silver, ceramic, or glass from around l680 to about 1720. Named after a Scotsman called Monteith who "wore the bottome of his cloake or coate so notched," they were used to chill glasses, which hung by their stems from the notches in the rim with their bowls in cold water. The earliest known hallmarked silver example dates from 1684.

Montelupo potteries   A group of Italian MAIOLICA potteries founded in the 14th century near Pisa. By the 16th century high-quality wares, depicting figures within a decorative band, were exported throughout Europe. Of a lesser quality are the brightly colored peasant wares decorated with animals and soldiers, which are typical of 17th-century output. Montelupo still produces pottery today.

Moon   A term applied to a small crescent mark or "tear" in the early porcelain body of CHELSEA, visible when held up to a strong light. Created from an imperfect mixture of ingredients and the expansion of air bubbles during the firing process, they also occur in porcelain from SÈVRES and TOURNAI.

Moonlight luster   A type of splashed or marbled pink or purple luster developed by WEDGWOOD between 1805 and 1815.

Moonstone   A bluish white gemstone with a characteristic milky sheen known

Modern movement
Isokon Penguin Donkey Mark II bookcase, designed by Ernest Race. c. 1963.

Mohair plush
English teddy bear, with gold mohair plush and jointed limbs.

Monkey Band
Meissen figure of a soloist from the Monkey Band, by J. J. Kändler. c. 1760.

Monteith
Monteith with scroll rim, by Hawksworth Eyre & Co. Ltd. 1901.

as adularescence. It was notably used in late 19th-century ARTS AND CRAFTS jewelry.

Moonstone glaze A trade name used by WEDGWOOD for a matt white glaze it developed in 1933. It has been used on wares designed by Keith MURRAY, animals designed by John Skeaping, NAUTILUS molded ware, and many other objects. It is employed without decoration, to emphasize the object's form.

Moorcroft, William (1872–1945) An English ceramicist who worked as a designer for MACINTYRE's in Staffordshire before leaving in 1913 to set up on his own. All his wares were handmade, with designs painted in raised slip. His patterns were largely floral, with their roots in ART NOUVEAU. After his death, his son, Walter Moorcroft, took over the business. The pottery is still active today and the designs have become more exotic but are still based on natural forms in characteristically rich colors. See TUBE-LINING

Moquette A textile woven with a wool pile in coarse imitation of silk velvet, which has been made in Europe from the Middle Ages, particularly in the Low Countries.

Morbier striking system A STRIKING SYSTEM found on COMTOISE CLOCKS in which the clock strikes on the hour and again two minutes after. It is named after a town in the Franche-Comté area of France, where such clocks were produced in the 18th century.

Mordan, Sampson (1790–1843) A notable English silver- and goldsmith and the founder of S. Mordan & Company, known for its production of high-quality small silver items, including VESTA cases, desk seals, and propelling pencils, a patent for which was registered by Mordan in 1822. During the late 19th century the firm supplied many, often novelty-shaped, articles to a number of notable retailers such as ASPREY & Sons and Walter Thornhill & Co. The company closed in 1941 and the name and rights were sold to Edward Baker.

Morgan, William Frend De See DE MORGAN.

Morion A HELMET used in the 16th and early 17th centuries by light cavalry and infantry. They often feature a large comb, although those from Spain are pear-shaped with a small "stalk" on the top.

Morris, William ■ (1834–96) An English designer, writer, romantic socialist, and printer. A foundation stone of the ARTS AND CRAFTS Movement, he was a major campaigner for the craft revival and was deeply opposed to factory production. In 1861 he cofounded Morris, Marshall, Faulkner & Company (renamed Morris & Co. in 1875), which made furniture and furnishings for domestic interiors until 1940. Morris commissioned his friends, including Philip WEBB and E. C. BURNE-JONES, to design for him and incorporated ceramic tiles by William DE MORGAN and lighting by W. A. S. BENSON into his interiors. He set up a printing press and published over 50 books.

Morris chair A type of 19th-century EASY CHAIR or armchair with an open wooden frame and loose seat and back cushions and a sloping adjustable back. Designed in 1883, it was manufactured by Morris, Marshall, Faulkner & Company. It was one of their most successful chair designs, which inspired many similar designs both in Britain and the US. See William MORRIS.

Morse ivory Walrus tusk used for carving functional, totemic, or decorative artifacts, often, for example, by 18th- and 19th-

M
257

MORRIS, WILLIAM

The primary sources of inspiration for William Morris's wallpaper, furnishing fabric, and tapestry designs are the pre-Industrial medieval, Gothic, and Oriental vocabularies of ornament. The resulting floral and foliage patterns are, however, uniquely Morris's in their understanding of the forms of Nature, their use of predominantly indigenous English plant-forms, and in their closely integrated and balanced compositions.

Birds in flowers and foliage

Armchair
Ebonized walnut armchair, designed by Philip Webb for Morris and Co. c. 1866.

Raised on brass casters

Tapestry
"Greenery" tapestry, designed by John Henry Dearle, in colored wools and mohair. 1892.

century sailors during long sea journeys. See SCRIMSHAW.

Mortise-and-tenon A type of furniture joint used widely by the late 15th century, in which two sections of wood are joined at a 90-degree angle, the projecting tongue (tenon) at the end of one section fitting exactly into a corresponding cavity (mortise) on the other. The mortise and the tenon are usually rectangular in shape. If the leading end of the tenon can be seen on the other side of the mortise, it is known as a "through" tenon; if not, it is a "blind" tenon.

Mosaic A technique in which decorative designs made from small, colored glass cubes, known as tesserae, are embedded in the walls and floors of buildings. It was known in ancient Greece and developed by the ancient Romans but is particularly associated with BYZANTINE churches. Mosaic glass is made from, or decorated with, pieces of colored glass that are heated until they fuse together without the colors mixing—a technique also known in ancient Greece. See PIETRA DURA, MILLEFIORI.

Mosaic jewelry ■ The fashion for MOSAIC jewelry centered on Rome and Florence, encouraged by the popularity of the GRAND TOUR to Italy in the 18th and 19th centuries. Visitors to Rome collected "micromosaics" with colorful scenes of Classical ruins and wildlife. Florentine mosaics were predominantly flower studies in colored

hardstone on a black marble field. Panels were brought home and made into jewelry. See PIETRA DURA.

Moscow porcelain See GARDNER'S PORCELAIN FACTORY.

Moser, Koloman ■ (1868–1918) An Austrian architect and designer associated with the VIENNA SECESSION and with establishing the WIENER WERKSTÄTTE in 1903. Moser was an influential designer working in painting, book illustration, jewelry, glass, textiles, and furniture, and became a professor at the School of Decorative Arts in Vienna in 1899.

Moser, Ludwig (1833–1916) A glass-engraver and founder of a Bohemian glasshouse in 1857 at Meierhofen (now Nove Dvory in the Czech Republic). His firm, Moser & Söhne, became one of the finest Bohemian glassworks, and is known for the production of colored glass with high-relief enameled decoration. It is still operating today.

Mote spoon A small silver spoon with a pierced bowl and a slender pointed stem, made from around 1690 to 1790. Mote spoons were probably used for straining tea leaves, or fishing specks, or "motes," from tea; the pointed end may have been for unclogging teapot spouts.

Mother-of-pearl The smooth, iridescent lining of various mollusk

shells, including ABALONE, NAUTILUS, pearl, and oyster. Also known as nacre, it has been used in jewelry, for MARQUETRY and INLAY work on furniture and other artefacts, and on PAPIER-MÂCHÉ furniture.

Motschmann, Charles A doll manufacturer from SONNEBERG who patented the "Motschmann" body in 1857. His dolls' heads, pelvises, and lower limbs are held together by strips of fabric, allowing movement between the parts. Motschmann was inspired by contemporary Japanese doll design.

Motto ware Table ceramics from the 19th and early 20th century, designed especially for children. Motto ware was made by the Staffordshire potteries, among others, and was typically transfer-printed, sometimes with hand tinting. Often very decorative yet educational, the designs included moralistic mottoes and religious quotes. See CHILDREN'S WARE.

Mold blowing A glassmaking technique known from Roman times and the method by which the vast majority of glassware is formed. The gather of molten glass is blown into either a full-size mold, to create a regular shape or decoration, or a smaller "dip" mold, to create a shape or decoration that can then be reblown and worked to the required effect and size.

Mold number A term commonly used in the manufacture of American toys. It is used

Mosaic jewelry
Onyx brooch, set with a micromosaic of the Colosseum in Rome. c. 1880.

Moser, Koloman
Wiener Werkstätte silver vase, with lattice decoration. 1905.

Moser
Stemmed amethyst glass, with an etched and gilded Amazonian frieze. c. 1920.

Molded pedestal stem
Engraved rummer, with a short stem and molded pedestal base. Early 19th century.

Molding
Parcel gilt Gothic cabinet, the molded cornice with a brass gallery. 19th century.

to identify the maker or model and is cast into the surface of the toy. Different finishes would then be applied, such as Fire Dept., Police, Taxi. The term is also applied to the incised or impressed numbers on the back of BISQUE, COMPOSITION, or PLASTIC doll heads, which can help identify the model and manufacturer.

Molded glass See PRESSED GLASS.

Molded pedestal stem ■ Having a pronounced shoulder, this popular 18th-century decorative device for glass, ceramics, and metalwork appears on a diverse range of objects, including drinking glasses, sweetmeat dishes, and candlesticks. In glassware it is also known as a Silesian stem.

Molding ■ One or more thin strips of wood, stone, plaster, or metal applied to a surface to make a uniform geometric profile, either as decoration or to conceal a joint. Moldings were used in ancient times on stone columns and FRIEZES. They became common on solid wood furniture in the 18th century, and on door and window frames, fireplaces, and cornices in interiors. Moldings may take many forms. See ASTRAGAL, CAVETTO, CHAMFER, FILLET, OGEE, and OVOLO.

Mount ■ A term used to denote metal HINGES, LOCKS, ESCUTCHEONS, and handles. It is used more specifically for the bronze, brass, gilt-bronze, or ORMOLU decoration on late 17th- and 18th-century

French furniture. Such mounts were introduced on French COMMODES in the late 17th century, and were initially used by such cabinet-makers as BOULLE for robustness and as protection for vulnerable extremities. Subsequently, mounts were used for purely decorative purposes. In France they were designed and cast separately by specialist craftsmen, and between 1745 and 1755 were stamped with a crown and the letter "C." Mounts were used by English and, later, American cabinet-makers on high-quality 18th-century furniture.

Mount Washington Glassworks ■ A large American glass manufacturer founded in South Boston, Massachusetts, in 1837, best known for ART GLASS produced from around 1876 until the 20th century. In 1869 it moved to New Bedford under the control of William LIBBEY. Mount Washington Glassworks specialized in satin-finished glass, with enameled decoration and silver-plated mounts made at nearby Connecticut factories. In 1894 it was acquired by the metal company PAIRPOINT. The factory closed in 1957.

Mourning jewelry ■ Jewelry of sentiment and remembrance, particularly fashionable in the 18th and 19th centuries. Georgian pieces tended toward the NEOCLASSICAL ideal and were heavily romanticized, such as a lady weeping by a tomb in an enamel and pearl frame. Most 19th-century mourning jewelry was black-enameled, engraved with the deceased's name or initials, and contained a

lock of their hair. The growth of the JET industry in England coincided with Queen Victoria's mourning after the death of Prince Albert in 1861.

Mouron, Adolphe See CASSANDRE.

Moustache cup ■ Popular in European porcelain or pottery at the end of the 19th century when luxuriant mustaches were fashionable. The cup had an inner rim with a narrow slit through which liquid could flow, so that the drinker's mustache could be kept dry and the wax from it did not flavor the tea.

Moustiers potteries ■ Now a popular tourist village in the Département of Var, France, Moustiers-Ste-Marie has long been a leading pottery producer. From 1679 to the 19th century it was one of the most important French FAIENCE towns, its wares being copied in Spain and Italy. The first factory, founded by Antoine Clerissy, began with earthenware but went on to make faience. It continued under Clerissy's son, Antoine II, and grandson, Pierre II. Pierre founded the Moustiers faience industry, building a flourishing business with the help of François Viry and his sons. In 1783 it was sold to Joseph Fouque, whose descendents ran it until 1852.

Earliest wares resemble ROUEN and NEVERS, decorated in UNDERGLAZE blue with figures, often after engravings by Tempesta, surrounded by finely painted

M

259

Mount
Louis XV *secrétaire à abattant,* with ormolu mounts. c. 1758.

Mount Washington Glassworks
Royal Flemish vase, decorated with winged dragon. c. 1894.

Mourning jewelry
Brooch showing two mourning ladies at an obelisk, on a white enamel ground. c. 1800.

Moustache cup
Edwardian pink luster moustache cup, with a view of The Pier, Hastings.

LAMBREQUIN borders in "style Bérain." The second factory was established in 1738 by Joseph Laugier and his brother-in-law, Joseph Olerys, who had worked at ALCORA in Spain; hence Moustiers ware can often resemble Alcora. The Laugier & Olerys factory used the *style Bérain* in early polychrome and had "LO" as a factory mark. It later painted MINIATURE mythological scenes in framed medallions and figures in a field of vegetation. Moustiers faience, still made today (the factory mark is an "X"), is usually light and finely potted. It can be difficult to differentiate from MARSEILLES.

Movement The complete timekeeping mechanism of a clock or watch, consisting of a set of wheels and PINIONS held between two brass or wooden plates and driven by the pull of weights, the force of a coiled spring, or by electrical power. See BACKPLATE.

Mucha, Alphonse (Alfons Maria) ■ (1860–1939) A Czech painter, poster-artist, and designer, who studied in Munich, Vienna, and Paris. He is popularly known for his posters, often with a flowing-haired woman, which are now regarded as the epitome of the ART NOUVEAU style. He designed jewelry for Georges Fouquet from 1898 to 1905, including some spectacular theatrical pieces for Sarah Bernhardt. From around 1903 he devoted himself to painting, living in the US from 1906 to 1910.

Muffineer A small CASTER of glass, POTTERY, SILVER, or TREEN, popular in the 19th century for sprinkling muffins with cinnamon or salt. It also refers to a round dish with a cover used for serving hot muffins.

Mughal The Muslim dynasty that ruled much of northern India between 1526 and 1857. Mughal decorative arts and architecture display a strong Persian influence, as the second ruler of the dynasty, Humayan (reigned 1540–54), spent some years in exile in Persia at a time when Islamic art reached a peak of refinement. In the Mughal courts the decorative arts flourished from the mid-16th to the mid-17th century, in particular during the reigns of Akbar (1556–1605), Jahangir (1605–28), and Shah Jahan (1628–58), who built the Taj Mahal. These enlightened rulers encouraged the fusion of Persian and native Indian artistic traditions, mainly Hindu, especially in carpet-weaving, hardstone carving, engraved and enameled metalwork, painted glassware, and illuminated manuscripts. Features of Mughal art include rich colors, naturalistic animals and figures in intricate patterns, and stylized flowers and leaves.

Mulberry Trees native to Europe (*Morus nigra* and *Morus alba*) that give a heavy, hardwearing, dark-streaked timber, varying in color from golden to reddish brown. Mulberry was supposedly used in the early 18th century as a VENEER for cabinet work and small boxes. However, it was often imitated and it is questionable how much genuine mulberry furniture was produced. Also, since these trees are used to feed SILK-producing moths, it is more commonly grown in silk-producing areas.

Mule chest ■ A term for a type of CHEST, a hybrid of a COFFER and a CHEST-OF-DRAWERS, made in England from the late 17th to the early 19th century. It has a hinged top and drawers in the base.

Mull ■ An ornamental SNUFF BOX, often Scottish, made of a ram's or sheep's horn, sometimes with a cork hinged to the horn as a stopper. As snuff-taking became widespread during the 18th century, snuff boxes were made in materials that were less costly than the traditional gold. However, some horn mulls have tooled silver mounts and use precious stones as decoration.

Müller Frères ■ One of the leading French makers of CAMEO GLASS, founded in 1895 at Luneville, near Nancy, by Henri Müller and associated with the SCHOOL OF NANCY. Müller had worked for GALLÉ and was later joined by his four brothers and sister. The factory was known for its high-quality landscape decoration on vases and lampshades. It made commercial glass and ART DECO lamps until 1933, with the glassworks closing in 1936.

Muntin A term in use since the 16th century for the vertical dividers of paneled frameworks

Moustiers potteries
Moustiers faience plate, decorated with a mythological scene. 18th century.

Mucha, Alphonse
One of a group of four decorative panels, entitled "Les Arts." 1898.

Mule chest
Oak mule chest. c. 1690.

Stained and polished horn

Mull
Scottish nickel-mounted horn snuff mull. c. 1820.

MULTI-FACE DOLL

Made from the 1860s onward, the Multi-face Doll was a novelty doll, with a two-, three-, or four-faced BISQUE or COMPOSITION head that rotated on a horizontal or vertical axle, allowing the doll to change moods at the twist of a knop or some other device.

Tinted red face

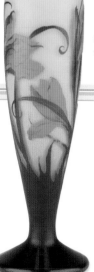

Bru doll
A two-faced Bru, marked No.4; the bonnet flips to reveal the second face of a crying child.

that lie between the STILES on the outside and connect the top and bottom RAILS.

Murano glass See VENETIAN GLASSHOUSES.

Murray, Keith ■ (1892–1981) A New Zealand-born architect and designer who designed glass for STEVENS & WILLIAMS from

1932 to 1939, and more notably, ceramics for WEDGWOOD that were produced from 1933 until the late 1960s. His MODERN ceramics are known for bold, clean shapes, often emphasized with horizontal banding and matt and semimatt glazes.

Murray, William Staite ■ (1881–1962) An English artist-potter who set up his own pottery in Rotherhithe (1919–24) and then at Whickham Road, London. Influenced by Chinese stoneware and technically able, his work is skillfully thrown and pieces are

often large or tall. He used rich glazes fired in kilns he built himself, and decoration was used sparingly to emphasize form.

Murrine ■ A small slice of a colored glass CANE or ROD. With patterns ranging from floral to abstract, murrines can be fused together into a form, or most often, picked up on a glass GATHER and blown and worked into a form. They are typically arranged in a mosaic pattern that eventually covers the whole body.

Mürrle, Bennett & Co. ■ A London jewelry wholesaler formed as a partnership in 1884 between the German-born Ernst Mürrle and an Englishman called Bennett. They worked in various styles in gold and silver, often with enamel. Well known for their ART NOUVEAU pieces, some are similar to LIBERTY & Co.'s CYMRIC range and include curving lines, sculptural forms, and Celtic motifs. Some pieces were produced in Germany. Mürrle was repatriated at the start of World War I and the factory closed in 1914.

Music box ■ A cylindrical musical box employing a metal cylinder revolving at a uniform rate with pins placed along it that strike metal teeth on a comb. The frequency of the sound produced is governed by the length and width of the teeth, and sounds from the succession of teeth produce the tune. Some music boxes employ bells and drums and sometimes AUTOMATA to produce and enhance the

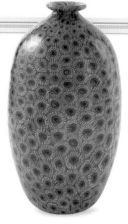

Müller Frères
Cameo glass vase, shaped as a stylized flower-bud, etched with budding crocuses. c. 1920.

Murray, Keith
Wedgwood footed oviform vase with lathe-turned ribbing. c. 1935.

Murray, William Staite
Stoneware vase, with a crackled celadon glaze and an impressed seal mark.

Murrine
Murano "Kiku" murrine vase, made at Fratelli Toso. c. 1930.

tune. A second type of music box uses revolving discs with punched slits and underhanging "pins" that again strike teeth on a horizontal comb. The first music box was made by the Swiss watchmaker Antoine Favre in 1796, and many fine examples of both types were manufactured by companies such as NICOLE FRÈRES in Switzerland and France from the early 19th to the early 20th century.

Music plate A type of dessert plate first appearing in the late 17th century with a song printed on it so that diners could sing together at the end of a meal. Music plates were made in many factories including DELFT, MOUSTIERS, and ROUEN.

Music stool A small stool designed for keyboard players. In the early 19th century it took the form of a lyre-backed stool or a stool with a circular upholstered seat that could be adjusted in height by means of a screw, often concealed inside a central pillar. By the mid-19th century these were largely superseded by rectangular stools, supported on four legs, with hinged, padded seat lids

that concealed a shallow compartment for storing sheet music.

Musical clock A type of clock emitting musical notes through bells, gongs, or a music box. They were first introduced in the late 16th century, but most of those seen today date from the 18th, 19th, and 20th centuries; they often combine musical work with elaborate STRIKING SYSTEMS or AUTOMATA such as figures of musicians.

Musical watch Mechanical music incorporated into watches. The first musical watches (mid-1700s) played on a nest of bells, the hammers lifted by a pinned barrel. With the invention of tuned tines by Favre, the watch could be made thinner and play more notes. See MUSICAL BOX.

Musket The general term for infantry shoulder firearms from the early 16th to the mid-19th century. It generally implies that the gun is smooth-bored.

Muzzle In firearms, the open front end of a gun's barrel from which the shot or bullet

exits. Up until the mid-19th century nearly all guns were loaded from the muzzle.

Myers, Myer (1723–95) An important early American silversmith of the COLONIAL period, active in New York City. Most recorded examples, marked with a single maker's mark only, are plain but may feature ROCOCO CHASING, or later be in the NEOCLASSICAL style. Myers's work is extremely rare.

Mystery clock A type of 19th-century French clock in which there is no apparent connection between the dial or pendulum and the MOVEMENT. One of the most popular designs was a brass or zinc figure holding a seemingly free-swinging pendulum. The movement in the base caused the figure to rotate imperceptibly, thereby swinging the purely decorative pendulum. There was another boom from the 1940s to the 1950s, where the mechanism in the base apparently had no connection to the hands, which were mounted on glass plates.

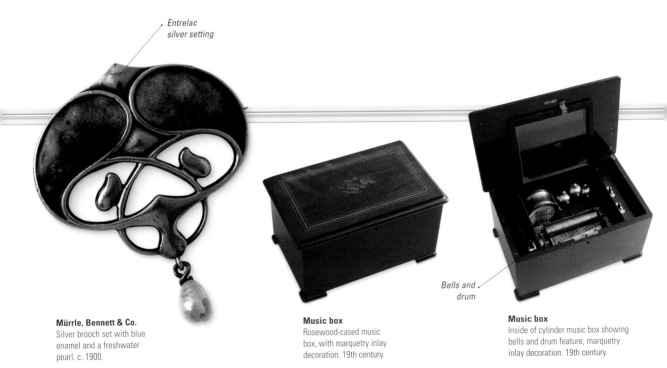

Entrelac silver setting

Mürrle, Bennett & Co.
Silver brooch set with blue enamel and a freshwater pearl. c. 1900.

Music box
Rosewood-cased music box, with marquetry inlay decoration. 19th century.

Bells and drum

Music box
Inside of cylinder music box showing bells and drum feature, marquetry inlay decoration. 19th century.

N

Nabeshima Japanese porcelain made from the second half of the 17th century until around 1870 at Okawachi near ARITA for the Lords of Nabeshima. The wares are mostly curved dishes with high FOOT RIMS and were used for formal banquets or as gifts to dignitaries. Designs were often derived from textiles, using DOUCAI and WUCAI techniques or painted in underglaze blue, sometimes in conjunction with a CELADON glaze. Fine Nabeshima of around 1720 is technically extremely high-quality porcelain.

Nail-head decoration The ornamental use of dome-headed brass nails to secure upholstery to chairs or leather to chests or trunks. It is sometimes called "close nail work."

Nailsea Glasshouse ■ The Nailsea Crown Glass Company was founded at Nailsea, near Bristol, in 1788, specializing in glazing glass. It is also reputed to have had a sideline of dark bottles, vases, and jugs with color-splashed decoration. Nailsea has become a generic term for similar glassware made at other factories in Bristol, Stourbridge, and Yorkshire. In 1824 its

owner, Robert Lucas Chance, took over a Birmingham-based glassworks, which became an important producer of glazing glass, undertaking the glazing of the Crystal Palace at the Great Exhibition of 1851. Nailsea produced the lenses for most of the world's lighthouses and made scientific, lighting, and domestic glass until the factory closed in 1981.

Nain A carpet-producing town in Central Persia. Weaving began around 1940 and continues today. Products are similar to carpets made in nearby ISFAHAN, with curvilinear floral designs and details often outlined in white silk. Ivory and blue are typical colors. See PERSIAN CARPETS.

Nakashima, George ■ (1905–90) Japanese-American architect and designer who trained in traditional Japanese carpentry while interned during World War II and later went on to become one of the leading figures in the American craft movement. Much of his now-iconic furniture is characterized by free-form organic shapes and perfectionism in every stage of construction. His signature pieces are large tables with tops made of irregularly shaped slabs of wood with smoothed surfaces but unfinished sides, raised on asymmetrical legs or supports.

Nancy School (École de Nancy) An alliance of French artists (*Alliance Provinciale des Industries d'Art*) working

in and around Nancy in Lorraine. Émile GALLÉ was president, and Louis MAJORELLE, Antonin DAUM, and Eugène Vallin were vice-presidents of the alliance. They organized courses to enhance the tradition of craftsmanship in Lorraine. The artists, all prominent ART NOUVEAU designers, were inspired by nature.

Nanking ware Blue and white CHINESE EXPORT PORCELAIN (also called Nankin ware) made in the 18th and 19th centuries at JINGDEZHEN. It was carried by river to Nanking and from there to Canton by sea. Pieces are often crude and decorated with Asian landscapes and repetitive border designs. See FITZHUGH PATTERN.

Nantgarw Porcelain factory ■ A factory founded in South Wales in 1813 by William BILLINGSLEY and his son-in-law, Samuel Walker. They moved to SWANSEA in 1814 but returned to Nantgarw in 1817. The factory mostly made plates, dishes, cabinet cups and saucers, and some services. Billingsley was known for his high-quality rose painting, but the richest decoration was done by decorators in London. Billingsley went to Coalport in 1819. The remaining stock was decorated by Thomas Pardoe until the factory closed in 1822.

Naples royal porcelain ■ The Fabbrica Reale Ferdinandea, founded by Ferdinand IV in 1771, began in the Royal Villa of Portici and moved to the Royal Palace in 1773. It made Neoclassical services with fine

Nailsea Glasshouse
Green glass jug, with white inclusions and loop handle. c. 1810.

Nakashima, George
Walnut conoid bench, with free edge seat and butterfly joint. c. 1975.

Nantgarw Porcelain factory
London-decorated Nantgarw plate, painted with a central flower bouquet. c. 1820.

Naples royal porcelain
One of a pair of Naples Monteiths, the rims applied with birds. c. 1795.

N

topographical scenes and charming figures. It became the property of a French firm in 1807 and finally closed in 1834. Marks are a crowned "N" or "FRF" with a crown for Ferdinand IV REX. The crowned "N" has since been used by a number of other factories. Genuine Naples porcelain is rare.

Nashiji ■ A Japanese lacquerwork technique in which gold dust is sprinkled onto a still-wet layer of LACQUER. Once dry, clear lacquer is applied and the surface polished to give a "pear skin" appearance. It is often used as a background to designs on INRO, boxes, and other decorative artifacts.

Native American pottery A generic term for pottery made by native cultures in North America, from prehistoric relics to modern tourist ware. Most sought-after examples are decorative and in original condition.

Natzler, Otto & Gertrud ■ An Austrian-born couple who emigrated to California in 1938 and became leading figures in a STUDIO POTTERY revival, which began in the late 1940s as a reaction to MODERNISM. Gertrude worked as the master potter and produced graceful, light earthenware that echoed VIENNA SECESSIONIST pottery. Otto specialized in the GLAZES, with notable examples from numerous innovations, including crater, lava, crystalline, and diverse lustrous glazes.

Nautilus cup ■ A standing cup, sometimes with a cover, of a type first imported into Europe from China in the 16th century. The bowl was made of a natural NAUTILUS SHELL held in place with silver-gilt or gold STRAPWORK mounts, often decorated with themes associated with the sea. Intended for display rather than use, they were fashionable in 16th- and 17th-century Europe, particularly in the Low Countries. The finest examples were made in late-16th- and early-17th-century Germany and were elaborately mounted in gold and silver.

Nautilus shell A large nacreous shell found in the Indian Ocean, used to make NAUTILUS CUPS. Exotic shells were carried to Europe by 16th-century travelers to satisfy MANNERIST curiosity.

Navajo ■ A large group of native weavers in North America who have for centuries produced FLAT-WEAVE textiles. These are created from a continuous thread, the thickness of which is often subtly varied, and have DYED bold geometric designs.

Nécessaire ■ A French term for a small item of silver, leather-covered wood, porcelain, or enamel, which carries everything necessary for a task. A *nécessaire à coudre*, for example, contains needles, bodkin, thread, thimble, and scissors.

Needlefire action A firearm whose mechanism incorporates a long needle that penetrates the base of a combustible CARTRIDGE to strike a priming pellet and fire the gun. It was perfected by the Prussian Nicholas von Dreyse in the 1830s.

Needlelace Lace made with a needle and single thread by working embroidered buttonhole stitches on a geometric grid (also called needlepoint). From the early 17th century it was made with a parchment pattern, releasing it from the geometric form. See PUNTO IN ARIA; VENETIAN, FRENCH, SPANISH, and ENGLISH NEEDLELACE. See RETICELLA.

Needlework See EMBROIDERY, STUMPWORK, CREWELWORK, SAMPLERS, and BERLIN WOOLWORK.

Needlework (or embroidered) carpets Made in Europe from the 16th to the 19th century with NEEDLEWORK stitches. Designs reflect the styles of the day and are based on patterns used in pile weavings. The technique permits greater definition of pattern than woven carpets.

Negretti & Zambra A London-based firm of scientific and optical instrument-makers and retailers, founded in 1850 by the Italians Enrico Negretti and Joseph Warren Zambra, and still operating today. They became

Floral-decorated, iridescent shell

Tiny veins of shimmering color

Nashiji
Namiki *maki-e* cigarette case, with a goldfish in *hiramaki-e* and *nashiji*. 1930s.

Natzler, Otto & Gertrud
Natzler tall bulbous vase, with blue crystalline glaze.

Nautilus cup
Continental nautilus cup on a gilt metal base. 19th century.

Navajo
Southwest Navajo weaving, using natural and commercially dyed wool. Late 19th century.

Nécessaire
French gold-mounted ivory nécessaire. Late 18th century.

NEOCLASSICAL STYLE

The development of the Neoclassical style was prompted by the rediscovery in the 1740s of the ancient Roman cities of Herculaneum and Pompeii, which had been buried by the eruption of Mount Vesuvius in 79 CE. Domestic items such as lamps, candelabra, small bronzes, and frescoed wall decorations were found.

These discoveries were publicized throughout Europe in *Le antichita di Ercolano esposti*, *Recueil d'Antiquités* by the Comte de Caylus, and *Antiquities of Athens* by James STUART and Nicholas Revett. Other factors were the popularity of the GRAND TOUR and its association with the democracy of ancient Greece and Republican Rome in the new republics of France and the US (see FEDERAL style).

From the mid-18th century, furniture became rectilinear with architectural forms such as pediments on mirror frames. Classical urns and two-handled vases were made in silver—for example, by Matthew BOULTON—and in ceramic at SÈVRES. A new tripod form for candelabra and perfume-burners was copied from ATHÉNIENNES found at Pompeii. Mythological themes dominated enamel painting and porcelain figures.

In the 1760s and 70s a lighter style emerged, using GROTESQUES, FESTOONS, HUSKS, ribbons, and medallions, of which the leading exponent was Robert ADAM. He also introduced the ETRUSCAN STYLE, which influenced WEDGWOOD's black BASALT and ROSSO ANTICO wares. Wedgwood's JASPER WARE was decorated to imitate ancient Greek and Roman hardstone CAMEOS. The apparent flimsiness of much Neoclassical silver in the 1770s and 80s was emphasized by the introduction of thin-gauge sheet silver, made by the new mechanical flatting mills, for oval and cylindrical teapots. In the 1790s Neoclassical furniture became more austere, especially in France during the DIRECTOIRE period. A more archaeologically exact style developed in the early 19th century as part of the REGENCY and EMPIRE styles. See also LOUIS XVI STYLE and GREEK REVIVAL.

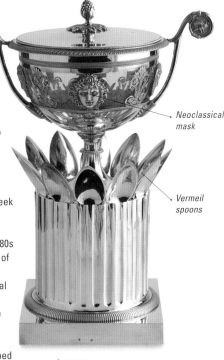

Neoclassical mask

Vermeil spoons

Jam pot
Silver *confiturier* (jam pot) in the form of an antique urn or perfume-burner, with 12 vermeil spoons. 1818–39.

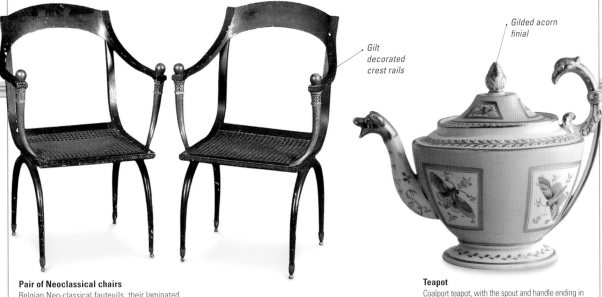

Gilt decorated crest rails

Gilded acorn finial

Pair of Neoclassical chairs
Belgian Neo-classical fauteuils, their laminated black, gilded and painted frames with putti, lyres, husks, and cornucopiae. Early 19th century.

Teapot
Coalport teapot, with the spout and handle ending in grotesques' heads, a typical English Neoclassical decoration. 18th century.

Opticians and Meteorological Instrument Makers to Queen Victoria.

Nelme, Anthony (fl. 1672–1722) An English silversmith apprenticed to Richard Rowley and Isaac Deighton, who was granted the freedom of the Goldsmith's Company in 1679. He may have had immigrants working for him, as his pieces show HUGUENOT influence. By the end of the 17th century Nelme had one of the largest establishments in London, gaining many commissions for large items and services. His later works are in the QUEEN ANNE style. When he died, his son, Francis, carried on the business.

Netsuke ■ A small, often figurative, carving used from the 16th century as part of traditional Japanese dress. *Netsuke* are popularly thought of as made in IVORY, but as elephants are not native to Japan, other ivory tusks (for example, from walrus and sperm whale), teeth, and stained and polished woods (such as CHERRY and BOXWOOD) were also used.

Kimonos were worn in Japan until the mid-19th century, and as they lacked pockets, men hung boxes known as INROS or pouches known collectively as *sagemono* from their OBIS. To stop the cord from slipping through the *obi*, *netsuke* was used as a toggle. A sliding bead or OJIME was strung on the cord between the *sagemono* and the *netsuke* to loosen or tighten the opening. As *inros* became more popular from the late 16th century, so did *netsuke*. Early *netsuke* are characterized by a simpler design, while later examples are more intricately carved. A wide variety exists, from the *manju* toggle formed as a simple rounded disk to more complicated designs taking the forms of animals, masks, and characters from Japanese legend or daily life. By the early 18th century, renowned *netsukishi* (*netsuke* carvers) existed whose signed works are highly prized, but many finely carved examples are not signed. Many reproductions exist, including late-19th- and early-20th-century examples, often with protruding parts that would not stand usage, made almost exclusively from ivory for export or tourist markets. More recently they have been made from resin or plastic.

Nevers ■ Italian potters working in the Italian MAIOLICA tradition arrived in Nevers, France, in the 16th century. The first to found their own factory in 1588 were the three Conrade brothers from Albisola near Genoa, who made strongly Italianate products such as ISTORIATO dishes and ewers. It was only in the mid-17th century that native French potters imposed their own style upon the Conrade tradition.

New FAIENCE factories started from around 1632 and the French owners gradually moved from RENAISSANCE styles to French BAROQUE. Nevers decorators painted Chinese-style figures and landscapes on the Baroque shapes, which suggests that they had Chinese porcelain originals to copy. Nevers also made large garden vases, much used in the Trianon de Porcelaine, the elaborate summerhouse built in 1670 at Versailles. Wares were painted in attractive tones of warm blue, soft orange, and pale yellow, usually outlined in soft purple. A style called BLEU PERSAN was also developed at Nevers. Nevers painters used engravings after Raphael, Nicolas Poussin, and Simon Vouet, and hunting scenes after Antonio Tempesta. In the 18th century they copied ROUEN and MOUSTIERS. They also made faience *patriotique* that depicted Revolutionary sentiments and were much collected in France. Pottery is still made in Nevers.

New England Glass Company ■ A large, important American glassworks founded by Deming Jarves and others in Cambridge, Massachusetts, in 1817, upon their purchase of the Boston Porcelain & Glass Manufacturing Company, which was founded in 1814. It was one of the first to develop the glass-pressing machine and made utility and ornamental wares, including PAPERWEIGHTS, much of it created by immigrant artisans from Europe. From the mid-19th century the company introduced numerous artistic lines, notably AMBERINA and Pomona, developed by Joseph LOCKE. The company moved to Toledo, Ohio, in 1888, and is still in existence today as the LIBBEY GLASS COMPANY. Products are unmarked.

New Hall Porcelain Factory ■ Founded in Staffordshire around 1781, the factory first made hybrid HARD-PASTE PORCELAIN developed from Richard

Netsuke
Ivory *netsuke* of a monkey picking fleas from a baby, signed "Kaigyokusai Masatsugu."

Nevers
Nevers maiolica model of a putto seated on a dolphin. 18th century.

New England Glass Company
Pressed amberina glass stork vase, designed by Joseph Locke.

New Hall Porcelain Factory
Tea bowl and saucer, "Boy and the Butterfly" pattern. c. 1795–1800.

Newlyn
Twin-handled copper vase, with applied beaten handles, and decorated with swimming fish.

CHAMPION's patent, but could not achieve a white body. Around 1815 the factory switched to producing BONE CHINA and concentrated on salable tea wares with simple Chinese-style floral patterns, some painted by Fidelle Duvivier. The factory closed in the 1830s.

Newcastle glassware Glass made at the many glasshouses established in Newcastle upon Tyne, since the time the city became a center of glass production in the 17th century. The area is known for its production of glass bottles in particular,

and in the mid-19th century became the center of British pressed-glass production.

Newlyn ■ A village in Cornwall that became known for its handmade copper wares in the ARTS AND CRAFTS style. In the late 19th century, makers followed the ethics of William MORRIS, and in 1890 the painter John McKenzie established the Newlyn Industrial Class that taught a variety of craft techniques. Vases, tea caddies, and jugs with hand-hammered, stylized REPOUSSÉ foliate or marine

designs are typical. Production ceased in 1939 at the outbreak of World War II.

Nickel silver See EPNS and SILVER. A silver-colored or white alloy of zinc, copper, and nickel, which is well suited to the manufacture of FLATWARE and is also used as a good base for electroplating.

Nicole Frères A Swiss manufacturer of cylinder MUSIC BOXES, started by the brothers Raymond and Francis Nicole in Geneva in 1815 and considered to be one of the finest makers of music boxes in the

NEWCOMB POTTERY

An American ART POTTERY workshop established at Newcomb College, New Orleans, in 1895, as a women's venture under the direction of Ellsworth Woodward. Until its closure in 1930, the

pottery specialized in matt-glazed vases with incised, floral decoration, the best examples of which are among the most highly prized of all American art pottery.

Pitcher
An early Newcomb College pitcher carved and painted by Marie de Hoa LeBlanc. c. 1905.

Decoration carved in shallow relief

Early Newcomb vase
An early Newcomb College vase, incised by Harriet Joor with magnolia blossoms on a blue ground. 1904.

Sadie Irvine vase
A Newcomb College vase, carved by Sadie Irvine, with Nicotina blossoms. 1922.

Bulbous vase
Newcomb College transitional bulbous vase, with yellow daffodils and green leaves on blue ground. 1910.

N

19th century. In 1881 they opened a retail branch in London. In 1906 they were taken over by the New Polyphon Company.

Niderviller Pottery and Porcelain Factory ■ A faience factory in Niderviller, Lorraine, France, founded by Jean-Louis, Baron de Beyerlé in 1754. From 1754 until 1779, its director was François Antoine Anstett, who was a painter and chemist. In 1766 the production of ivory-toned, delicately painted faience was abandoned. Porcelain, with clay at first from Passau and then from St Yrieix, was made on a large scale from 1768. In 1770 the factory was bought by Count Philibert de Custine, but when Custine was guillotined in 1793, Claude-François Lanfrey, his manager, became owner until his death in 1827. The factory then made tableware with German-style decoration and figures with brightly colored costumes. From 1827 porcelain-making was discontinued and the factory concentrated on cream-colored earthenware and faience. From 1886 it became known as S.A. Fayencerie de

Niderviller and produced copies from its 18th-century molds. It is still active. Custine's mark is two intertwined Cs under a crown.

Niello A powdered alloy of silver, lead, copper, and sulfur that gives a dark gray to black appearance on silver items. A silver body is engraved or incised with a pattern, and the niello powder sprinkled over it. The covered body is then heated to bond the metallic powder to the body. Once cool, the excess is removed, leaving the pattern picked out in dark gray or black. It has been used since ancient Egyptian times and was known throughout Europe in the Middle Ages and during the Renaissance. In Russia it is known as Tula work.

Nigoshide The Japanese term for "milky white." In Japanese ceramics it refers to the famed pure white porcelain body used for the finest KAKIEMON wares. It seems only to have been used for open forms such as plates, dishes, and bowls, and was never used in conjunction with underglaze blue.

Niloak Pottery Company ■ Located in Benton, Arkansas, and named after local deposits of KAOLIN (spelled backward), the Niloak Pottery Company was established by a group of local businessmen in 1911 and run by potter Charles Hyten. The company is best known for its "swirled" pottery, a pottery line made with colored swirls of clay. It was developed by the potter Arthur Dovey and came to be known as Mission Ware. It

comprised vases and other hollowware with a multicolored swirling pattern, usually left unglazed to highlight the natural colors and texture of the clay. Mission Ware remained the mainstay of production until the late 1920s when, after declining sales, Niloak turned to the production of cheaper stoneware and castware pieces. These were commercially less successful and production ceased in 1947.

Nock, Henry (c. 1741–1804) An English gunmaker whose patent BREECH designed in 1787 revolutionized firearms by improving ignition and ballistics. Nock was appointed Gunsmith-in-Ordinary to George III in 1789 and Master of the Gunmakers' Company in 1802. A maker of high-quality firearms, Nock is mainly remembered for his seven-barreled guns made for the Royal Navy.

Nocturnal A simple time-telling instrument used at night, usually made of BOXWOOD and occasionally of brass. It consists of two circular plates mounted one on top of the other, the larger outer disk having a long, shaped handle. To indicate the time, the pole star is viewed through the center hole and the pointer turned to be in line with certain boreal constellations that rotated around the pole star about once a day. The earliest known dated English example is 1637, and it began to fade from popular use in the 18th century.

Noritake ■ A Japanese HARD-PASTE PORCELAIN company established in 1904 near Nagoya, producing hand-painted tableware for export as well as decorative tea

Delicate "petit feu" polychrome enamels

Niderviller Porcelain
Figure symbolizing Fame, with *petit feu* polychrome decoration. c. 1780.

Niloak Pottery Company
Niloak Mission Ware cordial set of marbleized clay.

Noritake
Handpainted Noritake bowl, decorated with flowers and birds. 1930s.

Nove pottery and porcelain factories
Nove pottery dish decorated with pears. 19th century.

NYMPHENBURG PORCELAIN

ware, vases, candlesticks, and figures. It began by copying Victorian and Edwardian designs, but commissioned new patterns from eminent designers such as Frank Lloyd WRIGHT in the 1920s and 30s. Today Noritake is a large international business.

Northwood, John (1836–1902) An English glassmaker who trained at RICHARDSON's glasshouse, STOURBRIDGE. In 1860 he and his brother, Joseph, founded J. & J. Northwood, a glass-decorating business specializing in ACID ETCHING and engraving. He also created many superb pieces of CAMEO GLASS, including a copy of the PORTLAND VASE, made in 1876. His work was continued by his son, John Northwood II, and by George and Thomas WOODALL.

Nove pottery and porcelain factories

■ There were several FAIENCE factories at Le Nove, near Bassano in Italy. The first was founded by Giovanni Battista Antonibon in 1728, making dishes and tureens decorated in HIGH-TEMPERATURE COLORS. In 1752 a porcelain kiln was added to this prosperous MAIOLICA factory by Pasquale Antonibon, assisted by a worker from DRESDEN. It was used to make delicate tea ware and figures. Antonibon leased the maiolica business in 1774 for the next

30 years. From 1781 to 1802 the porcelain factory was leased to Francesco Parolin. The factory finally closed in 1832. The best porcelain was made from 1760 to 1780 and was grayish in color, like that produced by the COZZI PORCELAIN FACTORY. Le Nove is still an important center for ceramics, producing TIN-GLAZED EARTHENWARE painted with flowers in soft colors.

Nozzle The detachable flanged top section of a candlestick that facilitates the removal of candle stubs and serves as a drip pan. Also refers to the tapered end of a propelling pencil.

Nuremberg An important center of German FAIENCE and glass from the 16th century, Nuremberg is known for Hafuer wares (lead-glazed stoves, stove tiles, and vessels) attributed to Paul Preuning, and for a factory (1712–1840) managed by Johann Caspar Ripp, a potter from Ansbach. It made faience painted in blue (often on a grayish blue ground) and occasionally in red, manganese, and yellow. After, around 1750, it used ENAMEL COLORS. Specialties were jugs painted with tiny flowers and birds, jugs with pierced star-shaped rosettes, and dishes with six heart-shaped wells. Many HAUSMALER decorators also worked in Nuremberg, including Johann Ludwig Faber, Johann Heel, and Abraham Helmhack.

Nursery ware See CHILDREN'S WARE.

Nursing chair ■ A style of chair associated with the mid- to late 19th century, characterized by a low seat with no arms, designed for women nursing babies.

Nutmeg grater ■ In the 17th and 18th centuries, nutmegs were used to flavor food and drinks. They were, however, expensive, and warranted special boxes, often silver or treen, to contain them. These were inset with a hardened steel grater. Late 17th-century examples may be cylindrical. From around 1750, egg- and other shaped forms appeared.

Nymphenburg porcelain ■ Prince Maximilian Joseph of Bavaria founded a porcelain factory at Neudeck in 1747. In 1761 it moved to the premises of Castle Rondell, Nymphenburg, Munich, where it continues to operate today. J. J. RINGLER joined in 1753, and by 1757 the factory was making a fine white porcelain body but was in financial difficulty. When the FRANKENTHAL factory closed in 1799, some of its workers came to Nymphenburg. The factory began to flourish again, making good tea and dinner services. But it is most famous for the figures made by the Swiss modeler Franz Anton BUSTELLI. In 1862 the factory was leased to a private company making utility wares, but from 1888 it enjoyed new success. It continued the ROCOCO tradition, using original molds, and also kept pace with modern forms. It still uses the 18th-century mark of the checkered shield of Bavaria.

N
269

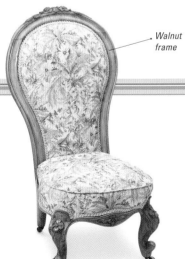

Nursing chair
Victorian nursing chair, with rounded rose-carved crest rail on short cabriole legs.

Walnut frame

Urn-shaped silver casing

Nutmeg grater
George III engraved silver nutmeg grater, in the form of a covered vase. 1804.

Nymphenburg porcelain
Porcelain figural group, "The Kiss on the Hand." c. 1865.

O

Oak  A hard, close-grained wood, generally pale honey-colored. Throughout the Middle Ages oak was used to make fine furniture, giving way to walnut in the late 16th century in France and a century later in England. It is the typical wood for GOTHIC STYLES, early Renaissance Flemish and German woodwork, the Tudor and Jacobean periods in England, and ARTS AND CRAFTS furniture on both sides of the Atlantic.

Oak-leaf jar  An APOTHECARY JAR decorated with stylized oak leaves in GOTHIC STYLE, often with heavily applied blue pigment, a pale buff body, and a creamy white glaze. This rare early Italian MAIOLICA is of uncertain origin but most probably comes from mid-15th-century Florence. Decoration is usually drawn in purple manganese outline and includes heraldic lions, birds, and human profiles.

Obelisk  A tall, tapering square or rectangular shaft of stone terminating in a pyramid. Originating in ancient Egypt, where its shadow was used to tell the time, the obelisk was brought to Europe during the Roman Empire. Admired during the Renaissance, it was adopted in Europe as FINIAL ornament from the late 16th century, when it also featured in Dutch and German architecture. During the 18th century it was adopted in England for garden ornament and tomb decoration. Miniature decorative obelisks made from marble became popular in the early 19th century.

Obi A Japanese term meaning "belt." It is a waist sash worn with a kimono.

Objet de vertu  A small accessory such as a SNUFF BOX, POMANDER, ÉTUI, or NÉCESSAIRE, made of luxury materials (for example, porcelain, gold, silver, gemstones, and enamel). They are valued for their workmanship and rarity rather than their function.

Occasional table A modern term for an all-purpose small table that can be easily moved from room to room. Occasional tables evolved in the 18th century to accommodate increasingly comfortable domestic interiors. Light and versatile, frequently with drawers, drop leaves, and mounted on casters, it was used for a host of leisure activities, from letter writing and reading, to serving tea and meals, to playing cards and games.

Octant A navigational instrument in the form of an eighth of a circle, usually made from ebony or mahogany and used widely from around 1750. Although largely made redundant by the introduction of the sextant after 1767, many octants were produced in the early 19th century. The arc, with a scale and VERNIER, measures angles up to 90°. It also has an index arm, colored filters, mirror, and a pinhole sight. Invented by John Hadley in 1731, it was an advancement of its predecessor, the BACKSTAFF and the cross-staff. See SEXTANT.

Oeben, Jean-François (c.1721–63) A German-born French ÉBÉNISTE, designer, and furniture-maker, who settled in Paris in the 1740s. A skilled metalworker and mechanic, his furniture is distinguished by elaborate MARQUETRY and ingenious mechanical effects. Under the patronage of Madame de Pompadour, Oeben was appointed *Ébéniste du Roi* in 1754. In 1760 he made the elaborately decorated *Bureau du Roi*, a large Louis XV cylinder-top desk now at Versailles. Although he was responsible for the design as well as the complex mechanism of this masterpiece, the desk was completed and signed after his death by his assistant, Jean-Henri RIESENER. Among Oeben's specialties are the elaborate multipurpose pieces known as *meubles à secrets* and *meubles à surprises*,

Formalized plant-form pattern

Oak
French oak wardrobe, with a molded cornice and central acanthus carving. c. 1780.

Oak-leaf jar
Italian apothecary jar. c. 1600.

Obelisk
Neoclassical-style, veneered marble obelisk, raised on bun feet and a square base.

Objet de vertu
French silver snuff box with enamel decoration, and gilt interior. c. 1880.

which became fashionable after 1750, along with the trend for smaller and more intimate rooms. In 1761 Oeben was appointed *Maître Ébéniste*, but he died bankrupt a few years later. His workshop continued under the direction of Riesener, who married Oeben's widow in 1768.

Off-hand glass See FREE BLOWING.

Ogee A continuous shallow, serpentine curve made up of convex and concave lines. From the 12th century the ogee form appeared in textiles, although it is most typical of GOTHIC STYLES. As an elaborate pointed arch, it was used as a MOLDING, for BRACKET FEET, or for the glazing bars of CABINETS and bookcases, and in bowls and drinking glasses from the mid-18th century. Ogee-headed panels occasionally feature as TRACERY on bookcase and cabinet doors, and on CASE FURNITURE in the GEORGIAN period.

Ogee clock See SHELF CLOCK.

Ohr, George E. ■ (1857–1918) One of the foremost American ARTS AND CRAFTS studio potters, active at the Biloxi Pottery, Mississippi, from around 1883 to 1906. Highly eccentric, he was known as "the mad potter of Biloxi." Ohr dug his own clays, mixed his own glazes, and even built his own kiln and pottery. Above all, he is

celebrated for the prescient modernity of his works, which in terms of form are characterized by thinly potted vessels with irregularly twisted and/or pinched bodies and irregularly folded and/or pucker and pinched rims. As a rule of thumb, the more extensively manipulated the piece, the more valuable it is. After around 1900 Ohr stopped applying glazes to his pieces—"God put no color in souls so I'll put no color in my pots"—and left them in BISQUE-fired simplicity. Prior to that, however, he made spectacular use of many highly innovative, multiple-color glazes. Typical yet unique examples would be a volcanic-like raspberry and white over a glossy dark blue ground, or a mottled and selectively iridescent combination of pink, red, black, metallic blue, and shades of brown.

Ojime The small bead in traditional Japanese costumes by which the cords binding together an INRO and NETSUKE were loosened or tightened.

Okimono ■ A small to medium-sized Japanese sculpture, often of ivory, made in the 19th century and later for display in an alcove or *tokonoma*. The intricately carved figurative or animal designs and forms were often based on the smaller NETSUKE.

Olbrich, Jose Maria ■ (1867–1908) A founding member of the VIENNA SECESSION and a prolific architect and designer of metalwork, textiles, and graphics. He also generated some

furniture designs, with clean-lined, unornamented forms in the ART NOUVEAU style. His friends included Koloman MOSER, Josef HOFFMAN, and Peter BEHRENS, through whom he had an influence on MODERNISM.

Old English pattern A silver FLATWARE pattern, very simple in form, with the ends of the stems turning down. The Old English pattern succeeded the HANOVERIAN PATTERN, and although still popular today, was most extensively produced from around 1775 to about 1830.

Old Hall pottery See MEIGH POTTERY.

Old Sheffield See SHEFFIELD PLATE.

Olive A hard, close-grained greenish yellow wood with dark, cloudy markings, originating in Southern Europe and used as a VENEER in PARQUETRY and for MOLDINGS from the late 17th century to the REGENCY period.

Omega Workshop A design company founded in 1913 in London by the art historian and critic Roger Fry. He aimed to apply the aesthetic of post-Impressionism to British design, which he felt had become debased. The Omega Workshop produced a broad range of painted furniture, textiles, and decorative objects, as well as lively and colorful interior designs, employing artists such as Vanessa Bell and Duncan Grant. The workshop closed in 1919

O

271

Oeben, Jean-François
Mahogany occasional table, with marble top and brass gallery. c. 1750.

Ohr, George E.
Tall vase with ribbon handles, covered in a red and green mottled glaze.

Okimono
Japanese ivory *okimono* of a musician playing a stringed instrument.

Olbrich, Jose Maria
Pewter candlestick, with flat relief ribbon decoration. c. 1902.

O

because of falling sales during World War I, but it set the fashion for abstract and geometric patterns that was taken up in the 1920s. See STAINED GLASS.

Onion pattern A popular design (also called Zwiebelmuster) of the MEISSEN porcelain factory, based on a Chinese blue and white original and produced from 1739. The rims of the plates were originally decorated with peaches, mistaken for onions by the Meissen painters. The design was copied in the 18th and 19th centuries by many other Continental factories and is still in production today.

Onondaga Shops See L. & G. STICKLEY.

Onslow pattern See ALBANY PATTERN. A silver FLATWARE pattern, the main distinguishing characteristic being the fanned-out ends of the stems that terminate in a scroll motif. It was produced from around 1750 and was probably named after the Parliamentary speaker Arthur Onslow.

Onyx A mineral of the chalcedony family and a form of quartz, onyx has been used since antiquity in jewelry and for artifacts such as CAMEOS and INTAGLIOS. It is distinguished by bands of coloring, ranging from white to almost every other color, except purple, blue, and black.

Opal ■ A gemstone celebrated for its unique play of rainbowlike colors. It was highly prized by the Romans, and in the Middle

Ages it was thought to have powers to predict disaster and cure ophthalmia (inflammation of the eye). The richest source of opal has traditionally been Czechoslovakia. Today the most valuable variety is the black opal, mined in Australia since the 1870s and displaying characteristic "harlequin" colors. Other notable varieties include the orange fire opal, mined in Mexico.

Opal glass A translucent white glass resembling opal. Opal glass was made in Venice in the 17th and 18th centuries, and from the late 17th to the 19th century in Germany and Bohemia, where it was also known as BEINGLAS.

Opalescent glass ■ An opal-like, milky blue glass, with subtle gradations of color in which opaque areas of thicker glass contrast with more translucent areas of thinner glass. It was first made by Venetian glassmakers in the 16th century, but is now closely identified with the luxury ART GLASS of the late 19th century and the ART DECO glass produced in France by celebrated glassmakers such as René LALIQUE and Marius Ernest SABINO. From the 1880s inexpensive PRESS-MOLDED opalescent glass was also produced in large quantities by British manufacturers. See PEARLINE GLASS.

Opalina See MILK GLASS.

Opaline glass ■ A semi-opaque glass, developed in France from around 1825,

achieved by adding BONE ASH to the glass mix. This results in the "fire" for which opaline is famed, where the color of the glass changes when held against light. It was produced in Britain from about 1840 and subsequently made throughout Europe. In the US opaline glass was made at the BOSTON & SANDWICH GLASS COMPANY.

Opaque glass Glass that does not transmit light, generally the opposite of transparent or translucent glass. In stained glass, it refers to any glass that is not translucent. See LITHYALIN.

Opaque twist stem A type of stem found in English glasses from about 1745 to 1780, consisting of a twisted rod embedded with threads of opaque white or colored glass. See AIR TWIST.

Open back setting See CLOSED BACK SETTING.

Open mouth ■ A BISQUE doll made from around 1890 with parted lips showing molded or inserted teeth.

Open-closed mouth An early BISQUE doll with lips that appear parted but in fact have uncut plaster between them.

Open-faced watch The earliest type of watch, produced from the late 16th century, where the dial is protected by glass only, rather than a cover.

Opal
Opal-set German Heinrich Levinger blue and *plique-a-jour* brooch. c. 1900.

Opalescent glass
Lalique "Perigord" vase, in opalescent glass, engraved "R. Lalique France." 1930s.

Opaline glass
Bohemian turquoise opaline glass beaker with gilded decoration. c. 1845.

Open mouth
Jumeau doll, with open mouth and molded teeth. c. 1890–1900.

Openwork One of the oldest techniques of metalworking, including methods such as piercing, saw cutting, or WIREWORK that create openings in the body of an object, allowing light to shine through and its beauty to be appreciated. Openwork was functional on items such as tea strainers, but has also been used both in Western countries and in East Asia since the 18th century purely as a decoration on silver items such as breadbaskets and fruit bowls.

Opus Anglicanum A term used in medieval Continental Europe for English embroidery that includes the use of intricately embroidered silver and gold threads. Considered some of the finest needlework ever made, this type of embroidery was mostly for ecclesiastical use.

Ormolu ■ Bronze gilded by the mercury or fire gilding processes and used, especially in 18th- and early 19th-century in France, as decorative mounts. The term is also used for a 19th-century gold-colored alloy of copper, zinc, and tin. Ormolu derives its name from the French *or moulu*, meaning "ground gold."

Orrefors Glassworks ■ A glassworks founded in Orrefors, Småland, Sweden, in 1898. The company began by producing bottles and tableware, but from the 1920s became increasingly renowned for its ART GLASS, which was often colorless and engraved with stylized designs. A number of noteworthy and influential designers

worked for the company, including Simon Gate, Edward Hald, Nils Landberg, and Sven Palmqvist. Vike LINDSTRAND also designed for them from 1928 to 1940, before leaving for KOSTA. Two techniques in particular gained the company an international reputation: GRAAL, developed from 1916, and ARIEL, developed from 1937. The company's reputation for such innovative processes was continued with the Ravenna, Kraka, and Fuga ranges. Orrefors became part of the Royal Scandinavia group in 1997 and still produces high-quality tableware and art glass today.

Orrery Originally a type of PLANETARIUM made in England in 1712 for the 4th Earl of Orrery, the word is now used to describe any tabletop demonstrational instrument showing the motion of the Earth around the Sun and the Moon around the Earth. Orreries were made until the mid-19th century, and prolific makers included Benjamin Martin, Bate, and W. and S. JONES.

Ortelius, Abraham (1527–98) A Dutch cartographer who produced several

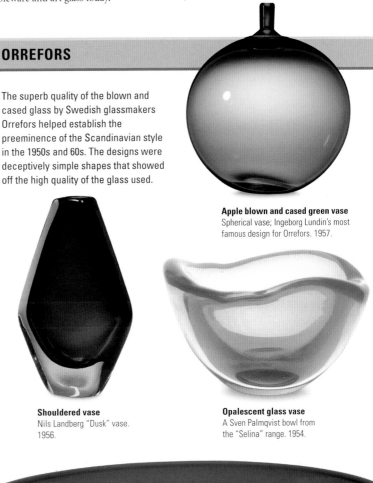

ORREFORS

The superb quality of the blown and cased glass by Swedish glassmakers Orrefors helped establish the preeminence of the Scandinavian style in the 1950s and 60s. The designs were deceptively simple shapes that showed off the high quality of the glass used.

Apple blown and cased green vase
Spherical vase; Ingeborg Lundin's most famous design for Orrefors. 1957.

Shouldered vase
Nils Landberg "Dusk" vase. 1956.

Opalescent glass vase
A Sven Palmqvist bowl from the "Selina" range. 1954.

Ormolu
French Empire bronze and ormolu cut-glass centerpiece. 19th century.

Spun blue glass charger
Large Orrefors "Expo" blown-glass charger, designed by Sven Palmqvist. 1962.

O
273

O

important maps before the publication in 1570 of his greatest work, the *Theatrum Orbis Terrarum* (Theater of the Whole World). This was the first true modern ATLAS, a collection of uniformly sized and styled maps of the countries and regions of the world, based on the latest geographical data. The *Theatrum* continued to be revised and reissued in different languages until 1612.

Osier ■ A pattern simulating basket weave (also called ozier), molded on the rims of porcelain plates, devised at MEISSEN in the 1730s. An early form was used on a service made for Count von Sulkowski designed by J. G. HÖROLDT in 1735. He also developed Altozierrand with radial rims and Neuozierran with four sets of spiraling ribs.

Osler, F. & C. (1807–c. 1940) An English glasshouse based in Birmingham that specialized in CUT-GLASS tableware and large-scale projects such as the huge—about 28-ft- (8.5-m-) high—glass fountain for the GREAT EXHIBITION in London in 1851.

Ostrich-egg cup The translucent cleaned egg of an ostrich set into a mount. Usually silver or gold, the mount is highly worked and decorated with figurative or floral and foliate motifs. It was an exotic, decorative curiosity made first in Europe in the 15th century, and more extensively in the 16th century through to the 17th century.

Ott & Brewer Porcelain Factory ■ An American factory founded in 1863 as the Etruria Pottery in Trenton, New Jersey, by William Bloor, Thomas Booth, and Joseph Otto. They were later joined by John Hart Brewer, and in 1873 the factory was renamed Ott & Brewer. Initially it made cream-colored earthenware and white GRANITE WARE. In the late 1860s it introduced PARIAN statuary and HOLLOWWARE, the best designed by Isaac Broome. Helped by William Bromley in the 1880s, the firm produced acclaimed American BELLEEK, some decorated by W. S. LENOX. The factory closed in 1893.

Ottoman A long, low, narrow upholstered sofa or bench without a back. Fashionable in the late 18th century, it was designed in imitation of the Turkish mode of sitting. In the REGENCY period it was synonymous with a divan, and in the 19th century it came to mean a COFFER with tapering sides.

Ottoman carpets ■ Ottoman carpets were made during the 16th and 17th centuries in the region that is modern Turkey. Early carpets have geometric GUL medallion designs. Some of these have been given names derived from Western painters who portrayed carpets in their paintings. For example, the Memling Gul was named after the 15th-century German painter Hans Memling and consists of an octagon enclosing a stepped, hooked medallion. The LOTTO design, after Lorenzo Lotto, is also a popular carpet.

In the mid-16th century a development of the Ottoman court style of carpet-weaving appears to have been derived from Cairo, which was colonized by the Ottomans in 1517. These rugs and carpets include such designs as the "cintamani" (three balls above a pair of wavy lines)—a design element that became one of the most popular in Ottoman art. Other patterns include bands of clouds, lotus PALMETTES from Chinese art, tulips, carnations, hyacinths, roses, and large leaves.

In the late 16th and 17th centuries other designs evolved, typically, the large "medallion" and "star" carpets from USHAK. Both these types show an endless repeating design cut by the borders. The medallion format, first seen in bindings of the Koran, was probably borrowed from contemporary Persian carpets from Tabriz, as artists from here were employed by the Ottoman court. These carpets have either red or blue as the background color, with a decorative vine design in another color. Other motifs such as flowerheads and ARABESQUE scrolls show Persian influence. The border designs included patterns such as KUFIC SCRIPT, cloudbands, palmettes with floral sprays, and floral CARTOUCHES. Most Turkish and a significant amount of Caucasian rug production, from the 18th century to the present, use designs developed or influenced by Ottoman carpet production of this time.

Oude Loosdrecht Porcelain Factory A Dutch factory founded in 1771 by Johannes de Mol using the stock from WEESP. The

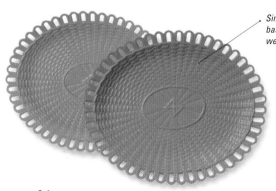

Osier
Osier pattern molded around the rim of plates.

Simulated basket-weave

Ott & Brewer Porcelain
Fine Belleek gourd-shaped pitcher, with gilded waterlily handle.

Ottoman carpets
Tabriz pictorial rug. c. 1930.

arcanist L. V. GERVEROT worked here in around 1777. It made fine-quality porcelain in the style of MEISSEN and SÈVRES. In 1784 the factory moved to Oude-Amstel but closed in 1820.

Outside decorator See HAUSMALER.

Overglaze A technique for decorating ceramics. After adding lavender oil and turpentine, enamels (color-bound metals or oxides held together by a flux, usually finely ground quartz, firestone, red lead, or bismuth oxide) are painted onto fired and glazed porcelain. They are then fired in a muffle kiln at about 1,380°F (750°C). See ENAMEL COLORS.

Overlay glass Glass made up of one or more layers of different colored glass, as in CASED, FLASHED, and CAMEO glass. In the UK this is known as "cased."

Overstuffed ■ Seat furniture such as chairs and sofas with upholstery completely covering the wooden frame, leaving only minor decorative woodwork exposed.

Ovolo A convex classical MOLDING, usually a quarter of a circle, often embellished with EGG AND DART or similar ornament. It was much used in RENAISSANCE decoration, on furniture CORNICES in the 16th and 17th centuries, and on JAPANNED and MARQUETRY mirror frames in the late 17th century.

Oxbow front ■ An American term describing the undulating front surface of a CHEST-OF-DRAWERS or other type of CASE FURNITURE with two convex curves flanking a concave one. It is the opposite of a SERPENTINE front.

Oxidized silver Silver whose surface color has been changed by a chemical reaction to create a decorative layer of metal oxide. It was produced from around 1850 to 1890 in France and England, especially on figurative and statuary silver. Many colors could be created and in England dark staining and shades of red were particularly popular.

Oyster veneer ■ Wood sliced in a diagonal cross-section from the smaller branches of trees such as walnut and laburnum and laid together to resemble oyster shells. Originating in Holland, it was popular on cabinets, drawers, and LONGCASE CLOCKS in the late 17th and early 18th centuries.

O

275

Overstuffed
An early 19th-century mahogany Biedermeier day bed, with overstuffed seat.

Oxbow front
Massachusetts Chippendale mahogany oxbow chest-of-drawers.

Oxbow front

Oyster veneer
Oyster veneer on the top of a Continental rectangular walnut table in 17th-century style.

P

276

Pad foot ■ A rounded foot resting on a circular base. Similar to the CLUB FOOT, but sometimes without the disk on the bottom, the pad foot was used mostly with the CABRIOLE LEG on furniture from the early 18th century onward.

Paddington bear ■ A character invented by Michael Bond in 1956. Paddington Bear first featured in the book *A Bear Called Paddington*, which was illustrated by Peggy Fortnum. In 1972 Shirley Clarkson of Gabrielle Designs made the first Paddington TEDDY BEAR, based on Peggy Fortnum's illustrations. Although still produced by Gabrielle Designs in the UK, the Paddingtons sold outside Britain are made by the American company Eden Toys.

Padouk A hard, heavy, well-marked red wood, ranging from a golden brown to a deep red or crimson color. Originating in the Dutch and Portuguese East Indies, padouk was used extensively by French *ébénistes* in the 18th century and in England for fretwork and for solid pieces of furniture.

Pagoda top ■ A motif representing a Chinese pagoda. Extensively featured in CHINOISERIE ornament, the pagoda top was adopted by furniture-makers in 18th-century England and France to lend an Oriental flavor to pieces such as cabinets, clocks, and mirrors.

Pair-cased watch ■ The term for watches made with an outer protective case. Usually made of the same material as the inner case, some cases are covered with SHAGREEN or TORTOISESHELL.

Pairpoint Corporation, The A metalware company founded in New Bedford, Massachusetts, in 1880, which produced functional and decorative household items. Many were combined with glass made by the MOUNT WASHINGTON GLASSWORKS. In 1894 the companies merged and the new company's products met with great success until 1929 and the Depression. Especially popular were the range of blown shades known as "Puffies," which were molded in high relief with f loral designs, hand-painted on the inside of the glass, and smaller "boudoir puffies." Ribbed and scenic shades were also produced. The metalware company closed in 1937 due to continued financial problems and less expensive competition from imports.

Paisley pattern A decorative pattern evolved from stylized images of pine cones (also known as BOTEH motif). A common

decorative device featuring a broad variety of vegetation such as the palm, cypress, and almond, it can be found throughout East Asia, although its origins remain obscure. By the mid-19th century, fabric patterned with this motif had become fashionable in both France and England. It was produced in quantity at Paisley, a Scottish wool-weaving town—hence the name.

Paktong A yellowish, silvery, durable alloy of copper, zinc, and nickel. Originating in China, possibly as early as the 1st century, it was not imported into Europe until the 17th century. A practical, inexpensive substitute for silver, it was used for fireplace furnishings, salvers, bowls, and candlesticks. It was superseded by the cheap nickel alloy German silver, making surviving examples scarce today.

Palissy, Bernard (c. 1510–90) A French HUGUENOT potter and glass-painter. In 1539 he settled at Saintes, Charente-Maritime, where he perfected various enamels and colored glazes using tin, iron, lead, antimony, copper, and Périgord stone. He made pottery with relief decoration that drew inspiration from nature, using motifs such as lizards, snails, and foliage, which became popular. His wares were imitated at Caldas da Rainha (1885–1908), Portugal's main FAIENCE factory, and he is credited

Pad foot
George I Virginia walnut fold-over tea table, with pad feet. c. 1725.

Paddington bear
Gabrielle Designs Paddington bear soft toy in a felt hat, coat, and Wellington boots.

Cabriole legs

Pagoda top
Mahogany display cabinet, with pagoda top.

with being a source of inspiration for MAJOLICA. In 1575 Palissy wrote a manual describing his potting techniques. He was arrested for heresy in 1586 and died in the Bastille.

Palladian A style of architecture and furniture inspired by the work of the 16th-century Italian architect Andrea Palladio and popular in England during the first half of the 18th century. The furniture designed by William KENT and John Vardy, among others, for Palladian houses is distinguished by solid, symmetrical, and Classical forms, ornamented with architectural-style PEDIMENTS, scrolled brackets, garlands and ACANTHUS leaves and swags. It is often heavily embellished with GILDING.

Palmette A decorative motif from antiquity, loosely based on the fan-shaped palm leaf. Frequently used with the ANTHEMION, the two forms are hard to distinguish, especially when interpreted in a florid style. Revived during the RENAISSANCE and NEOCLASSICAL periods, the Greek-style palmette (resembling honeysuckle flowers) was used on furniture, ceramics, and metalwork.

Panel ■ A flat surface sunk or raised within a framework, usually on furniture or as a wall covering. A FIELDED PANEL has a raised central flat surface, often with beveled edges. Panels could also be carved, with LINENFOLD, for example. Wall paneling developed in Northern Europe from the 15th century to meet the need for draft-free rooms, reaching great sophistication in 18th-century France.

Paneled chest A form of CHEST constructed with a framework of stiles and rails, held together by MORTISE-AND-TENON joints. One of the earliest types of furniture, the chest was usually decorated with simply carved or painted designs.

Panton, Verner ■ (1926–98) A Danish architect and designer of furniture, textiles, carpets, and lighting. In 1955 he designed the first all-in-one, plywood CANTILEVERED chair—the S-Chair—for the Swiss furniture company THONET. This was translated into plastic with the Panton Chair, designed from 1959 to 1960. It was produced by furniture company Herman Miller from 1962 and is still produced today by Vitra. Other iconic designs include the fabric upholstered, sculptural Cone (1958) and Heart (1959) chairs for Plus Linje. Panton developed his own color system for the textiles and room interiors that he designed. Some of the latter were lined with sculptural foam furnishings and "furniture" upholstered in bright fabrics of the day.

Pap boat A small, flat invalid feeder, with a spout for partaking of bread and milk (pap), used in the 18th and 19th centuries. It was usually made in earthenware with UNDERGLAZE blue printed patterns, but silver examples also exist.

Paperweight ■ Small, heavy, decorative glass objects used for holding down loose papers on a desk or table. Most have a circular base with a diameter of 2–4 in (5–10 cm)—glass weights with smaller or larger diameters are known as miniatures and magnums, respectively—and a decorative ground that is magnified by a high dome of clear glass. The type of decoration varies enormously, from densely packed MILLEFIORI canes to SULPHIDES, lampwork, fruit, flowers, vegetables, figures, snakes, and insects, or cameo portraits. The idea of enclosing a cameo in a ball of glass probably originated from France in the early 19th century, but the golden era of production was not until 1845 to 1850, when French glassworks such as BACCARAT, SAINT-LOUIS, and CLICHY made superb examples.

As the fashion for paperweights declined in France in the 1850s, French makers took their skills to such companies as the BOSTON & SANDWICH and NEW ENGLAND glassworks. In this way the US became the center of production of paperweights. British weights came to the fore in the 20th century, with weights made by Paul YSART for the MONCRIEFF and Caithness glassworks, the latter established in 1960 at Perth, Scotland.

Paperweight eyes Dolls' blown glass eyes with tiny threads running through the irises to create an illusion of depth.

Pair-cased watch
Gilt pair-cased verge pocket watch, within a plain outer case with key.

Gilt keywind and case

Panel
Oak stile "Joyned" chest, with four-paneled hinged lid above a carved frieze. 17th century.

Panton, Verner
Cone chair, by Verner Panton for Fritz Hansen. c. 1960.

Butterfly motif

Paperweight
Ken Rosenfeld "Monarch Ladybug & Floral" lampwork paperweight. 2003.

P

Papier-mâché A lightweight constructional material made from dampened pulped paper, glue, and chalk, and sometimes sand, which is molded to a desired shape, baked hard, and then decorated. Probably originating in East Asia, it was first used in the West in France in the 17th century and was developed and patented in Britain in 1772 by Henry Clay, with further developments in the early 19th century by JENNENS & BETTRIDGE. Used to make smaller domestic artifacts such as trays and tea caddies, as well as items of furniture, including chairs, it was mostly decorated by painting or JAPANNING, often augmented with GILDING or MOTHER-OF-PEARL inlay, or finished with DECOUPAGE.

Papier-mâché doll ■ A doll with its SHOULDER HEAD made of papier-mâché. Based on an established tradition in France, the German manufacturers rationalized the molding process, allowing MASS PRODUCTION of papier-mâché heads by around 1820. The shoulder heads have painted features and black, molded hair, reflecting changing fashions. The heads are attached to kid leather or cloth bodies and the lower limbs are carved from wood. Around 1870 PARIAN, china, and BISQUE dolls' heads became popular, but papier-mâché was still used for jointed dolls' bodies, which continued into the mid-20th century.

Parcel gilt ■ A form of GILDING in which the object, usually furniture or silverware, is selectively gilded, with the application usually confined to molded decoration or areas of carving.

Parian head doll PARIAN is a type of porcelain invented by COPELAND AND GARRETT. Parian head dolls, however, are not made of parian, but of a white untinted BISQUE. They were manufactured largely in Germany and were especially popular around 1860.

Parianware ■ A highly FELDSPATHIC porcelain named after the Greek island of Paros, which was famous for its white marble. Parianware was made in England in the mid-19th century at a time of great interest in museums and art and a growing middle class that was aware of "antique sculpture." Parianware gave them the opportunity to have affordable copies of ancient sculpture and marble models by the sculptors of the day. MINTON and COPELAND were important manufacturers and sold vast quantities of these busts and figures.

Paris potteries and porcelain factories ■ An area of provenance for a vast amount of ceramics made and decorated in Paris in the 19th century. Because SÈVRES, the Royal Factory, had been protected by a Royal Edict for so long (until 1784), there had been little room for other manufacturers. But after the Napoleonic wars, there was a burgeoning of ceramic activity. With the discovery of KAOLIN near LIMOGES, HARD-PASTE PORCELAIN was made in great quantities. Some of the porcelain made in Limoges was decorated in the Parisian workshops and some factories produced their own porcelain and earthenware.

French fashion influenced the taste of most of Europe in the 19th century. There were over 160 factories or decorating establishments in Paris, including P. L. DAGOTY in Boulevard Poissonnière from the end of the 18th century; Darte Brothers, a porcelain factory from 1795 and also a decorating studio in the Palais Royal; Dastin, a factory from 1810; Deck, a workshop for artistic FAIENCES founded by Theodore DECK in 1859; Pierre Deruelle, a factory at Clignancourt in 1771; Dihl, a factory founded in 1780 under the patronage of the Duc d'Angoulême; SAMSON, the great copyists; Rue Béranger, a decorating studio owned by Feuillet in Rue de la Paix from 1820; Fleury, in Rue de Faubourg St Lazare from 1803 to 1847; La Courtille, founded by J. B. Locre in 1771; brothers Pouyts, from 1808 to 1825; and Nast in Rue Popincourt.

Parisienne See FASHION DOLL.

Parquetry The INLAY of variously colored small pieces of wood veneer on the carcass of a piece of furniture to produce a geometric pattern. A variation on MARQUETRY that was employed most notably during the early period of walnut-veneered furniture in the

Papier-mâché doll
Papier-mâché head "Pauline" doll, on a kid leather body with wooden limbs. 1850–60.

Parcel gilt
Swedish parcel-gilt center table. c. 1820.

Parianware
Copeland Parian model of Marguerite in flowing robes. c. 1868.

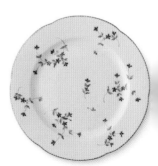

Paris porcelain
Plate with polychrome decoration from the Locre factory. Late 18th century.

17th century, parquetry mosaic was occasionally laid directly into the solid wood. By the mid-18th century the technique was used with great virtuosity, particularly on commodes in England and France.

Partners' desk A type of English pedestal desk or large library table, double-sized and double-sided to accommodate two people sitting opposite each other. Fashionable from the 1740s and throughout the 19th century, the desk was furnished with drawers and cupboards on both sides.

Partridge wood ■ A close and heavy straight-grained wood in varying tones of brown and red, with streaks resembling the feathers of a bird. Native to Brazil, it was used extensively in small INLAY and PARQUETRY work throughout the 17th century.

Parure A matching set of jewelry, usually comprising a necklace, a pair of bracelets, earrings, and a brooch. Parures were particularly common at the start of the 19th century, for example, in CANNETILLE jewelry with semiprecious stones. A demi-parure tends to comprise two components—a necklace and earrings, for example.

Pashmina From the Kashmiri *pashm* (wool). A type of fine shawl made from the silky underbelly hair of a Himalayan mountain goat. Much prized throughout Mughal history, these shawls were supposed to be so fine that they could pass through a finger ring.

Passing strike A type of STRIKING SYSTEM in which a clock strikes only once on the passing of the hour, usually found in late 19th-century SKELETON CLOCKS.

Paste ■ 1. Paste is a compound of glass that was principally invented by Frederic Strass, a French jeweler working in the 1730s. Strass discovered that a hard and versatile material is produced with many of the properties of real gemstones when selected oxides and minerals are added to FLINT GLASS. Paste jewelry in a wide variety of colors was worn in the 18th century, usually mounted in silver or gilt metal and FOILED to enhance the color and sparkle. Late 19th-century "French" paste lacked the quality of its 18th-century counterparts; much of 20th-century paste was painted with a gold-colored coating to intensify its appearance. 2. The "body" of porcelain, the mixture of clay and flux; it is used to describe both "true" (or HARD-PASTE) and SOFT-PASTE PORCELAIN (*pâte tendre*).

Pastille burner A ceramic receptacle that held a small perfumed tablet or pastille, which when lit gave off a fragrance in a room. These were necessary accessories in the 18th and 19th centuries when houses were often damp, personal hygiene not of a high standard, and the sewers of poor quality.

Patch mark A small, round mark, larger than a SPUR MARK, on the underside of DERBY porcelain in the 18th and early 19th centuries, left from the small "pads" of clay on which the piece stood in the kiln.

Patchbox ■ 1. A small box that originally held paper patches to cover smallpox scars. These patches became a fashion item in the 18th century and the boxes were decorated with enameling or were engraved. 2. A small, lidded compartment in the stock of a muzzle-loading RIFLE for the greased cloth patches that were wrapped around rifle balls for ease of loading and to make them spin for increased accuracy.

Pâte A rounded piece of cork or PAPIER-MÂCHÉ that covers the WIG APERTURE of a DOLL and gives a natural, rounded shape to the head. Also made of card or *carton*.

Pâte-de-verre ■ A French term for "glass paste." A technically demanding glass-making technique in which a paste is made from ground colored glass and a gelatin glue or water. This is then carefully applied into a mold before being fired, which melts and fuses the ground glass together. The resulting piece may then be carved after it has cooled. First used in ancient Egypt, the technique was revived in the 19th century by French glassmakers Amalric WALTER, François-Emile DÉCORCHEMONT, and Joseph-Gabriel ARGY-ROUSSEAU.

P

279

Partridge wood
Detail of a Regency partridge wood card table.

Paste
Prong-set ruby-paste earrings from a demi-parure that includes a matching pendant necklace. c. 1710.

Patchbox
Shallow enamel patchbox, depicting a rural scene and birds. c. 1775.

Pâte-de-verre
A Daum *pâte-de-verre* vide-poche by Almaric Walter. c. 1930.

P

Patek Philippe Swiss watchmaker founded in 1839, which produced and still produces some of the best and most finely made watches and mechanisms.

Patera The Latin term for the dish or wine holder used in religious ceremonies. The oval or circular medallion patera ornament is generally decorated with a formalized flower, rosette, or fluting. The patera was a popular motif in the NEOCLASSICAL period for silver and furniture.

Pâte-sur-pâte ■ The French term for "paste on paste." A technique introduced in SÈVRES around 1849 by the head of the painting department. White clay or "slip" is built up in layers on a dark background to give a striking effect of depth. The great exponent of *pâte-sur-pâte* was Marc Louis Solon, who worked at Sèvres and MINTON.

Patina (patination) A fine surface sheen and mellow appearance on silver and furniture. Years of handling, with an accumulation of polish and dirt, produce the attractive and desirable effect known as patination. A fine patina is a key ingredient looked for in a quality antique.

Pattern book Printed or engraved collections of designs by architects, artists, and craftsmen working in most mediums of the decorative arts. In widespread use from the 15th to the early 20th century, they were either published in bound-book form or as small collections of individual sheets, and played a major role in the national and international dissemination of new (or old) forms and styles in the days before instant communication. Notable among numerous influential and historically important examples are Thomas CHIPPENDALES's *The Gentleman and Cabinet-Maker's Director* (first published in 1754) and OWEN JONES's *The Grammar of Ornament* (first published in 1851).

Pattern number A system most usually used in English ceramics factories in the 19th century, although 18th-century pattern numbers are known. Some factory PATTERN BOOKS are still extant and give the year of the first introduction of a pattern. They may also have drawings of the shapes and give artists' names.

Paul Revere Pottery See SATURDAY EVENING GIRLS.

Pavé setting ■ A method of mounting diamonds and gems where each individual stone is "paved" in side-by-side with its neighbor, so that little or no setting is visible between. Pavé setting was often used in Georgian jewelry and in many postwar and contemporary diamond jewels.

Paw foot ■ Similar to the claw-and-hoof, the paw form usually decorates the base of a furniture leg. Originating in Classical antiquity, it was revived during the RENAISSANCE. Grotesque supporting figures with paw feet feature in the designs of MANNERIST engravers. A favored motif on the front of English and American chair legs from the early to mid-18th century, paws frequently embellish MONOPODIA.

Peach bloom A glaze derived from copper and ranging from red to green. First seen in Chinese KANGXI ware.

Peachblow ■ Late-19th-century opaque ART GLASS in shades of cream to light pink or deeper rose pink, in imitation of the Chinese PEACH BLOOM glaze. The majority were made in the US, notably by HOBBS, BROCKUNIER & CO., MOUNT WASHINGTON GLASS COMPANY, and the NEW ENGLAND GLASS COMPANY, who called their version "Wild Rose."

Peacock motif ■ A decorative motif since antiquity. In Classical ornament, the peacock was an emblem of immortality. In Christian iconography, it symbolizes immortality and Christ's resurrection. Peacock feathers were used on late 15th-century MAIOLICA from Faenza and often appeared on DELFTWARE apothecary jars of the mid-17th and 18th centuries. In the AESTHETIC MOVEMENT, the peacock symbolizing beauty appeared on William de Morgan ceramics, enamels, TIFFANY glass, and LIBERTY fabrics.

Pear See FRUITWOOD.

Pearline glass An opalescent PRESSED GLASS made by George Davidson & Co. in

Pâte-sur-pâte
A Minton *pâte-sur-pâte* peacock blue pilgrim bottle. c. 1880.

Pavé setting
One of a pair of "retro" earclips, with caliber-cut rubies and diamond accents. 1940s.

Paw foot
Paw foot carved in mahogany. Early 19th century.

Peachblow
Mount Washington Peachblow glass vase. 1886–88.

Gateshead, Northumberland, and typically used for tableware. Introduced in 1889, it shaded from transparent to opaque across the body or the design and was produced in various colors, including blue, made with the addition of cobalt, and yellow. See PRIMROSE GLASS.

Pearlware ■ English earthenware with a blue-tinted glaze, made from around 1770 to the first half of the 19th century. Usually printed, it was also painted in UNDERGLAZE blue and was quite often dated. Pearlware was made in Staffordshire, Yorkshire, and Wales, but is unmarked and impossible to attribute.

Pedestal In Classical architecture, the base that supports a column. Since the RENAISSANCE, decorative pedestals have been used to display vases, candelabra, lamps, and sculpture, and have sometimes been fitted with storage compartments.

Pedestal desk ■ Derived from the pedestal LIBRARY or WRITING TABLE made in the mid-18th century by a number of London cabinet-makers, including Thomas CHIPPENDALE. The flat desk, often with a leather top, rests on two side pedestals with drawers or folio cupboards. Made originally in walnut, pedestal desks in various woods have been popular from the 19th century to the present day.

Pedestal table A round or oval table supported on a single central pillar or

PEDIMENT

The triangular gable above the portico of a Classical temple, the pediment motif was adopted in Italy, France, and England from the 16th century for the tops of windows and doors and for the CORNICES on tall

CASE FURNITURE such as bookcases, BUREAUX, and LONGCASE CLOCKS. A broken pediment has a central break for a FINIAL; a swan-neck pediment consists of two opposing S-scrolls.

Pediment
Philadelphia Chippendale figured mahogany chest-on-chest, with broken arch pediment. c. 1770.

column, usually with spreading feet or a tripod base. First made in England in the 18th century, sometimes in pairs, pedestal library and dining tables have remained popular since.

Peepshow An enclosed box with a lit scene inside and a peephole for viewing. Some used a series of pictures to create a three-dimensional effect, while others had a lens that magnified the scene. They were often used by traveling showmen during the 17th and 18th centuries in Europe. Seaside peepshows with titillating subject matter were popular around 1900.

Peg doll See PENNY WOODEN.

Peg tankard ■ A tankard, usually of late 17th-century Scandinavian origin but common in other European countries as well, made of wood or silver with a row of applied pegs inside as a guide to the amount of liquid consumed.

Pegging See DOWEL.

Peking enamel Exquisitely painted enamel applied to copper-bodied items such as SNUFF BOTTLES and produced in the Imperial factories from the 18th century in Peking, China. Often grouped

Peacock motif
French Art Nouveau gold, enamel, and diamond peacock brooch or pendant.

Pearlware
Pearlware jug, inscribed "J.Cordal, 1832" in a heart beneath the spout.

Pedestal desk
Victorian mahogany pedestal desk with leather lined molded top over nine short drawers.

Peg tankard
Scandinavian burr wood peg tankard, with lion thumb piece. 17th century.

with CANTON ENAMEL ware, these pieces are of far higher quality.

Pellatt, Apsley (1791–1863) A glass chemist and manufacturer who inherited the Falcon Glassworks in Southwark, London, which his father had founded around 1790. He specialized in decorative wares and experimented with new glass-making techniques, including incorporating small, decorative Classical portrait panels known as sulphides, which he patented in 1819. He also revived ICE GLASS and other Venetian glass making techniques, was a pioneer of PRESSED GLASS, and exhibited at the GREAT EXHIBITION in London in 1851. In 1849 he published *Curiosities of Glass Making*—on the practice of glass making. The firm continued to make glass until the 1890s.

Pembroke table ■ An elegant, small OCCASIONAL TABLE with four legs—usually on casters—one or two frieze drawers, and two drop leaves supported by wooden brackets on hinges (known as

"elbows"). Believed to have been named after a Countess of Pembroke, the Pembroke table was produced in England from the mid-18th century. The tops were often elaborately inlaid with SATINWOOD, EBONY, and BOXWOOD. In the 19th century brass inlay became popular, and in the late 19th and early 20th centuries they were often painted in Revival styles.

Pendelfin ■ Hand-painted cast-stonecraft figurines made by Pendelfin of Burnley, Lancashire, from 1953 to the present day. The company name is derived from "Pendle," the infamous witch hill above the first workshop, and "elfin," the look of the early models. Although now best known for rabbit figures, the rare earlier wares, featuring myth and legend pieces, nursery rhyme characters, and ducks, are in much demand.

Pendulum A device controlling the timekeeping of a clock, developed in the mid-17th century by the Dutch scientist Christian Huygens. A brass, steel, or wooden rod is made to swing in a regular arc by a

flat or bulbous metal weight (bob) at one end. It is used with the ANCHOR ESCAPEMENT and VERGE ESCAPEMENT. The introduction of the pendulum in the mid-17th century dramatically improved accuracy, but the metal rod still expanded and contracted with changes in temperature. In the early 18th century, British clockmakers George Graham and John Harrison developed the temperature-compensating mercurial and gridiron pendulums, respectively. The mercurial pendulum has a mercury-filled glass jar as the bob—under heat, the expansion of the mercury counters that of the steel pendulum rod. The gridiron pendulum comprises alternating steel and brass rods—as they expand and contract at varying rates, the pendulum length remains the same.

Pennsylvania Dutch style ■ Referring to the folk traditions and styles of the mainly German, Central European, and Scandinavian communities, which settled in the Lancaster, Lebanon, and Buckinghamshire (Bucks) counties of

PENNSYLVANIA DUTCH STYLE

Furniture in this style is typically brightly painted, practical, and of simple construction from indigenous woods such as white or yellow PINE, MAPLE, or CHERRY. BLANKET CHESTS of the simple box type with a hinged lid were traditionally painted with panels of formalized folk imagery and may feature initials and dates (usually between c. 1750 and c. 1850) if they were originally presented as a marriage or dowry chest. Some pieces, such as tool chests, bowls, and small boxes, are also decorated with shallow carving and stippled surfaces.

Candlebox
Painted, decorated, and incised pine candlebox. Late 18th century.

Hand-painted polychrome imagery

Dower chest
Pennsylvania painted dower chest, inscribed with "Maria Stohlern 1788."

Pennsylvania from the 18th century onward. The style of furnishings and household items they made shared the forms and motifs of the Old World and suggest a nostalgia for it. The word "Dutch" is a corruption of Deutsch (German), although the influences and nationalities of the makers included those from Norway, Sweden, Austria, Holland, and Germany.

Pottery was typically crudely made, utility REDWARE, produced from the second quarter of the 19th century. The best examples were SGRAFFITO-decorated through a yellow or green glaze. It was rarely signed but may be attributable or dated. Tinware was typically simply made and coffeepots were common. Painted examples were often decorated with "gaudy" tulips. Textiles were typically bed QUILTS made in large numbers from the 18th century and often well preserved in BLANKET CHESTS as heirlooms. The best quilts were dated and had strong colors and rich decoration of figural or folk images. Other textiles included hooked wool rugs and, rarely, needlework SAMPLERS. HOOKED RUGS were mostly made in the 20th century and may have figural or geometric designs. Illuminated manuscripts, known by the German word FRAKTUR, typically recorded births or a family tree. The best examples feature vivid imagery and bold colors. Early (pre-1790) dates are not uncommon. Pennsylvania Dutch folk painting included landscapes depicting farming or

PENWORK

Decoration commonly applied to JAPANNED furniture such as tabletops, cabinet furniture, tea caddies, boxes, and trays, produced mainly in England in the late 18th and early 19th centuries. Furniture embellished with penwork was japanned black before being painted with decorative patterns in white japan. Details and shading were achieved with black Indian ink, using a fine quill pen.

Side cabinet
Penwork side cabinet, with single drawer. c. 1810–1820.

Detail of penwork
Delicate patterning painted on in white japan.

daily pursuits of the late 18th or early 19th centuries. Painting on furniture and on ceramics tended to be simple and stylized. Motifs derived from nature, especially tulips and birds, were popular. The spiraling rosette or "pinwheel" was also commonly used. The primary colors of red, blue, and yellow were particularly favored.

Pennsylvania tinware See TÔLEWARE.

Penny toy ■ A small toy made primarily in France and Germany in various materials from CAST METAL to wood, paper, TINPLATE, and CELLULOID, designed to be sold for a penny, usually by street vendors, between 1890 and 1935.

Penny wooden ■ Also known as a DUTCH PEG DOLL and produced in Germany and Austria since the 19th century, the Penny wooden is a roughly carved doll

Pembroke table
George III mahogany Pembroke table.

Square-section tapered and reeded legs

Pendelfin
"Squeezy Rabbit" Pendelfin figure, dressed in red. c. 1970.

Penny toy
German early lithographed tinplate "Early Flying Machine" Penny toy by Meier.

Penny wooden
American Penny wooden doll, with a painted face and jointed limbs. c. 1910.

P

284

with its head and torso in one piece, stick-like jointed arms and legs, crudely painted facial features, and center-parted black hair.

Pepperbox A pistol with four or more barrels revolving around a central pin. Pepperboxes first came into use around 1825 but became obsolete with the introduction of the true REVOLVER in 1836.

Percier, Charles (1764–1838) A French architect, interior designer, and decorator, who trained in Paris under the architect A. F. Peyre. In collaboration with Pierre-François-Léonard FONTAINE, Percier formulated the EMPIRE style in books, which were published in 1801. His studies of Classical and Renaissance architecture in Rome can be seen in his work. He became a set designer for the Paris Opéra, before joining Fontaine to create interiors and furniture for Napoleon I.

Percussion lock A system of ignition for firearms that uses a pressure-sensitive explosive compound, such as mercury fulminate, to set off the gunpowder charge. Percussion ignition was pioneered by the Reverend Alexander Forsyth from around 1800 to 1805. Copper percussion caps were available from about 1819 onward. The percussion cap revolutionized firearm design, paving the way for BREECH-LOADING and repeating guns.

Peridot ■ A yellowish green gemstone with a slightly "oily" luster found on St.

John Island in the Red Sea, Myanmar, and Australia. Formerly known as "olivine," peridot was a popular gemstone in VICTORIAN and ARTS AND CRAFTS gold jewelry, where it was frequently set with pearls.

Period A term referring to a distinct historical style or fashion, or used in a more general sense to refer to decorative arts displaying authentic features of a particular historical style. The Period Room, in which all the furnishings belong to one historical period, developed as part of museum displays in the late 19th century.

Perriand, Charlotte (1903–99) Influential French architect and designer best known for her work at LE CORBUSIER's studios, initially in the late 1920s and 1930s, where she made a major contribution to the introduction of a "Machine Age" aesthetic to interiors via her designs for steel, aluminum, and glass furniture.

Perry, Mary Chase See PEWABIC POTTERY.

Persian carpets ■ Persia (now Iran) is one of the most important countries for carpet-making. The golden age of carpet-weaving started in the 16th century under the Safavid dynasty (1501–1732). Persian carpet production continues today on a vast commercial scale. The earliest carpets are late 15th-century, from the city of Tabriz. These have a large medallion, often shaped

as a lotus flower, with stylized cloudbands (derived from Chinese art) and ARABESQUES. Some, called hunting carpets, show animals in combat. In the 17th century the city of ISFAHAN was the Islamic cultural center. Carpets displayed all-over designs of vine tendrils supporting large PALMETTES and saz leaves (shaped like the blade of a scythe). The background color was usually red in varying tones. In the city of Kirman in the 16th and 17th centuries, vase carpets, so called from their use of Chinese-style vases within an overall repeat of a vine lattice with palmettes and leaves, were produced. Another classic carpet is the "Polonaise," thought to have come from Poland, but in fact was made in Isfahan.

Fewer and poorer quality carpets were made in the 18th and early 19th centuries. But the mid-19th century boom in the European market and vogue for things Eastern led to a renewed interest. Town workshop-type carpets used curvilinear designs, emphasizing floral forms, palmettes, flowering vines and leaves, and sometimes people and exotic beasts. The format was either an overall repeat pattern or a central medallion design. Prayer rugs were also made, often including a tree of life. Tribal- and village-type production was quite different. Rugs were more often made than carpets because the looms were smaller (and more easily

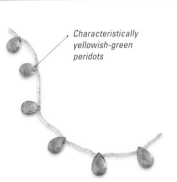

Characteristically yellowish-green peridots

Peridot
Victorian seed-pearl necklace, with peridot teardrops.

Persian carpets
Fine Ghashghai rug from southwest Persia. c. 1870.

Persian carpets
Tabriz prayer rug from northwest Persia. c. 1910.

Petit point
Louis XV walnut armchair, covered in 18th-century *gros* and *petit point* needlework.

transportable for nomadic tribes). Technical quality can vary. The best-known Persian tribes are the Afshar, the Khamseh, and the GHASHGHAI (Kashgai). Geometric designs were woven from memory along with stylized versions of the naturalistic town rugs.

Persian knot A knot (also called senneh or asymmetric knot) used extensively to create the pile in carpets from Central and Eastern Persia, India, and Central Asia.

Persian style Fascination for Persian art, particularly carpets, flourished in the West in the late 19th century and filtered into the decorative arts. The establishment of such firms as ZIEGLER & CO. exporting Persian goods to Europe and the US disseminated the Persian style, as did the exotic motifs illustrated in well-known pattern books such as Owen JONES's *Grammar of Ornament* (1856). MOTIFS such as serrated leaves, PALMETTES, cypress trees, pomegranates, peacocks, roses, carnations, and irises began to appear on Western carpets, textiles, and wallpapers; a characteristic Persian-influenced design is a brightly colored formalized pattern of leaves and flowers set against a cream or white ground, sometimes also used on ceramics and glass. Ceramic artists such as William DE MORGAN and French potter Eugène-Victor Collinot produced wares with floral designs and color schemes inspired by Persian or IZNIK ceramics.

Petit feu See ENAMEL COLORS.

Petit point Embroidery made up of short, finely worked stitches that generally cross only one warp or weft thread. *Petit point* is used to create upholstery, pictures, and cushions.

Petit, Jacob (1796–1865) A French porcelain-maker in Paris from around 1790, who copied MEISSEN but also had his own style. In the 1830s he acquired a factory at Belleville with his brother and bought the factory at Fontainebleau from Baruch Weil. Petit sold the latter in 1862. The mark "JP" was used at both factories on decorative wares, vases, and large figural scent bottles.

Petite sonnerie See STRIKING SYSTEMS.

Petuntse See CHINA STONE.

Pew group A primitive English STAFFORDSHIRE stoneware group, usually of three figures seated on a high-backed pew or bench and sometimes with an arched canopy overhead, made from around 1730 to the 1740s. The figures often wear "court" dress. Some examples are in white SALT GLAZE with details highlighted in dark brown; others have fine translucent green, ocher, and brown glazes. Pew groups are associated with John ASTBURY and Aaron WOOD.

Pewabic pottery An American ART POTTERY founded in Detroit, Michigan, in 1903 by Mary Chase Perry. The name is taken from a local Indian word for a river and means "copper color in clay." Pewabic specialized in matt-, iridescent-, or crystalline-glazed, thrown vases of robust shape with little decoration, as well as tiles and architectural ceramics. The pottery was active until the 1950s.

Pewter An alloy of tin and lead, often with small amounts of copper. Manufacture on a large scale developed in Europe from the Middle Ages. Durable, and much less expensive than silver or ceramics, pewter was mainly used for utilitarian domestic wares such as CHARGERS, FLAGONS, plates, tankards, and CANDLESTICKS. Not much early pewter has survived.

In the 16th century the French pewterer François Briot created ornate ewers and dishes decorated with MANNERIST ornament in low relief. "Display pewter" was also made in Germany at this time. Pewter was made in North America from the mid-17th century onward. Production of pewter declined in the 19th century with the introduction of BRITANNIA METAL and ELECTROPLATE. However, it enjoyed a revival in the ART NOUVEAU period—for example, in wares produced by WMF and KAYSER & SÖHNE in Germany, and the TUDRIC range of LIBERTY & CO. in England. Many pewter items are stamped with TOUCH MARKS.

Pezzato An Italian term for "patched." The name for a decorative glass technique

Petit, Jacob
French porcelain mantel clock, with an ornate base raised on bun feet. 19th century.

Pewabic pottery
Tall Pewabic baluster vase, covered in Persian blue mottled glaze.

Pewter
Philadelphia William Will pewter tankard, with a dome lid. Late 18th century.

Pezzato
Fulvio Bianconi-Venini Pezzato vase.

P

286

developed by VENINI in 1951. It is made up of large squares of colored and colorless glass, which are laid together in a patchwork pattern. These are then heated and fused together before being formed, while in a semimolten state, into an object such as a vase or bowl.

Phenakistoscope   A Greek term for "deceiving viewer." An optical toy invented in 1832 by Joseph Plateau that uses the principle of persistance of vision to create a "moving" image. A card or paper disk is printed with a number of slightly different images in successive actions, over which an identically sized disk with rectangular slots is laid. When spun at speed and viewed in a mirror, the images seen through the slots appear to show movement. See ZOETROPE.

Phonograph   A sound-recording and reproducing machine, invented by the American Thomas Edison in 1877. It uses a revolving wax cylinder to record vibrations caused by noise via a stylus attached to a diaphragm. Later variations such as the popular Gem played prerecorded cylinders, amplifying sound via a horn. See GRAMOPHONE.

Phrenology head ■   A representation of the head, usually ceramic, used in the 19th-century science of phrenology, a discredited nonscientific system that linked the conformation of the skull to character. The most famous phrenological heads were made by the American brothers Lorenzo and

Orson Fowler. Examples from the 19th-century are relatively scarce but have been much reproduced.

Phyfe, Duncan ■   This Scottish-born American furniture-maker was active in Brooklyn, New York City, from around 1792. He was one of the most prestigious and successful cabinet-makers of the Federal period, with over 100 employees operating from three premises at the height of his output around 1810.

Most of the furniture attributable to Duncan Phyfe is stylistically derived from English PATTERN BOOKS, particularly those of SHERATON and HEPPLEWHITE, which he typically rendered in the finest Honduras MAHOGANY, using elegant proportions and high-quality detail, especially in the carving. Phyfe's furniture tends to be more exuberant in form than the English prototypes. His success came at a time of rapid expansion in the US, particularly in New York, which by 1820 was the nation's largest city. New York's affluence made it ideal for furniture-makers and over 100 were active in the city by 1805, notably Michael ALLISON, who occupied premises a few streets away from Phyfe. Many, like

Allison, worked in the same style as Phyfe and it is difficult to attribute furniture directly to Phyfe's workshops, particularly as fewer than 20 labeled pieces exist, but his quality is outstanding. Phyfe was among the first American cabinet-makers to use factory assembly-line methods. He employed professional and apprentice carvers, turners, and upholsterers, each performing a specific task.

Piano baby (Piano doll) ■   A BISQUE FIGURE of a baby with molded hair and INTAGLIO eyes, intended for display on an upright piano. Most piano babies were produced by HEUBACH, between 1910 and 1920.

Picture back   A die-stamped image in low relief on the backs of the bowls of some late 18th-century silver spoons. Images included squirrels, birds, and flowers, or occasionally political or topical subjects.

Picture clock   A type of clock appearing on a tower, lighthouse, or windmill, in which the MOVEMENT is concealed behind a painting with a small aperture for the dial. They were made by BLACK

PHYFE, DUNCAN

Phyfe was always at the forefront of developing trends and interpreted them in a restrained, elegant way. Phyfe's name and his interpretation of the formal

English REGENCY style have remained popular in the US through extensive reproductions, which are generically referred to as "Duncan Phyfe style."

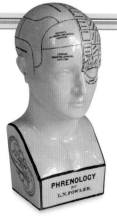

Phrenology head
Ceramic phrenology head, with annotated compartments. 19th century.

Phyfe, Duncan
Empire-style mahogany sofa, attributed to Duncan Phyfe. 1815–25.

Brass paws

FOREST clock-makers in the mid-19th century and often incorporate automata or musical work.

Piecrust A popular motif in the mid-18th century, typified by a multiple shaped and molded decorative edging, commonly seen on English furniture, especially circular tea tables, as well as silver SALVERS and STRAWBERRY DISHES.

Piecrust ware Pie dishes and TUREENS made in CANEWARE or a light brown EARTHENWARE, with the cover molded to simulate pastry. Piecrust ware was popular in England during the Napoleonic wars when wheat was in short supply and was made by various English factories, including WEDGWOOD. Piecrust borders also appeared on ceramic plates.

Pier A vertical, solid, often load-bearing masonry support found between window and door frames and other openings.

Pier glass ■ A tall, narrow mirror, popular in the 18th century, designed to hang on the wall between two windows (the PIER), often above a PIER TABLE.

Pier table A small side table designed to stand against a PIER—the wall between two windows. Fashionable from the 17th century, it was frequently surmounted by a PIER GLASS after the influential late 18th-century designs of the Scottish

architect Robert ADAM, who believed that furniture should be an integral part of the overall decorative scheme of a room. The table and mirror, which were designed to stand together, featured common decorative elements.

Pierced decoration Intricate OPENWORK decoration. The piercing was initially done with a sharp hand-chisel, then with a fretsaw, and finally by mechanical punches. The term also applies to the openwork carving of GOTHIC TRACERY, and in furniture, to the BAROQUE and ROCOCO detailing of chair backs, CRESTINGS, and APRONS. A popular metalware technique, pierced decoration was frequently interspersed with engraved and chased designs on silver baskets. It also served a functional purpose for strainers, caster covers, mustard pots, and salt cellars. Pottery and porcelain, especially pot pourri vases and bouquetières, were also decorated with pierced designs from the 18th century onward.

Pierotti Together with Augusta MONTANARI, Pierotti was the best-known manufacturer of poured WAX DOLLS in the middle of the 19th century. The family business was established in London around 1790 by the Italian Domenico Pierotti and was continued by successive generations until after 1925. The Pierottis were exceptionally skilled wax-modelers and were particularly famous for their

lifelike portrait dolls. Pierotti dolls often have a slightly turned head and tend to have shorter hair and more slender limbs than their Montanari counterparts.

Pietra dura ■ An Italian term meaning HARDSTONES, such as jasper, LAPIS LAZULI, AGATE, and chalcedony. *Pietra dura* was an expensive form of inlay, using thin slivers from a variety of semiprecious stones, and was initially reserved for small decorative objects. A highly developed technique in ancient Rome, it was revived during the Renaissance in Italy and perfected in the early 17th century. The most famous center of production was the Ducal workshops in Florence under the patronage of the Medicis, but Italian craftsmen also spread the technique farther afield in Europe. *Pietra dura* was lavishly employed for large vases, ewers, and bowls extravagantly mounted with gold, and for furniture such as table tops and display cabinets.

Piggin ■ A small, cylindrical drinking vessel, made of glass, ceramic, or silver in the shape of a half-barrel with a vertical stave for a handle. Glass versions were often used as dippers for milk and cream.

Pilaster An architectural term for a shallow pier or rectangular Classical column attached to a facade for decoration rather than structural support. Popular during periods of Classical revival, the pilaster generally appears along with other architectural MOTIFS such as

Piano baby (Piano doll)
Gebrüder Heubach Piano Baby, the tinted bisque doll in a seated pose.

Pier glass
Queen Anne giltwood and gesso pier glass, with shell and harebell molded frame.

Pietra dura
Pietra dura-mounted rectangular *bijouterie* box, with floral inlaid panels.

Piggin
Irish piggin, with diamond-cut bowl, serrated rim, and star-cut base. c. 1810.

P

ENTABLATURE and a flattened version of the appropriate column CAPITAL. Pilasters were carved on Tudor and Jacobean chests and bed heads, and in the 18th century they framed the doors of cabinets and cupboards, FLUTED with Corinthian or Composite capitals.

Pile The surface of a carpet when made with strands of wool, cotton, or silk that are secured to a foundation, tufted, and trimmed to the desired depth, which is determined by the fineness of the weave.

Pilgrim bottle A pottery gourd-shaped bottle with two loops at the sides for a strap to be threaded through to suspend the bottle. In primitive times they were made from goat skin, but they were later made in Italian MAIOLICA and silver. Pilgrim bottles were made all over Europe from the 16th century and sometimes decorated with a shell—the sign of a pilgrim.

Pilgrim chair A term used generically in the US to describe a stick-constructed, open armchair with a rush-woven seat and turned elements, comparable to provincial English chairs of the 17th and 18th centuries. Indigenous woods such as MAPLE, ASH, and hickory were used. The back pieces could be either turned or slats and the turned spindles and finials simple or elaborate. Generally, more massive turnings indicate an earlier date of production.

Pilgrim furniture An American term for furniture made for the first Puritan settlers in New England in the 17th century. Simply and solidly constructed, pilgrim furniture typically mirrors English furniture styles. Pieces were made from white oak and American ash, which were in plentiful supply.

Pilkington's Tile & Pottery Company ■ Known as Pilkington's and sometimes Royal Lancastrian (from 1913), the factory was founded near Manchester in 1891 by the Pilkington brothers to make architectural ceramics. They extended their range to include domestic vessels with distinctive glazes: Sunstone (1893), Eggshell (1896), luster (1906), mottled and matt "Cunian" (1927–28), and Lapis wares (1928). The company ceased making decorative ceramics in 1937 but continues to make tiles today.

Pillar-and-claw table See TRIPOD TABLE.

Pin box A porcelain box made in Europe during the late 19th and early 20th centuries. The covers often have FAIRING-type figures or animals. They were inexpensive SOUVENIR WARES.

Pinchbeck ■ An alloy of copper and zinc that closely resembles gold in appearance. It was invented in the early 18th century by Christopher Pinchbeck, a Fleet Street watchmaker, and was used to make jewelry and small items such as snuff boxes and shoe buckles until around 1854 when the sale of lower-carat gold became legal.

Pine ■ A straight-grained softwood, colored yellow or white, of the genus *Pinus*. The term frequently designates other coniferous woods such as fir, larch, and cedar. Ranging from relatively hard to very soft, pine was widely used by English furniture-makers from the early 17th century, especially for the linings and sides of drawers, the backs of carcasses, and as a foundation for gilding or veneers made of more expensive timbers. In the US, Scandinavia, and in Alpine areas, pine was the preferred wood for vernacular furniture and for cheaper pieces of furniture that was subsequently painted.

Pineapple motif ■ An ancient motif symbolizing fertility. From the late 17th century the pineapple motif appeared in both Europe and the US, used primarily on entrance architecture, such as gateposts, on guest beds, and as a table centerpiece. Cultivated as an exotic fruit in the 17th century after it was presented to Charles II by his royal gardener, John Rose, the pineapple is sometimes confused with pine-cone ornament. Decorative silver cups for display were made in the form of pineapples in 17th-century Germany. During the ROCOCO period the pineapple was typically appropriated for finials on furniture and silver. Josiah WEDGWOOD produced a range of tableware based on the pineapple form in the mid-18th century.

Pilkington's Tile & Pottery Co.
Vase by Gordon M. Forsyth, painted in ruby and copy luster, with bell flowers. 1912.

Pinchbeck
Shield brooch, with floral motifs, tassels, and emerald-paste cabochons. c. 1840.

Pine
Pine washstand, with two towel bars and original yellow paint on the rear. c. 1870.

Pineapple motif
Detail of majolica teapot cover, molded as a pineapple. 19th century.

Pinfire action A BREECH-LOADING firearm using a self-contained CARTRIDGE that incorporated a pin in its base. When this was struck by the hammer, it set off a percussion cap and fired the gun. The pinfire system was invented by Casimir LeFaucheaux in 1835, and although obsolete by around 1870, it survived into the early 20th century.

Pinion A small, toothed wheel acting as a gear in a clock MOVEMENT. The pinions, usually made of iron or steel but sometimes wood or brass, engage with larger wheels in the TRAIN.

Pinxton Porcelain Factory ■ An English factory founded near Derby in 1796 by William BILLINGSLEY with the help, and on the estate, of John Coke. They made a fine soft paste, copied shapes from DERBY and WORCESTER, and sometimes decorated wares with flowers and landscapes, some by Billingsley himself. The partnership was dissolved in 1799. John Coke carried on but closed the factory in 1813.

Pipe stopper ■ A pipe-smoker's tool (also called a pipe tamper) with a flat or rounded end used for pressing tobacco into the bowl of a pipe. It was made from the 17th century onward in various materials and forms.

Pique ■ A decoration (also called *piqué d'or*) on TORTOISESHELL or IVORY, developed in the mid-17th century by the Neapolitan jeweler Laurentini and used throughout the 19th century in jewelry, snuff boxes, and ÉTUIS. Small studs and strips of gold or silver were inlaid on the base material and secured in place by heating.

Pistol handle A style of knife shaft or handle that tapers outward from the blade end and curves around at the other end rather like the grip of a pistol. Produced from around 1715 to the end of the century, pistol handles can be plain or octagonal in section and made of silver, porcelain, ivory, or wood. The grip was occasionally found on forks.

Pitting The term used to describe the numerous, small, random indentations that can appear like pinpricks on the surface of metals such as chrome, certain plastics, and other materials. Pitting can be caused by corrosion or usage and is not usually removable.

Pivot A small spindle or shaft, usually made of steel, on which a wheel or pinion of the TRAIN in a clock or watch MOVEMENT rotates.

Plane A yellow-white, close-grained, durable wood. A variety of maple from Eastern Europe, plane was primarily used as an INLAY and VENEER in the 18th century. It was also used in country furniture for painted chairs and folding tables as a substitute for BEECH. A lacy FIGURE (known as lacewood) appears when it is quarter-sawn, which was popular in the ART DECO period.

Planetarium An expansion of the ORRERY, the planetarium is a complex instrument, often made of brass, which demonstrates the motions of the Sun, Moon, and planets. Ivory balls representing the planets are supported on wires with long rods attached to a central pivot and the instrument is generally cranked around by hand.

Planishing From the French *planir* (to smooth out). The action of giving a smooth or flat surface to a sheet of metal by using rollers or, more commonly, beating it with a planishing hammer (one with a broad, smooth, polished head) while the metal is supported on a stake.

Plank, Ernst ■ One of the most important 19th-century German manufacturers of TINPLATE toys, founded in 1866 in Nuremberg. The company was possibly the first to make a tinplate electric train in 1882. Steam trains, then clockwork, followed from 1890. Steam- and clockwork-driven boats were popular products, with steam cars produced from 1904. The initials "E.P." were used on many of its toys. The company was also well known for its production of MAGIC LANTERNS, particularly small versions for children.

Pinxton Porcelain Factory
Pinxton oval spoon tray, with gilt-lined rim and painted landscape scene. c. 1800.

Pipe stopper
Boxwood pipe stopper in the form of a greyhound. c. 1740.

Pique
Oval tortoiseshell snuff box, with gold pique-work decoration. c. 1715.

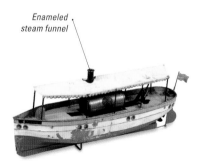

Enameled steam funnel

Plank, Ernst
German Ernst Plank hand-painted, steam-powered Jupiter river boat.

It was taken over in 1930, after which toy production ceased.

Plastic ■ From the Greek *plastikos* (plastic). A term applied to materials that can be molded and shaped. Although natural plastics such as tortoiseshell and shellac exist, plastics are primarily synthetic materials. The 19th century saw the birth of semisynthetic and synthetic plastics with CELLULOID, xylonite, and casein, but BAKELITE, invented in 1907 by the Belgian chemist Leo Baekland, is credited with being the first important completely synthetic plastic. Bakelite's patent expired in 1927, and from then until the late 1940s, plastics helped to free the world from the dominance of wood, ceramics, and metal, and ushered in a new age of style. This was linked with an increasing interest in design, and many plastic objects display key elements from ART DECO and Industrial Design movements.

Many famous 20th-century designers, including René LALIQUE, Henry DREYFUSS, Walter Dorwin Teague, Raymond Loewy, and Wells Coates, designed plastic objects. One household object that benefited from the invention of plastic was the radio—a simple wooden case changed to one of brightly colored Catalin (a phenolic resin) or Bakelite in a variety of modern and stylish designs. Domestic objects as well as desk accessories and jewelry were also made from an ever-increasing range of colored plastics. The adaptability to carving and casting and the low cost of plastics made them popular during the Depression years of the 1930s and later. After World War II the nature of plastics changed with the introduction of injection molding, acrylic, polythene, and VINYL (used particularly in toymaking). But public taste also changed, and the golden age of plastics was over.

Plate 1. An abbreviated form of SHEFFIELD PLATE. 2. A descriptive term corrupted from the Spanish *plata* to describe wrought gold and silver wares. 3. A shallow, usually circular, dish of any material on which food is served.

Plate bucket ■ A bucket-shaped wooden container with a brass handle, used for carrying plates between the kitchen and the dining room in 18th-century houses. Also called plate pails, plate buckets sometimes had fretwork sides to facilitate warming and a slot or open section for ready access to the plates.

Plate cameras ■ The term for any camera that uses a fixed, light-sensitive film or glass plate. Plate cameras date from about 1840, Louise Daguerre developed the sliding box camera. These were comprised of two rigid wooden boxes, one smaller than the other, and a brass-bound lens. The smaller box slid in and out of the larger one to focus the image. Collapsible fabric or leather bellows were introduced in 1851, and by 1855 folding plate cameras that could be folded flat had been introduced. The back of these cameras held a removable focusing screen and a wooden film plate. This held a glass plate that was coated with iodized collodion and sensitized with a solution of silver nitrate just before the photograph was to be taken. This time-consuming and time-sensitive process, called wet-plate photography, was practiced from about 1840 until the late 1870s.

Prepared dry-plate cameras were used from about 1878 after an English physician, Richard Leach Maddox, suggested the use of gelatin emulsions in 1871, instead of collodion, which gave off harmful vapor. By 1880, gelatin dry plates were on sale, and they were used widely for the next 70 years. The roll-film camera, introduced by George EASTMAN's Kodak in 1889, gradually replaced plate cameras by the 20th century. See Box BROWNIE.

Platform lever escapement A type of ESCAPEMENT in clocks, similar to the LEVER ESCAPEMENT in watches, that incorporates an oscillating balance wheel instead of a pendulum. From the early 19th century it was commonly mounted on a platform on the top of a CARRIAGE CLOCK. It enabled the clock to keep accurate time while in transit as it was not affected by movement.

Platinum ■ A silvery white metal more valuable than silver and gold because of its rarity. Discovered in Mexico in the 16th century, it was only used in Europe from the

Plastic
Italian Danese Pogo Pogo injection-molded ABS plastic vase. 1970s.

Plate bucket
Oak and brass-bound plate bucket, with a swing handle. c. 1800.

Plate cameras
Mahogany and brass folding plate camera, by Helios & Co. of Oxford Street, London.

19th century, reaching a high point in the ART DECO period when it was popular as a setting for diamonds. Malleable and ductile with high tensile strength, it is usually alloyed with palladium, another metal of the platinum family.

PLIQUE À JOUR

A technique by which translucent enamel is held in an unbacked framework to produce an effect similar to that of a stained glass window when light shines through it. It was developed in Russia during the 17th century and was used extensively by the jewelers of the ART NOUVEAU style.

Plique à jour
Floral Art Nouveau motif pendant, with silver-set *plique-à-jour*, clear crystal rhinestones, and faceted pink glass stones. c. 1900.

Playing cards ■ Thought to originate in ancient China, playing cards reached Europe via the Islamic Empire around 1380. The now standard pack of 52 cards evolved from a 16th-century French design. They gradually became more decorative and many idiosyncratic packs were produced in England in the 17th and 18th centuries. Germany and Austria were the chief 19th-century producers of playing cards.

Playworn ("loved") A euphemism for poor condition when describing the appearance of a TEDDY BEAR.

Pleydell-Bouverie, Katherine See STUDIO POTTERY.

Plum A FRUITWOOD of the *Prunus* genus, yielding a hard and heavy pinkish wood with a heart of deep brownish red. Plumwood was used from the 16th century for INLAY and turned work and for country CABINET furniture but fell out of fashion after the 17th century.

Plush ■ A soft natural material from the mountain goat (mohair plush) with cut pile that resembles fur, used to make TEDDY BEARS from the early 20th century. It was also used for late-19th-century tablecloths.

Plymouth porcelain The first HARD-PASTE PORCELAIN, made by a chemist William COOKWORTHY, by combining KAOLIN and CHINA STONE, in 1768 at Plymouth. Cookworthy was not an expert at

firing and the wares sometimes show distortion and a smoky, spotted glaze. In 1770 the factory moved to Castle Green, Bristol, and in 1774 it was taken over by Richard CHAMPION and ceased to be called Plymouth.

Plymouth Pottery Company Founded by William Alsop, this pottery in Plymouth, England, made blue-printed earthenware, marked with the Queen's Arms from 1856 to 1863.

Plywood A composition wood of three or more layers, each layer laid with the grain at right angles to the previous layer for strength. Used in furniture-making from the 18th century, it was appreciated by BIEDERMEIER craftsmen in Germany and Austria, who developed it in BENTWOOD chair backs in the 19th century. Plywood was popular into the 20th century, particularly in the US.

Pocket watch ■ The first watch small enough to be carried in a pocket, made around 1550. Early watches were more decorative than useful. With the introduction of the balance spring in 1675, the pocket watch became accurate enough to be used as a timekeeper. It was attached to a waistcoat with a FOB CHAIN from the early 19th century.

Point de neige A French word for "stitch of snow." Late 17th-century VENETIAN NEEDLE LACE with small-

P
291

Platinum
One of a pair of platinum- and diamond-set scroll-fan ear clips. 1930s.

Playing cards
Two playing cards, depicting a European monarch and a royal residence. c. 1890.

Plush
Gold plush Steiff bear, with original tag. 1950s.

Pocket watch
Patek Phillipe 18-carat gold open-faced pocket watch, with gold numerals. c. 1920.

scale design incorporating stylized scrolling and floral motifs, used for items such as gentlemen's cravats, ladies' headdresses, and LAPPETS.

P

Poker work Also known as *pyrogravure* or pyrography, the craft of creating formal patterns and pictorial scenes on light-colored wood such as holly, maple, chestnut, or linden, by scorching the surface with hot metal rods or needles. A decorative technique practiced from the 17th century in Italy, it was especially popular with artistic amateurs and ladies of leisure during the 19th century.

Polearm A weapon made up of a blade, head, or spike (sometimes elaborately worked) mounted on a wooden shaft. In the late 17th century, polearms were superseded by firearms, but they were carried by officers as symbols of rank until the early 19th century.

Polescreen ■ An adjustable FIRESCREEN on a pole with a platform or tripod base. The screen may be moved vertically and locked at various heights. In general use from around 1730 to protect the user from the heat of a fire.

Polyphon Musikwerke ■ A German manufacturer of clocks and clockwork music boxes, established in 1889 by Gustave Brachhausen. Polyphon Musikwerke produced clocks with

disc movements that were often coin-operated. Its music boxes included tabletop 15-, 19 5/8-, 22-, and 24-inch disc models in upright cabinets, often with disc bins beneath for storage. Larger examples were often free-standing and also coin-operated. The company is still in operation today.

Pomander ■ From medieval Latin *pomum ambrae*, and from Old French *pomme d'ambre* (apple of amber). A small container, usually spherical, made of silver gilt, gold, ceramic, and metal from the 16th century to the present day. These containers are divided into compartments for holding scents and spices. Originally worn on a chain, they were thought to protect the wearer from infections and diseases.

Pomegranate motif ■ A decorative Oriental and Classical device based on the fruit of the pomegranate tree, believed to symbolize fertility and plenty. Used in wood-carving, plasterwork, textiles, and silver, the pomegranate was a favorite naturally rendered motif in England during the JACOBEAN period and enjoyed a revival in the late 19th century.

Pomona glass A type of American MOLD-BLOWN, ART GLASS of colorless glass that was stained with colors (typically amber) and partly acid-etched before being decorated with amber or blue flowers and vines. Made by the NEW ENGLAND GLASS COMPANY, Pomona was developed by

Joseph LOCKE in 1884, patented in 1885, and mostly employed for stemware. The name was also used as a color—Pomona green—by the STEUBEN GLASSWORKS.

Pompeiian style A variant of the NEOCLASSICAL STYLE popular from the late 18th to the mid-19th century, inspired by antiquities and frescoes excavated at the ancient Italian cities of Pompeii and Herculaneum in the 18th century. The style is characterized by the use of a deep red color, called Pompeiian red, and delicate Neoclassical motifs such as PATERAE, HUSKS, and PALMETTES. It is found on SÈVRES porcelain made in the 1840s and 50s (though not always on Classically inspired forms), as well as on textiles, wallpapers, and painted furniture.

Ponti, Gio ■ (1891–1979) An Italian architect and designer of ceramics (for Richard Ginori from 1923 to 1930), furniture, textiles, lighting, and glass (for VENINI). Ponti was also a professor of architecture and a contributor to the magazines *Stile*, *Casabella*, and *Domus*, which he founded in 1928. As a designer Ponti drew on Italy's Classical heritage but combined it with MODERN design and all the advantages that modern industrialization had to offer, managing to maintain a balance between all aspects. Among his most celebrated furniture designs are the Superleggera chair for Cassina (1957) and his many designs in

Turned and leaf-carved support

Polescreen
Regency ebonized and parcel-gilt polescreen, with a panel depicting a young lady.

Polyphon Musikwerke
German walnut polyphon, playing interchangeable metal discs. c. 1870.

Pomander
George II pomander, the upper half with reticulated design and engraved crest. c. 1727.

Pomegranate motif
Pomegrante motif on "Vine and Pomegranate" wool curtain.

POOLE POTTERY

An English pottery in Poole, Dorset, founded by Jesse Carter, a potter and tilemaker. It became known as Carters in 1901, and in 1921, a subsidiary company known as Carter, Stabler & Adams, after the principal designers, was formed to make domestic artistic ceramics, hand-thrown and hand-decorated, often with stylized floral motifs in deep, subtle colors with predominant blue. The company went into receivership in 2006 and has since been bought out.

Vase
Carter, Stabler & Adams Ltd. earthenware vase, with "Leaping Deer" pattern, designed by Truda Carter. 1934–37.

mediums of advertising and comic books, and often emphasized the KITSCH or banal aspects of popular culture.

Poplar ■ A creamy white to yellowish gray softwood, commonly chosen for inlay in the 16th and early 17th centuries. It was sometimes stained before use to create decorative MARQUETRY for the veneers of cabinets, chests, and chests-of-drawers.

Porcelain Porcelain was first produced in China and is recorded as early as the Sui (581–671) and Tang (618–907) dynasties. The translucency of the ceramic material is the most distinctive feature of Chinese porcelain. Efforts to imitate Chinese porcelain in Europe led first to the development of SOFT-PASTE PORCELAIN, made from white clay and ground glass, before the true HARD-PASTE recipe was discovered in 1709 at MEISSEN. BONE CHINA, patented in 1748, is similar but has pure white BONE ASH added to the clay. Not much porcelain was made in the US before the 19th century. Porcelain is made from KAOLIN (china clay), QUARTZ, and FELDSPAR. In European hard-paste porcelain, the proportions are 40–65 percent kaolin, 12–30 percent quartz, and 15–35 percent feldspar. The feldspar and quartz act as a FLUX—they make the kaolin less plastic and reduce the firing and drying shrinkage.

collaboration with Piero FORNASETTI during the 1940s and 50s.

Pontil mark ■ An irregular or ring-shaped mark made on the base of a blown glass when the piece is taken off the PONTIL ROD.

Pontil rod The solid metal rod onto which the base of a part-formed glass piece is mounted using a GOB of molten glass so that the top can be worked and the piece completed. At this point, the glass piece is also removed from the blowing iron rod, which is typically attached to the top of the piece.

Pontypool ware A type of JAPANNED tinplated iron produced at the Pontypool

factory, founded by the Allgood family in Monmouthshire, Wales, from around 1680 to 1822. Wares typically included trays, boxes, and urns JAPANNED in black, brown, or tortoiseshell colors and hand-painted or gilded with CHINOISERIE, flowers, and later, landscapes and sporting scenes. Pontypool gave its name to similar wares made elsewhere.

Pop Art An art movement that emerged in Britain and the United States during the mid- to late 1950s, and spread to many other countries, most notably Spain and Japan. A reaction to abstract expressionism and elitism Pop Art, it was characterized by a return to a more readily understood representational art. For imagery and technique, Pop Art drew heavily on the

Ponti, Gio
Superleggera dining chair, with two horizontal backslats.

Pontil mark
Piontil mark on the base of a Murano zanfirico goblet.

Poplar
Pennsylvania tulip poplar corner cupboard, with bracket feet. c. 1830.

Porcelain flowers See VINCENNES.

Porcellaneous A porcelain-type stoneware made in China from the 6th century CE. It is like porcelain but less translucent. The Chinese do not distinguish between the two, calling both *ci* (tz'u). It was also made in Europe, particularly in the 19th century.

Porphyry From the Greek *porphyros* (purple). A hard volcanic rock, the color variations of which include gray, green, and red, but which is best known as the brownish purple porphyry found only near Mount Porphyrites in Egypt. Mined by the Romans, it became known as "Imperial Porphyry" because purple was the color of royalty and the emperors. It was employed in numerous prestigious building projects and monuments throughout the Roman and Byzantine empires. During the Renaissance, especially in Florence, many ancient pieces of porphyry were reworked into prestigious artifacts such as fonts and sarcophagi. In the late 19th century the Egyptian mines were reopened and new pieces of "Roman-style" porphyry came onto the market.

Porringer From the French *potager* (soup bowl). 1. A two-handled, cylindrical, slightly tapering cup with a curved base, with or without a cover. Made in silver, pewter, or ceramics from about 1650 to 1750, for soup. 2. In the US, a porringer is a shallow vessel with a flat, pierced handle. A similar vessel is called a BLEEDING BOWL in the UK. See CAUDLE CUP.

Portland Vase ■ The finest Roman CAMEO-GLASS vase surviving from antiquity and an important influence on English glass and ceramics manufacturers from the late 18th century. Made between the 1st century BCE and the 1st century CE, it was found in the late 16th century in a Classical tomb in Rome, from where it passed into the ownership of the Barberini family and was brought to London in 1784 by Sir William Hamilton, ambassador to the Court of Naples and an avid collector of artifacts. He, in turn, sold the vase to the Dowager Duchess of Portland (hence its name). In 1810 her son, the 4th Duke of Portland, lent the vase to the British Museum in London, where it remains today. From 1790 it was copied in JASPER WARE by the WEDGWOOD factory. An exact copy in cameo glass was not made until 1876, after 20 years of experiments by John NORTHWOOD. Other copies in cameo glass soon followed.

Portmeirion pottery ■ Named after the unique Italianate vacation village in North Wales—the setting for the cult TV series *The Prisoner*—Portmeirion tableware encapsulated the style and spirit of the 1960s. Founded between 1960 and 1961 by Susan Williams-Ellis and her husband, Euan Cooper-Willis, the company produced numerous, highly innovative TRANSFER-PRINTED patterns, mostly comprising abstract and geometric forms, and in many respects resembling textile designs. Notable examples include: "Totem" (1963 and re-launched in 2002); "Talisman" (1962); Black Diamond (1963); "Tivoli" (1964, named after the Tivoli Gardens in Copenhagen, Denmark); "Monte Sol" (1965, inspired by Oriental and Hispano-Moresque textiles); and "Moss Agate," dating to the early 1960s and inspired by engravings found in an 18th-century geological study showing different varieties and colors of the semiprecious stone moss agate.

Portrait doll ■ A doll that portrays a person, either real or fictitious, made by leading manufacturers from about 1870. Perhaps the most sought-after 20th-century

POSTER

Although letterpress posters have existed since the 15th century, posters as we now know them today date from the invention of LITHOGRAPHY in the 1860s.

Poster
Dubonnet poster, by Cassandre. 1950.

Poster
Zodiac poster, by Alphonse Mucha. 1896.

Portland Vase
Copy of the Portland Vase, the Classical figures in relief against the deep blue glaze. 19th century.

example is a doll depicting Queen Elizabeth II of Great Britain, age four, made in 1930 by Schönau and Hoffmeister and later by CHAD VALLEY and others.

Posset pot ■ A drinking vessel for posset (hot milk mixed with beer or wine and spices), made of TIN-GLAZED EARTHENWARE or GLASS with double handles, a cover, and a spout from which the posset was drunk. It was made in both England and Holland from the 16th to the 18th century.

Postcard The world's first postcard was issued by the Austrian Post Office on October 1, 1869, and in 1872, when the German Post Office allowed privately printed cards, the first picture postcards were published. The golden age of postcards is considered to be from 1902 to World War I, when the majority were printed by chromolithography or photographic methods. Today, collectors seek vintage examples from that era as well as more modern cards, particularly those featuring events and personalities that sum up the spirit of their time.

Poster ■ Brightly colored images could be printed cheaply and easily, leading to the production of commercial posters. The French artist Jules CHERET produced over a thousand poster designs, while Henri de TOULOUSE-LAUTREC, whose posters have now achieved the status of fine art, designed only 31, creating a series of

powerful images of Parisian night life in the 1890s. In the same period Alphonse MUCHA developed a series of extravagant ART NOUVEAU designs, initially for the theater, then for consumer products such as cigarettes and chocolate. Across Europe the style was adopted by such designers as T. Privat-Livemont in Belgium and Jan Toorop in Austria. The advent of World War I in 1914 saw the poster evolve into a propaganda tool for the military.

After World War I, the great age of automotive travel arrived. Posters promoted cars, trains, planes, and the latest routes offered by the great ocean liners such as the *Lusitania* and the ill-fated *Titanic* as well as immigrant shipping lines to Australia and New Zealand. Artists such as CASSANDRE and Ludwig HOHLWEIN created images that spoke volumes, and the power of the poster as an effective means of mass communication was realized in the way that we know it today. The poster continues to be judged as a work of graphic art and such examples as Bernard Villemot's work for the Swiss shoe company Bally in the 1970s are considered outstanding. In the category of movie posters, the impact of the movie is what determines value, as designers work "in house" and are consequently anonymous. Posters of classic films such as *The Mummy* (1932) and *Casablanca* (1942) have grown in popularity. More recently, Clint Eastwood's "cop" movies such as *Magnum Force* (1973) have produced striking posters, which look likely to become the antiques of the future.

Post-Modernism A style initiated in the late 1970s to the early 1980s in opposition to the stark surface content of Modernism. Generally, it aims to use ornament, past or present, to enhance furniture, furnishings, and architecture, and create, in the words of Robert VENTURI, "messy vitality over obvious unity." Italy was at the forefront of the Post-Modern style, with the work of Studio Alchimia and the MEMPHIS group leading the way.

Posy rings Originating in the 15th century and given as tokens of love (also called "poesy rings"). Early examples are simple gold bands with an engraved inscription such as "A loving wife, a happy life" or "God above increase our love."

Pot lid ■ A cover of a shallow circular or oblong earthenware box, dating from the 1840s to 1920s. These boxes held substances such as hair grease and ointments. The covers were transfer printed in colors or, rarely, in black and white, with a great variety of subjects (almost 300 have been estimated). There were numerous makers, but many of the best lids were PRATTWARE.

Pot metal See BASE METAL.

Potash glass A type of glass in which potash instead of soda has been used as the alkaline ingredient in the BATCH. The resulting glass, known as WALDGLAS in Germany and Bohemia and VERRE DE FOUGÈRE in France, was harder and more

P

295

Portmeirion pottery
Pair of Portmeirion "Talisman" pattern storage jars, transfer-printed. c. 1962.

Silk and velvet with tassel passementerie

Portrait doll
Jumeau portrait head doll on a shoulder plate attached to a kid leather body.

Posset pot
English delftware blue and white posset pot, inscribed "EIP" and dated "1689."

Pot lid
Staffordshire "Lady Brushing Hair" pot lid.

brilliant than SODA GLASS and better suited to cutting and engraving. See BOHEMIAN GLASS.

Potschappel See THIEME, Carl.

P

Pottery The craft of making wares from clay, developed from around 6000 BCE in the ancient Middle East. By about 3500 BCE the techniques of FIRING and using the wheel and turntable had been introduced, with LEAD GLAZES recorded in Mesopotamia from around 2000 BCE. These techniques spread to the Greek world, giving rise to Attic wares by 600 BCE. In China, pottery enriched by Greek influences dates from the Han dynasty (206 BCE– 220 CE). European pottery was fairly primitive until the Middle Ages and the arrival of Oriental and Islamic influences. The process of adding tin oxide to the basic lead glaze led to a form of TIN-GLAZED EARTHENWARE, brought by the Moorish invaders to Spain, resulting in the production of HISPANO-MORESQUE wares. Further developments included Italian MAIOLICA, French FAIENCE, German fayence, and by the mid-16th century, Dutch and British DELFTWARE. In the mid-17th century, Europeans took their pottery skills to the New World.

The craze for porcelain that swept the Western world from the early 18th century did not halt the development of the pottery industry. The simplicity of early forms was later rediscovered by ART and STUDIO POTTERS.

Pouffe A backless upholstered seat resembling a large round cushion with a wooden frame. It first appeared in France around 1845 and remained popular throughout the late 19th and 20th centuries.

Pounce 1. A fine powder of gum sandarach (pine resin) or cuttlefish bone, sprinkled on writing paper or parchment both before and after writing to prevent the ink from spreading, used from the Middle Ages until the end of the 18th century. 2. A form of stippled decoration made by pricking or hammering with a sharp pointed instrument onto SILVER, PEWTER, and other metals.

Pounce box A box (also called pot) with a PIERCED cover, made of silver or wood (TREEN) for POUNCE, either produced singly or fitted to silver or pewter INKSTANDS in the 17th and 18th centuries.

Poupard A French word for "baby doll." An all-in-one skittlelike doll, carved from a single piece of wood and painted to represent a baby in swaddling clothes. These dolls were made throughout Europe from the late 17th century onward.

Powder flask ■ A container with loose gunpowder in MUZZLE-loading guns from the early 18th century. Originally, leather bags were used, but it was soon found that cows' horns were safer. Flasks were later made in wood, metal, antler, and ivory. Most incorporate a spout, which measures the correct gunpowder charge. From 1800 to 1850, flasks were made from die-stamped metal, often incorporating decorative motifs. The metallic CARTRIDGE superseded powder flasks in the 1860s.

Powder-blue A traditional Chinese decorative technique for ceramics where, as an UNDERGLAZE decoration, powdered pigment is blown through a gauze onto an oiled surface, giving a fine, grainy appearance or effect. It was imitated in Europe from the 18th century, especially at MEISSEN, SÈVRES, BOW, and WORCESTER.

Powder-decorated glass A type of ART GLASS, patented in 1806 by the 19th-century Staffordshire earthenware and porcelain-maker John Davenport of Longport, also known as Davenport's Patent Glass. A paste of powdered glass was applied to an object and a design incised into it, commonly of a sporting scene or coat of arms. This was then fused onto the glass in the furnace. Powder-decorated glass was very fashionable; in 1806 and 1808 the Prince of Wales ordered extensive sets. It was made until 1811.

Powell, James & Sons See WHITEFRIARS GLASSWORKS.

Powolny, Michael ■ (1871–1954) An Austrian ceramicist and sculptor and one of the founders of the SECESSION and WIENER WERKSTÄTTE movements.

Powder flask
Silver-mounted Continental carved horn powder flask. 18th century.

Powolny, Michael
Figure of a boy riding a snail, by Michael Powolny. 1907.

Hand-painted polychrome decoration

Prattware
Prattware teapot. c. 1800.

Prayer rug
Silk Isfahan prayer rug, with a blue vase and palmettes and scrolling foliate vines.

Powolny specialized in white FAIENCE figures painted in black in Secession style, and influenced Austrian, British, and American ceramics of the 1930s, both as a teacher (Lucie RIE was a pupil) and a craftsman.

Prattware ◼ A type of pottery made at Lane Delph in Staffordshire at a factory founded around 1775 by William Pratt. It was copied by other factories such as BRISTOL. Prattware is similar to PEARLWARE, but is characterized by a strong high-temperature palette of blue, green, and yellow. In the mid-1840s the same factory, styled F. R. Pratt & Co., excelled in multicolored TRANSFER PRINTING, used to decorate tableware and POT LIDS until the 1880s.

Praxinoscope An optical toy (a development on the ZOETROPE) popular in the 19th century and patented by Charles Émile Reynaud in 1877. It consists of a cylindrical or polygonal box, which is open at the top, with a series of pictures printed on a paper band that is placed around the inside. Mirrors on a faceted central column inside the box reflect the images of the pictures. When the box is rotated, the reflections in the mirrors blend together, giving an illusion of movement. Subjects included galloping horses or somersaulting clowns. The praxinoscope is found in a variety of models, both hand-operated and

linked to a toy stationary steam engine, and topped by either a candle or an alcohol burner. They continued to be made until the early 20th century.

Prayer rug ◼ A name that refers both to a functional artifact used by Muslims and to a decorative design on a carpet. The composition is always directional and asymmetrical. Prayer rugs are made in curvilinear form in cities and in rectilinear form by tribal groups. When the rug is used, the pointed end of the MIHRAB is aligned in the direction of Mecca.

Preiss, Ferdinand (1882–1943) A Berlin-based ivory carver and sculptor. In 1906 he formed the company Preiss-Kassler, which produced bronze and ivory CHRYSELEPHANTINE figures in the Classical style. It closed during World War I but reopened in 1919, producing bronze and ivory statuettes in the ART DECO style in the 1920s and 30s. Typical subjects include athletic young women in elegant and graceful poses mounted on marble.

Press ◼ An archaic English term for a cupboard for storing clothes, linen, and books. Now generally reserved for a type of cupboard from the 16th and 17th centuries, with doors enclosing a large compartment below and two smaller compartments set side by side in the upper section. The term is also applied to a box for pressing linens in the 18th century.

Pressed glass ◼ A form of mass-produced glass made using a plunger to press molten glass into a mold. Although known since Roman times, the mechanical technique was developed in the US from the 1820s and in Europe, particularly France and Bohemia, from the 1830s. By the mid-19th century, most inexpensive mass-produced glassware was pressed. CARNIVAL GLASS and DEPRESSION GLASS are good examples.

Press-molding A technique of ceramic-making, where clay is pressed into or over a mold and then removed. It was used from the early 18th century onward in England, especially at the STAFFORDSHIRE POTTERIES. In glassmaking it is the process by which PRESSED GLASS is made.

Pricket ◼ An early form of CANDLESTICK made of bronze, brass, copper, or iron. It had a sharp metal spike set in the capital or top section and secured the candle by spearing it through the base. Found from the 12th to the 16th centuries, when it was replaced by the candlestick, the pricket was used in large houses, churches, and monasteries.

Prie-dieu ◼ A low-seated, armless chair, introduced to Britain from France in the 19th century. It has a tall, narrow back and often a wide top-rail shelf to hold a prayer book. Ostensibly designed for kneeling in prayer, it was also a popular occasional drawing-room chair. UPHOLSTERY was

Press
New Jersey applewood linen press, resting on straight bracket feet. c. 1790.

Pressed glass
Canadian clear pressed-glass "Beaver Band" pattern goblet. 1880.

Tapering octagonal shaft

Pricket
Wrought-iron double pricket candlestand on an arched tripod base.

Bold plant-form imagery

Prie-dieu
Victorian dark-stained beech *prie-dieu* on turned underframe with molded stretchers.

either plain or had BERLIN WOOLWORK embroidered with religious motifs. The cushioned seat is occasionally hinged to create storage for books.

Primrose glass A yellow version of Davidson's opalescent PEARLINE GLASS, made by the addition of uranium, which makes it glow green under ultraviolet light.

Print The oldest printed images are believed to be Chinese Buddhist scriptures and it was from China that the WOODCUT reached Japan by the 8th century. Printing methods fall into two categories: INTAGLIO (ETCHINGS, LITHOGRAPHS, AQUATINTS, and ENGRAVINGS), where an image is transferred from an indented surface; and relief (wood engravings and woodcuts), in which the printing surface is raised. Book printing, developed in Germany from the 15th century, has evolved into modern typography. Artists such as Rembrandt van Rijn, Pablo Picasso, and David Hockney have all used the same printing methods.

Print room A room used for displaying prints, fashionable in Britain from the 1760s to the early 19th century.

Printie A shallow, concave, circular or oval cut lenslike decoration used on glass from the early 18th century.

Prismatic cutting Cut-glass decoration in the form of abutting horizontal mitered grooves that catch the light. It was popular in the early 19th century, when it was used on the necks of decanters in particular.

Prisoner-of-war work ■ Domestic and decorative items such as COMPENDIUMS, ship models, and simple automata carved from bone by predominantly French prisoners of war in England during the Napoleonic wars (c. 1800–15).

Prouvé, Jean ■ (1901–84) A French architect, engineer, and metalworker, perhaps best known as the designer of some of the most innovative French MODERN furniture. He was the son of the painter Victor Prouvé, and cofounder of the ÉCOLE DE NANCY. Prouvé studied metalwork in Paris from 1916 to 1921 and opened a number of metalworks, the first being in Nancy in 1923. As an architect, he experimented with new materials, which influenced his bent- and welded-steel furniture designs.

Provenance A verifiable account or documentation accompanying a piece that identifies either its origins, or history, or both. An interesting provenance or one connected to a renowned maker, owner, location, or event can add desirability and often also value to a piece.

Prunt A blob of molten glass applied to a piece of glass and then often modeled as decoration. It was particularly associated

with drinking vessels such as the RÖMER, where it was applied to the stem and often modeled as raspberries.

Prutcher, Otto (1880–1949) Austrian architect and designer trained in the ARTS AND CRAFTS tradition, a pupil under Josef HOFFMAN, and whose progressive, early 20th-century designs—most of which were for the WIENER WERKSTÄTTE—included furniture, ceramics, glass, and textiles.

Ptolemy (Ptolomaeus Claudius) (C. 87 CE–C. 150 CE) The most influential of the ancient astronomers and geographers, Ptolemy dominated cartographic thinking for more than 1,400 years.

Pugin, Augustus Welby Northmore ■ (1812–52) An architect, designer, and leader of the GOTHIC REVIVAL in England. Following in the footsteps of his French immigrant father, Pugin designed furniture and silver until the 1830s, after which he turned to creating furniture that mirrored authentic medieval styles rather than simply decorating contemporary designs with Gothic ornament in the prevailing fashion. He also designed Gothic-style church plate, tiles, ceramics, and jewelry. He is perhaps best known for creating the interiors of the Houses of Parliament from 1836 to 1837.

Puiforcat, Jean (1897–1945) The most important French ART DECO silversmith, who learned his craft in his father's

Prisoner of war work
Bone spinning jenny, with two wheels and a figure. c. 1790.

Prouvé, Jean
Wardrobe, with two sliding doors and gold enameled metal panels and feet.

Pugin
Oak stool, the squared legs and seat rails of pollard oak, with Gothic panels. 1827–28.

Swagged floral border

Punch bowl
Large sterling silver punch bowl, by Charles Stuart Harris, London. 1893.

workshops and joined the family firm after World War I. From 1922, he produced solid yet simple silver tea sets, dishes, and bowls in cylindrical or rectangular designs, giving way in the 1930s to purer, sleeker shapes, which displayed his use of contrasting materials with silver. These textural and color contrasts included exotic woods, IVORY, AMBER, and JADE.

Pumpkin head A type of WAX OVER COMPOSITION, SHOULDER HEAD doll, popular in the third quarter of the 19th century and made by dipping a PAPIER-MÂCHÉ shoulder head in heated wax. The dolls are named for their large round faces and often have molded blonde hair.

Punch bowl ■ A large, often circular, bowl of silver, ceramic, or glass, used for mixing and brewing punch—an alcoholic beverage of water, spirits, spices, sugar, and citrus fruit, popular in England from the second half of the 17th century. Silver examples tend to be plain but some have engraved or embossed decoration, usually of bunches of grapes.

Punch glass ■ A type of small drinking glass with a handle that forms part of a punch set—a bowl with matching cups that were sometimes hung from the edge of the bowl.

Punched work ■ A form of decoration in which patterns and imagery are created on the surface or borders of metal wares—especially more malleable metals such as silver—by hammering with shaped steel punches.

Punto in aria An Italian term for "stitch in the air." The first true NEEDLELACE that was not worked on a woven fabric. Derived from RETICELLA and often using parchment as a temporary backing, early geometric motifs became more complex, involving animals, biblical scenes, and scrolls. It was used for ruffs and scalloped borders in the early 17th century.

Punty See PONTIL MARK.

Purdonium ■ A type of 19th-century coal-scuttle, named after a Mr. Purdon who was either its inventor or the first owner. It is made in a variety of materials, including wood and JAPANNED metal, and usually painted with elaborate scenes and shapes.

Puritan spoon A type of spoon (also called a slip-top spoon) with a slip-top handle—a hexagonal stem ending in a simple bevel, so called because it resembles an APOSTLE SPOON without the figure of an Apostle.

Purple heart ■ A dense hardwood from the Caribbean, of the genus *Peltogyne*, so called because of the violet or purplish color it becomes when freshly cut. In the 18th century it was used for INLAY and veneer border BANDINGS on furniture.

Push-along/pull-along mechanism Used in toys, usually for small children, where a movement within the toy is activated by moving the toy along the ground—for example, the nodding head of a dog on wheels.

Putto An Italian word for "cherub" or "boy." A chubby infant boy, widely used in ornament, deriving from angelic spirits. Used from the RENAISSANCE and popular in the BAROQUE period, the *putto* is typically depicted playing among scrolling foliage carrying FESTOONS and SWAGS.

Puzzle jug A jug with a pierced, cylindrical neck and a hollow handle that connects the lower part with a tube around the top, from which there are two or more "spouts." It is only possible to drink if one sucks at one of the spouts while blocking the others and a hole hidden under the top of the handle with one's fingers. The earliest dated example in DELFTWARE is 1653; it is also known in DELFT of the 17th and 18th centuries.

Pyrex A trade name for heat-resistant (borosilicate) glassware patented in 1915 by the CORNING GLASSWORKS, New York, and produced under license by manufacturers in Britain and elsewhere.

Pyrography A triangular gable above the portico of a Classical temple. The motif was adopted in Italy, France, and England from the 16th century for the tops of windows and doors and for the CORNICES on tall CASE FURNITURE, such as bookcases, BUREAUX and LONGCASE clocks. A broken pediment has a central break for a FINIAL; a swan-neck pediment consists of two opposing S-scrolls. See POKER WORK.

Punch glass
Imperial "Diamond Rings" pattern amethyst Carnival glass punch cup.

Punched work
Spanish steel thimble, with punched dot design and Toledo-work band. c. 1910.

Purdonium
Victorian octagonal *tole peint* purdonium, the hinged lid enclosing a lift-out liner.

Purple heart
George III Hepplewhite bow-front bowl stand, banded in purple heart. c. 1790.

Qianlong porcelain (Ch'ien Lung)
Chinese porcelain made in the reign of the Qing dynasty Emperor Qianlong (1736–95). The JINGDEZHEN kilns produced large quantities of CHINESE EXPORT PORCELAIN and fine Imperial wares, often in the MING or SONG dynasty style. See ARMORIAL WARE, CHINESE POTTERY AND PORCELAIN, FAMILLE ROSE, MANDARIN PALETTE.

Qing (Ch'ing) The Chinese dynasty (1644–1912) under the rule of the Manchus, which followed the native MING dynasty (1368–1644). The early years were marked by civil war, and the Imperial kilns at JINGDEZHEN, which were destroyed in 1673, were not rebuilt until the 1680s. Artistically, the three most important periods were under the Emperors Kangxi (1662–1722), Yongzheng (1723–35), and Qianlong (1736–95), and under their patronage, Jingdezhen witnessed a renaissance. New glazes were perfected, including peach bloom, ROBIN'S EGG, MIRROR BLACK, TEA DUST, and CLAIR DE LUNE. Classic shapes and styles from the SONG and Ming dynasties were revived. Production for the CHINESE EXPORT market increased greatly as Chinese goods and tea-drinking became fashionable in Europe. Export wares included FAMILLE VERTE, NOIRE, JAUNE AND ROSE porcelains, ARMORIAL WARES BLANC DE CHINE, YIXING stoneware, CHINESE IMARI, and large quantities of blue and white porcelain. Other goods exported during the Qing period include JADE, LACQUERWORK, IVORY, and furniture in BAMBOO and eastern hardwoods.

Quadrant An instrument used for navigation, surveying, or time-telling. Its name derives from its shape, a quarter of a circle, on which a scale of degrees from 0° to 90° is marked so that the angle of elevation can be read after aligning the sights with the sun or a star. Quadrants were invented in the Middle Ages and were superseded by the octant from around 1750. Gunter's quadrant was invented by the English astronomy professor Edmund Gunter in 1623, and pocket-sized brass or boxwood instruments of his design date from 1650 to 1750.

Quaich ■ A shallow silver, pewter, or wooden drinking bowl with two flat handles. It originated in medieval Scotland, probably in wood, and so can be considered as an example of TREEN. Early surviving examples date from the 17th and 18th centuries.

Quail pattern A decorative scheme painted on PORCELAIN, showing a pair of quails among rocks and foliage. This motif originated on KAKIEMON porcelain in Japan and was widely imitated on porcelain and TIN-GLAZED EARTHENWARE in Europe from the 18th to the 20th century.

Quaint Furniture See STICKLEY BROTHERS.

Quare, Daniel ■ (1649–1724) A renowned English clock- and watchmaker, known for his fine-quality workmanship and materials. He became master of the Clockmakers' Company in 1708 and produced LONGCASE and BRACKET CLOCKS and watches, often with extremely fine piercing and ENGRAVING on the BACKPLATES. He invented the REPEATER watch around 1680 and is also known for his elegant BAROMETERS, typically of columnar form.

Quarter striking A clock that strikes on the quarter hours as well as on the hour. See STRIKING SYSTEMS.

Quarter veneer ■ A technique whereby two matching sheets of veneer are sliced into two pairs. These are reversed and the pairs juxtaposed on the CARCASS of the furniture to form a decorative pattern. It was often used in walnut on table tops, chests-of-drawers, or desks in early 18th-century English furniture. It was revived in the mid-VICTORIAN period and was popular in satinwood.

Qing
A Qing Dynasty Chinese blue and white porcelain vase. 19th century.

Quaich
Scottish quaich on a spool foot, with shaped lugs. Mid-18th century.

Quare, Daniel
Watch, by Daniel Quare, with enameled dial. c. 1700–10.

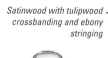

Satinwood with tulipwood crossbanding and ebony stringing

Quarter veneer
Sheraton Revival kidney-shaped dressing table, with quarter-veneered top. c. 1890.

Quartetto tables  A set of four small tables of graduated size that nest together, made primarily in MAHOGANY, ROSEWOOD, and SATINWOOD. The design originated in the early 19th century.

Quartz A group of gemstones and HARD STONES found throughout the world and used since antiquity for jewelry and small decorative artifacts. Crystalline quartz includes ROCK CRYSTAL (colorless), amethyst (purple), citrine (yellow to brown), smokey quartz (deep brown), rose quartz (pink), and aventurine (green with mica inclusions). Cryptocrystalline quartz, commonly known as chalcedony, includes chrysoprase (apple green), cornelian (reddish brown), bloodstone (green with red flecks), as well as AGATE, jasper, and ONYX.

Quartz glass An American term for opaque glass with the marbling simulating QUARTZ or HARDSTONE. The term was used as a trademark by the STEUBEN GLASSWORKS for a line of CLUTHRA glass with matte finish, including a pink-colored glass termed "Rose quartz."

Quatrefoil  Four-lobed GOTHIC TRACERY form resembling a four-leaved clover. Perhaps originating in architectural features found in Moorish and Asian mosques, the quatrefoil was used in the Gothic architecture of Venice. It survived into the RENAISSANCE in Italy and enjoyed renewed popularity as a decorative motif on GOTHIC REVIVAL furniture of the 19th century.

Queen Anne  The style of architecture and the decorative arts, especially silver and furniture, dominant in England during Queen Anne's reign (1702–14) and adopted in the US around 1725 with strong regional characteristics. The style favored restraint and limited ornament in contrast to the earlier BAROQUE style. Domestic silver by silversmiths such as Anthony NELME is devoid of decoration except for fine engraved ARMORIALS on some pieces. Walnut was the most fashionable wood, figuring, for example, in the use of burr walnut, and coloring was considered more important than applied ornament. Other characteristic features of Queen Anne furniture are the CABRIOLE LEG and chairs with vase- or fiddle-shaped slats forming their backs.

Queen Anne Revival A style of architecture and decorative arts popular in the late 19th and early 20th centuries in England, based on the QUEEN ANNE style. It was popularized by architects such as Richard Norman Shaw and Philip WEBB in their designs for red-brick town and country houses. The simplicity of Queen Anne furnishings appealed particularly to designers of the AESTHETIC MOVEMENT such as E. W. GODWIN. Direct reproductions of early-18th-century items were also popular during this period but their craftsmanship is rarely as fine as that of the originals.

Queen's Burmese See BURMESE GLASS.

Queen's pattern An ornate silver (and plated) FLATWARE design similar to KING'S PATTERN. The main differences are the heavier decoration on the Queen's pattern and the SHELL MOTIF on the top of the stem, which stands up in RELIEF, in contrast to the flatter or concave motif on the King's.

Queensware CREAMWARE made by Josiah WEDGWOOD from around 1765 and named after Queen Charlotte in honor of her visit to the Wedgwood factory.

Quervelle, Anthon G. (1789–1856). Born Antoine-Gabriel Quervelle in France, this eminent American cabinet-maker was active in Philadelphia, from 1817. Typical products include MAHOGANY and GILTWOOD PIER TABLES, comparable to contemporary FRENCH EMPIRE and English REGENCY examples.

Quezal glass  (1901–1925) A glassworks in Brooklyn, New York, that produced iridescent glass in the TIFFANY style. Founded by former Tiffany employees, the company derived its name from its use of feather patterns similar to the brilliant green, red, and white plumage of the quetzal bird.

Quilts  Textiles formed by joining together two layers of fabric with a third layer of wadding secured between them. Early

Quartetto tables
Quartetto set of crossbanded mahogany tea tables on slender supports with scroll feet.

Quatrefoil
Detail of a line of quatrefoils on the back of an English Gothic oak armchair. c. 1775.

Queen Anne
Philadelphia Queen Anne walnut side chair. c. 1760.

Quezal glass
Quezal vase, with pulled-feather decoration in gold and green on an ivory ground.

European examples were worked through two pieces of heavy linen. Parallel lines worked in backstitch create the design into which cords and braids are inserted. Known as a "whole-cloth" quilt, most early surviving quilts are of this type. In the 16th and 17th centuries, as trade between Europe and India increased, the ideas and fabrics of the East greatly influenced European quilt-making. Double-sided silk quilts from Portuguese India were imported for the first time, together with thinly wadded cotton quilts and painted and printed cotton chintzes. By the late 17th century these were being copied in Europe. Colorful chain-stitch designs against flat, quilted backgrounds became popular. By the 18th century quilted bed covers were fairly widespread. Carefully planned quilts with central panels and surrounding borders, known as "medallion quilts," were particularly favored. Some incorporated APPLIQUÉD detail and imported printed cotton into their designs; others were

whole-cloth quilts in plain cottons. In the 19th century, patchwork became more popular, although the two techniques were often combined. Decorative patchwork quilts became most closely associated with North America. Bed quilts served both a decorative and practical purpose and became an integral part of the social life of the women who worked them. Quilting bees were formed to make quilts in a sociable environment. Initially, patterns were based on English and Welsh designs, but gradually American forms emerged, the "block" pattern and its endless variations being a good example. ALBUM, autograph, or friendship quilts were worked extensively in the US; some of the most famous quilts known are mid-19th-century "Baltimore album" quilts.

Quimper A factory in Finistere, France, making peasant-type pottery painted in bright colors with figures in Breton costume. FAIENCE had been made here since the end

of the 17th century, but little of note was produced until the arrival of Pierre-Paul Causey, who ran the factory from 1743 to 1782, producing wares in the style of ROUEN. In 1853 Antoine de la Hubaudière took over the factory, and from this time, the wares of Quimper were marked with the monogram "HB." Other faience factories in the area making similar wares included Eloury-Porquier-Beau and Dumaine-Tanqueray-Henriot, the latter established in 1778. By the beginning of the 19th century, faience production in France had nearly ceased and CREAMWARE had taken over. However, because of its isolated Breton position, Quimper persisted. The factory continues to produce traditional-style faience today.

Quizzical bird A comical STONEWARE bird with a long beak and heavy-lidded eyes, made by the MARTIN BROTHERS at the end of the 19th and beginning of the 20th century.

QUILTS

Simple quilting methods have been used since the earliest times for clothing and furnishings. It is believed that quilting first came to Europe from the East, with the earliest references being to quilted garments in the 12th century. Decorative quilting is recorded with increasing frequency from the 14th century onward.

Pieced quilt
Pennsylvania German or New Jersey pieced and appliquéd cotton quilt, with Mariner's Compass motif. c. 1845.

Appliqué quilt
Ohio appliqué quilt, with calico flowers and leaves.

R

Race, Ernest ■ (1913–64) An English furniture and textile designer who founded Ernest Race Inc. with Noel Jordan in 1945. Early designs were governed by rationing restrictions after World War II—for example, the BA chair (1946) was made from aluminum from scrapped war planes. In 1951 Race designed the Antelope chair for the Festival of Britain.

Racinage A 19th-century technique for MARBLING leather with acid. It was not widely used as it tended to damage the leather.

Rack clock A clock in which the power source is the weight of the clock itself. The clock gradually descends a toothed vertical rack and is then pushed back up to the top. Rack clocks were popular from the 17th century in Germany and Austria and were reproduced in England in the mid-20th century. See GRAVITY CLOCK.

Radiogram A combined radio receiver, gramophone, and loudspeaker. Radiograms were popular from 1950 to the early 1970s and were often housed in a wooden cabinet in the size and form of a sideboard.

Raeren potteries An important German center of STONEWARE production near Aachen from around 1560 to the 17th century. Initially, it produced COLOGNE-style brown-glazed wares and later gray stoneware with blue reliefs similar to WESTERWALD ware. Less notable wares were produced throughout the 19th century.

Rag doll Originally a homemade fabric toy. From the second half of the 19th century, rag dolls were also mass-produced in kit form, as printed fabric patterns to be cut out, sewn, and stuffed. They can be made of cotton, linen, felt, or stockinette.

Raggedy Ann ■ The trademark registered in 1918 in the US by John B. Gruelle for a RAG DOLL character taken from stories written and illustrated by Gruelle, based on a doll owned by his daughter. Raggedy Ann and her male companion, Raggedy Andy (introduced in 1920), have flat faces with a wide smile, round eyes with lower lashes, and a shock of red yarn hair. First produced under Gruelle's guidance, the dolls were taken over by Volland and Co. from 1920 until 1934, and then by the Georgene Novelty Company. Raggedy Anns are currently made by Hasbro.

Rail The horizontal member in the framework or CARCASS of furniture such as the seat rail of a chair, intended to support the vertical members.

Raising A technique used by silversmiths to create HOLLOWWARE out of sheet metal by hitting the metal with a round-headed hammer over an anvil or stake.

Raku ware ■ A type of Japanese pottery made for TEA CEREMONY use. Raku is named after a seal mark, meaning "enjoyment," which is found on early examples. It was first made around 1580 by Chojino, a Korean potter living near Kyoto. Chojino took the name Raku, which was passed down through generations. Many other small-scale potters also worked in the Raku tradition. Wares were modeled by hand (rather than thrown) and were asymmetric and uneven, with a thick LEAD GLAZE, usually in black or brown but occasionally reddish, green, white, or yellow. Raku is particular to the Japanese taste, with the finest pieces held in high regard. Raku firing techniques are employed today to create the unique look of Raku pottery using a specialized second firing process known as post-fire reduction.

Ramsden, Omar ■ (1873–1939) An English ARTS AND CRAFTS metalworker, silversmith, and artist craftsman who worked from 1898 to 1919 in partnership with Alwyn Carr, and ran a small workshop until he registered his own mark in 1919. Ramsden's workshops produced a large quantity of work, much of it ecclesiastical,

Race, Ernest
Ernest Race BA3 cast-aluminum armchair, covered with cotton velour upholstery.

Raggedy Ann
American cloth Volland Raggedy Ann and Raggedy Andy doll. c. 1930.

Cloth body

Raku ware
Tim Andrews Raku vase, incised with a cross-hatched design, and with impressed seal mark.

Sinuous Art Nouveau curves

Ramsden, Omar
Silver cream jug, with a turquoise enamel cabochon on the handle. 1904.

civic, and corporate. He produced many presentation pieces and private commissions. Many of his silver, metalwork, and jewelry designs were reinterpreted from Tudor and Celtic styles, often featuring hand-hammered finishes and colored enamels, with an emphasis on quality and applied decorative detail. He is also well known for his ART NOUVEAU pieces. Ramsden's work often features the inscription *"omar ramsden me fecit"*—Omar Ramsden made me.

Randall, John (1810–1910) An English porcelain decorator who began as an apprentice to his uncle, Thomas Martin RANDALL, at his china works at Madeley, Shropshire. He left in 1833, and in 1835 went to the COALPORT factory where he decorated plates, vases, and other items. He specialized in finely painted exotic birds, first in imitation of SÈVRES and later in his own highly naturalistic style. In 1851 Coalport displayed Randall's French-style vases at the GREAT EXHIBITION in London, where they were much admired. Randall remained at Coalport for 40 years and retired in 1881.

Randolph, Benjamin (c. 1745–c. 1805) A celebrated American furniture-maker who was active in Philadelphia, Pennsylvania, from 1770. Randolph was a superb exponent of the AMERICAN CHIPPENDALE style (it is known that he owned a copy of Chippendale's *The Gentleman and Cabinet-Maker's Director*). His

flamboyant solid mahogany furniture, featuring ROCOCO details such as intricate openwork, acanthus carved knees, and ball-and-claw feet, is comparable in quality and value to pieces by his contemporaries Thomas AFFLECK, William SAVERY, Hercules Courtenay, and Thomas Johnson.

Rapier ■ Derived from the Spanish words *espada ropera*, meaning *dress sword*, the rapier is a slender, straight, sharp-pointed sword used primarily for thrusting attacks. With a blades up to 48 in (122 cm) long, some of which also had sharpened sides for cutting strokes, and elaborate hilts to protect the wielding hand, they were in widespread use, most notoriously for dueling, from the late 15th to the late 17th century—from which point they were generally supplanted by the SMALLSWORD.

Ratafia glass A type of slender drinking flute with a tall, narrow, funnel-shaped bowl blending into the stem. It was developed in the mid-18th century for drinking ratafia—an almond-flavored liqueur.

Rat-tail spoon ■ A type of spoon common in the late 17th to early 18th century with a tapering rib (resembling a rat's tail) from the handle to the back of the bowl to reinforce the joint.

Rattan See CANE.

Ravenscroft, George (1632–83) An English glassmaker who developed FLINT

GLASS (or LEAD CRYSTAL) with Italian glassmaker da Costa in London. In 1676, during experiments to counter CRIZZLING, he added lead to the batch and created a new glass that was softer, easier to cut, and more brilliant than any that had previously been available.

Ravilious, Eric William (1903–42) An English artist, designer, engraver, and war artist (he was killed flying with Coastal Command). His design work for WEDGWOOD included a dinner service decorated with the "Travel" pattern (1937) and a limited-edition (only 200 were made) Boat Race Bowl (1938).

Reading chair A chair with an adjustable device for supporting a book. The basic form had been established by the 18th century, and most examples had the bookrest attached to the TOP RAIL at the back of the chair, which meant the occupant sat astride the seat facing the rear if he or she wished to read, but could also sit the "right way around" if using the chair just for sitting. By the middle of the 19th century, many examples featured swivel bookrests supplemented with candle brackets for illumination.

Realism In painting, sculpture, architecture, and applied arts, the naturalistic representation of humans, animals, birds, or plants. Attempts at realism have been a feature of all arts throughout history, but were especially

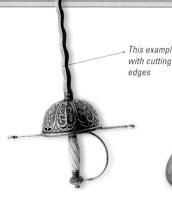

Rapier
Spanish rapier. Late 17th century.

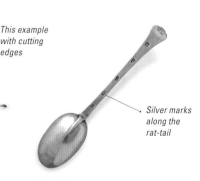

This example with cutting edges

Rat-tail spoon
Rare James II large silver trifid spoon, with a plain, molded rat tail. 1686.

Silver marks along the rat-tail

Réchampi
Gustavian armchair, with carved decoration gilded against a white ground.

Red stoneware
Meissen red stoneware tea canister. c. 1710.

evident in applied arts in the 19th century, when new technical advances allowed more accurate depictions of the natural world.

Rebate Also called a rabbet. A rectangular recess cut into the edge of a piece of wood in order to insert another piece. The adjoining STILES of cabinet doors were often rebated together to form a dustproof joint and the bottom edge of drawer fronts was generally rebated to provide secure lodging for the bottom boards.

Réchampi ▪ A decorative technique in which ornamentation is picked out in gold or a color that contrasts with the ground color—for example, chairs with carved decoration gilded against a white ground.

Red stoneware ▪ Wares made in China at Yi-Hsing in the 17th century and exported to Europe. Red stoneware was copied at MEISSEN and known as BÖTTGER stoneware. In England it was made by David and John ELERS at Fulham in London around 1693 and at Bradwell Wood in Staffordshire in 1698. It was also made in Holland by Ary-de-Milde and at Plaue-an-der-Havel in Prussia, but these examples tend to have softer bodies than the hard Böttger stoneware.

Red ware An American term used to describe RED STONEWARE and, generally, provincial pottery with a porous red body, typically decorated with colored LEAD GLAZE and trailed SLIP or SGRAFITTO

work. Most red ware was made during the 17th and 18th centuries.

Reed, Henry Gooding (1810–1901) An American silversmith and pioneer of ELECTROPLATING in the US. He was active in Taunton, Massachusetts, from 1834. His firm became Reed & Barton in 1840 and is still active as a prolific maker of silver and plated ware.

Reed-and-tie molding REEDING loosely bound together with crisscrossed straps or ribbons, lending it the appearance of rods that have been tied together. An elaborate variation on the popular reed molding, reed-and-tie (or reed-and-ribbon) was used to ornament silver from the 1770s, and on furniture was applied as cast-brass edging or to decorate the legs of chairs.

Reeding ▪ Fine parallel convex molding derived from the decoration on Classical columns. The opposite of FLUTING, reeding has been popular at various times since the 15th century, whenever Classical orders were in fashion. Used to decorate fireplace and door surrounds, silver, and parts of furniture such as chair and table legs.

Refectory table A long, narrow, rectangular hall or dining table, usually made of oak. The term was coined in the 19th century after the dining room used by monks during the Middle Ages. Early versions were constructed from planks of

wood joined with pegs to a frame, with legs connected by a framework of rails and joined at the bottom by heavy stretchers. Found chiefly in prosperous households, by the late 17th century the refectory table had been largely superseded by the gateleg table, although they are still made today.

Reform ware ▪ Ceramic jugs, bowls, and flasks made in England around the time of the 1832 Reform Bill. Made from salt-glazed stoneware or STAFFORDSHIRE pottery, they were decorated with molded or transfer-printed portraits of the leaders of Parliamentary reform, including Earl Grey and Lord John Russell. Reform ware also often bore relevant inscriptions.

Regard jewelry ▪ Sentimental and romantic jewelry popular in the first quarter of the 19th century, in which the first letter of a line of gemstones spells a message such as REGARD (Ruby, Emerald, Garnet, Amethyst, Ruby, Diamond) and DEAREST (Diamond, Emerald, Amethyst, Ruby, Emerald, Sapphire, Topaz).

Régence style ▪ The French decorative arts and interior design named after the regency of Philippe, Duc d'Orléans (1715–23) and popular until the introduction of the ROCOCO style around 1730. Representing the transition between the BAROQUE and Rococo, Régence forms are still symmetrical and rectilinear but with curving and serpentine lines and lighter, more fantastical ornament such as

R

305

Reeding
Reeded columns carved on the sides of a Pennsylvanian chest-of-drawers. c. 1755–60.

Reform ware
Pearlware Reform Bill mug, printed in pink with four figures holding a scroll. c. 1830.

Regard jewelry
Regency gold "regard" locket, the applied flowerhead set with gems. c. 1825.

Régence style
Régence carved fruitwood commode from southwestern France. Early 18th century.

ARABESQUES and GROTESQUES derived from the designs of Jean BÉRAIN. In furniture the style is epitomized by the work of the ÉBÉNISTE and sculptor Charles CRESSENT, whose pieces feature light-colored wood and elegant gilt-bronze mounts.

R

Regency style ■ This opulent style of architecture and decorative arts was popular in England from around 1784 to about 1830. It was named after the Regency (1811–20) of George, Prince of Wales (the Prince Regent), later George IV (1820–30), who commissioned magnificent interiors at Carlton House, London, and the Royal Pavilion, Brighton. The style was established by the Prince of Wales's architect and interior designer, Henry Holland. In

England the archaeologically exact approach was adopted by Thomas HOPE, who inspired a vogue for the Greek KLISMOS chair that Holland had introduced and X-framed stools and thrones with SABER LEGS, SPHINXES, CARYATIDS, herms (armless male or female busts), or GRIFFINS. Cabinet-makers George SMITH and George BULLOCK imitated Hope's style.

The simple rectilinear forms in Thomas SHERATON'S *The Cabinet-Maker* and *Upholsterer's Drawing Book* (1793–94) were also influential. Mahogany remained the most popular wood, but ROSEWOOD, SATINWOOD, ZEBRAWOOD, and AMBOYNA were also used. Silversmiths such as Paul STORR and Benjamin SMITH created copies of, for example, the

WARWICK VASE, in silver or silver-gilt. The trend for massive, ornate forms also appeared in English and IRISH GLASS. Exotic fashions such as TURKISH, INDIAN, and CHINOISERIE motifs in the early 19th century anticipated Victorian ECLECTICISM. The EGYPTIAN STYLE was popular after Nelson's victory at the Battle of the Nile (1798), leading to a fashion for hieroglyphics, scarabs (winged beetles), winged disks, and stylized lotus flowers. Classical motifs included PALMETTERS, ANTHEMIONS, winged lions, eagles and CARYATIDS, GUILLOCHE, FASCES, and GREEK KEY patterns, together with exotic emblems.

Registry marks See DESIGN REGISTRATION.

REGENCY STYLE

A late development of the NEOCLASSICAL STYLE, Regency forms were larger and more solid, curvaceous, and richly ornamented than those of the late 18th century. Luxurious materials were much used, such as brass inlay and figured woods on furniture and IVORY and EBONY handles and finials on silver. The style was influenced by the EMPIRE STYLE in France, which favored historically accurate copies of Greek and Roman furniture prototypes rather than just applying Classical motifs to

contemporary designs. Regency pieces can be distinguished from their French Empire counterparts by the absence of Napoleonic emblems, such as "BEES" and "Ns," and heavy GILT-BRONZE mounts.

Sofa table
Regency mahogany sofa table, on reeded legs with brass caps and casters.

Canterbury
Regency rosewood Canterbury, with three open compartments and base drawer with acanthus carving and acorn finials.

 brass caps and casters

Chair
Mahogany X-frame chair, Thomas Hope design. c. 1800.

Regulator ■ A precise timekeeper made from the 18th century and used to regulate other clocks. Produced in Britain, France, the US, and especially Austria, such clocks were of both LONGCASE and wall type, generally with extremely plain cases (although French types often feature ORMOLU mounts). To ensure extreme precision, regulators were equipped with a gridiron, wood-rod or mercurial compensated PENDULUM, and DEADBEAT ESCAPEMENT with JEWELED bearings to reduce friction. The chapter ring usually displays minutes, with subsidiary dials for hours and seconds. See VIENNA REGULATOR.

Reign mark ■ An Imperial Chinese mark regularly used on ceramics and other works of art from the beginning of the MING DYNASTY (1368–1644). They were written as either six or four characters, in regular script (*kaishu*) or seal form (*zhuanshu*), which became popular from the YONGZHENG reign (1723–35).

Reijmyre glasbruk A Swedish glasshouse established in Östergötland in 1810. In the 19th century it was one of the major producers of tableware, including pressed glass and cut-glass dinner services. In the early 20th century it employed numerous designers, many producing

CAMEO GLASS and designs inspired by GALLÉ. Other designers such as Monica Bratt were employed from 1940s onward and colored decorative and functional designs were produced. The factory is still active.

Relief ■ A type of molded, carved, or stamped decoration raised above the background of a surface. Various styles of carving can be identified by the type of relief—high, low, or medium—which depends upon the amount of background that has been removed to allow the design to emerge. The carving may be further modeled by UNDERCUTTING. In Europe the refinement of the early RENAISSANCE gave way to the robust, high relief of the late period, paving the way for the flamboyant BAROQUE STYLE. Relief carving later became more subtle (lower), ranging from foliage in the ROCOCO period to the delicate relief ornament by Robert ADAM in the NEOCLASSICAL period. The Victorian taste for excess led to more ornate relief decoration, followed by a return to lower relief, in general, in the 20th century.

Reliquary ■ A receptacle designed to hold sacred objects or relics of a saint or a holy person, often made of precious materials such as silver or gold, and mounted with rock crystal or gemstones. Few English examples have survived the Reformation, but they were, and still are, an important part of the Catholic Church throughout Europe.

Remington, Eliphalet (1793–1861) An American firearms manufacturer. He first made firearms in 1816, built his factory on the Erie Canal in New York State in 1828, and became a major competitor of COLT. Remington is best known for a series of simple and robust revolvers and an archetypal double-barreled DERRINGER. Another major success was the rolling-block rifle, which was produced from 1864 to 1933.

Remontoire A device in a precision timekeeper, such as a CHRONOMETER, to supply constant force to the ESCAPEMENT despite changes in the power source. It consists of a small weight or a spring wound at intervals by the mainspring.

Renaissance ■ A French term meaning "rebirth." The revival of interest in the culture of ancient Greece and Rome that began in Florence, Italy, in the 15th century, and in the following century, spread throughout Europe. Significant developments included the European exploration of the Americas and Asia, the expansion of trade, advances in science, mathematics, medicine, and law, and the increasing power of the urban merchant classes. Painting, architecture, and sculpture were dominated by the introduction of linear perspective and greater naturalism. The Renaissance style was also stimulated by the court patronage of the Medicis in Florence, the papacy in Rome, Francis I of France, and Henry VIII of England.

R

307

Regulator
Small one-month duration mahogany longcase regulator. c. 1800.

Reign mark
Yongzheng mark on the base of a blue and white double phoenix dish.

Relief
Arts and Crafts terra-cotta relief wall plaque, depicting the Virgin and Child with angels.

Reliquary
Engraved and gilded brass reliquary, with pyramid-shaped colver and lobed foot. 1551.

The decorative arts are characterized by symmetry and strongly architectural and sculptural forms, decorated with motifs derived from Classical buildings and sculpture. These include architectural orders, columns, CAPITALS, ACANTHUS leaves, TROPHIES, and human and mythological figures. The discovery of ancient Roman wall paintings in buried ruins—for example, the Golden House of Nero in Rome in 1488—resulted in the introduction of GROTESQUES, combined with MASKS, ARABESQUES, SCROLLWORK, SWAGS, and WREATHS. This wealth of ornament was circulated throughout Europe in engravings, made possible after the invention of the printing press in the 15th century, and adapted on Italian MAIOLICA at Urbino and Faenza, LIMOGES enamels, metalwork, and textiles.

Renaissance Revival ■ The 19th-century revival of forms and ornament associated with the arts of the RENAISSANCE. Popular in Europe and the US, it appeared in architecture from the 1820s, with buildings in the style of 16th-century Italian villas and town palaces. It remained in vogue until the 1880s as one of the main revivalist styles. In Britain the ELIZABETHAN REVIVAL is an adaptation of the Renaissance Revival style. It is distinguished by the loose interpretation of Classical motifs such as SCROLLS, FLUTING, SWAGS, oval panels, and STRAPWORK, often derived from MANNERIST and BAROQUE designs

and combined with GOTHIC and ROCOCO motifs. The movement had a big impact on late 19th-century glass, particularly through engrave motifs.

The style was widely favored in Italy, where it was known as "Dante-esque." Italian furniture of the 1860s and 70s often feature IVORY and bone inlay and PIETRA DURA plaques inspired by 16th-century originals. Renaissance Revival furniture was also produced in France and the US. Renaissance-inspired MEISSEN and SÈVRES porcelain featured gray and white decoration of Classical figures, GROTESQUES, and swags on colored grounds imitating 16th-century LIMOGES ENAMELS. The Italian glassmaker Antonio SALVIATI made glass in the Venetian Renaissance style, featuring winged and serpent stems and lampwork decoration on TAZZAS, goblets, and other wares. In jewelry, the HOLBEINESQUE style combined gold, ENAMEL, and GARNETS.

Rennes potteries Lead-glazed EARTHENWARE was made here in Ille-et-Vilaine, France, from the 16th century. A FAIENCE factory, called Manufacture Forasassi di Barberino, operated from 1748 to the end of the century. Statuettes of the Virgin Mary and local saints have been attributed to this factory. In 1749 François-Alexandre

Tutrel founded another factory, Manufacture Tutrel, which closed in 1770.

Rent table See DRUM TABLE.

Rep A corded textile used in curtains and upholstery.

Repairer The craftsperson who assembles the separately cast parts of a ceramic figure such as the legs, arms, head, and torso before it is fired.

Repeater A mechanism in a clock or watch that repeats the strike of the past hour, the quarter hour, and subsequent minutes, to enable the owner to tell the time without looking at the dial. The mechanism is activated by pulling a cord or lever or pressing a button and is found mainly on watches and CARRIAGE CLOCKS.

Repoussé work ■ A French term for the relief decoration on malleable metals that have been embossed by hand-hammering the relief design from the back or inside of the body. See CHASING and EMBOSSING.

Reserve ■ 1. An area of a design, especially in textiles, porcelain, and glass that is left uncolored or unworked. SÈVRES porcelain often features white reserve panels painted with figurative motifs such as birds or flowers. 2. An auction term referring to the minimum amount of money required by the seller (not including a deduction for the

Renaissance
Fragment of Renaissance Brussels tapestry, showing the Twelve Ages of Man. Early 16th century.

Acanthus foliage moldings

Renaissance Revival
One of a pair of Renaissance Revival ewers, in patinated bronze on a red marble base.

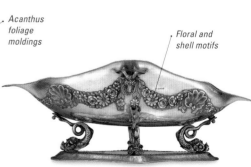

Floral and shell motifs

Repoussé work
Silver-plated bowl, decorated with extensive repoussé swags.

auctioneer's commission), below which the auctioneer is not allowed to sell the object.

Resist luster ■ A ceramic decoration in which parts of an object are temporarily "resisted" with a wax or paper cut-out so that the LUSTER solution applied to the whole does not affect those areas.

Restauration style ■ The decorative arts popular in France from around 1815 to 1830 during the restoration of the monarchy under Louis XVII (1814–24) and Charles X (1824–30). The French royal family continued to employ craftsmen such as Pierre FONTAINE and François JACOB-DESMALTER, who had enjoyed the patronage of Napoleon I. Furnishings made in this period are largely in the EMPIRE style, but in more restrained designs. Restauration furniture used light-colored wood and eschewed elaborate mounts. On SÈVRES PORCELAIN, flowers, birds, and views replaced scenes of battles and the life of Napoleon. The furniture of Pierre-Antoine BELLANGÉ introduced RENAISSANCE and GOTHIC REVIVAL motifs.

Restoration style The decorative arts popular in England from the restoration of the monarchy in 1660 to the late 1680s, also known as the CAROLEAN style after Charles II (reigned 1660–85). The return of the King and his court from exile on the Continent led to the replacement of the Puritan severity of the CROMWELLIAN style with a taste for magnificence and opulence and to the introduction of Dutch and French artistic influences. These were evident in furniture in the use of floral MARQUETRY, walnut instead of oak, twisted, turned supports and legs, exotic veneers, cane seats and backs on chairs, sumptuous tapestry and velvet upholstery, and ornate carved and gilded scrolling bases for cabinets. Restoration silver is characterized by embossed motifs of tulips and naturalistic fruit and leaves. New types of furniture introduced in this period include CABINETS-ON-STANDS, CHESTS-OF-DRAWERS, armchairs and WING CHAIRS, DAY BEDS, and SETTEES.

The growing power of the British EAST INDIA COMPANY resulted in increased imports of exotic commodities from China and Japan, including tea, porcelain and LACQUER, and CHINTZES from India. This led to a craze for CHINOISERIE, reflected in the development of imitation lacquer (JAPANNING), blue and white decoration on ceramics, flat-chased scenes of Chinese-style figures and landscapes on silver, new forms of silver such as teapots, as well as colorful Indian-style CREWELWORK bed-hangings and curtains. Other developments in the Restoration period were the emergence of the English glass industry, following the perfection of LEAD GLASS by George RAVENSCROFT around 1676, and the manufacture of SLIPWARE by Thomas Toft. After the accession of William III and Mary II in 1689, Restoration style was superseded by WILLIAM AND MARY STYLE.

Reticella An Italian term for the decorative geometric grid designs created by drawing out and cutting away threads from a woven linen ground and then filling the spaces with complex designs worked in a variety of detached buttonhole stitches. Made primarily from the early 15th to the late 18th century and the forerunner of NEEDLELACE, it was made popular in the 16th century by the fashion for heavily starched collars and ruffs. Reticella is still made in the traditional way, mainly for domestic use, in Italy, Greece, and Cyprus.

Reticello glass The Italian term used to describe glass incorporating thin threads of opaque white or colored glass arranged in a crisscross pattern to form a fine net. Small, trapped air bubble inclusions may also appear. See FILIGRANA.

Reticulated A pattern in the form of a network or web, either open or filled in (blind reticulation). On glass, the most common technique is RETICELLO, but the pattern may also be applied by cutting and engraving or by blowing the glass bubble into a wire mesh so that the glass bulges out through the spaces between the wires. It is also used for ceramics and metal. See PIERCED DECORATION.

Reveillon, Jean-Baptiste ■ (died 1811) An important French wallpaper designer and manufacturer. Starting out as a retailer, in 1765 he founded a factory at Faubourg Saint-Antoine and worked with original

Reserve
Sèvres cache pots, painted with scenes of romantic dalliance on gilt reserves. 19th century.

Resist luster
Pearlware ovoid jug, with angular loop handle, decorated in silver resist. c. 1815.

Restauration style
Restauration pendulum clock, with engraved and gilded bronze mounts.

Reveillon, Jean-Baptiste
Piece of Indian-style wallpaper, with flowers, strawberries, lily of the valley, and lovebirds.

designs. A great innovator and perfectionist, Reveillon used quality paper and insoluble colors, producing wallpaper for three markets: elaborate luxury papers for the wealthy aristocracy; block-printed papers for the bourgeoisie; and simple one-color papers for those of humble means. His factory was destroyed in 1789 during the French Revolution.

Revere, Paul ■ (1734–1818) An American patriot, silversmith, and folk hero of the Revolutionary War. He is famous for his dramatic midnight ride from Boston to Lexington in 1775, warning his countrymen that the British were on the march. Revere was the son of a French HUGUENOT silversmith, Apollos Rivoire. He began work as a silversmith in Boston before 1760, but was largely unsuccessful until after the war, supplementing his income with work as a print-engraver. His best pieces were made under the patronage of a wealthy American elite and can be compared to the work of contemporaries Joseph Richardson in Philadelphia and Myer MYERS in New York City. Revere's career spans the American COLONIAL and FEDERAL periods and his style changes accordingly. Pieces made before the Revolutionary War are rare and highly prized.

His postwar work, much of which was carried out for wealthy Boston families, is generally more refined, featuring BRIGHT CUT DECORATION and engraved motifs. In the 1780s Revere became involved in

other businesses, including a foundry and a copper rolling mill.

Reverse painting See MIRROR PAINTING.

Revolver A repeating firearm with a multi-chambered cylinder rotating around a central axis, perfected by SAMUEL COLT in 1836. In firing, each chamber is aligned and locked with the firing mechanism and barrel.

Revolving chair ■ A chair with a swivel seat. The earliest examples date to the 16th century, but the concept did not come into vogue until the 18th century and the fashion for adjustable height MUSIC STOOLS. Revolving chairs for invalids became relatively commonplace by the end of the 19th century. However, it was not until after World War II that the concept was really exploited (for both domestic and office use). Notable exponents included Charles EAMES, Eero SAARINEN, and Arne JACOBSEN. Eames's lounge chair No. 670, a traditional armchair mounted on a metal swivel base, combined masculine good looks with comfort. Along with Saarinen's swivel Tulip chair, it remains much admired and is still replicated today.

Rhead Family ■ Three generations of English ceramicists. George Woolliscroft Rhead Sr. worked for BROWN, WESTHEAD, MOORE & CO. and MINTON. He had three sons: George

Woolliscroft, who worked at Minton Art Studio and FOLEY POTTERIES; Louis John, who was an artist, illustrator, and successful American poster artist; and Frederick Alfred, a potter, designer, teacher, and writer, who worked for W. Brownfield, Minton, WEDGWOOD, SHELLEY, Cauldon Potteries, and ROYAL WORCESTER PORCELAIN CO. Frederick Alfred had three children who followed in the family tradition: Frederick Hurten RHEAD; Harry G. Rhead, who worked for a number of potteries in the US before starting the Standard Tile Co. in Zanesville, Ohio, in 1923; and Charlotte Rhead, who trained under her father and was a designer and skilled TUBE-LINE decorator for many pottery ranges, including CROWN DUCAL.

Rhead, Frederick Hurten (1880–1942) An English-born potter active in the US from 1902, where he worked at the Weller Pottery in Zanesville, Ohio (1888–1948), and was art director of the ROSEVILLE Pottery. In 1911 he joined AREQUIPA pottery, where he remained for two years. From 1913 to 1917 he ran a pottery with his wife in Santa Barbara. He designed the extremely successful American tableware Fiesta, first produced in 1936. He later concentrated on research, teaching, and writing. Rhead's designs feature incised decoration and are signed with a monogram.

Rhineland stoneware (or Rheinish) ■ Heavy salt-glazed wine jars and tankards made in several places along the Rhine River

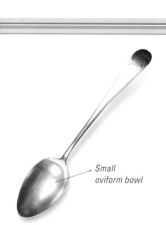

Revere, Paul
Boston silver spoon, bearing the touch of Paul Revere II. Late 18th century.

Small oviform bowl

Revolving chair
Arts and Crafts mahogany revolving chair, with slatted back and tripulitic legs. c. 1881.

Rhead Family
Bursley ware vase by Charlotte Rhead, with stylized flowers, fruit, and printed marks.

Rhineland stoneware
Salt-glazed brown stoneware Bellamine jug, with an old man's face. c. 1660.

in Germany for the Rhenish wine trade, from the late 16th to the 18th century. Vessels often have a bearded mask near the rim and a small loop handle, and are called BELLARMINES or Bartmanns.

Rhinestone ■ Originally a type of clear quartz dug from the Rhine River in Germany and used for COSTUME JEWELRY. It is now a commercial term usually referring to colorless PASTE or rock crystal imitating diamonds. It can also broadly apply to many imitation gems in jewelry made after the 1930s.

Rhodium A brilliant silvery-white metal, similar to PLATINUM, discovered in 1803. It is durable, resistant to corrosion, and is used mainly for plating metalwork, precious jewelry, and COSTUME JEWELRY.

Rhyton ■ A drinking horn or cup in the form of a stag's antler. Originally made from horn, but later made all over Europe and China in silver, pottery, and porcelain.

Ribbing A ridged or raised line formed by introducing a coarser yarn into a woven textile. The term also describes the same effect on knitted fabric created by the alternation of plain and purl stitches.

Ribbon plate An inexpensive porcelain plate made widely in Europe in the late 19th and early 20th centuries with pierced rims, either for decorative fruit sets or to be threaded with a ribbon and hung on a wall.

German and British examples often had lithographed views.

Ribbon-back A style of chair back in which the backsplats are carved to resemble ribbons tied in bows. Essentially a ROCOCO motif, the decoration was employed on a number of CHIPPENDALE and Chippendale-style chairs.

Rice-grain A perforated decoration used on porcelain in Asia from the 12th century and popular on 18th-century Chinese QIANLONG wares. The body is pierced with small holes resembling grains of rice. The transparent glaze that covers the vessel fills in and seals the pierced work, which remains faintly visible.

Richardson's An English glass dynasty established near the town of STOURBRIDGE, West Midlands, in 1829, and taken over in 1930 by Thomas WEBB & Sons. Richardson's was one of the greatest British glassmakers of the mid-Victorian era. They developed a range of colors never before used in Britain and were used by the household of Queen Victoria to furnish the royal glass pantries.

Richardson, Henry Hobson (1838–86) An influential American architect and designer, active in New York City and Brookline, Massachusetts, from 1867. He studied at Harvard and in Paris, where he worked briefly for the NEOCLASSICAL architect Jacques-Ignace Hittorf. The "Richardsonian"

style is comparable to the work of Edward William GODWIN. Richardson also designed typically heavy, solid furniture for many of his buildings.

Ridgways A factory set up by Job Ridgway at Cauldon Place, Staffordshire, in 1802. It produced blue and white STONE CHINA (Cauldon ware). Job's sons, John and William, continued after his death, exporting quantities of Cauldon ware to the US, some of it decorated specially for this market. Rare porcelain marked "Ridgway & Sons" dates from 1808 to 1814. The firm was run by the Ridgway family until 1964, when it was absorbed by Allied English Potteries.

Rie, Dame Lucie ■ (1902–95) A studio potter born in Vienna who trained under Michael POWOLNY at the Kunstgewerbeschule. She went to England as a refugee in 1938 and made glass buttons at a friend's workshop while setting up her own studio in London. Rie produced mainly domestic wares, in both stoneware and porcelain. She was a friend of Bernard LEACH, but her style is less Oriental and more European. Hans COPER began his career as Rie's assistant.

Riedel, Gottlieb Friedrich (1724–84) A German porcelain painter of landscapes and birds and designer of services and figures. He was a decorator at the MEISSEN factory from 1743 to 1756, at FRANKENTHAL from 1756 to 1759, and from 1759 to 1779 worked as chief

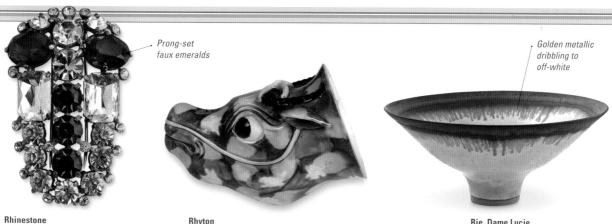

Rhinestone
Eisenberg Original fur clip, set with emerald and clear crystal rhinestones. 1940s.

Prong-set faux emeralds

Rhyton
A Kangxi biscuit porcelain rhyton, in the form of a buffalo head.

Golden metallic dribbling to off-white

Rie, Dame Lucie
Footed conical stoneware bowl, with golden metallic glazing around the rim.

R

decorator at LUDWIGSBURG, designing a set of miniature figures and stalls of the annual "Venetian Fair" in Württemberg. As an engraver, he published transfer patterns for porcelain decorators.

Riemerschmid, Richard (1868–1957) A German painter, architect, and designer of glass, metalware, furniture, ceramics, and textiles. He was a founder of the Vereinigte Werksätten für Kunst im Handwerk in Munich (1897) and also of the Deutsche Werkbund (1907), two important institutes that encouraged artists, designers, and manufacturers to work to the mutual benefit of all.

Riesener, Jean-Henri ■ (1734–1806) A German-born French furniture-maker celebrated for elegant design and exceptional craftsmanship. He joined the workshop of Jean-François OEBEN after 1754, becoming the manager after his patron's death and marrying his widow. By 1767 he had been appointed a *maître ébéniste*, completing the famous Bureau de Roi, originally commissioned from Oeben and now in the palace of Versailles. As well as being a gifted designer, he also made his own furniture. Hallmarks of his style include elaborate floral marquetry panels, richly sculptured gilt-bronze mounts, and careful treatment of the carcase. Following his appointment as *ébéniste* to Louis XVI, Riesener produced

sumptuous COMMODES, secretaires, and mechanical furniture for an illustrious coterie of patrons. He began as an earnest advocate of the ROCOCO tradition, but also adopted the elegant, rectilinear style becoming fashionable in architecture and the decorative arts. His ability to accommodate changes in taste served him well in the economy campaign of 1784. Many of his pieces made in the 1780s—plain mahogany veneers embellished with slender fillets of gilt bronze—seem austere by comparison to his earlier work. Riesener survived the Revolution and was employed to remove royal emblems from furniture in 1794. He purchased many of his own pieces at the Revolutionary sales and continued in business until 1801. His work under the Directoire and Consulate lacked the originality and distinctive quality upon which his reputation rests.

Riessner, Stellmacher & Kessel's See AMPHORA POTTERY.

Rietveld, Gerrit ■ (1888–1964) A Dutch architect and designer and member of the De Stijl group of painters and designers, whose work was based on geometric shapes, the use of primary colors, and the eschewing of all ornament. He is best known for his Red-Blue Chair (1918), Zig-Zag Chair (1932), and the Truus Schröder-Schrader House (1924–25) and its interior.

Rifle A firearm in which the bore is cut with spirally twisting grooves. On firing,

the bullet engages with the grooves and this makes it spin, thus increasing its accuracy. Rifled firearms were known as early as the 16th century, but were not perfected until the mid-19th century.

Rinceau ■ A French term for a continuous spiraling or wavy ornament, usually composed of scrolling vine foliage or ACANTHUS leaves. A popular decorative motif in the 18th century, the *rinceau* was adopted by ornamental designers for carved, molded, and painted decoration.

Ringler, Joseph Jacob ■ (1730–1802) An Austrian porcelain-maker who worked in the Imperial factory in VIENNA from 1744, where he became an ARCANIST, learning about making porcelain and building kilns. He left Vienna and was a porcelain-maker at HÖCHST in 1750, STRASBOURG in 1752, briefly in Neudeck, NYMPHENBURG, from 1753 until 1757, and Ellwangen from 1753 until 1758. Ringler moved to LUDWIGSBURG in Germany in 1759 and settled there as director for over 40 years.

Risenburgh II, Bernard van (c. 1700–65/7) A French furniture-maker, who was the son of a *maître ébéniste* of Dutch origin. Until 1957, when his full name was discovered, he was known only by his stamp, "BVRB." Risenburgh worked exclusively for Parisian dealers, through whom his elegant and refined furniture was supplied to a distinguished clientele that included Louis

Riesener, Jean-Henri
Louis XVI parquetry semainier, veneered in tulipwood and purplewood. c. 1780.

Rietveld, Gerrit
Red-Blue Chair—this example made under license by Cassina. c. 1980.

Rinceau
Murano glass mirror, the frame richly engraved with *rinceau* and leaves. c. 1800.

Scrolling and spiraling forms

Ringler, Joseph Jacob
Unusual Meissen model of Cupid with two dachshunds. c. 1899.

XV, his mistress, Madame de Pompadour, and the German courts. A *maître ébéniste* himself by 1730, Risenburgh specialized in furniture decorated with MARQUETRY designs of naturalistic flowers, or veneered in Oriental or imitation Japanese gold and black LACQUER, and occasionally in VERNIS MARTIN. He was the first furniture-maker to apply SÈVRES porcelain plaques to furniture, a practice popularly revived in the late 19th century.

Roanne potteries There were several FAIENCE factories in Roanne, France, the first to be documented founded by Richard Teste around 1632. Its 17th-century products include tiles and large dishes. There were nine factories active in the area before the French Revolution, making tableware and larger pieces such as stoves and wall fountains. During the Revolution, *faience patriotique* was made. One of the last factories to remain active was the Faiencerie Sebastian Nicolas, in operation from 1772 until 1866.

Robbia, Luca della The most important member of a family of Florentine RENAISSANCE sculptors, who were the first to use a ceramic medium for sculpture and gave their name to a type of TIN-GLAZED EARTHENWARE (della Robbia ware). They made many representations of the Virgin and Child and other religious subjects, in frames formed of wreaths of fruit, leaves, and flowers. They also made vases with realistically modeled and colored fruit and flowers for decorating churches and houses.

Andrea della Robbia, nephew to Luca, worked exclusively in tin-glazed earthenware and made many RELIEFS, the most famous of which are the babies in swaddling clothes on the facade of Brunelleschi's Loggia degli Innocenti in Florence.

Robin's-egg glaze An opaque speckled pale blue or turquoise glaze used on Chinese porcelain from around 1720, particularly on wares of archaic form.

Robineau, Adelaide Alsop ■ (1865–1929) An American STUDIO POTTER, active in Syracuse, New York, making porcelain from 1903. Her work is rare and mostly consists of small, ovoid vessels decorated with pale, CRYSTALLINE GLAZES and stylized flora in the manner of the French caddy ceramicist Taxile Doat. Later, she used Chinese and Mayan motifs. Prized examples feature RETICULATED decoration. Her company closed in 1928.

Robinson & Leadbeater ■ A factory in Stoke-on-Trent from 1864 to 1924 that made inexpensive PARIANWARE figures and busts. Early examples are unmarked and are of better quality than the later ones, which were sometimes marked with "R & L" in an oval, or with the full name.

Robinson, Gerrard (1834–91) An English woodcarver who was born in Newcastle-upon-Tyne, where he remained for most of his working life. Robinson is best known for his massive carved oak SIDEBOARDS.

His accomplished furniture was suited to the popular taste and was displayed at numerous international exhibitions.

Robsjohn-Gibbings, Terence Harold (1905–76) An English-born furniture designer, writer, and interior decorator who had his own showroom on Madison Avenue, New York, and designed furniture for John Widdicomb Co. He moved to Athens in 1964, where he designed the Classically inspired KLISMOS chair (1961).

Rocaille ■ A French term meaning "rockwork" and the iconic decorative motif of the ROCOCO STYLE. It derives from the rock and shell forms used in GROTTO decoration. The jagged asymmetrical shapes provided a backdrop for motifs such as SCROLLwork, CHINOISERIE, and flowers.

Rock & Gräner A toy manufacturer in Biberach, Germany, that was one of the earliest producers of TINPLATE toys. The company was established around 1813 by Christian Gottfried Rock and his brother-in-law, Gottfried Wilhelm Gräner. Rock & Gräner specialized in well-crafted, hand-painted dollhouse furniture, forts and castles, railroad locomotives, boats, and dioramas. The company exhibited at the 1851 GREAT EXHIBITION.

Rock crystal ■ A clear, colorless form of QUARTZ used from antiquity for forming into *objets d'art* and jewelry. One of the most luxurious substances known to

Robineau, Adelaide Alsop
Porcelain vase, with the artist's "AR" medallion carved on its side.

Robinson & Leadbeater
White parian portrait bust of British prime minister Arthur Balfour.

Detail of rocaille

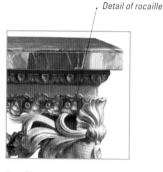

Rocaille
George II console table, with a band of rocaille running below the cornice. c. 1745.

Rock crystal
Victorian rock crystal pendant, surmounted by a crown set with diamonds and pearls.

mankind that has been carved into the most splendid vessels, gems and objects for thousands of years. Collected by many of the great figures of history, including LOUIS IX.

Rocking chair ■ A chair mounted on curved BENDS between the front and back feet, introduced in the US and Britain in the 1760s. It was particularly popular in the US, with several unique types such as the BOSTON ROCKER, derived from the WINDSOR CHAIR. It was adapted in the UK in the Victorian period in a diverse range of designs. A bentwood version was pioneered by THONET from the mid-19th century. A later version stands firmly on the floor while the seat rocks on springs.

Rockingham glaze The name given in the US to a rich, lustrous, brown glaze, sometimes called treacle glaze. It was obtained by the use of MANGANESE and applied to American, British, and other earthenware from about 1870 to 1920. The ware was produced at numerous potteries, but is particularly associated with the United States Pottery Co. of BENNINGTON, Vermont. Typical products in the glaze include pitchers, Toby jugs, mantelpiece dogs and other animals, and spirit flasks.

Rockingham Pottery and Porcelain Factory ■ Possibly founded as early as 1745 on the estate of the Marquess of Rockingham at

Swinton in Yorkshire, England. In its early period, the factory produced EARTHENWARE similar to that of LEEDS and some with a treacle-like glaze, including the lidless CADOGAN TEAPOT. From 1826 until its closure in 1842, it produced high-quality BONE CHINA in ROCOCO REVIVAL style, especially tea and dessert services with rich floral decoration. It also produced well-modeled animal figures. The Rockingham mark (the griffin of the Rockingham family) was widely imitated.

Rockingham ware ■ A name used generically in the US to describe earthenware decorated with a ROCKINGHAM GLAZE, made in several states of the US, Britain, Australia, and Canada from around 1830 to the end of the 19th century. The most valued items are pre-1840 American pieces of interesting form such as bottles shaped as coachmen, attributable to specific factories, especially BENNINGTON.

Rococo ■ Originating in France in the early 18th century, the Rococo style swept Europe and then reached the US. Seen in all branches of the decorative arts, its characteristics include ornaments of shells and other naturalistic forms, extravagantly carved, gilded, and engraved.

The beginnings of the Rococo style can be traced to the work of Jean BÉRAIN in the early years of the 18th century. By the RÉGENCE of the Duc d'Orleans in 1715, a new lightness and curvaceousness

of form in the decorative arts was apparent. Designs by the French court silversmith Juste-Aurèle MEISSONIER as early as 1724 are asymmetrical and soon afterward this had become a well-defined feature of the new and rapidly evolving style that was to sweep Europe, arriving in England around 1735.

Rococo furniture has curving CABRIOLE legs, often inlaid with MARQUETRY of exotic woods, and embellished with pierced and gilded foliate and curving mounts. The emergence of Rococo coincided with the development of the European porcelain industry, and the style was taken up enthusiastically by factories such as MEISSEN, NYMPHENBURG, SÈVRES, BOW, and CHELSEA. Leading silversmiths such as Paul de LAMERIE produced tureens, candelabra, and other wares with cast ornament of shells, flowers, and fruit. During the mid-18th century, a reaction against the Rococo style emerged, and it was gradually replaced by the more austere NEOCLASSICAL STYLE of the 1750s.

Rococo Revival ■ A style of decorative arts and interior design popular from the 1830s to the early 1900s throughout Europe and the US, reviving the forms and motifs of the 18th-century ROCOCO style. One of the most popular of the 19th-century Revival styles, it emerged in the 1820s and 30s as part of a vogue for "Old French" styles and remained popular for much of the century. All the

Rocking chair
Canadian rod-back Windsor rocking chair, with raised comb piece. c. 1830.

Sprigs of flowers

Rockingham pottery
Rockingham porcelain Rococo-style teapot, cup, and saucer, decorated with flowers.

Rockingam ware
Rockingham ware with mottled brown glaze. 19th century.

Rococo Revival
Louis XV-style silver candelabra of ornate Rococo scroll form. 19th century.

decorative arts, but especially furniture, porcelain, and metalwork, feature larger, heavier, and more sinuous forms than in 18th-century originals, with a greater profusion of ornament, typically shells, flowers, and scroll work. The brighter colors and shinier gilding distinguish Rococo Revival porcelain made, for example, at MEISSEN and SÈVRES, from authentic Rococo pieces, even though at such leading factories, 18th-century molds were reused for casting. In the US the style was popularized by John Henry BELTER in his patented molded and laminated ROSEWOOD furniture, decorated with elaborate OPENWORK and carving.

Rod A term used in glassmaking for a cylindrical length of glass that can be monochrome, colored, polychrome, or contain smaller threads of glass arranged in a decorative pattern. Also known as a CANE. The glass can vary in width and may be used in lengths as decoration in glass STEMS or as part of the BODY of an object. It can also be cut into slices and used as decoration in PAPERWEIGHTS or on vases or bowls, where the slices are known as MURRINES. Rods were first widely used in VENETIAN GLASS.

Rod bear An early TEDDY BEAR, made for only one year, from 1904 to 1905, by STEIFF. Rod bears are jointed by means of two firm horizontal metal rods at the shoulder and hip level and one vertical rod through the neck and head, holding the bear together with movable limbs. Rod bears can be identified by X-rays or by a hand-sewn seam on the top of their head between the ears. Disk-jointing replaced rod-jointing in 1905.

Rodney decanter A decanter shape named after the British naval hero Admiral Rodney, who defeated the French fleet at Cape Saint Vincent in 1780. Typically, it has a large broad base, suitable for the cabin of a ship's officer.

R

315

ROCOCO

The term is probably derived from the French *rocaille* (rockwork) and *coquillage* (shellwork), referring to the scrolling ornament of shells and rockwork, which is one of the most distinctive features of the style. Other characteristics include complex arrangements of C- and S-SCROLLS, fantastic and exotic marine forms, naturalistic flowers, and an emphasis on movement. Forms are small in scale, delicate, and elegant, in sharp contrast to the massive, symmetrical shapes of the BAROQUE. Chinese and Indian motifs are also common. The Rococo style is exemplified by the work of Charles CRESSENT in France and Thomas CHIPPENDALE in England. The designs of the latter had a particularly strong influence on American cabinet-makers and carvers, especially Thomas AFFLECK, James Reynolds, and Hercules Courtenay.

Sucrier
Sèvres *sucrier*, decorated with garlands of flowers on an *oeil de perdrix* ground. 1767.

Mirror
Louis XV mirror, the gilded frame carved with typical Rococo scrolls and foliage.

Clock
A Louis XV-style gilt metal table clock, 1863.

Roentgen, David ■ (1743–1807) A German furniture-maker who had outlets in Berlin, Vienna, and Paris. His sumptuous, heavily Germanic furniture is characterized by *trompe l'oeil* pictorial MARQUETRY, elaborate mechanical devices, and an architectural monumentality. His marquetry designs were celebrated for their technical virtuosity and skilled composition, using delicate INLAYS of variously colored woods. Roentgen's Paris depot supplied finely crafted furniture to the French royal palaces and he was given the unique title of *Ébéniste-méchanicien du Roi et de la Reine* by Louis XVI. He joined the Paris guild and was made a maître in 1789, taking the stamp "DAVID," although he rarely signed or stamped his work. Roentgen also supplied a vast quantity of furniture to the Empress Catherine II of Russia, and in 1791 was appointed court furnisher to Frederick William II in Berlin. His fortunes as the most famous *ébéniste* in Europe came to an abrupt end with the French Revolution in 1789, when his workshops were pillaged and his Paris depot confiscated. Although Roentgen tried to reestablish his business in the early 19th century, he was unsuccessful.

Rogers Brothers A firm of American silver-plate manufacturers, active from 1847 in the silversmithing towns of Hartford and Meriden, Connecticut, which made the first successful ELECTROPLATE wares in the US. In 1856 it was absorbed into the Meriden Britannia Co., the largest silver-plate maker in the US, now known as the International Silver Co., although the name "Rogers" continued to be used for some years.

Rogers group An American plaster genre group made from designs by the sculptor John Rogers in New York from 1859 to 1893. Most were painted in pale gray but some were polychromed in realistic colors.

Rohde, Gilbert ■ (1894–1944) Son of a cabinet-maker, designing furniture from 1927, inspired by the work of the French avant-garde BAUHAUS and ART DECO. Rohde established an office in New York in 1929 and from there designed furniture for Heywood-Wakefield, THONET, and Herman Miller. His typically simple, well-constructed forms appealed to the modern lifestyle, with storage units, sectional sofas, and the Living-Dining Group. His Design for Living House was displayed at the 1933 Century of Progress exhibition in Chicago, and his interiors were shown at the 1934 Machine Art exhibition at the Museum of Modern Art in New York. He also exhibited work at the 1939 New York World's Fair. Rohde was head of industrial design at New York University's School of Architecture from 1939 to 1943.

Rohde, Johan ■ (1856–1935) A Danish painter and designer who approached Georg JENSEN to make some FLATWARE and HOLLOWWARE pieces in 1907. The resulting collaboration worked well and he designed for Jensen from 1907. His work included the popular Konge (Acorn) pattern cutlery and the notable Pitcher No. 432A, with its curvaceous, MODERN styling, designed in 1920.

Rohlfs, Charles ■ (1853–1936) An American ARTS AND CRAFTS furniture designer who opened the Charles Rohlfs Workshop in Buffalo, New York (1898–1928). His distinctive style combined Arts and Crafts solidity with ART NOUVEAU ornament and Norwegian craft influences. His furniture was mostly made from OAK with FRETWORK decoration and carved motifs.

Rolex ■ A wristwatch manufacturing company set up in London by Hans Wilsdorf in 1905 and still functioning today. It specialized in importing watch movements from Switzerland. Wilsdorf was convinced that wristwatches would become popular and persisted in promoting them. The name "Rolex" was chosen in 1908 because it sounded more or less the same in many different languages. In 1926 the name "Oyster" was patented and used for the innovative water-resistant case that became the foundation of the company's success.

Rolled gold Imitation solid gold created by fusing a thin layer of gold to a base metal such as copper and then rolling it into sheets, in a method similar to that used for SHEFFIELD PLATE. It was used for inexpensive jewelry and small decorative objects in the 19th and early 20th centuries.

Roentgen, David
Mahogany, rosewood, and maple marquetry table, by David Roentgen. c. 1770.

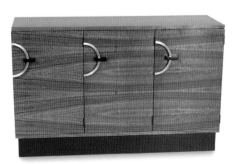

Rohde, Gilbert
East India laurel sideboard, the doors with chrome and black-enameled wood pulls.

Rohde, Johan
Georg Jensen water jug, designed by Johan Rohde. Design No. 432A. c. 1925.

Rolled paperwork A technique used in the Victorian period for decorating small items such as boxes using small scrolls of paper.

Rolling ball clock See CONGREVE CLOCK.

Roman pottery ■ Ceramics produced in various parts of the Roman Empire from the 1st century BCE until the 4th century CE. The most distinctive type of Roman pottery is Arretine ware and its provincial equivalent, Terra Sigillata or Samian ware. This red, glossy pottery was typically relief-molded. In the provinces and in the later stages of the Roman Empire, decoration gradually became more abstract and in Northern Europe took on a CELTIC flavor. The technique of lead glazing, introduced from Asia Minor to Italy, reached Southern Gaul by the middle of the 1st century CE and the Rhineland and England by the 3rd century CE, producing handsome jugs and other vessels with a greenish yellow glaze. The eastern provinces of the Empire developed a type of pottery from powdered QUARTZ that had originated in Egypt, characterized by glassy, brilliantly colored turquoise blue glaze, which remained popular from the 1st until the 3rd century CE. Vessels made of each of these types of pottery were exported in great quantities to other parts of the Empire from their sites of manufacture.

Roman striking system A mechanism invented by the 17th-century English clock-

ROMAN GLASS

Made across the Roman Empire from around 100 BCE until its collapse in the 4th century CE. Wares in Roman glass included quantities of CORE-FORMED, free-, and MOLD-BLOWN glass bottles, AMPHORAS, and flasks, as well as luxurious CAMEO and MOSAIC glass. Prolonged burial gave excavated pieces an IRIDESCENT appearance, which inspired the work of TIFFANY.

Mottled iridescence

Roman glass
Roman unguentarium in honey-colored glass. 1st to 3rd century CE.

maker Joseph KNIBB. This system aimed to reduce the number of hammer blows and thus the power storage of the weight. One bell strikes for the Roman numeral I and another for V—for example, the hour VII may be struck by one low note then two high ones.

Romanesque Revival A 19th-century style inspired by ROMANESQUE architecture. It was largely confined to architecture, in particular the work of Henry H. Richardson in the US, but it is also seen on furniture. Wardrobe and cabinet doors were decorated with carving of round-headed arches in the style of Romanesque buildings, and in the 19th century jewelry featured brightly colored CHAMPLEVÉ enamels. The style was also used by eclectic 20th-century designers such as Piero FORNASETTI.

Romanesque style The architecture, painting, manuscript illumination, sculpture, and decorative arts from the mid-11th century to the end of the 12th century, when it was supplanted by the GOTHIC style. Inspired by Classical Roman architecture, it is characterized by the use of round-headed arches, arcading, naturalistic birds and animals, geometric motifs such as CHEVRONS and LOZENGES, and CLOISONNÉ and CHAMPLEVÉ enamels.

Römer (röemer) ■ A traditional German or Dutch drinking glass. Derived from 15th-century BEAKERS, early examples took the

R

317

Rohlfs, Charles
Rare and early Charles Rohlfs Arts & Crafts stained oak settee, with signature mark. 1900.

Rotating bezel

Rolex
Stainless steel Rolex Comex Sea Dweller, Ref: 1665, with plastic face. 1970s.

Roman pottery
Roman buff pottery mug in the form of the head of Dionysus.

R

form of a low, cup-shaped bowl on a hollow stem decorated with PRUNTS and a short, coiled foot. On later examples the stem became shorter and the foot wider. Derivatives and variants are still commonly made today and are used for drinking white wine.

Rookwood Pottery ■ An American ART POTTERY founded by Maria Longworth Nichols in 1880 in Cincinnati, Ohio, and named after her old childhood home. One of her decorators was her friend Mary Louise Mclaughlin. William Watts Taylor joined Rookwood as a partner in 1883 and took over the pottery when Maria remarried in 1890. Maria had been impressed by the Japanese ceramics at the Philadelphia Centennial Exposition in 1876 and many Rookwood art wares have an Oriental feel. In 1888 a Japanese artist, Kataro Shirayamadani, was taken on. Recognizing the commercial potential for good glazes, a chemist, Karl Langenbeck, was employed in the same year. Silver appliqué (overlay) was introduced in 1892. Portraits, figures, animals, and birds were made from 1897, and tiles from 1901. Taylor died in 1913 and the pottery continued with a board of trustees until it failed in 1941. After World War II, Rookwood reopened with new owners and less time was spent on art wares. After 1971 various owners came and went, and revivals using old molds were tried. In 1982 Arthur Townley of Michigan Center bought Rookwood and a limited number of pieces have since been made from old molds.

Rörstrand Pottery and Porcelain Factory ■ The most important Swedish FAIENCE factory, along with MARIEBERG, with which it merged in 1782. It was founded in 1726, near Stockholm, under royal patronage. The earliest wares were blue and white, based on German and DELFT models, and after 1745 it was one of the first Northern European factories to use the BIANCO-SOPRA-BIANCO technique. By the 1760s wares were influenced by French FAIENCE and were mostly in ROCOCO style. By 1771 the factory was making CREAMWARE, and faience manufacture was discontinued in 1797. In the 19th century Rörstrand produced a variety of ceramics, including copies of PARIANWARE and LIMOGES ENAMELS, as well as porcelain showing Swedish scenes. Under the direction of Alf Wallander, the factory embraced ART NOUVEAU, making use of PÂTE-SUR-PÂTE and FLAMBÉ glazes. In the 1920s and 30s leading designers such as Edward Hald reflected contemporary Swedish design. A modern Swedish style was maintained through the 1940s and 50s. In 1964 Rörstrand became part of the Upsala-Ekeby group. See ORREFORS GLASSWORKS.

Rose amberina See AMBERINA.

Rose du Barry A term used by 19th-century English porcelain factories for "rose Pompadour," a pink ground

color used on SÈVRES porcelain. It was not called by either of these names in the 18th century; the Sèvres factory records refer only to "roze"—a delicate rose red ground said to have been discovered in 1757 by the decorator Xhrouet. Madame de Pompadour was the mistress of Louis XV and a patron of the factory.

Rose Pompadour See ROSE DU BARRY.

Rose, John (1772–1841) The founder of the porcelain factory that later became the COALPORT AND COALBROOKDALE PORCELAIN FACTORY. Both Rose and his brother, Thomas, trained at CAUGHLEY. In around 1796, he began porcelain production at nearby Coalport, and in 1799 acquired Caughley itself. Early Coalport wares were mostly copies of Chinese patterns, but Rose also supplied independent china-painters with plain white porcelain. By 1803 John Rose & Co. was one of the leading porcelain manufacturers in England, and in 1814 it also acquired the factory of Anstice, Horton & Thomas Rose, partly owned by Thomas Rose.

Rosenthal Porcelain Factory ■ Founded by Philipp Rosenthal in 1879 as a decorating studio. In 1889 Rosenthal opened a factory in Selb, Bavaria, to make his own ceramics to decorate. He also employed well-known designers and modelers. From 1900 a group of pieces with marbled and luster finishes were designed by Adolf Oppel in the ART

Römer
German römer, with applied berries on a trumpet-shaped hollow stem. 18th century.

Rörstrand Pottery
Rörstrand porcelain vase, with manta-ray decoration and handles.

Rosenthal Porcelain Factory
Rosenthal porcelain figure of a dancer, by Lore Friedrich-Gronau. 20th century.

Rosette
Rosette carving on the side of an 18th-century New Mexico pine chest.

NOUVEAU style. In the 1920s and 30s, strong figurative designs were produced, and in the 1950s Rosenthal produced pieces by Beate Kuhn and the American industrial designers Raymond Loewy and Richard Latham. In 1961 Rosenthal introduced their Studio Line, producing high-quality pieces by leading designers (for example, Tapio WIRKKALA). The company continues today, making traditional and modern pieces.

Rosette ■ A circular patera or disk ornament in the shape of a rose, sometimes with formalized roselike petals. An ancient decorative motif, the rosette was adopted from the early RENAISSANCE as a standard enrichment for architecture, furniture, metalwork, and ceiling ornament. Occasionally rosettes cover the joints on

LATTICEWORK patterns and also feature in continuous patterns such as ribbon moldings, GUILLOCHES, and FRETS.

Roseville Pottery Co. Founded in 1890 in Roseville, Ohio, under the directorship of George F. Young, for the production of utilitarian STONEWARE. By 1910 the factory had moved to Zanesville, Ohio. The company's reputation is based on their art wares produced from 1900 to 1920, including vases with richly colored glazes, marketed as Rozane ware. The factory closed in 1954.

Rosewood A hard, heavy, evenly grained tropical wood from the *Dalbergia* tree, so named because, when cut, it smells of roses. The wood is colored from light hazel to deep reddish brown and is richly marked

with dark streaks. From the 18th century, it was used in fine European furniture for VENEERS, INLAYS, and BANDINGS, frequently combined with other contrasting woods. Rosewood enjoyed widespread popularity in the 19th century, especially during the REGENCY period, when it was used to make solid pieces of furniture.

Rosso antico The name used by WEDGWOOD for the unglazed red stoneware that was an improvement on similar ware introduced by the ELERS BROTHERS in the late 17th century. Decorations were based on Greek and Roman designs—hence the "antico."

Rouen potteries ■ Rouen had become a prominent French center for FAIENCE by

R

319

ROOKWOOD POTTERY

The Rookwood Pottery is famous for its glazes; the Rookwood Standard Glaze (color applied with an atomizer) was the idea of one of Rookwood's artists, Laura Fry, in 1883; another popular glaze, Tigers Eye or Goldstone (streaks or flecks of gold), appeared in 1885. It exhibited at the Exposition Universelle in Paris in 1889 and at the World Columbian Exposition in Chicago in 1893.

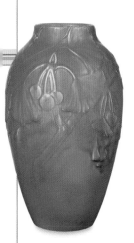

Ovoid vase
Carved matte ovoid vase, by Kataro Shiriyamadani, with relief work. 1905.

Sea green vase
Sea green vase, by Matthew A. Daly. 1894.

Scenic vase
Iris glaze scenic vase, by Kataro Shiriyamadani. 1907.

Silver-overlaid vase
Silver-overlaid standard glaze two-handled vase, by Kataro Shiriyamadani. 1898.

the end of the 17th century. This was due to its location on the banks of the Seine, its proximity to Paris, and access to good local clays. The large-scale melting down of silver ordered by Louis XIV in 1709 to pay for foreign wares also promoted the production of pottery. The first phase of production dates from around 1530, when the potter Masseot Abaquesne produced fine, tin-glazed Italian-influenced wares until his death in 1564. The second phase began in 1644, when a 50-year monopoly for making faience in Normandy was granted to Nicolas Poirel, Lord of Granval, who transferred it to Edmé Poterat. The Poterat family maintained the monopoly until 1694, during which time typical wares were still Italian influenced, decorated in blue and white or polychrome. When the monopoly ended, the industry expanded, with 18 factories working concurrently.

At the height of its fame (around 1695–1725), Rouen produced a wide range of wares, some typically decorated with scrollwork in *style rayonnant* (literally, radiating style), that is, with a close-knit pattern radiating from a focal point. This was widely copied by other French manufacturers. Later wares are in the ROCOCO style and show Chinese influence. By the end of the 18th century the industry was suffering from competition from England. The industry declined, the last factory closing in 1847. Today the manufacture of faience has been revived in Rouen, mostly for the tourist trade.

Rouleau vase ■ The name for a Chinese porcelain vase with cylindrical body and neck of slightly smaller diameter than the body, made from the KANGXI period (1662–1722). The Dutch equivalent term is *Rolwagen*.

Rousseau, François-Eugène (1827–91) A French glass retailer and designer who experimented with the effects of internal CRACKLING and also made glass imitating JADE. He owned a combined workshop and retail outlet in Paris, where he sold ceramics and glass designed both by himself and other notable artists such as Marc-Louis SOLON, many reflecting the fashion for JAPONAISERIE.

Roux, Alexandre (active 1837–81) One of the most accomplished of 19th-century American furniture-makers, active in New York City. Many Roux pieces are of a grand scale with rich MARQUETRY and Louis XVI-style ORMOLU mounting, but those that show an understanding of the AESTHETIC MOVEMENT are more popular today.

Royal Copenhagen porcelain See COPENHAGEN PORCELAIN FACTORY.

Royal Crown Derby Porcelain Co. See CROWN DERBY.

Royal Dutch Glassworks (Koninklijke Nederlandse Glasfabrik) Founded in 1765, the factory's reputation is based on its 20th-century glass, in particular ART DECO pieces designed by Andries Dirk Copier, who joined in 1927. Commonly known as Leerdam after the factory's location, it is still in existence today.

Royal Dux A porcelain factory founded at Dux (or Duchcov) in Bohemia in 1860. The factory copied ROYAL WORCESTER, especially in its matt ivory and bronze finishes. Dux became part of Czechoslovakia in 1918, but continued to use "Bohemia" in the mark. The factory made some good ART DECO figures in the 1930s, and is still producing today.

Royal Flemish ■ A highly decorative range of glass made from 1890 and patented in 1894 by the MOUNT WASHINGTON GLASS CO. A light, semitransparent glass body with a matt acid finish is decorated with an intricate, rich gold and colored enamel design. Patterns include Asian designs, birds, and foliate and floral motifs.

Royal Winton The trade name for a group of potteries in Stoke-on-Trent, including Grimwades, whose name was included in the Royal Winton mark until 1930. Royal Winton is particularly noted for its domestic wares and MAJOLICA, with bright colors and luster glazes, and popular CHINTZWARE. It has seen several changes of ownership since 1979 and is today based at Longton, Staffordshire.

Royal Worcester porcelain See WORCESTER PORCELAIN CO.

Rouen Potteries
Rouen tureen, decorated with polychrome chinoiserie scenes. c. 1730.

Rouleau vase
Famille verte Rouleau vase, depicting a woman and scholar on horseback. 20th century.

Royal Flemish
Vase, with mauve and tan geometric background and raised gold enamel lines.

Rozenburg Pottery
Earthenware vase, decorated with red, purple, and yellow flowers. c. 1900.

Roycroft See HUBBARD, ELBERT.

Rozenburg Pottery and Porcelain Factory ■ Founded by Baron Wilhelm von Gudenberg in 1883 in The Hague, Netherlands. It first produced ART NOUVEAU earthenware, and from 1899, under the direction of Jurriaan Kok, produced EGGSHELL PORCELAIN, hand-painted with naturalistic motifs. It closed in 1916.

Ru ware A Chinese northern SONG (960–1279) ware (formerly Ju ware) made for Imperial use from 1107 to 1127. The most coveted of all Song ceramics, Ru ware has a gray-blue glaze with a close crackle and a buff stoneware body. Until a kiln site was found in 1986, fewer than 40 examples were known.

Rubber band mechanism A device in mechanical toys where a rubber band is wound up by hand and used to power items such as propellers on flying model airplanes and some plastic cars.

Ruby glass ■ A red glass colored with the red stain produced by Friedrich EGERMANN and the pinkish red and brilliant red glass developed by Frederick CARDER at STEUBEN GLASSWORKS.

Ruhlmann, Jacques-Emile ■ (1879–1933) One of the finest furniture-makers and designers of the 20th century and one of the most revered French ART DECO designers of his generation. His first designs were shown at the Salon d'automne in Paris in 1913 (furniture, fabric, and lamps), and in 1919 his firm merged with Pierre Laurent to become Ruhlmann & Laurent. In 1923 he opened his own cabinet-making company, employing the finest craftsmen and draftsmen. His forms are modern, clean, and sophisticated, exquisitely crafted in rich, exotic woods and other materials.

Rummer ■ An English drinking glass from the 1770s in the form of a goblet, with a large bowl, short stem, and sometimes with a domed or square foot. The name may derive from the German RÖMER (wine glass), as it was used for drinking wine rather than rum.

Rundell, Philip (1743–1827) An English silversmith, born at Widcombe, Bath, and apprenticed to William Rogers, a jeweler. He arrived in London around 1768 as shopman to Theed and Picket, silversmiths in Ludgate Hill, and acquired sole ownership of the business in 1772. He took John Bridge, then later his nephew, Edmund Rundell, into partnership. From 1805 the firm was known as Rundell, Bridge & Rundell. In 1797 the firm was appointed Goldsmith and Jeweler to King George III and the royal family. Paul STORR came into the partnership from 1807 to 1819. After his departure, the plate produced bears the marks of Philip Rundell until 1823, when he probably retired. The firm employed the French artist J. J. Boileau, who introduced a severe Greek style to their work as well as the Egyptian motifs that were popular on French silver of the 1780s. Rundell's work, particularly during the REGENCY period, is characterized by outstanding craftsmanship and Classical design excellence.

Runner (or bar) foot A type of foot commonly employed on chairs and tables in the RENAISSANCE. Horizontal side-bars connect the front and rear legs at ground level.

R

321

Runner ■ 1. The name given to long, narrow rugs. Designed by size, the length can vary but the width should not exceed 4 ft (1.2 m). They are made in most Eastern rug-producing countries in urban workshops as well as by tribal groups. 2. A strip of wood sliding in a groove in CASE FURNITURE. In the 16th and 17th centuries a runner supported the leaves of DRAW-LEAF TABLES. The term also refers to the strips of wood added along the side, and in the 18th century, the bottom edge of a drawer, allowing it to slide. The runners that support the flaps of BUREAUX and SECRETAIRES when open are known as lopers.

Running dog See VITRUVIAN SCROLL.

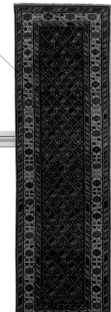
Geometric pattern borders

Ruby glass
Large Venetian ruby glass goblet and matching dish. c. 1900.

Ruhlmann, Jacques-Emile
Ivory-inlaid rosewood cabinet of *demi-lune* form. c. 1919.

Rummer
Rummer engraved with fruiting vine, and wine lemon squeezer base. c. 1780–90.

Runner
Shirvan runner, with an overall floral and diamond design and multiple border. c. 1910.

RUSH WORK

R
322

Rush work Braided stems of marsh plants used to form seats for chairs and stools. The use of rush developed in the Low Countries in the late 16th century. Chair seats consisting of a square wooden frame in which rushes were woven from side to side were popular from 1700 in France, England, and North America. William MORRIS designed rush seat chairs and they remain popular today.

Ruskin Pottery ■ Founded by William Howson Taylor in 1901 in West Smethwick, England, this pottery was called Ruskin Pottery in honor of the ARTS AND CRAFTS champion John Ruskin after their work was on show at the 1903 Arts and Crafts Exhibition. Taylor was a glaze specialist and developed his own clay BODY to take his renowned high-fired glazes. He produced luster, crystalline, and high-fired glazes with vibrant colors. Shapes may be Chinese in inspiration. The pottery closed in 1935.

Ruskin, John See ARTS AND CRAFTS.

Russell, Sir Gordon ■ (1892–1980) An English furniture-maker who began his career around 1911. His firm became

known as Russell & Sons after World War I. Russell was influenced by the work of Ernest GIMSON and the BARNSLEYS and he followed the ARTS AND CRAFTS ideal of handmade furniture. However, in the mid-1920s he introduced machine tools and made some pieces in batches to reduce costs. The firm also offered a modern alternative to traditional styles with the designs of Richard Drew Russell (Gordon Russell's younger brother), Eden Minns, and Marion Pepler. During the 1930s Russell designed and manufactured cabinets for Murphy Radios. He became a government adviser during World War II (working on UTILITY FURNITURE), and in 1947 became Director of the Council of Industrial Design. In 1956 he opened the Design Centre in London.

Russet A technique for producing a brown finish on iron and steel by chemical action. Also known as browning, the subsequent finish is not only decorative but also impedes corrosion.

Rust spotting A blemish that develops when the layer of TINPLATING on steel oxidizes in moisture. LITHOGRAPHED or

paint decoration offers little protection and the condition cannot be reversed.

Rustic furniture ■ Rough, handmade functional furniture, usually of common materials, for farmhouses and cottages. Pieces include kitchen sideboards, benches, and cupboards, and WINDSOR chairs or Yorkshire LADDER-BACK chairs. The term also refers to garden furniture carved in imitation of tree roots and branches, made in England from the mid-19th century. The latter was popularized by the designs of Thomas CHIPPENDALE and Robert Mainwaring, among others, and was intended to furnish arbors, hermitages, and other follies in a landscape garden. The most famous American rustic furniture was made in the late 19th century in the Adirondacks in upstate New York, and included the work of Ernest Stowe.

Ryijy rug A coarsely knotted pile rug made in Scandinavia with a large number of wefts (5–20) between each row of knots, first mentioned in 1420 at Vastena Monastery in Sweden. The pile is thick and about 1 in (25 mm) long. Most examples are 18th- and 19th-century, made in gray, black, and white.

Everted rim

Ruskin pottery
High-fired flambé glazed Ruskin vase, including red "sang-de-boeuf" glaze. 1910.

Russell, Sir Gordon
"Ilmington" cherrywood dressing table, designed by W. H. Russell. c. 1935.

Rustic furniture
East Anglian rustic Windsor reclining chair. Early 19th century.

S

Sabino, Marius-Ernest (1878–1961) An Italian-born French glassmaker who first trained as a woodcarver. He established a company to make light fixtures after World War I and soon began to work increasingly with glass. Sabino made a variety of lamps and small decorative objects in a range of techniques, developing his OPALESCENT GLASS from 1925. He is best known for his sculptures, lamps, and vases in the ART DECO style. His company closed in 1939 but reproductions of his wares using original molds have been made since the 1950s.

Sabot A French term for "shoe." A metal shoe, often brass, fitted to the end of a CABRIOLE LEG.

Saber leg A chair leg with a gentle concave curve. It was a popular form in Western Europe, especially England, in the first half of the 19th century. The saber leg commonly featured on chairs and sofas made in the English REGENCY and American FEDERAL styles.

Saddle seat A wooden, often elm, chair seat that has been scooped away at the sides and back from a central ridge resembling the pommel of a saddle. Shaped to prevent the sitter from sliding forward, the saddle seat was adopted for WINDSOR CHAIRS in the 18th century.

Sadler & Green A Liverpool-based company established in 1756 that decorated ceramics using a TRANSFER-PRINTING process invented by John Sadler. Sadler and his partner, Guy Green, decorated pottery for several factories, notably WEDGWOOD, printing over the glaze in black, green, and red. The company closed in 1799.

Sagger A box of fireproof clay designed to hold porcelain ware securely in the kiln.

This was done by stacking the saggers in layers in the kilns once they were loaded with items for firing.

Sailors' valentines Octagonal or sometimes rectangular cedarwood cases enclosing colored shells arranged in geometric patterns under glass, made in the late 18th and 19th centuries in the West Indies. Some examples have wording such as "Home again" or "Forget me not." Shellwork was often bought by English and American sailors as a memento for the loved ones they left behind.

Saint-Clément ■ A French ceramics factory founded in 1757 by Jacques Chambrette as an offshoot of LUNEVILLE. From 1772 it was run by the architect

SAARINEN, EERO (1910–61)

A Finnish-born architect and designer who moved to the US with his parents in 1923, Eero Saarinen studied sculpture in Paris and architecture at Yale, and worked for a short time in Finland. He practiced a Humanist approach to design, perhaps influenced by his Scandinavian heritage. He worked with Charles EAMES from 1937 and together they won an award for their molded plywood shell armchair in 1940. Saarinen designed his famous Womb chair (produced by KNOLL ASSOCIATES) in 1948 and the Tulip chair in 1956. He also undertook some large architectural commissions, the most famous being the TWA terminal at New York's JFK Airport (1962). Some of his furniture designs are still being made today.

Tulip chairs
Pair of Tulip chairs in molded white fiberglass on an enameled white base. 1956.

Chair and footstool
Womb chair and footstool, with upholstered fiberglass, for Knoll International. 1950s.

Saint-Clément
Jardinière-bouquetière, with polychrome decoration and gilding. 19th century.

Richard Mique. It produced FAIENCE and BISCUIT figures, but is best known for its tableware with enamel decoration. The factory declined at the end of the 18th century, but was revived in 1824 by Germain Thomas and remained in production until the late 19th century.

Saint-Cloud ■ A ceramics factory founded in 1666 by François Reverend. In 1674 it was rented by Pierre Chicaneau, who discovered the process for SOFT-PASTE PORCELAIN. He died in 1677. In 1679 Berthe Coudray, his widow, married Henri Charles Trou, and in 1702 Louis XIV granted a privilege to her and her children for the manufacture of porcelain. Saint-Cloud made the first commercially viable European porcelain. Much of its early ware is derived from Oriental porcelain, but later it produced more individual pieces, including wares with an overlapping leaf pattern and teapots with animal-head spouts. It also made small objects such as SNUFF BOXES. The factory closed in 1766. St Cloud was also a notable early–mid-19th century glassworks.

Saint-Louis Glassworks ■ A French glassworks established at Saint-Louis, Alsace-Lorraine, in 1767. It underwent several changes of ownership and name and is now known as the Compagnie de Cristalleries de Saint-Louis. It was the first French glassworks to produce LEAD CRYSTAL in the late 18th century, and during the 19th century was one of the leading producers of high-quality CUT-GLASS tableware, in addition to OPALINE GLASS and PAPERWEIGHTS.

Saint-Porchaire A French ceramics factory established from 1525 near Bressuire, Deux-Sèvres. It produced elaborately ornamented ware formerly known as Henri Deux. Fine white EARTHENWARE was decorated by impressing with bookbinders' stamps and then filling the hollows with a contrasting colored clay, usually dark brown but occasionally green, black, or blue. Saint-Porchaire made a variety of wares, including TAZZE, CANDLESTICKS, SALTS, and EWERS. These are very rare, with around 50 known pieces only. The factory closed in 1560. Saint-Porchaire ware was greatly admired in the 19th century and copied by many, including AVISSEAU in France and by WEDGWOOD and Toft at MINTON in England.

Salem secretary An American form of the SECRETARY, comparable to a late George III bureau bookcase, made in Salem, Massachusetts, in the late 18th century. Features include a FALL FRONT writing surface concealing a pull-out desk compartment of a type known in Britain as a SECRETAIRE.

Salopian The old name for Shropshire, England. Although the CAUGHLEY factory marked its wares with the word "Salopian," it should not be confused with the Salopian Art Pottery Company of Shropshire. Working from 1882 to around 1912, the factory made EARTHENWARE and MAJOLICA and marked its wares "SALOPIAN," which it registered in 1882.

Salt A receptacle for table salt. The scarcity of salt during the Middle Ages gave it great social significance and the position of the salt container on the table separated the host and principal guests from the less important diners. Salts have been produced in all materials from ceramics to SILVER GILT or gold.

Salt glaze ■ A thin, glassy coating on STONEWARE, produced by throwing common salt into the kiln at the end of the firing.

Salt, Ralph (1782–1846) A potter active in Hanley, Staffordshire, in the late 18th and early 19th centuries with his son, Charles. They made brightly colored naive figures, usually with BOCAGE background, often marked with the word "SALT" on a small ribbon panel on the back of the base. Charles Salt also made PARIAN ware.

Salver A flat, handleless dish with a border for serving food or drink. A salver usually, but not always, has small feet. When it is elevated on a single foot or pedestal, it is known as a TAZZA or "footed salver." The term usually applies to silver or plated wares.

Stylized foliate decoration

Saint-Cloud
Cane handle, decorated *en camaieu* in blue. Early 18th century.

Saint-Louis Glassworks
Vase in blue and white cut crystal, decorated with stylized plants. c. 1930.

Salt glaze
Nottingham brown salt-glazed stoneware cylindrical mug, with scrolling flowers. c. 1723.

Salviati
Salviati green glass vase. c. 1960.

Salviati ■ A Venetian glasshouse established at MURANO in 1859 by Dr. Antonio Salviati. It specialized in VENETIAN GLASS in historical styles and in MOSAICS. Handmade mosaic tesserae were used in such prestigious projects as the Albert Memorial in London. The factory also produced reproductions of ancient Roman glass. Dino Martens designed for the company from 1932, and the 1950s were dominated by the designs of the painter Luciano Gaspari. Designer-led ranges continued to be produced from the 1960s to the 1980s. In 1988 the company was sold and the factory closed and moved production elsewhere. In 1995 the name was acquired by a French company, JG Durand, which still uses it to market decorative glass and tableware.

Samadet Pottery A French FAIENCE factory founded in 1732 that made wares such as fountains, TUREENS, and jugs in the style of MOUSTIERS and MARSEILLES. After the Revolution (1789) it produced only simple village crockery. It closed in 1836.

Sampler ■ A Latin *exemplum* (example or model). Originally a record of stitches and patterns made as a reference tool by professional and amateur needleworkers. Although few survive, 16th-century samplers included border patterns and spot motifs worked in colored silks on linen. These were gradually superseded by printed PATTERN books, and by the 17th century samplers were used to show the embroiderer's skill. Samplers still included border patterns and spot motifs, but WHITEWORK, DRAWN THREAD WORK and NEEDLELACE techniques, and the occasional name and date also started to appear. Increasingly, alphabets, inscriptions, and pictorial elements began to feature, and with the exception of specific forms such as map or darning samplers, these elements became ubiquitous on 18th-century samplers. As education for women became more common, sampler-making became less important, and in the 20th century it became primarily an adult leisure activity.

Samson et Cie A ceramics firm founded by the French porcelain maker Edmé Samson, who began by making exact copies of European and Oriental porcelain for collectors and museums. His son, Émile, also made reproductions of 18th-century SÈVRES, MEISSEN, and CHINESE EXPORT ware. Wares carried Samson et Cie's own monogram—an entwined "S" or a dissected cross—alongside that of the factory they were imitating. The Samson et Cie factory openly sold reproductions that were often almost better than the originals and can still fool inexperienced collectors today. Only when they copied English and French soft-paste pieces did the hard paste used by Samson betray the pieces' origins. Samson also made copies of pieces in ORMOLU, DELFT, FAIENCE, and ENAMELS. The firm closed in 1970.

Sancai ■ A Chinese term for "three-colored wares." These include Chinese TANG (618–906 CE) wares decorated with green, amber, and cream lead glazes, and other colors

SAMPLER

The most detailed examples of samplers were often stitched by young girls and included moral or religious verses. During the 19th century the pictorial element became increasingly dominant in samplers and the variety of stitches reduced until often only CROSS STITCH featured.

Silk linen needlework sampler
Needlework with alphabets, inscription, and verse in the center and wide borders, with urns issuing flowering vines and a house, trees, and deer below. c. 1822.

English band sampler
Crewelwork depiction of Adam & Eve, with alphabet and trailing vine above. 1744.

Sancai
Tang dynasty Sancai camel, glazed in runny tones of amber and green.

used for burial figures and boxes. The glazes might be splashed (streaky), mottled, or controlled with RESIST designs. The term is also associated with MING (1368–1644) Fahua ware and the enamel decoration on BISCUIT PORCELAIN.

Sand glass See HOURGLASS.

Sand molding Also known as sand casting, it comprises a mold created in damp, compacted sand, sometimes by impressing it with a carved, wooden block. Molten glass or metal is then poured into the mold and removed when cool. It is sometimes treated to remove any residual marks, although a pitted surface incorporating sand particles is often desired. This was a common technique in postwar Scandinavian glass.

Sand picture ■ A picture, often depicting a landscape, made from colored sands glued to a wooden or canvas surface or built up in layers in a bottle. Benjamin Zobel was perhaps the best-known maker and worked for George III. Sand pictures continued to be popular throughout the 19th century.

Sand blasting Fine grains of sand, crushed flint, or powdered iron are blasted or propelled at high speed under compression against the surface of the glass that has a masked-out design. Invented by Benjamin Tilghman in the US in 1870, the technique gradually superseded ACID ETCHING as a way of producing matt decoration, especially on tableware, or

carving away areas of glass in the CAMEO GLASS technique during the 20th century.

Sanderson, Elijah (1751–1825) An American cabinet-maker who worked with his brother, Jacob, in Salem, Massachusetts. They began in the AMERICAN CHIPPENDALE period but worked mainly in the FEDERAL style. Some pieces feature carving attributed to Samuel MCINTIRE.

Sandwich glass A generic term given to a type of American glass made by the BOSTON & SANDWICH GLASS CO. and other New England factories from the 1820s until the 20th century. Most American colored pressed and "fancy" glass of all types is referred to as "Sandwich." Famous designs include dolphin-stem candlesticks, which have been widely reproduced.

Sang de boeuf ■ A French term for "ox blood." A brilliant red or plum-colored glaze used for Chinese monochrome wares from the KANGXI period. It is derived from copper fired in a reducing atmosphere. The glaze tends to run, collecting at the shoulders and foot of the object and leaving a streaky effect with pale greenish areas or pink markings. It was also used in 20th-century STUDIO POTTERY by factories such as DOULTON.

Sanson, Nicolas (1600–67) The foremost French cartographer of the 17th century, Sanson laid the groundwork for his nation's future cartographic preeminence. His major work, the *Cartes Générales de*

Toutes les Parties du Monde (General Maps of All Parts of the World), published in 1658, includes the first MAPS to show all of the North American Great Lakes and to name lakes Superior and Ontario. Less ornamental than contemporary Dutch maps, Sanson's finely engraved maps are distinguished by their clarity, simplicity, and elegant decorative tide CARTOUCHES.

Sapphire ■ The blue variety of corundum. It also occurs in several other colors, of which pink, yellow, and a rare peach shade called *padparadschah* are the most valuable. The highest prized sapphires come from Kashmir in northern India. Other principal sources include Burma, Thailand, Sri Lanka, Australia, and Africa.

Sapwood The wood from between the bark and heart of a tree trunk. Still living tissue when the tree is felled, it is softer than the heartwood and tends to be susceptible to woodworm attacks.

Sarcophagus An often richly decorated stone coffin from Classical antiquity. A common motif in funerary ornament in the late 18th century, the distinctive shape of the sarcophagus was adopted for wine coolers, cellarets, and tea caddies from the NEOCLASSICAL period, but mainly in REGENCY and GREEK REVIVAL styles.

Sarreguemines A FAIENCE factory established during the French Revolution in Sarreguemines in Alsace-Lorraine, France.

Sand picture
American sand picture in a bottle, with ship *Wm. H. Cook* and patriotic eagle. 1888.

Sang de boeuf
Chinese *sang de boeuf* glazed vase.

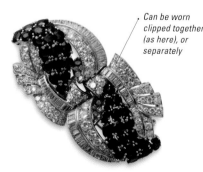

Can be worn clipped together (as here), or separately

Sapphire
One of a pair of Art Deco sapphire and diamond double clips. c. 1930.

Satin glass
Mount Washington mother-of-pearl satin glass vase, with muslin airtrap pattern.

By the mid-19th century the factory was employing 2,000 workers and was producing around 4 million pieces, including porcelain wares, annually. From 1870 to 1918, when Alsace-Lorraine was annexed by Germany, markings often included the claim "Made in Germany." Porcelain and MAJOLICA production ceased in 1945 and the company was eventually bought out in 1979. The range and diversity of Sarreguemines ware was considerable and included many decorative and utility wares not dissimilar to those of the English factories WEDGWOOD, DOULTON, and MINTON. However, the best known are the fantasy majolica wares comprising dishes and pots with molded in-relief designs of fruits, berries, vegetables, nuts, and leaves.

Sasha dolls Designed by the Swiss sculptor Sasha Morgenthaler in an attempt to produce a doll that would appeal to children of all races. Sasha dolls were produced in vinyl and have dark skin and calm, wistful expressions. The British company Trendon Toys was the first to produce them commercially from 1965 to 1986, and since 1994 they have been made by the German toy company Götz.

Satin birch See BIRCH.

Satin glass ■ Glass with a fine matte finish created by ACID ETCHING or light SAND BLASTING. It is also known as *verre de soie* (silk glass), a term coined by

STEUBEN GLASSWORKS for a popular range of decorative glass with a silky, slightly iridescent finish made from 1905 to 1930. Nearly all satin glass is CASED with an opaque white interior layer, and common colors include pink, blue, and yellow.

Satinwood ■ A hard-textured, fine-grained, honey-colored wood from several species of trees native to the West Indies, Sri Lanka, and India. From the late 18th century it was used as a VENEER and INLAY as well as in the solid. It was suitable for furniture of the period—the solidity of CHIPPENDALE and the lighter designs of HEPPLEWHITE and ADAM.

Satsuma potteries ■ Established by immigrant Korean potters in the late 16th century in the Satsuma province of Kyushu island, Japan. They made simple wares in the Karatsu style for the tea ceremony, often with thick, dark glazes. The name has since become a generic term for Japanese cream-colored pottery made for export to the West from around 1870. With a clear, yellowish, finely crackled glaze, it is often decorated with figures, flowers, and butterflies, in polychrome enamels and gilding. Much of this later Satsuma was made at Kyoto and elsewhere. The quality of Satsuma pottery varies enormously. See JAPANESE POTTERY AND PORCELAIN, KINKOZAN, MEIJI PERIOD.

Saturday Evening Girls The Saturday Evening Girls Club began in 1906 when a

group of immigrant girls gathered weekly to decorate pottery that could be sold in support of the settlement house activities. They studied the basics of ceramics and learned how to glaze and fire their wares with the help of an experienced potter. The club grew into a highly successful enterprise, moving to larger premises and adopting the name of the revolutionary war hero Paul Revere. It continued to train young women to work as ceramic decorators, although it was rarely profitable. The Paul Revere pottery closed in 1942.

Sauceboat Made in ceramic or silver to adorn the dining table and contain flavoured sauces or gravy. Early 18th-century sauceboats were double-lipped, boat-shaped vessels with a handle on each side and a central foot. By the 1730s these were superseded by single-lipped, single-handled examples, usually on three feet.

Savery, William (1721–87) A furniture-maker of the AMERICAN CHIPPENDALE period. His best pieces are among the most valuable of all American furniture and feature high-quality carving and sweeping ROCOCO lines. Savery was a chair specialist (who also made CASE FURNITURE) and traded from The Sign of the Chair on Second Street, Philadelphia, from around 1740.

Savings bank ■ This toy money-saving device, usually of painted cast iron or lithographed TINPLATE, falls into two

Satinwood
George III satinwood cellaret, with elongated octagonal body on splayed square legs.

Satsuma potteries
Pottery bowl, decorated with a procession of figures and a view of Mount Fuji beyond.

Undulating petal-shaped rim

Satsuma potteries
Bowl, with shaped rim and a profusion of immortals painted on the interior and exterior.

Savings bank
Hubley painted cast-iron "Circus Elephant" still bank.

S

categories—the mechanical, which performs a function or trick, and the still bank. The first mechanical bank, the Hall's Excelsior, appeared in the US in 1869, patented by John Hall and made by J. E. Stevens & Co. Other noted makers include Shepard Hardware Co., Kyser & Rex, and W. S. Reed. Many banks were made by companies as a sideline or promotion of their main product. They were at their most popular from around 1869 to 1910, declining by the beginning of World War I, after which tinplate banks became popular in the US and Europe (in particular in Germany, the center of tinplate toy production). Many reproductions have been made.

Savona potteries ■ An Italian center for MAIOLICA, which was made at Savona and at nearby Albisola from the 16th to the 18th centuries. The earliest wares were in the BAROQUE STYLE with embossed, ornament and blue-painted decoration. In the second half of the 17th century APOTHECARY JARS and dishes were made, generally with Roman cavalry but also PUTTI, marine views, and biblical subjects. The potteries were numerous and the products are hard to distinguish. The shield mark of Savona is commonly used. Conrade of Albisola was an important potter, and he used his initials beneath a ducal crown as a mark. At another factory, G. Levantino used the lighthouse of Genoa as a mark, while a pentagram mark is known for Siccardi or Satomini.

Savonnerie Carpet Factory ■ A French carpet factory at Chaillot, near Paris, founded in 1627 by Louis XIII (1610–43). It was set up on the site of a former soapworks. Production under Louis XIII is characterized by blackish brown grounds with rich, naturalistic floral patterns in various colors. The style was deliberately non-Oriental, reflecting instead contemporary French artistic tastes. The factory's greatest success was under Louis XIV (1643–1715), when 13 carpets were made for the Apollo Gallery in the Louvre, and 92 for the Great Gallery connecting the Louvre to the Tuileries Palace, the latter never being used. Carpets were also made for the palaces at Versailles, Fontainebleau, and Choisy-le-Roi. During the ROCOCO period the designer Pierre Josse Perrot created bold patterns with exuberant colors. In the EMPIRE period (1804–15) designs were inspired by Classical antiquity and military emblems. During the mid-19th century, under LOUIS-PHILIPPE (1830–48), the carpets became more intricately patterned with stronger colors; the colors softened during the SECOND EMPIRE (1848–70). The Savonnerie factory combined with the GOBELINS at their premises in 1826. The company is still producing carpets.

Sawbuck table An American term for a rustic TRESTLE TABLE made by communities such as the PENNSYLVANIA DUTCH, in which a long plank top rests on X-form supports like sawbucks or saw horses. Most are of 19th- or 20th-century origin.

Scagliola ■ A substitute for marble or PIETRA DURA mixed from gypsum or plaster of Paris, chips of marble or granite, and various pigments. Originating in ancient Rome, it was revived in Italy in the early 17th century and was in widespread use all over Europe during the 18th century for interior columns, pedestals, and wall panels, and for the tops of tables and commodes.

Scale pattern ■ Overlapping circles that resemble the scales of a fish. The pattern originated in Greco-Roman architecture and reappeared during the Italian RENAISSANCE. It was used to decorate glass and MAIOLICA in the late 15th and early 16th centuries. It took a more delicate form on 18th-century European porcelain, molded in relief at SAINT-CLOUD and ENAMELED on wares made at MEISSEN, BERLIN, VIENNA, and WORCESTER. Scale cut glass was popular from the mid-18th to the late 19th century and was a very common form of decoration for decanter necks at that time. The pattern also features on 18th-century woodwork as carved or pierced surface decoration on chairs, SETTEES, and CONSOLE TABLES in the style of William KENT.

Scales (balance) A horizontal beam supported at the exact center, with a dish or hook hanging from each end, one for weights and the other for the item to be

Scagliola (faux marble) top

Savona potteries
Savona maiolica tazza, painted with a winged putto in Italianate landscape. 18th century.

Savonnerie Carpet Factory
Savonnerie carpet seat cover. 19th century.

Scagliola
Louis XIV-style giltwood table, with scagliola top. 19th century.

weighed. Scales vary in size from small sets in 18th-century medicine chests to large grocers' scales. Handheld coin balances are known from the late 15th century. Apothecaries' balances are distinguished by glass pans and jewelers' balances are mounted on a stand. Chemical balances, made from around 1700, required high precision. Letter scales were used by the postal service in Great Britain from 1840.

Scallop shell See SHELL MOTIF.

Scalloped ■ An edge or border cut or modeled in a continuous series of curves, resembling the shape of a scallop shell. It was a favored design on furniture, textiles, ceramics, and metalwork and was particularly popular on British glass from around 1720.

Scarificator A medical instrument used to pierce the skin to aid blood-letting. Developed in the late 17th century but still available in the late 19th century, it was usually made out of BRASS or silvered metal. It had a series of horizontal slots from which 4 to 12 sharp blades protruded when triggered, to make several incisions at the same time. A screw governed the depth of the cut.

Sceaux Pottery and Porcelain Factory ■ The factory at Sceaux, near Paris, was managed from around 1748 by Jacques Chapelle, who was its proprietor from 1759 to 1763. He originally made SOFT-PASTE PORCELAIN but in 1749, due to the monopoly of VINCENNES, he started making high-quality FAIENCE, known as *faience japonné*. In 1763 the factory was acquired by Joseph Jullien and Charles-Symphorien Jacques and soft-paste porcelain was reestablished. Richard Glot, under the patronage of the Duc de Penthièvre, owned the factory from 1772 until the French Revolution, and Antoine Cabaret owned it from 1796. The factory produced only common household wares in its last years, in the early 19th century.

Scent bottles See PERFUME BOTTLES.

Schäper, Johann (1621–70) A German pottery and glass decorator born in Hamburg. He worked as a HAUSMALER in Nuremberg, where he developed SCHWARZLOT.

Scherenschnitte A German term for "scissor cuts." A form of FOLK ART where decorative patterns are cut into paper sheets. It originated in Germany in the 15th century and was brought to North America, particularly Pennsylvania, by German immigrants in the 18th century. Motifs tend to be geometric and symmetrical, and may include natural motifs such as flowers and animals. Some early examples are embellished with painting. The technique is still practiced today.

Schinkel, Karl Friedrich (1781–1841) A German architect, painter, and designer who settled in Berlin in 1805, creating delicate furniture that anticipated the BIEDERMEIER period. His contemporary style drew on historical motifs but did not overemphasize them. Among his innovations were daring designs in CAST IRON. The outstanding qualities of his furniture were solidity, practicality, comfort, and simplicity.

Schleswig pottery A German FAIENCE factory founded in 1755 by J. C. L. von LÜK and acquired by Johann Rambusch in 1758, who ran it until 1773. Its finest products were made in this period. Wares included bowls in the shape of a bishop's miter and ROCOCO tureens. Its marks are "OS ," " S ," and "SR," often with the marks of decorators such as Conrad Bade, Abraham Leihamer, and Johann C. Ewald. The pottery closed in 1814.

Schmelzglas A German term for "enamel glass." A type of opaque glass with a marbled surface that resembles HARDSTONES. It was first made in Italy in the late 14th century, where it was known as *calcedonio*, and was imitated in Germany from the 16th century. See LITHYALIN GLASS and AGATE glass.

Schneegas & Sons A producer of high-quality wooden doll's house furniture in Waltershausen, Thuringia, Germany. Production began in the 1840s with BIEDERMEIER-style pieces, in imitation rosewood, and continued until World War I.

Schnelle ■ The German term for a tall, tapering TANKARD, usually

Scale pattern
Sèvres hard-paste saucer, with gilt scales and a band of flowers. 19th century.

Border with alternating solid and cross-hatched grounds

Scalloped
Caughley scalloped plate, painted with flowers and a butterfly. c. 1768.

Sceaux Pottery and Porcelain Factory
Sceaux plate decorated with a landscape scene. c. 1760.

Schnelle
Altenburg Perlhumpen tankard in brown salt-glazed stoneware. c. 1733.

made of STONEWARE or FAIENCE, often with a PEWTER cover. It was of the typical shape used by the SIEGBURG potters of the 16th century and was often decorated in relief with biblical or mythical subjects. Imitations were made in the 19th century.

Schofield, John A prominent English silversmith who worked in London from around 1776 to 1794, first in partnership with Robert Jones and then alone from 1778. His work displays a Classical elegance and he is best known for his Adamesque cruets, candlesticks, and candelabra.

School of Nancy See NANCY.

Schreiberhau Glasshouse (Schreiberhau Glashutte) A leading German glasshouse established around l840 at Marienthal, near Schreiberhau. Directed by Franz Pohl, it produced MILLEFIORI PAPERWEIGHTS, vases, and enameled and IRIDESCENT GLASS. In 1923 it joined with two other glasshouses. Now based in Poland, the company is still active.

Schuco ■ The trademark of Schreyer & Co. (1912–77) of Nuremberg, makers of high-quality mechanical, often TINPLATE, toys and teddy bears. The Tricky (or Yes/No) bear with a movable head was introduced in 1921 and was soon followed by a variety of PLUSH animals incorporating PERFUME BOTTLES, compacts, or lipstick holders. The most successful products of the 1920s were reissued in the 1950s.

Schwarzburg Porcelain Factory Founded in Schwarzburg-Rudolstadt, Thuringia, in 1908, by Max Adolf Pfeiffer. The factory was known for its white porcelain Russian peasant figures, designed by the sculptor Ernst Barlach. It merged with a factory in Volkstedt in 1913.

Schwarzlot ■ German for "black lead," the term is used to describe a type of monochromatic, handpainted decoration in black or brown enamels applied to glass and ceramics and especially popular on bowls and beakers from around 1650 to 1750. The technique was improved by Johann SCHÄPER in Nuremberg from the mid-17th century and soon spread to Bohemia and Silesia. There it was used mainly for landscape and battle scene designs on glass BEAKERS, flasks, and ceramic domestic ware by such notable exponents as Ignaz Preissler. Schwarzlot was revived at the end of the 19th century.

Sconce ■ A wall candleholder associated with the early 17th to early 18th century, but manufactured into the 20th century. A sconce consists of an arm or bracket with a candle socket for and a backplate to magnify and reflect the light, usually upward. Architecturally, sconces are found in churches and palaces such as the Medici Palace in Florence for holding torches.

Scrapbook A book with colorful paper images of sentimental or souvenir value fixed to the pages. First made in the early 19th century, by the mid- to late 19th century scrapbooks had become such a popular pastime that printed and often embossed SCRAPS were commercially produced. Scrapbooks are popular to this day.

Scraps ■ Small, color LITHOGRAPHED diecut paper objects made for collecting in a SCRAPBOOK or to embellish small boxes or small items of furniture such as table tops or screens. Originating in Germany where they were initially used to decorate cakes, they peaked in popularity from the 1860s to the 1930s. Sentimental, festive, floral, and animal themes are typical.

Scratch blue A style of decoration on early 18th-century English STONEWARE. The design is scratched onto the surface with a pointed tool and filled in with blue pigment.

Scratch built The term used to describe a model or working machine such as a steam-powered model train that has not been built using parts from a specially designed commercial kit. Instead, stock materials such as plastic, metal, and wood are crafted by the modeler, who builds the model from scratch.

Screen ■ Originating in China around the 2nd century CE and introduced to Japan in the 8th century CE, screens appeared in Europe in the 16th century, after trade with the East began. Made in Europe from the 17th century, they served various practical purposes—to block

Schuco
Tinplate combination car No.4003, with clockwork operation and key.

Original box enhances value

Schwarzlot
German goblet with Schwarzlot decoration. c. 1730.

Sconce
One of a pair of gilt-bronze wall sconces. 1887.

Scraps
Victorian scrap of cricketers.

out drafts, to protect modesty, or (the majority) to shield from the direct heat of fires (see FIRESCREEN and POLESCREEN). As decorative devices, screens were excellent for displaying carving and needlework. By the 18th century, screen panels decorated with prints, paintings, imported Chinese wallpapers, embroidery, and filigree paper were highly fashionable. Ladies of the house also created BERLIN WOOLWORK and BEADWORK panels. From arond 1750 it was considered *de rigueur* to match screen panels with the fabric of upholstery and wall hangings.

Screw Early screws with hand-filed, uneven threads and uncentered slots were made of brass and used together with brass pins to fasten hinges. From the late 17th century, tapering metal screws with slotted heads appear in furniture construction. Lathe-made screws were introduced from around 1760, securing hinges of folding tables, including GATELEG TABLES. By the mid-19th century, machine-made screws with centered slots and milled threads were a common feature of furniture construction.

Scrimshaw ■ A 19th-century FOLK ART produced by sailors on whalers, in which the bone, teeth, and tusks of whales, walruses, and other marine animals were used to make decorative objects. After extraction, the surface was scraped smooth and then a design was often pricked out with a needle. The pricked-out dots were then joined together with black ink, soot, or tar to reveal, for example, a whaling scene or portraits of ships. There are many replicas on the market, most made from resin. As a general rule, these are often heavier than the originals and have a milkier, waxier finish without the natural veining of tooth or ivory.

Scroddled A collective term for pottery made from scraps of different colored clays, which produce a mottled, abstract, polychromatic finish.

Scroll foot ■ The foot of a CABRIOLE LEG, which terminates in a tight, upturned scroll or spiral form. The "French" scroll foot, derived from the 17th-century French BAROQUE scroll leg, became fashionable on furniture in the mid-18th century, in imitation of the French taste that began to assert itself in the 1730s. Scroll feet were popular in English glassware from around 1865 to 1885.

Scroll handle See C-SCROLL, S-SCROLL. A handle of a piece shaped to resemble the letter "C" or "S."

Scroll top See SWAN-NECK PEDIMENT.

Seal Used universally from ancient times, the seal is a relief image of an emblem, coat of arms, or crest made in sealing wax and fixed to a document, letter, or charter. It serves as a mark of authentification or a warrant. The term also applies to the matrix that is impressed into the wax on which the devices are engraved in reverse (or INTAGLIO). Seal matrices can be cut from ivory, silver, gold, or HARDSTONES. They may be for personal use, set into rings or handles, or may have wider importance, such as the Great Seal of Scotland or those used in a borough or corporation.

Seal bottle ■ A glass bottle used to collect wine from a vintners, impressed with a molded SEAL that was marked with the date, a monogram, coat of arms, or initials, which identified either the owner, the glassworks where it was made, the tavern, or the contents. Dark free-blown "shaft and globe"-shaped bottles were made in Britain from around 1650, developing to onion-shaped examples in the early 1700s. Seal bottles remained popular until the mid-19th century, by which time they were cylindrical in shape and were made in dark brown and dark green glass.

Seal box See SKIPPET.

Seal-top spoon A silver or base metal spoon characterized by a SEAL-shaped terminal or finial soldered to the end of the stem. Early examples from the late 15th century have squat finials, whereas 17th-century examples have more elongated baluster terminals. By around 1670 they were no longer fashionable.

Seams The visible lines along which two separate pieces of a material (or two ends

Screen
Robert Winthrop Chanler Art Deco three-panel screen, painted with zebras. 1928.

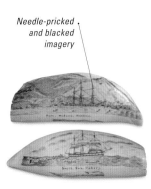

Needle-pricked and blacked imagery

Scrimshaw
Large, engraved whale's tooth, depicting "South Sea Fishery." Early to mid-19th century.

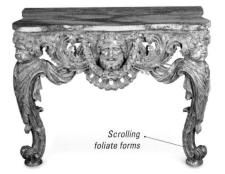

Scrolling foliate forms

Scroll foot
George II carved giltwood console table, with scroll feet. c. 1740.

Seal bottle
Early English onion-shaped dark green glass wine bottle, with a seal. c. 1690.

SECESSIONIST MOVEMENT

A society of avant-garde artists, designers, and architects founded in 1897 as a breakaway group from the conservative Academy of Fine Arts in Vienna, the leading members of the Secessionist Movement included Josef HOFFMANN and Koloman MOSER, who founded the WIENER WERKSTÄTTE in 1903, architect-designer Otto Wagner, and the painter Gustav Klimt. They exhibited the work of MACKINTOSH and the GLASGOW SCHOOL, which inspired the rectilinear and geometric designs of the Wiener Werkstätte. The term is now used to describe the Austrian variant of ART NOUVEAU.

Cabinet
Secessionist mahogany cabinet, with exotic wood and mother-of-pearl inlay. c. 1910.

Nest of tables
Nest of four black-lacquered tables, attributed to Josef Hoffmann.

Vase
Minton Secessionist vase, tube-lined with stylized tulips and swags.

---

of the same) have been joined together. It is seen, for example, in silver when a sheet of silver is curved around to form a cylinder and joined to form a visible solder seam.

Seat rail The horizontal structural member of a chair supporting the seat. The seat rail can be situated across a chair seat at the back, front, or sides.

Seaweed glass A term used to describe clear-cased glass with an internal decoration of air bubbles that resembles seaweed. Well-known exponents include Andries Dirk Copier, who used the

technique in the Serica limited edition range of vases, which he designed for the LEERDAM glassworks and the Austrian glassworks LOETZ.

Seaweed marquetry ■ A type of decoration resembling seaweed and consisting of intricate and delicate leaf patterns of richly figured HOLLY or BOXWOOD on a WALNUT background. Originating in Italy, it was further developed in England and Holland in the late 17th century. This design was frequently applied

to the fronts of LONGCASE CLOCKS, CHESTS-OF-DRAWERS, SECRETAIRES, and CABINETS.

Second The term used to describe an object that does not meet the minimum level of quality set by the maker or company, perhaps due to a manufacturing flaw or error. Royal Doulton incises a line through their standard printed mark to mark seconds. Alternatively, a company may not apply its standard mark, or any mark, to a "second." Such pieces will usually be sold more cheaply than standard pieces.

Holly or boxwood "seaweed" on walnut ground

Seaweed marquetry
Detail of an Indo-Portuguese cabinet with seaweed marquetry. Late 17th century.

Second Empire
Louis XV-style kingwood vitrine, of serpentine form with gilt metal mounts.

Secretaire
George III inlaid satinwood- and mahogany-banded secretaire bookcase. c. 1790.

Secrétaire à abattant
Louis XV ormolu, tulipwood, amaranth, and marquetry *secrétaire à abattant*. c. 1758.

Second Empire ■ A term describing the variety of styles popular in France during the reign of Emperor Napoleon III from 1848 to 1870. It does not refer to a revival of the early 19th-century EMPIRE style of Napoleon I but to the increasingly eclectic mix of forms and ornament and overall effect of opulence, characteristic of mid 19th-century French decorative arts. The LOUIS XVI style was dominant, owing to the Empress Eugenie's interest in the life and times of Queen Marie Antoinette, and was manifest in Classical forms with GILT-BRONZE mounts and BRASS INLAY. The RENAISSANCE REVIVAL was also popular, and high-quality furniture in both styles was made by Louis-Auguste-Alfred Beurdeley. Interiors were filled with large, richly upholstered and tasseled armchairs, SOFAS, and OTTOMANS. From the 1860s, with the opening up of trade between the West and Japan, the taste for JAPONAISERIE was also evident.

Secretaire ■ The French term for a freestanding writing cabinet, popular from the late 18th century. The vertical-fronted cabinet of the secretaire is enclosed by a deep top drawer that, when pulled out, drops down to create a flat writing surface. Behind this FALL FRONT are recessed drawers, cupboards, and pigeonholes where papers can be safely stored and locked away. Frequently, the upper section of a secretaire features a bookcase or a glazed display cabinet.

Secrétaire à abattant A tall French writing cabinet, first made in the 17th century and especially favored in late 18th-century France. It resembles a cupboard with a thin drawer at the top, a panel below, and three drawers or a pair of cupboard doors enclosing drawers. The top usually has a FALL FRONT, which encloses small drawers and pigeonholes and provides a larger writing surface when open.

Secretary ■ An American term for a tall writing desk, comparable to the English BUREAU bookcase. Popular from around 1750, they were made in two parts for ease of moving and often had brass carrying handles. Most pieces were fashioned in the NEOCLASSICAL STYLE.

Sedan chair An enclosed portable chair borne on two long carrying poles. Sedan chairs first emerged in Italy at the end of the Middle Ages. The popular appeal of this mode of transport—often elaborately decorated and upholstered with luxurious fabrics—rapidly spread alongside a growing taste for luxury from the 16th until the 18th century.

Sedan clock A type of clock intended for use when traveling in a SEDAN CHAIR or coach. Made mainly in the late 18th century, its circular, square, or octagonal form has a metal or wooden case fitted with a verge watch MOVEMENT.

Seddon, George ■ (c. 1727–1801) An English cabinet-maker who established his workshop in London in around 1760. By the 1780s it had become celebrated for a large and varied output of high-quality furniture. His business flourished until the mid-19th century, following the opening of a new West End branch in 1826. From 1827 until 1833 the firm provided furniture for Windsor Castle, in partnership with Nicholas Morel.

Seeds ■ A term used to describe the tiny fragments of clay that break from the inner lining of the glass furnace pot and into the bath of raw materials melted within it. These can be found most commonly in early glass, typically in examples from the 18th century. The term is also used to describe tiny bubbles contained in some glass, either accidentally or intentionally.

Segmental pediment ■ An unbroken, curved PEDIMENT formed from the arc of a circle and derived from Classical architecture. Toward the end of the 18th century it was adopted for bureaux, cupboards, cabinets, and bookcases.

Seguso Vetri d'Arte Founded in Murano in 1933, the glassworks produced Art Glass until the 1990s. It established an international reputation in the 1930s, 40s and 50s for a series of innovative designs by artistic director Flavio Poli, many early examples of which were executed by master glassblower and designer Archimede Seguso.

Secretary
New York Federal cherry two-part secretary. c. 1815.

Seddon, George
Satinwood breakfront bookcase in the manner of Seddon. Early 20th century.

Seeds
Archimede Seguso stained petrol blue and clear glass vase, with gold and air bubbles. c. 1960.

Segmental pediment
Victorian burr ash breakfront wardrobe, with inlaid panels and central segmental pediment.

Notable examples included sculptural animal figures; the clear-bubbled and colored underlay "Bulicante" range; and diverse SOMMERSO art glass. Several members of the Seguso family are still making glass on Murano.

Self-loading pistol A repeating pistol whose action relies on either recoil or gas operation to reload it after each CARTRIDGE has been fired. Effective self-loaders date from the 1890s and were readily adopted for military use by most of the major powers. They are still in use today and most are based on the patents of gunmaker John Moses Browning.

Selvedge The edge of a length of woven fabric that has been finished to prevent fraying (also called selvage). The term is also used for the over-bound edges on a rug, made by joining together one or more warp threads and then overcasting in wool, cotton, or silk.

Semainier A French term for a narrow CHEST or CHIFFONIÉR made from the 18th century. With seven drawers, it was originally intended to hold a fresh supply of personal linen for every day of the week. The term is also applied to a case or rack with seven divisions or drawers.

Semi-flat A metal figure such as a toy soldier, cast in a mold usually with lead, made by small factories in Europe and the US from the late 19th century. Often unpainted and with no maker's mark, they are classed today as the cheaper cousin of FLATS and HOLLOW-CAST FIGURES.

Semiprecious stones A group of gemstones, often occurring in large sizes and of a lesser value than PRECIOUS STONES. The term "semiprecious" is not precisely defined, but PERIDOT, AQUAMARINE, TOURMALINE, SPINEL, and ZIRCON are usually included.

Senneh knot See PERSIAN KNOT.

Serpentine ■ A wavy or undulating curved surface on a piece of furniture. From the mid-18th century, serpentine curves were adopted for furniture in place of rectangular shapes. The new style based on elegant outlines demanded the talents of highly skilled craftsmen for construction and the laying of VENEERS. Typically, COMMODES, CHESTS-OF-DRAWERS, and clothes presses were made with serpentine fronts. The form was also applied to SEAT-RAILS and STRETCHERS and the FRIEZES of SIDE TABLES through the 19th century. See BOMBÉ.

Seto Pottery An early Japanese pottery center around Seta in the Owari province, Honshu island. It is the earliest and the most important of the "Six Old Kilns" of Japan. The earliest wares of the Heian period (898–1184 CE) include large jars with natural ash glazes. In the Kamakura period (1185–1358 CE), Chinese CELADON wares were copied, using a coarse STONEWARE body. The celebrated Flower Seto, incised or stamped with floral designs, and TEMMOKU-glazed wares were also from the same period. Tashiro was considered the greatest Seto potter in the 13th century, but very little is known of individual early kilns or potters. By the mid-15th century Seto produced wares for TEA CEREMONY use. Throughout the 17th and 18th centuries, wares for daily use continued to be produced. In the 19th century, domestic and decorative porcelain, often of low quality, was made in large quantities for the export markets. Today Seto has over 900 pottery factories. See JAPANESE POTTERY AND PORCELAIN.

Settee ■ A light, open seat with a back and open arms, sometimes with a padded seat, and large enough for two or more persons. More comfortable than a settle and more formal than a SOFA—encouraging one to sit but not lounge—it was adopted in England from the 17th century in various forms, from the LOVE SEAT to the French *causeuse*. In the first quarter of the 18th century, the hall settee—an enlarged hall chair with a solid wooden seat—became popular, although by the 19th century the form had largely been abandoned in favor of the more comfortable sofa.

Setting ■ The various methods of securing a gemstone in the mount (often referred to as the gallery) include CLAW SETTING, closed and open back setting, COLLET SETTING, PAVÉ SETTING, gipsy setting (sunk into the metal surround), and star

Serpentine
Mahogany serpentine *bombé* commode. 18th century.

Settee
Mahogany Empire revival settee. Late 19th century.

Setting
Trifari plant motif pin, with pavé-set clear rhinestones. c. 1940.

Settle
Box settle, with paneled back and bracket feet. 18th century.

setting (gipsy setting with engraved lines radiating from the stone itself).

Settle ■ The earliest chair designed to seat two or more persons and comprising a bench with a back and curved open arms. Constructed entirely of wood, usually oak, with solid ends and occasionally a wooden hood, the settle remained popular from Tudor times until the 19th century, mainly for taverns and farmhouses. Sometimes built solid to the floor, with a hinged seat positioned over a box, it was the forerunner of the SETTEE. Valued for its rustic appeal, the settle was revived in the late 19th century by designers such as William MORRIS.

Seville potteries The Moors made well-heads, oil and water jars, and vases in this Spanish town from the 11th century. After the Christian reconquest in 1248, TILES became the most important product. In the 15th century tiles were exported to other parts of Europe. Pictorial tile panels in Italian RENAISSANCE style were made in the 16th century, and in the 17th and 18th centuries colorful domestic wares

were also produced in an Italianate style, with later inspiration coming from CHINESE EXPORT PORCELAIN. In the 19th century several industrial potteries were founded. Around 1840 the English industrialist Charles Pickman built a pottery at the disused Cartuja Convent, producing "china opaca," TRANSFER-PRINTED wares, and imitations of HISPANO-MORESQUE tiles. The pottery remained in operation on the same site until 1982, when it relocated to a new out-of-town factory.

Sèvres Porcelain Factory ■ The factory started in VINCENNES, outside Paris, around 1738. In 1745 Louis XV backed it up by prohibiting all foreign porcelain imports, except for Chinese goods. He prevented other French porcelain factories from decorating in more than one color and forbade their use of gilding. In 1753 the King styled the factory Manufacture Royale de Porcelaine, cementing its privileges. Sèvres had the advantage of the best painters and modelers and the encouragement of the King's mistress, Madame de Pompadour. In 1756 the factory moved to Sèvres, where it is still in business.

The products of the 18th century are in pure French ROCOCO style. Delicate CABARETS, vases in startling color combinations, and JARDINIÈRES were among the ornaments made. Porcelain plaques were created to be inserted in pieces of furniture and BISCUIT figures were produced.

The Sèvres factory is renowned for the brilliance of its ground colors such as *gros bleu* (a deep underglaze blue), *bleu celeste* (turquoise), yellow, pea green, and pink, later called ROSE POMPADOUR. Outlined and scrolled with delicately tooled gilding, these colors surrounded cartouches of pastoral scenes. Once Sèvres started making HARD-PASTE PORCELAIN in 1768, new colors such as brown, black, tortoiseshell, and another dark blue were developed.

The state monopoly was discontinued in 1780 and following the French Revolution

SÈVRES

Prior to the 1770s, Sèvres porcelain was dominated by the ROCOCO STYLE. Thereon, until the early years of the 19th century, the NEOCLASSICAL style dominated. In contrast, and up until the advent of ART NOUVEAU, Sèvres's subsequent 19th-century output was highly eclectic and dominated by historical revivals ranging from GOTHIC, to RENAISSANCE, to Classical revivals.

Sucrier
Lobed oval *sucrier* and cover; the porcelain of 18th century, the decoration of a later date.

Pastoral scene in gilded floral cartouche

Cup, cover, and stand
Two-handled cup, cover, and stand, painted with garlands of flowers and gilt leaf fronds. 1761.

Cup and saucer
Cup and saucer, decorated with garlands of flowers on an *oeil de perdrix* ground. 1767.

Factory mark
Sèvres mark.

(1789–99), the factory lost its aristocratic custom and royal patronage. However, in 1800 a new period of prosperity began and it became the Imperial Factory in 1804.

After 1847 copies of 18th-century pieces were made, and FAIENCE and ENAMEL work on copper were introduced. The ceramist Joseph-Théodore DECK was Director from 1887 to 1891. He had been one of the first ART POTTERS and this taste was reflected in some of the individualistic pieces created around 1900. In the 20th century Sèvres produced ART DECO pieces in porcelain. Cristalleries de Sèvres was a notable glassmaking side of the business in the 20th century.

Sewing table See WORK TABLE.

Sextant ■ A navigational instrument, still used today, in the form of a sixth of a circle, based on the concept of the OCTANT, but introduced over a quarter of a century later in 1767. The arc has a scale divided from 0° to 120°, an index arm, vernier, filters, telescope, and magnifier. Sextants often come in a wooden case with two additional telescopes. Examples from the mid-19th century onward are made of brass, with later examples showing a black crackle finish.

Seymour, John (c. 1738–1818) An important English-born American cabinet-maker of the FEDERAL period, active in Boston from 1794. Together with his son, Thomas, he was patronized by wealthy New England merchants. His elaborate and complex furniture in the English NEOCLASSICAL taste was inspired by George HEPPLEWHITE and Thomas SHERATON. The best pieces feature INLAY, delicate BANDING, and the use of exotic woods.

S.F.B.J. (Société Française de Fabrication de Bébés et Jouets) ■ A syndicate founded by French dollmakers in 1899 in an attempt to compete with the fast-growing German doll industry. S.F.B.J.'s most common mold numbers are 60 and 301. Its 200 series of character dolls is the most sought-after of its products. The syndicate closed down in 1950.

Sgraffito The Italian term for "little scratch." A term that denotes inscriptions or drawings scratched or carved onto a pottery (or rock) surface. The pottery decoration is incised through a contrasted coating of SLIP to expose the color of the body beneath. The term was used first in England in 1862. Italian writers refer to such decoration as a *stecco*.

Shagreen ■ Derived from the Persian word *saghari* (ass's skin), shagreen originally referred to roughened, untanned animal skins, often dyed green and used for sword and dagger handles and book bindings. However, from the 17th century onward, shagreen was used in Europe to describe leather made from shark or rayfish skin. Covered with calcified papillae (roughened, rounded, pale protrusions) and also typically dyed green, it was used as a decorative covering on flasks, diverse boxes, and cases.

Shaker crafts The Shaker community was a religious sect for whom furniture-making and other crafts sprang naturally from their spiritual approach to life. They left a lasting legacy in craft and design. The Shakers, so called because of a dance they performed in worship, or The United Society of Believers, as they were formally known, followed a path of peaceful, celibate coexistence inspired by the life of Christ. The community was founded by Ann Lee, a 39-year-old English woman who left Manchester, England, for North America with eight founding followers in 1774. However, she did not live long enough to see the expansion of the movement.

The Shaker community was large enough to create a successful environment that was peaceful, fulfilling, and efficient. Without any worldly distractions, the artisans devoted their time and energies to their crafts, either for the community or for trade or sale outside.

Shako ■ A military hat, generally cylindrical with a peak, plume, or pom-pom. Shakos appeared around 1800 and were superseded by the *képi* and spiked helmet at the end of the 19th century.

Shakudo ■ A Japanese alloy, traditionally comprising 96 percent copper and 4 percent

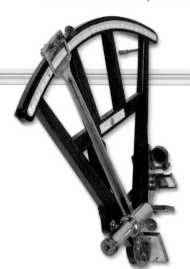

Sextant
Mahogany sextant, by Gregory & Wright, London. 1783–89.

S.F.B.J.
French S.F.B.J. mold 301 Bébé, wearing original clothes.
c. 1900.

Shagreen
Shagreen and silver-mounted draftsman's instrument case.
c. 1810–20.

Shako
Pattern shako of Lieutenant of the 24th Regiment. 1869.

SHAKER CRAFTS

The greatest period in Shaker craft, in terms of growth of the community and therefore artifacts made, was from around 1820 to 1860, and is known as the Classic period, with a total membership of over 5,000.

Shaker design is based on function, economy, and proportion, with no added ornamentation. Any decoration was in the construction or making and in this sense is similar to the work of the ARTS AND CRAFTS designers. The Shaker way of life meant that every task, however small, was executed to the best of the individual's ability and without haste.

Materials were simple, usually locally available timber such as MAPLE or OAK, and usually unpainted. The details of the joinery work were left visible and were regarded as beautiful in themselves. The attention to detail meant that even small utilitarian pieces such as the oval steamed storage boxes and coat racks were attractive. Other craft items included braided rag rugs, baskets, brooms, and metalware.

Shakerism declined in the late 19th century. The Shakers did not set out to create a style. However, the simple elegance of their designs has become increasingly popular and many reproductions are now available. Some harmonize better than others with the original Shaker values.

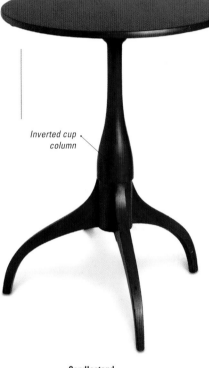

Inverted cup column

Candlestand
Cherrywood candlestand, with dark stained finish. New Lebanon, New York. c. 1825–40.

Boxes
Set of 11 shaker boxes in different sizes. Late 19th century.

Ladder-back form

Rocking chair
Tiger maple rocking chair, with original varnish finish, beiged taped seat, curvilinear arms, and tall finials. New Lebanon, New York. c. 1840.

Sewing case
Maple and cherry sewing case, with breadboard top and original varnish finish. Hancock, New York. c. 1840.

Chest-of-drawers
Butternut and poplar chest-of-drawers, with fine double-beveled top board and cherrywood threaded knobs.

S

gold, used for sword, guards, and hardware during the EDO period. Shakudo objects are generally inlaid with gold, silver, or brass and have a distinctive purple-black patina.

Shamshir A Middle-Eastern sabre with a curved blade, often anglicized to "scimitar." They usually do not have a FULLER and are often decorated with calligraphic inscriptions from the Koran. Made from the Bronze Age onward, *shamshirs* became popular in Europe after Napoleon's campaign in Egypt from 1798 to 1801.

Shang dynasty The Chinese historical period (c. 1500–1028 BCE) following the Neolithic period and noted for the quality and variety of its bronze ritual vessels. Among the best-known ritual shapes are the "ding," "tsun," "hu," "li," "ju" and "gu." They are decorated with complex designs, often incorporating monster masks called "taotie." There are two notable types of Shang pottery: a high-fired ware with a FELDSPATHIC GLAZE, which represents a considerable technical advance for the time, as it made porous vessels watertight, and a thickly potted white ware. Wares include ritual vessels imitating bronze shapes and decorative and domestic red-, gray-, or buff-colored pottery, often continuing earlier Neolithic styles. The Shang dynasty was succeeded by the Zhou (Chou) dynasty (c. 1028–221 BCE).

Shearer, John (active c. 1800–17) An American furniture-maker of Martinsburg, West Virginia. Shearer's furniture was of provincial type, typically in WALNUT or CHERRY. His work is distinctive and identifiable by its carved or inlaid detail, which shows his British sympathy in the use of the "federalist knot" (elongated quatrefoil), symbolic of presumed Federalist support of the British monarchy.

Sheffield plate ■ Another term for Old Sheffield that refers to English fused plate made between about 1742 and 1840. The process was invented by a Sheffield cutler, Thomas Bolsover, who discovered that a sheet of copper could be fused with a thin sheet of silver (or fused in a sandwich between two thin sheets of silver) and that articles could be constructed from this bimetallic sheet, giving the outward appearance of silver while reducing the cost of the raw materials. Seams and edges on these articles were disguised with silver wires and borders, the lapping over of edges, and the judicious placing of handles, spouts, and decoration to conceal the copper core. In Continental Europe, the products are referred to as fused plating rather than Sheffield plate. With the advent of commercial ELECTROPLATING in about 1840, the more skilled and labor-intensive Sheffield plate industry continued for a short period, and then ceased.

Shelf clock ■ A type of inexpensive, mass-produced American BRACKET CLOCK made from the early 19th century, which was slim enough to sit on a narrow shelf. Cases, made in a wide range of styles such as plain rectangular, "steeple," and "acorn," were mostly of softwood with a mahogany veneer and simple glass-paneled doors, sometimes incorporating decorative VERRE ÉGLOMISÉ panels.

Shell motif ■ The scallop or cockleshell is the most common shell form used as ornament, especially for Italian and Spanish furniture from the RENAISSANCE. The ROCOCO style is partially based on shell ornament, and the form was used in silver and ceramics for sauceboats, salt cellars, dishes, and tureens throughout the 18th century. In furniture, the shell featured as carved ornament on Queen Anne CABRIOLE LEGS and as a central theme in the work of Thomas CHIPPENDALE. Inlaid wood furniture of the late 18th and early 19th centuries often features the conch shell.

Shellac 1. A secretion of the lac insect (*Coccus lacca*) native to parts of Asia, which when dissolved in various blends of alcohol, provides a durable, shiny coating for wood. It was introduced to Europe in the 16th century, via Venice, and from the 18th century onward became a key component of colored varnishes such as VERNIS MARTIN, and later, FRENCH POLISHING, devised to imitate Oriental LACQUERS. 2. During the second half of the 19th century a PLASTIClike compound of

Shakudo
One of a pair of Japanese daisho shakudo tsuba. Late Edo period.

Sheffield plate
One of a pair of George II Sheffield plate candelabra. c. 1795.

Shelf clock
Pine- and maple-cased transitional shelf clock, with *églomisé* panel. c. 1830.

Shell motif
Shell motif carved on a George I side chair. c. 1720

shellac was also used to mold objects such as picture frames, boxes, jewelry, and early records.

Shelley Pottery ■ A Staffordshire company, originally Wileman & Co., then Foley Pottery. Joseph Shelley joined the firm in 1872 and his son, Percy Shelley, continued the business. After 1925 the firm traded as Shelley's, and from 1929 as Shelley Potteries Ltd. until it closed in 1966. They became well known for their BONE CHINA tea sets, and during the 1920s their ART DECO wares were reknowned for their practicality and innovative design. The company's lasting popularity is owed largely to such designers as Susie COOPER and Eric Slater (who introduced two new Modernist ranges), the illustrator Mabel Lucie ATWELL, and painters Duncan Grant and Dame Laura Knight.

Shepherd's-crook arm ■ The arm of a chair carved in a curving form, resembling a shepherd's crook. The form found in English furniture of the QUEEN ANNE period (officially 1702–14, but applied generally to the period up to the 1730s), is fashioned in both WALNUT and MAHOGANY.

Sheraton, Thomas ■ Thomas Sheraton was born in Stockton-on-Tees, Durham, and settled in London in 1790. His influential publications have given his name to furniture that is characterized by lightness, elegance, and the extensive use of

INLAY. He clearly trained as a cabinet-maker, although no furniture by him has been identified and it is unlikely that he owned a workshop. He is celebrated above all for his books of designs, especially the *Cabinet-Maker & Upholsterers Drawing Book* of 1791–94. These were aimed at the cabinet-making trade, with practical advice and up-to-date designs for cabinet-makers.

The patterns in his *Drawing Book* show a preference for simple outlines, delicately inlaid or painted, and emphasize the

qualities of wood grain VENEERS. He also freely adopted the antique ornaments favored by Robert ADAM. He produced two additional books: *Cabinet Dictionary* in 1803 and the incomplete *Cabinet-Maker, Upholsterer, and General Artist's Encylopedia* in 1805. After his death, a selection of plates from the three pattern books was issued as *Designs for Household Furniture* in 1812.

Sheraton's style returned to favor in the late 19th century, when the elegant forms of Neoclassicism were resurrected. Together

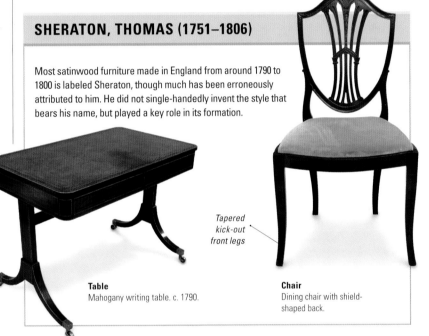

SHERATON, THOMAS (1751–1806)

Most satinwood furniture made in England from around 1790 to 1800 is labeled Sheraton, though much has been erroneously attributed to him. He did not single-handedly invent the style that bears his name, but played a key role in its formation.

Tapered kick-out front legs

Table
Mahogany writing table. c. 1790.

Chair
Dining chair with shield-shaped back.

Shelley Pottery
Mark of Shelley Pottery.

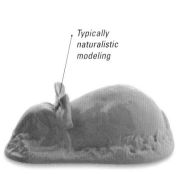

Typically naturalistic modeling

Shelley Pottery
Shelley jelly mold, in white, in the form of a crouching rabbit.

Shepherd's-crook arm
Dutch walnut and floral marquetry elbow chair, with shepherd's-crook arms.

Sherrat, Obadiah
Staffordshire cow and snake on a rainbow base. c. 1830.

with the designs of ADAM and HEPPLEWHITE, this gave birth to the Edwardian style. Inexpensive imitations existed alongside high-quality reproductions.

Sherrat, Obadiah ■ A master potter working in Burslem, Staffordshire, from around 1815 to the late 1830s. Perhaps the maker of some of the unmarked pottery groups that bear his name, which are naive and brightly painted, with themes such as fair grounds or bull-baiting.

Shibuichi The Japanese name for an alloy of copper and silver (approximately 70 percent copper and 30 percent silver), inlaid with gold or silver and treated to produce a pewter gray patina. Like SHAKUDO, it was used for sword fittings in the EDO PERIOD and for elaborate metalwork in the MEIJI PERIOD (1868–1912), up to the present day.

Ship in a bottle A wood, bone, or ivory ship model, complete with masts, sails, and rigging, inserted into a bottle. The masts and sails are then erected by pulling strings. Popular in the 19th century, these were commonly made by sailors.

Shiraz A historic city in southwest Iran whose name is used for rugs in the tribal tradition of the region, especially prayer rugs. They are generally of medium pile and thickly knotted, in dark reds and blues, with stylized motifs of animals, birds, and human figures. Shiraz examples can be found from the early 19th century. Today Shiraz produces rugs using modern techniques.

Shirvan A rug-making district to the south of the Caucasus mountains and one of the most prolific weaving areas in the region during the 19th and 20th centuries. Products tend to be finely woven, incorporating a wide variety of stylized geometric, floral, and animal motifs in jewel colors. The pile is close-clipped with high knot counts.

Shi-shi See DOG OF FO.

Shoe A projecting bar rising from the back RAIL of a chair seat, into which the base of the central SPLAT has been slotted.

Shoulder The sloping part of a vase or decanter above the body and below the neck.

Shoulder head ■ A type of doll where the head and shoulders are cast together, made from the 1830s to the 1880s.

Shoulder plate Part of the SHOULDER HEAD of a doll, comprising shoulders and front and back chest plates.

Sicilian potteries A group of potteries in Sicily, Italy, producing MAIOLICA wares from the late 16th century onward. The main centers were Caltagirone, Palermo, Sciacca, and Trapani. The Caltagirone wares were made in the CASTEL DURANTE style, with figures of saints, military arms, and foliage in part-colored compartments. The style was continued into the 18th century. All the centers produced ALBARELLI of the typical tall, waisted shape and also large oviform jars in the Venetian style. Potteries still exist in Sicily today.

Side (single or upright) chair A chair without arms, designed to stand against a wall, frequently resembling a dining chair. Originating in the BACK STOOL, and later

SHIBAYAMA

A type of Japanese INLAY, Shibayama was developed by the farmer Onogi Senzo from 1770 to 1780. Popular in the MEIJI period (1868–1912), it employs a variety of materials, including TORTOISESHELL, IVORY, glass, and shell, carved and usually set into a gold lacquer or ivory ground. It was used on both *objets d'art* and furniture.

Ivory rather than gold lacquer gold

Visiting-card cases
Ivory visiting-card cases, with Shibayama scenes of storks in a garden and a basket of flowers hanging from a tree. c. 1880.

Shoulder head
Wagner and Zetzsche bisque shoulder head doll.

having upholstered seats and backs, they were traditionally made in sets. Side chairs were made in the UK and Europe from the late 17th century, and in the US from the early 18th century.

Side cabinet See CHIFFONIÉRE.

Side table A simple table designed to stand against a wall. Dating from the 16th century, side tables were used for serving food, for writing, or as dressing tables. The LOWBOY was a form of side table popular in England from around 1700 to 1760.

Sideboard ■ A piece of dining furniture, comprising a number of drawers for the storage of cutlery, table linen, and condiments, invented for use as a serving table in the early 1760s by Robert ADAM. In the late 18th and early 19th centuries sideboards were frequently designed en suite with other dining furniture, and could incorporate knife boxes, plate-warmers, and wine-coolers.

Siegburg potteries ■ A group of potteries in the area of Siegburg, near Bonn, Germany, producing some of the best German STONEWARE from the 15th to the early 17th century. The most typical wares were SCHNELLEN—tall, tapered tankards decorated with shallow reliefs molded separately and sealed onto the sides. Decorative motifs were often taken from contemporary engravings or were modeled in German RENAISSANCE style.

The industry declined at the beginning of the 17th century, but Siegburg wares have been extensively copied from the 19th century.

Sileh A type of FLATWEAVE carpet incorporating embroidery on a KILIM base. More specifically, the term refers to a design made up of S-motifs representing stylized dragons. Silehs were normally woven in two halves and joined together. They were made in vibrant colors, mainly during the 19th century, and were produced in the Caucasus. See SOUMAK.

Silhouette ■ A profile portrait, usually in black paper fixed to a white background, but sometimes also painted. The earliest silhouettes are French and date from the late 17th century. The word is derived from the reputation for parsimony gained by one of Louis XV's finance ministers, Etienne de Silhouette, whose inexpensive hobby was to cut paper "shadow portraits." They were popular in the 18th and 19th centuries in the UK and the US until the arrival of photography. Artists included Augustin Edouart and John Field, and the Americans William King and Charles Polk.

Silicon ware ■ A hard, smooth, high-fired stoneware with a thin glaze made by the DOULTON pottery and porcelain factory from around 1880 to 1912, with typical decoration of light blue and white on a buff and brown body.

Silk A natural fiber obtained from the cocoon of the mulberry silk moth of China. Its cultivation originated in China around 4000 BCE and spread slowly westward along the Silk Route (the trading route between China and the West), arriving in the Byzantine empire around 300 CE. By the 4th century, silk was being produced in Constantinople. Silk produced in the East was known in northern Europe by the 8th century. In the 11th century, silk-weaving was established in Europe, introduced first in southern Italy by the Arabs and then in Spain by the Moors. Silk was cultivated in Italy by the 13th century and by the 14th century had reached a high standard in the centers of Lucca, Florence, and Venice. By the mid-17th century, French silk production had begun to challenge that of Italy and Spain, and by the late 17th century and into the 18th century the main silk workshops were in France and England. After the Napoleonic Wars (1799–1815) France continued to produce high-quality silks while England concentrated on the lower end of the market. Experiments to manufacture artificial silk began at the end of the 19th century, and together with the economic, social, and political changes of the early 20th century, it meant that by 1945 the European silk industry had effectively ended.

Silk-screen printing A 20th-century term for a printing technique, also known as screen printing, in which ink is forced over a stencil that is supported on a very

Sideboard
George III mahogany sideboard on six square tapering legs and spade feet.

Siegburg potteries
Rare cylindrical tankard, with tapering body molded with three vertical panels. 1274.

Silhouette
Augustin Edouart study of a child playing with a ball in cut silhouette. 1827.

Silicon ware
Doulton Lambeth *jardinière*, pierced and decorated with foliate and rosette friezes.

fine mesh or screen (originally made of silk). The image can be built up by the application of a succession of different colors over a series of carefully aligned stencils.

Silver gilt ■ Silver that is covered with a thin film of gold. On antique pieces (and certainly on those before 1840), this was done by MERCURY GILDING, superseded around 1840 by electrogilding. See VERMEIL.

Silver table ■ A square table with a galleried edging, first designed by Thomas CHIPPENDALE in 1754. Silver tables were used for serving tea or displaying objects. They were decorated on all four sides and were designed to stand in the center of the room. See TEA TABLE.

Silver-electroplated glass A type of ART GLASS, the surface of which was decorated with a design of silver deposits, using an electrical current. It was popular from around 1890 to 1920, when it was made by Loetz (see LOETZ GLASS), and in Britain by companies such as STEVENS & WILLIAMS.

Silveria glass ■ A type of English ART GLASS, in which silver foil was embedded between layers of clear or colored glass to give a silvery effect. It was developed by John NORTHWOOD around 1900. In the early 20th century, Silveria glass was made by STEVENS & WILLIAMS.

SILVER PLATE

Silver is a brilliant, grayish white metal that is the most malleable and ductile after gold. It can be hammered, worked, shaped, stretched, beaten, and cast, making it an extremely useful commodity since early times. It is one of the least reactive of elements and therefore suitable for most domestic and culinary purposes.

Teapot
A William IV silver teapot by Joseph and John Angell, London. c. 1834.

Silvering ■ A technique for decorating woodwork and furniture with silver leaf instead of gold. Used from ancient times, it was favored in France and England from the mid-17th century for the lavishly carved BAROQUE furniture of the LOUIS XIV period. The term is also used to describe the method of backing mirror glass with a deposit of silver. The technique was perfected by the Venetian glassmakers of the 19th century, who replaced an amalgam of tin and mercury with silver nitrate.

Simmance, Eliza See DOULTON.

Simon & Halbig ■ A porcelain factory founded in 1839, in Grafenhain, Thuringia, which manufactured BISQUE dolls' heads from 1869. Its best product is a range of CHARACTER DOLLS and ethnic dolls— for example, the Dolls of Four Races (1890–1910). Simon & Halbig also supplied dolls' heads to other factories such as JUMEAU and particularly KÄMMER & REINHARDT, whose dependence on Simon & Halbig for their heads led them to buy the company in 1920. Most Simon & Halbig heads are incised with the factory's name or initials as well as a mold number.

Silver gilt
Silver-gilt grape scissor, with high-relief grape vine and bunch designs. 1835.

Silver table
George III mahogany silver table.

Silveria glass
Stevens & Williams Silveria glass pitcher.

Silvering
George III mahogany cabinet on an 18th-century Venetian gilt and silvered wood stand.

Singerie An ornament incorporating monkeys, frequently dressed in clothes. Monkeys figured in European art from the Middle Ages but were most popular in the 18th century during the fashion for CHINOISERIE. They were painted on walls, porcelain, and FAIENCE by ornamentistes such as Claude AUDRAN and Jean BÉRAIN, worked in PIQUÉ and MARQUETRY, engraved on to glassware, and embroidered and printed on textiles until the early 1800s. See MONKEY BAND.

Siphon barometer Invented in the late 17th century, this type of BAROMETER has its tube bent in a "J" with the short arm open to the atmosphere. Siphon barometers continued to be made, more often in Europe than in England, until they were superseded by the ANEROID barometer in the mid-19th century.

Sitzendorf Porcelain Factory A 19th-century German porcelain factory making copies of MEISSEN porcelain. It was founded in Thuringia by the Voigt brothers in 1850. Its marks include two parallel lines crossed by a third line, imitating the crossed swords of Meissen, and a crown. They made vast quantities of decorative porcelain such as large baskets encrusted with cupids and flowers in delicate pastel shades.

Size gilding A technique used in early ceramic painting for applying gold leaf to designs painted in gold size or animal glue when it was partly dried. The technique is usually seen on Italian MAIOLICA and some early FAIENCE and on English SOFT-PASTE PORCELAIN such as BOW. It is particularly vulnerable to rubbing and general wear and tear.

Skean dhu A Gaelic term for "black knife." A small knife, similar to a DIRK, tucked into the top of the hose in the Scottish Highland dress. This practice was unknown before the 19th century and is probably a Victorian affectation.

Skeleton clock ■ A type of clock with a pierced or fretted, usually brass frame or case revealing the MOVEMENT. Intended to display the skill and ingenuity of the clockmaker, most examples date from the mid-19th century and are set on a marble or wood base. Some frames are modeled on well-known medieval cathedrals with Gothic spires and arches.

Skillet A bronze, iron, brass, or ceramic medieval cooking vessel in the form of a cylindrical or rounded bowl with three or four short legs and a long handle. Some English silver examples surviving from the 17th century have a vertical scroll handle, similar to the one on a tankard.

Skippet A box made to contain a SEAL when it is attached by a cord or ribbon to a document, protecting it from wear. It was used since the advent of seals, but circular silver or SILVER-GILT examples with detachable covers are associated with the 17th and 18th centuries.

Sklo Union ■ A group of established glass factories in Czechoslovakia that were amalgamated into a national glass company in 1965, when the country was under Communist rule. Tableware and decorative pieces were produced in MOLD-BLOWN, CUT, and PRESSED glass. The company employed a number of talented designers, including Frantisek Vizner, Adolf Matura, and Rudolf Jurnikl.

Slag glass ■ A type of inexpensive, opaque, colored press-molded glass with purple-streaked patterns, first made by SOWERBY of Gateshead and taken up by other glassmakers, particularly in northeast England from around 1875 to 1900, and also by John Derbyshire and Co. in Manchester (closed 1877). It used a mixture of slag from local iron foundries in the batch, which resulted in a marbled appearance. Also known as Malachite glass.

Slat-back chair A type of simple chair made from the late 17th century, with horizontal slats across the back. The LADDER-BACK chair is a more elaborate derivative of it.

Sleeper A dealers' term used to describe a piece of either great interest or value, and often both, that has not been recognized as such by the owner, seller, or auctioneer.

Bisque head

Simon & Hablig
Detail of a doll's head incised with the factory name and a mold number.

Simon & Hablig
Simon & Hablig Bébé dressed in elegant French clothes, including elaborate bonnet. c. 1890.

Skeleton clock
Giant wheel skeleton clock of passing strike, with an enamel dial in a glass dome.

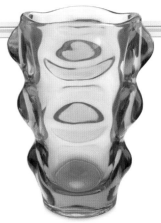

Sklo Union
Sklo Union blue egg vase.

Sleeping eyes ■ Dolls' eyes that can open and close. In dolls produced after 1880, this movement is usually mediated by a lead-weighted rod inside the head. The eyes are linked by a metal bar with weights. If the doll is upright, the weight hangs down and the eyes open. If the doll is placed in a horizontal position, gravity causes the weight to move backward, thus closing the eyes.

Sleeve vase A type of Chinese vase with a cylindrical body and slightly waisted neck, popular in the TRANSITIONAL period around 1640.

Sleigh bed A type of bed based on the LIT EN BATEAU, with a scrolled head and foot, curved wooden sides, and occasionally a canopy. The style was popular in Europe in the REGENCY and EMPIRE periods from around 800 until about 1840.

Slip 1. A homogeneous mixture of clay and water, usually finer and richer than the BODY it covers. Slips are used for coating clay bodies to give color and a smooth, textured surface. 2. An embroidered motif cut out and applied to a ground fabric, commonly heavy silk and velvet bed- and wall-hangings in the 17th century.

Slip glaze A GLAZE that contains over 50 percent clay and is applied as a SLIP to the raw ware.

Slip-casting A technique for molding pottery. Liquid clay is poured into plaster of

Paris molds that absorb some of the water from the SLIP. A layer of clay builds up to give a cast. When the excess slip is poured out, the cast is left in the mold. The cast is allowed to stiffen, removed from the mold, and fired in the usual way.

Slip-trailing ■ A type of ceramic decoration. Different colored SLIPS are trailed onto the first surface slip when it is dry, in much the same way as icing a cake.

Slipware Pottery with one or more coatings of a more refined clay, which is then decorated with designs trailed on in different colored SLIPS. The name of the potter and the date may be added. The lead glaze finish gives a characteristic yellowish coloring. The technique was used by the Romans and was widely popular from the 17th to the mid-19th century—for example, in WROTHAM WARE. Imitations are still made.

Slit head A type of wax-over-composition SHOULDER HEAD in DOLLS, popular in England around the second quarter of the 19th century, produced by dipping a shoulder head in liquid wax. Slit heads, sometimes called "Crazy Alices," are named after the slit in the crown of their head into which strands of hair were inserted.

Slop bowl ■ An uncovered bowl in 18th- and 19th-century tea services, intended to hold the used tea leaves from the teacup. They were used throughout Europe and made by all the major porcelain factories.

Slump glass ■ The term used to describe glass that has been formed by heating sheets of glazing glass over a mold until it is soft and malleable, resulting in its "slumping" into the mold beneath and taking its form. Chance Brothers of Smethwick, Birmingham, were a leading exponent, with their Fiesta range and series of "handkerchief" vases.

Smallsword A light civilian sword that was worn from the 1680s to around 1790. Their HILTS are often lavishly decorated with engraving, chiseling, precious metals, stones, and porcelain. See RAPIER.

Smalt A pigment made by in the 18th century by grinding together cobalt oxide, potassium carbonate, and white QUARTZ to make a powder. It was used to color glass a deep blue.

Smith and Wesson American firearms manufacturers, Horace Smith and Daniel Wesson, remembered mainly for their REVOLVERS. The firm was founded in 1856 and is still in business today. They produced the first practical CARTRIDGE REVOLVER in 1857 and became a major rival of COLT. A small number of their revolvers were fitted with grips made by TIFFANY.

Smith, Benjamin (1764–c. 1822) An English silversmith who worked in Birmingham with Matthew BOULTON as a chaser and silversmith. Smith entered his

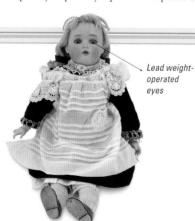

Sleeping eyes
Kammer & Reinhardt/Simon & Halbig bisque doll, with sleeping eyes.

Lead weight-operated eyes

Slip-trailing
Pennsylvanian redware plate with pie-crust edge, slip-trailed with yellow lines.

Gilt-bordered polychrome imagery

Slop bowl
George Grainger miniature round slop bowl. c. 1830.

SNUFF BOX

A box for holding a small quantity of snuff (finely ground scented tobacco) and keeping it fresh and dry. Most snuff boxes were small and portable, but larger presentation pieces were made for use at the table or ceremonies. They were made in PORCELAIN, IVORY, PAPIER-MÂCHÉ, TORTOISESHELL, TREEN, and gold and silver (or SILVER GILT), in particular. The decoration varied from bright-cut engravings that sparkled as they caught the light to detailed depictions of hunting, pastoral scenes, or Classical myths. They were fostered by the trend of taking snuff in Europe from the late 17th to the mid-19th century, after which their popularity declined. SNUFF BOTTLES were used in China.

Snuff bottle
Chinese *famille rose* enameled glass snuff bottle and stopper.

Shell snuff box
George III cowrie-mounted shell snuff box. c. 1770.

Shell snuff box detail
Detail of engraved coat of arms on the cover.

Naturalistic carved flowerhead motif

Wood snuff box
Dutch carved fruitwood snuff box in the shape of a shoe. 18th century.

first mark in 1802 as partner to Digby Scott in London and then registered his own mark in 1807. He manufactured silver almost solely for Rundell, Bridge & Rundell (as did Paul STORR), including many fine pieces for the Royal Collection.

Smith, George ■ 1786–1826) An important English furniture designer of the REGENCY period who owned a sizable London cabinet-making business. Smith popularized the circular dining table and the OTTOMAN in England. His interpretations of the Grecian

and Egyptian styles disseminated by Thomas HOPE emphasized comfort rather than historical accuracy, but he used Classical motifs such as MONOPODIA and claw feet. Smith published several volumes on design, including: *A Collection of Designs for Household Furniture and Interior Decoration* (1808); *A Collection of Ornamental Designs after the Antique* (1812); and *The Cabinet Maker and Upholsterer's Guide* (1826).

Smocking A decorative embroidery using a variety of stitches such as chain, feather, and

herringbone, over a tightly pleated ground applied to shirts, shifts, and childrens' clothes.

Snakewood ■ A hard, durable, pale brown wood with serrated figuring. Native to Brazil, snakewood was used occasionally as INLAY in the 17th century; in the 18th century it was used primarily for MARQUETRY and BANDING and as a VENEER in REGENCY cabinetwork.

Snaphaunce A variant of the FLINTLOCK mechanism, dating from the mid-16th

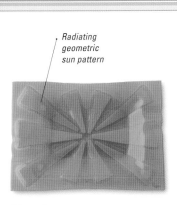

Radiating geometric sun pattern

Slump glass
Higgins Mandarin ashtray in slumped sandwich glass.

Smith, George
Regency rosewood-veneered card table, in the manner of George Smith.

Snakewood
Regency snakewood games table.

century, in which the flint was attached to a spring-loading arm. Less expensive than the WHEEL LOCK, it was gradually superseded by the true flintlock during the 17th century.

Snuff bottle ■ A small Chinese bottle for snuff, usually with a stopper to which a tiny spoon is attached. Typically cylindrical or of flattened ovoid form, they were made in porcelain, glass, lacquer, amber, coral, ivory, jade, agate, and other hardstones. They were made throughout the 18th century, but most date from the Daoguang period (1821–50) and later.

Snuffer See CANDLE SNUFFER.

Soap box A silver box of spherical or rectangular form, sometimes on a spreading base with a hinged cover. They contained a soap ball and were part of toilet services from the early 18th century, but are scarce today.

Soapstone ■ A metamorphic rock also known as steatite and largely composed of the mineral talc. It is whitish in color and has been employed as a component of porcelain, notably at the WORCESTER factory in England. However, in its primary role as a medium for carving, it has been in use since antiquity.

Socket head A doll's head with a neck that ends in a ball shape. This ball neatly fits into a specially designed socket, a cup-shaped opening between the shoulders of the torso, thus enabling the head to rotate from side to side.

Soda glass A type of GLASS in which soda is added to the batch as the FLUX and lime is added as a stabilizer. Various materials were used to provide the soda, including the ashes of burned salt-marsh plants and seaweed. The resulting glass, often slightly yellowish or brown-tinged, is fragile. It was well suited to the intricate designs seen on early Venetian and FAÇON DE VENISE glass because it cooled rapidly and so prevented applied ornament from sagging.

Sofa A long, informal, fully upholstered SETTEE. Made from the 1690s, the sofa usually resembled a double chair until the mid-18th century, when it was lengthened. Unlike the settee, the sofa invited the user to lounge or recline upon it and this "comfort factor" gradually saw the sofa replacing the settee from the 19th century.

Sofa table ■ A table for use while sitting on a sofa. Popular from the late 18th century until the 1840s, the sofa table generally contained a drawer that had compartments for storing cards or gaming counters. Sofa tables had rectangular tops and hinged flaps and rested on trestle- or plinth-type supports. During the early 19th century, elegant sofa tables were decorated with fine VENEERS of exotic woods and occasionally embellished with EBONY or BRASS inlay. More elaborate

specimens had lyre-shaped end supports, MONOPODIA, or lion masks on the drawer handles.

Soft-paste porcelain A substitute for true porcelain made of ground-up glass or FRIT (to give translucency) blended with white clay, soapstone, and lime. It was fired at a relatively low temperature (2, 192°F/1,200°C), was costly to produce, and suffered heavy kiln losses.

Softwood A collective term for timber from coniferous trees such as pine, hemlock, and spruce. The wood is often of a more open grain and softer than that of HARDWOOD.

Solid china A term referring to an all-in-one porcelain doll's figure, for example, the FROZEN CHARLOTTE.

Solids See FLATS. Early lead toy figures cast completely solid. The process was superseded by HOLLOW-CAST figures. The term is usually applied to toy soldiers.

Solitaire See CABARET.

Solon, Marc-Louis ■ (1835–1912) A French modeler and decorator who developed the technique of *pâte-sur-pâte* and *pâte d'application* at the SÈVRES factory from 1862 to 1871, after which he went to England and worked at the MINTON factory.

Soapstone
Mottled dark gray soapstone depiction of "The Migration," by Joe Talirunili.

Sofa table
Regency sofa table. c. 1810.

Mahogany top with hinged flaps

Solon, Marc-Louis
One of a pair of Minton ovoid vases, designed by Marc-Louis Solon.

Sommerso
Murano *sommerso* vase in four colors. c. 1955.

Sommerso ■ The Italian term for "submerged," used to describe CASED GLASS produced on the island of MURANO.

Song dynasty ■ A Chinese period (960–1279 CE) notable particularly for ceramics, especially stoneware in simple and elegant shapes with monochrome glazes. CELADON wares with semitranslucent greenish glazes were made for the court. Some early pieces made when the court was at Kaifeng in northern China (960–1126) have molded floral decoration. Later Song wares include ivory porcellaneous DING WARE, Qingbai ware with a pale-blue glassy glaze, and CIZHOU WARE with bold incised or painted decoration in black and white slip. The simplicity of Song ceramics was influential on 20th-century STUDIO POTTERY.

Sonneberg A town in Thuringia, Germany, and a leading doll- and toy-producing center in the 19th and early 20th centuries. Except for the porcelain heads, most components were made by outworkers and sold to the Sonneberg companies to be assembled. Many dolls, bears, and toys were bought by American buyers to import to the US.

Sottsass, Ettore Jr. ■ (born 1917) An Austrian-born Italian architect and designer who established his own office in Milan in 1947 and was appointed art director of Poltronova, the Italian design company, in 1957. He began to turn away from the ethics of the MODERN MOVEMENT during the late 1960s and became one of the most influential figures of the POSTMODERN Movement from the late 1970s onward and a major player in the establishment of the MEMPHIS group. He was a versatile designer, creating glass and ceramic pieces, office machines for Olivetti as well as more expressive pieces of colorful furniture for Memphis from 1981, especially in the "new" colored plastic laminate materials and in medium density fiberboard (MDF).

Soumak A flat-woven rug with the weft wrapped around a number of warp threads. Made in the Caucasus, southwest Persia, Turkey, and by the Baluch on the Afghan-Persian borders from the 19th century to the present day. Designs tend to be geometric and finely woven.

South Jersey glass American glass made at small glasshouses in southern New Jersey around Milville and Williamstown, including that of Caspar WISTAR, from the mid-18th century through the 19th century. The first products were crude, free-blown green glass, made by German immigrants and resembling Bohemian forms. Jugs (pitchers) and sugar bowls are typical. Early examples are rare and were reproduced in the early 20th century.

Southwark potteries London factories producing TIN-GLAZED EARTHENWARE in the 17th century. Production probably began with the Dutchman Christian Wilhelm in the 1620s, who petitioned several times for a monopoly of the manufacture of smalt (cobalt pigment). His pottery was known for blue and white wares similar to DELFT.

Souvenir ware ■ A term mostly applied to inexpensive small objects in ceramics, wood, and glass, often with inscriptions naming the vacation resort in which they were purchased. Souvenir ware includes MAUCHLINE WARE, Bohemian glass trinkets sold in SPA TOWNS and engraved with the word "Andenken" (souvenir or memory), and Goss porcelain items with the town's name or coat of arms.

Sowerby ■ An English glassworks established at Gateshead by John Sowerby for a year in 1847, and reopened in 1850. The glassworks introduced many new techniques such as Vitro-porcelain (1877) and Queen's Ivory (1878), and in the late 19th century was one of the leading manufacturers of PRESSED GLASS, SLAG GLASS, and wares decorated with enameling or iridized glass. It was Victorian Britain's leading pressed glassmaker. Its products can be distinguished by the inclusion of a peacock logo on most of its output. The factory supplied world markets with all types of domestic ware, including nursery ware inspired by the designs of Walter CRANE. It closed in 1972.

Soy frame A CRUET frame made from around 1775 to 1830, usually of silver or Old Sheffield plate for stoppered, cut-glass,

Graduated annular rings and cylinders

Song dynasty
Song/Jin Henan tea bowl.
c. 13th century.

Sottsass Jr., Ettore
Bitossi Totem hand-painted ceramic sculpture, with 11 components bolted together.

Souvenir ware
Tunbridgeware view of the Pantiles, Tunbridge Wells, in tesserae frame.

Sowerby's Ellison
Sowerby's white milk glass basket.

S

gilded, or plain bottles used for soy and other condiments.

Spa towns In the 18th and 19th centuries, "taking the waters" was both fashionable and deemed healthy in spas and resorts such as Carlsbad, Warmbrunn, and Franzensbad in Bohemia, Baden-Baden and Wiesbaden in Germany, Aix-en-Provence in France, and Bath and Tunbridge Wells in England. The visitors were wealthy, often nobility or royalty, and wares were made to cater to their taste and included spa glass, tumbler and carafe sets, and vases. Many pieces were decorated by distinguished engravers such as Dominik BIEMANN. Others were made of colored glass such as LITHYALIN or STAINED or CASED glass decorated with local views or suitable inscriptions.

Spade foot A rectangular form of foot that slightly tapers from the top, suggesting the outline of a spade. The spade foot was used in England from the latter part of the 18th century by such influential furniture designers as Thomas SHERATON and George HEPPLEWHITE.

Spandrel An architectural term referring to the triangular space on either side of a central arch or the space between one arch and another in an ARCADE, which is frequently favored for decorative ornament. It may also refer to the decoration in the four corners of a clock dial. Spandrels may be embellished with patterns or paired figures such as angels or CHERUBS.

Spanish colonial ■ A term given to the art and architecture of the Spanish colonial Americas, including parts of the southern US, from the 16th to the 19th century. Decorative arts include painted wood *santos* (saints) figures and painted and carved primitive wooden furniture.

Spanish foot See BRAGANZA FOOT.

Sparrow-beak jug A small milk jug, part of a tea set, with a pear-shaped body and a pointed spout like a bird's beak, found in 18th-century pottery and porcelain, especially WORCESTER and CAUGHLEY.

Spatter (or spangled) glass Glass made in Europe and the US decorated with a pattern of multicolored spots or blobs. Variations of the glass were made by HOBBS, Brockunier & Co., J. S. Irwin, and SOWERBY. Also known as color-splashed glass.

Spatterware See SPONGE WARE.

Specimen chest ■ A chest designed to contain a collection of coins or other precious objects such as shells, medals, or semiprecious stones. The WELLINGTON CHEST, named after the Duke of Wellington, was originally created as a specimen chest in the early 19th century.

Speed, John (1552–1629) An English cartographer of the early 17th century. Drawing on the work of Christopher Saxton as well as his own research, Speed published an English county atlas, *Theatre of the Empire Great Britaine*, in 1611, which continued to be reissued well into the 18th century. In 1627 he published *A Prospect of the Most Famous Parts of the World*, the first world atlas produced by an Englishman. Speed's maps are noted for their flowing script and rich decoration.

Spelter ■ A term for zinc or an alloy of zinc and lead or aluminum, used as a substitute for bronze. It was popular in the 19th century for small, mass-produced, inexpensive cast items such as candlesticks, or for larger pieces like figures.

Sphinx ■ A mythological winged creature with the body of a lion and the head of a woman. Although a royal and religious symbol in ancient Egypt, it was the Classical interpretation of the sphinx that became popular throughout Europe. The original function of the sphinx as a guardian of temples and tombs inspired its use as a support for SARCOPHAGI during the Italian RENAISSANCE and as a garden ornament from the BAROQUE period. In 18th-century France the sphinx was even more widely adopted, originating in the designs of Jean BÉRAIN and further popularized by Napoleon's Egyptian campaign. It was found in overmantel decoration, gilt-bronze FIRE-DOGS, and images of court beauties. In the NEOCLASSICAL period it was also used to decorate chair arms, vases, side tables, and architectural brackets. In mid-18th-

Spanish colonial
Painting on tin of the Madonna and Child, probably from Mexico. Late 19th century.

Specimen chest
Early Victorian rosewood specimen chest.

Spelter
Art Nouveau "L'Ame des Fleur" patinated spelter figure, signed "A. Foretay."

Sphinx
One of a pair of Louis XVI gilded bronze sphinx andirons. c. 1790.

century England, porcelain figures of famous actresses as sphinxes were produced at CHELSEA and BOW. The sphinx continued to be used as a decorative motif throughout the 19th and 20th centuries, and is still employed in the 21st century.

Spice box A small box or cupboard designed for exotic spices. In the 18th century, wooden spice cupboards were made as miniature cabinets. TREEN examples were made in the form of towers. Silver spice boxes were procuced as dining table accessories, with several compartments and sometimes incorporating a nutmeg grater. Small examples were sometimes included in traveling dining sets. Porcelain spice boxes were made from the early 18th century at SAINT-CLOUD and MENNECY.

Spider leg table ■ A rectangular gateleg OCCASIONAL table, popular from the late 18th century and made primarily in MAHOGANY. The name "spider" derives from the table's six slender legs.

Spill vase ■ A vase, usually cylindrical with a flared rim, used on the mantelshelf in pairs to hold "spills" of paper or cut wood slivers to light candles and lamps from the fire. They were made in many materials, including ceramic, BRASS, glass, and PAPIER-MÂCHÉ.

Spindle A slender piece of wood turned on a lathe, often used as an upright member or horizontal stretcher

on a chair. Turned spindles sawn in half—known as "split spindles"—were commonly applied as decoration to the flat, framed faces of chests in the 17th century. See BALUSTER.

Spinel A gemstone found in several colors, including red, blue, and green, although red is the most used commercially. Found in Sri Lanka, Burma, and Thailand, the stone was popular in India, where it was particularly prized by the Mughal emperors and was frequently set in necklace and turban jewels. Synthetic blue spinel is a common imitation of AQUAMARINE.

Spinner, David (1758–1811) An American folk potter active in Buckinghamshire County, Pennsylvania. His work, with its animated decoration often depicting horses, is considered typical REDWARE of PENNSYLVANIA DUTCH type.

Spitalfields silk factories In the East End of London, Spitalfields became the center of the English silk industry from around 1700. Although silk-weaving was already known in England, it was given new impetus from immigrant HUGUENOT weavers after the revocation of the Edict of Nantes in 1685. In the first half of the 18th century dress silk was the main product. Designers such as James Leman and Anna Maria Garthwaite contributed to the growth in both the home and export market. Government legislation,

including the 1721 prohibition of printed calicoes and the 1766 ban on imported French silks, together with the Spitalfields Acts on rates of pay, helped the industry to prosper. Spitalfields continued to prosper until 1824, when legislation once again permitted free trade, and imported French silks flooded the market, causing Spitalfields to go into a steep decline. In the late 19th century a number of new factories produced furnishing silks for the growing interior design market, but the last one left the area in 1895.

Spittoon ■ A receptacle for tobacco chewers to spit into, made in the 18th, 19th, and early 20th centuries in pottery, porcelain, or metal (usually brass). They were either small and handheld or larger and designed to rest on the floor. Examples from WORCESTER and CAUGHLEY have a spherical body and sloping rim. They were also made at SÈVRES and as CHINESE EXPORT WARE, and by factories across the US.

Splat ■ The central vertical member of a chair back, generally shaped, and either left solid or decorated with carving, piercing, veneering, or inlay. From the early 18th century, splat shapes were produced in a variety of designs.

Splint seat Chair seat with thin, interlaced strips of OAK or HICKORY wood that have been woven into it. In use since the 18th century, splint seats are largely a rustic North American feature.

Spider leg table
George III mahogany spider leg drop-leaf table. c. 1800.

Spill vase
Porcelain spill vase. c. 1830.

Spittoon
Zanesville spittoon, painted with orange chrysanthemums on a shaded brown ground.

Splat
Queen Anne walnut arm chair, with a vasiform splat. 1750.

S

Spode ◼ From 1776, Josiah Spode of Stoke-on-Trent produced well-made pottery across a wide range: white STONEWARE with applied or sprigged designs in relief, black BASALT WARE copying WEDGWOOD, and most importantly, blue printed EARTHENWARE. The Caramanian and Indian Hunting series of prints are famous and much collected. In tune with the REGENCY designs of the time, the pottery used brilliantly colored Japanese patterns with excellent gilding. Harry Daniel was in charge of decoration but left in 1822 to set up his own factory. Spode continued its rich Regency patterns throughout the 1820s. Pattern 1166 is well known, with colored sprays of flowers painted on a dark blue ground gilt with an all-over scale pattern. The PATTERN BOOKS of the factory give information on shapes and decoration. Tableware, vases, desk sets, candlesticks, pastille burners, and cabinet wares were produced. In 1833 the firm was taken over by William Copeland and Thomas Garrett, who had been managers in Spode's London retail shop. The firm traded as COPELAND & GARRETT, and aware of the growing competition, endeavored to introduce up-to-date designs. Its Statuary Porcelain busts, figures, and groups—better known as PARIANWARE— sold in large quantities. In 1847 Garrett retired and Copeland took sole charge. He spent much time in London, becoming an alderman and Lord Mayor, but still managed the factory. He retired in 1867, leaving the firm to his four sons. The factory

continues today, having reverted to its name of Spode in 1970, and still makes its 19th-century patterns.

Sponge ware ◼ Cheaply decorated ware in which the color was applied with a sponge, creating a blurred effect. Dating from the beginning of the 19th century and common on Staffordshire pottery, it is called SPATTERWARE in the US.

Spoon tray ◼ A small, shallow, usually silver or porcelain tray, often with fluted edges, made from aound 1700 to 1760, before saucers were common. These trays held teaspoons and stopped tea drips from soiling furniture, clothing, or tablecloths.

Spoon warmer ◼ A Victorian invention in the form of a vessel or container for hot water in which one or more serving spoons could

SPODE

Spode made high-quality overglaze designs using the bat-printing technique. Early pieces have the Spode mark impressed or painted with the pattern number. Spode is generally credited with the invention of BONE CHINA from around 1796 to 1797.

Dish
Dish printed with the "Battle between a buffalo and a tiger" scene from the "Indian Sporting" series.

Pastel burner and cover
Porcelain campana-shaped pastel burner and cover. c. 1820.

Sponge ware
Blue, green, and red rainbow-striped sponge ware plate.

Sponge ware
Blue sponge ware paneled pitcher, with double-sided tulip leaves and buds.

Spoon tray
Worcester lozenge-shaped spoon tray, painted in *Compagnie des Indes* style.

Spoon warmer
Turquoise Burmantofts Art Pottery spoon warmer in a seated toad shape. c. 1895.

balance with their bowls heating in the water. Often made from silver-plate or silver, these items exist in various novelty forms and generally have a nautical theme or shape such as shells or a life buoy.

Spot motif See SAMPLERS.

Spratling, William ■ A silver and metalware designer who opened a shop, La Aduana, in 1931 in Taxco, Mexico, a town known for its production of silver. By 1935, he had met with success and opened a larger shop, Taller de las Delicias, and also exported his work to the US. Many of his designs combined Mexican motifs with a MODERN aesthetic. After briefly forming an alliance with the Silson company, Spratling resigned from his company, which went bankrupt in 1945. Thereafter, he studied Alaskan and North West styles, but died in 1967 while still active. The Ulrich family acquired the company and is still producing today.

Sprig ■ A decorative technique for ceramics, whereby ornament is molded or stamped separately and attached to the BODY of an object or vessel.

Sprimont, Nicholas (1716–71) A leading practitioner of English ROCOCO in silver and porcelain. A Flemish HUGUENOT, he apprenticed as a silversmith and arrived in England in the early 1740s, entering his mark in London in 1743. He specialized in decoration inspired by, and in some cases

cast from, sea creatures such as shells, crabs, and dolphins—even naturalistic crayfish salts, which he produced both in porcelain and silver. Sprimont also decorated objects with finely modeled human figures. In 1749 he became manager of the CHELSEA PORCELAIN FACTORY.

Spring clock See TABLE CLOCK.

Spur mark The small mark on the underside of a plate left from the "spurs" or pegs that support them in the SAGGER in the kiln. They are noticeable on CHELSEA and JAPANESE PORCELAIN.

Squab cushion A removable stuffed cushion for a chair or stool. Originating in France, squab cushions were a popular feature of chairs and stools from the 17th and 18th centuries. Occasionally the term was used to designate a large, padded seat.

S-scroll ■ See C-SCROLL, VOLUTE. A decorative scroll form carved or applied in the shape of a continuous or broken "S." It often featured as an apron or corner ornament in the BAROQUE and ROCOCO styles.

St. Ives Pottery A ceramics studio in St. Ives, Cornwall, founded in 1920 by the English studio potter Bernard LEACH in collaboration with the celebrated Japanese potter

Shoji HAMADA. After Leach's death, the pottery was run by his widow until 1999 and is still in operation today.

St. Petersburg Imperial porcelain factory ■ A Russian factory established around 1720 by Peter the Great. In the early years it was unsuccessful, but in 1744 the Empress Elizabeth engaged Christoph Hunger, an ARCANIST, who helped turn it into a viable concern. Hunger left in 1748, but the factory continued under the patronage of Catherine the Great. The earlier wares show MEISSEN influence, but Catherine encouraged Russian traditions. Its products included imposing NEOCLASSICAL dinner services, porcelain with military motifs, and a series of peasant figures and portrait busts. After the 1917 Revolution, the factory became the property of the people. Since 1925 it has been called the Lomonosov State Porcelain Factory.

Staffordshire figure ■ A ceramic "portrait" figure, produced throughout the 19th century. The trend grew from around 1840 to the early 20th century for portraits of contemporary figures. Staffordshire figures depict people from all walks of life— the royal families of Europe, politicians, soldiers and sailors, actors and actresses, circus performers, sports personalities, people who achieved fame or notoriety, and even famous animals. Many of the potters would never have seen these people, but the likenesses were produced from prints in newspapers and show bills. It is also

Scrolling foliate forms

Spratling
Art Deco William Spratling tortoise and sterling Modernist hand necklace.

Sprig
Wedgwood black jasper two-handled urn and cover. Late 19th century.

S-scroll
Louis XV gilded bronze clock "A L'Amour," with extravagant S-scrolls.

St. Petersburg
Plate with eagle crests, gilt monograms, and flower panel details. Early 19th century.

certain that many figures of soldiers and politicians had the same mold for the body but a different head. Many of them were FLATBACKS, designed to stand on the mantelshelf. Some have the name of the person depicted molded on the base (not always correctly). Much research has been done to identify the figures. Queen Victoria and her family were popular. So were generals such as Wellington, Napoleon, and Garibaldi, the Italian patriot, who made two visits to England and captured the people's imagination. The American circus performer van Amburgh featured in pottery after Queen Victoria went to see his wild animal act twice in 1838. The opera singers Jenny Lind (the Swedish Nightingale) and Maria Malibran were portrayed, as was the perpetrator of the "Murder in the Red Barn," William Corder, and his victim, Maria Marten. Even the elephant Jumbo, who was killed by a train and plunged the nation into mourning, was captured in ceramic immortality.

Staffordshire potteries The "Five Towns" of the Staffordshire potteries—Stoke, Burslem, Hanley, Longton, and Tunstall—were the heartland of British ceramics. In the 19th century there were more than 1,000 firms working at various times, a few all through the period, such as WEDGWOOD, SPODE, and RIDGWAY. These were the great "potting families," but innumerable small concerns made a fleeting appearance. There were factories at Longport, Fenton, Cobridge, Shelton, Lane Delph

(now called Middle Fenton), and Lane End. Largely because of Josiah Wedgwood and the canal system, and, in the last half of the 19th century, the railroads, English ceramics spread far and wide. The port of Liverpool also helped, supplying the vast export trade to the Americas and to India. Staffordshire became the pottery supplier to the world. Besides figures, most factories also made tea and dinner sets for everyday use, which were sold through china shops. These shops did not wish the makers to mark their products with their own names. Naturally, the shops wanted clients to come back to them for repeat orders, and as a consequence, it is hard to attribute much Staffordshire pottery to specific makers.

Stained glass ■ A term for colored, stained, or enameled glass held together by lead strips in an abstract or figurative design, set in an iron framework, and used in an architectural context, usually a window or as a decorative panel. The process was used in the Middle Ages, when first monastic and then guild workshops made windows from glass—usually blue, green, gold, and brown—colored with metallic oxides. Details of drapery, features, and decoration were painted onto the surface and then fired. Some of the finest stained glass cathedral windows from the 13th and 14th centuries were made using this technique. From the late 15th and through the 16th century, stained glass windows were often made of rectangular panes of clear glass painted with colored enamels. During the 17th and 18th centuries, the art of stained glass fell into abeyance, but it was revived in the 19th century with the GOTHIC REVIVAL, under the influence of William MORRIS and the Pre-Raphaelite painters. Stained glass windows, doors, and panels became a feature of ART NOUVEAU and ART DECO interiors. In the US TIFFANY produced panels and screens for domestic interiors and adapted the technique for lampshades. In the 20th century leading artists such as Henri Matisse, Marc Chagall, and Patrick Heron designed stained glass windows, while glass workshops and individual

Stained glass
Leaded glass panel, depicting a medieval maiden collecting flowers.

STAFFORDSHIRE FIGURE

Several factories in the "Five Towns" of the Staffordshire potteries made portrait figures. They are a fascinating record of the Victorian period seen through the lives of the famous and the infamous.

Gilt collar

Model
Seated spaniel, with a basket of fruit at its feet. c. 1860.

Selectively polychrome enameled and gilded

Male figure
Crimean figure of Admiral Sir Deans Dundas. c. 1854.

Female figure
A Staffordshire pottery figure of a young woman, standing, with a plumed hat and holding a riding crop. c. 1860–70.

makers used the technique for decorative pieces such as jewel boxes.

Staining ■ Oil-based vegetable and spirit stains have been used to darken or color the original appearance of some woods, sometimes with the intention to deceive, since the 17th century. The green husks of walnuts were used to stain BEECH to achieve the look of highly prized WALNUT furniture. PEARWOOD was often ebonized during the Victorian period. In the 18th century, oxide of iron was applied to SYCAMORE MAPLE to produce greenish gray HAREWOOD. MAHOGANY was reddened and imitated using alkanet root. Staining was useful in INLAY and MARQUETRY work, where colors were used to render flower and foliage designs realistically.

Stainless steel A corrosion-resistant alloy of STEEL with chromium and nickel, developed simultaneously in Germany and Sheffield, England, in the early 20th century. Although used for cutlery and tableware before World War II, it was only after the war that it became the predominant material in cutlery manufacture.

Stalker, John, and George Parker The authors of *A Treatise on Japanning and Varnishing* published at Oxford in 1688. The book was a welcome source for European copiers, from female amateurs to well-established craftsmen, of the rare and highly expensive Chinese lacquered furniture that was fashionable from the late 17th century. With 24 plates of CHINOISERIE designs—bamboo foliage, rocks, temples, insects, cranes, HO HO birds, and mandarins—Stalker and Parker's book illustrates a variety of patterns originating in Japanese LACQUERWORK, which have been adopted as decoration for a host of objects, including cabinet furniture, picture and mirror frames, and toilet articles.

Stam, Mart (Martinus Adrianus ■ (1899–1986) A Dutch architect and designer closely identified with the BAUHAUS designers in Germany, where he worked in the 1920s, and with Russian Constructivists. He is best known as the inventor of the tubular steel CANTILEVER CHAIR, celebrated for its simplicity of construction, with two supports rather than four legs that relied on the strength of tubular steel. His seminal design of 1924, which was not fully realized until 1926, coincided with a similar tubular steel cantilever chair produced by Ludwig MIES VAN DER ROHE. The pioneering form was adopted and popularized by designers such as Marcel BREUER.

Stamping The practice of impressing a mark into a piece of metalwork, ceramics, or furniture with a stamp. It also describes pressing low-relief ornament onto a ceramic body.

Standee ■ An advertising piece, typically of cardboard, with a folding stand to make the board stand upright on a counter or store floor. The front was decorated with a color LITHOGRAPHED design, often using the same imagery, motifs, and branding as larger advertising posters. Standees were popular from the late 19th century into the 1960s, but can still be found today, and are used particularly to advertise movies.

Standing cup (or hanap) A silver or gold cup, usually with a cover, where the bowl is raised up or literally standing on a pedestal or extended foot. The term is mainly used for larger, important, ceremonial cups dating from the medieval period, through the Reformation, and up to and including certain examples from the early 18th century.

Standish See INK STAND.

Stangl Pottery ■ Having worked for the FULPER pottery of Flemington, New Jersey, from 1910, the ceramics engineer Martin Stangl bought Fulper in 1929 and changed its name to Stangl. After retreating from art pottery production and concentrating on simpler utility wares with matt glazes, Stangl began to specialize in handpainted bird figurines. These included, from 1940, a naturalistic line based on the *Birds of America* prints of John James Audubon. Many new ranges were introduced until 1955, but competition from European imports caused a decline in production, which ceased in 1978.

Staining
Scottish school Arts and Crafts stained and carved beech settle.

Stam, Mart
Chair by Thonet, with ebonized molded plywood and steel cantilever frame. c. 1930.

Standee
Amalgamated Lithographers Majestic polar bears refrigerator diecut standees.

Stangl Pottery
Stangl porcelain red-headed woodpeckers, marked.

STARCK, PHILIPPE (BORN 1949)

A French designer, Philippe Starck trained at the École Camondo in Paris as an interior architect. In 1969 he worked for Pierre Cardin and designed 65 pieces of furniture. He achieved celebrity status after he and four other designers were asked to design for the president's private apartments at the Elysee Palace in Paris (1983). A good self-publicist with a strong personality, he set up his own company, Starck Products, in 1980 to manufacture his designs. In 1985 Starck won a competition to design the street furniture for the *Parc de la Villette* in Paris. His interiors for the Costes Café in Paris, the Starck Club nightclub in Dallas, and the Royalton and Paramount Hotels in New York, have all added to his reputation as one of the finest designers of his generation.

Square-section tapered front legs

Vase
French limited-edition Daum teardrop-shaped "Etrangeté 66" glass vase or display piece, with matt finish. 1988.

Chair
Philippe Starck-Aleph chair, from the Royalton Hotel in New York.

Stanhope ■ A small souvenir formed in metal, plastic, or carved wood or bone, produced from the mid-19th to the mid-20th century in various novelty shapes. It is held close to the eye to view a tiny, transparent microphotograph (invented by J. B. Dancer) showing up to twelve tourist scenes through a miniature lens (invented in the late 1700s by the third Earl of Stanhope). René Dagron was the first to set the lenses and micro-photographs into miniature objects and mass-produce them from the mid-1860s onward.

Steam mechanism See LIVE STEAM MECHANISM.

Steiff ■ The Steiff factory was founded in 1877 by Margarete Steiff, a seamstress who sold felt clothing from her shop in Giengen, Germany. In 1880 she made a felt elephant pincushion for a friend. An overwhelming success, this was soon produced on a larger scale in her workshop. In 1886, over 5,000 elephants were made, and in 1892 Steiff distributed her first catalog. The Steiff soft toy business was registered in 1893. At the Leipzig Spring Trade Fair of 1903, Steiff showed its first animals with movable limbs. One was a TEDDY BEAR called 55PB. Three thousand bears were ordered for export to the US and soon other orders followed. Bear 55PB was joined by 35PB in 1904 and 28PB in 1905. Jointing evolved in these two years from twine to twisted wire over rods to disk joints. To distinguish its products from those of its competitors,

Celtic motifs carved in bog oak

Gold plush fur

Stanhope viewing lens

Stanhope
Stanhope view of Ryde Pier before the installation of the "electric tramway." c. 1880

Stanhope
Carved Celtic cross charm with views of Kilarney, Ireland, through a Stanhope lens. c. 1890.

Steiff
Gold plush Steiff bear, with original tag. 1950s.

Steiff devised its trademark "button in ear." At first the button was embossed with an elephant. A blank button was used between 1904 and 1905 and from then onward the button bore the name "Steiff." Until 1908, most of Steiff's bears were exported to the US. Later, English and the German markets followed, resulting in a teddy bear craze that lasted into the late 1930s. Some of Steiff's best known bears of that period are its "original" bear, the teddy clown, the Petsy bear, and the teddy baby. Teddies typically had a characteristic humped back, elongated limbs, and a shaved muzzle. The firm also made other animal toys such as monkeys. World War II put a stop to the factory's output, but production resumed in 1947. As MOHAIR was difficult to obtain, bears of artificial and wool plush were made. In the 1950s, some of the prewar models were slightly modified and produced again. The "original" bear was reintroduced with a larger, rounder head, shorter snout, and stubbier limbs on a plumper body with a less pronounced hump. A popular Steiff bear of that time is the Zotty bear, a super-soft bear with great appeal for children. In the following years, Steiff's bear designs were made safer, washable, more hygienic, and child-friendly, but perhaps lost their appeal to grownups. In 1980 the factory started producing replicas of their old models, for collectors.

Steiner (Société) ■ A French maker of BISQUE-headed BÉBÉS, founded by Jules Nicholas Steiner, a former clockmaker,

in Paris in 1855. The company patented over 24 innovations, many of them CLOCKWORK, including the *bébé premier pas*, which could walk while being held by one arm, a baby that kicked and cried, and a dancing lady. Following Steiner's death in 1901, the company continued to use his name until 1903, when it was taken over by Edmond Daspres. It closed in 1908. Some Steiner dolls are marked "Bourgoin," the name of a Parisian retailer.

Steiner, Herman A company making BISQUE-headed dolls, in SONNEBERG, south Germany. Founded in 1911, the company still produces toys today. Most Steiner dolls are marked with the company's initials "HS."

Stem ■ The vertical structure that joins the bowl of a drinking vessel to the foot. Stems vary in length, thickness, and decoration, from the PRUNTS on RÖMER to serpent-stemmed Venetian goblets. They also vary in types and combinations of KNOPS on BALUSTER and BALUSTROID glasses and the AIR TWIST on 18th-century English drinking glasses.

Stem cup ■ A Chinese ritual vessel, otherwise called a *gaozu*, with a wide, shallow bowl raised on a tall, slender stem that flares toward the base. Some of the best MING DYNASTY examples from the Xuande reign (1426–35) are pure white, decorated with three fish painted in underglaze copper red. Stem cups were also

made in LACQUER and decorated with Buddhist motifs.

Stem winding See KEYLESS WATCH.

Stencil ■ A method of decoration known from ancient times in which paint is dabbed through a design cut in a template that can be used repeatedly to reproduce the pattern. Stenciling can be done by hand on wall surfaces or furniture, or as a form of printing on fabrics or wallpaper. It was widely adopted, especially in the US in the 18th and 19th centuries, and was also used to achieve the effects inspired by JAPONAISERIE and for the geometric shapes and heraldic ornament of the GOTHIC REVIVAL. The fashion also spawned imitations with fabrics, ceramics, and wallpaper simulating stenciled designs created by designers from the late 19th century.

Stereoscope A device for viewing two images (stereographs) placed side by side that appear to be identical but are in fact subtly different, each image having been taken from a slightly different viewpoint along the horizontal. Through a stereoscope, each eye is directed to one of the images and thus the combined single image gains depth and appears to be three dimensional. Initially described by the English scientist Charles Wheatstone in 1832, the idea was applied to photography by David Brewster in 1849 and presented at the 1851 GREAT EXHIBITION in London.

S

355

Steiner (Société)
Doll, with pressed bisque socket head on fully-jointed composition body.

Air twist decoration

Stem
Wine glass, the stem with central swelling knop.

Stem cup
Chinese blue and white Kangxi stem cup.

Stencil
Double-tiered dressing table in yellow and green, with black stencil decoration. c. 1840.

STERLING SILVER

S

356

Sterling silver Silver with a standard of purity equal to 925 parts of silver to 75 parts alloy, or 92.5 percent. It is possibly named after "Easterlings," who were mint workers from East Germany, brought to England by Henry II (1154–89) to improve the coinage of the realm. Sterling silver became the accepted purity or standard in Britain from 1300 (excluding the BRITANNIA period, from 1697 to 1720) and the standard for some other countries, including the US. See HALLMARKS.

Steuben Glassworks ■ An American glassworks founded in Corning, Steuben County, New York, in 1903, and incorporated as a division of the CORNING GLASSWORKS in 1918. Under the Directorship of Frederick Carder, an English glassmaker and chemist, it introduced a broad range of artistic lines, many in response to contemporary American or European glassmakers. One of the most popular ranges was Aurene, an IRIDESCENT GLASS, made from 1904 to about 1933. It also made the bubbly CLUTHRA and Intarsia glass ranges. In 1932 Steuben developed "10M," a pure, high-quality colorless crystal glass that was highly suitable for ACID ETCHING, cutting, and engraving. This was in response to shapes and decorative forms pioneered at ORREFORS GLASSWORKS. It soon dominated production, with colored glass being discontinued after 1933. John Monteith Gates, the sculptor and architect Sidney Waugh, and George Thompson were

employed during the 1930s as designers, many producing strongly ART DECO designs. At the end of the 1930s, the glassworks began to commission designs from leading artists (Henri Matisse, Salvador Dali, Marie Laurencin, Jean Cocteau, Paul Manship, and Eric Gill) and continued this practice through the 1950s and beyond. The company is still active, producing tableware and decorative pieces such as vases and sculptures.

Stevengraph ■ A brightly colored woven silk picture, with scenes depicting horse races, transport, and famous people, used to decorate GREETING CARDS and bookmarks. Made in England on JACQUARD LOOMS from around 1879 to 1940, when the factory was bombed, they were named after their manufacturer, Thomas Stevens.

Stevens & Williams ■ An English glasshouse established in 1846 at Brierley Hill, near STOURBRIDGE, West Midlands, which became known as Stevens & Williams in 1847, and was known as Royal Brierley from 1919 after receiving a royal warrant. The company developed new types of ART GLASS such as ALEXANDRITE and SILVERIA under John NORTHWOOD and Frederick CARDER, and made fine engraved glass (at the end of the 19th century) and CUT GLASS, enhanced by the designs of Keith MURRAY in the 1930s. Royal Brierley went bankrupt in the late 1990s, but the name was still used in

association with Dartington, under the control of the American conglomerate Enesco Inc.

Stick-back ■ A chair back that is composed of SPINDLES or small members. The stick-back form is a characteristic feature of the WINDSOR CHAIR.

Stick barometer ■ The earliest and simplest type of barometer, made from around 1750 but largely dating from the 18th century, in which a glass tube of mercury ending in a cistern of mercury is contained in a narrow upright case (often walnut or mahogany) about 3 ft (1 m) high.

Stick furniture Rustic wooden furniture, sometimes made with the bark of the wood left on, and sometimes from green (unseasoned) wood.

Stick pin See TIE PIN.

Stickley Brothers ■ Born to German migrant parents in Wisconsin, the five Stickley brothers—GUSTAV, Charles, Albert, Leo, and John George—achieved various degrees of artistic and financial success as manufacturers of American ARTS AND CRAFTS furniture. The first furniture company founded by

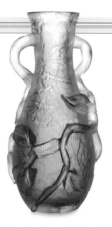
Steuben Glassworks
Crystal quartz glass vase, with *Mat-su-no-ke* acid-etched flowers and leaves. 1930–32.

Stevengraph
General George Washington and a verse, by L. Steven of Coventry .

Stevens & Williams
Tall Stevens & Williams silver-mounted claret jug. c. 1895.

Stick-back
Victorian elm and beech stick-back kitchen elbow chair.

Stick barometer
Rosewood-cased stick barometer. 19th century.

members of the Stickley family was Stickley Brothers, based in Binghamton, New York, and inaugurated in the 1880s. This early venture involved Charles, Albert, and Gustav, although Charles left to work with John George in Michigan during the early 1890s. After Gustav's departure, Albert was left at the helm of the original family firm. The features that define Stickley Brothers furniture are similar to those used by other members of the family, including unadorned oak and mahogany surfaces. Albert's "Quaint Furniture" trademark was also applied to more decorative items inspired by members of the Scottish School. Albert Stickley's furniture is generally rigidly rectilinear with conspicuously exposed structural elements, including through-tenoned stretchers and rails. He applied a number of stained finishes to his work, ranging in tone from rich mahogany red to a yellow-tinged limed oak color.

Stickley, Gustav (1857–1942) A prominent American ARTS AND CRAFTS furniture-maker. In the 1870s Gustav and his younger brothers, Charles and Albert, worked in their uncle Jacob Schlager's chair factory in Pennsylvania. After a visit to England, Gustav was converted to the ARTS AND CRAFTS style, and in 1898 he founded the Gustav Stickley Company, making furniture inspired by William MORRIS. In 1901 he began to publish a monthly magazine, *The Craftsman*, and renamed his business United Crafts. In 1904 the name of the business changed again to The Craftsman

Workshops. Most Stickley furniture is made of quarter-sawn oak with the MORTISE AND TENON joints exposed. It is solid and comfortable and generally without ornament. Panel and frame construction was also used and any metalwork was bold and hand-wrought. He employed the talented architect and designer Harvey Ellis from 1903 until his death in 1904, who introduced a slightly lighter style with small, inlaid motifs. Gustav's business expansion in New York led him into difficulties at the beginning of World War I. In 1916 his other brothers, Leopold and John George, took over and ran the company as L. & J. G. Stickley. In 1974 the company passed out of the family's hands, but it still retains the Stickley name. See MISSION STYLE, GRAND RAPIDS.

Stickley, L. & J. G. ■ When they set up business together in Fayetteville, New York, in 1904, Leopold and John George Stickley used the name Onondaga Shops for two years before rebranding themselves as Handcraft. The name Onondaga was that of a tribe of American Indians from the upstate New York area. Leopold and John George became successful by producing more economical versions of the MISSION STYLE furniture made by GUSTAV STICKLEY. They took advantage of their brother's relaxed attitude to issues of copyright—he often encouraged architects and designers to customize and thus appropriate his plans and scaled his designs down, making them more cost-effective.

They also turned out work from designs by Frank Lloyd WRIGHT. Following the success of their Onondaga shops, Leopold and John George reincorporated their firm as L. & J. G. Stickley and unveiled their first line of furniture at a 1905 trade show in GRAND RAPIDS, Michigan. They marketed their product as "simple furniture built along mission lines," in a clear nod to the work of their brother, Gustav. Unlike Gustav, they had little time for the costly business of handcrafting, instead opting to produce furniture mechanically. L. & J. G. Stickley was financially successful in a way that Gustav never was, thanks to their better business acumen. In the early 1920s the firm referred back to traditional New England and Pennsylvania furniture design as inspiration for a new range called the "Cherry Valley Collection." A marriage of vernacular American form with native American wood was achieved by using black cherry sourced from the Adirondack Mountains.

Stickwork ■ A term for small objects, similar to TUNBRIDGEWARE and TREEN, made in the 19th century. Sticks of colored wood were glued together into rods that were then either sliced into veneers to decorate items or turned on a lathe to make eggcups, SNUFF BOXES, chessmen, pens, and sewing implements.

Stiegel, Henry William See AMERICAN FLINT GLASSWORKS.

Stickley Brothers
Tea table, with circular overhanging top and flaring legs.

Stickley, L. & J. G.
Sideboard, with copper strap hardware on two doors and five drawers.

Stickwork
Tunbridgeware stickware vesta, modeled as a capstan with tesserae mosaic top.

Stile The upright or vertical members of the framework of a chair back or a piece of PANELED furniture such as a chest or cupboard.

Still bank See SAVINGS BANK.

Stinton, Harry See WORCESTER PORCELAIN FACTORY.

Stipple engraving Engraved decoration on glass in which the design is built up from tiny shallow dots made by striking the surface with a diamond or other hard point. Glass is the perfect medium for this technique, as the design is visible on both sides. Stipple engraving was developed in the early 17th century in Holland, and Dutch craftsmen remained the major exponents of the technique in the 18th and 19th centuries, using it often on goblets. In the 20th century the technique was revived in Britain by Laurence Whistler and others.

Stippling ■ A decorative technique in which color is applied with repeated dabs of the point of a brush, to produce a mottled effect. In ceramics, the same technique is also used to build up a detailed design with dots, rather than lines, of color—both by hand, and in TRANSFER PRINTING.

Stirrup-cup ■ A drinking vessel of SILVER, SILVER-GILT, glass, ceramic, or Old SHEFFIELD PLATE, intended to be used on horseback. These cups have a curving or shaped base and no foot, so they cannot be put down unless they are empty. Many silver examples are formed as fox, hare, boar, or greyhound heads. They are still made today, but were most popular between 1770 and 1820 and enjoyed a revival in the late 19th century.

Stobwasser und Söhn ■ The German japanner Johann Heinrich Stobwasser (1740–1829) was noted for his PAPIER-MÂCHÉ SNUFF BOXES, which were intricately and finely painted, often with scenes inspired by paintings by great artists. His factory opened in Braunschweig in 1763 and closed just after World War I.

Stone china ■ See IRONSTONE CHINA. A type of STONEWARE that approaches porcelain in hardness and may be slightly TRANSLUCENT. It was first developed by John TURNER around 1800. Turner sold the patent to Josiah SPODE, who used the formula to make tableware.

Stoneware ■ A type of ceramic that shares characteristics of EARTHENWARE and porcelain. The BODY is made of clay mixed with a fusible stone (that is, capable of being melted at sufficiently high temperatures, around 2,372°F/1,300°C), usually FELDSPAR. This vitrification renders the ware watertight, although salt glaze or LEAD GLAZE are also added. It was produced in China during the SHANG DYNASTY but was developed independently in Germany in the Middle Ages and spread to other European countries. It was not known in England until the late 17th century and was at the height of its popularity with WEDGWOOD in the 18th century.

Stool The most common type of seat furniture until the 19th century, the stool was used in ancient Egypt and was adopted by the Greeks and later by the Romans. Unlike a bench, the stool seats only one person. It is distinguished from the chair as it lacks arms and a back. From antiquity, the stool was constructed in two forms, one that was supported on four straight legs, and the other that was supported on four legs arranged crosswise. It remained more or less unaltered until the late Middle Ages, when a three-legged version with a circular or polygonal top, known as the Strozzi stool, was introduced in Italy. Later stools are largely variants of the original two basic types, with the decoration of the supports and the treatment of the padded or hard top being the only innovations.

Stopper A shaped piece of glass, ceramic, or metal that fits into, and so closes, the mouth of a vessel such as a DECANTER, bottle, or CRUET, designed to hold liquid that might otherwise evaporate or become tainted. They were made in a wide variety of shapes, sizes, and colors, usually in a style complementing the vessel.

Storr, Paul ■ (1771–1844) England's most celebrated 19th-century silversmith and a

Stippling
Scheier coupe-shaped vase with a stippled celadon glaze bordering a band of incised abstract-organic motifs.

Stirrup-cup
Staffordshire porcelain stirrup-cup.

Stobwasser und Söhn
Papier-mâchè snuff box, signed Stobwasser. c. 1830.

Stone china
Spode stone china soup tureen.

brilliant businessman, Storr was apprenticed to the Swedish-born NEOCLASSICAL master Andrew Fogelberg in Soho, London. He had a short-lived partnership with William Frisbee from 1792 to 1796, when he entered his first mark alone. By 1807, styled as Storr and Co. and having registered his fourth mark, he was producing most of his work for the Royal Goldsmiths Rundell, Bridge & Rundell, forming a sub-partnership with them in 1811. This partnership ended in 1819 when Storr took premises in Clerkenwell, London. In 1822 he went into partnership with John Mortimer, thus benefiting from his retail premises in New Bond Street, and succeeded in recruiting various excellent craftsmen who had previously worked for Rundell. Storr and Mortimer then employed Storr's nephew, John Hunt, as a chaser.

Storr retired in 1838 and the firm continued under the name Mortimer & Hunt. Storr's early silversmithing (before 1800) was generally unremarkable and rather domestic, both in design and quality, although the workshop produced some highly competent pieces. It was perhaps his apprenticeship with Fogelberg and his dalliance with Neoclassical ornamentation, coupled with the timing of Britain's Industrial Revolution and burgeoning wealth, that led to his success. His astute association with the Royal Goldsmiths and his contact with some of the most eminent

sculptors and artist-craftsmen of the period, including John FLAXMAN, helped to build the solid foundation of what became a mighty business. It was under Storr's direction that his business produced the vast array of magnificent REGENCY silver and SILVER GILT that adorned the tables and sideboards of the wealthiest households in Britain, though it is not known how much of the silver was made by Paul Storr himself.

Stourbridge A British town in the Midlands that was the center of the British fine glass industry from around 1860 until its demise in the 1990s. The first in the area were established by HUGUENOT refugees in the early 17th century. They specialized in flat glass, but began to produce decorative and colored glass in the mid-18th century. By the 19th century Stourbridge had become home to a number of small decorating workshops as well as many of the major English manufacturers, including RICHARDSON'S, STEVENS & WILLIAMS, STUART & SONS, and Thomas WEBB & SONS, who made all types of glass, including CAMEO GLASS.

Straightlace See BOBBIN LACE.

Straining spoon A silver spoon with a pierced divider running down the center of the bowl. Also known as a gravy spoon, it was used for straining vegetables or sauces. Most were made in Ireland in the late 18th century, with some also being made in the late 19th century.

Strapwork An ornament reminiscent of leather straps or carved FRETWORK, used either alone in interlacing bands or teamed with GROTESQUES, first designed in the late 16th century by Rosso Fiorentino and Primaticcio to frame some paintings at Fontainebleau. Originating in antique motifs and distorted for expressive purposes by Italian RENAISSANCE artists, strapwork spread to the rest of Europe through the ENGRAVINGS of designers such as Hans Vredeman de Vries and Cornelis Floris. It was used extensively in the Low Counries, England, Germany, and France for metalwork, furniture, moldings in plaster, STUCCO, and carved wooden panels. Strapwork appeared in increasingly elaborate variations throughout the 17th and 18th centuries, embellished with jewels, ROSETTES, pyramids, and NAIL-HEADS, or combined with foliage and scrollwork.

S

359

Strasbourg pottery and porcelain factories ■ Carl Hannong founded a FAIENCE factory in Strasbourg, France, in 1721, together with Johann Wachenfeld, who left after a short time. The faience produced was particularly fine, with well painted plates, mugs, and pots, some decorated with botanically accurate plants. The factory also made TROMPE L'OEIL plates applied with realistic models of fruit and vegetables, and specialized in large

Stoneware
Staffordshire salt-glazed stoneware bear-baiting jug and cover. c. 1760.

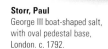

Applied armorial shield

Storr, Paul
George III boat-shaped salt, with oval pedestal base, London. c. 1792.

Strasbourg pottery and porcelain factories
Strasbourg plate. c. 1870.

S

tureens in the form of wild boars' heads or fish. The Prince de Rohan had a palace in the city, so there was a rich market for such extravagant creations.

In 1724 Hannong founded another faience factory in Haguenau, France, (near the source of the clay), and when he retired in 1732, he left the two factories to his sons. Balthasar ran Haguenau and Paul-Antoine took over Strasbourg, where faience table services, large clock cases, fountains, and bidets were made, decorated in HIGH-TEMPERATURE COLORS. In 1751 Paul-Antoine went into partnership with J. J. RINGLER. They were soon making quality porcelain, decorated in bright OVERGLAZE ENAMELS. In 1754 Louis XV, determined to protect the monopoly of SÈVRES, passed a royal decree forbidding any other

porcelain manufacturer to use gilding or more than one color. As a result of this, the porcelain-making side of the business was moved to FRANKENTHAL, where Paul-Antoine enjoyed the patronage of the Elector Carl Theodor von der Pfalz. Following Paul-Antoine's death in 1760, the faience factories at Haguenau and Strasbourg passed to his sons, Pierre-Antoine and Josef Adam, who resumed porcelain production in 1766. However, by 1781 the business was in financial ruin, Josef Adam was declared bankrupt, and the factories were closed.

Strass, Georges Frédéric (1702–73)
A Parisian jeweler who invented a form of PASTE, also known as "strass," that effectively imitated precious gemstones,

especially diamonds. He set up his own business in 1730 and made a fortune, becoming jeweler to Louis XV in 1734.

Straw marquetry A decorative technique mainly used on mirror frames, tea caddies, caskets, and small pieces of furniture, in which strips of bleached and colored straw are applied to create landscapes, figures, animals, or geometric patterns. Also called straw work, it was practiced in Europe from the 17th century. It was especially popular in France in the late 18th and 19th centuries as a veneer for tabletops and cabinets and for little boxes known as *petits hoîtes de l'amitié*.

Strawberry Hill Gothic See GOTHIC STYLE, GOTHIC.

STREAMLINING

An aerodynamic design style strongly associated with the Art Deco Movement, Streamlining was fashionable in the 1920s and 30s. It reflected a preoccupation with travel, especially speed, following the invention of gasoline-, oil-, and electric-powered motors as well as the growth of rail and air travel and car ownership. Promoted by American designers like Norman Bel Geddes, streamlined shapes and motifs originally designed for moving vehicles were transferred to all manner of furnishings and domestic artifacts. Curved forms, parallel lines, and wing motifs abounded, often enhanced by the use of brilliant materials, most notably chrome.

Andiron
One of a pair of American Art Deco andirons, the relief design featuring a water fountain motif, cast of solid, polished aluminum and bronze. c. 1930.

Molded Bakelite base (and shade)

Desk lamp
Jumo streamlined late Art Deco Bakelite desk lamp for Brevette. c. 1940s.

Poster
Poster of the streamlined *Patria* cutting a graceful wave in green water, by Anton Ottomar.

Strawberry-dish ■ A silver, SILVER-GILT, or ceramic bowl of shallow circular form with a scalloped rim, flat base, and fluted, upcurved sides, associated with the serving of strawberries, particularly in England during the first half of the 18th century.

Stretcher The horizontal rail or bar joining the legs of tables, stools, and chairs, designed to strengthen the construction. The stretchers may be left plain or may be embellished by turning or decorative carving.

Striations Irregularities in glass in the form of fine, parallel or swirling lines. They are usually caused when the glass is manipulated into shape.

Strike/silent A device, usually in the form of a lever or small handle set against a SUBSIDIARY DIAL marked "strike" and "silent," used to turn the striking mechanism of a clock on or off. Such devices are often set in the dial arch on the dials of 18th-century LONGCASE CLOCKS.

Striking system Sounds made by the bell or gong of a clock to indicate the passing of the hours and often also the half- or quarter- hours. Before the late 17th century, the striking TRAIN was activated by the COUNT WHEEL, which allowed the hours to be sounded only in succession. If the mechanism was altered, the strike did not synchronize with the hands on the dial. This problem was solved in 1676 by Edward

Barlow, who invented the rack-and-snail system, which linked hand movement with striking.

Stringing Fine, inlaid lines of wood or metal applied as a decorative border for furniture, especially around the edges of table tops or drawers. The technique was especially popular in the late 18th century, coinciding with the fashion for SATINWOOD and other exotic veneers, which furnished an accommodating ground for this decorative device. American furniture produced in New England at this time featured stringing frequently composed of small, geometric patterns.

Strut clock A small traveling clock with a shallow case supported by an easel-like strut. Most date from the 1850s onward. They were a specialty of Thomas COLE.

Stuart & Sons Ltd. ■ An English glasshouse established in STOURBRIDGE in 1787 by Richard Bradley and known as the Red House glassworks. In 1881 Frederick Stuart bought a lease on the factory, and in 1885 it became known as Stuart & Sons. It patented "medallion cameo" glass in 1887, but is best known for fine-quality, clear CUT GLASS made in the 20th century. The designer Ludwig Kny produced highly MODERN designs from 1918 to 1937. He was succeeded by Reginald Pierce, and then John Luxton in 1948. The factory took over Strathearn in 1980, and also produced some MOLD-BLOWN ART

GLASS during the 1980s and continued until it was closed by its owner, WATERFORD, in 2001.

Stuart, James (1713–88) An English architect and designer. Coauthor of *The Antiquities of Athens* in 1762 with Nicholas Revett, James Athenian Stuart championed the GREEK REVIVAL in England. He worked only sporadically as an interior designer at Kedleston Hall in Derbyshire and at Spencer House in London in a florid interpretation of the Classical style that influenced the early work of Robert ADAM. Stuart's greatest success was his ability to adapt Roman temple furniture such as altars and tripods to household use. See ATHÉNIENNE.

Stucco A slow-setting plaster used for interior moldings, especially on ceilings, and for exterior rendering and sculptural purposes. Containing marble or stone dust, it mainly comprises gypsum, sand, and lime. Stucco spread in the 18th century from Italy, where it had been used since the Classical Roman period.

Studio glass ■ One-of-a-kind, LIMITED EDITION, or LIMITED PRODUCTION glassware, designed and made by one or more glass artists in small workshops, or made under their direct supervision. Studio glass was made in France in the 19th and early 20th centuries by such designers as François DÉCORCHEMONT and Maurice Marinot, but from 1962 saw the start of the

Strawberry-dish
George Jones majolica strawberry-dish. 1875.

Stuart & Sons Ltd.
Vase, designed by John Luxton for Stuart & Sons. c. 1952.

Studio glass
Studio glass vase, by Wes Hunting.

movement as it is known today. Experiments took place in Germany and Communist Eastern European countries, but developments in the US in 1962 by Dominick Labino and Harvey Littleton are generally credited with starting the movement. Their techniques spread to the UK by 1966 and also to Europe. Dale Chihuly is one of the most notable and best-known late 20th-century studio glassmakers. Studios of thousands of artists are now in existence.

Studio pottery ■ The work of independent artist-potters working in individual studios or with other like-minded potters wishing to express their artistry without commercial pressures. Studio potters are responsible for all aspects of pottery production. Leaders of the trend include John Mason, Peter Voulkos, and Betty Woodman in the US, and Michael CARDEW, Bernard LEACH, Lucie RIE, Hans COPER, William Staite MURRAY, and Raoul Dufy in Europe.

Studio, The An English monthly art periodical published from 1893 to 1988 (also in the US), subtitled *An Illustrated Magazine of Fine and Applied Arts*. In the early years, it acted as a newsletter for the ARTS AND CRAFTS Movement.

Stumpwork A term widely used for a form of 17th-century embroidery, also known as raised work, in which padded motifs are raised from a satin ground fabric to form a three-dimensional image. Frequently featuring a variety of stitches and materials, it was often the work of young girls. From around 1650 to 1680 stumpwork was a fashionable decoration on small-scale pictures, caskets, and mirror frames.

Style rayonnant A manner of ceramic decorative painting, first developed in the late 17th century at ROUEN, France. The patterns, which radiate inward from richly decorated borders on plates and dishes, resemble engraved embroidery designs and are comprised of LAMBREQUINS, scrolls, FESTOONS of flowers and leaves, lacy ARABESQUES, and FERRONNERIES. It was taken up at influential French factories for the decoration of FAIENCE and porcelain. A similar motif is seen on English silver cups from around 1650 to 1750. It remained a popular decorative motif until the 1740s.

Subsidiary dial A small dial set in a clock's main DIAL PLATE, inside the CHAPTER RING or in the dial arch on break-arch dials, showing the seconds, date, phases of the moon, or STRIKE/SILENT indication.

Sucket fork These delicate silver (and SILVER-GILT) utensils have two prongs or tines at one end and a spoon bowl (teaspoon size) at the other. They were used for sweetmeats and candied fruit. Both engraved and plain, they were produced during the second half of the 17th century, but only a few fully hallmarked examples exist from before 1670.

Sugar tongs (nips) ■ A small silver utensil used for conveying sugar chips to a cup. The earliest type, resembling small ember tongs and dating from around 1680, were superseded around 1700 by tongs that had a pivot instead of a spring "U" section. As sugar became more affordable around 1770, sugar nips evolved into scissorlike items with ring handles and shell grips. Larger sugar nips were often made of brass for kitchen use. They still formed part of silver tea utensils in the 19th and into the 20th century.

Sulphides Small ornaments, often medallions or cameo portraits, made of a white porcelain-like material and encased in colorless glass. They were incorporated into pieces such as drinking glasses, perfume bottles, PAPERWEIGHTS, plaques, and marbles. First developed in France in the late 18th century, Apsley PELLATT patented his "cameo incrustations" in Britain in 1819. In the US, fine sulphides were made from around 1814 by the Pittsburgh Flint Glass Manufactory. They were also made by John Ford in Edinburgh in the 1870s.

Sumakh See SOUMAK.

Summers, Gerald (1899–1967) A British engineer and designer who worked for Marconi before forming his own company, Makers of Simple Furniture, in 1933, having initially designed the furniture for his own home. He made furniture from molded sheets of plywood. The firm closed during World War II due to rationing of materials.

Studio pottery
John Maltby studio pottery pedestal tankard. 1970s.

Sugar tongs
Pair of late Victorian cast novelty sugar tongs, by Charles James Fox, London.1899.

Sunburst motif
Louis XIV-style carved giltwood and gessoed sunburst mirror.

Sunflower motif
Louis XVI *table à ecrire*, with rectangular top inlaid with flowerheads. c. 1780.

Sunburst motif ■ A motif featuring the sun encircled by sunrays. A popular theme for 17th-century BAROQUE ornament, it appears frequently in furniture and interior decoration as the central point for ceiling decoration and the gilded surround for a mirror, clock, or barometer. In the 19th century it was used for decorating light fixtures and American mold-blown glass flasks. It was also favored by ART DECO designers. Later, a more formalized sunrise motif was popular in the 1920s.

Sunderland ware Pottery made in Sunderland, northeast England, in the 19th century, mostly by Dixon, Austen & Co. Large jugs, plates, and mugs, typically with pink and copper luster borders, are TRANSFER-PRINTED with images of the iron bridge over the Wear River, ships, and plaques with religious verses.

Sundial An instrument for measuring the passage of time from the shadow of a pointer (the GNOMON) cast by the sun on a graduated plane. Sundials were the principal method of judging time before the spread of mechanical clocks and watches in the 16th and 17th centuries.

Sunflower motif ■ A symbol of remembrance, gratitude, and constancy, widely used as a decorative device from the 17th century. In the early 1750s sunflower-shaped dishes and lidded pots were produced in England by the CHELSEA porcelain factory. Sunflowers also figure in the QUEEN ANNE revival of the 1870s and in the AESTHETIC MOVEMENT.

Supper set A set of four or five shaped dishes that fit together to form an oval or circle and stand on a tray. Popular in Britain from the late 18th century, they were made from silver, Old Sheffield plate, porcelain, or pottery.

Sussex chair ■ A rush-seated ARTS AND CRAFTS chair designed by MORRIS & CO. Made from around 1865, it had its roots in the turned spindle-back country chair. Elegantly proportioned, this simple form was produced in a host of variations, including a corner version, a SETTEE, and a Rossetti armchair. Its popularity continued well into the 20th century.

Sutherland table ■ A small, narrow, lower version of the DROP-LEAF, GATELEG dining table used for taking tea or card playing. This early equivalent of the coffee table was made in England in great numbers from the 1880s until around 1914, and was reputedly named after the Duchess of Sutherland who served as Queen Victoria's Mistress of the Robes. Though practical, the Sutherland table enjoyed limited popularity. It was made mainly in mahogany or oak, occasionally decorated with inlaid borders, foliage, or formalized NEOCLASSICAL patterns.

Suzuribako A Japanese term for a writing box containing tools for calligraphy or writing, including brushes, an ink stick, a stone slab to rub the ink stick on to make ink, and a pot for water. They are often lacquered with scenes or natural motifs.

Swag ■ A decorative ornament similar to a FESTOON, made up of fruit, flowers, nuts, leaves (often LAUREL), or shells. Unlike the festoon, a swag may also be composed of a pendant loop of cloth drapery. Originally a Classical motif, the swag was adopted in the NEOCLASSICAL period for architecture as well as for silver, glass, and ceramics and carving or painting on items of furniture.

Swan-neck handle A curved, hanging brass handle introduced in the early 1760s on the drawers of CASE FURNITURE and on glass ewers.

Swan-neck pediment ■ A PEDIMENT (known as scroll top in the US), derived from Classical architecture, in which two S-curves almost meet in scrolls. They were a popular decorative feature on early 18th-century English furniture, especially bookcases, cabinets, cupboards, mirrors, and bureaux.

Swansea Pottery and Porcelain Factory A pottery, which became known as the Cambrian Pottery, was established in the 1760s in Swansea by William Coles. He made salt-glazed stoneware and creamware

S

363

Sussex chair
Morris & Co. ebonized beech chair, with spindle-filled back, rush seat, and turned legs.

Sutherland table
Victorian burr walnut oval Sutherland table.

Swag
Ormolu laurel swag tied with ribbon.

With raised urn finial

Swan-neck pediment
Chippendale-style mahogany highboy, with swan-neck pediment. Late 19th century.

resembling WEDGWOOD. Some of this was painted with realistic botanical designs by William Pardoe between 1795 and 1809. Coles died in 1779 and the factory was run by his descendants before being taken over by William Dillwyn in 1801, followed by his son, Lewis Weston Dillwyn. Porcelain was produced in 1813 after William Billingsley joined the factory from WORCESTER in 1813. He and his son-in-law, Samuel Walker, worked at NANTGARW, then moved in 1814 to Swansea. Billingsley and Walker produced beautiful porcelain but had severe kiln losses. The wares were finely decorated in the factory in the latest Paris fashion with figures, birds, and flowers, and in London by OUTSIDE DECORATORS. Billingsley and Walker left in 1817 and the factory was taken over by Bevington Brothers. It closed in 1870.

Swastika A Sanskrit term for well-being. In many cultures the swastika represents the sun's course and the rotation of the heavens. The swastika was widely used as a symbol of prosperity in early Greece and was adopted as a cross form in early Christian art. On Chinese ceramics, the swastika, signifying longevity, appears in border patterns.

Sweetmeat dish ■ A shallow silver, SILVER-GILT, glass, or ceramic dish, usually lightly constructed, with one or two handles, and with or without a stem. These dishes could be decorated with fluting on the rim or with embossed or punched work. They were made in large numbers from the 1630s to the 19th century to hold candied fruits, preserves, and pastries.

Sweetmeat set A central star-shaped or small circular dish surrounded by four or six shaped dishes. Known in English DELFTWARE from around 1730 to 1760, and in salt glaze and creamware into the 19th century.

Swivel-head A variation on the SHOULDER HEAD that allows the head of a doll to move from side to side, independent of the breastplate. The ball-shaped underside of the neck fits neatly into a cup-shaped indentation in the SHOULDER PLATE. This type of head was commonly used for PARISIENNES between 1860 and 1880.

Sycamore maple ■ A light-colored, close-grained, durable wood native to Western Europe. Sycamore maple was used by turners and joiners from the Middle Ages, especially for the tops of country tables. The grain is interlocking, so that the wood does not split straight and is difficult to work. It was a popular VENEER in 18th-century England and was used for MARQUETRY in Europe. Sycamore maple veneer dyed greenish gray is known as HAREWOOD and is often found alongside SATINWOOD on late 18th-century furniture.

Syllabub glass A small glass vessel for drinking syllabub, first introduced into Britain in the early 18th century. A version of the JELLY GLASS, sometimes with a flared top, also known as a pan top, with either a single or no handle.

SylvaC ■ Shaw and Copestake made earthenware in Staffordshire from 1901, bearing various printed marks with the trade name SylvaC. Most frequently seen pieces are molded rabbits glazed in blue, brown, or green. Production ceased in 1982.

Syng, Philip (1703–89) An American silversmith of the COLONIAL period, active in Philadelphia. Syng was a personal friend of Benjamin Franklin and other prominent citizens and made the inkstand used for the signing of the Declaration of Independence, on July 4, 1776. His work, with ROCOCO decorations, resembles George II silver and is extremely rare and historically significant.

Synthetic gem An affordable, artificially manufactured copy of a real gemstone. Almost every gem has been synthesized, some more successfully than others. Synthetic gems tend to possess different internal characteristics from their natural counterparts. Synthetic ruby and sapphire provided a viable alternative to natural stones and were widely used in the 1920s and 30s.

SYP teapot Standing for "Simple yet Perfect," a novelty teapot made by WEDGWOOD from 1895, in which the leaves could be separated from the liquid. They were small pots on three peg feet with blue printed floral decoration.

Sweetmeat dish
Pair of Bow sweetmeat figures finely decorated in enamels. c. 1758.

Sycamore
Table and bar, with the interior veneered in contrasting mahogany. c. 1930.

SylvaC
Fawn rabbit, stamped "MADE IN ENGLAND 1026B" and printed "SYLVAC."

SylvaC
Detail showing the SylvaC mark.

T

Tabako-ire A Japanese tobacco pouch or box, usually on a cord with a NETSUKE counterweight. Metal or lacquerwork examples from the 19th century are sometimes highly ornate.

Tabernacle clock A type of early clock produced principally in Germany from the late 16th to the late 17th century. They had square brass cases enclosing a MOVEMENT made entirely of steel. Larger versions, often in elaborate GOTHIC architectural styles, feature dials or CHAPTER RINGS on all four sides.

Tabernacle mirror An American giltwood mirror form popular from the early FEDERAL period until the late 19th century. They were of portrait shape, often with engaged half columns. The glass was divided into a lower large looking glass and an upper section resembling an entablature, with a molded CORNICE (earlier examples had applied balls) and decorated (normally églomisé) glass.

Table ambulante ■ The French term for any small, portable table. From the mid-18th century these were used for various items of domestic life such as books or cups of tea.

Table center Known as ÉPERGNE in French, an elaborate silver, porcelain, or glass centerpiece for a dining table, often fitted with candle sockets and CRUET bottles. Table centers were popular in the 19th century.

Table clock A type of spring-driven clock produced from the late 16th century in Germany, with a drum-shaped, square, or hexagonal case on which the dial was set horizontally. Such clocks usually have three or four elaborate feet and the case is of gilt-brass decorated with silver, glass, or rock crystal panels. The MOVEMENT is also often ornately pierced and engraved.

Tabouret ■ The French term for a low, upholstered footstool, originally drum-shaped. Tabourets played an important role during the reign of Louis XIV—rigid court etiquette dictated who was permitted to use the stool, which made it a privilege that was highly sought-after. In the 18th century a tabouret referred to a stool of any shape with fixed, upright legs.

Tabriz ■ One of the leading centers of Persian carpet making in the 16th-century. Production declined after around 1650 until the latter years of the 19th century, when the industry was reestablished on a massive workshop basis. The carpets are sometimes difficult to identify, as their design repertoire is very varied, incorporating geometric and curvilinear patterns. Many pieces use a restricted color palette with shades of terracotta, ivory, and blue. The quality of the carpets varies enormously from extremely fine to rather coarse.

Talavera de la Reina potteries A group of factories producing tin-glazed earthenware in Castile, Spain, from the mid-16th century. The most important of the factories made 24,800 tiles for the Escorial (the palace of Philip II of Spain) in 1570. Although they also made large pictorial panels, tiles were the major product until the 17th century. An edict of 1601 restricted the use of silver and so increased the demand for household pottery. Small plates and helmet-shaped ewers and basins were made decorated with hunting scenes and bullfights. Modern wares of the Talavera de la Reina potteries imitate those made by it in the 17th century.

Talbert, Bruce James ■ (1831–81) An architect and designer of furniture, wallpaper, and metalwork, born in Dundee, Scotland. His designs reflected the prevailing mid-19th century reaction against the Neo-Gothic excesses of William BURGES and Augustus PUGIN. His "GOTHIC dressoir" earned him a silver medal at the Paris Exhibition of 1867, which was followed closely that year by the publication of his *Gothic Forms Applied to Furniture, Metal Work, and Decoration For Domestic Purposes*. Talbert is best known for his "reformed" Gothic style, combining massive rectilinear forms with shallow panels of geometric

Table ambulante
For Herman Miller, a folding table by Charles Eames.
c. 1955.

Tabouret
Louis XIV-style tabouret chaise longue, with a padded rectangular stuff-over seat.

Tabriz
A large Tabriz garden carpet.

inlays and reliefs, exemplified by Talbert's celebrated "Pet Sideboard," made by GILLOWS, rather than the florid, deeply carved ornament favored by PUGIN.

Talking doll A doll that makes sounds. The simplest method to make a doll squeak uses bellows in the doll's torso. It is activated by exerting pressure on the belly or by pulling strings to the side. A more realistic sound can be produced by means of a phonograph, used from about 1890 onward.

Tallboy See CHEST and HIGHBOY.

Tallcase clock A term used in the US for a LONGCASE CLOCK or grandfather clock. Produced from the late 18th century, tallcases are similar in style to European longcases, but are often distinguished by the use of native woods such as MAPLE for case veneers. As BRASS was a scarce commodity in the US, most dials are made of white-painted iron.

Tambour ■ A flexible sliding shutter or door constructed of thin strips of wood laid side by side and glued to a piece of stiff fabric such as linen or canvas, with the ends slotting into grooves cut in the wood. Tambours were used as curved sliding tops for roll-top writing desks or for the sliding doors on the fronts of cupboards, mainly in furniture made in England, France, and the US from the last quarter of the 18th century.

Tambour hoop The name given to a frame of two concentric hoops over which fabric was stretched in order to make the popular 18th-century hooked embroidery known as TAMBOUR WORK.

Tambour work ■ A fine chain-stitch embroidery produced originally on muslin or net stretched over a TAMBOUR HOOP or frame, using a very small hook to work threads from beneath. Imported from India in the late 18th century with muslin for ladies' aprons and sleeve ruffles, the embroidery was used on machine net for veils in Ireland, England, and elsewhere throughout the 19th century. Tambour work was also produced by machine.

Tamper See PIPE STOPPER.

Tang ■ A Chinese dynasty (618–906) that saw great cultural and economic prosperity, with ceramic art reaching a high status. The dynasty is famed for the pottery burial wares that revived traditions of the Han dynasty (206 BCE–220 CE). Burial wares were made of a soft, absorbent pottery (modern copies are usually harder). A wide variety of objects was produced, and glazed or decorated with earth pigments. The best examples are powerfully modeled horses, camels, and guardian figures decorated with SANCAI glazes, which were splashed or poured over the piece's upper section and allowed to drip and run. The use of sancai became widespread in the reign of the Tang dynasty. YINGQING, one of the earliest Chinese porcelains, was developed in this era.

Tankard ■ A drinking vessel resembling a mug, sometimes with a hinged cover. Tankards are made of silver, pewter-mounted ceramic, ivory, horn, wood, hardstone, or glass, and are generally used for beer or cider. The small silver-gilt tankards from the late 16th and early 17th centuries were sometimes used for wine.

Tantalus ■ A silver-plated or mounted wooden frame fitted with two or three CUT-GLASS spirit decanters that can be locked inside the frame to prevent theft but remain tantalizingly visible. Although still made today, the design dates from the mid-19th and early 20th centuries.

Taperstick A type of silver, plated, or brass candlestick, made from the end of the 17th until the end of the 18th century. Smaller than the candlesticks of the period, they were designed to hold a single taper or slender candle used to melt sealing wax at a desk.

Tapestry A weaving technique in which colored weft threads are woven into undyed warp threads to form a decorative or pictorial design. The different colored weft threads are wound on bobbins and woven as far as the warp thread that marks the edge of a particular area of color. Thus each part of the design is built up independently. The term also applies to the wall hangings and furnishings made by this method of weaving by factories such as GOBELINS and ARRAS.

Talbert, Bruce James One of a pair of Gothic Reform hall chairs. c. 1850.

Tambour Ormolu-mounted George III tambour lady's writing desk. c. 1775.

Tambour work French hand-beaded evening purse, decorated with flowers in tambour work. 1940s.

Tang Camel of the Tang dynasty.

Tapissier A French term for a tapestry weaver, also sometimes used in countries outside France.

Tarnishing The dulling or discoloration of silver or other metals, including Old SHEFFIELD PLATE and ELECTROPLATE, caused by exposure to air or moisture, which leads to slight surface oxidation of the metal. Cleaning removes this oxidized layer.

Tarsia See INTARSIA.

Tartan ware Small wooden domestic items such as boxes and napkin rings and small pieces of furniture decorated with a distinctive printed tartan (plaid) pattern, typically in red and green. With Scotland becoming a fashionable Victorian vacation destination from the 1850s, this SOUVENIR WARE boomed in popularity. It was made primarily by the MAUCHLINE WARE manufacturer W. & A. Smith from 1810 to 1939.

Tassie ■ A portrait medallion, rather like a cameo molded from white glass paste, which was applied to a flat glass surface. Named after the Scotsman James Tassie, who invented the technique.

Tastevin A French silver wine taster for sampling and examining the color of wine, usually in the form of a small, shallow, circular bowl. With a ring handle at one side, often formed as a coiled serpent, and sometimes with a thumbpiece, extant examples are known from the early 18th century and often have engraved or embossed decoration. Tastevins are still used today.

Tatami A woven rice straw mat—a type of modular floor covering—used in a traditional Japanese house.

Tatting A technique for knotting thread, usually cotton or linen, to produce a fabric similar to lace, using a metal shuttle. Developed in the 19th century as a domestic craft, tatting was used to produce such items as collars and lace-edged handkerchiefs.

Tavern clock A type of English wall clock intended for use in taverns and other public buildings. Made from around 1720 to the early 19th century, it had a relatively large, square, shield-shaped or round wooden dial with gilt numerals and sometimes CHINOISERIE, scroll, or flower decoration. A long trunk housed the pendulum and weights. The case was sometimes decorated with appropriate vignette scenes. Such clocks are sometimes erroneously described as "Act of Parliament" clocks following a tax on clocks and watches instituted by the British Parliament in 1797.

Tazza ■ From either Arabic *tassah* (basin) or the Italian *tazza* (cup). A form deriving from Venetian 15th- and 16th-century glass in which a shallow saucerlike drinking cup or bowl is raised on a single pedestal foot. Later examples were made of silver, ceramics, enamel, or glass. The tazza was found in Europe and North America from the 16th to the 19th century. In the 19th century, light, engraved, heavy CUT GLASS, and delicate VASELINE glass were used to make tazza.

Tea bowl A small, handleless bowl or cup, originally made in China and exported to the West along with Chinese tea. They were also produced by many European factories in the 18th century, with or without saucers. Tea-drinking became fashionable in the late 17th and early 18th centuries, and both tea and tea bowls were expensive. Portraits of people drinking tea show the various ways they held this handleless cup.

Tea caddy ■ A metal or wood container for storing tea, often lined with lead foil. Caddy is derived from the Malaysian word *kati* and is used in China for a unit of weight equal to about one and a half pounds (0.67 kg). Incorporated within a tea chest, caddies sometimes had a small sugar bowl in the center, and some 18th-century examples—dating from the period when tea was relatively expensive—also had locks. Wooden tea chests used in England usually had two compartments for green and Bohea tea, flanking a central glass mixing or sugar bowl.

Tea canister ■ A small Chinese as well as European porcelain container for tea and an integral part of an 18th-century tea service. Early MEISSEN examples are usually upright and rectangular in shape, but from the latter part of the century most are ovoid. Canisters were superseded by

T
367

Tankard
George II silver tankard, by Richard Bayley of London.

Tantalus
Victorian carved oak tantalus and games box.

Tassie
White-paste tassie of Lord Daer in mid-relief, in an oval ebonized pearwood frame. c. 1794.

Tazza
Arts and Crafts silver tazza, by John Reilly, with Sheffield hallmarks. 1904.

T

caddies during the late 18th century, although they continued to be made during the 19th century.

Tea ceremony ware Ceramic vessels used in the Japanese tea ceremony or *Cha no yu*. This Buddist ceremony, which is thought to have arrived in Japan from China in the 15th century, became an important part of Japan's social and cultural life. A specific protocol was developed by Tea Masters who favored humble coarse pottery so as not to distract from the ceremony. From the 16th century this influenced most areas of Japanese ceramics as well, as STUDIO POTTERY wares were produced to cater specifically to the tastes of the Tea Masters. Tea ceremony wares include tea bowls, jars, trays, dishes, flower vases, braziers, whisks and KOGO. See JAPANESE POTTERY AND PORCELAIN; BIZEN; KARATSU; KENZAN; RAKU; SATSUMA; SETO; TEMMOKU.

Tea dust glaze ■ A brown opaque glaze with a speckled greenish appearance created when iron oxide is fired. It was used on Chinese porcelain from the QIANLONG period (1736–95), often for pieces in the SONG DYNASTY tradition.

Tea kettle A large silver vessel on a stand with a lamp or alcohol burner beneath to provide boiling water for tea or coffee. First appearing during the late 17th century, early examples were plain with low, separate stands, later giving way to light, three-legged

stands attached to the body of the kettle with a hinge to aid pouring. They were largely superseded by tea urns around 1760.

Tea table A small table for the service of tea, popular in the 18th and 19th centuries. The fashionable beverage of tea gave rise to an afternoon ceremony with a whole paraphernalia of equipment, including tea kettle stands, TEAPOYS, and TEA CADDIES, which in turn needed a tea table to accommodate them.

Tea urn ■ A large urn-shaped vessel, plated or made of silver or other metal, with two handles, a detachable cover, a pedestal base, a spigot or tap, and a heating apparatus (often an internal compartment to take a red-hot iron). These vessels, introduced in the mid-18th century, were more convenient than tea kettles but did not completely replace them.

Teague, Walter Dorwin (1883–1960) A leading American designer and founder of the American Society of Industrial Designers in 1944. An exponent of functionalism and STREAMLINING, Teague founded his first studio as a graphic designer in 1912, which was followed by an INDUSTRIAL DESIGN company in New York in 1926. Teague's vast portfolio of designs included redesigning the box brownie camera for Eastman Kodak, glass for STEUBEN GLASSWORKS, a lamp for Polaroid, radios for Sparton, and the Marmon Model 16 car.

Teak ■ A species of tropical hardwood (*Tectona verbenaceae*) with a density and an oily composition that make it resistant to insect infestation and fungal growth, and therefore particularly suited to garden furniture. It has been used in the West since the 18th century, with a notable revival inside the home as a central component of Danish furniture in the 1950s and 60s.

Teapot ■ A pot in which tea is infused. In the late 17th century, teapots were made of silver, Chinese red stoneware, and Chinese porcelain. By the beginning of the 18th century they were made of stoneware and porcelain in Europe. Teapots made in soft paste often cracked, as boiling water caused the glaze to crack, and many English factories experienced this difficulty, as did SÈVRES. Teapots have been made in many shapes and with different types of decoration over a very long period.

Teapoy ■ A small tripod table or stand for the storing and mixing of tea. Popular during the first half of the 19th century, the teapoy was designed for use in the drawing room. The top was usually constructed as a lockable lidded wooden box above the pedestal base and often contained two small caddies and two glass bowls—one for sugar and one for mixing the tea leaves.

Tear A tear- or drop-shaped bubble of air accidentally or deliberately enclosed in a glass stem or a similarly

Tazza
Arts and Crafts silver tazza, by John Reilly, with Sheffield hallmarks. 1904.

Tea canister
Qianlong tea canister. c. 1760.

Tea dust glaze
Chinese porcelain double-gourd vase, with tea dust glaze.

Tea urn
Sheffield part-fluted round tea urn. Early 19th century.

TEDDY BEAR

Teddy bears appeared between 1902 and 1903 and were produced in Germany and the US. By the 1920s, the German companies had regained their position as leaders in teddy bear production and innovation.

Steiff bear
Steiff teddy bear seated upright. c. 1907.

Petz Company bear
Petz Company; seated bear with glass chest button, brown mohair plush fur. c. 1950s.

Mohair bear
Scarce and early gold mohair American teddy bear, possibly by Ideal. c. 1905–1910.

shaped trail of glass applied to the outside of a vessel.

Teco Pottery An American ART POTTERY founded in Terra Cotta, Illinois, in 1881 by William D. Gates. The Teco line (a shortened form of terra-cotta) was introduced in 1902 and produced until the mid-1920s. The French sculptor Frederick Moreau brought the ART NOUVEAU style to the pottery in 1904. Later wares were modern in style and included vases, tiles, or garden ornaments of architectural form, usually with a pale green matt glaze, which is characteristic of Teco.

Teddy bear Two companies claim to have been the first to produce plush, jointed teddy bears. In 1902 Morris Michtom, a Russian migrant in New York, was inspired by a cartoon in the *Washington Post* that showed Theodore "Teddy" Roosevelt refusing to shoot a bear cub. Michtom's wife made a brown plush bear to display in the window of their shop, alongside the cartoon. The toy, labeled "Teddy's Bear," was an instant success. Michtom went on to establish the IDEAL NOVELTY AND TOY COMPANY.

The German company STEIFF also claims to have invented the teddy bear. Around 1884, Margarete Steiff, a

seamstress, included a bear standing on all fours in her range of toys, which she sold at local fairs. Her nephew Richard Steiff devised a jointed version, which was exhibited at the Leipzig spring trade fair in 1903. Although the toy did not become popular at first, Borgfeldt of New York ordered 3,000 pieces, fueling a teddy bear craze in the US. The ban on German imports during World War I helped to boost the English industry. Companies such as CHAD VALLEY and J. K. FARNELL added teddy bears to their toy ranges. SCHUCO introduced miniature bears in unusual colors that concealed lipsticks, compacts, and perfume bottles. World War II

Teak
Detail of teak sideboard, by Russell of Broadway. 1950s.

Formalized plant-form imagery

Teapot
Worcester "Spinning Maiden" teapot, in *famille rose* palette in Chinese style. c. 1770. AA

Teapoy
Regency mahogany and ebony lined teapoy.

Tekke
Tekke rug, from central Turkestan. c. 1880.

T

disrupted toy production in Germany and England, but during the 1950s bear production recovered to its prewar volume. New models appeared with rounder features, shorter snouts, and stubbier limbs. Plastic eyes and noses and synthetic fibers like Dralon were introduced. Well-known products of the 1950s include Steiff's Jackie and Zotty bears, MERRYTHOUGHT's Cheeky bear, and Dean's Tru-to-Life. Unjointed bears, first introduced on a large scale by Wendy Boston, were popular in the 1960s, resulting in bears like Steiff's Cosy Teddy and Schuco's Biggo Bello. In the 1970s, cheap bears made in East Asia flooded the market.

Teheran A central Persian carpet-producing town. Few rugs were made here before 1900. Weaving is generally of fine quality, displaying intense floral curvilinear designs similar to those on ISFAHAN rugs. Colors are similar too, although many have a distinctive rust red tone.

Tekke ■ An important carpet-weaving tribal group in the 19th century in West Turkestan. They were prolific weavers whose products range from carpets to functional artifacts. Their carpets are often incorrectly described in the West as BOKHARA. Background colors range from a soft terra-cotta in earlier examples to shades of plum and bright red in early-20th-century examples. The pattern is characteristically made up of GUL motifs, sometimes known as "elephant's foot," arranged within a black grid.

Telescope An instrument for viewing distant objects. Of the two forms of telescopes, the refracting telescope, which uses a series of lenses and is popularly credited to Galileo, was first made in 1608 by the Dutch lensmaker Hans Lippershey. The reflecting telescope, which uses polished metal mirrors and is ideal for astronomical uses, was first made by the Scottish astronomer James Gregory in 1663. Early refracting telescope lenses were affected by chromatic aberration distortions, which were corrected by the invention of the ACHROMATIC LENS in the 18th century. Both types of telescopes are still made today.

Temmoku glaze ■ A Japanese term, used originally to describe a streaky black-brown glaze on Chinese stoneware cups made at Jian (Fujian province) during the SONG DYNASTY. They were favored by the Japanese on TEA CEREMONY WARES. Named after the Tianmu Mountains in China, the term is now used to describe almost any pottery or stoneware with a thick black-brown glaze.

Tenon See MORTISE AND TENON.

Tent stitch A plain diagonal or horizontal fine stitch (also known as PETIT POINT) across one thread of ground fabric, usually canvas. The term is also used to describe tapestries using this stitch. It was widely used in France in the 17th and early 18th centuries.

Teplitz amphora ■ A collective term for amphora ware, a form of art pottery made during the late 19th and early 20th centuries in the Turn-Teplitz region of Bohemia (now Czechoslovakia). The basic amphora form was originally derived from large, ancient Greek storage vessels of that name, with oval-bodies tapering toward the base and two handles extending from just below the lip to the shoulder. However, the Teplitz forms and decorations reflected the then-prevailing styles of the ART NOUVEAU (JUGENSDTIL) and SECESSIONIST movements. These innovative shapes included many figural forms, notably female busts (sometimes of monumental proportions), and designs incorporating animals, birds, and reptiles. Although there were many manufacturers producing amphora wares in the Turn-Teplitz region, it is generally accepted that Reissner, Stellmacher & Kessel (R.S.K), the first of the manufacturers founded in 1892, was the best. Indeed, its amphora pottery is often simply referred to as "Teplitz."

Terra-cotta ■ An Italian term meaning "baked earth." An unglazed EARTHENWARE of reddish clay, often used for architectural purposes such as ornamentation, tiles, and facing. It has been used throughout the world since

Temmoku glaze
David Leach stoneware charger, with temmoku glaze.

Teplitz amphora
Amphorawerke Riessner, Stellmacher & Kessel large porcelain vase. c. 1900.

Pendant medallion

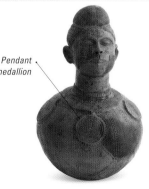

Terra-cotta
Zande terra-cotta vessel from Sudan, potted by Mbitim.

Tessuto
Murano Venini & Cie tessuto glass vase, designed by Carlo Scarpa. c. 1940.

ancient times, for practical items and for sculpture, toys, ritual objects, decorative pieces, and even furniture. When glazed, it is known as FAIENCE.

Tessuto ■ A technique developed by VENINI, similar to FILIGRANA, where glass CANES are flattened to form narrow bands or stripes. These may then be twisted or manipulated to give a wavy appearance or arranged to create woven fabriclike patterns.

Tester ■ From the French *tête* (head). "Tester" originally described the headboard of a four-poster bed, but from the 16th century it generally referred to the canopy above it. A half-tester has a canopy that extends only halfway over the bed.

Tête-à-tête See CABARET.

Thaumatrope A simple optical toy consisting of a circular diskthat had two related images drawn on either side, such as a bird on one side and a cage on the other. The disk may be rotated rapidly by means of attached threads. As it spins, the eye sees the two images simultaneously and in the same place, creating the illusion of movement. It was introduced in 1825 and is generally attributed to London physicist Dr. John Paris.

Thebes stool ■ A type of X-frame stool, popular in the REGENCY period and based on a prototype from Classical antiquity. Generally made of ROSEWOOD, the form appears in the design books of Thomas HOPE and George SMITH.

Theodolite ■ An instrument used by surveyors for measuring both horizontal and vertical angles. The most common form is a transit theodolite in which a TELESCOPE, which could revolve through 360° degrees on a vertical axis, is mounted over a circular horizontal plate marked with a scale and containing a COMPASS. The theodolite was invented in the mid-16th century, improved in the 18th century, and is still in use today.

Thieme, Carl ■ The founder of a porcelain factory in 1872 in Potschappel, Thuringia (near Dresden), which imitated MEISSEN. Typical wares were large vases, candelabra, and clockcases, encrusted with bright flowers, fruit, and birds. The original mark—a "T" over a cross—was similar to that of Meissen. From 1900 the factory became known as Sächsische Porzellanfabrik, and in 1972 it was reorganized as VEB Sächsische Porzellanmanufaktur Dresden.

Thimble A cap worn since Roman times to protect the finger when sewing. Many silver examples are found in 18th-century ÉTUIS. Earliest known porcelain examples were made by MEISSEN from around 1725 to 1730, decorated with CHINOISERIES in the style of HÖROLDT. Early metal examples, often from East Asia, tend to have pronounced domes and irregular, hand-punched dimples. Charles Horner and Iles were two notable 19th-century manufacturers.

Thompson, Robert (1876–1955) An English furniture-maker from Kilburn, Yorkshire, who is often known as the "Mouseman" because his work is signed with the carved figure of a mouse. He used oak for well-made pieces, with a distinctive adzed finish to give a subtle rippled effect to the surface. The firm he founded still exists today.

Thread and shell pattern A decorative variant of FIDDLE and OLD ENGLISH PATTERN made in silver and plated ware since the early 19th century. Similar to these patterns, the thread and shell pattern has a border of THREADING and a shell in relief at the top of the stem.

Threading A decorative motif on silver, also known as a threaded edge, which consists of fine lines engraved around the border of the handle of a fork, spoon, or other small article of silver. It was common from the early 19th century.

Throne ■ A ceremonial seat, primarily for a sovereign or an ecclesiastical dignitary. The term derives from the Greek *thronos* and Latin *thronus* meaning an elevated seat, and as such its main purpose was

T

371

Tester
Rococo Revival half-tester bed. Mid-19th century.

Thebes stool
Stained-wood Thebes stool, probably retailed by Liberty.

Theodolite
Cook, Troughton & Simms brass theodolite.

Thieme, Carl
Rococo-style wall bracket, painted with a romantic scene.

to raise the occupant above the level of other people.

Throwing A term used in potting to describe making a vessel by hand on the potter's wheel. A lump of well-kneaded and prepared clay is placed in the center of the revolving wheel. It is then sprinkled with water to keep it pliable for shaping by hand as the wheel revolves.

Thumb-piece ■ An area where the thumb can be placed to aid in holding or steadying an article—for example, a silver TASTEVIN. On a drinking vessel, it is usually on top of the handle. On a SNUFF BOX, it takes the form of a protruding lip designed to give the thumb purchase for opening of the box or a vertical protrusion on the cover.

Thuyawood A golden brown or brown-red close-grained wood from North Africa with a mottled, bird's-eye figure. It was used in the 18th and 19th centuries for small turned ware and veneer.

Tiara A woman's semicircular jeweled headdress for formal occasions, popular from the 18th century onward. The tiara was probably the most significant of all the jewels in a collection and often the finest gems were reserved for such a piece. Mid- to late 19th-century tiaras could usually be

broken down and converted into individual brooches or a necklace; original components are an important element when assessing tiaras today. Firms such as GARRARD and CARTIER produced tiaras for an aristocratic clientele from the 1880s to the 1950s. The tiara is also an item of papal regalia.

Tie pin ■ An accessory (also called stick pin) worn mainly by men since the 18th century and still made today. Tie pins with diamond-studded animals, rare fancy-colored gemstones, and novelty or political subjects are avidly sought-after. Many late Victorian designs were mass produced in Britain.

Tiffany ■ Founded in 1837, Tiffany & Co. of New York became the leading American manufacturer of silver, jewelry, and glass. Charles Louis Tiffany, the founder's son, started his career with a "fancy goods" store in New York. A manufacturer with a keen sense of the spending power of America's burgeoning wealthy class, he expanded his business rapidly, especially into the areas of jewelry and silver.

On Charles's death, his son, Louis Comfort Tiffany, became vice-president of Tiffany & Co. (as the company was called after 1853) and its first art director. He brought an artist's eye and an enthusiasm for the emerging Art Nouveau style into the wares. He became a designer of glass, jewelry, stained glass, silver, metal, and ceramics, and the creator of magnificent lamps and windows.

Louis Tiffany's first business venture was as an interior designer, and in 1880 he founded Louis C. Tiffany & Associated Artists. He experimented increasingly with innovative glassmaking techniques and in the same year patented his famous glass with its characteristic iridescent finish, sold under the trade name of FAVRILE (from the Old English *fabrile*, meaning "belonging to a craftsman or his craft"). His reputation and business grew and his lamps and other bronze and metal items were made at, and marked, "Tiffany Studios." He received

Upholstered armrests

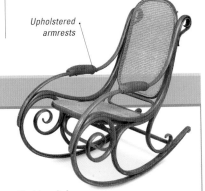

Rocking chair
Model No.1 stained beechwood rocking chair, with original canework. c. 1888.

THONET BROTHERS

A family firm of German furniture-makers comprising Michael Thonet (1796–1871) and his four sons, Thonet Brothers perfected the BENTWOOD process for chair-making and pioneered the mass production of standardized furniture. Born in Boppard, southern Germany, Thonet established a cabinet-making business in 1819, specializing in PARQUETRY. By the 1830s his experiments with bentwood led to the invention of a revolutionary process in which solid lengths of beechwood were boiled or steamed in water, then bent to form long, curved rods for chair frames, which were inexpensive, light, flexible, yet remarkably durable, thus eliminating the need for hand-carved joints.

Throne
One of a pair of Indian hardwood thrones, with applied brass and steel incised panels.

Eared back rest

Whatnot
Model No.4 beechwood whatnot. c. 1904.

international acclaim after he exhibited wares at the Exposition Universelle in Paris in 1900.

Tiffany Studios closed in 1932, but during the interwar years the original company, Tiffany & Co., continued to produce silver, jewelry, and glass of outstanding quality. In the 1950s there was a move to simpler forms by innovative contemporary artists, which continues today.

Tiffany, Louis Comfort See TIFFANY.

Tigerware ■ A word used in Elizabethan England for Rhenish stoneware, especially jugs with a mottled brown glaze over a grayish body. Similar ware was made by John DWIGHT, who started a factory in Fulham, London, toward the end of the 17th century.

Tigerwood See ZEBRAWOOD.

Tiles ■ Earthenware tiles with various types of decoration and glaze have a long history. In Islamic countries they were used from the 8th century for walls, floors, and the domes of mosques. In Europe they were made by Cistercian monks, often using the ENCAUSTIC method. In Spain the *cuerda seca* (meaning literally "dry cord") method was used to produce tiles with colored glazes enclosed by lines of grease. In Portugal tile-making has been an important industry since the Middle Ages and still is. FAIENCE

tiles (*azulejos*) were built up into large panoramic views on walls. Tiles were a huge part of DELFT production in Holland, either made to form a continuous pattern, or with a single motif on each tile. The Dutch workmen who came to England with William and Mary around l680 brought their tile-making techniques with them. Tiles of the 17th century were usually hand-painted both in blue and in polychrome, often with naive renderings of biblical and mythological subjects. Toward the end of the 18th century, English tiles were also TRANSFER PRINTED with NEOCLASSICAL subjects (see SADLER & GREEN) and theatrical images.

During the 19th and early 20th centuries, tiles became popular again. They were decorated with Japanese themes by designers of the AESTHETIC MOVEMENT such as William DE MORGAN, inspired by Japanese exhibitions in London and Paris in the mid-19th century. Designers in the ART NOUVEAU and ART DECO styles also created tiles, and in Staffordshire, factories such as MINTON and DOULTON made them industrially. Tile factories in the US such as the Low ART TILE WORKS in Massachusetts also flourished.

Tilt-top table A table with a top hinged to the base or pedestal so that it can be tipped to a vertical position. Originating in medieval times, the tilt-top table had become highly developed by the 18th century and was popular in Britain and the US. The ingenious construction allowed

the decorative features of the top to be displayed and also allowed the table to be stored neatly against a wall when not in use. It also meant that the table could act as a FIRESCREEN when necessary.

Timepiece A clock or watch that shows the passing of time but does not have a striking or chiming mechanism.

Tin A brittle white metal, the main constituent of PEWTER and, alloyed with COPPER, of BRONZE. Tin has also been used as a protective coating to prevent oxidization or corrosion on objects made from other base metals such as iron and steel and on the interiors of copper and BRASS cooking vessels.

Tin glaze ■ The process by which MAIOLICA, FAIENCE, and DELFT were produced. After a first firing, the pottery was dipped into a glaze of oxides of lead and tin, which produced a porous white surface. It was then decorated with HIGH-TEMPERATURE COLORS, which were absorbed by the glaze, before being fired again, possibly with the addition of a LEAD GLAZE. In this way, the decoration was fused into the substance of the piece and could not later be altered. The technique was first used in the Middle East in the 9th century and was later brought to Europe via Spain by the Moors in the 13th century. In 18th-century Germany, extra decoration was added when ENAMEL COLORS were used over the tin glaze.

Stylized leaf form

Thumb-piece
Rare French silver water jug by Dufrenes, with leaf-shaped cover and thumb-piece.

Tie pin
Horse-shaped platinum and gold tie pin, set with diamonds, rubies, and sapphires. c. 1920.

Tigerware
Bellarmine, with a mask and lion medallion applied to the neck and side. Late 17th century.

Tiles
Rare Dutch Delft tile showing a Roman warrior. c. 1630.

Tinderbox A small metal box used from the 15th to the 19th century that held a piece of flint, a section of steel, and tinder (such as dry wood). Striking the flint against the steel produced sparks that ignited the tinder. Later tinderboxes were sometimes decorative and quite elaborate in mechanism. The tinderbox was the forerunner of the lighter, invented in the late 19th century and perfected by Wise and Greenwood in what became the Dunhill Unique lighter.

Ting A Chinese ceramic or bronze cooking vessel made from the SHANG and early Zhou dynasties (around 1500–1000 BCE) onward. It generally comprises a rounded or rectangular bowl set on three or four feet with loop handles on the rim.

Tinplate toy ■ A toy made from thin sheet steel that was coated with tin or a tin alloy to counter rust. Early tinplate toys were painted by hand, but from around 1900 they were more commonly decorated using color transfers produced with LITHOGRAPHY.

Tinsel picture Formed from hand-colored prints embellished with applied colored

metallic foil, often on portrait engravings. They were especially popular in the 1830s and 1840s, depicting actors and actresses and historical personalities. They were often sold in sets with maple frames.

Tinworth, George ■ See DOULTON.

Tired An expressive term used to describe a piece, often with a practical function, that is in poor or worn condition due to heavy usage through the years.

Toasting fork Usually made of silver or Sheffield plate with a long, turned wooden handle (sometimes these could be telescopic or collapsible) and deeply curved tines that allowed a slice of bread or the muffin to be held vertically in front of an open fire so that it toasted evenly. Silver examples exist from the late 17th century.

Toasting glass A tall glass with a small trumpet bowl and thin, elongated stem, introduced in the 17th century and much used in the 18th century in England and Holland. Tradition has it that such wineglasses were used to drink toasts,

after which the stem was snapped to ensure that the toast could not be broken.

Toastmaster's glass A drinking glass used throughout the 18th and early 19th centuries. The apparently full-sized bowl was, in fact, made of very thick glass in order to reduce capacity and thus allow the toastmaster to repeatedly down the contents and still remain sober.

Tobey Furniture Company A furniture-making and decorating firm founded in Chicago by Charles and Frank Tobey in 1875, producing architectural-style furniture inspired by the work of local architects Louis Sullivan and Frank Lloyd WRIGHT. The company closed in 1954.

Toby jug ■ The name given to the pottery jugs that were first made by Ralph WOOD in the 1760s and imitated throughout

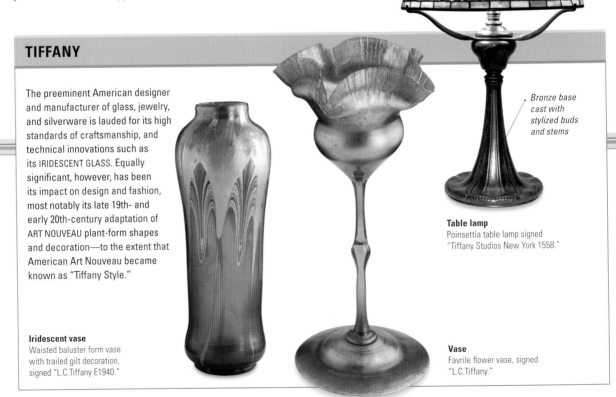

TIFFANY

The preeminent American designer and manufacturer of glass, jewelry, and silverware is lauded for its high standards of craftsmanship, and technical innovations such as its IRIDESCENT GLASS. Equally significant, however, has been its impact on design and fashion, most notably its late 19th- and early 20th-century adaptation of ART NOUVEAU plant-form shapes and decoration—to the extent that American Art Nouveau became known as "Tiffany Style."

Bronze base cast with stylized buds and stems

Table lamp
Poinsettia table lamp signed "Tiffany Studios New York 1558."

Iridescent vase
Waisted baluster form vase with trailed gilt decoration, signed "L.C.Tiffany E1940."

Vase
Favrile flower vase, signed "L.C.Tiffany."

Staffordshire and elsewhere in England from the late 18th century until the present time. The name probably comes from the title of an engraving of an obese drinker, "Sir Toby Philpott," who was depicted sitting down holding a mug of foaming ale in one hand and a glass or a pipe in the other. There were many variations, including the Squire, the Thin Man, Martha Gunn, the Brighton Bathing Machine Lady, and the Snuff Taker. See CHARACTER JUGS.

Toddy lifter A glass vessel used for transferring liquid such as punch from a large bowl to a small drinking glass, made in Britain in the 18th and 19th centuries. A toddy lifter was shaped like a small, long-necked decanter with a small hole in the base. The lifter was plunged into the punch bowl and the liquid entered through the hole. The punch was held in place by closing off the neck opening with the thumb to create a vacuum, and then released into the drinking glass by removing the thumb and allowing the liquid to flow out.

Toftware SLIP-decorated earthenware dishes bearing the names of James Toft, Ralph Toft, or Thomas Toft. Some examples have dates as well as the names on the front of the dishes. On some dishes, the name of the potter is part of the decoration. Thomas Toft's work is the most common—over 30 signed examples are recorded. It is the only known SLIPWARE of this kind that displays the potter's name in such a way.

The dishes are usually large, with a trellis border on the rims, some bearing the Royal Arms in the center.

Toile A French term for "cloth" given to single-color designs in red, blue, or sepia printed onto cotton. First made in the 18th century, early toiles were printed on cloth imported from India. In 1759 the French textile designer and industrialist Christophe-Philippe Oberkampf set up his factory in Jouy-en-Josas near Versailles, producing what have become the best-known toiles, *toiles de jouy*. These were rollerprinted, using copper plates engraved with Classical or pastoral scenes (often allegorical). Many were designed by J. B. Huet, Oberkampf's chief designer.

Tokoname Potteries A large and productive Japanese pottery, one of the celebrated "Six Ancient Kilns." Located south of Nagoya, Tokoname's early phase—along with SETO, Shigaraki, Tamba, BIZEN, and Echizen—was from the 12th until the late 16th century. Their production consisted of unevenly formed and undecorated wares—either partially or entirely covered with natural wood-ash glazes—as well as the highly prized vessels associated with the TEA CEREMONY. In the late 19th and early 20th centuries it produced accomplished imitations of early Japanese wares and Chinese YIXING teapots.

Tôleware A term for *tôle peinte* or painted tinware, used for lampshades and hollowware. Most tôleware in the US was imported during the 19th century, but some was made as Pennsylvania tinware. The process is similar to JAPANNING, although that is done on a wider variety of materials.

Tomimoto, Kenkichi (1886–1963) A Japanese potter who studied under Kenzan VI with Bernard LEACH, then established his own workshop at Ando (Nara) in 1915. He is best known for his very pure white porcelain decorated, especially with landscapes, in underglaze blue or enamel colors. One of the leaders of the Mingei Movement—founded to foster an appreciation of traditional Japanese folk art—Tomimoto was a very influential teacher, and from 1958 was Principal of the Municipal College of Fine Arts in Kyoto.

Tompion, Thomas (1639–1713) An English clockmaker, admitted to the Clockmakers' Company in 1671. Tompion was the leading London maker of ebony-veneered LONGCASE and BRACKET CLOCKS and watches in the late 17th century. Tompion introduced a number of features in clock-making, including a wider, more legible CHAPTER RING, a larger hour hand, small subsidiary dials for striking mechanisms, and the locking of the pendulum while the clock was transported. He also developed an early CYLINDER ESCAPEMENT in 1695 and a REPEATER mechanism.

T

375

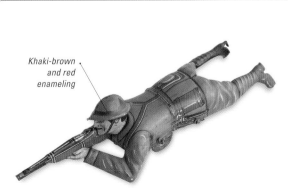

Tinplate toy
German tinplate clockwork rifleman, in prone position with sparking gun.

Khaki-brown and red enameling

Tinworth, George
Doulton Lambeth stoneware menu holder, modeled as two mice playing instruments.

Detachable hat forms the lid

Toby jug
Davenport Toby jug, typically modeled seated and holding a foaming jug of ale. c. 1840s.

Tongue and groove A method of creating paneling by jointing boards side by side with a tongue on one panel fitting into a groove on the adjacent one.

Toning ■ The term used to describe the cloudy PATINA that may build up on a coin, particularly a silver coin, over time. It is caused by exposure to air and humidity, and varies from grays to brighter colors. Visually appealing toning can add value to a coin, and many collectors prefer to see toning, as it usually indicates that the coin is in its original state from the mint.

Tooling A technique employed to give ornamental decoration to LEATHER and employed on bookbindings and on leather-covered furniture. It employs various other techniques such as STAMPING, GILDING, PUNCHING, or INCISING.

Tootsietoys ■ An American toy manufacturer established by Charles Dowst in Chicago. Starting out as a publisher, he and his brother, Samuel, began to manufacture metal novelties in 1893, and the first three-dimensional DIECAST lead toy car was released in 1911. A Model T Ford was released in 1915 and the range grew in the 1920s and 30s. The trade name "Tootsietoy," named after one of the Dowst brothers' granddaughters, "Toots," was registered in 1924. They had the diecast field to themselves and introduced zamac (an alloy of zinc) in 1933. Their best-known achievements were cars, including the

Graham Paige, but they also made trucks and planes. Although it was eclipsed by DINKY, MATCHBOX, and CORGI after World War II, Tootsietoys continued to produce toys and is still in business, now owned by the Strombecker corporation.

Top plate A term used to describe the plate uppermost when looking into the back of a watch. This is usually where the maker signs his name and puts any relevant information. All the wheels are held between the top and bottom plate. The term is also used to describe the metal plate on the top of cameras to which the dials and shutter button are fixed.

Topaz ■ A gemstone found in several colors, brown being the most desirable and a rich, golden brown from Brazil, called "Imperial" or "Sherry" topaz, the most valuable. Topaz was used extensively in 18th- and 19th-century jewelry, particularly in sets of pink topaz and chrysolite in CANNETILLE frames.

Top rail ■ The highest horizontal bar on the back of a chair.

Topsy-turvy ■ A type of RAG DOLL, popular in the early 20th century, with two heads, one on each side of the torso. One is concealed by clothing while the other is on view.

Torchère (candle stand) ■ A portable stand for a candle or lamp, usually a tall table with a small top. From the mid-17th

century they were frequently made en suite to flank a SIDE TABLE with a mirror above. Torchères are found in many 18th-century design books and the form was especially suited to the NEOCLASSICAL style of Robert ADAM.

Torquay Terracotta Company Figures, plaques, and vases were made at Hele Cross, Torquay, Devon, in the local terra-cotta from 1875 to 1909. It used an impressed or printed mark of the name in full, and from 1900 to 1909 the name appears within a double circle.

Tortoiseshell ■ The mottled dark brown or reddish brown shell of the hawksbill turtle. Flattened and joined under pressure and heat-molded or carved, it was traditionally used for INLAY work, notably on English and French furniture during the 17th, 18th, and early 19th centuries (see BOULLE), as well as for jewelry, boxes, and other *objets de vertu*. Because the hawksbill turtle is an endangered and protected species, tortoiseshell nowadays is usually imitated in celluloid or other plastics.

Tortoiseshell glass A type of 19th- and 20th-century clear cased ART GLASS, in which a layer of brown mottling was enclosed between two layers of clear glass, made throughout Europe and in the US. It was made by rolling the first GATHER in shards of brown glass before forming the final shape.

Toning
Crown, minted by George IV, with attractive rainbow toning. 1819.

Two-tone blue enamel

Tootsietoy
American Tootsietoy car.

Topaz
Early Victorian cruciform brooch, with four arms of oval mixed-cut Imperial topaz.

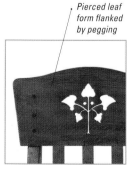

Pierced leaf form flanked by pegging

Top rail
Leon Jallot oak and purplewood chair, the top rail with pierced stylized leaf decoration. c. 1908.

Tostrup, Jacob (1806–90) A Norwegian silversmith working in Christiania (now Oslo) from the early 19th century who promoted mechanized production and manufacturing techniques to compete within the European marketplace. In the 1830s he installed powered machinery in his workshops and thus stimulated the revival of silversmithing in Norway. The company made pieces in historical revival and ART NOUVEAU styles.

Touch mark The mark of a pewterer, stamped on his wares. From the 16th century, most European pewterers were required to register their mark on a touch plate held by the local guild. Some pewterers added imitation HALLMARKS.

Touchpiece A coin or medal given out by a monarch when curing the disease of scrofula (TB of the lymph glands), known as "the king's evil." In medieval times it was thought that the monarch could cure this disease by touching the sufferer.

Toulouse-Lautrec, Henri de (1864–1901) A French artist and printmaker renowned for his paintings and posters, which usually depicted the circuses, night clubs, music halls, and theaters of *fin-de-siècle* Paris, especially the Montmartre area. *Moulin Rouge: La Goulue* (1891) was Toulouse-Lautrec's first LITHOGRAPH poster.

Tourmaline A gemstone found in a range of colors of which a dark bluish green and deep pink variety (known as rubellite) are the most popular. Tourmaline was rarely used before 1900, but was employed extensively in the 20th century, mounted in bold gold and silver jewelry.

Tournai Porcelain A factory founded in Tournai, in what is now Belgium, by François-Joseph Peterinck in 1751, under the patronage of the Holy Roman Empress Maria Theresa. It made a creamy, soft paste, resembling that of SÈVRES, and the products were completely French in tone. The factory employed Henri-Joseph Duvivier as chief decorator from 1763 to 1771. He also later worked in England. In 1787 it made a famous service for the Duc d'Orléans, painted with birds after Buffon's *Natural History*, probably by Jean-Ghislain Mayer. But it also produced a great deal of cheap blue and white tableware. The factory closed, but was reopened in 1840 by Maximilian Bettignies, who moved it to St Armand les Eaux, where he made good copies of SÈVRES, CHELSEA, and WORCESTER until the factory closed for good in the mid-19th century.

Tournai tapestry factories ■ Weaving was known in Tournai from the 14th century and the town became an important tapestry-weaving center in the 15th century. Through merchants such as the highly influential Pasquier Grenier (working in Tournai from around 1447 to 1477), high-quality tapestries were sold to the Dukes of Burgundy and to the Church as well as to European royalty. Competition from Brussels together with the plague of 1513 saw a marked decline in Tournai's fortunes, although fine tapestries were still being produced. They are often recognizable because from 1544 weavers were obliged to include the city arms in the design. During the 16th and 17th centuries, Tournai's continued use of old cartoons meant that Brussels and Antwerp became more fashionable, with the last factory in Tournai closing in 1712.

Toy 1. See AUTOMATA, DIECAST, DOLLS, TEDDY BEAR, TINPLATE, TRAIN. 2. A small inexpensive item made in the 18th and 19th centuries in various materials, but especially in porcelain or metal. Items included cane handles, PERFUME BOTTLES, and ÉTUIS.

Tracery Delicate lattice shapes consisting of lines and bars with spaces for glass or openings. Derived from GOTHIC windows and ornament, tracery was used in architecture and adapted for use in furniture, especially during the GOTHIC REVIVAL of the 19th century.

Trailing A type of decoration on glass in which plain or colored glass in molten strands of varying thickness is dripped

Mythological figures in a pastoral setting

Topsy-turvy
Bruckner topsy-turvy doll.

Torchère
Adam period giltwood torchère. c. 1790.

Tortoiseshell
Tortoiseshell-covered box.

Tournai tapestry factories
Fragment of a Tournai tapestry. c. 1700.

and trailed or wound onto the handle, foot, or body. First employed on ROMAN GLASS, the technique is still used today.

Train A set of interlocking toothed wheels and pinions in the MOVEMENT of a clock or watch. TIMEPIECES have only one train, but other clocks require a separate train for striking the hours. A third train is used to activate more complex striking.

Train (model) ■ Replicas made to common scales—for example, 0-gauge and 00-gauge—and usually powered by steam, clockwork, or electric motors contained within the locomotives. Production started in the 1860s with rather crudely modeled push-along examples. Accurate representations followed by 1900. MÄRKLIN, BASSETT-LOWKE, and HORNBY are the best-known European model train makers. The focus has been on smaller gauges since 1950. Many early examples in TINPLATE or CAST IRON were unmotorized.

Transfer printing ■ A process for decorating ceramics in which an engraved copper plate is covered with ink, prepared with metallic oxides. The engraved design is transferred to paper, which is then pressed onto the surface of the object while the pigment is still wet. The design is then fixed by firing. Transfer printing was much used at the BATTERSEA ENAMEL FACTORY (around 1753), BOW (around 1756), WORCESTER (from 1756), and on earthenware at LIVERPOOL by John Sadler

from 1756. Subsequently, most English factories used the process. In the rest of Europe, it was not popular as a commercial means of decoration until FAIENCE had been abandoned for cream-colored EARTHENWARE. One exception was at RÖRSTRAND, where Anders Stenman, who discovered the process independently, used it from 1766. He took it to MARIEBERG. Berthevin tried it at FRANKENTHAL but without much success. At the end of the 18th century it became common on earthenware at many factories, including CREIL, Sarreguemines, Montereau, ZURICH, Proskau, ALCORA, Sargadelos, and METTLACH.

Transitional ware ■ Chinese porcelain made around the transition from the MING DYNASTY to the QING DYNASTY (c. 1620–50). The blue and white Transitional style is characteristically well painted with naturalistic images of flowers, foliage, animals, and figures. Narrative subjects illustrating scenes from Chinese Classical literature were also popular. Pieces often have flat, unglazed bases and ANHUA border designs. WUCAI, BLANC-DE-CHINE, KRAAK PORCELAIN and Ko-sometsuke wares (for the Japanese market) were also made in this period.

Translucency True porcelain usually allows light to pass through to a certain

TREEN

An Old English word for "tree" or "wood," treen refers to small wooden objects, often of domestic use, turned on a lathe or carved in a variety of woods, including FRUITWOOD and HOLLY. Pieces include love spoons and small boxes. Early pieces date from the 17th century.

Carved and cut decoration

Snuff box
English fruitwood snuff box, the double-headed man depicting good and evil. Mid-18th century.

extent, but most pottery does not. The translucency of the porcelain depends on the thickness of the porcelain and on the firing temperature, which produces a degree of vitrification.

Train model
Clockwork-powered Hornby 0-gauge No.2 tender locomotive. Mid- to late 1920s.

Green and gilt livery

Transfer printing
Creamware teapot, printed with Harlequin, Columbine, and Pierrot. c. 1765.

Transitional ware
Transitional blue and white vase, painted with a figure riding a water buffalo. c. 1640.

Tranter, William (1816–90) An English FIREARMS designer and manufacturer. Active from 1840, Tranter was granted some 16 patents for improvements to firearms. He is best known for his REVOLVERS, which were well-made and reliable. His factory at Aston Cross near Birmingham produced all types of firearms, many of which were for the armed forces and other services.

Trifid A silver FLATWARE pattern, probably derived from the TREFOIL, developed during the 1660s and popular until around 1700. The terminals of forks and spoons are hammered out and given either two projections or two notches, making a tripartite splay, visually dividing the end of the piece into three sections.

Trefoil A GOTHIC decorative motif consisting of three lobes and resembling a stylized clover leaf. Occasionally used as a symbol of the Christian Trinity—like other three-part devices—the trefoil was widely adopted in the late 19th century for geometric GOTHIC REVIVAL designs for metalwork, wall decorations, and furniture INLAYS.

Trek A painted outline in dark blue, sometimes in black or manganese, on Dutch DELFT WARE, filled in with blue or other colors.

Trelliswork From the French *treillage* (latticework) An elaborate trellis motif constructed with a false perspective, giving the illusion of a building, archway, or niche. Well-known examples of trelliswork include garden screen niches at Versailles in France and at Sans Souci at Potsdam.

Trembler (tremblant) ■ Naturalistic diamond and gem-set spray brooches worn in the 18th and 19th centuries in which the principal flowerhead was mounted on a coiled spring, causing the brooch to "tremble" when worn. Such a mechanism was described as *en tremblant* and was later also employed on some 20th-century COSTUME JEWELRY.

Trembleuse ■ A saucer with a circular, and often pierced, gallery in the center to hold the cup and prevent it from "trembling" or spilling the contents.

Trencher A medieval term for a slab of wood from which food or bread was eaten. Post-medieval receptacles made in silver that served the same purpose were also known as trenchers, but the term became outmoded. By the 16th century they were known as plates. See CHARGER.

Trencher salt ■ A low, open receptacle without feet having a hollowed top section to contain salt. Trencher salts were designed for use by individual diners and originally accompanied the TRENCHER. They were often made in sets from silver, ceramic, or enamel from the early 17th century to around 1730, when they were superseded by glass SALTS, sometimes in CRUETS.

Trestle table The earliest type of dining table, made of large boards of oak or elm resting on a series of "trestles" or central supports. The tops were detachable, making it easier to remove the entire table following a meal. Trestle tables were made for dining from the Middle Ages through to the 17th century.

Tri-ang ■ In 1919 William, Walter, and Arthur Lines left their father's firm, LINES BROS., and set up their own firm in Merton, London, and adopted a triangular trade mark, registering the name Tri-ang in 1924. They made everything for children, including carriages, dolls, pedal cars, nursery furniture, ships, dollhouses, TINPLATE clockwork vehicles, and more. They began making soft toys in 1937 and registered the name "Pedigree" for their dolls in 1938. By focusing on finish and quality, they became Britain's most successful general toymaker, even rescuing MECCANO in 1964 before it eventually succumbed to poor trade conditions. Since 1983, Sharna Tri-ang Ltd., now in Manchester, has produced toys based on childrens' TV programs.

Tribal art ■ The functional, ceremonial, or ritualistic work of the peoples of Africa, Oceania, South East Asia, and the Americas. Although tribal art has been produced for centuries, climate conditions and constant use has meant that few pieces earlier than the late 19th century have survived. The items produced for

Trembler (tremblant)
Victorian *en tremblant* butterfly brooch, with diamond, sapphire, and ruby flower stem. c. 1840.

Trembleuse
Louis XVI Viennese cup and trembleuse saucer. c. 1780

Trencher salt
Dutch Delft blue and white trencher salt. Mid-19th century.

Tri-ang
Minic 85M clockwork transport van, with original box.

decorative purposes from the late 20th century onward, such as figurines or jewelry intended to be exported or sold to tourists, are different, although the term has been extended to include these.

Tricoteuse A term used in the 19th century to designate a small WORK TABLE. Originally the term referred to a table at which one could *tricoter*, or knit.

Tridarn A type of Welsh PRESS cupboard constructed in three stages. The two lower stages are enclosed by doors while the upper stage remains open.

Tripod table A small OCCASIONAL table, often with a round top supported on a slender central three-legged pillar. The tripod table was widely adopted in the second half of the 18th century for the informal serving of tea, supper, desserts, and other refreshments. Many tripod tables have a TILT-TOP and sometimes a BIRDCAGE SUPPORT.

Trivet ■ A stand with three legs (sometimes four), usually made of wrought iron but also of brass or bronze, for supporting cooking vessels and other domestic utensils such as a kettle in front of an open fire. Used from early times, the trivet commonly has a decorative pierced top, a long wooden handle, and perhaps also hooks for attaching it to the bars of a firegrate. The CAT was a similiar object.

Troika ■ A pottery established in 1963 in St. Ives, Cornwall, England, by Benny Sirota, Leslie Illsley, and Jan Thomson. In contrast to the prevailing ethos of the STUDIO POTTERY movement of the time (as exemplified in the works of BERNARD LEACH), they pursued a vision of pottery as art, without any particular regard to its function. Sold to summer tourists and via prestigious outlets such as Heals in London, Troika produced two main ranges: rough-textured and smooth-glazed. The former were more numerous and remain the most popular, whereas the latter are rarer and therefore more desirable to many current collectors. The pottery moved to Newlyn in 1970 and closed in 1983.

Trompe l'oeil ■ A French term meaning "trick the eye." A type of decoration designed to imitate a surface or texture to create the impression of three-dimensional objects, or create patterns in two dimensions. Different effects such as MARBLING or GRISAILLE were used to transform wood, stone, or plaster. The other form of *Quodlibet* produced an image of objects lying on a surface. In the mid-18th century, some influential German porcelain was painted with flowers with *trompe l'oeil* shadows.

Trophy A motif that originated as a memento celebrating a victory and consisting of arms and armor. In the 17th century, it was popularly adopted as decoration for related themes such as hunting. Its usage expanded throughout the

18th century, particularly in France, to embrace a variety of themes—love, music, the seasons, astronomy, and ecclesiastical designs. No longer confined to architectural ornament, the trophy was applied to MARQUETRY, textiles and embroidered patterns. In the NEOCLASSICAL period, it returned to its roots as a military motif.

Troubadour style A French variant of the GOTHIC REVIVAL style, popular from around 1815 to the 1840s. It was introduced during the RESTAURATION period as it was favored by the Duchesse de Berry, a member of the French royal family. It was also popularized by the translations into French of Sir Walter Scott's historical novels at this time. Elements of GOTHIC architecture such as PINNACLES, CROCKETS, and arches were applied to furniture, tapestries, mirrors, glass, clocks, and ceramics, often combined with other Classically inspired components of the RESTAURATION such as ACANTHUS scrolls and LAUREL wreaths. In this way, the style was a continuation of the ornamental gothic rather than the historically accurate Gothic Revival. The troubadour fashion declined in the mid-19th century with the growing enthusiasm for the RENAISSANCE REVIVAL style.

Troy weight A unit of measurement used for weighing precious metals such as silver, gold, and platinum, named after the town of Troyes in France. One troy pound equals 5,760 grams, 240 penny weight, or

Tribal art
Yoruba figure from Nigeria. Early 20th century.

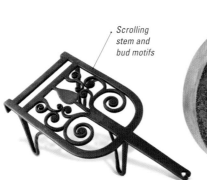

Scrolling stem and bud motifs

Trivet
Artificers' Guild wrought-iron trivet.

Troika
Pottery "Wheel" vase, modeled in relief with face design, and painted marks.

Trompe l'oeil
Japanese Nasco ceramic "smoking" ashtray, with *trompe l'oeil* decoration. 1950s.

12 ounces. One troy ounce equals 31.3 grams. It is slightly heavier than the ordinary (*avoirdupois*) weight measurement where one ounce equals 28.3 grams.

Trumpeter clock ■ A variant of the CUCKOO CLOCK, featuring mechanically propelled figures of trumpeters instead of a cuckoo and with the hour (and sometimes the quarter hour) sounded on a tiny trumpet operated by bellows.

Tsuba ■ The plate mounted on a Japanese sword between the blade and the handle, acting both as a counterbalance to the blade weight and as a hand guard. Most commonly made from metal, they are often highly decorated.

Tube-lining ■ A ceramic decoration in which thin trails of SLIP are applied as outlines to areas of colored glaze, a technique used extensively at MOORCROFT. See SLIP-TRAILING.

Tubular bell See BELL.

Tucker Porcelain Factory An American porcelain works founded in 1827 and the earliest to enjoy commercial success. Established by William Ellis Tucker, the factory

produced a wide range of HARD-PASTE PORCELAIN comparable to contemporary French porcelain. Most Tucker is sparsely decorated but may be painted with floral sprays or simple landscapes in polychrome, sepia, or gilt. Some decoration can be attributed to Thomas Tucker, the chief decorator. Few pieces are signed but may be attributed by form, painting style, and distinctive FOOT RIMS. Ambitious pieces include pairs of scenic vases or pieces with historically significant decoration. The firm became Tucker & Hemphill in 1831 but the factory closed in 1838.

Tudor Revival A revival of forms and motifs of the 16th-century TUDOR STYLE in 19th-century English decorative arts. Typical elements include richly carved bulbous supports on tables and other furniture, the use of the stylized Tudor rose and LINENFOLD paneling, as well as RENAISSANCE and MANNERIST motifs such as STRAPWORK, GROTESQUES, ARABESQUES, and roundels. Thus the Tudor Revival was closely related to, and often combined with, the GOTHIC, ELIZABETHAN, and RENAISSANCE REVIVALS, and integrated with Elizabethan and JACOBEAN ornament to create the eclectic JACOBETHAN STYLE.

Tudor style The architecture and applied arts dominant in England during the 16th century, named after the ruling Tudor dynasty (1485–1603). The style is characterized by medieval English forms combined with

RENAISSANCE and MANNERIST ornament, introduced by Continental European artists working at the court of Henry VIII (for example, Hans Holbein), and later, with the advent of printing derived from Flemish, French, and German PATTERN BOOKS. Typical ornament includes portrait roundels, ARABESQUES, and GROTESQUES, and in the late 16th century STRAPWORK and CHERUBS. Such motifs are found on oak furniture characterized by large, rectilinear forms with rich carving, ceremonial silver such as STANDING CUPS, salt cellars, and silver and silver-gilt mounts on exotic items such as coconuts and hardstones. ELIZABETHAN STYLE specifically denotes the Tudor style of the reign of Elizabeth I (1558–1603).

Tudric ■ The trade name for table and decorative ware made from 1903 in a type of PEWTER with a high proportion of silver, marketed by LIBERTY & Co. to accompany its silver CYMRIC range. Made by William H. Haseler of Birmingham, it was inspired by the CELTIC and ART NOUVEAU styles and featured ENTRELACS, stylized leaves and flowerheads, and vitreous enamel in blueish green. Forms include chalices, clocks, and vases. Many pieces were designed by Archibald KNOX.

Tula work Steel furniture, candlesticks, caskets, and fireplace furnishings made at the ironworks at Tula, near Moscow, founded by Peter the Great in 1705. Made in traditional Russian and Western

Stepped and molded pediment

Trumpeter clock
Large Black Forest trumpeter mantle clock.

Tsuba
One of a pair of Japanese shakudo tsuba, of mokko form, with dragons in gilt relief.

Tube-lining
Large Moorcroft Florianware vase, tube-line decorated with irises in shades of blue.

Tudric
Liberty Tudric hand-polished pewter ice bucket, designed by Archibald Knox. c. 1903.

NEOCLASSICAL styles, these items feature cut-steel and inlaid metal decoration. The term also applies to small silver and NIELLO objects, such as snuff boxes, made at other Russian factories from the early 19th century.

Tulip ware A generic term given to American pottery of PENNSYLVANIA DUTCH origin, decorated with stylized tulips in SGRAFFITO through a yellow or green glaze. Originally made by 18th- and 19th-century German immigrants, tulip ware has been widely reproduced.

Tulipière A vase, especially DUTCH DELFT, specifically meant to hold tulip bulbs while they grow. Such vases were ancillary to the bulb-growing trade. Tulips were imported from Turkey in the 17th century, and "tulipmania" became an obsession, with rare species reaching high prices.

Tulipwood ■ A hard, dense, light-colored wood with a pronounced red grain similar in appearance to striped tulips. Related to ROSEWOOD, it was imported to Europe from Brazil and Peru in the 18th century and used with amaranth by French furniture-makers. In France it is called *bois de rose*.

Tulwar A name for the Indian SABER, particularly the type with a curved blade. The most common of Indian swords, its HILT generally features a disk-shaped pommel.

Tumbler ■ A type of domestic drinking glass without a stem or foot and with a cylindrical, tapering, waisted, or barrel-shaped body on a flat base. They were made in various sizes, styles, and decoration in ceramic, horn, metal, and glass. See MILDNER GLASS, KOTHGASSER, ZWISCHENGOLDGLAS.

Tunbridgeware ■ Small wooden domestic objects such as stamp- and workboxes, rulers, picture frames, games boards, and rarely, work tables. The surfaces are decorated with patterns created from an intricate mosaic of thin geometric slivers of colored wood. Although the technique was used from the late 17th century, most Tunbridgeware seen today was produced from the 1830s until the end of the 19th century. It was made in and near Tunbridge Wells, England, often as souvenirs of this town, a popular spa resort in the 19th century. Geometric borders typically surrounded flora and fauna designs, people, buildings, and views.

Tureen ■ A deep vessel with a lid, two handles, and an oval or circular outline. Large tureens are for soup and small ones are for sauce. They were made in sets or pairs. Originally ceramic, soup tureens appeard in silver in the 1720s, and sauce tureens appeared from around 1760.

Turin pottery and porcelain factories
There were several MAIOLICA factories in Turin whose typical products were pierced baskets of BIANCO DI FAENZA, made in the 1570s. The first factory, founded before 1562, employed painters from URBINO. The Regio Parco factory, established in 1646, was notable in the 17th century for blue and white wares similar to those of SAVONA. A factory founded in 1725 by Giorgio Rossetti di Macello and his two nephews peaked in the 1750s. It made good French FAIENCE wares painted in HIGH-TEMPERATURE COLORS with ROCOCO subjects. Similar wares were also made in the factory of Giovanni Antonio Ardizzone from around 1765 to 1771. Rossetti experimented with porcelain-making from 1757 but very few examples are known. Two busts are in the Museo Civico in Turin. In 1824 his factory was bought by Jacques-François Richard and Frédéric-Louis Dortu. It made porcelain printed with landscapes until it closed in 1878.

Turkey work ■ A type of needlework, fashionable in England in the late 16th century, simulating the pile rugs imported from the Middle East. It was made by pulling heavy wool through canvas or coarse linen, knotting it, and cutting the ends to form a pile. Rare carpets were used as tablecovers in the same way as Oriental rugs of the same period. Turkey work was also used for cushions, bed hangings, and upholstery.

Graduated annular knops

Tulipwood
French tulipwood jewelry box, with watercolor on lid and two drawers.

Tumbler
Plain glass tumbler of gently tapered form. c. 1750.

Tunbridgeware
Occasional table, with octagonal tilt top inlaid with perspective cubes.

Turkish carpets ■ With its beginnings in the 16th century, an industry emerged producing carpets on a large scale, mainly to meet Western demand and a growing export market. Carpets woven in Turkish towns are similar to Persian carpets, using floral curvilinear designs in a formal format. Wool, as opposed to cotton, is often used for the foundation. Ghiordes was one of the main towns in the 19th century, making prayer rugs with patterns recreated from earlier Classical designs. Ladik and Konya were also important centers for prayer rugs. Extremely fine carpets were made in Hereke and in the Armenian quarter of Istanbul, known as Kum Kapi, from the end of the 19th century and into the second quarter of the 20th. Designs were inspired by the Ottoman court style and the Classical 16th-century Persian rugs of the Safavid period (1501–1732). Many such pieces were signed by master weavers such as Zareh Penyamian, Hagop Kapoudjian, and Toussonian. These rugs are mostly small and are woven in fine silk. Some include metal-thread brocading. The PRAYER RUG format is frequently seen.

Large decorative carpets were produced on a huge scale toward the end of the 19th century, particularly at USHAK. Carpets from here and other towns were often made to order by stores such as LIBERTY & Co. in London. Some are extremely fine and compare favorably with their Persian counterparts; others can be extremely coarse and loosely woven. Color combinations range from monochromatic to brightly colored. Products of village-based or cooperative rug-making are similar to CAUCASIAN and some Persian rugs in design inspiration, construction, and tradition. Geometric design elements are predominant, woven on a woolen foundation and made with the TURKISH knot. The medallions or GULS are similar to those found in TURKOMAN rugs. Influence of the earlier Classical pieces is seen in rugs that display Holbein medallions. Production by nomadic groups is virtually nonexistent; only the Yoruk and the Kurds weave while on migration. Rugs woven by these two groups share similarities with their Caucasian neighbors and use strong colors and bold geometric designs. Human forms are not seen in either village or nomadic carpets.

Turkish knot Also known as Ghiordes knot, a type of symmetrical knot used for making the pile in handmade rugs, named after Ghiordes, an Anatolian town. It was used throughout Turkey, Persia, the Caucasus, and Europe and was well suited to creating geometric patterns.

Turkish style ■ From the 16th century, Turkish architecture and art inspired a style of decorative arts and interior design throughout Europe. The Turkish style reflects Western fascination with exotic motifs and decoration and was later combined with CHINOISERIE and the ARABIAN STYLE.

The influence of Turkish art was a result of the proximity of the Ottoman Empire (which at its height in the 16th century extended from Hungary to Egypt to Western Europe) as well as the introduction in the 16th century of imported TURKISH CARPETS. These were highly prized and feature in many TUDOR portraits. European carpet-makers adapted the predominantly geometric motifs of the carpets for use in their own work, while TURKEY WORK was popular until the late 17th century. In the 18th and early 19th centuries, publications such as Charles de Ferriol's *Les Differents Nations du Levant* (1714) stimulated growing interest in Ottoman art. A fashion for entire rooms decorated in the Turkish style, with richly tasseled and fringed upholstery and ornament such as crescents, stars, and stylized flowers, became popular among royalty and aristocracy, especially in France. Similarly, the growth of smoking in the mid-19th century led to the development of smoking rooms furnished with divans and OTTOMANS, upholstered in richly figured and colored materials. Some artists attempted to produce wares based more closely on Turkish originals, in particular William DE MORGAN, who in the late 19th century designed tiles with intertwined floral patterns, long serrated leaves, and rich coloring of blue, turquoise, red, green, and purple, adapted from IZNIK POTTERY.

Turkoman carpets A collective term for the carpets woven by the tribes of West Turkestan, an area

T

383

Tureen
Nanking cargo "Lattice Fence" tureen, with finely crafted pomegranate finial. c. 1750.

Turkey work
Victorian carpet chair, by John Taylor & Sons Edinburgh, with Turkey carpet panels.

Turkish carpets
Carpet from the Konya area of Turkey. Late 18th century.

Turkish style
Very rare Bohemian overlay bottle for the Turkish or Islamic market. c. 1860–85.

T

bordered by Iran, Afghanistan, and China. The best-known tribes are the Tekke, Yomut, Salor, Ersari, Beshir, Saryk, and Baluch. Most products date from the 18th century or later and as a group are relatively easy to recognize. They have a limited color palette. Red is used as a background in shades ranging from bright terra-cotta to burgundy, brown, and eggplant. The geometric patterns are defined in shades of white, brown, blue, yellow, crimson, and green. The GUL motif is a distinguishing feature. By the end of the 19th century, colors were less harmonic and designs more stereotyped.

Turner & Co.
A STAFFORDSHIRE POTTERY started by John Turner, who was apprenticed to Thomas WHIELDON. Turner set up on his own in 1755, making JASPER WARE, CREAMWARE, and BASALT WARE. He exported to Holland and France, but his sons, John and William, suffered ruinous losses in 1806 because of the repercussions of the French Revolution.

Turning ■
A technique for shaping legs, spindles, and other members of pieces of furniture (and staircase components such as balusters) in the round that allows similar pieces to be cut in a variety of decorative shapes—for example, BARLEY SUGAR TWISTS or BALUSTER. If the piece of wood is turned on a face-plate, hollow items

such as bowls and small boxes with or without lids such as TREEN can be made. Pole lathes, in which the power was supplied by the spring action of a whippy pole, and treadle lathes have been widely used since the Middle Ages, especially by country chair bodgers who worked on green wood. As these pieces dry, they often distort to an oval rather than a round section.

In various Eastern and North African countries, craftsmen still use lathes powered by their feet while they sit on the ground. ISLAMIC woodwork includes great quantities of elaborate turnings. Treadle lathes were superseded by electric-powered lathes at the end of the 19th century and now computer-controlled lathes enable turners to produce unlimited runs of identical pieces.

Turquoise ■
An opaque, waxy gemstone that varies in color from sky blue to pale green. Turquoise has been used in jewelry and ornament since ancient times. The finest turquoise is found in Iran; other sites include New Mexico, the Sinai Peninsula, and Egypt. Turquoise was used extensively in 19th-century jewelry such as sentimental rings and lockets, where it represented forget-me-nots, or gold serpent necklaces studded with turquoise CABOCHONS.

Turret clock
A type of weight-driven wall clock, developed from the earliest medieval mechanical clocks, usually made of iron and named from its position on the tower of a church or other public building.

Twist stem ■
A type of drinking glass stem made by twisting glass RODS or CANES embedded with bubbles of air, threads of opaque or colored glass, or a combination of these. Introduced around 1735, the twist stem was popular until around 1775.

Tyg
A large earthenware mug with three or more handles dividing the rim into sections for several drinkers. A favorite drinking vessel in the 16th and 17th centuries, it is known in both SLIPWARE and LEAD-GLAZED examples. Tygs were made in large quantities at WROTHAM in Kent and in many STAFFORDSHIRE POTTERIES.

Tyneside potteries ■
The earliest EARTHENWARE factory on the Tyne River, near Newcastle, was founded by John Warburton around 1730, making BROWN WARE until 1750 when he moved to Gateshead. By 1827 there were around 20 factories producing household wares in blue-printed earthenware, LUSTERWARE, CREAMWARE, and MOCHA. In the early 19th century, C. T. Maling moved his factory to Tyneside from Sunderland, where the Maling factory was established around 1762. Maling was very successful and produced enormous quantities of earthenware, including pink-splashed luster until the factory closed in 1963. Other factories include Richard Davis, which made tiles in the 1830s, and Thomas Fell & Co., active from 1817 to 1890.

Turning
Canadian Louis XV birch armchair, with slats flanked by block and urn turned stiles over seat.

— Turned stiles

Turquoise
Early Victorian serpent brooch, with graduated turquoise cabochons and garnet eyes.

Twist stem
Wine glass, with drawn trumpet bowl and double-series opaque twist stem. c. 1765.

Tyneside potteries
Pratt-type cow creamer, Newcastle-Upon-Tyne. c. 1810.

U

Unaker The Cherokee name for a form of KAOLIN from colonial Virginia and used for the earliest COLONIAL porcelain in the 17th century, of which very little survives. It was also imported to England for early English porcelain made at BOW.

Uncirculated The term used to describe paper money (bills) and coins that have not been in public circulation, which leads to wear and damage. As such, they are in the same condition as when they left the mint, hence the term "mint condition."

Undercut A type of carving on wood that hollows out or cuts away the wood. The technique, perfected on furniture in the 17th and 18th centuries by carvers such as Grinling GIBBONS, was used on mirrors and other furniture to give a light, refined impression.

Underglaze Decoration painted onto a BISCUIT body. As the colors have to withstand the full heat of the kiln, the palette is restricted. Cobalt blue is the main color, although chrome, nickel, and iron oxides can also be used. After the decoration has been put onto the body, it is glazed and then fired again. The Chinese used copper oxide to produce a red color, but it was not discovered in Europe until the end of the 18th century. See HIGH-TEMPERATURE COLORS.

Union Glass Company A large American glassworks that began as a factory founded in Somerville, Massachusetts, in 1851 by Amory and Francis Houghton. After they left in 1864, the factory became the Union Glass Company under Thomas Dana, specializing in clear CUT, PRESSED, and blown glass until its closure in 1924. Although tableware and functional items such as kerosene lamps formed the main body of its production, it is best known for its KEW BLAS range.

Union Porcelain Works ■ A large American porcelain factory founded in 1861 by Thomas Carll Smith (1815–1901) in Brooklyn, New York, on the site of an earlier works operated by William Boch & Brothers, and close to the rival works of Charles Cartlidge (1848–56). Much of the porcelain was of a Continental hard-paste type with a German feel to the decoration. Union produced inexpensive robust ware, including door plates and knobs, but is best known for the Century commemorative vases made for the CENTENNIAL Exposition in 1876, a range of innovative and whimsical ware modeled by Karl L. H. Müller (1820–87), and oyster plates. Some pieces are marked "U.P.W." The factory closed in the 1920s.

United States Pottery Co. See BENNINGTON POTTERY.

URANIUM GLASS

The yellow- or green-tinted Uranium glass is made by adding uranium oxide to the batch, which causes the glass to fluoresce under ultraviolet light. It was first made in the 1830s by Josef Riedel (active 1830–48) in Bohemia, who developed Annagrün (greenish yellow) and Annagelb (yellowish green) glass, named after his wife. It was subsequently made by other glassworks, including some in STOURBRIDGE. Uranium was used in the 19th century for making VASELINE GLASS. Uranium glass was later found to be mildly radioactive and the process was abandoned. See also BOHEMIAN and PEACHBLOW glass.

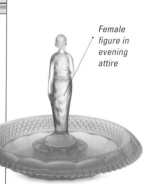

Centerpiece
Czech pressed Uranium glass centerpiece.

Female figure in evening attire

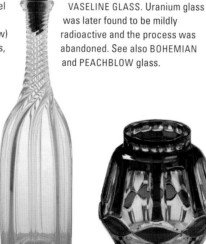

Decanter
English Arts and Crafts Uranium glass decanter. c. 1920.

Vase
Val St Lambert vase, cased in amethyst over pale straw-colored Uranium glass. 1930s.

Stepped conical cover

Union Porcelain Works
Large urn in polychrome enamels.

U

Upholstery This term has specifically come to mean the covering and padding of seat furniture, but originally referred to all textile decoration and furnishings in a room. By around 1600 some chairs began to be upholstered in the more modern sense. Padded furniture was often commissioned from saddlers. In the late 16th century, craftsmen known as "upholsterers" were employed in large households as decorators. Independent upholsterers soon appeared in cities and large towns. By the 18th century most seat furniture was upholstered (CHIPPENDALE gives guidelines in his *The Gentleman and Cabinet-maker's Director*). Upholstery with springs was introduced in the early 19th century; patents for them were obtained in Vienna by Georg Junigl in 1822 and in London by Samuel Pratt in 1825. BUTTONING, a characteristic of Victorian furniture, was also introduced in the early 19th century.

Urban, Joseph An Austrian architect and furniture designer, trained in Vienna and active in the US as a theatrical set designer from 1911. He founded and ran the short-lived New York WIENER WERKSTÄTTE showrooms from 1922 to 1924. His architecture, including the New School building on West 12th Street, Manhattan, shows distinctive modern Viennese roots. His luxury furniture is considered among the best examples in the American ART DECO style.

Urbino potteries ◼ An important group of Italian MAIOLICA potteries from 1477, patronized by the Dukes of Urbino. Known 16th-century potters include Guido Durantino, Francesco Xanto Avelli, the Patanazzi family, and Nicola da Urbino. From the 1520s Urbino specialized in ISTORIATO ware painted in blues, yellows, and oranges. Also typical are Belle Donne dishes, from around 1520, depicting the heads of women. From the 1560s, GROTESQUE decoration, following the style of the Italian painter Raphael, was used. In the 18th century, maiolica was made on a smaller scale in Urbino, as other pottery centers in Europe had become more important.

Urn stand ◼ A small table for a tea kettle and burner, often with a pull-out teapot stand, made from around 1720 to 1780.

Ushak ◼ A Turkish weaving center, known for 16th- and 17th-century (see OTTOMAN) and late 19th-century (see TURKISH) carpets. The best examples have soft color palettes; the worst are harsh and abrasive.

Utility ◼ A British government program introduced in 1941 in an attempt to ration resources during World War II. Initially applied to clothing, it was gradually imposed on all decorative arts. For example, ceramic manufacturers were compelled to restrict production to simple tableware in plain white or cream, while furniture manufacturers were limited to just 20 standardized, functional, albeit well-detailed, designs that were conceived by a committee of top designers overseen by Gordon Russell. The program wound down in 1953, but the surviving pieces have acquired a certain utilitarian chic for many present-day collectors.

Urbino potteries
Patanazzi studio Urbino platter, painted with a religious scene. c. 1580.

Urn stand
Satinwood checker-banded and ebony-strung urn stand.

Ushak
Large Ushak carpet, with large salmon pink palmettes on a turquoise field.

Designed by Eric Olsen

Utility
Copeland Spode Utility plain white Winston Churchill Toby jug. c. 1942.

V

Valadier, Luigi (1726–85) An Italian bronze-founder and official silversmith to Pope Pius VI from the late 1770s. He produced a variety of ecclesiastical and domestic silver, particularly ornate ÉPERGNES with representations of Classical sculpture and architecture. He also made NEOCLASSICAL BRONZE MOUNTS for furniture and CAMEOS. His mark was "LV" with three FLEURS-DE-LIS. He was succeeded by his son, Guiseppe.

Valencia potteries A Spanish center for LUSTERWARE. Before 1400, it was based in MALAGA. The finest 15th-century lusterware is thought to have been made in the Valencia suburb of Manises. No marked pieces are known, and as designs remained unchanged throughout the 15th century, chronology and origin are difficult to ascertain. The finest examples are dishes (16–20 in/40–50 cm diameter) made for the aristocracies of France, Italy, and Spain, decorated with coats of arms and prancing beasts on a ground of foliage or DIAPER in rich golden luster with touches of blue. ALBARELLI and jugs were also made and are seen in paintings of the time—for example, a Hugo van der Goes painting in the Uffizi Gallery, Florence, shows a lustered albarello. Tiles were also made in large quantities with heraldry, arabesques, and inscriptions in Arabic or Gothic script. The wares continued to be made at Valencia, but by the 16th century, it was beginning to lose to Italy, which had started making its own MAIOLICA. In the 17th and 18th centuries the quality of the painting declined. Later wares have a harsh, burnished copper tone, while early wares show a soft gold to rich reddish purple luster. Potteries still produce wares at Valencia today.

Valenciennes A French or Belgian BOBBIN LACE center that made very fine straightlace, typically with no cordonner (raised outline threads) and complex patterns. In the early 18th century, it was densely patterned with flowers, snowflakes, and OEIL DE PERDRIX, and was used for high fashion LAPPETS and ruffles. Later, the pattern had a braided round mesh ground. In the 19th century it was sparsely patterned with a diamond mesh.

Valentine card ■ Commercial examples first appeared in the early 19th century and derived from the centuries-old custom of sending love verses. By the middle of the 19th century, improvements in the manufacture of paper as well as the development of chrimolithography resulted in highly decorative cards, often made of embossed and diecut paper, satin, and lace. They were hugely popular, had great sentimental value, and were widely collected in Britain and the US.

Val Saint Lambert, Cristallerie de ■ Belgium's most important glasshouse, founded just outside Liège in 1825 by Francois Kemlin and Auguste Lelievre. It is best known for its strongly colored CUT GLASS in the ART NOUVEAU and MODERNIST styles. It also made some paperweights. Léon Ledru was the chief designer from 1886 to 1926, followed by Joseph Simon, and then Charles Graffart (from 1929). The firm also collaborated with designers such as Samuel HERMAN. It exhibited at the Paris Exhibition in 1925 and the Milan Triennale in 1957, winning prizes at both.

Van Briggle, Artus ■ (1869–1904) An American ART POTTER, active as a decorator at the ROOKWOOD POTTERY, but best known as the founder of a pottery in Colorado Springs in 1899, where he made a range of ART NOUVEAU, matt-glazed vessels. His widow sold the factory in 1912, but it is still in operation, making copies of his original wares.

Van Cleef & Arpels ■ A French firm of jewelry designers and manufacturers founded in 1906 by the brothers Alfred

Valentine card
Late-19th-century valentine card.

Val Saint Lambert
Vase on a pedestal in straw-colored glass cased in amber. 1930s.

Van Briggle, Artus
Vase embossed with cornflowers under a superior burgundy and blue-green glaze. 1903.

Van Cleef & Arpels
Unique triple rope-twist necklace, with gem-set center. c. 1950s.

and Charles Van Cleef, the former being married to Estelle Arpels. It produced elegant and colorful diamond and gem-set jewels from the 1920s to the 1940s, including innovative calibré-cut (cut to fit a particular shape) sapphire and ruby flower studies with no apparent setting between the stones, described as "invisible setting." Many pieces were designed by René Lacaze as well as members of the founders' family. The company opened in the Rockefeller Center in Manhattan in 1939, and still produces fine jewelry today.

Van de Velde, Henry ■ (1863–1957) A Belgian architect and ART NOUVEAU designer, with ideals midway between ARTS AND CRAFTS craftsmanship and the industrial severity of the MODERN MOVEMENT. Originally a painter, he turned to the decorative arts and architecture around 1893, influenced by the writings of William MORRIS. In 1894 he designed his own house, "Bloemenwerf," near Brussels, creating all the furniture, fixtures, silver, and cutlery in an undecorated, elegant style, influenced by C. F. A. VOYSEY. His 1896 interior design for Samuel BING'S Paris shop La Maison de l'Art Nouveau brought him recognition throughout Europe. In 1908 he became Director of the School of Arts and Crafts at Weimar, the precursor of Walter GROPIUS'S BAUHAUS in 1919. Van de Velde's furniture is sculptural with little applied decoration; chairs have slender SPLATS, outcurving legs, and studded UPHOLSTERY.

Van Doren, Harold (1895–1957) An American industrial designer active from the late 1920s. Along with Raymond LOEWY and Norman BEL GEDDES, his designs were concerned with STREAMLINING, identifying the function of an item, representing it aesthetically, and creating an overall attractive product. He was a pioneer of plastics and in 1940 he published *Streamlining in Industrial Design*. Two examples of his designs are the Skyscraper Air King radio and the Ensign Ful-Vue camera.

Van Erp, Dirk ■ (1860–1933) A Dutch-born ARTS AND CRAFTS metalworker, active in the US from 1886. From 1908 he worked in Oakland, near San Francisco, California, where he founded his Copper Shop. He worked in the Dutch medieval style, specializing in hammered copper with exposed riveting. Typical products included vases, writing-table equipment, and table lamps with conical shades of mica panels, which are highly prized today. His son, William, carried on his studio until 1944. Modern reproductions are now common.

Vandyke rim A decorative scalloped rim used on glass and ceramics (often on MONTEITHS) and named after the scalloped lace collars depicted in portraits by Anthony van Dyck.

Vargueño ■ A type of Spanish drop-front writing cabinet (also called

barqueño) that rests on a chest or a trestle stand. The interior was often elaborately carved, painted red and gold, or decorated with TORTOISESHELL, IVORY, EBONY, or other INLAYS in a variety of intricate geometric patterns. The vargueño was popular throughout the 16th and 17th centuries.

Varnish A wood-finishing material, consisting of gum dissolved in linseed oil, which is applied in layers by brush or spray to protect and enhance the appearance of wood surfaces. The technique of varnishing, which had been known in ancient times, was lost during the medieval period and was replaced by oil and wax that could be absorbed into the wood. Although no reliable records exist to indicate that varnish was made again before the mid-19th century, in some form it was probably the basis of VERNIS MARTIN. Early varnishes had a sticky, glazed appearance, but improved quality today produces a fine, satiny gloss.

Vasart See YSART; SALVADOR & SONS.

Vaseline glass ■ A type of OPALESCENT, yellowish green glass with a "oily" appearance, hence the name. No maker ever called it "Vaseline glass," using names such as CANARY GLASS or yellow glass instead. It is made by adding uranium oxide to the BATCH, which causes it to fluoresce under ultraviolet light. It was first made by the

Van de Velde, Henry
Lady's writing table, designed by Henry Van de Velde. 1903.

Van Erp, Dirk
Hammered copper vessel, with rolled rim covered in a fine, original dark patina.

Vargueño
Spanish Baroque-style inlaid walnut vargueño-on-stand. 19th century.

Vaseline glass
Powell Vaseline vase. 1904.

Romans and Chinese, but reached the height of its popularity from the 1850s to the 1890s. Vaseline glass was produced up until the 1930s. Manufacturers included James Powell at WHITEFRIARS and Lloyd & Summerfield in the UK and BOSTON SANDWICH COMPANY and Gillinder & Sons in the US. Blue, yellow, green, and the very rare red Vaseline glass were made by adding tiny quantities of uranium and metal oxides to the batch. When it was reheated in the furnace, the clear glass turned opaque and milky.

Vauxhall glasshouses A group of English glasshouses active in Vauxhall, London, from the mid-17th century until the end of the 18th century. The first firmly documented Vauxhall glasshouse was founded by the Duke of Buckingham around 1663, which produced MIRROR glass.

Vauxhall Porcelain Factory ■ An early English porcelain factory founded at Vauxhall, London, in 1752 by Nicholas Crisp, a jeweler and one of the founders of the Society of Arts. It was not recognized officially until 1988, when the Museum of London excavated the site. In 1753 Crisp joined John Sanders, a Lambeth DELFTWARE potter, and together they advertised "Porcelain Ware made of English materials" (they used a soap-rock formula similar to that used by WORCESTER) for sale in Vauxhall. They made blue and white wares that were influenced by CHINESE EXPORT PORCELAIN. Some polychrome

examples with CHINOISERIE decoration are known, but these are very rare. The factory closed in 1763.

Vechte, Antoine (1800–68) A French artist-craftsman who was exceptionally talented and skilled at REPOUSSÉ WORK, producing highly complex silver designs in very high relief in the MANNERIST and Classical styles. Originally working in Paris, Vechte left France to work in London for Hunt & Roskell, and the firm received a medal at the GREAT EXHIBITION of 1851 for work executed by him. He was also commissioned to produce silverware for Queen Victoria. Vechte taught many pupils, some of whom went on to become great silversmiths in their own right, such as L. Morel-Ladeuil (see ELKINGTON).

Veilleuse ■ A receptacle designed to keep food or drink warm on a bedside table. It consists of a hollow cylindrical stand with pierced vents surmounted by either a covered food bowl or a small teapot. The heat source is oil burned by means of a floating wick located in a tiny bowl at the bottom of the stand. Known in POTTERY and PORCELAIN, WEDGWOOD and CREAMWARE, the veilleuse was popular in the 18th and early 19th centuries, especially in Paris.

Veneer ■ A thin layer of fine wood, IVORY, or TORTOISESHELL applied to the surface of a furniture CARCASS that was made of a coarser, cheaper wood. Widely used from the second half of the

17th century, the technique of veneering was used to decorate all kinds of furniture in a wide range of imaginative designs. Originally, veneers were cut by hand, but machine-cutting has been employed since the early 19th century.

Venetian glass ■ Glass made in Venice and the neighboring island of MURANO. Although glass had been made in Venice from the 5th century CE, the industry really began to develop in the 13th century with the establishment of a glassmakers' guild. This was followed by an ordinance in 1292 that prohibited Venetian glassmakers from divulging their trade secrets and relocated most glasshouses to the island of Murano to protect Venice from the fire risk posed by the furnaces. In the 15th century, the sack of Damascus led to an influx of skilled Syrian glassmakers. By midcentury the development of CRISTALLO glass, new and revived techniques such as GILDING, ENAMELING, TRAILING, and thread decoration (see FILIGRANA, LATTICINO), and the use of AGATE, IRIDESCENT, and ICE GLASS had made Venice the world's leading glassmaking center.

Despite their guild restrictions, many Venetian glassmakers traveled widely in the 16th and 17th centuries, and as a result,

V
389

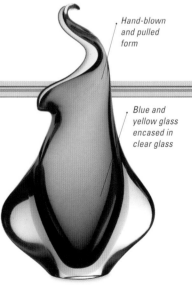
Hand-blown and pulled form

Blue and yellow glass encased in clear glass

Vauxhall Porcelain Factory
Vauxhall saucer, painted in the Imari palette. c. 1760.

Veilleuse
English creamware veilleuse. c. 1800.

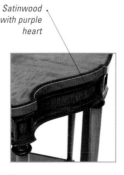
Satinwood with purple heart
Veneer
Satinwood veneer on a George III English side table. c. 1790.

Venetian glass
Triple-cased "Sommerso" free-form Venetian glass vase. 1950s–60s.

V

FAÇON DE VENISE ("Venetian-style") glassware was made throughout Europe in forms such as the TAZZA, serpent-stemmed drinking glasses, and covered goblets. In the 18th and 19th centuries, Venetian glassware was overshadowed by the new LEAD glass, but its fortunes revived in the 20th century through the efforts of leading companies such as SALVIATI & Co. and designers and makers such as Paolo VENINI, who revived and introduced forms, color, and decoration—much as the early Venetian glassmakers had done—and did much to reestablish the reputation of Venetian glass.

Venetian needlelace The name given to various types of NEEDLELACE made in Venice from the 17th century. The most flamboyant of these is GROS POINT, which has large flower and foliage motifs linked by rows of buttonhole stitching, decorated with padding and raised picots on bars. POINT DE NEIGE, made between 1650 and 1700, is the most intricately worked of all laces and is also the rarest and most sought-after. Other types of Venetian needlelace include *point de rose*, a fine 17th-century lace that was revived in the 19th century, and *point de Venise à réseau*, a flat, mesh-based lace that was made in the 18th century.

Venice porcelain Venice was a center of porcelain-making from the 18th century. Important factories included VEZZI, COZZI, Le NOVE, ESTE, and Trevison.

Porcelain was also made by Nathanial and Maria Dorothea Hewelcke, who came to Udine (then in Venetian territory) from MEISSEN. In 1757 they petitioned for a monopoly for making porcelain, which was granted in 1758. They worked at Udine from 1758 to 1761 and in Venice from 1761 to 1763. The Cozzi factory was the last to produce porcelain around 1812.

Venice pottery MAIOLICA was made in Venice from around 1515. Early wares were inspired by imported Chinese blue and white porcelain and use a tin glaze stained with cobalt to a pale lavender gray decorated in dark blue or opaque white. This unique glaze, known as *berettino*, distinguishes Venetian pottery from other Italian pottery of the time. From around 1540, there were many workshops producing maiolica in various styles, including ARMORIAL WARES and ISTORIATO pieces. Important workshops included those of Maestro Lodovico at San Polo, Iacomo da Pesaro at San Barnabas, Domenigo da Venezia, and the Bertolini and Manardi brothers. In the 17th and early 18th centuries wares decorated with Classical PUTTI and Roman ruins were produced.

Venini, Paolo (1895–1959) ■ A Venetian lawyer turned glassmaker who became a partner in a Venetian glassworks in 1921, known from around 1925 as Venini & Co. This became the leading post-war Italian glassworks,

producing decorative colored glassware that was usually signed. It revived many traditional Venetian techniques, and Venini, together with other leading designers, such as Gio PONTI and Fulvio BIANCONI, developed new forms and decoration in glassware, including the handkerchief vase. Examples include the PEZZATO technique and the FAZZOLETTO form. From 1959 the firm was run by Venini's widow and son-in-law, but in 1985 it was sold to the Ferruzzi and Gardini families. Since 1988 it has traded as Venini s.p.a.

Verdigris An Old French term for "green of Greece." The greenish, powdery deposit (copper carbonate) that forms naturally on the surface of copper or brass articles when exposed to moisture. It can be removed by polishing. Verdigris is also produced artificially and used as a pigment.

Verge escapement A type of ESCAPEMENT used in most clocks until the invention of the more accurate ANCHOR ESCAPEMENT in the 1670s. It was first drawn up by Giovanni da Dondi, a Paduan professor, in 1364. It comprises a toothed wheel and a verge (shaft), with two pallets released in turn by a foliot (large horizontal bar) or a balance (wheel).

Vermeil The French word used to describe silver that has a thin outer layer of gold. It is produced in two ways: by fire-gilding or electroplating. In fire-gilding a mixture of gold and mercury is first applied to the

Venini, Paolo
Venini *fasce orrizontali* decanter and two glasses, by Fulvio Bianconi.

Vernis Martin
Louis XVI-style D-shaped mahogany vitrine, with *vernis Martin* painted panels.

Verre églomisé
Needlework picture of a native American, with a *verre églomisé* frame. c.1800.

Vesta case
Silver vesta case, with shield design and hallmarks for Birmingham. 1909.

silver body. The piece is then heated so that the mercury evaporates, leaving behind the gold. Electroplating uses electricity to cause gold ions in a solution to deposit over the silver body. See SILVER GILT.

Vermiculé From the Latin *vermis* (worm). A type of decoration, usually gilding, that is wavy and sinuous and reminiscent of worm tracks. It is often seen on the gilding of SÈVRES porcelain.

Vernier scale Invented by Pierre Vernier in 1631, a graduated scale of units with an auxiliary sliding scale, allowing further subdivision of the reading from the principal scale to the tenths and then to the hundredths. It was used to show minute sections of an arc on navigational instruments such as a SEXTANT, or on a bar beside the mercury tube on a BAROMETER.

Vernis Martin ■ A generic name for an 18th-century French JAPANNING method for wood. Named after Guillaume Martin and his brothers—but covering similar work by other craftsmen—this varnishing technique was invented during the reign of Louis XIV (1643–1715). Although less durable than the Oriental LACQUERING that inspired it, the attractive brilliance and depth of *vernis Martin* made it highly fashionable during the 18th and 19th centuries for indoor paneling, furniture, small boxes, and even carriages.

Verre de fougere The French term for "fern glass" or "bracken glass." An early type of glass, popular during the 14th century, in which potash from burned bracken or ferns was used as the alkali FLUX. The French equivalent of WALDGLAS, it shares the same green, brown, or yellow color and was used for simple forms, occasionally with shallow cut decoration.

Verre églomisé ■ A type of glass decorated with a layer of gold or silver leaf on the reverse. A design is cut or engraved into the leaf, sometimes accompanied by REVERSE PAINTING, and covered with a protective layer of varnish or glass. The technique dates from the 13th century, but is named after a Parisian frame-maker, Jean-Baptist Glomy, who employed it in the 18th century.

Vesta case ■ A small, portable box made in a great variety of forms with snap-shut covers to contain vestas (short matches) and keep them dry. Produced extensively from around 1890 to 1920, they coincided with an explosion in the popularity of smoking. Most were made of inexpensive materials but some were produced in precious metals or were enameled. They often have a rough or serrated panel for striking the matches.

Vezzi Porcelain Factory The Venetian goldsmiths Francesco and Giuseppe Vezzi, helped perhaps by C. C. Hunger from MEISSEN, first made porcelain around 1720 with KAOLIN smuggled from Aue in Germany. Hunger returned to Meissen in 1725. Vezzi made translucent HARD-PASTE PORCELAIN with a clear, wet-looking glaze, often using silver shapes, until 1727. Decoration included CHINOISERIES and coats of arms. Some wares have BLANC-DE-CHINE-style

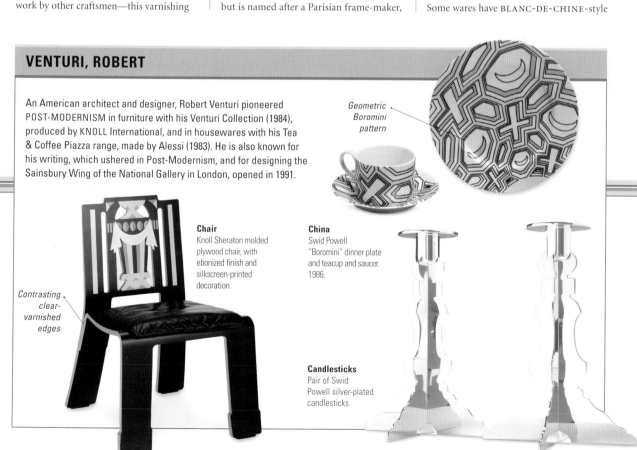

VENTURI, ROBERT

An American architect and designer, Robert Venturi pioneered POST-MODERNISM in furniture with his Venturi Collection (1984), produced by KNOLL International, and in housewares with his Tea & Coffee Piazza range, made by Alessi (1983). He is also known for his writing, which ushered in Post-Modernism, and for designing the Sainsbury Wing of the National Gallery in London, opened in 1991.

Geometric Boromini pattern

Chair
Knoll Sheraton molded plywood chair, with ebonized finish and silkscreen-printed decoration.

Contrasting clear-varnished edges

China
Swid Powell "Boromini" dinner plate and teacup and saucer. 1986.

Candlesticks
Pair of Swid Powell silver-plated candlesticks.

V

Prunus blossoms. A distinctive Venetian shape is a gondola lamp with Bérainesque designs.

Victorian style ■ The term Victorian style describes the characteristics of architecture and the decorative arts during the reign of Queen Victoria (1837–1901) in Great Britain. It is sometimes used more broadly to refer to similar trends in 19th-century European and American decorative arts and the revival of NEOCLASSICISM in the reign of Edward VII (1901–10). The quest for novelty was an important factor in the development of fresh decorative styles, many of them revivals.

As a result of the Industrial Revolution, this era was dominated by the growth of industrialization and MASS PRODUCTION for the increasingly prosperous middle classes. Technology advanced rapidly in the Victorian period. A wide range of oil, gas, and eventually electric lighting was produced, and unusual materials such as molded PAPIER-MÂCHÉ and glass were used for furniture. This Victorian mastery of technology, combined with the expansion of international trade, encouraged the development of international exhibitions. The first and most important of these was the GREAT EXHIBITION of 1851.

Vienna porcelain ■ Viennese porcelain was produced by a number of enterprises, many of which used the Bindenschild mark taken from the arms of the ruling Hapsburgs, although it should only rightfully have been used by the first

Austrian porcelain factory, founded in 1718 by Claudius du Paquier. Du Paquier had tried to make porcelain in 1716 but had failed. In 1717 he lured Christoph Conrad Hunger, an enameler and gilder, from MEISSEN. In 1719 Samuel Stolzel, another defector from Meissen, joined him. They produced porcelain similar to that of BÖTTGER in Meissen. Stolzel and Hunger soon left and du Paquier continued on his own until 1744, when he sold the factory to the state, staying on as Director for a year.

Under state ownership from 1744 to 1784, the factory showed the influence of BAROQUE, and later, that of Sèvres. In 1784, due to financial difficulties, the directorship was transferred to Konrad Sorgenthal, a textile manufacturer who brought a flurry of success with pieces in the NEOCLASSICAL style. However, by 1820 the factory was beginning to decline, and in 1864 the emperor closed the factory. Molds from the factory were sold in 1900 to the enterprising retailer Ernst Wahliss and to HEREND in Hungary. Augarten was founded in 1922 to carry on the tradition of the state-owned factory. It used the shield mark of the original factory with various additions. The Bock factory, founded in 1828, made table, coffee, and tea services until 1933. From around 1880 to 1930, Franz Dorfl ran a studio where he decorated porcelain. In 1885 the GOLDSCHEIDER Porcelain Works and Majolica Factory was founded. It made metallized TERRA-COTTA in the ART NOUVEAU style. The factory closed in

1953. Other factories and decorating studios used forms of the Vienna banded shield mark, taken from Hapsburg armorial bearings. See Michael POWOLNY.

Vienna regulator A type of REGULATOR produced in Austria during the first half of the 19th century. Generally weight-driven, it is either of the LONGCASE or wall-mounted type, with a wooden case, glass panels on the front and sides, and a pediment at the top. The MOVEMENT is finely made with a compensated PENDULUM. In the late 19th century, poor imitations were produced in the US and in the BLACK FOREST region of Germany.

Vienna Secession ■ An alliance of artists, designers, and architects who broke away from the Viennese Society of Visual Artists in 1897. Josef HOFFMANN was a founder of the alliance. Members included Otto Wagner and Gustav Klimt. They favored Symbolism and the ART NOUVEAU style.

Vietnamese pottery and porcelain ■ Wares made at Annam, modern-day Vietnam, usually referred to as Annamese ware. For over 1,000 years (3rd century BCE to the 10th century CE), Annam's major cultural influence was China. Excavations in north Vietnam have uncovered pottery contemporary with China's Han and SONG

Scrolled plant-form handle

Vienna porcelain
Circular plaque, painted with central roundel "Der Gebrochene Krug."

Vienna porcelain
Vienna porcelain cup and saucer from the Sorgenthal period. 1800.

Vienna secession
Minton Secessionist twin-handled, tube-lined vase.

Vietnamese porcelain
Annamese blue and white ewer, with openwork panels. Early 16th century.

VICTORIAN STYLE

There was no one definable Victorian style; instead, a general fascination with a range of historical styles and exotic motifs derived from INDIAN, Chinese, Japanese, PERSIAN, TURKISH, and ISLAMIC art, among others, combined extremely realistic depictions of nature that were fashionable at the time. A greater emphasis on comfort and the display of wealth, required by the newly affluent industrialists and entrepreneurs, resulted in heavier, more curvaceous, and richly upholstered, braided, and tasseled furniture, together with a liberal sprinkling of ornament.

Porcelain vase
English Rococo Revival porcelain vase, encrusted all over with relief flowers and foliage.

V
___
393

Serpentine and scrolled gilt apron

Centerpiece
German silver centerpiece, the circular foot framed by vines and the stem with vines and a cherub. c. 1875.

Tripod table
Painted papier-mâché tripod table, with mother-of-pearl. c. 1860.

Ram's head
Scottish mounted ram's head table snuff mull. 1894.

Screen
Four-fold rosewood screen, each fold with pierced strapwork cresting and panels of needlework and tapestry.

Tureen
Staffordshire soup tureen and "Cambridge College, Massachusetts" cover.

Vase
Unsigned Webb red and white cased cameo vase.

V

DYNASTIES, variously decorated with SLIP, CELADON, or brown glazes. The finest Annamese wares date from the 12th to the 15th century and closely follow the Chinese YUAN and MING originals. Annamese wares have a coarse, heavily potted, grayish body, usually painted in UNDERGLAZE blue or occasionally in polychrome enamels. Wares include bowls, vases, KENDI, and boxes that were exported throughout southeast Asia. They are similar in type to the Thai ceramics of Sawankhalok.

Vignette ■ From the French *vigne* (vine). A carved ornament—traditionally dating to the medieval period—featuring a continuous design of grapevine leaves and tendrils. The term also refers to a photograph or drawing in which the edges are shaded off.

Vile & Cobb Leading English furniture-makers of the mid-18th century. William Vile established a London workshop in partnership with John COBB. In addition to interior decorating, they made some of the finest ROCOCO- and ADAM-style furniture produced for George III and Queen Charlotte, among others.

Villeroy & Boch See METTLACH POTTERY.

Vinaigrette ■ A small box produced from around 1770 up to around 1900, generally made of silver with a hinged cover and grille, behind which was a sponge soaked in aromatic vinegar that could be inhaled to mask bad smells or counteract faintness.

Vincennes ■ The "nursery" of the SÈVRES factory. Orry de Fulvy, an official at the Treasury, helped by the Dubois brothers from CHANTILLY, started experiments in porcelain-making in the Chateau de Vincennes, France, from around 1740. By 1745 their wares had become commercially acceptable. Typically, decoration was sparse, consisting mainly of scattered sprigs of flowers—a far cry from the sumptuous colors and gilding of later Sèvres porcelain. In 1755 the company moved to its new factory at Sèvres, with King Louis XV acquiring ownership of it in 1759.

Vineland Flint Glass Works See DURAND.

Vinovo Porcelain Factory Founded under royal patronage by Giovanni Vittorio Brodel and Paul Anton Hannong in 1776, in the castle of Vinovo, near Turin in Italy. When Hannong left in 1780, Vittorio Amadeo Gioannetti took over and the factory began to produce utility wares and a variety of figures and groups, especially in the style of COMMEDIA DELL'ARTE. The French invasion of 1796 ended the prosperous period and the factory never recovered. It closed in 1826.

Vinyl ■ Discovered by Waldo Sermon in the 1920s, polyvinyl chloride (PVC) is a light, durable PLASTIC that remains in widespread use to this day. Resistant to light, chemicals, and corrosion, PVC can be flexible or rigid and translucent or opaque in any color, and therefore has been employed extensively by toy manufacturers.

Violet wood See KINGWOOD.

Vitrifiable colors A term applied to glazed colors, primarily with enamels. It also refers to the hard, fixed, and glassy colors achieved when porcelain, earthenware, or glass is fired. Vitrifiable colors are achieved at 930–1,650°F (500–900°C) for enamels, and at 1,470–1,830°F (800–1,000°C) for pottery and porcelain.

Vitrine ■ A cupboard with large, glazed panels. Originally made in the 18th century as bookcases, vitrines designed especially for the display of ornaments did not become common until the latter part of the 19th century. Vitrines with mirror backs were popular from the mid-19th century, as they made it possible to view both sides of the objects displayed.

Vitro-porcelain A shiny, opaque glass that resembles porcelain. It was produced in several colors and was a popular medium for late 19th-century inexpensive press-molded domestic glass and novelties. See MILK GLASS.

Vitruvian scroll A Classical ornament of repeated VOLUTES, usually on a FRIEZE. Also known as a running dog

Vignette
Samson shaped box and hinged cover, painted with vignettes of a picnic. Late 19th century.

Vinaigrette
Victorian vinaigrette, by Yapp & Woodward, Birmingham 1847.

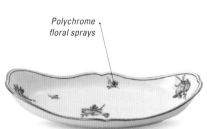

Polychrome floral sprays

Vincennes
Oval dish, painted with flower sprays within a gilt dentil and blue line border. 1764.

Vinyl
Ideal Little Miss Revlon hard vinyl doll, with clothing and accessories. c. 1958.

or wavescroll, it was revived in the early RENAISSANCE period and was used extensively to embellish 18th-century architecture and silver and early Georgian furniture.

Vizagapatam ■ A town in southeast India producing Anglo-Indian furniture and smaller pieces for the British market in the 18th and 19th centuries. Although essentially English in form, the decoration is a fusion of Indian and English styles—for example, hardwood INLAID or covered with IVORY.

Volkmar, Charles ■ (1841–1914) An American studio potter who trained in France as a barbotine (underglaze painting) artist. He founded a studio in Brooklyn, New York, in 1895, and moved to Metuchen, New Jersey, in 1903. Volkmar's work is technically and artistically advanced and may be marked with an incised "V" or "CV."

Volkstedt ■ A porcelain-making center in Thuringia, Germany. The oldest factory, founded in 1762 under the protection of the Prince of Schwarzburg-Rudolstadt, used crossed hayforks as a mark. In the 19th century, many new factories sprang up, making ornamental porcelain, which are now often called "DRESDEN." Among them was Richard Eckert & Co., which revived the hayfork mark in 1895. Many of these factories continue to produce porcelain today.

VOYSEY, CHARLES

An English architect and designer, Charles Voysey (1857–1941) was influenced by William MORRIS and was central to the ARTS AND CRAFTS Movement. He joined the ART WORKERS GUILD in 1884 and showed furniture with the Arts and Crafts Exhibition Society in 1893. His furniture, mainly in oak, has a simple, almost RUSTIC appeal. He also designed metalwork, wallpaper, textiles, and pottery.

Paddle arms

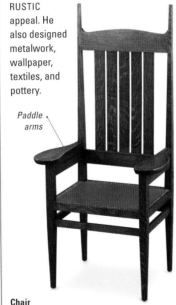

Chair
C. F. A. Voysey hall chair. c. 1895.

Volute A spiral scroll typically found on an Ionic CAPITAL, supposedly derived from the horns of the ram. The volute was taken from Renaissance ornament and architecture and used on ceramics, silver, and furniture.

Voulkos, Peter (1924–2002) An American artist, Voulkos began his career producing functional dinnerware and went on to produce Abstract Expressionist ceramic sculptures in the mid-1950s, for which he is best known. Of free-form construction and conveying a sense of weight, they are decorated by pounding, tearing, and gouging, or by glazing or hand-painting.

Vulcanite A durable form of rubber discovered by Charles Goodyear in around 1839 and patented in 1843. Hardened by curing with chemicals (originally sulfur), it is mostly black in color (although a dark red was also produced) and acquires a brownish tone through exposure to the atmosphere. Often used as a substitute for JET in Victorian MOURNING JEWELRY, it also remained popular until the 1930s for molding VESTA CASES, pipes, buttons, combs, and fountain pens.

Vulliamy family An English family of clock-makers. The earliest known member, Justin Vulliamy, arrived in London from Switzerland in 1730. His son, Benjamin, made LONGCASE and BRACKET CLOCKS and the regulator for George III's observatory in London. His son, Benjamin Lewis, was a leading clockmaker in the early 19th century.

Vitrine
Louis Phillipe walnut and gilt brass-mounted vitrine, with mahogany banding.

Vizagapatnam
Indian ivory workbox. c. 1780.

Volkmar, Charles
Underglaze-painted charger with an American Indian chief.

Volkstedt
Figurine of a stag. c. 1800.

Wain, Louis William ■ (1860–1939)

An English illustrator famous for his illustrations of anthropomorphic cats with human features and emotions. His work was immensely popular, and from 1901 to 1925, he published a *Louis Wain Annual*. Averaging 600 drawings a year, many for postcards, the market for his work saturated and eventually declined. He was certified insane in 1924 and later died in poverty in an institution.

Wainscot chair ■ From the Germanic

wain (wagon) and *schot* (crossbar). A 17th-century oak joined chair with arms, the wainscot chair originated in Britain, although variations were made throughout Northern Europe. The paneled back was often decorated with carved leaves, LOZENGES, roundels, and LUNETTES. The scroll-carved TOP RAIL might be inscribed with names and dates. The solid seat was fitted with a SQUAB CUSHION. The front supports were ring-turned, a popular decorative technique at that time, and the legs were joined by STRETCHERS. Wainscot chairs were made until the end

of the 17th century and survive in some numbers today. They were also made in the 19th century revival.

Waiter See SALVER.

Waldglas A German term for "forest glass." A type of early glass in which burned wood provided the alkali potash FLUX. The green color of the glass resulted from natural impurities in the ingredients or batch—it was made in the heavily wooded areas of central and northern Europe from the Middle Ages until the late 17th century.

Wall clock ■ Any type of clock that can be mounted on a wall. One of the earliest domestic wall clocks was the LANTERN CLOCK. From the mid-18th century, simple DIAL CLOCKS were used in public buildings and offices. Other types of wall clocks include French CARTEL CLOCKS with elaborate brass or bronze cases, TAVERN CLOCKS, and many types of REGULATOR CLOCK.

Wall pocket ■ A flat-backed vase, made in pottery and porcelain and pierced to hang on the wall, made widely in Europe from the beginning of the 18th century until the present day.

Walnut ■ A HARDWOOD ranging from light golden to dark brown. Burr walnut is highly prized for veneers and for turning. In Europe, walnut was a popular choice for

furniture-making, both solid and as a VENEER, from the mid-17th century until the introduction of burr walnut mahogany in the early 18th century. In the early 18th century, walnut was exported to Europe from Virginia.

Walter, Victor Amalric (1859–1942) A French glass artist renowned for his PÂTE-DE-VERRE work, which he made initially for DAUM FRÈRES, who helped him introduce more color into his work. He also produced sculptural pieces and plaques. Some pieces were created in collaboration with the glass technician Henri Berge. In 1919 he set up his own studio at Nancy.

Waltham Watch Company An American watchmaking company in Waltham, Massachusetts, from 1851, which merged in 1859 with Appleton, Tracy, & Co. It underwent several name changes, reemerging as the Waltham Watch Company in 1925. It was the first American company to mass-produce watches, and by 1957, when production ceased, it had made over 34 million watches.

Wanli porcelain ■ Chinese porcelain made in the reign of the MING DYNASTY Emperor Wanli (1573–1619). Large quantities of blue and white KRAAK PORCELAIN were made for export to Europe. The finest porcelain decorated in the WUCAI palette was made in this period. See CHINESE EXPORT PORCELAIN.

Wain, Louis William
"Missed," study of a cat taking a wild swing at a ball.

Wainscot chair
Oak chair, with acanthus frieze on the crest and coat of arms on central panel.

Wall clock
Victorian mahogany wall clock, with enamel dial marked "Honeybone Nottingham."

Wall pocket
English creamware wall pocket. c.1785.

Wardrobe A closed cupboard for the storage of clothes. Usually fitted with drawers, shelves, and pegs or hooks for hanging, wardrobes began to replace the PRESS, with its horizontal sliding trays, by the mid-19th century. Although Thomas SHERATON had designed a cupboard with a rail and arms to hang clothes on in the 1790s, rails and coathangers did not appear until the 1870s, and were not universally used until after 1900. From the late 19th century, wardrobes were usually made as part of bedroom suites, often with a built-in mirror.

Waring & Gillow See GILLOWS.

Warming pan A circular brass or copper pan containing hot embers, for warming a bed. Made from the 15th century, it usually has a long, carved or turned wooden handle and a decorative pierced, embossed, or engraved hinged lid. It was superseded in the 19th century by copper or earthenware hot-water bottles.

Warwick cruet frame ■ An English silver condiment stand with a cinquefoil (five-lobed) base and handle, fitted with three silver casters and two CUT-GLASS bottles. Named after an example made by Anthony Nelme for the Earl of Warwick in 1715.

Warwick vase A large ancient Greek marble vase purchased by Sir William Hamilton for his nephew, the Earl of Warwick, after it was unearthed at Hadrian's villa in Rome, in around 1770. Scaled-down copies were produced in bronze, silver, and ceramics by such makers as Paul STORR and RUNDELL & Bridge.

Washstand Although known from the medieval period, the washstand was not common until the mid-18th century. Washstands vary in shape from simple tripod stands to small cabinets holding wash basins and jugs, with drawers for toiletries. During the late 19th century large washstands with marble tops were made en suite with bedroom furniture.

Watch stand A stand made in wood, metal, or ceramic, the latter often with figures, to hold a POCKET WATCH, either at night or on a mantelpiece as a substitute for a clock. Popular in STAFFORDSHIRE pottery but also made in fine porcelain—for example, at SÈVRES.

Watcombe Pottery A pottery founded near Torquay, Devon, in 1867 by G. J. Allen to make use of the local red clay. Christopher DRESSER provided some designs for their wares, which included terra-cotta pieces for domestic use, often SLIP CAST and sometimes decorated with turquoise enamels. In 1901 it merged to become Royal Aller Vale & Watcombe Potteries. The pottery closed in 1962.

Water clock A type of clock used in ancient Egypt, Greece, and Rome in which time is measured by the flow of water into or out of a calibrated container. In the 17th and 18th centuries water clocks with a drum filled with mercury or water and mounted on an axle were produced, the falling weight of the drum driving the clock. It is also known as a *clepsydra* (water thief) in Greece.

Water gilding ■ A type of exceptionally smooth wood GILDING in which the gold leaf is laid onto damp GESSO.

Waterford Glasshouse An Irish glasshouse founded in 1783 at Waterford in County Wexford. One of the best-known producers of IRISH GLASS, the company's international reputation was built on its heavy, deeply cut glassware that included decanters, fruit bowls, honey jars, finger bowls, and jugs. The company closed in 1850 due to financial problems and taxation, but was relaunched in 1947 as Waterford Crystal. By the 1960s its traditional, deeply cut designs had met with great success. John Rocha was employed as a designer in 1997 and the company is still active today.

Watteau figures Pastoral lovers, based on the paintings of the French ROCOCO artist Jean-Antoine Watteau. In the 18th century they were copied by MEISSEN and SÈVRES, among others, and were called "Watteau pictures."

Carved fish and birds

Two glass cruets with three silver casters

Walnut
Detail of a German Baroque Revival carved walnut side cabinet. 19th century.

Wanli porcelain
Wanli blue and white jar. c. 1600.

Warwick cruet frame
George III silver Warwick cruet frame, by Samuel Wood, with London hallmarks. 1754.

Water gilding
Victorian giltwood and gesso pier glass and table, with oil and burnished water gilding.

Wax dolls The heads and sometimes the limbs of dolls have been made from wax—either poured into a mold or carved—throughout Europe since ancient times. The process was commercialized around the middle of the 19th century by firms such as PIEROTTI and MONTANARI. The SHOULDER HEADS may either be of solid or hollow wax. Solid heads with molded hair and black bead eyes were popular in the early 19th century. After 1840, hollow heads were favored, with inserted glass eyes and rooted hair. The fashion for wax dolls began to wane from around 1870.

Wax jack ■ Also known as a taper stand, it comprises a brass, silver, or Old Sheffield plated frame to hold a long coil of wax, the end of which is secured between spring-loaded grips. On lighting the wax wick, wax dripped onto the back of an envelope to seal a letter, often impressing a SEAL into the blob. They were made in various forms from around 1680 to 1850.

Wax over composition ■ A doll-making technique, popular in the mid-19th century, in which SHOULDER HEADS of a material such as PAPIER-MÂCHÉ are dipped into molten wax to create a skinlike effect.

Waywiser An instrument consisting of a wheel attached to an arm with a handle, and a dial with scales used to measure the distance covered by the wheel. Also known as an odometer, perambulator, or surveyor's wheel, it is known to have been used by the Romans and was reintroduced in the 17th century.

Webb, Philip ■ (1831–1915) An English architect and designer who opened his architectural practice in 1856. He designed the Red House in Bexley, Kent, for William MORRIS in 1860. Webb was the chief designer for Morris, Marshall & Faulkner and then Morris & Co. until 1900 and was responsible for many interiors, particularly furniture. Around 1860 he also designed a suite of glass tableware for James POWELL & Sons.

Webb, Thomas & Sons ■ English glassworks founded by Thomas Webb in 1837, near Stourbridge, West Midlands. From 1863 it was managed by his sons and produced a wide range of decorative glass. The range included CAMEO GLASS by John NORTHWOOD and Thomas and George WOODALL, and new types of ART GLASS such as ALEXANDRITE, IRIDESCENT GLASS, and QUEEN'S BURMESE. The company won the Grand Prix for glass at the Paris Exposition Universelle in 1878. It also produced CUT GLASS in traditional and modern designs. After various takeovers and mergers, the company closed in 1990.

Wedgwood ■ Josiah Wedgwood was apprenticed to a potter, but ill health forced him to quit the thrower's bench. Instead, he began to learn to mold wares and experiment with clays and metallic oxides. In 1754 he joined Thomas WHIELDON, devoting himself to improving colored glazes. In 1759 he started on his own, making all kinds of pottery similar to contemporary STAFFORDSHIRE wares. The business grew and in 1762 he met Thomas Bentley, a Liverpool merchant, who imbued him with a love of the Classical. They became partners in 1768 and built a new factory, house, and village named Etruria. Here Wedgwood worked on improving the black EARTHENWARE he called black BASALT and finding new material to make the white reliefs used to decorate JASPER WARE. From the beginning, Wedgwood also produced AGATEWARE knife handles, SALT-GLAZED STONEWARE, and green-glazed wares with relief-molded leaves. He also created CREAMWARE, which he re-named QUEENSWARE after securing the patronage of Queen Charlotte. His creamware swept across Europe, completely swamping the DELFT and FAIENCE markets. In PEARLWARE, created around 1779, the cream tinge of creamware was counteracted by a minute quantity of cobalt blue.

In the early 19th century the firm continued the 18th-century styles and patterns but gradually lost its leadership of the Staffordshire industry. In the early 19th century LUSTER decoration began to be used as well as RESIST and MOONLIGHT decoration. Chinese FAMILLE ROSE-style painting on black basalt (Capri ware) was also briefly in vogue. Wedgwood made BONE CHINA

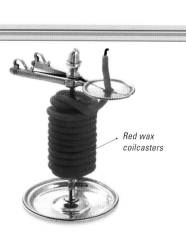

Wax jack
George III silver wax jack, with a wax coil, crested by Burrage, Davenport, London. c. 1783.

Red wax coilcasters

Wax over composition
Wax-head doll, with cloth body, typical turned-in feet, and original clothes. c. 1820–30.

Webb, Philip
Large Morris & Co. mahogany dining table, designed in the 1860s by Philip Webb.

from 1812 to 1816. In the 20th century, Wedgwood employed many innovative designers, including Daisy Makeig-Jones (who produced FAIRYLAND LUSTER), Keith MURRAY, and Eric RAVILIOUS. Traditional ware was still produced—for example, copies of 18th-century Jasper ware. In 1989 Wedgwood merged with WATERFORD GLASS to form the Waterford-Wedgwood Group.

Weesp Porcelain Factory The first successful Dutch porcelain factory, founded by the Irish ARCANIST D. McCarthy in 1757 and taken over in 1759 by Count Gronsveldt-Diepenbroek, helped by the German arcanist Nikolaus Paul.

The factory, which made good-quality HARD-PASTE PORCELAIN with a clear glaze, moved to Oude Loosdrecht in 1771, to AMSTEL in 1784, and finally closed in 1820.

Wegner, Hans ■ (born 1914) A Danish furniture designer who worked with Arne JACOBSEN before founding his own workshop in 1943. Many of his designs were produced by Johannes Hansen and Carl Hansen. His most notable designs include the Model JH501 Round chair, known as The Chair (1949), and the Model No. JH250 Valet chair (1953). Representing Scandinavian design ethics of the period, Wegner's designs were often modern takes

on traditional styles and were always simple, well balanced, and finely crafted.

Weisweiler, Adam ■ (1744–1820) A German furniture-maker who began his career in the workshop of David ROENTGEN. He moved to Paris, becoming

W

399

WEATHERVANE

Also known as a windvane, the weathervane is a metal construction mounted on a building to show wind direction with an arrow. Since the 18th century, most arrow pointers are balanced with a larger flag or motif to point upwind. Motifs include cocks, ships, mottoes, and figures.

Hand-painted in shades of red, orange, and black

Gilt-bronzed-iron mount

Eagle
American eagle weathervane, by Fische & Co., with original iron rod, from the Federal Building in Buffalo, New York. c. 1893.

American Indian
American cut-tin weathervane, with original paint decoration. Late 19th century.

Webb, Thomas & Sons
Three-color cameo vase. 1889.

Wedgwood
Large Wedgwood blue jasper-dip campana vase. 19th century.

Wegner, Hans
Rare Johannes Hansen Valet chair, by Hans Wegner.

Weisweiler, Adam
Louis XVI mahogany architect's table, stamped "A. Weisweiler." c. 1790.

a *maître ébéniste* by 1778, and worked primarily for furniture dealers such as Dominique Daguerre, who supplied furniture for Marie Antoinette and the Prince of Wales. Weisweiler specialized in small, light pieces such as BONHEURS-DU-JOUR, CONSOLES, and SECRETAIRES, and is celebrated for clean, elegant lines, flawless construction, and delicate floral mounts. He used plain mahogany veneers, lacquer, SÈVRES plaques, or PIETRA DURA panels. His furniture features tapering legs with barley-sugar inlay, interlaced stretchers, and legs shaped like spinning tops.

Weller Pottery See RHEAD; FREDERICK HURTEN.

Wellings, Norah An English fabric doll-maker who, after working for CHAD VALLEY, ran her own soft toy company with her brother in Wellington, Shropshire, from 1926 to 1960. Her dolls have characteristic molded fabric faces with side-glancing eyes and are marked with a label on one foot. They were widely copied.

Wellington chest ■ A narrow CHEST-OF-DRAWERS popular in England and France from 1820. They have up to 12 drawers and a single locking mechanism in which a hinged flap runs down one side of the chest and locks over the drawers. See CAMPAIGN CHEST, SPECIMEN CHEST.

Welsh dresser See DRESSER.

Wemyss ware ■ Distinctive pottery from the Fife Pottery in Kirkcaldy, Scotland, established around 1790. It was run by Robert Methver Heron from 1833 to 1906, which was the main period of production of Wemyss ware (named after Wemyss Castle in Fife). In 1883 he put Karel Nekola from Bohemia in charge of the painting shop. Nekola introduced the brightly colored underglaze motifs typical of Wemyss. Wares included jug-and-basin sets, large pig doorstops, tableware, inkstands, and candlesticks, hand-painted with fruit, cabbage roses, birds, and cats. Commemorative souvenirs for Queen Victoria's Diamond Jubilee and George V's coronation were also made. Some wares were commissioned by Thomas Goode & Co. In 1930 the rights and molds were sold to the Bovey Tracey pottery in Devon, where Nekola's son, Joseph, continued to paint traditional Wemyss ware until his death in 1942.

West German Ceramics ■ The name given to the SLIP-MOLDED ceramics produced during the postwar period from the 1950s to the 1970s. Pieces were hand-decorated, with styles of the 1950s consisting primarily of curving forms decorated with abstract patches or bands of bright color, sometimes with black lines.

The 1960s saw the introduction of bubbling, textured glazes that often resemble brightly colored lava and are typically randomly dripped over the body. Factories included Scheurich, Ruscha, Ceramano, Jopeko, and Bay.

Westerwald potteries A group of German stoneware factories at Adendorf, Grenzau, and Grenzhausen, established in the Middle Ages in the Rhineland. In the 17th century a distinctive type of jug appeared with an oviform body and narrow neck, stamped with reliefs of lion masks, flowers, and rosettes, and with cobalt blue or manganese purple glaze. They had an extensive export trade, especially with England. Stoneware continued to be made in the area throughout the 19th century and is still made there today.

Whatnot See ÉTAGÈRE.

Wheat-ear motif ■ A symbol of fecundity and fertility since ancient times, the wheat ear was a popular decorative motif from the 17th to the 19th century. It was used on glassware and ceramics as well as on furniture, particularly chair backs.

Wheel barometer Invented in around 1650 by the British scientist Robert Hooke. It comprises a U-shaped tube filled with mercury, and a float attached to a pointer on a dial, which measures changes in atmospheric pressure. See BANJO BAROMETER.

Pilaster-shaped locking flap

Wellington chest
Highly figured walnut Wellington chest with seven drawers. c. 1850.

Wemyss ware
Medium-sized pig, decorated with roses.

West German Ceramics
Otto Keramik small bun-shaped bowl.

Sgraffito decoration

Wheat-ear motif
North Dakota School of Mines cabinet vase, carved in sgraffito, with sheaves of wheat.

Wheel engraving ■ A technique for decorating glass and metal. The object is against a rotating wheel, using disks of stone or copper and a fine abrasive paste to create an INCISED design. Known in Roman times, it was revived by Caspar Lehmann for use on BOHEMIAN GLASS and remained popular until it was largely superseded by the ACID ETCHING technique.

Wheel lock The first gunlock to strike its own sparks to ignite the gunpowder. The mechanism was invented in southern Germany in around 1500 and was used until the mid-18th century. A notched steel wheel, powered by a spring, is released by the trigger against a flint to create the spark.

Whieldon, Thomas ■ (1719–95) A STAFFORDSHIRE potter and apprentice to John ASTBURY. From 1740 he made stoneware and agateware, cauliflower- and pineapple-molded vessels, and animal and human figures, using semitranslucent green and yellow as well as TORTOISESHELL glazes. In 1749 he employed Josiah SPODE, and from around 1755 he was in partnership with Josiah WEDGWOOD.

Whitby jet See JET.

White metal 1. A term sometimes used for unmarked silver, unmarked alloys with unknown levels of silver, or silver that does not bear British hallmarks. 2. See BRITANNIA METAL.

Whitefriars Glassworks ■ A London glasshouse founded in the 17th century. In 1834 it was acquired by James Powell and was known as James Powell & Sons until 1962, after which it reverted to the name Whitefriars Glassworks, before closing in 1980. In the 19th century, production included designs for William MORRIS, windows for Pre-Raphaelite painters, and hand-blown glass in historical styles. In the 20th century glass was made in ART DECO designs, with innovative colored and textured MOLD-BLOWN glass, designed by Geoffrey Baxter, being made in the 1960s and 70s.

Whitework A technique, known from medieval times, in which white linen thread is embroidered onto a white linen ground. The term also describes SAMPLERS worked solely in white, which often include NEEDLELACE techniques.

Wickerwork The weaving of flexible RODs, or shoots, of fibrous material (usually of willow, cane, or rattan), known from ancient times. Surviving examples dating before the 17th century are rare. It was fashionable for outdoor use in the 18th century, but achieved greater recognition through the SECESSION designers of the 19th century. LLOYD LOOM made by weaving created a surge in its popularity from 1920 to 1940.

Wiener Werkstätte ■ (1903–32) Workshops founded in Vienna by Josef HOFFMANN, Koloman MOSER, and Fritz Warndorfer as an association of craftsmen based on C. R. ASHBEE's Guild. By 1910 they had been joined by Joseph Olbrich, Gustav Klimt, Dagobert Peche, and Otto Prutscher. The 100 workers, including 40 "masters," made a wide range of furniture, metalwork, and glass of progressive design.

Wig aperture An opening in the crown of a BISQUE doll's head into which the PÂTE is inserted. It allows access for stringing and the insertion of the SLEEPING EYE mechanism.

Wig stand A shaped wooden or, more rarely, ceramic support for storing wigs, made from the 17th to early 19th century.

Wilkinson, A. J. Ltd. A pottery founded in Burslem, Staffordshire, in 1885, making earthenware and ironstone ornamental pieces and tableware. It took over the Newport Pottery in 1920 and is best known for Clarice CLIFF's work. In 1964 it was taken over by Midwinter, and in 1970 it became part of the WEDGWOOD group.

Wilkinson, Norman ■ (1878–1971) An English marine painter, poster artist, and printmaker. He illustrated travel posters in the 1920s and 30s for British railroad companies. He also developed camouflage techniques during both world wars and painted a series of pictures for the nation about the wars at sea.

Wheel engraving
Flemish soda glass goblet, with engraved crowned armorial shields. Mid-18th century.

Whieldon, Thomas
Whieldon-type miniature teapot. c. 1780.

Whitefriars Glassworks
Whitefriars kingfisher blue coffin vase, designed by Geoffry Baxter.

Ribbed bowl with undulating rim

Wiener Werkstätte
Purple bowl, by Josef Hoffmann. 1910–20.

WILLOW PATTERN

Designed by Thomas MINTON in around 1780, the willow pattern is a CHINOISERIE design that was printed on ceramics, probably for the CAUGHLEY pottery. It was later used by a large number of STAFFORDSHIRE factories throughout the 19th and 20th centuries. The willow pattern comprised a willow tree, a Chinese temple, a bridge with figures on it, a boat, birds in flight, and a distant island.

Ale measure
Willow-pattern quart ale measure. c.1900.

Cow creamer
White glazed Staffordshire willow-pattern cow creamer.

William & Mary Style ■ Decorative arts and architecture associated with the reign of William III and Mary II in England (1688–1702). It was influenced by the French LOUIS XIV style due to the HUGUENOT refugees coming to England via Holland (where William ruled as Stadholder). The designer Daniel MAROT created unified schemes of interior decoration, featuring motifs such as LAMBREQUINS and ACANTHUS. Developments in furniture included the introduction of BOULLE marquetry, silver furniture, and JAPANNING. Huguenot silversmiths introduced new types of decoration such as CUT-CARD work, and new wares such as ECUELLES and HELMET-SHAPED EWERS.

Willow A flexible and tough wood that was chiefly used in Europe for basket- and furniture-making from early times to the present day. In the 17th and 18th centuries it was also dyed black to imitate EBONY for INLAY work as well as for applied ornament. Willow pegs were also used in early English oak and country furniture.

Wilson, Henry ■ (1864–1934) An English ARTS AND CRAFTS goldsmith and metalworker who used polychrome enamel in jewelry and *objets d'art* influenced by ecclesiastic or medieval styles. He employed major Arts and Crafts figures such as John Paul Cooper and H. G. Murphy.

Wilton A center for carpet production in Wiltshire, England, from the second half of the 19th century and still active today. After a fire destroyed the AXMINSTER factory, its looms were transferred to Wilton in the 1830s. Designs were inspired by the French carpets of the period—AUBUSSON and SAVONNERIE—although the quality and colors were generally less sophisticated.

Wincanton Delft Pottery Founded in the small town of Wincanton, near Bristol, by Nathaniel Ireson and Thomas Lindslee. Apart from a few marked pieces, ranging in date from 1737 (on a plate in Edinburgh Museum) to 1748 (a jug in the Glaisher Collection, Cambridge), the products of this factory cannot be differentiated from those

Wilkinson, Norman
War Savings Are Warships, published by National Savings, printed by J. Weiner.

William & Mary Style
Modern reproduction walnut bureau in William and Mary style. 20th century.

Wilson, Henry
Arts and Crafts silver altar crucifix, with a central painted enamel panel. c. 1908.

Window seat
Regency rosewood and brass-mounted window seat, in the style of William Trotter.

of a number of others. However, a particular lilac-manganese "powdered" border with reserved panels decorated in blue is often attributed to the Wincanton Pottery.

Winchester, Oliver F. (1810–80) An American gunmaker and entrepreneur. Winchester was a successful shirt manufacturer who invested his profits in the Volcanic Repeating Arms Company. He hired B. Tyler Henry as his expert designer, and in 1866 the first Winchester repeating rifle was born. Operated by a lever and fed by a tubular magazine, the Winchester rapidly became an American icon and was in heavy demand during the westward expansion of the US in the last decades of the 19th century. In 1866 the company was renamed the Winchester Repeating Arms Company. Although the Winchester company remains in business, production of the classic lever action rifle ceased in 2006.

Winding mechanism Mechanical clocks and watches rely on a spring to power the MOVEMENT. The earliest watch springs were wound directly with a key. In the 1650s the FUSÉE was introduced, connected to the spring barrel by a cord or chain. This continued until Thomas Prest invented the KEYLESS winding mechanism in 1822.

Window seat ■ A bench, usually with low arms and sometimes upholstered, which was designed to fit into the recess beneath a window. Fashionable from around 1825, especially in the US, the window seat was often raised on long legs or on carved (often scrolled) supports.

Windsor chair ■ A provincial wooden chair with the legs, arms, and spindle back doweled into the shaped seat. Made in Britain from the early 18th century, these chairs were traditionally created by wood-turners using ash, yew, beech, and birch, with an elm seat. Early examples were painted and intended for outdoor use. So named because it was said to have originated around the town of Windsor and the Thames Valley, the main center of the Windsor chair industry was High Wycombe, Buckinghamshire, although the form was adopted for provincial chairs made throughout Britain and the US. Since the late 19th century, Windsor chairs and their variant styles have been mass-produced.

Wine cooler ■ A container for cooling bottled wine (in ice if available) made in silver, porcelain, or wood with a lead lining (CELLARET). In English porcelain, they were generally of a deep U-shape with small handles. In SÈVRES they were usually oval-shaped and were called *seaux à bouteilles* or *seaux à liqueurs ovales* and were meant to cool pairs of liqueur bottles.

Wine funnel ■ A silver, plated, and sometimes ceramic funnel with a strainer bowl or a provision for a muslin strainer used for decanting wine. The funnels were made in large quantities from around 1775 to 1825, but earlier examples are known.

Wine label A small label, also known as bottle ticket, made from around 1745 in large numbers and in an infinite variety of forms in silver, Old Sheffield plate, enamels, and porcelain. These labels were hung by a chain or wire around the neck of a bottle or decanter to indicate its contents.

Wine table A small occasional table in the form of a tray on a stand for the informal serving of wine. Produced from the mid-18th century, it usually had a semicircular horseshoe shape, sometimes with drop leaves, and was fitted with a pivoted arm and coaster that could swing across to pass the bottles to any point of its radius.

Wine taster A small, silver and parcel-gilt saucerlike bowl, usually with two wire handles and with a polished domed center, for tasting and examining the clarity and color of wine. It is the English form of a TASTEVIN. Wine tasters date from the 17th century and are sometimes decorated with punched work.

Wine waiter An open wagon or case supported on legs, designed to contain bottles or decanters of spirits or wine. Possibly of Irish origin, the wine waiter was sometimes fitted with a CELLARET and casters to allow easy movement around the room.

Wineglass cooler See MONTEITH.

Horsehair and wadding squab

Windsor chair
George IV yew and elm Windsor chair.

Wine cooler
Regency octagonal mahogany wine cooler, with lead-lined interior.

Wine funnel
George III part-fluted wine funnel with gadrooned and molded borders. 1810.

Wing chair  An upholstered armchair with "wings" added to the sides of the chair back to keep out drafts. Originally designed for the elderly and infirm, wing chairs were derived from French sleeping chairs with adjustable backs dating to the 1670s. They were first made in England in the late 17th century and described in contemporary inventories as "easie" chairs. They have been in production ever since.

Winston, Harry (1896–1978) One of the most successful American jewelers of the 20th century. He worked in New York, where he quickly established a reputation from 1932 for buying antique estate jewelry, remounting the stones into superb new settings, and selling to a clientele that included royalty, movie stars, and millionaires. Winston owned many famous jewels, including the Hope Diamond, which he donated to the Smithsonian Institute. The company is still running today.

Winter, Friedrich (*fl.*)1685–c.1710) A German glass-engraver working at the end of the 17th and the beginning of the 18th century. He used a water-powered cutting mill to produce cameo reliefs (HOCHSCHNITT) in bold BAROQUE designs exclusively for his patron, Graf Christopher Schaffgotsch.

Wirework  A technique whereby small articles such as fruit baskets or toast racks are formed from wire, usually of silver or gold, of different sizes bent into a lattice.

Wirkkala, Tapio  (1915–85) A Finnish designer in wood, metal, and glass who worked for factories in Finland and other European countries such as the ROSENTHAL porcelain factory in Bavaria, the CHRISTOFLE silver factory in France, and the IITTALA glassworks in Finland. His work is characterized by a respect for the intrinsic nature of his materials and is typically inspired by organic forms found in nature.

Wistar, Caspar (1696–1752) A German-born American glassmaker and founder of the SOUTH JERSEY glasshouse in Wistarburg, New Jersey, in 1739. Products resembled German WALDGLAS, were often decorated with applied TRAILS and loops, and are difficult to attribute. The works closed in 1780 but former employees the Stanger Brothers established an important glassworks in nearby Glassboro, New Jersey.

Wit, Federick de (1630-1706) A prominent map-engraver and publisher in Amsterdam, Federick de Wit produced sea charts, world ATLASES, and "town books" of European town and city plans. He was known for the high quality of his engravings and his use of color.

Witch ball  A colored glass ball, primarily in blue, red, or green, and often with a silvery lining that made them opaque and reflective. They were traditionally hung in windows to ward off evil spirits or prevent disease, and were derived from small glass containers containing holy water used in 17th-century England for the same purpose. They were popular during the 19th century, but modern reproductions are known.

Wogden, Robert (1734–1813) An English gunmaker active from 1748, famous for his high-quality and innovative FLINTLOCK DUELING PISTOLS.

Wolfsohn, Helena  (died c. 1872) A porcelain decorator whose workshop in Dresden (established in 1843) used SECONDS from MEISSEN and white porcelain from other factories. One of her specialties was imitating the Meissen pattern of WATTEAU FIGURES alternating with flower patterns. Her workshop marked wares with the Meissen "AR" until 1881, when it was stopped by legal action; thereafter, a crown over a "D" was used. The firm was bought by Walter Stephan in 1919.

Wood, Aaron (1717–85) A Staffordshire ceramics modeler and brother of Ralph WOOD. He worked for WHIELDON and other factories and made models for household wares and ornaments.

Wood, Enoch (1759–1840) The son of Aaron WOOD. He ran a factory with his

Wing chair
American New England carved walnut wing chair, upholstered in yellow fabric.

Wirework
Citrine and agate pendant of wirework scroll form.

Wirkkala, Tapio
Iittala cut glass vase, designed by Tapio Wirkkala. 1950s.

Spiraled red glass cane

Witch ball
Victorian glass witch ball with red swirl. c. 1880.

cousin, Ralph WOOD II, from 1783 to 1790, and with James CALDWELL from 1790 to 1818. His wares included blue printed ware, BASALT WARE, and JASPER WARE. He was joined by his sons, who continued the business after his death until 1846.

Wood, Ralph I ■ (1715–72) The most important member of a distinguished family of Staffordshire potters. He owned the Hilltop factory in Burslem, and made figures—some modeled by John Voyez, others adapted from the Belgian modeler Paul-Louis Cyme—as well as TOBY JUGS and models such as the Vicar and Moses.

Wood, Ralph II (1748–95) The son of Ralph Wood I, who inherited his factory and continued making figures. He initiated the use of ENAMEL COLORS.

Woodall, George (1850–1925) **and Thomas** (1849–1926) British glass-engravers and cutters who were apprenticed to John NORTHWOOD until 1874. They produced a number of finely toned, intricately carved CAMEO pieces, including vases and plaques for Thomas WEBB & SONS.

Woodcut ■ A type of printing that originated around 860 CE in Asia. It developed in Europe in around 1400 and was the earliest means of printing illustrations. The image is cut in low relief with a sharp knife on wood sawn along the grain. Ink is applied to the relief image, which is then pressed onto paper.

Wooden doll ■ Dolls have been made from wood by most civilizations since the earliest times. In early English examples, the heads and torsos are turned or carved out of one piece of wood, to which arms are nailed or tied and legs are jointed. In the 18th century doll-carving centers emerged in Austria and Germany at GRÖDNERTAL, SONNEBERG, Oberammergau, and Berchtesgaden. Mass production resulted in the PENNY WOODEN dolls.

Wool picture A picture in which the chief embroidery thread is wool. Good examples of the genre are 19th-century pictures of boats embroidered by sailors and BERLIN WOOLWORK pictures popular from the mid-19th century.

Worcester Porcelain Factory ■ A factory founded in Worcester, England, in 1751, by Dr. John Wall and the apothecary William Davis. After initial failures, the partners bought the BRISTOL porcelain factory, which gave them a source of SOAPSTONE and new kilns, and by 1752 they were making PORCELAIN. They started by making utility wares, decorated in UNDERGLAZE blue in the Chinese style.

From the mid-18th century Worcester pioneered the technique of TRANSFER-PRINTING. In the 1760s Worcester also made polychrome designs in the Chinese FAMILLE ROSE style to compete with imported MEISSEN wares and introduced colored grounds. The defection of Thomas Turner in the mid-1770s to run his factory

at CAUGHLEY was a blow, but Worcester struggled on until it was bought by Thomas Flight in 1783 for his sons. John Flight managed the company and abandoned the unprofitable blue and white in favor of the latest French styles.

In 1789 the CHAMBERLAIN family, who had supervised the decoration at Worcester, also left to set up their own business. After John Flight died in 1791, his brother, Joseph, was joined in 1792 by Martin Barr, and the firm traded as Flight & Barr, making products for the top end of the market.

In 1840 the firm was forced to merge with its rivals and the partnership traded as Chamberlain & Co. When W. H. Kerr joined the factory in 1852, the firm was named Kerr & Binns, but in 1862 was reborn as the Worcester Royal Porcelain Company. After 1901 more everyday wares were produced, but grand porcelains such as those by the Stinton family were still made.

In 1978 the company merged with SPODE. It continues its tradition of producing high-quality porcelain in both historical and contemporary styles.

Work (or sewing) table ■ A small, low table used by ladies to store needlework, made from the mid-18th century and popular in France, England, and the US. They had built-in drawers or shelves and a pouch for silks, bobbins, and needles. Some had hinged lids, while others had a hinged flap top and pull-out sides.

Wolfsohn, Helena
Porcelain box and cover.
Late 19th century.

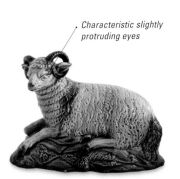

Characteristic slightly protruding eyes

Wood, Ralph
Finely detailed
color-glazed ram.

Woodcut
Edward Burne-Jones woodcut,
for the frontispiece of *Dream of John Ball* by William Morris.

Wooden doll
German wooden Grödnertal
doll, with fine painted hairstyle
and comb in her hair. c. 1830.

WORCESTER

The Worcester porcelain factory embraced the prevailing fashionable styles of ornament. Thus, from the 1750s to the 1770s CHINOISERIE and ROCOCO style wares dominated. They were gradually supplanted by NEO-CLASSICAL forms and then, by the early 19th century, by a less austere REGENCY style, and a hybrid Neo-classical-Rococo style.

Vase
Royal Worcester ovoid vase and cover, painted by John Stinton.

Jug
Baluster-shaped sparrowbeak jug, with notched loop handle, painted in the "Warbler" pattern. c. 1755.

Plate
Worcester Barr, Flight & Barr plate, printed with a view of Port Mahon in Menorca. c. 1804–13.

Wreathing Spiral marks in the "paste" of a ceramic BODY made when the vessel was turned on the wheel. Particularly seen on BRISTOL HARD-PASTE PORCELAIN.

Wrigglework ■ A form of engraved zigzag or wriggly lines as border decoration on metals, particularly PEWTER and SILVER boxes and HOLLOWWARE. It was widely used in the NEOCLASSICAL period.

Wright, Russel ■ (1904–76) An American industrial designer who is best known for his American Modern ceramic dinnerware, designed in 1937 and produced from 1940 to 1961 by the Steubenville Pottery, which sold in huge quantities. He later designed Casual China for Iroquois, which was promoted for its durability; if it chipped or broke, it was replaced free of charge. His glass designs include Flair, for Imperial Glass in 1949, and a few designs for Morgantown. He also designed cocktail shakers and pitchers as well as furniture. His forms are typically MODERN and combine ART DECO styles with awareness of an object's function.

Wristwatch Although earlier bracelet-type watches exist, the wristwatch did not begin to supersede the pocket watch until World War I, when wristwatches were issued to servicemen and their popularity spread. Although the earliest examples look more like POCKET WATCHES with a strap, the basic design of the watch with a strap or bracelet has changed little over the last century.

Writing table ■ A flat-topped desk, inspired by the French BUREAU PLAT.

Work or sewing table
William IV tortoiseshell work table, with hinged top, silk pleated box, and square stem.

Wrigglework
Samuel Pamberton silver caddy spoon, with wrigglework ribbons. c. 1800.

Wright, Russel
Steubenville American Modern coral teapot, designed by Russel Wright.

WRIGHT, FRANK LLOYD

A student of architecture and, briefly, engineering, Wright worked in the Chicago practice of Louis Sullivan and was also the practice specialist in designing homes for Adler & Sullivan. In 1893 he started his own practice in Chicago and evolved a unique style that became the cornerstone of the so-called PRAIRIE SCHOOL. He designed many houses, mostly around Chicago, which had dominant horizontal lines mirroring the contours of the land, clearly reflecting the influence of the surrounding prairie and his appreciation of Japanese design. His STAINED GLASS designs also have echoes of the Japanese paper screen. His reputation as a furniture designer derives from the pieces he designed for these buildings.

He was a major supporter of the Chicago Arts and Crafts Society, which he helped found in 1897. His interior designs were in the ARTS AND CRAFTS style, and his high-backed chairs were probably influenced by British examples. His work relied on geometric forms, and, coupled with a positive attitude toward the machine, it anticipated the MODERN MOVEMENT.

The range of Wright's commissions grew along with his reputation. In 1916 he designed the furniture and tableware (made by NORITAKE) for the Imperial Hotel in Tokyo. This was followed by the stunning house, Fallingwater in Bear Run, Pennsylvania, built over a waterfall. From 1936 to 1939 he masterminded the S.C. Johnson Administration Building in Racine, Wisconsin. His final building was the Solomon R. Guggenheim Museum in New York, with its distinctive spiral focal point.

Double-doored breakfront cabinet

Console
Console table, designed by Frank Lloyd Wright.

Buffet
Mahogany buffet, designed by Frank Lloyd Wright for Heritage Henredon.

Oak top with molded edges

Armchair
Cassina reissue barrel armchair, designed by Frank Lloyd Wright.

Chair
One of a pair of dining chairs. 1950.

Side table
George Mann Neidecken side table. c. 1910.

WÜRTTEMBERG METAL FACTORY

A German firm founded by Daniel Straub in Geislingen in 1853 was renamed WMF as an amalgamation of several firms in 1880. It was particularly known for its ART NOUVEAU metalware and the Art Nouveau maiden that decorated some of the most popular pieces. In the 1920s, it introduced ART DECO-style Ikora metalware and a range of glass, including the iridescent Myra glass and the heavier Ikora glass, decorated with colors and bubbles. WMF still produces metal tableware today.

Iridescent Ikora Red Kristall

Card tray
Art Nouveau pewter card tray.
c. 1906.

Glass tazza
Ikora glass tazza. c. 1930.

Various types were made, with drawers and baize or leather-covered tops. Desks with two pedestal chests-of-drawers came into use in the late 17th century and were popular from the 1740s. Writing tables of this and other types continued to be made through the 19th century and are still made today. See CARLTON HOUSE DESK, PEDESTAL DESK.

Wrotham pottery A small village pottery in Kent, making simple SLIPWARE

in the late 17th century, with trailed decoration in yellow on a dark brown ground. Potters included Henry Ifield, George Richardson, John Green, and Nicholas Hubble.

Wrythening ■ A type of decoration consisting of diagonally twisted ribbing, used on early Venetian glass and 18th-century ALE GLASSES. It was revived in the late 19th century, notably by the WHITEFRIARS GLASSWORKS.

Wrythening was also used in metalwork—for example, to make cutlery handles.

Wucai ■ A Chinese term for "five colored." A type of decoration on Chinese porcelain related to the earlier DOUCAI style but with washes of UNDERGLAZE blue and OVERGLAZE colored enamels. Outlines are usually in red or black. The finest pieces date from the WANLI period.

Cabriole leg with bronze sabot

Writing table
Kingwood and floral marquetry writing table.
Late 19th century.

Wrythening
Unusual Wrythen decanter, engraved "Brandy" and with blown stopper. c. 1900.

Wucai
Chinese Wucai baluster vase, painted with panels of lotus on an iron red ground. c. 1650.

XYZ

X-chair ◼ Chairs with X-shaped frames were known in the ancient world. In medieval Italy the X-chair was a type of folding chair that had a frame like an "X" when viewed from the front or the side. Also known as a Savonarola or Dante chair in Italy and a Luther chair in Germany, the X-chair was a light and practical form that was popular throughout Renaissance Europe. In England the GLASTONBURY CHAIR made an X-shape by crossing the front and back legs, while in Spain X-chairs were inlaid with ivory and metals in Moorish designs. The woodwork was nearly always covered with silk or velvet, and the seat made up of loose cushions resting on the webbing between the side rails of the frames. The form was revived in the NEOCLASSICAL period and features in Thomas SHERATON's *The Cabinet Directory*. It continued through the 19th century as a portable folding chair used during campaigns or other outdoor pursuits. See THEBES STOOL.

Yangshao culture The Neolithic culture in China from around 5000 BCE to about 1500 BCE. It was noted for its coiled bulbous earthenware in red, black, and white, with impressed cord patterns. Purple or black geometric designs were also used. These items were possibly conceived as gifts for the dead.

Yellow metal A term sometimes used for unmarked gold, unmarked alloys, including unknown levels of gold, or gold that does not bear British hallmarks.

Yew ◼ A hard and close-grained wood of reddish brown color, which was used from an early period for small articles and TREEN and for the backs of WINDSOR CHAIRS.

Yingqing (Qingbai) ◼ Early Chinese porcelain made in the JINGDEZHEN area. Literally meaning "shadowy blue," it obtained its name from the bluish tinge of the glaze. Yingqing was introduced in the TANG DYNASTY and continued to be made throughout the SONG DYNASTY. Wares included bowls and vases with naturalistic carved, molded, or incised decoration.

Yixing Chinese kilns in the Jiangsu province dating back to the SONG DYNASTY. They produced red and brown STONEWARE, tea ware, and other small items, usually unglazed, known in China as *zisha* ware. They were exported to Europe from the 17th century.

Yomut A tribal group of West Turkestan who were prolific producers of carpets in the 19th century. Designs often have geometric motifs. The distinguishing GUL often has hooked edges that are arranged diagonally. Colors include shades of brown and eggplant with bright reds, yellows, blue, and ivory.

Yongzheng porcelain Chinese porcelain made in the reign of the QING Emperor Yongzheng (1723–35), including some of the most technically perfect Chinese porcelain. SONG DYNASTY and MING DYNASTY shapes and styles were revived, and REIGN MARKS were written using seal (*zhuanshu*) script alongside the regular (*kaishu*) script. The FAMILLE ROSE palette was also widely adopted.

Ysart, Salvador (& Sons) ◼ (1878–1955) A Spanish-born glassmaker who with his son, Paul, created MONART glass from 1924 at the MONCRIEFF GLASSWORKS. In 1947 he set up Ysart Bros. in Perth, Scotland, with his sons, Augustine and Vincent, and made Vasart, a colored glass range similar to Monart. All pieces were designed by Elizabeth Moncrieff. Specialties were vases, bowls, baskets, and some paperweights. The company became Strathearn Glass in 1965 and in 1980 was acquired by STUART & SONS LTD. Paul Ysart is known as one of the best paperweight makers of the 20th century,

Yu (or you) A Chinese bronze wine jar and cover with a bulbous body and swing

X-chair
Italian walnut savonarola-type X-shaped folding chair. 18th century.

Yew
Section of burr yew veneer.

Yingqing (Qingbai)
Chinese Song dynasty Yingqing water dropper. 1127–1279.

Ysart, Salvador (& Sons)
Paul Ysart paperweight, with polychrome canes on a green ground. Mid-20th century.

ZANFIRICO

A corruption of the name of an early 19th-century Venetian glass dealer, Antonio Sanquirico, zanfirico refers to a glassmaking technique in which thin white or colored glass threads or ribbons are twisted together within a casing of clear, colorless glass. The resulting composite CANE can then be used to decorate the bodies of vessels or can be used in combination to form bodies. The technique was widely practiced by glassmakers on the island of MURANO.

Dolphin-shaped stem

Goblet
Murano zanfirico goblet, the dolphin-shaped ornamental stem with gold foil inclusions. 2004.

Zeisel, Eva ■ (born 1906) A Hungarian-born ceramics designer known for her influential MODERN yet practical designs. Her first workshop was founded in Hungary around 1925, and she subsequently worked for a number of notable factories, including Majolika-Fabrik Schramberg and Christian Carstens in Germany from 1927 to 1932 and Lomonosov and Dulevo in Russia from 1932 to 1937. In 1938 she fled to the US, where she designed tableware for Hall China and Sears, Roebuck & Co., among others. In 1943 she designed the iconic Museum range for the Museum of Modern Art in New York, which was manufactured by Castleton China from 1946.

Ziegler ■ A British-Swiss firm making carpets around 1885 in Sultanabad in northwest Persia. It responded to the needs of European clients and created a new and distinctive style. The carpets tend to have large-scale motifs in a vine lattice, usually with an overall repeat pattern within large borders. Terra-cotta shades and ivory are most frequently seen for the main field color and pale or dark blue are seen for the borders. The carpets were not finely woven, but lustrous fine-quality wool was often used.

Zircon ■ A gemstone with a high degree of brilliance, which in its colorless state can be mistaken for a diamond. Blue and brown zircons were used in late 19th-century jewelry, particularly in bold rings and stylized spray brooches in the 1940s to 1950s.

handle, made from the 13th to the 9th century BCE. See SHANG DYNASTY.

Yuan ■ The Chinese Mongol dynasty (1260–1368) founded by Kublai Khan. Production of ceramics at JINGDEZHEN flourished, CELADON wares exported, and UNDERGLAZE blue introduced.

Yuruk (Yoruk) A widespread Turkish nomadic tribal group and weavers of rugs whose design repertoire is close to that of the CAUCASUS. Yuruk rugs tend to be narrower and the designs are essentially geometric, based on stylized floral forms with somber color combinations.

Zebra wood ■ A general term used for several tropical hardwoods with vivid and pronounced dark brown stripes. Zebra wood was mainly used as a veneer in the late 18th and early 19th centuries.

Radiating ribbed bowl

Yuan
Yuan dynasty Longquan celadon charger. 13th century.

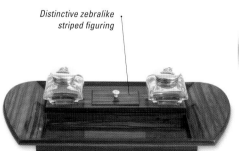

Distinctive zebralike striped figuring

Zebra wood
Asprey zebra wood inkstand, with silver hallmark and family crest on the ink bottles.

Zeisel, Eva
Geometric-patterned decanter and plate, by Eva Stricker-Zeisel. c. 1929.

Zoetrope ■ From the Greek *zoe* (life) and *tropos* (turn). An optical toy, one of the forerunners of the art of animation. It was first described by William George Horner in 1834, as a "Daedalum" (wheel of the devil) but was not properly introduced until the 1867, when it was patented in the US by William F. Lincoln and in the UK by Milton Bradley. At this point, it was renamed and became a popular 19th-century children's toy. It is a modification of the slotted disk device in which a series of images on a strip of paper are placed in a hollow metal drum that can be rotated on a stand around a horizontal axis. The images are viewed through slots in the side of the drum.

The eye sees a succession of momentary images, which together give the impression of movement.

Zsolnay ■ A ceramics factory established around 1865 in Pécs, Hungary, by Vilmos Zsolnay. Until the 1890s, it produced ornate ceramics inspired by Islamic pierced wares, but after 1893, when the chemist Vincse Wartha became art director, Zsolnay began to specialize in simple ART NOUVEAU organic forms and shapes, often with low-relief molding and

decorated with a wide range of marbled, shaded, and crystalline glazes, the most successful of which was a lustrous, iridescent, greenish glaze called eosin.

Zürich pottery and porcelain factory Started in 1763 as a joint stock company in Schonen, on Lake Zurich, and directed by Adam Spengler, who had been at HÖCHST. At first it made FAIENCE and SOFT-PASTE PORCELAIN. From around 1765 it made finely painted tableware in HARD-PASTE PORCELAIN, typically with elaborate scrolled handles. The chief modeler in the 1780s was Valentin Sonnenschein, who created charming models of Swiss people. A series of figures of street vendors was called "The Cries of Zurich." The painter Heinrich Fussli worked at the factory from 1771 to 1781. In 1793 the factory was bought by Spengler's son-in-law, Mathias Nehrache, the first of several changes of ownership until its closure in 1897. In the 19th century the firm produced faience and cream-colored earthenware. The factory mark was a "Z."

Z
411

ZWISCHENGOLDGLAS

The German term for "gold between glass," Zwischengoldglas is a type of decorative glass in which gold leaf was applied to the outside of a glass, engraved with a design, and then overcased by a close-fitting outer sleeve, which was sealed at the top and bottom. The ancient technique was revived in Bohemia and was popular in the 1730s and 40s, used primarily on beakers and goblets. It was revived again at the end of the 18th century by Johann Josef Mildner.

Glass goblet
Kaiser Karl Zwischengoldglas drinking glass. c.1743.

Ziegler
Ziegler Mahal Wagireh rug from west Persia. Late 19th century.

Gold-washed butterfly

Zircon
Flower spray brooch, set with zircon, amethyst, and citrin. 1965.

Zoetrope
French zoetrope, *Les Images Vivantes*, with cardboard body. c. 1910.

Zsolnay
Vase with the figure of a maiden. c. 1900.

DEALERS AND AUCTION HOUSES

Dorling Kindersley and the Price Guide Company would like to thank the following dealers and auction houses for permission to use images.

Abbreviations: TR=top right; C=center; TL=top left; TC=top center; BL=bottom left; BR=bottom right; BC=bottom center.

Albert Amor,
37 Bury Street, St James's,
London, SW1Y 6AU
Tel: 020 7930 2444
www.albertamor.co.uk
63 C, 66 C, 129 TL TR R, 317 T, 350 CR, 364 L, 369 CL,

Andrew Lineham Fine Glass,
P.O. Box 465, Chichester, PO18 8WZ
Tel: 01243 576 241
www.antiquecolouredglass.com
10 CR, 144 CL, 160 L, 197 CL, 343 CR, 356 C, 385 CL,

Antique Glass @ Frank Dux Antiques
33 Belvedere, Lansdowne Road,
Bath, BA1 5HR
Tel: 01225 312 367
www.antique-glass.co.uk
109 L, 160 C, 169 TR, 190 L

Antique Textiles and Lighting
34 Belvedere, Landsdowne Road,
Bath, BA1 5HR Tel: 01225 310 795
www.antiquetextilesandlighting.co.uk
21 CR, 35 R, 70 R, 72 R, 192 L

Auction Team Köln
Postfach 50 11 19, Bonner Str. 528-530,
D-50971 Cologne, Germany
Tel: 0049 221 38 70 49
www.breker.com
119 CR, 164 C, 207 L, 252 R, 411 CR

Auktionshaus Dr Fischer
Trappensee-Schößchen, D-74074
Heilbronn, Germany
Tel: 0049 71 31 15 55 70
www.auctions-fischer.de
16 R, 41 R, 54 T R, 60 CR R, 153 R, 161 R, 174 L, 194 C, 215 L, 221 CL, 229 C, 258 C, 330 CL, 408 TL

Auktionshaus Kaupp
Schloss Sulzburg, Hauptstrasse 62,
79295 Sulzburg, Germany
Tel: 0049 7634 5038 0 www.kaupp.de
125 R, 133 L, 211 CL, 249 T L R, 253 CR, 269 R, 270 L, 318 L CR, 393 TR

Auktionshaus Bergmann
Möhrendorfestraße 4,
91056 Erlangen, Germany
Tel: 0049 9 131 450 666
www.auction-bergmann.de
9 CR, 13 L, 18 CL, 36 C, 45 R, 53 R, 58 R, 64 CR,

143 C, 222 L, 235 R, 250 L, 300 CR, 304 R, 379 CL, 395 R

Auktionshaus Metz
Friedrich-Eber-Anlage 5,
69117 Heidelberg, Germany
Tel: 0049 6221 23571
www.Metz-Auktion.de
53 T, 63 R, 166 R

Barry Davies Oriental Art Ltd
PO Box 34867, London, W8 6WH
Tel: 020 7408 0207
www.barrydavies.com
189 R, 266 L

Beaussant Lefèvre
32, rue Drouot, 75009 Paris, France
Tel: 00 33 (0)1 47 70 40 00
www.beaussant-lefevre.auction.fr
48 L, 271 L, 307 R, 315 C

Bébés et Jouets
c/o Lochend Post Office, 165 Restalrig
Road, Edinburgh, EH7 6HW
bebesetjouets@tiscali.co.uk
26 L, 188 R, 210 L, 244 CL, 336 CL

Bernard and S Dean Levy
24 East 84th Street, New York,
NY 10028, USA
Tel: 001 212 628-7088
12 R, 115 CL

Bertoia Auctions
2141 Demarco Drive , Vineland ,
NJ 08360, USA Tel: 001 856 692 1881
www.bertoiaauctions.com
22 CR, 128 L, 193 R, 245 L, 261 T, 283 CL, 289 R, 327 R, 355 L

Beth, Unit GO43/4, Alfies Antique Market
13 Church Street, Marylebone
London, NW8 8DT
Tel: 020 7723 5613
100 CR, 113 R

Bloomsbury Auctions
Bloomsbury House, 24 Maddox Street,
London W1 S1PP
Tel: 020 7495 9494
www.bloomsburyauctions.com
141 CL CR, 291 CL, 376 L

Branksome Antiques
370 Poole Road, Branksome,

Poole, Dorset, BH12 1AW
Tel: 01202 763 324
84 CL, 197 C, 299 L, 371 CR

Brookside Antiques
44 North Water Street, New Bedford,
MA 02740, USA
Tel: 001 508 993 4944
www.brooksideartglass.com
266 C, 280 R, 326 R

Brunk Auctions
Post Office Box 2135, Ashville
NC 28802, USA
Tel: 001 828 254 6846
www.brunkauctions.com
51 T, 99 CL, 205 CL, 308 R

Bucks County Antique Center
Route 202, 8 Skyline Drive, Lahaska,
PA 18914, USA
Tel: 001 215 794 9180
63 CL, 177 CL, 218 R, 377 L, 399 TL

Bukowskis
Arsenalsgatan 4, Box 1754, 111 87
Stockholm, Sweden
Tel: 00 46 8 614 08 00
www.bukowskis.se
24 L, 139 C, 304 CR

Charlotte Sayers FGA
313–315 Grays Antique Market,
58 Davies Street
Tel: 020 7499 5478
sayers@grays.clara.net
16 CL, 52 CR, 111 CR

Cheffins
Clifton House, 1 & 2 Clifton Road
Cambridge CB1 7EA
Tel: 01223 213 343
www.cheffins.co.uk
40 R, 59 CR, 81 CL, 82 L, 107 R, 117 CR, 132 R, 144 R, 165 C, 187 R, 196 CR, 211 R, 215 CR, 236 R, 237 L, 246 L, 248 CL, 292 CL, 294L, 347 R, 367 L, 379 CR, 396 CR, 401 L

Chiswick Auctions
1–5 Colville Road, London W3 8BL
Tel: 020 8992 4442
www.chiswickauctions.co.uk
145 L, 226 R, 326 CL

Christopher Sykes Antiques
The Old Parsonage, Woburn, Milton
Keynes, MK17 9QJ

Tel: 01525 290 259/ 290 467
www.sykes-corkscrews.co.uk
112 L, 151 L, 331 R, 367 CL

Clevedon Salerooms
The Auction Centre, Kenn Road, Kenn,
Clevedon, Bristol, BS21 6TT Tel: 01934
830 111 www.clevedon-salerooms.com
130 L, 172 R, 217 L, 301 L, 402 TR

Craftsman Auctions
333 North Main Street, Lambertville, NJ
08530 USA Tel: 001 609 397 9374
www.ragoarts.com
147 CR, 149 L, 225 T, 332 TC, 395 T, 400 R

David Bowden
Stand 07 Grays Antique Markets,
58 Davies Street, London W1K 5LP
Tel: 020 7495 1773
91 CR, 198 R, 216 R, 366 R, 409 CR

David Rago Auctions
333 North Main Street, Lambertville,
NJ 08530, USA
Tel: 001 609 397 9374
www.ragoarts.com
23 CL, 25 CT, 28 C, 49 L, 50 CR, 71 CR, 79 L, 95 R, 117 R, 121 C, 125 CL CR, 137 TL, 141 L, 165 L, 166 C, 167 T L C, 176 CR, 181 L C R, 185 CR, 186 CR, 203 CL, 213 L, 214 R, 216 C, 219 T C, 224 CL, 242 CR, 247 R, 267 T L C R, 268 CL, 271 CL, 274 C, 285 CL, 301 R, 313 L, 319 L CL CR R, 344 C, 346 CR, 349 CR, 353 R, 357 L CL, 385 R, 387 CR, 388 CL, 395 CR, 407 TL R

Decodame.com
Tel: 001 239 514 6797
www.decodame.com
351 L, 360 R

Derek Roberts Fine Antique Clocks & Barometers
25 Shipbourne Road, Tonbridge, Kent
TN10 3DN
Tel: 01732 358 986
www.qualityantiqueclocks.com
43 CR, 84 R, 307 L

Dreweatt Neate (Formely Hamptons)
Baverstock House, 93 High Street,
Godalming, Surrey GU7 1AL
Tel: 01483 423 567
www.dnfa.com/godalming
72 CR, 153 C, 207 CR, 271 CR, 280 C, 305 CR, 396 CL

Dreweatt Neate
Bristol (formerly Bristol Auction Rooms),
St John's Place, Apsley Road, Clifton,
Bristol BS8 2ST
Tel: 0117 973 7201
www.dnfa.com
50 L, 248 CR, 363 CL

Dreweatt Neate
Donnington Priory Salerooms,
Donnington, Newbury, Berkshire
RG14 2JE
Tel: 01635 553 553
www.dnfa.com/donnington
*11 CL, 18 L, 22 R, 25 L, 33 B, 38 BL, 43 L, 44 C,
45 L, 52 R , 60 CL, 65 L, 66 TR, 67 C R, 73 L, 74
L, 76 CR, 80 R, 83 CL, 87 CR, 89 L CL, 96 CR, 97
R, 104 R, 106 C, 108 R, 109 CR, 111 L CL, 112 C,
114 CL R, 116 L, 120 CL, 123 R, 126 CR, 128 CR,
131 C, 135 CL CR, 136L, 144 L, 149 R, 151 BC,
152 CR, 156 C, 164 L R, 168 R, 172 L, 177 L, 178
T, 183 R, 188 CR, 191 CR, 196L, 197 CR, 205 CR,
223 CL, 239 L, 241 L, 248 R, 258 CR, 266 CL,
274 L, 275 C, 284 R, 295 CR, 299 CR, 300 R, 310
CR, 327 CL, 328 L, 339 CR, 350 TL TR, 351 CL,
352 TR C, 355 CL, 358 R, 368 R, 375 C R, 376
CR, 380 CL, 381 CL, 382 C, 384 R, 386 CL, 394 L,
403 R, 408 L, 409 L*

Dreweatt Neate
Tunbridge Wells (formerly Bracketts),
Auction Hall, The Pantiles, Tunbridge
Wells, Kent TN2 5QL Tel: 01892 544 500
www.dnfa.com
347 CR, 357 R, 367 R, 368 L

Early Technology
Monkton House, Old Craighall,
Musselburgh, Midlothian, Scotland,
EH21 8SF
Tel: 0131 665 5753
www.earlytech.com
290 R

Fellows & Sons
Augusta House, 19 Augusta Street,
Hockley, Birmingham B18 6JA
Tel: 0121 212 2131
www.fellows.co.uk
109 CL, 126 CL, 276 C, 287 L, 404 CL

Festival
136 South Ealing Road
London W5 4QJ
Tel: 020 8840 9333
127 R, 252 T, 295 L

Freeman's
1808 Chestnut Street
Philadelphia, PA 19103, USA
Tel: 001 215 563 9275
www.freemansauction.com
*13 CL, 17 R, 18 R, 21 R, 31 R, 32 CR, 34 L, 42
BR, 55 CR, 58 C, 62 CR, 71 CL, 73 TR, 85 L, 87
CL, 91 R, 98 L R, 105 CR, 115 L, 116 C, 119 L,
133 T, 148 L C, 149 CR, 150R, 152 R, 157 CL BL
BC, 158 R, 172 CR, 188 C, 216 L, 227 CR, 231
CR, 232 R, 242 L CL, 247 CR, 263 CL, 274 R, 279
R, 280 L, 282 R, 285 L, 287 CR, 292 R, 293 R,
297 CR, 298 R, 305 L, 314 R, 320 CL, 323 C, 330
CR, 334 R, 349 L R, 361 R, 363 R, 390 CR, 393
TL, 397 L, 402 CL, 403 CL, 410 L, 411 L*

Galerie Hélène Fournier Guérin
18, rue des Saints-Pères,
75007 Paris, France
Tel: 0033 (0)1 42 60 21 81
*236 CL, 237 CL, 250 R, 278 R, 320 L, 324 L, 329
CR*

Galerie Maurer
Kurfurstenstrasse 17,
D-80799 Munchen, Germany
Tel: +49 89 271 13 45
www.galerie-objekte-maurer.de
250 CR, 290 L, 347 CL

Galerie Olivia et Emmanuel
Village Suisse, Galeries 24 et 58,
78, avenue de Suffren,
75015 Paris, France
Tel: 0033 (0)1 43 06 85 30
www.artface.com/olivia
48 CR, 244 CR, 265 T

Galerie Vandermeersch
Voltaire Antiquités-Vandermeersch SA
21, quai Voltaire, 75007 Paris, France
Tel: 0033 (0)1 42 61 23 10
260 L, 268 L, 315 L, 335 R

Gallerie Koller
Hardturmstrasse 102, Postfach
8031 Zürich, Switzerland
Tel: 00 41 1445 6363
www.galeriekoller.ch
*49 CR, 133 C TC, 155 CR, 221 L, 277 L, 348 R,
351 CR*

Gardiner Houlgate
Bath Auction Rooms, 9 Leafield Way,
Corsham, SN13 9SW
Tel: 01225 812 912
78 R, 194 R, 343 L, 381 L, 403 CR

Geoffrey Diner Gallery
1730 21st Street NW,
Washington
DC 20009, USA
Tel: 001 202 483 5005
www.dinergallery.com
213 C, 317 L

Gillian Neale Antiques
P.O. Box 247, Aylesbury HP20 1JZ
Tel: 01296 423754
www.gilliannealeantiques.co.uk
112 CL, 173 R, 281 R

Goodwins Antiques Ltd
15 & 16 Queensferry Street,
Edinburgh EH2 4QW
Tel: 0131 225 4717
12 CR, 30 CR, 169 L, 258 L, 342 L

Gorringes
15 North Street
Lewes, East Sussex, BN7 2PD
Tel: 01273 472 503
www.gorringes.co.uk
*63 CR, 72 CL, 73 C, 120 R, 137 TR, 151 TL, 180
CL, 225 TCR, 233 CL, 241 CR, 253 R, 256 CL CR,
261 CL, 264 R, 269 L, 273 R, 297 R, 281 CR, 309
L, 329 CL, 341 CR, 344 L, 367 CR, 368 CL, 383 R,
406 L, 409 R*

Halcyon Days
14 Brook Street, London, W1S 1BD
Tel: 020 7629 8811
www.halcyondays.co.uk
56 CL, 77 CL, 152 CL, 279 CR

Hampton and Littlewood
The Auction Rooms, Alphin Brook Road,
Alphington, Exeter, Devon, EX2 8TH
Tel: 01392 413100
www.hamptonandlittlewood.co.uk
59 L, 92 R, 292 CR

Harpers General Store
301 Maple Avenue, Mt. Gretna
PA 17064
Tel: 001 717 865 3456
www.harpergeneralstore.com
291 CR, 303 CL, 354 R, 370 TL, 345 L, 406 R

Hermann Historica OHG
Linprunstrasse 16,
80335 Munich, Germany,
Tel: 0049 895 237 296
www.hermann-historica.com
132 CR, 153 L, 193 CR, 304 L

Hope and Glory
131A Kensington Church Street,
London W8 7LP Tel: 020 7727 8424
71 R, 386 R

Hugo Ruef
Gabelsbergerstraße 28,
80333 Munich, Germany
Tel: 0049 89 52 40 84
www.ruef-auktionen.de
74 CL, 188 L

Imperial Half Bushel
831 N Howard Street,
Baltimore,
MD 21201, USA
Tel: 001 410 462 1192
www.imperialhalfbushel.com
58 L, 78 CR, 135 L

James D Julia Inc
PO Box 830, Fairfield,
Maine 04937 USA
Tel: 001 207 453 7125
www.juliaauctions.com
*15 CL, 26 CR, 34 CR, 57 R, 75 CR, 114 L, 225 R,
254 T, 259 CL, 356 CL, 374 R, 393 C, 399 L*

Jean Scott Collection
Stanhope Collectors' International,
www.stanhopes.info
8 L, 29 C, 354 L CL

Jeanette Hayhurst Fine Glass
32A Kensington Church St.,
London W8 4HA
Tel: 020 7938 1539
www.antiqueglass-london.com
*15 R, 77 R, 93 CL, 126 C, 186 L, 200 R, 203 CR,
251 L, 255 CR, 321 CR, 361 C, 384 CR, 390 L,
408 C*

Jill Fenichell, Inc.
Suite 333, 55 Washington Street
Brooklyn, NY 11238
Tel: 001 718 237 2490
jfenichell@yahoo.com
214 CL

John Bull (Antiques) Ltd
139A New Bond Street,
London W1S 2TN
Tel: 020 7629 1251
www.jbsilverware.co.uk
www.antique-silver.co.uk
68 L, 80 CR, 159 CL, 244 R

John Howard @ Heritage
Heritage, 6 Market Place
Woodstock, Oxon, OX20 1TA
Mob: 07831 850 544
www.antiquepottery.co.uk
*14 C R, 111 T, 118 R, 320 CR, 339 R, 389 CL,
396 R, 404 R, 405 CL*

John King
74 Pimlico Road, London, SW1W 8LS
Tel: 020 7730 0427
170 R, 283 T, 306 R

John Nicholsons
The Auction Rooms, Longfield
Midhurst Road, Fernhurst
Haslemere, Surrey GU27 3HA
Tel: 01428 653727
www.johnnicholsons.com
185 L, 311 R, 322 L, 324 R, 355 CR

Jonathan Wadsworth
Wadsworth's, Marehill, Pulborough
West Sussex, RH20 2DY
Tel: 01798 873 555
www.wadsworthsrugs.com
*12 CL, 31 R, 38 L, 170 L CL, 209 CL, 284 CL CR,
369 R*

Joseph Bonnar
72 Thistle Street, Edinburgh, EH2 1EN
Tel: 0131 226
2811 151 TR, 411 CL

Juwelier Pütz
St Aspern Straße 17–21,
50667 Cologne, Germany
Tel: 00 49 221 257 49 95
25 TL, 373 CL

Lankes Triftfeldstrasse 1
95182 Döhlau, Germany
Tel: 0049 92 869 5050
www.lankes-auktionen.de
56 R, 57 L, 83 CR, 243 CR

Law Fine Art Ltd.
Ash Cottage, Ashmore Green, Newbury
Berkshire, RG18 9ER
Tel: 01635 860 033
www.lawfineart.co.uk
*11 T, 13 CR, 30 C, 43 R, 59 CL, 90 C, 95 L, 116
R, 135R, 170 CR, 171 L CR, 172 CL, 187 CR, 202
C, 223 CR, 225 CR, 309 CL, 335 T, 339 CL, 344
R, 406 TL TC*

Lawrences' Auctioneers
Norfolk House, High Street,
Bletchingley, Surrey, RH1 4PA
Tel: 01883 743 323
24 CL, 256 R, 327 CR

Lawrence's Fine Art Auctioneers
The Linen Yard, South Street,
Crewkerne, Somerset TA18 8AB Tel:
01460 73041 www.lawrences.co.uk
41 L, 106 L, 154 L, 262 R

Leigh Keno American Antiques
127 East 69th Street, New York

NY 10021, USA
Tel: 001 212 734 2381
110 C

Lempertz
Neumarkt 3, 50667 Cologne, Germany
Tel: 0049 221 925 72 9 0
www.lempertz.com
42 TC, 54 L, 220 L

Lennox Cato
1 The Square, Church Street, Edenbridge
Kent TN8 5BD
Tel: 01732 865 988
www.lennoxcato.com
*183 CR, 226 L, 235 C, 290 C, 341 L, 389 CR, 402
R 403 L*

Lillian Nassau Ltd
220 East 57th Street, New York
NY 10022
Tel: 001 212 759 6062
www.lilliannassau.com
200 L, 220 R, 243 L, 401 R

Lost City Arts
18 Cooper Square, New York,
NY 10003 USA
Tel: 001 212 375 0500
www.lostcityarts.com
25 BR, 185 R, 201 L, 277 CR, 365 L

Lotherton Hall
Lotherton Lane, Aberford
Leeds, LS25 3EB
Tel: 0113 281 3259
74 R, 76 R, 298 CR

Lyon and Turnbull Ltd.
33 Broughton Place,
Edinburgh EH1 3RR
Tel: 0131 557 8844
www.lyonandturnbull.com   *8 T, 10 R, 11
CR, 15 CR, 19 CL, 20 C, 25 TR, 28 T, 31C, 32 L,
36 CL R, 38 CR, 39 R, 40 CR, 42 TL, 52 CL, 67 T,
68 R, 69 CL, 70 CL, 75 CL, 80 L, 81 R, 84 L CR,
85 R, 87 L R, 91 C, 92 CL, 93 C, 103 R, 106 R,
107 L, 108 CR, 112 CR, 115 R, 116 CL, 119 CL,
121 L R, 122 T L R, 123 C, 124 CR R, 125 L, 126
L, 127 CR, 128 R, 137 TC, 138 L, 139 L, 142 L,
143 R, 146 C, 148 R, 149 CL, 152 L, 156 R, 159
L, 176 L, 183 CL, 184 R, 186 R, 191 CL, 203 L,
211 L, 212 L, 219 R, 220 CL, 221 CR, 226 CL,
227 R, 230 T, 232 T, 233 L, 235 L, 237 CR, 238
TL TR L C R, 245 CR, 247 CL, 253 CL, 255 L, 256
L, 257 L, 266 R, 275 R, 276 R, 277 CL, 283 L,
287 CL, 292 L, 293 L, 296 R, 300 CL, 303 R, 306
T L, 307 CR, 313 R, 314 CL, 322 C, 327 L, 328 R,
332 TL CL, 333 CL R, 334 L CL, 341 R, 342 CL R,
345 R, 348 CL CR, 353 L, 356 R, 363 L, 365 R,
369 CR, 372 L, 381 CR, 383 CL, 386 CR, 390 CL,
392 L, 393 TCL TR, 395 L, 396 L, 397 CR R,
398 R*

Mallett
141 New Bond Street, London, W1S 2BS
Tel: 020 7499 7411
www.mallettantiques.com
154 CL, 218 CL, 385 CR, 387 CL

Leigh Keno American Antiques
127 East 69th Street, New York

Marie Antiques
G107 & 136–137 Alfies Antique Market
13 Church Street, Marylebone,
London, NW8 8DT
Tel: 020 7706 3727
www.marieantiques.co.uk
123 L, 145 BR, 278 CL, 288 CL

Mary Ann's Collectibles
c/o South Street Antiques Centre
615 South 6th Street, Philadelphia
PA 19147–2128 , USA
Tel: 001 215 923 3247
*79 C R, 126 R, 167 R, 182 CR, 240 C, 281 L, 318
CL, 320 R, 326 CR, 373 L, 374 L C*

Mostly Boxes
93 High Street, Eton, Windsor,
Berkshire, SL4 6AF
Tel: 01753 858 470
260 R, 382 L, 410 C

N. Bloom & Son (1912) Ltd.
Tel: 020 7629 5060
www.nbloom.com
99 L, 291 L, 379 L, 387 R

Nagel
Neckarstrasse 189–191, 70190
Stuttgart, Germany
Tel: 0049 711 649 690
www.auction.de
*61 CL, 195 L, 199 CL, 206 C, 212 CR, 316 L, 338
L, 383 CR*

Noel Barrett Antiques & Auctions Ltd
PO Box 300, Carversville, PA 18913
USA
Tel: 001 215 297 5109
www.noelbarrett.com
73 R, 229 R, 245 CL

Northeast Auctions
93 Pleasant Street, Portsmouth
NH 03801, USA
Tel: 001 603 433 8400
www.northeastauctions.com
*36 CR, 42 BL, 50 R, 110 T R, 112 R, 157 TL TR,
159 CR, 163 L, 173 C, 174 CR, 189 L, 200 CR,
209 L, 241 R, 275 L, 393 L, 404 L*

Onslows
The Coach House, Manor Road,
Stourpaine, Dorset
DT11 8TQ
Tel: 01258 488 838
www.onslows.co.uk
86 R, 402 L

Palais Dorotheum
Dorotheergasse 17, 1010 Vienna,
Austria Tel: 0043 1 515 600
www.dorotheum.com
193 CL, 230 L, 241 CL, 258 CL, 372 T R

Pantry & Hearth
994 Main Street South, Woodbury, CT
06798 Tel: 001 212 532 0535 www.
nhada.org/pantryhearth.htm
39 CR, 55 CL, 69 L, 116 CR, 405 L

Partridge Fine Arts Plc
144–146 New Bond Street,
London, W1S 2PF
Tel: 020 7629 0834
www.partridgeplc.com
*9 L, 10 L, 23 L, 42 TR, 52 L, 61 CR, 65 CL, 68 CL,
83 R, 86 CL, 101 C, 108 CL, 119 R, 145 TL, 146
L, 158 L, 171 CL, 178 L R, 180 L, 182 CL, 195 CR,
200 CL, 209 R, 210 CR, 232 L, 233 CR R, 234 TL
TR L R, 243 CL, 259 L, 312 L, 313 CR, 331 CR,
332 R, 362 R, 363 CR, 366 CL, 399 R*

Pendulum of Mayfair
King House, 51 Maddox Street,
London, W1S 2PH
Tel: 020 7629 6606
www.pendulumofmayfair.com
34 R, 38 R, 131 R, 192 CL, 224 CR, 231 L

Pook & Pook
463 East Lancaster Avenue,
Downingtown PA 19335
USA
Tel: 001 610 269 4040/ 610 269 0695
www.pookandpook.com
*17 CR, 59 L, 110 L, 157 C, 163 R, 164 T, 192 R,
201 CL, 239 CR, 243 R, 255 R, 281 T, 282 L, 285
CR, 297 L, 301 CR, 302 R, 310 L, 314 CR, 321 R,
325 C, 333 L, 350 L CL, 384 L, 399 TR*

Puritan Values
The Dome, St Edmund's Road,
Southwold, Suffolk IP18 6BZ
Tel: 01502 722211
www.puritanvalues.co.uk
19CR, 137 BC, 257 R, 310 CL

Quittenbaum
Hohenstaufenstraße 1,
D-80801 München, Germany
Tel: 0049 859 33 00 75 6
www.quittenbaum.de
*27 R, 46C, 50 CL, 54 C, 74 CR, 103 CL, 127 C,
162 CR, 190 CR R, 195 C R, 225 TL, 228 R, 261
L, 271 R, 296 CL, 323 R, 370 R, 388 L, 411 R*

R & G McPherson Antiques
40 Kensington Church Street, London,
W8 4BX Tel: 020 7937 0812
www.orientalceramics.com
*18 CR, 127 CL, 155 L, 202 R, 205 L, 206 T L, 209
CR, 222 R, 223 R, 307 CL, 347 L, 397 CL*

Richard Gardner Antiques
Swan House, Market Square, Petworth,
West Sussex GU28 0AH
Tel: 01798 343 411
www.richardgardnerantiques.co.uk
*20 L, 40 L, 43 CL, 62 L, 139 R, 169 C, 276 R, 299
R, 346 CL, 400 L*

Ritches Auctioneers & Appraisers
288 King Street East, Toronto, Ontario,
Canada, M5A 1KA
Tel: 001 416 364 1864
www.ritchies.com
91 L, 120 L, 393 TCR

Rogers de Rin
76 Royal Hospital Road, Paradise Walk,

Chelsea, London SW3 4HN
Tel: 020 7352 9007
www.rogersderin.co.uk
247 L, 289 CL, 298 L, 345 TR, 358 CR, 400 CL

Rosebery
74–76 Knight's Hill, West Norwood,
London, SE27 0JD
Tel: 020 8761 2522
www.roseberys.co.uk
13 R, 175 C, 336 CR, 360 C

Rossini SA
7, rue Drouot, 75009 Paris, France
Tel: 00 33 (0)1 53 34 55 00
www.rossini.fr
33 T, 161 L, 309 R, 328 C

Salle des Ventes Pillet
1, rue de la Libération, B. P. 23, 27480
Lyons la Forèt, France
Tel: 0033 (0)2 32 49 60 64
www.pillet.auction.fr
147 L, 308 C, 323 L

Sampson & Horne Antiques
120, Mount Street, London, W1K 3NN
Tel: 020 7409 1799
www.sampsonhorne.com
*21 C, 40 CL, 55L, 61 R, 90 R, 95 CR, 109 R, 118
TR, 161 CR, 166 L, 179 R, 270 CL, 296 CR, 310
R, 373 R, 401 CL*

Sidney Gecker
226 West 21st Street, New York, NY
10011, USA
Tel: 001 212 929 8789
92 CR, 355 R

Sign of the Tymes
12 Morris Farm Road, Lafayette, NJ
07848 USA
Tel: 001 973 383 6028
www.millantiques.com
353 CR, 370 TR

Skinner
63 Park Plaza, Boston, MA 02116, USA
& 357 Main Street, Bolton, MA 01740,
USA
Tel: 001 617 350 5400/001 978 779 6241
www.skinnerinc.com
*8 R, 14 L, 24 R, 48 CL, 63 L, CL, 76 L, 99 CR, 103
C, 157 R, 192 R, 210 CL, 259 CR, 264 CR, 302 L,
325 L, 326 L, 331 CL, 337 TL, 338 CR, 348 L*

Sloans & Kenyon
7034 Wisconsin Avenue, Chevy Chase,
Maryland 20815, USA
Tel: 001 301 634 2330
www.sloansandkenyon.com
*143 L, 179 L, 300 L, 362 CR, 365 C, 368 CR,
392 R*

Sollo:Rago Modern Auctions
333 North Main Street, Lambertville,
NJ 08530, USA
Tel: 001 609 397 9374
www.ragoarts.com
8 CL, 22 CL, 35 L, 61 T, 88 R, 142 T R, 151 BR,

*223 L, 252 L, 264 CL, 285 R, 293 CL, 298 CL, 316
C, 331 L, 354 TR, 358 L, 391 L R, 399 CR, 407 C*

Somlo Antiques
7 Piccadilly Arcade, London, SW1Y 6NH
Tel: 020 7499 6526
www.somlo.com
68 CR, 85 CR, 291 R

Special Auction Services
Kennetholme, Midgham, Nr. Reading,
Berkshire RG7 5UX
Tel: 0118 971 2949
www.invaluable.com/sas
253 L, 295 R, 313 CL

Steppes Hill Farm Antiques
Stockbury, Sittingbourne, Kent,
ME9 7RB Tel: 01795 842 205
66 L, 115 CR, 180 R, 231 CL

Stockspring Antiques
114 Kensington Church Street, London
W8 4BH Tel: 020 7727 7995
www.antique-porcelain.co.uk
129 L, 359 R

Sumpter Priddy III, Inc.
601 S. Washington Street, Alexandria,
Virginia 22314 Tel: 001 703 299 0800
www.sumpterpriddy.com
57 CL, 239 R

Swann Galleries Image Library
104 East 25th Street, New York, New
York 10010 Tel: 001 212 254 4710
www.swanngalleries.com
*25 BC, 82 CL, 96 L, 159 R, 191 L, 260 CL, 294 C,
360 L*

Sworders
14 Cambridge Road, Stansted
Mountfitchet, Essex, CM24 8BZ
Tel: 01279 817 778
www.sworder.co.uk
*71 L, 140 TL TR, 160 CL, 162 CL, 203 R, 286 L,
311 C, 322 R, 325 R, 332 CR*

Sylvie Spectrum
372, Grays Antique Market,
58 Davies Street, London, W1K 5LP
Tel: 020 7629 3501
246 CL, 284 L, 390 R

T.C.S. Brooke
The Grange, Wroxham,
Norfolk, NR12 8RX
Tel: 01603 782 644
186 CL, 236 L, 265 R, 358 CL, 406 TR

The Blue Pump
178 Davenport Road, Toronto,
Canada, M5R 1J2
Tel: 001 416 944 1673
297 CL

The Design Gallery
5 The Green, Westerham,
Kent, TN16 1AS
Tel: 01959 561 234

www.designgallery.co.uk
16 CR, 91 CL, 175 R, 366 L

The Graham Cooley Collection
grahamcooley_ffc@hotmail.com
69 CR, 86 CR, 176 R, 400 CR

The Silver Fund
1 Duke of York Street,
London SW1Y 6JP
Tel: 0207 839 7664
www.thesilverfund.com
204 TL TR L R, 316 R

The Thomas Dreiling Collection
9 CL, 78 CL, 83 L, 356 L

The Watch Gallery
129 Fulham Road, London, SW3 6RT
Tel: 020 7581 3239
info@thewatchgallery.co.uk
103 CR, 317 C, 165 R, 337 TR L C R

Thos. Wm. Gaze & Son
Diss Auction Rooms, Roydon Road,
Diss, Norfolk, IP22 4LN
Tel: 01379 650 306
www.twgaze.com
127 L, 175 L, 259 CL, 362 L, 375 L

Titus Omega
www.titusomega.com
27 C, 213 R, 408 TR

Van Den Bosch
24–25 The Mall, Camden Passage,
Islington, N1 0PU
Tel: 020 7226 4550
www.vandenbosch.co.uk
*29 CR, 30 L, 73 TR, 77 L, 122 C, 225 TCL, 262 R,
272 L, 402 CR*

Vectis Auctions Limited
Fleck Way, Thornaby, Stockton on Tees
TS17 9JZ Tel: 01642 750 616
www.vectis.co.uk
44 L, 70 R, 97 L, 114 CR, 132 L CL, 330 L

Vetro & Arte Gallery
Calle del Capeler 3212, Dorsoduro
30123, Venice, Italy
Tel: 0039 041 522 8525
www.venicewebgallery.com
261 R, 293 CR

Victoriana Dolls
101 Portobello Rd, London,
W11 2BQ
Tel: 01737 249 525
*64 CR, 72 R, 95 CL, 134 L, 136 R, 180 CR, 205 R,
272 CR, 278 L, 295 CL, 343 L, 398 L, 405 R*

Von Zezschwitz
Friedrichstrasse 1a,
80801 Munich, Germany
Tel: 0049 89 38 98 930
www.von-zezschwitz.de
35 CL, 62 CL, 155 CL, 158 CL, 199 CR, 333 CR

Waddington's
111 Bathurst Street, Toronto,
Ontario, Canada M5V 2R1
Tel: 001 416 504 9100
www.waddingtons.ca
161 CL, 314 L, 346 L

Wallis and Wallis
West Street Auction Galleries, Lewes,
East Sussex BN7 2NJ
Tel: 01273 480 208
www.wallisandwallis.co.uk
*39 CL, 47 C, 67 L, 75 L R, 128 CL, 160 R, 187 CL,
189 CL, 193 L, 201 R, 215 R, 224 R, 225L, 246 R,
296 L, 336 R, 340 R, 378 L, 379 R*

**Wiener Kunst Auktionen –
Palais Kinsky**
Freyung 4, 1010 Vienna, Austria
Tel: 00 43 15 32 42 00
www.palais-kinsky.com
32 R, 47 CR, 85 CL, 103 L, 392 CL

William Walters Antiques Ltd
London Silver Vaults, Chancery Lane,
London, WC2A 1QS
Tel: 020 7242 3248
www.williamwalter.co.uk
30 R, 338 CL

Woolley and Wallis
51–61 Castle Street, Salisbury,
Wiltshire SP1 3SU
Tel: 01722 424 500
www.woolleyandwallis.co.uk
*12 R, 21 CL, 23 CR, 26 CL, 29 L CL, 32 CL, 34 CL,
35 CR, 47 CL, 49 C R, 56 L, 57 CR, 62 R, 66 R, 77
CR, 78 L, 89 R, 92 L, 93 L R, 96 CL, 100 CL R,
105 L CL R, 106 CL, 107 T C, 108 L, 113 C, 117 L
CL, 118 L C, 120 CR, 124 C, 140 L, 141 R, 145
TR,147 CL R, 150 L, 154 CR R, 158 CR, 162 L,
168 L, 171 R, 174 TR, 176 CL, 177 CR, 187 L,
188 CL, 189 CR, 190 CL, 197 L, 198 C, 199 L R,
201 CR, 202 TL TR L, 203 C, 205 C, 206 R, 207
R, 208 L R, 211 CR, 212 R, 215 CL, 218 L CR,
221 R, 225 TR, 226 CR, 227 CL, 230 R, 231 R,
236 CR, 244 R, 246 CR, 251 R, 254 L R, 258 R,
261 CR, 263 CR R, 269 C, 278 CR, 279 L, 280
CR, 281 CL, 288 L R, 289 L CR, 303 CR, 304 CL,
305 CL, 315 R, 321 L, 324 CR, 329 L, 335 L, 341
CL, 342 TL, 345 TL TC C, 351 R, 352 L, 359 L C,
361 L, 362 CL, 370 L, 371 CL, 373 CR, 378 C R,
380 CR, 384 CL, 389 L, 394 CL CR, 398 C, 399
CL, 406 C, 408 R*

Additional Picture Credits
*24 L © DACS 2007; 100 R © ADAGP, Paris and
DACS, London 2007; 182 R © DACS 2007;
191 L © DACS 2007; 193 CL © DACS 2007;
219 C CL CB CR © ADAGP, Paris and DACS,
London 2007; 222 R © FLC/ADAGP, Paris and
DACS, London 2007; 273 CR © DACS 2007;
298 CL © ADAGP, Paris and DACS, London
2007; 312 CL © DACS 2007; 407 CL CR BCL
BC BCR © ARS, NY and DACS, London 2007.*

All other images © Dorling Kindersley
and The Price Guide Company Ltd.

ACKNOWLEDGMENTS

From the author

The authors would like to thank the following people for their substantial contributions to the production of this book: George Archdale, Fiona Baker, Miles Barton, John Benjamin, Alexis Butcher, Nicholas Couts, Jonathan Darracott, Nicholas M. Dawes, Audrey Field, Joseph Gonzalez, Leigh Gotch, Jeanette Hayhurst, Charles Kewley, Ann Knox, Jo Marshall, Mike and Sue Richardson, Rebecca Scott, Jeremy Smith, Catherine Southon, Michael Turner, and Jonathan Wadsworth.

Photographer Graham Rae for his patience, humor, and wonderful photography. Bob Bousfield for his workflow and technical assistance and Nick Croydon for his business advice.

All of the dealers, auction houses and private collectors for kindly allowing us to photograph their collections, and for taking the time to provide a wealth of information about the pieces.

The team at DK, especially Nicola Hodgson and Silke Spingies for editorial and design coordination.

From the publisher

Dorling Kindersley would like to thank: Stephanie Jackson; Simon Shaw and Daniel Mirzoeff at the BBC; Angela Wilkes and Neil Lockley for editorial assistance; Tim Lane for jacket design; and Caroline Hunt for proofreading.